The Elusive Quest

The Elusive Quest

*America's Pursuit of European Stability
and French Security, 1919–1933*

by Melvyn P. Leffler

The University of North Carolina Press
Chapel Hill

© 1979 The University of North Carolina Press
All rights reserved
Manufactured in the United States of America
ISBN 0-8078-1333-8
Library of Congress Catalog Card Number 78-9782

Library of Congress Cataloging in Publication Data

Leffler, Melvyn P., 1945 –
    The elusive quest.

    Bibliography: p.
    Includes index.
        1. United States—Foreign Relations—France.
2. France—Foreign relations—United States.
3. Europe—Politics and government—1918–1945.
4. United States—Foreign relations—Europe.
5. Europe—Foreign relations—United States.
6. United States—Foreign relations—20th century.
I. Title.
E183.8.F8L43   327.73   78-9782
ISBN 0-8078-1333-8

To
P. J. K. L.

Table of Contents

Preface   [*ix*]

Acknowledgments   [*xiii*]

Abbreviations   [*xv*]

 1. *From Versailles to Washington, 1919–1921*   [*3*]

 2. *Economic Diplomacy Takes Shape, 1921–1923*   [*40*]

 3. *German Rehabilitation
    and French Security, 1923–1925*   [*82*]

 4. *Toward Monetary Stability, 1924–1926*   [*121*]

 5. *Economic Diplomacy Falters, 1927–1928*   [*158*]

 6. *Changing Times,
    Old Approaches, 1929–1930*   [*194*]

 7. *Crisis, Action, and Uncertainty, 1931*   [*231*]

 8. *Hoover and the Failure
    of Economic Diplomacy, 1932*   [*273*]

 9. *Roosevelt and the
    Dilemmas of Policymaking, 1933*   [*316*]

10. *Conclusion*   [*362*]

Bibliography   [*369*]

Index   [*395*]

Preface

This book seeks to bridge the gap between revisionist and traditionalist studies of American foreign policy. It does so by presenting a comprehensive analysis of American policy toward France and western Europe in the years between the Paris Peace Conference of 1919 and the London Economic Conference of 1933. Without overemphasizing the importance of foreign markets to American policymakers, this book depicts the economic and financial imperatives that compelled American officials to take an active interest in European affairs. Likewise, without disregarding the political and strategic considerations that precluded the assumption of military obligations in the Old World, it portrays the ongoing efforts of American officials to play an influential part in the European stabilization process. Too frequently, accounts of this period have tended to highlight either the politically isolationist elements of American foreign policy or the economically expansionist aspirations of American officeholders and businessmen. Such a dichotomy simplifies rather than clarifies reality. In fact, American policymakers were torn by conflicting impulses as they sought to play a constructive role in postwar Europe. They wanted to remain aloof from Europe's wanton game of power politics and concentrate on balancing the budget, avoiding inflation, and protecting the domestic market. Yet, they also sought to expedite the rehabilitation of Germany and enhance the security of France. Many of these objectives were contradictory. Nevertheless, American officials from Wilson to Roosevelt struggled to find suitable mechanisms that would enable them to contribute to Europe's stabilization without compromising the nation's domestic priorities or its freedom of action. The attempts of American policymakers to balance conflicting diplomatic goals and reconcile foreign and domestic economic priorities constitute the heart of the present study.

Throughout this volume I have focused on American policy toward France. Yet, this book is not intended as a traditional study of a bilateral relationship between two nations. Indeed, I have alluded to the policymaking process in France only when American perceptions of French foreign policy help to explain the nature of American decision making. In other words, the Washington-Paris relationship is used here as a framework for elucidating the dynamics of American efforts to reconstruct and stabilize all of western Europe in the aftermath of the Great War. The focus on France is made necessary by the fact that policymakers in Washington almost always singled out that nation as the greatest roadblock to the achievement of American goals. Hence, American officials had to contend with French anxieties and demands within the larger context of American foreign policy objectives. This was no easy task, and American officials were never able to submerge Franco-American differences in behalf of a successful assault on all the sources of European instability.

Although most of this book deals with an analysis of Republican foreign policy, it begins with a chapter on Wilsonian diplomacy and concludes with an examination of Roosevelt's policymaking from his election to the London Economic Conference. Woodrow Wilson's decisions to include the League of Nations covenant in the peace treaty, to sign a guarantee pact with France, and to struggle for ratification of the Treaty of Versailles without reservations affected the subsequent course of American diplomacy in the interwar era. By personalizing the treaty issue and intensifying partisan rifts, he helped create a legislative stalemate and a policymaking impasse. When the Republicans assumed office in 1921, they did not turn their backs on the Old World. But, having witnessed the consequences of Wilson's struggle with the Senate and having developed misgivings about the efficacy of Wilson's handiwork, they decided to subordinate the questions of military guarantees and political entanglements, to accentuate the importance of economic and financial affairs, and to concentrate on establishing policymaking instruments that would accommodate America's foreign economic interests without undermining her domestic priorities. This Republican approach to European affairs I have labeled economic diplomacy. With certain modifications and alterations, the assumptions and instruments devised under the rubric of economic diplomacy characterized Republican foreign policy in times of prosperity and depression. When Roosevelt was elected in 1932, he was determined to throw off the shackles of the past. But, though it was easy to jettison the techniques and practices of economic diplomacy, it was considerably more difficult to devise alternative policies capable of balancing the New Deal's domestic programs with Roosevelt's internationalist predilections. In short, the dilemmas of American policymaking were not easily resolved. The quest for European stability and French security had to be abandoned while the Democratic president dealt with the internal exigencies of the Great Depression.

By focusing on the goals, tactics, and techniques of American foreign policy, this book seeks to elucidate the complexities of the policymaking process in the United States. Accordingly, no effort is made in this volume to study the decision-making processes in European capitals. Although I have used a considerable number of printed foreign documents to better understand the international context of American diplomatic activity, I have carefully sought to maintain my emphasis on developments in Washington. Fortunately, my research has been greatly facilitated by the availability of the records of the State, Commerce, Treasury, Navy, and War departments, by the opening of the archives of the Federal Reserve Bank of New York, and by the accessibility of several dozen private manuscript collections in the United States. Such an abundance of archival materials has allowed me to explore the origin, the functioning, and the interrelationships of key policymaking agencies. Although there is no indication that military officials played a decisive role in shaping policy during this era, their views on Franco-German rivalries, French security questions, and American strategic priorities help to explain why civilian officials were so reluctant to increase American commitments on the Continent. With this vast array of documentation, it should now be possible to present a new and more penetrating examination of the American approach to European affairs in the era after the First World War.

Acknowledgments

In writing a book of this nature one cannot help but be indebted to the many scholars who have preceded him and whose works have set the limits for subsequent debate. I am especially grateful for the writings of William A. Williams, George F. Kennan, Robert E. Osgood, Arno J. Mayer, N. Gordon Levin, Carl P. Parrini, Robert H. Ferrell, Joan Hoff Wilson, L. Ethan Ellis, and Robert Freeman Smith. Their books and articles on American foreign policy stimulated my interest in the interwar era and inspired me to conduct my own study of American diplomacy in the aftermath of World War I. If my own work can serve others as their writings have served me, I shall feel that my efforts have been rewarded.

Almost a decade ago, Marvin R. Zahniser, my graduate adviser at Ohio State University, suggested that I undertake a study of some aspect of Franco-American relations in the interwar era. Although this project subsequently took on a dimension that neither of us foresaw, his advice, criticisms, and encouragement over many years have been a source of great satisfaction to me. I was fortunate as well to have had a number of instructors at Ohio State University whose enthusiasm for historical analysis and respect for historical evidence left a lasting impression upon me. I hope that Mary E. Young, John C. Burnham, Andreas Dorpalen, and Peter Larmour will find the quality of this book commensurate with the high standards they set in their classrooms and in their own writings. My years in Columbus would not have been so pleasant nor my interest in foreign policy so intense if not for the scores of hours spent with Charles Robinson. On the tennis court and in the seminar room our discussions of the role of economic factors in the shaping of American foreign policy never ceased to be meaningful and productive.

One of the joys of doing historical research is the acquaintances one makes and the friendships one develops in a community of scholars working on similar questions. Over the years my understanding of interwar diplomacy has been enormously enriched by extensive discussions with Frank Costigliola, Joan Hoff Wilson, Michael J. Hogan, Robert Van Meter, and Denise Artaud. Their willingness to exchange ideas with me, their concern with my work, and their continual encouragement of my efforts have been greatly appreciated.

Many historians, librarians, and institutions have helped bring this work to fruition. At various times I have received friendly advice and constructive criticism from Jules Davids, William Becker, Samuel F. Wells, Ellis W. Hawley, Kermit Hall, and Hans Trefousse. At a critical moment in the preparation of this book, my colleague, Charles F. Delzell, took time from a busy schedule to read my manuscript with care. I shall always be grateful to him for his aid. Although I have received courteous attention and expert advice wherever I have carried on my research, I particularly want to express my gratitude to Thomas T. Thalken and Robert S. Woods of the Herbert Hoover Presidential Library. They went out of their way to make my visit to West Branch, Iowa, a pleasant and productive experience. In addition to the many individuals who have been so generous with their time, I also wish to thank the Vanderbilt University Research Council, the American Council of Learned Societies, and the Mershon Foundation for being equally generous with their funds. Grants from these institutions greatly facilitated the research and writing of my manuscript.

From the inception of this book, my wife Phyllis has been an invaluable partner. Frequently, she has deferred work on her own manuscript in order to aid me. Although she has not always been content with the rapidity of my progress, she has always had confidence in my ability to bring this project to a conclusion. An historian in her own right, she has urged me to deal with the larger questions of interpretation and has prodded me to place technical financial questions in clear perspective. More than anything else, however, she has never allowed me to forget that the pursuit of historical knowledge is but one way to fulfill the human spirit.

Abbreviations

AAA	Agricultural Adjustment Act
ABA	American Bankers Association
AEA	American Economic Association
AFBF	American Farm Bureau Federation
BFDC	Bureau of Foreign and Domestic Commerce
BIS	Bank for International Settlements
CCUS	Chamber of Commerce of the United States
CNO	Chief of Naval Operations
DBFP	Documents on British Foreign Policy
DDB	Documents diplomatiques belges
DDF	Documents diplomatiques français
FR	Papers Relating to the Foreign Relations of the United States
FR, PPC	Papers Relating to the Foreign Relations of the United States: The Paris Peace Conference
FRBNY	Federal Reserve Bank of New York
HHCD	Herbert C. Hoover Commerce Department Papers
HHPL	Herbert Hoover Presidential Library
HHPP	Herbert C. Hoover Presidential Papers
HHPPP	Herbert C. Hoover Post-Presidential Papers
IBA	Investment Bankers Association
MID	Military Intelligence Division
NAM	National Association of Manufacturers
NFTC	National Foreign Trade Council

NIRA   National Industrial Recovery Act
ONI   Office of Naval Intelligence
PCF   Presidential Case File
PPC   Paris Peace Conference
PPF   Presidential Personal File
RFC   Reconstruction Finance Corporation
RG   Record Group
WDC   World War Foreign Debt Commission
WFC   War Finance Corporation
WPD   War Plans Division

The Elusive Quest

[*1*]

From Versailles to Washington, 1919–1921

The Great War decimated the population of Europe. It devastated enormous tracts of land, disrupted the economic life of nations, and accentuated social unrest. It magnified nationalist fervor, intensified ideological differences, and bequeathed a legacy of hate. During peace negotiations the leaders of the Allied and Associated powers sought to lay the basis of a stable and secure world while combating the forces and destroying the roots of bolshevism. Accordingly, they assumed the tasks of establishing new nations, redrawing national boundaries, imposing sanctions, distributing relief, and creating a new international organization. Their labors, arduous as they were, demanded compromise and conciliation. No leader was entirely satisfied with the terms of the peace negotiated at Paris. Yet, European economic turmoil and social strife impelled action; a formal peace seemed an indispensable prerequisite of the stability of Europe, the security of France, and the well-being of the United States.

Wilsonian Peacemaking and French Security

At the Paris Peace Conference, President Woodrow Wilson was beleaguered by conflicting impulses and contradictory pressures. On the one hand he sympathized with the French quest for security and appreciated their "sense of danger."[1] He understood the particular dilemmas faced by French statesmen as they endeavored to protect their homeland against the demographic and industrial superiority of Germany. Addressing the French Senate on 20 January 1919, the American president declared that France stood "at the frontier of

1. Senate, Committee on Foreign Relations, *Treaty of Peace with Germany*, p. 544.

freedom'' and would ''never again'' have to face ''a lonely peril'' or have to ''ask the question who would come to her assistance.'' Frenchmen had to be assured, Wilson insisted, ''that the same thing will happen always that happened this time, that there shall never be any doubt or waiting or surmise, but that whenever France or any other free people is threatened the whole world will be ready to vindicate its liberty.''[2]

Yet, though he sympathized with the French quest for security, Wilson did not wish to provide for such security through a return to traditional balance-of-power politics. The balance of power in his view was part of the old order, inherently unstable, and the source of competitive armaments and international rivalries.[3] The president did not want the United States to become part of such a system. Accordingly, he frowned upon the traditional alliance system, emphasized America's historical aloofness from European politics, and renounced any intention to play the role of broker or balancer in Europe's wanton game of power politics.[4] Nor did Wilson wish to enhance French security through the dismemberment of Germany or the emasculation of her economic and industrial potential. Such attempts, he maintained, were certain to be countereffective and dangerous to French interests over the long run.[5] A harsh peace he could accept; but an unjust peace, Wilson warned, would drive Germany into the hands of the Bolsheviks or engender an atmosphere of lasting enmity and permanent revenge. The president wanted Germany to pay for her mistakes, but he also wanted to reintegrate Germany into a postwar liberal capitalist order that would be both prosperous and stable. Wilson assumed that, once a participant in such an order, Germany would be peaceful and cooperative, French security would no longer be jeopardized, and American economic interests would be enhanced.[6]

There was considerable tension between Wilson's sympathy for France and his desire to reintegrate Germany into a prosperous world order, between his concern for French security and his antipathy toward balance of power politics, and between his desire to preserve Allied unity and his aversion to alliances. He believed, however, that these apparent inconsistencies and contradictions could be reconciled

2. Woodrow Wilson, *The Public Papers of Woodrow Wilson*, 5:393, 406–7.
3. See, for example, ibid., p. 342.
4. Ibid., p. 354.
5. Ray Stannard Baker, *Woodrow Wilson and World Settlement*, 2:10–12.
6. Paul Mantoux, ed., *Les Délibérations du conseil des quatre*, 1:28–29, 41, 71–72; Wilson, *Public Papers*, 5:635–36. See also N. Gordon Levin, Jr., *Woodrow Wilson and World Politics*, pp. 123–53.

through the creation of the League of Nations. Wilson considered the League to be the keystone of all his work because it provided a mechanism for maintaining French amity while coopting Germany into a new order, for guaranteeing French security while sublimating alliance systems, and for preserving Allied unity while minimizing American embroilments in European politics.[7]

Wilson believed that the League could accomplish such diverse objectives without obligating the United States to dangerous strategic commitments. This was the result, he insisted, of his careful framing of the covenant to safeguard America's independence in military matters.[8] Although he championed Article 10 of the covenant, which obligated League members to protect the territorial integrity of one another against external aggression, Wilson refused to allow specific sanctions to be tied to this article and considered it a strictly moral obligation.[9] Within the League Commission, he labored to preserve the veto, safeguard the Monroe Doctrine, and oppose binding arbitration.[10] Furthermore, he objected to proposals calling for the creation of an international army and a military planning staff.[11] These actions reflected Wilson's efforts to balance his desire for French security with his reluctance to compromise independent American decision making in military matters.

French Premier Georges Clemenceau did not share Wilson's enthusiasm for the new international organization. The French premier was preoccupied with guaranteeing future French security. Clemenceau believed in the efficacy of traditional balance-of-power methods to accomplish this goal and distrusted new and untried experiments.[12] Although Wilson and Colonel Edward M. House, one of the American

7. For Wilson's views on the League of Nations, see, for example, Wilson, *Public Papers*, 5:330, 353–54, 395–97, 408, 446, 452–53, 523, 544–49, 575–79; see also Edward M. House, *The Intimate Papers of Colonel House*, 4:279–83, 410. For Wilson's eagerness to bring Germany into the League of Nations, see Department of State, *Papers Relating to the Foreign Relations of the United States: The Paris Peace Conference*, 6:157–58, 11:219 (hereafter cited as FR, PPC).

8. See, for example, Wilson's press interview, 10 July 1919, Woodrow Wilson Papers, Series 2, Reel 103; Wilson, *Public Papers*, 5:575–79, 593–98, 611–14, 631–33; Senate, Foreign Relations, *Treaty of Peace with Germany*, pp. 509–11, 515, 535–38, 548–49.

9. For Wilson's opposition to linking sanctions to Article 10, see David Hunter Miller, *The Drafting of the Covenant*, 1:170, 177–82; for Wilson's emphasis on Article 10 as a moral obligation, see Wilson, *Public Papers*, 5:579; see also Lloyd E. Ambrosius, "Wilson's League of Nations," pp. 369–78.

10. Ambrosius, "Wilson's League," pp. 376–79, 385–87.

11. Miller, *Drafting of the Covenant*, 2:290–97, 320–22, 344–47.

12. John Hampden Jackson, *Clemenceau and the Third Republic*, pp. 189–90;

peace commissioners, tried to convince him that the League, in general, and Article 10, in particular, were aimed at providing security for France, Clemenceau remained dubious. He realized that although Wilson ostensibly committed the United States to safeguarding the peace of Europe, the president's multifaceted conception of the League did not fully guarantee the security of France nor insure the prompt and complete collaboration of the United States in deterring aggression.[13] Similarly, Clemenceau recognized that Wilson's antipathy toward commissions to enforce the armaments provisions of the peace treaty and his readiness to invite a reformed Germany into the new organization conflicted with the French premier's desire to perpetuate the wartime coalition as an instrument for enhancing French security against Germany in the postwar era.[14]

Clemenceau eventually acquiesced to French participation in a new international organization, but he would not entrust the safeguarding of French security to it, especially as long as there were no provisions for an international army and a military planning staff.[15] When Wilson returned to Paris in mid-March after a brief trip to the United States, he was confronted with a concerted effort by the French delegates to achieve more concrete guarantees of French security. The French wanted to establish a separate Rhineland state, occupy the Rhine bridgeheads for thirty years, demilitarize both the left and right banks of the Rhine, and limit German land and naval armaments. In a long memorandum on these issues André Tardieu, one of the French plenipotentiaries at the peace conference, explained that the League did not afford France a "zone of safety" comparable to the physical guarantees enjoyed by Great Britain and the United States. Nor did it insure France against another invasion since there would be an interval of time before League members, especially the United States, could provide tangible aid to defeat Germany. Thus, the only way France could

---

Jacques Chastenet, *Histoire de la Troisième République*, 5:22; Walter Allan McDougall, "French Rhineland Policy and the Struggle for European Stabilization," pp. 26–33.

13. For the arguments of Wilson and House, see Wilson, *Public Papers*, 5:407–8; House, *Intimate Papers*, 4:254–55, 270; Baker, *Woodrow Wilson*, 1:288; for Clemenceau's doubts and French anxieties, see Mantoux, *Conseil des quatre*, 1:42–45; Baker, *Woodrow Wilson*, 1:320–39; Miller, *Drafting of the Covenant*, 1:442–50, 2:290–97, 372–73.

14. Baker, *Woodrow Wilson*, 1:363–65; FR, PPC, 6:158; McDougall, "French Rhineland Policy," pp. 3–4.

15. For French demands for an international army and military planning staff, see Miller, *Drafting of the Covenant*, 2:290–97, 320–22, 344–47; FR, PPC, 3:219–24; see also Mantoux, *Conseil des quatre*, 1:15.

achieve certainty against another German attack was by establishing an independent Rhenish republic.[16]

Wilson understood French worries that in an emergency the League might not function quickly enough to prevent another invasion of France.[17] But, like British Prime Minister David Lloyd George, the president feared that dismemberment of Germany and occupation of her territory would embitter her citizens, plant the seeds of another conflict, and violate the self-determination principles of the Fourteen Points. Consequently, he supported Lloyd George's suggestion that Great Britain and the United States offer strategic guarantees to France in return for the latter's abandonment of her aims in the Rhineland. Such an arrangement, the president hoped, would insure French security without permanently alienating Germany, foreclosing the eventual reintegration of that nation into a new order. His offer of an American security guarantee in mid-March represented his own effort to conciliate the French and expedite the proceedings at Paris at a time when the rumblings of revolution throughout central Europe were growing more ominous and the demands in America for a more rapid demobilization from the Continent were growing more strident.[18]

Clemenceau discussed the offer of an Anglo-American security guarantee with his closest advisers, Tardieu, Louis Loucheur, and Stephen Pichon. They were eager to extract long-term strategic commitments from their allies, but were unwilling to relinquish unilateral physical guarantees. Too many imponderables raised doubts about the efficacy of foreign political guarantees. How permanent would they be? How effectively would they operate? The French, therefore, modified their demands for physical guarantees but did not abandon them altogether. Clemenceau withdrew his plea for a separate Rhenish republic in return for the Anglo-American guarantee pacts, but he still insisted on the demilitarization of the right and left banks of the Rhine. Moreover, he wanted a permanent commission established to insure Germany's compliance with the demilitarization and disarmament clauses of the Versailles treaty. Clemenceau demanded that any

16. André Tardieu, *The Truth about the Treaty*, pp. 125–201, especially pp. 147–67. The quotation is on p. 157. See also Baker, *Woodrow Wilson*, 2:1–83; McDougall, "French Rhineland Policy," pp. 32–35.

17. House, *Intimate Papers*, 4:205; Louis Allmond Richard Yates, *United States and French Security, 1917–1921*, p. 45.

18. Baker, *Woodrow Wilson*, 1:314–39, 2:8–22, 33–38, 53–57, 122–23; House, *Intimate Papers*, 4:391–96; Mantoux, *Conseil des quatre*, 1:41–51; David Lloyd George, *Memoirs of the Peace Conference*, 265–66; Yates, *United States and French Security*, pp. 44–52.

violation of these provisions be interpreted as an act of aggression that would entitle France to reoccupy parts of the Rhineland and activate the Anglo-American guarantees. In addition, the French still insisted on Allied occupation of the Rhine bridgeheads for thirty years. Accordingly, France launched a campaign to increase the amount and extend the duration of Germany's reparation payments and claimed that the prolonged occupation was necessary to enforce these treaty provisions. Finally, the French premier asked the British and Americans to recognize the enlarged French frontier of 1814 and allow France to occupy the Saar coal basin.[19]

As the issues of the occupation and demilitarization of the Rhineland, the payment of reparations, the administration of the Saar, and the granting of strategic guarantees became increasingly interrelated, the peace conference reached an impasse. Wilson and Clemenceau became infuriated with one another. The French premier charged that Wilson was pro-German and stormed out of a meeting of the Council of Four. The American president, exasperated and ill, contemplated leaving the conference.[20] The French press unleashed a bitter attack against Wilson for disregarding France's strategic anxieties and for discounting French claims on the Rhine.[21] Meanwhile, European conditions worsened. On 4 April, Secretary of State Robert Lansing noted that central Europe was "aflame" with anarchy. The red armies were advancing westward. "Hungary," he wrote, "is in the clutches of revolutionists; Berlin, Vienna and Munich are turning toward the Bolsheviks."[22]

Domestic and international political, economic, and social factors demanded that Wilson and Clemenceau resolve their differences. Under Colonel House's prodding Wilson retreated on the reparations issue and agreed to leave both the amount of the indemnity and the number of annuities unspecified. He consented to the demilitarization of the Rhineland but succeeded at confining the demilitarized area to fifty kilometers on the right bank. He accepted French economic control of

19. Ministère des Affaires Etrangères, *Documents relatifs aux négociations concernant les garanties de sécurité contre une agression de l'Allemagne (10 janvier 1919–7 décembre 1923)*, pp. 32–35; Tardieu, *Truth about the Treaty*, pp. 176–209; Louis Loucheur, *Carnets secrets, 1908–1932*, pp. 71–73; Mantoux, *Conseil des quatre*, 1:50–51, 63–65, 89–91; Keith L. Nelson, *Victors Divided*, pp. 79–85; McDougall, "French Rhineland Policy," pp. 53–58.

20. Baker, *Woodrow Wilson*, 2:23–58; House, *Intimate Papers*, 4:396.

21. William G. Sharp to American Mission, 31 March 1919, Woodrow Wilson Papers, Series 5B, Reel 398.

22. Confidential memorandum, 4 April 1919, Lansing Papers, Box 66.

the Saar and the political alienation of that region from Germany for fifteen years. Wilson insisted, however, that the administration of the Saar be turned over to the League of Nations, and he resisted French attempts to regain part of this territory. He reluctantly assented to a fifteen-year, inter-Allied occupation of the Rhineland, but he persuaded the French to evacuate the occupied area in stages beginning after five years. Finally, Wilson accepted a separate treaty obligating the United States to aid France in case of unprovoked aggression and defining any violation of the demilitarized zone as a *casus belli*. The president also agreed that this guarantee pact would remain in force until the Council of the League of Nations acknowledged that the League provided adequate security.[23]

Wilson's concessions, although substantial, were by no means unilateral. Clemenceau abandoned the French demand for a separate Rhenish republic, renounced French efforts to establish the 1814 frontier, acquiesced to a League of Nation's administration of the Saar, accepted a fifteen (rather than thirty) year occcupation period, and compromised on a fifty-kilometer demilitarized zone on the right bank of the Rhine.[24] He relinquished what many Frenchmen considered to be a strategic frontier on the Rhine to preserve Allied unity and gain the Anglo-American security guarantees.[25] His concessions were bitterly resented by Raymond Poincaré, president of the Republic, and Marshall Ferdinand Foch, commander of the Allied armies. They criticized Clemenceau for putting too much faith in Anglo-American promises and commitments—promises that might be repudiated by the appropriate legislative bodies in either nation; commitments that might be implemented tardily while France was bled white.[26] The French premier recognized the risks inherent in a course of action that relied exclusively on foreign aid. Consequently, he refused to abandon all the physical guarantees and sought a provision, incorporated into Article 429 of the Treaty of Versailles, that allowed the evacuation of troops in the Rhineland to be delayed more than fifteen years if guarantees

23. For the gradual resolution of Franco-American differences during the first two weeks of April, see Mantoux, *Conseil des quatre*, especially 1:41–51, 63–75, 89–95, 143–46, 151–65, 168–78, 193–94, 203–7, 214–22; Baker, *Woodrow Wilson*, 2:59–83; House, *Intimate Papers*, 4:396–408; Tardieu, *Truth about the Treaty*, pp. 182–217; Nelson, *Victors Divided*, 80–91; Yates, *United States and French Security*, pp. 44–97.

24. See note 23 above.

25. Georges Clemenceau, *Grandeur and Misery of Victory*, pp. 195, 234–39; Jackson, *Clemenceau*, pp. 211–12.

26. Raymond Poincaré, *Au Service de la France*, 11:363–64; Ministère des Affaires Etrangères, *Garanties de sécurité*, pp. 35–38, 52–55; Jere Clemens King, *Foch versus Clemenceau*, pp. 47–48; Pierre Miquel, *Raymond Poincaré*, pp. 381–403.

against unprovoked aggression were not considered adequate by the Allied and Associated governments. Thus, Clemenceau tried to insure France's strategic defenses, should the United States or Britain renege on their commitments. For the French premier, the Rhineland occupation still constituted the critical guarantee of Germany's compliance.[27] Although Foch and Poincaré remained critical of Clemenceau's compromises, their attempts to muster public and parliamentary support of their position failed. In general, the French people seemed to feel as did Clemenceau: the treaty did not meet France's maximum needs, but it was the best that could be had in a very trying situation.[28]

Among the American peace commissioners, however, there was a strong feeling that Wilson had gone too far to placate French apprehensions and had failed to adequately balance French demands, German needs, and American commitments. Secretary of State Lansing bitterly condemned French policies and deplored Wilson's efforts to conciliate the French. Lansing criticized the League as an instrument designed by the mighty to preserve a dangerous and inherently unstable status quo. Like his fellow peace commissioners General Tasker H. Bliss and Henry White, he voiced grave reservations about the separate security pact with France. Lansing felt that an alliance with France was "extremely unfortunate, and absolutely fatal to the League of Nations." The secretary of state contended that Wilson did not realize that the security pact would increase the anxiety of eastern Europeans, since Germany would seek to expand in their direction. Moreover, Lansing believed that the separate treaty with France would be badly received in the United States where the tradition of nonentanglement remained strong.[29]

President Wilson, although contemptuous of his secretary of state, shared some of Lansing's misgivings. Wilson acknowledged that he had made major concessions pertaining to the reparation, territorial, and occupation clauses of the Versailles treaty that were likely to complicate subsequent efforts to integrate a reformed Germany into a prosperous liberal capitalist order. Yet, this was the price he had to pay to preserve Allied unity and gain French adherence to a revised League covenant. Wilson was not unaware of the political pressures bearing

27. Clemenceau, *Grandeur and Misery*, pp. 195, 236–38, 243; Tardieu, *Truth about the Treaty*, pp. 210–17; McDougall, "French Rhineland Policy," pp. 65, 75–76.
28. Pierre Miquel, *La Paix de Versailles et l'opinion publique française*, pp. 215–419, especially pp. 283–387.
29. For Lansing's views, see confidential memoranda, 20, 28 March, 5, 8 May 1919, Lansing Papers, Box 66; FR, PPC, 11:124, 126, 133.

on his principal antagonist, Clemenceau, and he feared that further attempts to wring concessions might delay the consummation of the peace and postpone reconstruction efforts.[30]

Wilson, however, remained apprehensive about the ramifications of the security pact with France. He worried that the Anglo-American guarantee might overcommit the United States, violate the principles of the League of Nations, and depart too radically from precedents. Therefore, he equivocated on its meaning. While in Paris the president refused to state publicly whether German violations of the demilitarization provisions, Articles 42 and 43 of the Treaty of Versailles, obligated the United States to send immediate aid to France. Instead, he let it be announced that in the event of unprovoked aggression the United States would provide help.[31] When subsequently asked what constituted unprovoked aggression, Wilson ambiguously retorted that he could not define it but "would know it when I saw it."[32] Moreover, after he returned to the United States, the president subordinated the issue of French security. He did not submit the guarantee pact to the Senate on 10 July at the time that he presented the Treaty of Versailles. When compelled to submit the separate treaty later in the month, Wilson warmly supported it but spoke of it as a temporary commitment, subordinate to the new international organization and rendered inoperative by the effective functioning of the latter.[33]

Wilson's attempt to minimize American commitments under the guarantee pact paralleled his effort to limit the nature of American obligations under Article 10 of the League covenant. The president reiterated that the covenant did not legally bind the United States to use force to deter aggression. Certain provisions, he explained, did obligate the United States to implement an economic boycott but did not demand the automatic application of military force. Wilson defined Article 10 as "a very grave and solemn moral obligation. But it is a moral, not a legal obligation, and leaves our Congress absolutely free to put its own interpretation upon it in all cases that call for action. It is binding in conscience only, not in law."[34] Though Wilson acknowl-

---

30. For Wilson's misgivings about the treaty and his decision to go ahead with it, see Baker, *Woodrow Wilson*, 2:1–123; FR, PPC, 11:218–22.

31. FR, PPC, 5:474–76, 485–86, 494–95.

32. Press interview, 10 July 1919, Woodrow Wilson Papers, Series 2, Reel 103.

33. Wilson, *Public Papers*, 5:549–50, 555–57; see also press interview, 10 July 1919, Woodrow Wilson Papers.

34. Wilson, *Public Papers*, 5:579; see also, for example, pp. 597, 611–13; press interview, 10 July 1919, Woodrow Wilson Papers.

edged that a moral obligation might be superior to a legal obligation, he nevertheless stressed that a moral commitment implied discretion. Therefore, he said that the United States would not have to use force either under Article 10 or under the guarantee pact until it was convinced that unprovoked aggression had occurred. The United States in other words might disagree with other nations on whether aggression had taken place and might act accordingly. Moreover, the president asserted that under Article 10 the territorial integrity of nations was not violated by armed intervention but only by the retention of territory.[35]

In his defense of Article 10 and the guarantee pact, Wilson emphasized that he was not compromising America's right to independent judgment nor jeopardizing its right to independent action. When Senators Warren G. Harding and Frank B. Brandegee inquired whether American commitments constituted much of a deterrence to aggression if the United States could interpret these obligations unilaterally, the president scorned this line of questioning. Fundamentally, Wilson believed that good judgment would enable the American government to reconcile its desire for aloofness from European politics with its desire to afford protection to France.[36] He did not think the commitments he had entered into endangered the nation, because he believed that the experience of the recent war demonstrated that the United States would become embroiled in a European conflict regardless of whether these obligations existed or not. Indeed, Wilson hoped that their existence would serve to deter aggression and preserve peace.[37] Thus, somewhat paradoxically, while narrowly defining American commitments under Article 10, the president considered it "the very backbone of the whole Covenant"; while minimizing the implications of the alliance with France, Wilson emphasized that Senate ratification would "be one of the handsomest acts of history."[38]

There was much uncertainty in Wilson's rhetoric about how the League could alleviate German grievances, yet preserve the territorial status quo. Equal ambiguity existed about how the guarantee pact

35. Senate, Foreign Relations, *Treaty of Peace with Germany*, pp. 510–11, 515–16, 535–39; for Wilson's careful modification of his commitments toward France, see Lloyd E. Ambrosius, "Wilson, Clemenceau, and the German Peace Problem," pp. 69–81.

36. Senate, Foreign Relations, *Treaty of Peace with Germany*, pp. 515–16, 535–39, 549–51.

37. Ibid., pp. 535–36; see also, for example, Wilson, *Public Papers*, 5:594, 597, 612–15.

38. Wilson, *Public Papers*, 5:579; Senate, Foreign Relations, *Treaty of Peace with Germany*, p. 544.

and Article 10 could satisfy France's quest for security, yet leave America's freedom of action unimpaired. Wilson's desires to enhance French security, to rehabilitate a liberal Germany, and to circumscribe American strategic commitments in the Old World were constantly at odds with one another. His belief that contradictory impulses could be reconciled through the instruments he had fashioned was an act of faith.[39] Despite his exhaustive defense of his work at Paris, he never satisfactorily answered the enigma of how Article 10 could provide effective security to France and other nations without either compromising America's independence of action or embroiling the nation in disputes unrelated to its vital interests. Rather than face this dilemma he preferred to stress the efficacy of economic boycotts and to disregard the question of what the United States would do militarily in case of violations of Article 10 of the covenant or Articles 42 and 43 of the treaty.[40]

Wilson's attempt to balance inherently contradictory goals through the League mechanism exposed him and his work to criticism from all directions. Liberals, like Senators Robert M. LaFollette and George W. Norris, accused him of betraying the Fourteen Points and of engineering a vindictive and oppressive peace. Conservative nationalists, like Senators Brandegee and Philander C. Knox, condemned him for sacrificing the nation's realistic interests, negotiating too lenient a treaty, and disregarding France's legitimate demands. Isolationists, like Senators William E. Borah and Hiram W. Johnson, denounced him for compromising the nation's independence of action and ignoring Washington's dictum against entangling alliances. Faced with such disparate criticism and believing that there was no alternative means of balancing conflicting imperatives, Wilson was determined not only to thwart his irreconcilable opponents but also to defeat all substantive reservations proposed by Senator Henry Cabot Lodge and other Republican critics. The president believed that he had the support of the American people, that he could tap this latent grass roots sentiment, and that he could subject wavering senators to popular pressure.[41]

39. For a perceptive critique of the ambiguities inherent in the League of Nations, see Roland Stromberg, "Uncertainties and Obscurities about the League of Nations," pp. 139–54.

40. These generalizations are based on an analysis of Wilson's speeches in defense of the treaty and the League. See, for example, Wilson, *Public Papers*, 5:590–645, 6:1–416.

41. For the motivations and tactics of Wilson's irreconcilable opponents, see Ralph Stone, *The Irreconcilables*; for Wilson's approach to the struggle over the ratification of the treaty, see, for example, Thomas A. Bailey, *Woodrow Wilson and the Great Be-*

Wilson embarked upon an ambitious speaking tour during which he was stricken with a cerebral thrombosis. This affliction seemed to toughen his stand. Lacking sufficient access to information and unable to assess the extent of Senate opposition, he was less inclined than ever to make substantive concessions. His rigidity played into the hands of his opponents. Although the vast majority of senators supported the Versailles treaty in some form, Wilson's refusal to compromise with the reservationists allowed the irreconcilables to defeat the entire treaty in November 1919.[42]

As soon as the treaty was defeated, Wilson permitted Lansing to withdraw the remaining American peace commissioners from Paris and to terminate formal American participation in the Supreme Allied Council. Although these moves were intended to dramatize the ramifications of the Senate's action and influence the votes of Republican reservationists,[43] they had a more noticeable effect on French opinion. As the controversy over ratification reached a climax in November, the French remained worried but circumspect.[44] Once America's departure from Paris seemed imminent, however, there was an outburst of anti-American sentiment. On 6 December Ambassador Hugh Wallace reported that "disappointment concerning America and the reported revival of German militarism which is laid at America's door have produced a distinct nationalist and militarist reaction."[45] Shortly thereafter, the new French government of the Bloc National under Premier Alexandre Millerand embarked upon a more independent foreign policy. Exasperated by Germany's failure to deliver her monthly coal quotas, the French toughened their occupation policy and in April

trayal, pp. 1–15, 72–207; John Chalmers Vinson, *Referendum for Isolation*, pp. 24–34, 86–100; Arthur C. Walworth, *Woodrow Wilson*, 2:333–94; Denna Frank Fleming, *The United States and the League of Nations*, pp. 232–401; for Wilson's belief that he had public opinion behind him, see, for example, Wilson, *Public Papers*, 5:444; for an appraisal of press sentiment toward the League, see "Nation-Wide Press Poll on the League of Nations," *Literary Digest* 61 (5 April 1919):13–14.

42. For the impact of Wilson's illness, see Edwin A. Weinstein, "Woodrow Wilson's Neurological Illness," pp. 324–51; for information on the Senate's vote against the treaty, see note 41 above.

43. FR, PPC, 11:695–96, 681–82, 692; see also Daniel M. Smith, *Aftermath of War*, pp. 35–37.

44. See the reports on French opinion emanating from the American embassy in Paris. Hugh Wallace to secretary, 10 November 1919, Records of the American Commission to Negotiate Peace, Record Group 256, File No. 851.9111/18; Warrington Dawson to secretary, 11 November 1919, General Records of the Department of State, Record Group 59, File No. 763.72119/8147 (hereafter cited as RG).

45. Wallace to secretary, 6 December 1919, RG 256, 851.9111/19.

1920 moved into Frankfurt. Millerand insisted that the latter action was prompted by the illegal entry of German troops into the demilitarized zone and the consequent violation of Article 43 of the Treaty of Versailles.[46]

American officials became exasperated with French policy. Since German troop movements had ostensibly been aimed at preserving order and preventing revolution, the French response seemed inappropriate. Wilson lost all confidence in the French. "What has evidently happened," he wrote, "is that Foch has at last gained his object. He showed, while I was in Paris, a perfect obsession with regard to the Rhine provinces, and at last he has been indulged in his desire to get a hold upon them. He will not be dislodged except by the most vigorous action of the French Government."[47] The president always had maintained that European stability depended upon reconciling France's security needs with Germany's economic and political rehabilitation. The guarantee pact had been aimed at protecting France without dismembering Germany. Now, ironically, France was alluding to the guarantee pact to justify her punitive actions in the Rhineland.[48] Such logic did not appeal to Wilson. Ignoring the impact of the United States Senate's actions on French behavior, he insisted that French policies had greatly diverged from his own position at Paris. Therefore, he considered it wise to stay aloof from European affairs. He made no effort to secure Senate ratification of the guarantee pact, even though there had initially been substantial Republican support for a separate alliance with France.[49]

Paradoxically, while Wilson increasingly condemned "the follies of Europe,"[50] he still insisted on ratification of the Treaty of Versailles without reservations. After the Senate's initial defeat of the treaty in November, some of the president's closest advisers at Paris—including

46. Department of State, *Papers Relating to the Foreign Relations of the United States*, 1920, 2:290–326 (hereafter cited as FR). See also Nelson, *Victors Divided*, pp. 144–73; McDougall, "French Rhineland Policy," pp. 99–104.

47. Wilson to Bainbridge Colby, 8 April 1920, Colby Papers, Box 2; FR, 1920, 2:297–326.

48. FR, 1920, 2:312–14.

49. Wilson to Colby, 17 April 1920, Colby Papers, Box 2; see also Wilson to Colby, 12 November 1920, ibid., Box 3B; Smith, *Aftermath of War*, pp. 50–55; for Republican support of the guarantee pact, see Lloyd E. Ambrosius, "Wilson, the Republicans, and French Security after World War I," pp. 341–52; Yates, *United States and French Security*, pp. 136–38; for the reaction of the public and the press, see Glenn Howard Coston, "The American Reaction to the Post-First World War Search of France for Security, 1919–1930," pp. 108–39.

50. Wilson to Colby, 4 October 1920, Colby Papers, Box 3B.

Colonel House, Norman H. Davis, Bernard M. Baruch, and Herbert C. Hoover—urged him to compromise.[51] Meanwhile, Senators Gilbert Hitchcock and Furnifold Simmons carried on negotiations with Lodge and other reservationists trying to work out a mutually acceptable formula.[52] Some progress might have been possible had Wilson been willing to compromise, especially with regard to the proposed reservation to Article 10 of the League covenant. This reservation would have specified that the recommendations of the League Council would not become binding until approved by Congress. Wilson had always concurred that the United States could not act legally under Article 10 without the consent of Congress. But he refused to make this explicit in the form of a reservation. During the winter and spring of 1920 the president contended that such a reservation would eliminate the moral obligation of the United States to deter aggression and would betray America's allies, invite new aggression, and undermine the structure of peace.[53]

Wilson's arguments were not very convincing. For the most part the proposed reservation to Article 10 did not create new ambiguities in the treaty. Hence, it is understandable why many American internationalists disagreed with his intransigent position.[54] When the president charged that the reservation would weaken the moral obligations inherent in Article 10 and therefore invite aggression, he was overestimating the efficacy of moral guarantees as well as disregarding his previously stated belief that moral obligations did not obviate America's duty to use its discretion in applying military sanctions.[55] When he argued that reservations would betray America's allies, Wilson also ignored the fact that Frenchmen were already aware of possible gaps between American promises and American actions and between French and American conceptions of French security.[56]

Clemenceau, in fact, had never believed that American obligations

51. House to Wilson, 24 November 1919, Woodrow Wilson Papers, Series 2, Reel 105; Davis to Joseph Tumulty, 1 December 1919, ibid.; Hoover to Wilson, 19 November 1919, ibid.; Walworth, *Woodrow Wilson*, 2:383–94.

52. Bailey, *Great Betrayal*, pp. 226–32; Fleming, *United States and the League of Nations*, pp. 402–16; Vinson, *Referendum for Isolation*, pp. 96–109.

53. Wilson, *Public Papers*, 6:453–56, 460–61, 484; see also Vinson, *Referendum for Isolation*, pp. 86–109.

54. Warren F. Kuehl, *Seeking World Order*, pp. 298–331.

55. Senate, Foreign Relations, *Treaty of Peace with Germany*, pp. 510–11, 515–16, 535–39.

56. See, for example, Miller, *Drafting of the Covenant*, 2:374; McDougall, "French Rhineland Policy," pp. 65–66.

under Article 10 and the guarantee pact fully insured French security. Having observed Wilson's efforts to balance various American goals at Versailles, Clemenceau attached more importance to preserving Allied unity than to the precise form of American guarantees, which he knew would remain unpredictable in any case. Consequently, he became exasperated when Wilson refused to accept reservations. Several French newspapers discussed the same points and traversed the same course as Clemenceau. Since ratification of the unamended treaty would not necessarily overcome the practice of America's political aloofness, they concluded that it made little sense to insist on ratification without reservations. Not surprisingly, even before the United States Senate voted, Clemenceau and his opponents were considering the wisdom of taking independent action in the Rhineland to enhance French strategic interests.[57]

Thus, Wilson's position was not based on a hardheaded and pragmatic assessment of the political situation at home or of diplomatic realities abroad.[58] In March 1920 he refused to allow his supporters to vote for reservations. As a result, the treaty went down to a second defeat.[59] Even then Wilson did not regret his policies. "The dead treaty," he wrote, "lies very heavy on the consciences of those who killed it and I am content to let it lie there until those consciences are either crushed or awakened." He called upon the Democratic party to make the League issue the focal point of the forthcoming election. He hoped to be vindicated in a great national referendum. Meanwhile, he vetoed congressional resolutions that would have ended the technical

57. For Clemenceau's concern with the preservation of Allied unity and his disgust with Wilson's position regarding reservations, see Clemenceau, *Grandeur and Misery*, pp. 199, 233–39, 259; for the importance of preserving Allied unity, see Tardieu's defense of the treaty before the Chamber in Ministère des Affaires Etrangères, *Garanties de sécurité*, pp. 61–62; for Clemenceau's recognition that the treaties were not perfect, see Yates, *United States and French Security*, pp. 103–4; for the prospect of independent French action in the Rhineland, see McDougall, "French Rhineland Policy," pp. 80–88; for references to the French press, see Wallace to secretary, 10 November 1919, RG 256, 851.9111/18; Wallace to secretary, 12 December 1919, ibid., 851.00/50; see also Bailey, *Great Betrayal*, p. 241.
    58. Historians have disagreed about whether the reservations to Article 10 constituted a significant weakening of the powers of the League of Nations. For a brief analysis that differs with my viewpoint, see Kuehl, *Seeking World Order*, pp. 337–38.
    59. There seems to be an emerging consensus among historians that Lodge and other Republican reservationists would have accepted the treaty had it been modified to suit their demands. See, for example, Vinson, *Referendum for Isolation*, pp. 110–20; Kuehl, *Seeking World Order*, pp. 332–45; Stone, *Irreconcilables*, pp. 128–77; John A. Garraty, *Henry Cabot Lodge*, pp. 357–91; James E. Hewes, "Henry Cabot Lodge and the League of Nations."

state of war that still existed between the United States and Germany.[60]

The United States was neither at peace nor at war. This ambivalent status enormously complicated the implementation of an effective postwar economic policy toward France and western Europe. But such concerns did not influence Wilson's behavior on the League or treaty issues. Wilson did not act as he did because he denied the importance of European economic reconstruction to American self-interest. Rather, Wilson's personality, his illness, and his passionate attachment to Article 10 and the League covenant warped his judgment. As a result, he subordinated the problems of economic reconstruction at home and abroad and ignored the inconsistency between his refusal to accept reservations, lest they betray the Allies, and his own actions, which already were upsetting both France and Britain.[61] Wilsonian peacemaking, therefore, failed to achieve its goals of enhancing French security, expediting Germany's reintegration into a liberal capitalist order, and clarifying America's strategic obligations to the Old World. In fact, these larger concerns were partly obscured by the controversy over Article 10 and the League covenant. Meanwhile, plans for the economic reconstruction of Europe had taken a back seat.

Economic Reconstruction Thwarted

At the peace conference Wilson focused much more attention on political issues than on economic ones. Afterwards, he felt awkward when he emphasized the economic advantages of the treaty.[62] But he was always aware of the complex interrelationships between the restoration of peace, the reconstruction of Europe, and the preservation of domestic stability and prosperity. When he returned from Europe in July, Wilson recognized both the nation's preoccupation with the high cost of living and the widespread fear of a slack in the postwar economy. Alarmed by the social strife he had observed in the Old World, the president was no less cognizant of the prevailing domestic labor unrest and internal social turmoil. Yet, Wilson presented no plan for the conversion of a wartime economy to peacetime. Instead, he

60. For the quotation, see Wilson to Colby, 2 April 1920, Colby Papers, Box 2; see also Wilson, *Public Papers*, 6:455–56, 483–85, 492–94.

61. For the impact of the stroke on Wilson's personality and actions, see Arthur Link's comments in John A. Garraty, ed., *Interpreting American History*, 2:140; for Wilson's personality, see Alexander L. George and Juliette L. George, *Woodrow Wilson and Colonel House*.

62. Walworth, *Woodrow Wilson*, 2:334–35; Wilson, *Public Papers*, 5:640–41.

emphasized that the consummation of the peace, the ratification of the Treaty of Versailles, and the establishment of the League of Nations were the necessary prerequisites of internal social tranquility and orderly economic progress.[63]

The revitalization of America's best markets in the Old World depended upon the implementation of coherent policies relating to reparations, war debts, private loans, exchange fluctuations, and customs duties. Foreign demand could be boosted, as many of the president's advisers realized, if the United States supplied sufficient capital, deferred interest on the war debts, or increased imports. Yet, each of these tactical alternatives affected important domestic priorities: an expansion of credit might fuel inflationary tendencies; a generous policy on the war debts might defer the reduction of high wartime taxes, delay the consolidation of the national debt, and postpone the balancing of the budget; a lowering of tariff duties, especially at a time of widespread currency depreciation, might harm domestic-oriented manufacturers. Thus, policy had to be molded adroitly. Careful attention had to be paid to the domestic repercussions as well as to the foreign ramifications of any action.[64]

The problem was that Wilson's insistence on ratification without reservations engendered an atmosphere that made effective American policymaking on these difficult economic and financial issues almost impossible. A quick return to normalcy in Europe was unlikely under any circumstances; the ravages of the Great War had taken an unparalleled economic, financial, demographic, and spiritual toll.[65] But the legislative-executive impasse in the United States and the stalemate over ratification of the peace treaty further complicated American attempts to expedite financial and economic readjustments in the Old World in the immediate postwar years.

63. For Wilson's views, see, for example, Wilson, *Public Papers*, 5:559–71, 6:428–42; for Wilson's failure to present a plan for domestic reconversion, see Burt Noggle, *Into the Twenties*, pp. 31–65; see also Link's comments in Garraty, *Interpreting American History*, 2:138; for government policy and domestic economic and social developments, see also John D. Hicks, *Rehearsal for Disaster*; Robert K. Murray, *Red Scare*.

64. Several recent studies have analyzed the Wilson administration's search for foreign markets and European stability, but these accounts have not focused on the tension between domestic priorities and diplomatic goals. See Carl P. Parrini, *Heir to Empire*; Burton I. Kaufman, *Efficiency and Expansion*; Michael J. Hogan, *Informal Entente*, pp. 1–37; Robert H. Van Meter, "The United States and European Recovery, 1918–1923."

65. For an excellent study of European efforts to restore stability in the postwar era, see Charles S. Maier, *Recasting Bourgeois Europe*.

At Paris the financial and economic experts attached to the American peace delegation considered the reparations issue critical to Europe's postwar reconstruction. From the first tentative assessments of the indemnity to the final review of the peace terms, Paul Cravath, Thomas W. Lamont, Norman H. Davis, Vance C. McCormick, John Foster Dulles, and Bernard M. Baruch emphasized the importance of fixing the indemnity at a reasonable amount within Germany's capacity to pay. An excessive or indefinite reparations levy, they argued, would incapacitate Germany's economic potential, undermine her ability to consume, increase the chances of revolution, and ultimately reduce the amount she could pay. Furthermore, they maintained that a reasonable indemnity was essential to the rehabilitation of the credit of the Allies since they would try to use German reparation bonds as collateral for their own borrowings. If German obligations were too large, no one would have any confidence in these bonds, and they would not be able to serve as a basis for Allied credit.[66]

The president understood the importance of setting a fixed and reasonable indemnity to be liquidated within thirty years. Although he sacrificed the American position on these issues in order to gain French concessions, Wilson still hoped to exercise American influence within the newly created Reparation Commission.[67] The Reparation Commission was charged with assessing Germany's legal obligations and with arranging for the payment of appropriate indemnities. Lamont emphasized to the president that the commission would have enormous powers both to influence economic developments in Germany and to determine the course of financial affairs throughout Europe.[68] Accordingly, Wilson assumed that with quick ratification of the Treaty of Versailles, the American delegate would take a seat on the commission

66. For the views of the reparation experts as they began their work, see, for example, FR, PPC, 2:585–607, 619–21; for the development of their views, see the indispensable documents in Philip Mason Burnett, ed., *Reparation at the Paris Peace Conference from the Standpoint of the American Delegation*; see also, for example, Bernard Baruch, *The Making of the Reparation and Economic Sections of the Treaty*; Thomas W. Lamont, "Reparations," in Edward Mandell House and Charles Seymour, eds., *What Really Happened at Paris*, pp. 259–90; Ronald W. Pruessen, "John Foster Dulles and Reparations at the Paris Peace Conference, 1919," pp. 381–412.

67. One can follow the proceedings pertaining to reparations in the Council of Four during the crucial days of late March and early April, in Mantoux, *Conseil des quatre*, 1:15–17, 24–44, 58–62, 85–91, 151–65, 168–81, 214–22; see also House, *Intimate Papers*, 4:268–71, 381–83, 398–405; for Wilson's refusal to reopen the reparations issue at the close of the conference, see FR, PPC, 6:146, 156–57, 261–64, 11:198–205, 218–22.

68. Lamont to Wilson, 18 July 1919, Woodrow Wilson Papers, Series 2, Reel 103.

and play a leading role in its affairs. In this way the United States would not only be able to assure the payment of a reasonable German indemnity but also be able to oversee Germany's industrial revival and her economic reintegration into a western liberal capitalist community.[69]

Once the Senate defeated the treaty in November, however, Wilson's plans for effective American representation on the Reparation Commission collapsed. When the commission was established in December, the French and British arranged a deal giving the chairmanship of the commission to the former and the general secretaryship to the latter. American policymakers were dissatisfied but acknowledged their inability to protest, given the Senate's failure to ratify the Versailles treaty.[70] Subsequently, unofficial American representatives looked on futilely as decisions were made regardless of the American viewpoint. More significantly, State Department officials lamented the growing tendency of French and British officials to usurp authority from the commission and resolve key issues at summit conferences.[71] The United States, of course, had the opportunity to participate officially in the meetings at San Remo, Hythe, Spa, Boulogne, and Brussels.[72] Wilson, however, overruled the State Department's inclination to attend these conferences. He wanted to demonstrate his dissatisfaction with Allied policies and avoid additional conflict with the Senate while he sought ratification without reservations. The result of his actions, however, was to reduce American influence in the emerging reparation settlements.[73]

Meanwhile, officials in the State and Treasury departments observed the accords emanating from these conferences with keen dissatisfaction.[74] Deploring the way Britain and France were handling reparation matters, Secretary of State Bainbridge Colby considered submitting a formal protest to the Allied governments. After consulting with his colleagues, however, Colby decided that such a protest would expose the differences among the Allies and encourage Britain and France to

69. Wilson, *Public Papers*, 5:635–36.
70. Albert Rathbone to Davis, 15 December 1919, RG 59, 763.72119/8928.
71. For American discontent with the decisions and actions of the Reparation Commission, see, for example, FR, 1920, 2:382–85, 390–91, 399–400, 421–29, 433, 439.
72. For events at these conferences, especially as they related to reparations, see Etienne Weill-Raynal, *Les Réparations allemandes et la France*, 1:543–92.
73. See Wilson to Colby, 17 April 1920, Colby Papers, Box 2; Wilson to Colby, 29 May 1920, ibid., Box 3A; for the impact of America's absence from the Reparation Commission, see Carl Bergmann, *The History of Reparations*, pp. 22–24.
74. See, for example, Nicholas Kelley to secretary of the treasury, 11 October 1920, Records of the Bureau of Accounts, RG 39, Box 49.

sound out official American opinion, which could not be given because "of the state of mid-air suspension in which Congress has left the whole question of peace." Colby bemoaned the fact that he had no effective way of exercising American influence. If the peace treaty had been ratified, he remonstrated, the United States could have exercised a veto within the Reparation Commission.[75] Now, there was nothing he could do but watch the dismal sequence of events in Europe as the Allies bickered among themselves and quarreled with Germany over coal deliveries and indemnity payments. In February 1921, exasperated by the impotence of the American position and embarrassed by the outcome of the presidential election, the administration decided to withdraw its unofficial representative on the Reparation Commission.[76] Although convinced of the need to fix a reasonable indemnity within Germany's capacity to pay, the struggle over the League precluded the effective implementation of policy by the United States.

The French presented the greatest impediments to the conclusion of a reparations settlement according to American guidelines. France had contracted an enormous debt during the war and faced gigantic expenditures to reconstruct her devastated areas. The French government considered German reparation payments critical to the financial rehabilitation of their country. When Clemenceau and his finance minister, Louis-Lucien Klotz, encountered American opposition to their reparation plans at the peace conference, they developed an alternative strategy to alleviate French financial problems: the pooling of the costs of the war.[77] Accordingly, during 1919 and 1920 the French increasingly sought to link the issues of war debts and reparations. After Clemenceau left office, Millerand reluctantly agreed to modify French demands regarding German coal deliveries. But long-term French concessions on reparation matters, Wilson was informed, depended on a more lenient American policy on the war debt obligations owed to the United States government by her wartime Allies.[78]

From the onset officials in the Treasury Department asserted their

75. Colby to Wilson, 4 February 1921, Colby Papers, Box 4.
76. FR, 1921, 1:6–9.
77. For French tactics regarding the war debts at the peace conference, see testimony of Davis, House, Committee on Ways and Means, Executive Session, *Foreign Loans*, RG 39, Box 60, pp. 7–8; for French opinion, see Miquel, *Paix de Versailles*, pp. 419–94; George B. Noble, *Policies and Opinions at Paris*, 1919, pp. 394–97, 415–16; see also Wallace to secretary, 4 October 1919, RG 256, 851.00/40.
78. See Senate, Committee on Foreign Relations, Executive Session, *Credits to Foreign Governments*, RG 39, Box 218, p. 66; see also the testimony by Secretary of the Treasury David Houston, ibid., pp. 31–33; for Millerand's policies, see Maier, *Recasting Bourgeois Europe*, pp. 194–209.

authority over the war debts.[79] They opposed cancellation. During the peace conference Assistant Secretary Albert Rathbone warned the French that further machinations in behalf of debt cancellation or debt reapportionment would mean an immediate halt to additional American loans.[80] Treasury officials opposed cancellationist schemes because they believed that financial rehabilitation could take place if European nations curtailed their expenditures, reduced their armaments, balanced their budgets, settled the reparations controversy, and terminated discriminatory commercial practices. Moreover, these officials worried about the impact of war debt cancellation on domestic fiscal and economic policies. Wilson himself repeatedly emphasized the great importance of reducing taxes to foster orderly economic growth, and he was acutely aware that a generous policy on the war debts might jeopardize this domestic priority.[81]

Despite their stand against cancellation, Treasury officials were not inflexible in their approach to war debt questions. In the autumn of 1919 they decided to defer interest payments on the war debts for three years provided that European governments agreed to discuss the conversion of their demand obligations into long-term certificates of indebtedness. Secretary of the Treasury Carter Glass explained to the House Ways and Means Committee that European nations were financially incapacitated by the war. If compelled to make interest payments, their ability to purchase American goods would be undermined and their long-term ability to pay would be harmed.[82] While Glass did not indicate a readiness to cancel the war debts, Rathbone did acknowledge a willingness to make additional concessions to France. His was not a policy of generosity, he maintained; it was enlightened self-interest. The United States, he explained, had a substantial stake in the financial rehabilitation of France and the restoration of financial stability throughout Europe.[83] In other words, despite their opposition to cancellation, Treasury officials still hoped to formulate a war debt

79. See, for example, FR, PPC, 2:537–38, 544–46, 556.

80. World War Foreign Debt Commission (WDC), *Combined Annual Reports of the World War Foreign Debt Commission*, p. 66; House, Ways and Means, *Foreign Loans*, pp. 7–8.

81. For Treasury views, see, for example, Department of the Treasury, *Annual Report of the Secretary of the Treasury*, 1926, pp. 67–69; see also Denise Artaud, ''Le Gouvernement américain et la questions des dettes de guerre au lendemain de l'armistice de rethondes, 1919–1920,'' pp. 211–15; for Wilson's views, see Wilson, *Public Papers*, 5:317–18, 490–91.

82. Senate, Committee on Finance, *Refunding of Obligations of Foreign Governments*, 4:96–99.

83. Rathbone to secretary of the treasury, 4 November 1919, RG 39, Box 49.

policy flexible enough to accommodate domestic priorities and European reconstruction needs.

Congress, however, increasingly interfered with and objected to Treasury plans. This behavior constituted part of the larger postwar assertion of congressional authority in the wake of the League fight. In the autumn of 1919, for example, Paul M. Warburg, governor of the Federal Reserve Board, returned from Europe with a plan for reconstruction that called for, among other things, a partial cancellation of the war debts. Initially, he found Norman Davis, assistant secretary of the treasury and a highly prized adviser to the president, sympathetic to his plans. But as the struggle over the League intensified, Davis withdrew his support and dissociated himself from any statement calling for partial cancellation.[84] When he appeared before a closed door session of the Ways and Means Committee in February 1920, Davis was clearly on the defensive. Democratic representatives, like Claude Kitchin and James Garner, attacked him for postponing Allied interest payments and for sacrificing the interests of American taxpayers.[85] Davis was clearly impressed with the intransigence of Congress. He cautioned other administration officials not to raise false hopes.[86] Thereafter, British and French requests for a reconsideration of American policy were rebuffed. In fact, with executive-legislative relations at an impasse and with the elections immediately forthcoming, the official public position of the Democrats toughened still further. Wilson wrote Lloyd George in October 1920 that there would be no cancellation and no linkage of the war debt and reparation issues.[87]

Such a rigid stand was countereffective. American officials knew it but could do nothing about it. The French, although willing to be somewhat malleable on the indemnity question, refused to consider conversion of their demand obligations while the Americans ignored the apparent link between reparations and war debts. Davis acknowledged that the two matters could not be entirely separated and Treasury officials intimated to their French counterparts that if the demand obligations were converted, interest payments might be deferred longer than three years.[88] But Congress precluded further concessions. In

84. See Paul M. Warburg, "History of the European Memorandum," n.d., in "Post-War Europe," Paul M. Warburg Papers; for Wilson's confidence in Davis, see Wilson to Colby, 2 April 1920, Colby Papers, Box 2.

85. House, Ways and Means, *Foreign Loans*, pp. 24, 31–35, 39–40, 43.

86. Davis to Rathbone, 28, 30 April 1920, Leffingwell Papers, Box 15.

87. For official correspondence on the war debts, see WDC, *Combined Annual Reports*, especially pp. 70–71, 72–74.

88. Ibid., pp. 71–72; Kelley Memorandum, 15 December 1920, RG 39, Box 49.

February 1921 the Senate Committee on the Judiciary launched an aggressive investigation of the Wilson administration's foreign loan practices with a blistering attack on its supposed violations of wartime legislation.[89] Under such conditions it was impossible for the administration to mold a permanent and sophisticated war debt policy that would offer relief to France and other needy debtors without compromising domestic priorities. Legislative interference with postwar debt policy might have eventuated regardless of the League fight. But the wounds from that battle made things more difficult than they would have been otherwise. Not coincidentally, it was Senator James A. Reed of Missouri, one of the two Democratic irreconcilables, who was at the center of the Judiciary Committee's attack on Wilsonian loan and debt policies.[90]

While Wilsonian reparation and war debt policies floundered, the French need for American loans intensified, especially as the expectation for immediate large indemnity payments proved illusory. In October 1919 at the International Trade Conference in Atlantic City, Baron du Maurais, vice-chairman of the French economic mission, outlined France's predicament. His nation was in desperate need of foodstuffs and raw materials. Bad crops and a shortage of manpower, he contended, had exacerbated the problems wrought by war and demobilization. Meanwhile, as a result of her depleted equipment and the demands of reconstruction, France could not immediately regain her place in the world's markets. In 1920 alone France needed to borrow hundreds of millions of dollars to pay for cotton, copper, oil, gasoline, and essential foodstuffs.[91] To raise this money French officials and bankers explored various alternatives with their American counterparts. The French sought government credits and private loans; they inquired whether French securities could be made tax exempt in the United States; they explored the possibility of listing French *rentes* on the New York Stock Exchange; they considered using the assets of entire industrial groupings as collateral for the extension of credits. No

89. Senate, Committee on the Judiciary, *Loans to Foreign Governments*, Senate Document No. 86; Senate, Committee on the Judiciary, unpublished hearings, *Repeal of Wartime Legislation*, RG 39, Box 218.

90. For Reed's investigation and the efforts of executive officials to meet his demands, see Houston to Colby, 26 February 1921, RG 59, 800.51/226; Colby to Houston, 3 March 1921, RG 59, 800.51/237b; for a differing opinion on the influence of Congress, see Artaud, "La question des dettes."

91. Chamber of Commerce of the United States (CCUS), *International Trade Conference*, pp. 226 ff.

possibility was ignored by the French in their relentless search for American financial aid.[92]

The United States Treasury Department was initially sympathetic to French needs. In February Carter Glass appealed for legislation that would allow the granting of government credits both to expedite European reconstruction and to facilitate the overseas sales of American foodstuffs and raw materials. But as the year progressed two developments altered the Treasury's support for government loans. First, Congress demonstrated its antipathy to postwar government lending and circumscribed the Treasury's authority to make foreign loans.[93] Second, Treasury officials themselves, including Glass and Assistant Secretary Russell C. Leffingwell, reappraised their priorities and focused primary attention on halting the upward spiral of domestic prices. Accordingly, they sought to limit government borrowings, curtail credit, and stabilize financial markets. Anxious to see the War Finance Corporation (WFC) go out of business in early 1920, Leffingwell saw nothing "to justify the Government's increasing its floating debt in order to stimulate exports to Europe." Minimizing the amount of destruction wrought by the war, emphasizing the vast recuperative powers of the Old World, and insisting on greater self-discipline in European finance ministries, Treasury officials maintained that the private sector could and should accommodate European financial needs.[94] By rejecting government involvement in international finance, Wilsonian officials hoped to mobilize private American capital for European reconstruction without engendering domestic inflation, sacrificing conservative fiscal policies, compromising antistatist principles, or risking the politicization of economic relationships.[95]

92. Wallace to secretary, 7 November 1919, RG 256, 851.00/46; Davis to Rathbone, 1 December 1919, RG 39, Box 49; H. H. Harjes to Dean Jay and Lamont, 1 February 1920, ibid.; Leffingwell to Rathbone, 10 December 1919, ibid.; Eugene Meyer to Leffingwell, 31 March 1920, ibid.; William Heaton to Meyer, 31 March 1919, ibid.; C. P. Snow to P. B. Kennedy, 20 September 1919, Records of the Bureau of Foreign and Domestic Commerce (BFDC), RG 151, File 640.

93. For Treasury requests and congressional restrictions, see Senate, Judiciary, *Loans to Foreign Governments*, pp. 5–8, 277–79; see also Parrini, *Heir to Empire*, p. 48.

94. For the quotation, see Leffingwell to Meyer, 16 April 1920, Leffingwell Papers, Box 15; see also Glass to Wilson, 25 August 1919, ibid., Box 12; Rathbone to secretary of state, 23 October 1919, RG 39, Box 49; Rixey Smith and Norman Beasley, *Carter Glass*, pp. 185–89; David F. Houston, *Eight Years with Wilson's Cabinet*, pp. 62–63, 114–15.

95. See Hogan, *Informal Entente*, pp. 1–37; Paul P. Abrahams, "American Bankers and the Economic Tactics of Peace: 1919," pp. 572–83; Parrini, *Heir to Empire*, pp. 47–137.

Significantly, the private sector was already focusing considerable attention on meeting the financial requirements of Europe. During 1919 and 1920 the Investment Bankers Association (IBA), the Chamber of Commerce of the United States (CCUS), the National Association of Manufacturers (NAM), and the American Economic Association (AEA) studied the problems of furnishing European nations with capital. They all explicitly recognized the implications of America's becoming a creditor nation. They emphasized that if the nation were going to sustain its export trade, it would have to expand its foreign lending. But they feared that the granting of additional credits might augment total purchasing power and stimulate further increases in the cost of living. Hence, the CCUS concluded that "the most immediate and important problem for this country is how to extend further credit to foreign nations without bringing about inflation at home." The task was complicated by investors' unfamiliarity with foreign securities and by their preference for tax-exempt municipal bonds, which offered a higher return and were less risky.[96] Not surprisingly, foreign flotations, including French and British loans, performed dismally on American markets during 1919. Leading Wall Street financiers, like Thomas Lamont of J. P. Morgan and Company and Otto Kahn of Kuhn, Loeb, and Company, grew increasingly agitated. They realized that some mechanism had to be established that would serve to mobilize dollars for European reconstruction without generating internal inflation or shortchanging the capital requirements of the domestic economy.[97]

In late 1919 there was great hope among Treasury officials, international bankers, and export-oriented businessmen that the legislation introduced by Senator Walter Edge of New Jersey would solve the problem. The Edge amendments to the Federal Reserve Act provided for the establishment of a new type of federally chartered private banking institution designed to finance America's export trade and satisfy Europe's demand for long-term capital. So much confidence

96. For the quotation, see CCUS, Report of National Committee, "European Finance," Kent Papers, Box 4, p. 20; see also Investment Bankers Association of America (IBA), *Proceedings of the Annual Convention*, 1919, pp. 150–52; American Economic Association, "Report of the Committee on Foreign Trade," 9 January 1920, RG 151, File 721A; National Association of Manufacturers (NAM), *Proceedings of the Annual Convention*, 1920, pp. 5–9.

97. For the performance of foreign loans and the concerns of Kahn and Lamont, see Baron de Neuflize to Kahn, 9 November 1919, Kahn Papers, Box 115; De Neuflize to Reboul, 18 November 1919, ibid.; Kahn to H. C. Cutting, 25 November 1919, ibid., Box 114; Lamont to Leffingwell, 18 November 1919, RG 39, Box 49.

was placed in the efficacy of the new banks that several months after the Edge amendments were enacted, the WFC ceased its overseas financial operations.[98] Despite all the enthusiasm for the Edge banks, however, they never lived up to expectations. Theodore Laurent, the French metallurgical manufacturer, explained to W. S. Kies, chairman of the First Federal Foreign Banking Association, that the Edge banks concentrated on providing commercial credits for six to nine months while most French industrialists sought ten- to fifteen-year loans, hoping that the eventual appreciation of the franc would ease the problems of repayment.[99] American bankers and investors, however, continued to be reluctant to make long-term loans while the nation remained in a technical state of war and the conditions of peace were uncertain. As early as November 1919 Paul Warburg had warned the White House of this possibility. Expressing the same apprehensions, Herbert Hoover had implored Wilson to accept reservations but to no avail.[100]

Predictably, then, as the treaty fight dragged on throughout 1920, Europe's capital needs were only partially met. In September the French government successfully floated a $100 million loan, but the interest rate was a high 8 percent.[101] Meanwhile, French officials estimated that they would need at least $225 million in additional funds during 1921.[102] Acknowledging the inadequacy of existing credit facilities, representatives of America's most prominent business and banking organizations met in December 1920 to discuss the problem. Frightened by the recent decline in American exports, the fluctuation of European currencies, and a slackening in the American economy, business leaders once again emphasized the importance of reproductive long-term foreign lending. Yet, they realized that little could be done until the terms of peace were made permanent, differences between European nations were resolved, and intergovernmental debt obligations were fixed.[103] As a temporary expedient, Congress overrode Wilson's veto and authorized the WFC to resume its financing of for-

98. For more on the Edge banks, see Parrini, *Heir to Empire*, pp. 79–100; Abrahams, "American Bankers," pp. 575–81.
99. W. C. Huntington to R. S. MacElwee, 14 October 1920, RG 151, File 600.
100. Warburg to Tumulty, 18 November 1919, Woodrow Wilson Papers, Series 2, Reel 105; Hoover to Wilson, 19 November 1919, ibid; see also War Finance Commission (WFC), Monthly Report, 23 December 1919, RG 151, File 151.2.
101. "Bankers Prepare for a Big Year in Foreign Financing," *The Annalist* 17 (17 January 1921):107–8.
102. Kelley, Memorandum, 15 December 1920, RG 39, Box 49.
103. See "Mr. McHugh's Address," *Journal of the American Bankers Association*, 13 (January 1921):461.

eign agricultural exports.[104] But permanent machinery for effectively mobilizing private capital for European reconstruction, institutionalizing cooperation between the public and private sectors, and reconciling internal and external priorities still awaited the settlement of the treaty and League issues.

With no permanent solutions to the reparation and war debt issues in sight and with foreign loans lagging, European currencies, including the franc, began depreciating and fluctuating in value once they were unpegged from the dollar in the spring of 1919. These developments alarmed not only Democratic officials but also American businessmen, many of whom consistently alluded to European exchange problems as the major impediment to a steady growth of American exports. There was considerable understanding both in business and official circles that one means of expediting the stabilization of European currencies, fostering American exports, and cultivating international trade was through an increase in American purchases of foreign goods.[105] In several messages to Congress in 1919 and 1920, President Wilson emphasized this point and recommended commensurate action with regard to American tariff policy. "If we want to sell," he explained, "we must be prepared to buy. Whatever, therefore, may have been our views during the period of growth of American business concerning tariff legislation, we must now adjust our own economic life to a changed condition growing out of the fact that American business is full grown and that America is the greatest capitalist in the world."[106]

As on other matters Wilson's advice was not heeded by Congress. When agricultural prices broke in July 1920 and began a dramatic slide downward, one response was a call for an increase in customs duties. Widely disparate agricultural interests in Congress joined together to push through an emergency tariff bill that increased duties on a diversified group of agricultural products. The president, pointing out how inconsistent the tariff bill was with America's creditor status and how ineffective it would be in remedying farm problems, vetoed the legislation.[107] Although the veto was sustained, the battle was just begin-

104. James H. Shideler, *Farm Crisis, 1919–1923*, pp. 71–72.
105. See, for example, NAM, *Proceedings*, 1920, pp. 9–10, 115, 237; "Mr. McHugh's Address," pp. 460–61; National Foreign Trade Council (NFTC), *The American Trade Balance and Probable Tendencies*, pp. 26–27, 39–40; Minutes of Thirty-fourth Meeting, State Department Economic Liaison Committee, 19 November 1919, RG 151, File 151.2.
106. Wilson, *Public Papers*, 6:431.
107. Ibid., pp. 530–35; for farmers and the tariff, see Shideler, *Farm Crisis*, pp. 73–75.

ning. As foreign currencies continued to depreciate, sentiment mounted among some businessmen for increased protection to prevent low-priced foreign goods, especially German products, from flooding the American market.[108] Innovative methods would evidently have to be devised to reconcile the expansionist and protectionist tendencies in American economic life and alleviate the exchange problems of European nations without resorting to statist practices or jolting the well-entrenched interests of small manufacturers and businessmen. Although ideas were emerging on how to reconcile these divergent objectives,[109] no progress could be made while executive-legislative relations were at an impasse and the nation was waiting for a new Republican administration to take office.

For almost a year and a half the deadlock over the League and treaty issues and the acrimony between Wilson and his Republican opponents thwarted American attempts to establish diplomatic machinery and policymaking instruments capable of balancing divergent pressures emanating from the domestic and European economies. With reparation, war debt, and foreign loan policies in a state of confusion, currency problems and exchange fluctuations went unresolved, American exports began to encounter increasing competition abroad, and foreign goods began to compete more effectively in the domestic market. The president could do little about these developments. His health made him unable to resume a full work routine. Consumed by the League struggle, he continued to hope for ultimate vindication. Thus, only after Harding achieved a landslide victory in the 1920 election and assumed office in March 1921 did prospects rise for the implementation of long-term foreign economic policies. The legislative-executive impasse over the ratification of the Treaty of Versailles, however, still had to be broken.

Republican Peacemaking and French Security

Upon taking office Republican officials were intent on quickly resolving the impasse that had stymied effective policymaking. During the campaign Harding had equivocated on his position regarding

108. Even export-oriented groups recognized the dangers of foreign currency depreciation. See IBA, *Proceedings*, 1919, p. 152; John H. Williams, "German Trade and the Reparation Payments," *Journal of the American Bankers Association* 14 (March 1922):605–10.

109. See Senate, Select Committee, *Investigation of the Tariff Commission*, 5:604–11, 628–31.

the League and the treaty.[110] Both Secretary of State Charles Evans Hughes and Secretary of Commerce Herbert C. Hoover urged the new president to waste no time in delineating the administration's stand on these issues. They believed that "peace was urgent in a world shaking with political and economic instabilities."[111] Businessmen and bankers felt similarly, and their sentiments reverberated in Congress where legislators of all political persuasions acknowledged the economic importance of making peace with Germany.[112] Harding immediately began to ascertain whether senators were amenable to ratifying the existing treaty with reservations. Both Hughes and Hoover, his two key foreign policy advisers, were on record supporting this approach.[113]

Meanwhile, the French viewed the Republican accession to power with trepidation. Commenting on Harding's inaugural address, many French newspapers noticed his lack of emphasis on European affairs, and they predicted that the United States would return to its prewar policy of nonintervention in the Old World.[114] Fearful that the new administration would ignore the problem of French security, sign a separate peace, and indirectly encourage Germany to violate treaty provisions, French Premier Aristide Briand sent René Viviani on a goodwill mission to Washington. Ostensibly, Viviani's intention was to express French gratitude for American aid during the war and emphasize the pacific character of French foreign policy. But his real purpose was to plead his nation's case for a continuation of Allied cooperation. Arriving at the end of March, Viviani implored Harding, Hughes, and other Republican officials to seek ratification of the Treaty of Versailles in whatever form was necessary to win Senate approval. He emphasized that even Article 10 of the League covenant could be modified. This was of no consequence to the French, he maintained, because they always believed that the guarantees provided for in this article would not work in practice.[115]

110. For Harding's position during the campaign, see Randolph C. Downes, *The Rise of Warren Gamaliel Harding, 1865–1920*, pp. 562–98.
111. Herbert C. Hoover, *The Memoirs of Herbert Hoover*, 2:37.
112. Van Meter, "United States and European Recovery," pp. 285–90.
113. See [Henry C. Beerits Memorandum], "Separate Peace with Germany, the League of Nations, and the Permanent Court of International Justice," Hughes Papers, Box 172, pp. 15–19; see also Hoover, *Memoirs*, 2:36–37; Gary Dean Best, *The Politics of American Individualism*, especially pp. 121–79.
114. For French press reaction to Harding's inauguration, see the newspaper clippings in Harding Papers, Presidential Case File, Box 193 (hereafter cited as PCF).
115. For Viviani's mission, see FR, 1921, 1:962–67; George Harvey to Harding, [March 1921], Harding Papers, Presidential Personal File 60 (hereafter cited as PPF).

Republican policymakers were not unsympathetic to the problems faced by France in the postwar era. But the real dilemma from the official Republican viewpoint was how to avoid another confrontation with Congress over the treaty issue while still working to reconcile French security demands with the imperatives of European stabilization. Hughes and Hoover worried that the treaty might retard Germany's reconstruction, that the League might delay necessary revisions in the peace treaty, and that Article 10 might provide illusory guarantees of French security.[116] Before assuming office Hughes had discussed these matters with French Ambassador Jules Jusserand. Hughes subsequently asked Viviani for concrete suggestions on what the administration might do. When the French offered no constructive alternatives and the irreconcilables warned that they would wreck the administration if Wilson's treaty were submitted in any form, Hughes and Harding decided to abandon the Treaty of Versailles altogether, sign a separate peace, and proceed with alternative steps toward European stabilization.[117]

Accordingly, on 12 April 1921 the president announced his opposition to the League, warned against the dangers of incurring unknown strategic commitments, and declared his support of a congressional resolution terminating the technical state of war. It was evident that this was the first step toward signing a separate peace with Germany in which the United States would preserve all rights and privileges under the Treaty of Versailles while renouncing all obligations and commitments. Harding emphasized that this action did not signify an end to American involvement in Europe's economic restoration. To demonstrate that he was not withdrawing the United States from a constructive role in the international arena, Harding proclaimed his readiness to work with other nations to reduce armaments.[118] Although divergent considerations prompted the administration to call for a disarmament

116. For the views of Hoover and Hughes on the League and the treaty, see, for example, Hoover, *Memoirs*, 2:10–13, 36–37; [Beerits Memorandum], "Separate Peace with Germany," pp. 27–31; Hughes to A. Lawrence Lowell, 20 July 1922, Hughes Papers, Box 31.

117. For Hughes's meeting with Jusserand, see "Note," n.d., Hughes Papers, Box 172; for Hughes's talk with Viviani, see FR, 1921, 1:966–67; for the opposition of the irreconcilables and the decision to abandon the Treaty of Versailles, see [Beerits Memorandum], "Separate Peace with Germany," pp. 15–19; see also Hughes to Hamilton Holt, 13 July 1922, Hughes Papers, Box 172; Kurt and Sarah Wimer, "The Harding Administration, the League of Nations, and the Separate Peace Treaty," pp. 13–15.

118. For Harding's speech, see FR, 1921, 1:xvii–xx; for the separate peace, see [Beerits Memorandum], "Separate Peace with Germany," pp. 19–21; FR, 1921, 2:1–36.

conference, Republican officials were very hopeful that an agreement limiting armaments would ease the burden on European budgets, abet the Old World's financial stabilization, and spur a growth in American agricultural exports.[119]

By concurrently negotiating the Treaty of Berlin with Germany and preparing a conference on arms limitation, Republican officials were intensifying strategic apprehensions in France, while embarking on what they considered a pragmatic course toward meeting Europe's financial needs and America's commercial imperatives. The French were in a vulnerable position. Increasingly divided from the British over the question of reparations, they now feared that their other major wartime ally, the United States, might not only absolve Germany from responsibility for the war in a separate treaty but also press France to reduce her military superiority over Germany.[120] Although Briand could do nothing to forestall the separate treaty, he hoped to turn the disarmament conference to France's advantage by cultivating a better image of France in America and by drawing the United States more actively into European affairs. The French premier did not expect to secure an actual American endorsement of French security. But he did seek to revive American interest in French strategic problems and to associate Germany with the results of the conference. Moreover, Briand assumed he would have some leverage at the conference because he anticipated that the United States and Britain would reach an impasse over naval reductions; hence, they would need France to help compromise their differences.[121]

Republican officials, however, felt no incentive to reconsider the matter of strategic guarantees. Assessing Germany's military potential on the eve of the disarmament conference, the General Board of the Navy concluded that the former enemy would not be able to wage an aggressive war against a major power during the lifetime of any con-

119. For Hughes's interest in land as well as naval armaments, see FR, 1922, 1:21–22; for an incisive analysis relating the preparations for the disarmament conference to the financial problems of Europe and the search for new American export markets, see Van Meter, "United States and European Recovery," pp. 295–300; for the standard work on the Washington Conference, see Thomas H. Buckley, *The United States and the Washington Conference, 1921–1922*; see also Roger Dingman, *Power in the Pacific*.

120. For French fears that a separate treaty might absolve Germany from responsibility, see the memorandum of the interview between Hughes and Prince de Bearn, 23 August 1921, Hughes Papers, Box 174.

121. For Briand's views, see Georges Suarez, *Briand*, 5:251–52, 267 ff.; Raymond Escholier, *Souvenirs parlés de Briand*, pp. 172–78; Chastenet, *Histoire*, 5:88–89; Buckley, *Washington Conference*, pp. 104–5; extract of letter from Nicholas Murray Butler to the president, 13 July 1921, Hughes Papers, Box 14.

ceivable arms limitation agreement. American naval officials, therefore, cautioned against support for French policies on the Continent that "might involve us in embarrassing situations."[122] Even more significant in dissuading the administration from incurring a new set of commitments was the waning of public support for an alliance with France. In the autumn of 1921 the *Literary Digest* conducted a nationwide poll of newspaper editors asking what the American government should do to protect France from another attack. The vast majority of respondents (228 out of 273) favored military and financial aid to France in case of unprovoked aggression. But fewer than a quarter of them thought it wise to sign a formal treaty guaranteeing French security.[123] Most businessmen felt the same way. A special committee of the National Foreign Trade Council (NFTC) concluded that "in Western Europe, the French fear of future military aggression by a rehabilitated Germany influences the whole problem." But there was no consensus even among export-oriented businessmen that it was either wise or desirable for the United States to alleviate French apprehensions through the assumption of strategic commitments. No matter how interested they were in restoring European markets, not many businessmen urged the American government to offer military guarantees as a means of creating the necessary political framework for the economic reconstruction of the Old World.[124]

Not surprisingly, then, Hughes decided to avoid the complex problem of land disarmament and American military commitments at the Washington Conference. In his opening speech he proclaimed that "if there is to be economic rehabilitation . . . competition in armament

122. W. L. Rodgers to secretary of the navy, 12 September 1921, Records of the General Board of the Navy, File 438, Serial no. 1088; Rodgers to secretary of the navy, 12 November 1921, ibid., Serial no. 1088–z.

123. For the poll, see "What Will We Do if France Is Attacked Again," *Literary Digest* 71 (31 December 1921):5–7. In 1919 there had been some public opposition to the guarantee pact, but the majority of commentators seemed favorable. See Coston, "American Reaction," pp. 108–39; for Republican support of the guarantee pact in 1919, see Ambrosius, "Wilson, the Republicans, and French Security," pp. 341–52; for changing public attitudes toward France, see Elizabeth Brett White, *American Opinion of France from Lafayette to Poincaré*, pp. 283–302; for additional press concern with France's strategic problems, see "France to Disarm, If—" *Literary Digest* 71 (22 October 1921):5–6.

124. For the quotation, see Special Committee of the National Foreign Trade Council (NFTC), "Report on European Conditions," *Official Report of the National Foreign Trade Convention*, 1923, pp. 9, 23–25; see also "European Problems Affecting American Business," *Nation's Business* 9 (5 October 1921):4–6. Most internationalists had always been opposed to the incursion of strategic commitments and political obligations. See Kuehl, *Seeking World Order*, pp. 339–44.

must stop." He then went on to propose specific guidelines for the limitation of naval vessels.[125] Immediately thereafter he entered into secret negotiations with the British and Japanese delegates. They worked out an agreement limiting capital ships virtually without consulting the French. Not only were the French deprived of an opportunity to mediate Anglo-American differences, but their own naval requirements were disregarded as the three great naval powers struggled to reach an accord among themselves. France wanted equality with Japan in capital ships but was compelled to accept parity with Italy instead.[126] When the French delegates considered rejecting the Anglo-American-Japanese proposal, Hughes threatened economic retaliation. "At this point," he wrote Briand, "when we are anxious to aid France in full recovery of her economic life, it would be most disappointing to be advised that she was contemplating putting hundreds of millions into battleships." The secretary of state emphasized the economic benefits that would accrue to France and other nations as a result of an agreement limiting naval armaments. Such an accord would save taxpayers' money, facilitate the balancing of budgets, promote currency stability, and stimulate world trade. Hughes reminded Briand that the secretary of state had not raised the issue of land armaments, but he could not allow France to upset a naval agreement.[127]

Briand submitted to American pressure and accepted the accord on capital ships. In making this concession the French premier wrote Hughes that it would be impossible for the French government to accept proportionate reductions in auxiliary craft, especially submarines.[128] The British then adroitly manipulated the French position on submarines to justify Britain's reluctance to limit cruisers and destroyers. As a result the conference ended in February 1922 without any agreement on auxiliary craft. In the American press the French were portrayed as the militaristic villains of the drama and the intransigent foes of a comprehensive accord.[129] Ironically, Briand had attended the opening of the conference hoping to resuscitate the image of France in

125. Charles Evans Hughes, *The Pathway of Peace*, pp. 24–31.
126. For developments at the Washington Conference, see Buckley, *Washington Conference*, pp. 63–126, 107–18; Suarez, *Briand*, 5:296–308; for France's isolation, see also Chastenet, *Histoire*, 5:89–90; Georges Bonnet, *Le Quai d'Orsay sous trois ré-publiques, 1870–1961*, pp. 47–48.
127. FR, 1922, 1:130–33; see also Suarez, *Briand*, 5:298–302; Ministére des Affaires Etrangères, *Conférence de Washington (juillet 1921–février 1922)*, pp. 52–63.
128. FR, 1922, 1:135–36; Suarez, *Briand*, 5:303.
129. Donald S. Birn, "Open Diplomacy at the Washington Conference of 1921–1922," pp. 297–319.

America. The conference closed with France's reputation at a postwar low. Commenting on the terrible publicity his nation had received at Washington, the French ambassador wrote that "such a complete misunderstanding aggravated by acerbic, sour, and persistent criticism I have rarely seen."[130]

The events at Washington discredited France among top Republican officials and influential senators. They increasingly felt that French military policies and reparation demands were incompatible with the requirements of Europe's economic reconstruction. While Harding simply registered his disappointment with French policy, Hoover bitterly assailed French military expenditures and called for a ban on private loans to that nation.[131] Meanwhile, on 25 January 1922 Borah reaffirmed America's interest in Europe's economic restoration and denounced the French view that their security "depends upon the destruction of Germany as a great economic unit." This statement by the well-known irreconcilable senator revealed that many Americans were acutely aware of the importance of stabilizing Europe but were increasingly inclined to subordinate the issue of French security and highlight the importance of Germany's reintegration.[132] Significantly, both Harding and Hughes had already acknowledged that the "only way for France to obtain real security is by taking Germany into camp."[133] At a time of deepening recession and multiplying calls for new export outlets, this self-serving orientation identified French security with Germany's economic restoration. Such a policy obviated the need for the United States to incur military commitments but still held out the prospect of revitalizing European markets for American goods.

The French were well aware of the miserable publicity engendered by their performance at the Washington Conference. Their expectations had been too high and their disappointment was great indeed.[134]

130. Jules Jusserand to Lamont, 16 February 1922, Thomas W. Lamont Papers, Box 94; White, *American Opinion of France*, pp. 292–94.

131. For Harding's disappointment, see Harding to Harvey, 6 January 1922, Harding Papers, PPF 60; for Hoover's view, see Fred Dearing to Hughes and Henry Fletcher, 30 December 1921, RG 59, 851.51/233.

132. For Borah's statement, see Senate, *Congressional Record*, 67th Cong., 2nd sess., 1922, 62, pt. 2:1684–85; for growing American concern with European stability, see chapter 2.

133. The quotation is from a letter from Harvey to Harding, 3 October 1921, Harding Papers, PPF 60. Harding and Hughes concurred. See Harding to Harvey, 24 October 1921, ibid.; Hughes to Harding, 25 October 1921, ibid.

134. For the French reaction to developments at Washington, see Edouard Bonnefous, *Histoire politique de la Troisième République*, 3:264–66; see also Birn, "Open

The Washington Conference highlighted the different interests and policies of the powers, exposed the weakness of France's position, and confirmed America's readiness to pursue her own goals regardless of French desires. If the repudiation of the Treaty of Versailles constituted a negative demonstration of America's departure from the wartime alliance, the conclusion of the Treaty of Berlin and the signing of the Washington naval accords were positive indications that the United States would pursue an independent diplomatic course subordinating French strategic interests to the larger imperatives of American foreign policy. Thereafter, in official American circles the French security issue would be subsumed under the rubric of Germany's reintegration.

While the Washington Conference was still in progress, Briand returned to France. He was aware that for a variety of reasons French ties with both Great Britain and the United States had become terribly strained. He was also exasperated by Germany's persistent attempts to circumvent her financial commitments and evade her disarmament obligations. Under these circumstances the French premier tried to improve relations with the British and elicit a new and more comprehensive set of security guarantees. But while meeting with Lloyd George at Cannes, Briand was assailed by his political opponents for his alleged willingness to shortchange French financial and strategic needs. Parliamentary criticism prompted his resignation.[135]

President Millerand immediately asked Poincaré to form a new government. The new premier had always doubted the value of the guarantees secured at Versailles and had deplored Clemenceau's concessions to Wilson. Now Poincaré confided that "even an Anglo-American Pact of Guarantees, duly ratified by the Federal Senate . . . would not suffice entirely to relieve France of anxiety." Although Poincaré was not eager to pursue a bellicose course toward Germany, he wished to resolve the ambivalence in French policy, secure German respect for the treaty, and elicit more comprehensive guarantees from Britain.[136] With the closing of the Washington Conference and with

---

Diplomacy,'' pp. 301–7; Myron T. Herrick to Harding, 14 February 1922, Herrick Papers, Box 11.

135. Stephen A. Schuker, *The End of French Predominance*, pp. 14–20; Sally Marks, *The Illusion of Peace*, pp. 38–42; McDougall, ''French Rhineland Policy,'' pp. 175–78.

136. For the quotation, see Viscount Edgar Vincent D'Abernon, *An Ambassador of Peace*, 2:15. Recent writing based on the newly opened materials in the French archives has minimized the differences between Poincaré and Briand. See McDougall, ''French Rhineland Policy,'' pp. 175–90; Schuker, *French Predominance*, pp. 17–19; for Poin-

the accession to power of Poincaré, important developments were about to unfold in both the United States and France.

Conclusion

At Versailles Wilson tried to balance several contradictory goals. He wanted to enhance French security and expedite Germany's rehabilitation without entangling the United States in Europe's traditional game of power politics. In an effort to accomplish these goals, he assumed the ambiguous commitments inherent in Article 10 of the League covenant, signed a guarantee pact with France, and modified America's traditional insistence on independent diplomatic action. The president was not happy about the concessions he had to make, but he believed them indispensable to the creation of a stable world order conducive to the limitation of armaments, the reconstruction of Europe, and the reintegration of Germany into a liberal capitalist community.

After almost two years of fruitless debate, during which time the imperatives of European reconstruction were submerged, the Republicans came to power. They shared the Democrats' goals for a stable world order. Like Wilson, the Republicans were not indifferent to France's strategic predicament. But responding to political considerations, congressional warnings, and diplomatic imperatives, the Republicans decided to follow the line of least resistance and pursue their foreign policy goals without incurring strategic commitments. This course of action reflected Republican doubts about the efficacy of the Versailles treaty and the League covenant. The Republican policy avoided another clash with Congress, accorded with the predilections of most American internationalists,[137] and placed a higher priority on pragmatic accomplishments than on idealistic aspirations.

As the preparations for the Washington Conference got underway, the task of protecting French security was subordinated to the more pressing problems of ending the state of war with Germany, curtailing an incipient arms race, and establishing a new framework for Europe's economic reconstruction and financial stabilization. As far as Republican officials were concerned, this framework did not have to include the League of Nations, Article 10, or the guarantee pact with France.

---

caré's attitudes, see also Miquel, *Raymond Poincaré*, pp. 403–41; Ministère des Affaires Etrangères, *Garanties de sécurité*, pp. 113–24.

137. Most internationalists in the 1920s continued to oppose the assumption of strategic obligations. See Charles DeBenedetti, "Alternative Strategies in the American Peace Movement," pp. 69–78.

Indeed, the proceedings of the Washington Conference suggested to Republican policymakers that a successful foreign policy could be pursued through a combination of diplomatic finesse, astute bargaining, moderate concessions, and financial leverage. That French strategic interests had to be disregarded while other problems were tackled seemed a regrettable but unavoidable result of the domestic controversy over the Treaty of Versailles. Thereafter, Republican officials hoped that the task of reconstructing Europe could take place within a basically economic context—a framework designed to maximize America's financial leverage and minimize her strategic commitments. Although this orientation placed enormous pressures upon the French, it was founded upon the assumptions that a republican and prosperous Germany would be a peaceful nation and that a defeated and constrained Germany would be a militarily incapacitated power, at least for the short run. Meanwhile, a new era of economic diplomacy was about to begin for the United States.

[2]

Economic Diplomacy
Takes Shape, 1921–1923

During the Washington Conference, American officials resisted French pleas for additional guarantees of their security. Nevertheless, the Americans remained greatly concerned about European developments. President Harding indicated that he was waiting for the propitious moment to exert a helpful hand in European affairs, and Secretary of State Hughes emphasized that the United States wanted stability abroad in order to have prosperity at home.[1] But it was Secretary of Commerce Hoover who pondered the interrelationships between European stability and American well-being most carefully and who explored the prerequisites of Europe's reconstruction most systematically. In a memorandum to the president in January 1922, Hoover concluded that the crux of Europe's problems rested "in the economic relationships of France and Germany alone." He contended that the restoration of stability in western Europe depended upon the resolution of the reparations controversy, the balancing of governmental budgets in France and Germany, the stabilization of the franc and the mark, and the reduction of land armaments. If these objectives could be achieved, Hoover predicted that European social chaos would be reduced, artificial European competition in the world's marketplaces curtailed, and American exports expanded.[2]

The steep economic downturn of 1920–21 made many economic interest groups as well as government officials increasingly aware of

1. Harding to George Harvey, 3 May 1922, Harding Papers, Presidential Personal File 60 (hereafter cited as PPF); Charles Evans Hughes, "Deal Only with Upright States," *Nation's Business* 10 (5 June 1922):12.
2. Hoover to Harding, 23 January 1922, Herbert C. Hoover Commerce Department Papers, Box 21 (hereafter cited as HHCD); Herbert Hoover, "A Year of Cooperation," *Nation's Business* 10 (5 June 1922):12.

the interdependence of the European and American economies. In October 1921, for example, the President's Committee on Unemployment reported that the business cycle was a worldwide phenomenon and that the difficulties plaguing the agricultural and raw material sectors of the American economy were attributable to foreign developments. Large percentages of the total production of cotton (61.5 percent), rice (53.2 percent), rye (46.5 percent), tobacco (44.5 percent), wheat (23.5 percent), copper (51.5 percent), and tin plate (17.8 percent) were exported abroad. In fact, 11 percent of the nation's domestic agricultural production was shipped directly to Europe.[3] Consequently, when exports to the Old World fell by almost 60 percent between 1920 and 1922,[4] farm leaders as well as business and financial spokesmen increasingly concurred that "our interests are indissolubly united with the interests of Europe, and until we have a reorganized, a sound, a normal condition of affairs in Europe . . . we shall not have normal healthy times at home."[5]

Even when recovery began to take place in 1922, Americans continued to indicate growing apprehension over the deterioration of European financial, social, and political conditions. Democrats and Republicans, bankers and farmers, internationalists and isolationists clamored for resolution of the incessant strife between France and Germany. There was a growing consensus that something had to be done to settle the war debt and reparation questions, reduce land armaments, stabilize European currencies, mobilize American capital for European reconstruction, and create the conditions for a flourishing international trade. In February 1923 even Senator Borah exclaimed that "we are drifting, drifting, while the most serious conditions the world has ever experienced are calling for bold and determined action.

3. Conference on Unemployment, *Report of the President's Committee on Unemployment*, pp. 147, 158–59; Department of Commerce, *Annual Report of the Secretary of Commerce*, 1922, p. 20.
4. Department of Commerce, *Commerce Yearbook*, 1922, p. 520.
5. The quotation is from George Wickersham's introductory remarks to Frank A. Vanderlip, "The Allied War Debt to the United States," *Consensus* 7 (February 1922):3; for the interest of farm leaders and agricultural groups in European stability, see American Farm Bureau Federation (AFBF), *Report of the Executive Secretary, The Federation's Third Year*, pp. 15–20; James R. Howard, "Europe the Farmers' Market," *Nation's Business*, 10 (5 June 1922):24–26; J. S. Wannamaker to Harding, 3 December 1921, Harding Papers, Presidential Case File, Box 197 (hereafter cited as PCF); for business and financial interest in European reconstruction, see, for example, "Final Declaration," National Foreign Trade Council (NFTC), *Official Report of the National Foreign Trade Convention*, 1921, p. viii; proceedings of the 1922 convention of the Chamber of Commerce of the United States (CCUS), *Nation's Business* 10 (5 June 1922); NFTC, *Official Report*, 1922.

. . . We are verging . . . upon another World War, and even if it does not result in war, it will result in such utter economic chaos as would have a more destructive effect upon civilization and upon peoples than war itself.''[6]

The real dilemma facing Republican officials was how to make an American contribution to European stability without jeopardizing domestic priorities. As important as European developments were to American self-interest, President Harding still believed that it was his duty ''to prosper America first.'' In his opening address to Congress in April 1921, the president emphasized that the reduction of taxes, the liquidation of the public debt, and the protection of American industry were the most immediate goals of his administration. Republican officials considered these measures, together with the adequate provision of credit, the stabilization of the domestic construction industry, and the thorough collection and dissemination of statistical data, to be the primary prerequisites of the rejuvenation of the American economy.[7] This orientation placed important constraints on the extent to which the Republicans could contribute to stability in the Old World. The desire to reduce the public debt and lower taxes circumscribed the extent to which the United States could decrease the European war debts or involve itself in the dispute over reparations. Commitment to the protective tariff restricted European imports and retarded American efforts to stabilize European currencies. Concern with domestic liquidity during the credit crunch of 1920–21 temporarily limited the availability of American capital for European reconstruction. In sum, domestic policies aimed at restoring internal economic activity often collided with the selfishly enlightened desire to play a helpful role in mitigating Franco-German differences and in rehabilitating Europe.

6. For Borah's statement, see Borah to Robert J. Thomson, 5 February 1923, Borah Papers, Box 227; for the growing preoccupation with European instability in Congress, the press, and the business community, see, for example, ''A Golden A. E. F. to Save Europe Again,'' *Literary Digest* 75 (30 December 1922):5–7; [William R. Castle], ''Two Years of American Foreign Policy,'' p. 18; ''A Summary of Views on Cancellation of Inter-Allied Debts,'' *Congressional Digest* 2 (December 1922):77–83; ''The Balance Sheet of Europe: Reparations and International Debts,'' *Consensus* 8 (January 1923); Special Committee, ''Report on European Conditions,'' NFTC, *Official Report*, 1923; National Association of Manufactures (NAM), *Proceedings of the Annual Convention*, 1923, p. 311; AFBF, *Federation's Third Year*, pp. 15–20; Russell C. Leffingwell, ''War Debts,'' pp. 22–40.

7. For Harding's speech, see Department of State, *Papers Relating to the Foreign Relations of the United States*, 1921, 1:vii–ix (hereafter cited as FR); see also Department of Commerce, *Annual Report*, 1922, pp. 31–32; Conference on Unemployment, *Report*, pp. 159–60; Hoover, ''Drafts,'' January 1922, HHCD, Box 21; see also, for example, Robert K. Murray, *The Politics of Normalcy*, pp. 46–47.

American policymakers recognized the often conflicting, yet inter-locking, demands of the domestic and European economies.[8] In the midst of a complex interplay of interest-group pressures, bureaucratic rivalries, partisan conflicts, and legislative-executive encounters, the Americans sought to put together a matrix of economic policies and decision-making instruments that would prove capable of balancing the needs of the domestic economy with the requirements of European stabilization. During the initial years of the Republican ascendancy, therefore, American policy toward France evolved in the larger context of American efforts to aid in the rehabilitation of Europe. But since the American contribution to Europe's reconstruction was limited to the financial and economic spheres, circumscribed by domestic consider-ations, and influenced by the perceived value of European stability to American self-interest, the brunt of American policy often fell upon the French.

Equality, Flexibility, and American Commercial Policy

When the Harding administration assumed office in March 1921, the nation's commercial situation demanded immediate attention. Export-oriented associations, like the NFTC, called for an expansion of foreign markets, while other business organizations, like the Home Market Club of Boston, sought still higher tariffs. Agricultural spokesmen, meanwhile, clamored for both tariff protection and export expansion. Ironically, whether interested in protecting the internal market or cul-tivating new markets abroad, business and farm leaders often cited European developments, especially European monetary disorder, as a major source of their problems.[9]

The new administration moved quickly to respond to these diverse pressures. Convening a special session of Congress in April, Harding reaffirmed his commitment to the protective tariff principle, cited his belief in the primacy of internal development and the home market, and called for the enactment of emergency tariff legislation.[10] Several weeks later the president signed the Emergency Tariff Act, which raised the duties on agricultural staples, imposed a temporary embargo on

8. See Harding's comments in FR, 1921, 1:vii.
9. For an excellent discussion of divisions within the business community, see Joan Hoff Wilson, *American Business and Foreign Policy, 1920–1933*, pp. 65–100; for ag-ricultural demands, see AFBF, *Federation's Third Year*, pp. 15, 19, 25; Howard, "Europe the Farmers' Market," pp. 24–26.
10. FR, 1921, 1:ix.

foreign dyes and chemicals, and contained antidumping provisions.[11] He also appointed to the United States Tariff Commission Thomas O. Marvin and William Burgess, well-known protectionists.[12] The president and his advisers, however, did not ignore the concomitant demands for commercial expansion. Hoover reorganized the Bureau of Foreign and Domestic Commerce (BFDC), expanded its activities, and recruited trained professionals to foster the sale of American goods overseas. The administration initiated conversations with bankers regarding the adequacy of credit facilities for the nation's export trade. During the summer, Harding put his influence behind the Emergency Agricultural Credits Act, which, among other things, empowered the WFC to extend loans to foreign purchasers of American farm products.[13]

These initial actions set the background for the protracted controversy over the implementation of long-term commercial policy. While the Emergency Tariff Act was being enacted, the House Ways and Means Committee was already working on a permanent tariff measure. During the committee's review of the rate structure low-tariff proponents were overwhelmed by the influence of small- and medium-sized manufacturers and by the spread of protectionist sentiment into the South and West, the Democratic party, and the major farm organizations.[14] As a result in July 1921 the House passed the Fordney Bill. This legislation raised most tariff rates, imposed almost insurmountable duties on new chemical and dyestuff products, and incorporated the highly protectionist principle of American valuation for computing ad valorem duties. In addition sections 301 and 302 of the bill reaffirmed the policies of reciprocal concessions and special bargaining as the underlying basis of America's commercial relations with the rest of the world.[15]

At the same time that the House of Representatives was deliberating

11. Robert K. Murray, *The Harding Era*, pp. 206–7; Wilson, *American Business*, pp. 70–73.
12. Wilson, *American Business*, p. 87.
13. For Hoover's efforts, see Herbert C. Hoover, *The Memoirs of Herbert Hoover*, 2:79; for the reappraisal of credit facilities, see Memorandum on western bankers' dinner and conference at the White House, 23 June 1921, Harding Papers, PCF, Box 88; for the Emergency Agricultural Credits Act, see Murray, *Harding Era*, pp. 208–11.
14. Frank W. Fetter, "Congressional Trade Theory," p. 418; Charles M. Dollar, "The South and the Fordney-McCumber Tariff of 1922," pp. 45–66; James R. Connor, "National Farm Organizations and United States Tariff Policy in the 1920's," pp. 32–43; Frank William Taussig, *The Tariff History of the United States*, pp. 451–77; Wilson, *American Business*, pp. 74–79.
15. Murray, *Harding Era*, pp. 271–72.

over the Fordney Bill, members of the Commerce Department, the State Department, and the Tariff Commission began meeting to consider the more fundamental principles of United States commercial policy. Rather than focusing on the protectionist rates emerging in the Ways and Means Committee, their major concern was with ending foreign discrimination against American goods, expanding American exports, and promoting stable commercial relations. William S. Culbertson of the Tariff Commission and Wallace M. McClure and W. W. Cumberland of the Department of State became convinced that the best means of achieving these objectives was by rejecting the practice of reciprocity and by adopting the equality-of-treatment or most-favored-nation principle in its unconditional form.[16]

In the early summer of 1921 Culbertson assumed the initiative within the executive branch on the matter of United States commercial policy. In a twenty-one-page memorandum submitted to the State and Commerce departments, he attacked the reciprocity and bargaining features of the Fordney Bill. Culbertson insisted that these features would lead to chronic haggling between nations and to the erection of discriminatory trade barriers.[17] He advocated the adoption of a nonnegotiable tariff structure that would apply equally to the goods of all nations. In order to pressure other nations to abide by the principle of strict equality and to reject the practice of granting special favors, Culbertson emphasized that the president should have the power to impose penalty duties on the products of those nations discriminating against American commerce. Implicit in this orientation was the belief that, given the ability to compete on equal terms, American producers would rapidly expand their exports. But Culbertson reiterated that the equality principle would contribute to world peace and stability as exporters in various nations would know that for a certain period of time they would be competing on equal terms within specific market areas.[18]

16. "Minutes of Meeting of Representatives of the Departments of State and Commerce and of the Tariff Commission," 26 May 1921, General Records of the Department of State, RG 59, File No. 611.003/841; Wallace McClure to Hughes, 27 May 1921, ibid.; W. W. Cumberland to Fred Dearing, 18 June 1921, ibid., 611.003/842; Cumberland to Dearing, 29 June, 14 July 1921, ibid., 611.003/844, 843; Carl P. Parrini, *Heir to Empire*, pp. 226–33.

17. William S. Culbertson, Memorandum on reciprocity and bargaining provisions of the Fordney Tariff Bill, 16 July 1921, Culbertson Papers, Box 46.

18. For Culbertson's views, see "Minutes of Meeting," 26 May 1921, RG 59, 611.003/841; Cumberland to Dearing, 18 June 1921, ibid., 611.003/842; William Culbertson, *International Economic Policies*, pp. 60–63, 78–80, 87–88, 96–101. Culbertson's ideas were based on a Tariff Commission study undertaken in 1919. See Tariff Commission, *Reciprocity and Commercial Treaties*.

While executive officials discussed the basic principles of United States commercial policy, the Senate Finance Committee initiated its own hearings on the Fordney Bill on 25 July 1921. The committee immediately became immersed in the protracted controversy over the nature and extent of protectionism. High-tariff proponents insisted on American valuation; that is, the computation of duties on the basis of the wholesale price of competitive goods in the United States. More moderate members of the committee urged that duties continue to be levied according to the foreign market value. Meanwhile, the tariff issue became linked to the concurrent legislative debates over the war debts, tax policy, the veterans' bonus, and agricultural relief. Since the president was still reluctant to intervene forcefully in legislative affairs and was uncertain how to proceed on commercial policies, no meaningful action was taken by the Senate Finance Committee during the special session of Congress.[19]

This delay provided Culbertson with an opportunity to muster additional support in Congress and the administration for his viewpoint. Culbertson had been raised in Emporia, Kansas. He had developed a close association with William Allen White, the well-known progressive editor from his home town, and had cultivated the friendship of the Kansas delegation in Congress. During the summer and autumn of 1921, Culbertson adroitly used these contacts to establish relations with important members of the Senate Finance Committee and gain access to the White House. In numerous memoranda and several personal meetings with the president, Culbertson championed the equality-of-treatment principle in its unconditional form and warned of the dangers inherent in the system of American valuation. He feared that prevailing economic circumstances might lead to the imposition of excessively high tariffs. Therefore, he urged the president to adopt a flexible tariff policy. Such a policy, Culbertson emphasized, would allow the president to correct abuses in congressional rate making, equalize the costs of production at home and abroad, and adjust the American economy to changing world economic conditions.

Culbertson's systematic campaign to mold American commercial policy was sustained by his ambition to become chairman of the Tariff Commission, his desire to aggrandize the powers of the institution to which he belonged, and his conviction that revolutionary changes in

19. Murray, *Harding Era*, pp. 272–75; Murray, *Politics of Normalcy*, pp. 36–78; Wilson, *American Business*, pp. 82–84.

the nation's economic position demanded new initiatives. Conscious of the transition of America from debtor to creditor status and of the growing importance of American exports, yet fearful of the impact of unrestricted imports on domestic industry, Culbertson hoped that the principles of equality and flexibility, if independently administered by an apolitical commission, would enable the United States to reconcile competing pressures in behalf of protection and expansion.[20]

Throughout the prolonged debate stretching from December 1921 to September 1922 Culbertson lobbied, cajoled, and pleaded for administrative and senatorial support of the principles of equality, flexibility, and foreign valuation. As coordinator of the economic work being done for the disarmament conference, Culbertson developed a cordial relationship with the secretary of state, convinced Hughes of the value of his own position on commercial policy, and encouraged the secretary to press these matters with the president.[21] Even more significantly, during the winter of 1921–22 Culbertson cultivated a working relationship with Senator Reed Smoot, second-ranking Republican on the Finance Committee. He gradually persuaded Smoot that the adoption of the principles of flexibility and equality and the rejection of American valuation were prerequisites of the maintenance of international commercial stability and the expansion of American trade. During the winter of 1921–22, Smoot proposed amendments to the Fordney Bill incorporating many of Culbertson's recommendations. Shortly thereafter Culbertson acknowledged that "if anyone had told me six months ago that I would now be sympathetically working with Senator Smoot . . . , I would have rolled over and croaked."[22] At the same time, Culbertson persuaded Harding to support the principle of flexibility. In his annual message to Congress on 6 December 1921 the

20. This discussion of Culbertson is based largely on material in Culbertson Papers, Box 46. See especially Culbertson to William Allen White, 14 March, 25 July, 12, 13, 15 October 1921, ibid.; Culbertson to Harding, 28 October 1921, ibid.; see also Culbertson to Dwight W. Morrow, 9 February, 10 September 1921, Morrow Papers; J. Richard Snyder, "William S. Culbertson and the Formation of Modern Commercial Policy, 1917–1925," pp. 397–406.
21. Culbertson to White, 5, 8 January 1922, Culbertson Papers, Box 47.
22. For Culbertson's relationship with Senator Reed Smoot, see Culbertson to White, 20 January 1922, ibid.; see also Culbertson to White, 14 December 1921, ibid., Box 46; Culbertson to White, 13 March 1922, ibid., Box 47; Culbertson, "The Plan Submitted by Senator Smoot," 21 January 1922, ibid.; Smoot to White, 1 February 1922, ibid.; Culbertson to Smoot, 17 February, 24 March, 20 April 1922, ibid., Box 46; see also Senate, Select Committee, *Investigation of the Tariff Commission*, 5:619–23, 632.

president called for a flexible tariff that would not prohibit imports and that would aid American exports.[23]

The struggle over the shaping of commercial policy, however, was not over. Protectionists continued lobbying for ever higher rates, championing American valuation, and challenging the idea of flexibility. Culbertson fought back and pressed his case with a wavering president, sympathetic members of the cabinet, ambivalent leaders of the farm bloc, and other members of Congress.[24] As a result the tariff legislation that was finally passed incorporated, though sometimes in ambiguous and uncertain language, many of the principles that Culbertson had championed. Sections 315, 316, and 317 of the Fordney-McCumber Act replaced sections 301, 302, and 303 of the original Fordney Bill. Section 315 provided the president with flexible authority to increase or decrease tariff rates by up to 50 percent to equalize costs of production. Section 317 empowered the president to impose penalty duties on the products of nations that discriminated against American commerce. Moreover, the traditional method of computing duties according to foreign market or export value was maintained; American valuation was accepted only as an alternate means of calculating duties. Finally, the Tariff Commission was authorized to conduct studies of comparative production costs, investigate foreign discriminatory practices, and submit its findings to the president.[25]

The principles of equality and flexibility upon which American commercial policy was based during the Republican ascendancy were in large part the result of the unremitting efforts of Culbertson. Although officials in the State and Commerce departments supported his efforts, their limited conception of the role of the executive branch in tariff matters and their fear of congressional accusations of executive interference in legislative concerns made them reluctant to press their views in the House Ways and Means Committee and the Senate Finance

23. For Harding's message, see FR, 1921, 1:xxvi–xxvii; for Culbertson's efforts, see Culbertson to Harding (including proposed amendments to Fordney Bill), 28 October 1921, Culbertson Papers, Box 46; Senate, Select Committee, *Investigation of the Tariff Commission*, 5:628–33; for the significance of Harding's speech, see Cumberland, Memorandum, 19 January 1922, RG 59, 611.003/991.

24. For the struggle between Culbertson and his opponents, see Culbertson to White, 21 October 1921, Culbertson Papers, Box 46; Culbertson to White, 13 March, 14, 24, 28 April, 24 June, 24 July 1922, ibid., Box 47; Culbertson, Memorandum for the president, 24 April 1922, ibid.; Culbertson to Harding, 23 June 1922, ibid.; Culbertson, Memorandum, 10 August 1922, ibid.; Culbertson to Arthur Capper, 17 July 1922, ibid.; Culbertson to Smoot, 20 April 1922, ibid., Box 46.

25. For a fine but critical assessment of the legislation, especially of the flexible tariff provision and cost-of-production formula, see William B. Kelly, Jr., "Antecedents of Present Commercial Policy, 1922–1934," pp. 14–25.

Committee. Consequently, they usually relied on Culbertson to argue their case.[26] Similarly, while business organizations like the NFTC and CCUS officially endorsed the ideas of equality and flexibility, key officials within these associations viewed them with misgivings and did not lobby strenuously in their behalf. During a critical time in the tariff debate, for example, O. K. Davis, secretary of the NFTC, went on vacation, returned to find the automobile industry very upset, admitted his uncertainty on basic issues, and informed Culbertson he would leave matters to Culbertson's discretion.[27] This incident reflected the uncertainty among most businessmen about what ought to be done to sustain the nation's economic and commercial needs in an increasingly interdependent world economy. Culbertson exerted a decisive influence because he successfully integrated prevailing ideas and developed a clear vision of the types of administrative machinery that might resolve the conflicting demands for protection and expansion and reconcile the divergent needs of the national and international economy.[28]

Culbertson and other executive officials expended considerably less energy and experienced much less success in setting tariff rates. When duties had to be established on each of thousands of particular items, the overall well-being of the American economy seemed rather remote. Meanwhile, special-interest groups were directly affected and clamored for as much protection as they could get. The result was a duty structure that executive officials considered unnecessarily high but which they were prepared to accept because of the recent economic recession, the rise in foreign customs duties, the depreciation of foreign currencies, the massive amount of congressional logrolling, and the divisions within the Republican party.[29]

26. See, for example, Cumberland to Dearing, 29 June 1921, RG 59, 611.003/844; Stanley K. Hornbeck to Arthur N. Young, 1 September 1922, ibid., 611.003/1165; Cumberland to Young, 30 August 1922, ibid.; Young to Leland Harrison, 1 September 1922, ibid., 611.003/1166. Hughes presented the department's case only after his views were solicited by Senator Porter McCumber. See McCumber to secretary, 20 July 1922, ibid., 611.003/1083; Hughes to McCumber, 21 July 1922, ibid.

27. O. K. Davis to Culbertson, 8 March, 22, 28 August 1922, Culbertson Papers, Box 47; Culbertson to Davis, 26, 29 August 1922, ibid.; see also the correspondence between Culbertson and C. P. Snow (of the Foreign Commerce Department of the CCUS), 20, 22 May 1922, ibid.

28. There were, of course, enormous problems in implementing the flexible tariff provisions and in determining costs-of-production. But these received little attention in 1921–22. For the problems, see Senate, Select Committee, *Investigation of the Tariff Commission*, 1:9 ff.

29. For the considerations influencing the level of customs duties, see Culbertson, Memorandum for the president, 24 April 1922, Culbertson Papers, Box 47; Culbertson to White, 18 September 1922, ibid.; Tariff Commission, *Depreciated Exchange and International Trade*, p. 8; Department of Commerce, Bureau of Foreign and Domestic

Republican policymakers, however, did recognize the interrelation-ships between American import duties, the well-being of the interna-tional economy, and the expansion of American commerce. Like many leading businessmen, they realized that, as a creditor nation, the United States had to increase imports.[30] In early 1923 Hoover noted with satisfaction that the nation's merchandise export surplus had been de-creasing steadily since mid-1920, and that imports, measured quanti-tatively, had been increasing more rapidly than exports.[31] At the same time the Commerce Department's assessment of the anticipated impact of the new Fordney-McCumber duties convinced Hoover that they would not constitute a barrier to additional imports.[32] Moreover, he argued that whatever export balance did exist could be offset by foreign loans, tourist expenditures, and immigrant remittances.[33] Therefore, Hoover, Culbertson, and other members of the administration believed that the new tariff duties could be reconciled with the well-being of the world economy and the expansion of American exports.

Republican officials thought that whatever faults existed in the new tariff structure would prove self-correcting. Harding emphasized that the success of the Fordney-McCumber tariff depended upon the effec-tive functioning of the flexible tariff provisions.[34] Culbertson, Smoot, and other framers of the legislation assumed that these provisions would be used to lower rates. As soon as the tariff act was passed, Culbertson exhorted the Tariff Commission "to plunge boldly into its work." He maintained that reductions emanating from the imple-mentation of the flexibility principle would be well received by the

Commerce (BFDC), *Foreign Tariff Legislation*, pp. 5–7; see also Murray, *Harding Era*, pp. 272–80.

30. For the emphasis on increasing imports, see, for example, NFTC, *The American Trade Balance and Probable Tendencies*, pp. 26–27, 39–40; NFTC, *Official Report*, 1922, p. vii; NAM, *Proceedings*, 1920, p. 10; Lester V. Chandler, *Benjamin Strong*, pp. 264–65; Culbertson to Morrow, 9 February 1921, Morrow Papers; see also Harding's address, FR, 1921, 1:xxvi–xxvii.

31. Department of Commerce, *Annual Report*, 1922, pp. 17–19; for the depart-ment's recognition of the need for increased imports, see also Department of Com-merce, *Commerce Yearbook*, 1922, pp. 450–51, 456; see also, Hoover to Senator George W. Pepper, 19 February 1922, HHCD, Box 292.

32. J. Hohn to Louis Domeratzky, "Effect of New Tariff," 28 September 1922, 2 October 1922, HHCD, Box 293; "Memorandum on the Probable Effects of the New Tariff on Our Import Trade," n.d., ibid., Box 292; Hoover to Oswald Knauth, 23 December 1922, ibid.

33. For Hoover's emphasis on the so-called invisible items, see his foreword to "The Balance of International Payments of the United States in 1922," BFDC, *Trade Informa-tion Bulletin*, 144:2; see also Department of Commerce, *Annual Report*, 1922, p. 17.

34. Murray, *Harding Era*, pp. 275–77.

American public, redound to the benefit of the Republican party, and lead to the institutionalization of scientific rate making. In early 1923 he appealed to the State Department and the Commerce Department for support in his efforts to persuade the protectionists on the Tariff Commission to utilize the flexible provisions effectively.[35]

At the same time, Culbertson prodded his colleagues in the executive branch to interpret the new tariff legislation as an endorsement of the most-favored-nation principle in its unconditional form.[36] Section 317, though calling for equality of treatment, did not specifically authorize a departure from the conditional interpretation of this principle. But State Department officials, like Wallace McClure and Stanley K. Hornbeck, were as eager as Culbertson "to revise our entire commercial policy along the lines of the open door" and to construe the Fordney-McCumber legislation as authorizing a new set of commercial treaties. Believing that additional foreign markets were "a sine qua non to continued industrial expansion," they reiterated that the unconditional interpretation of the most-favored-nation principle would eliminate foreign discrimination, expand exports, and stabilize the international commercial environment.[37] In early 1923 Hughes and Culbertson were able to convince both President Harding and Senator Lodge of the wisdom of an unconditional interpretation and of its essential compatibility with the new congressional tariff act.[38] Thus, while Culbertson was endeavoring to activate the flexible tariff provisions, State Department officials launched a campaign to overhaul the nation's commercial treaties to gain universal acceptance of the principles of equality and nondiscrimination.

Policymakers immediately recognized that, with the exception of the British system of intraimperial preferences, France presented the greatest threat to the new commercial policy of the United States.[39] In

35. Culbertson, "Proposed Policy of the Tariff Commission for the First Six Months of 1923," 28 December 1922, RG 59, 611.0031/181; Culbertson, "Domestic Tariff Policy," 30 January 1923, ibid.; Culbertson to Hoover, 22 March, 5, 7 April 1923, HHCD, Box 294; for the expectation that tariff duties would be lowered, see also Senate, Select Committee, *Investigation of the Tariff Commission*, 3:259, 5:570, 639, 648–51.

36. Culbertson to Hughes, 29 September 1922, RG 59, 611.003/1141; Young to William Phillips, 29 August 1922, ibid., 611.0031/179; Culbertson to Hughes, 14 December 1922, Culbertson Papers, Box 47.

37. McClure and Hornbeck, "The Department of State and the Tariff Act of 1922," 30 October 1922, RG 59, 611.003/1188; Young to Hughes, 21 October 1922, ibid., 611.003/179; White to Harrison, 29 December 1922, Culbertson Papers, Box 47.

38. FR, 1923, 1:121–32; [Beerits Memorandum], "The Commercial Treaty with Germany," Hughes Papers, Box 172, pp. 4–6.

39. See, for example, McClure and Hornbeck, "Tariff Act of 1922," 30 October 1922, RG 59, 611.003/1188.

the immediate aftermath of World War I, France sought new foreign markets and adopted a commercial policy based on reciprocity and protection. French producers were agitated that French exports usually encountered higher duties than did goods entering France. French businessmen and government officials were unimpressed by explanations that this discrepancy occurred because French exports tended to be specialty items and luxury goods. The reciprocity formula adopted by the Chamber of Deputies in 1919 was designed to secure better treatment of French exports in high-tariff nations like the United States. The French maintained a two-column tariff structure, including a maximum and minimum schedule of duties. But after 1919 any reductions from the maximum rates were considered favors exchanged for equivalent foreign concessions. This policy underscored a bargaining approach to tariff matters, deviated from the nonnegotiable, single-column tariff policy of the Harding administration, and multiplied the distinctions in the treatment accorded the products of different nations in the French market.[40]

Although even before the war France had not granted her minimum rates to all American goods, this unequivocal postwar commitment to reciprocity constituted a fundamental threat to American commercial interests and principles. Studies conducted by the Department of State and the Tariff Commission in 1922 and 1923 concluded that France "openly and palpably" discriminated against American goods, especially industrial products. According to American officials there was no justification for such discrimination because French goods received the same treatment in the United States as the goods of all other nations. Most worrisome, however, was the fact that French policies reflected a general European departure from the principle of strict equality. One State Department official summed up the situation for his colleagues by insisting that "if our policy is to prevail that of France must be overthrown. It is believed that the commerce of both the United States and France and the commerce of the world generally would greatly benefit by the elimination of the present French policy. Perhaps extreme measures against it would, under these circumstances, be justified."[41]

40. This brief outline of French tariff policy is based on the following sources: Graham Stuart, "Tariff Making in France," pp. 98–106; Frank W. Taussig, "The Tariff Controversy with France," pp. 177–84; H. Van V. Fay, "Commercial Policy in Post-War Europe," pp. 456–57; William F. Ogburn and William Jaffe, *The Economic Development of Post-War France*, pp. 441–550; BFDC, *Foreign Trade Legislation*, pp. 5, 9.
41. McClure to Harrison, 17 July 1923, RG 59, 611.0031/188; McClure and

Yet, most American policymakers hesitated to activate section 317 and impose penalty duties on French imports. They realized that the new, high tariff duties of the United States constituted a serious problem for foreign exporters. Jules Jusserand, the French ambassador, had already complained bitterly about the increases in duties on French goods. Commerce Department officials had heard rumors of impending French retaliatory measures. Under these circumstances McClure and Hornbeck acknowledged that "an increased rate might provoke unreasoning hostility and reprisal rather than a cessation of the discrimination against which it is aimed."[42] Thus, no immediate action was taken under section 317. Instead, American officials were left to find some appropriate means, perhaps the flexible tariff provisions, to alleviate French retaliatory measures. Under these circumstances McClure and Hornbeck acknowledged that "an increased rate might provoke unreareciprocity and accept the most-favored-nation principle in its unconditional form.

By early 1923 the basis of American commercial policy had been laid, and France had emerged as a leading antagonist. Congress had increased duties far in excess of what the administration considered desirable. Yet, Harding and his key advisers, believing in the protective principle, were willing to acquiesce to the tariff schedule. They insisted, however, on the incorporation of the flexible tariff provisions. With the use of section 315 they hoped to redress legitimate foreign grievances, adjust the nation's duty structure to the needs of the world economy, and entice foreign nations into granting American goods unconditional most-favored-nation treatment. If countries like France remained recalcitrant, however, section 317 could be implemented to exert additional pressure. Policymakers hoped that the Tariff Commission and the president would be able to use sections 315 and 317 in an objective and scientific manner to reconcile the conflicting imperatives of the American economy and inaugurate a regime of commercial stability in the Old World.

Hornbeck, "Tariff Act of 1922," 30 October 1922, ibid., 611.003/1188; United States Tariff Commission, Memorandum on French tariff discriminations, June 1923, ibid., 611.0031/188; McClure and Hornbeck, Memorandum, 19 July 1922, ibid., 611.0031/1380.

42. McClure and Hornbeck, "Tariff Act of 1922," 30 October 1922, ibid., 611.003/1188; for French complaints, see Jules Jusserand to secretary, 20 December 1921, 28 February 1922, ibid., 611.003/960, 993; Henry Chalmers to chief, Foreign Service Divisions, 13 October 1922, Records of the BFDC, RG 151, File 3266.

Exchange Instability and Central Bank Cooperation

The instability of European exchange rates and the depreciation of European currencies complicated the formulation of American commercial policy. Business leaders and farm spokesmen feared that European exports, benefiting from depreciating exchange rates, would flood the American market and undersell American goods. They also worried that the appreciation of the dollar would force Europeans to cut back their purchases of American products.[43]

These concerns found expression in several branches of government. In the autumn of 1921 the House Committee on Banking and Currency held hearings on the impact of exchange-rate fluctuations on American commerce and the American economy. At about the same time several United States senators wrote letters to the president urging him to take action to ameliorate the European exchange situation. Harding, Hoover, and Secretary of the Treasury Andrew W. Mellon had already consulted with leading bankers on how to frame a loan policy that would expedite the stabilization of exchange rates. The restoration of exchange stability was recognized in official circles as prerequisite to the expansion of American exports, the well-being of the American economy, and the reconstruction of Europe.[44]

Real impetus toward developing a coherent administration policy awaited the visit to the United States in August 1921 of Montagu Norman, governor of the Bank of England. Norman's aim was to inform American officials of the critical world financial situation and the need for immediate international action to deal with the particularly grave financial problems besetting central and eastern Europe. While Norman was in Washington, Benjamin Strong, governor of the Federal Reserve Bank of New York (FRBNY), was invited to participate in the high-level talks. During the ensuing discussions, Secretary of Commerce Hoover assumed a leading role. He emphasized that "the economic rehabilitation of these 100,000,000 people [in central and eastern Europe] is vital to our commerce, not only directly with them but also with the other states [of western Europe] whose prosperity so much depends

43. See, for example, NFTC, *Official Report*, 1921, p. vii; Howard, "Europe the Farmers' Market," pp. 24–26; address, by F. C. Schwedtman, NAM, *Proceedings*, 1922, p. 350.
44. House, Committee on Banking and Currency, *Exchange Stabilization*; Senator Gilbert Hitchcock to Harding, 30 June 1921, Harding Papers, PCF, Box 88; Senator John F. Shafroth to Harding, 14 January 1922, ibid., Box 307; Memorandum on western bankers' dinner and conference, 23 June 1921, ibid., Box 88; Strong to S. Parker Gilbert, 23 May 1921, Strong Papers, 012.5.

upon them. In the last analysis the rebuilding of economic life among these people is of daily importance to every worker or farmer in our country and the whole world." According to Hoover the only means of rehabilitating currencies and promoting recovery was through "the healing power . . . of private finance and commerce." Belittling the efficacy of political action and government initiatives, he urged Strong to consult with bankers in the United States and Europe regarding the possibility of devising a plan "of purely private character" to restore currency stability and generate economic progress.[45] Hoover had little faith in government loans because he believed that they would be based upon political criteria rather than economic facts, that they would be vulnerable to the conflicting demands of ethnic groups in the United States, that they would lead to undesirable political entanglements abroad, and that they would politicize international financial transactions and intensify political friction among nations.[46]

Although these initial talks between the administration and Strong did not lead to concrete developments, the framework for subsequent action had been established. The first task, Hoover wrote Harding in January 1922, was for European nations, especially France and Germany, to stop inflation and balance their budgets.[47] These steps would create the necessary preconditions for cooperative international action of a nonpolitical, nongovernmental character; that is, cooperation among private American and European bankers, especially between the FRBNY and the central banks of England and France. Such cooperation would remove the entire matter of exchange stabilization from the realm of domestic and international politics and place it in the hands of experts who wished to resurrect the prewar gold standard as a means of automatically insuring currency stability.

Strong was eager to assume the task envisioned for him by the administration. For several years he had been contemplating collaborative efforts between the Bank of England, the Bank of France, and the FRBNY.[48] In the spring of 1922 he told Hoover that his major goal was

45. Hoover to Strong, 30 August 1921, Strong Papers, 013.1; Strong to Pierre Jay, 29 August 1921, ibid., 320.115; Montagu Norman to Strong, 15 September 1921, ibid., 1116.2.
46. Herbert Hoover, "Momentous Conference," *Journal of the American Bankers Association* 13 (January 1921):462–63; Hoover, *Memoirs*, 2:13–14; Parrini, *Heir to Empire*, pp. 185–91; Wilson, *American Business*, pp. 105–13.
47. Hoover to Harding, 4 January 1922, Harding Papers, PCF, Box 5.
48. Memorandum of conversation between Strong and Sir Arthur Salter, 25 May 1928, Strong Papers, 1000.9; Stephen V. O. Clarke, *Central Bank Cooperation, 1924–1931*, pp. 40–41.

to facilitate the restoration of the gold standard and the resumption of free gold payments. Some progress had been made. But currencies could not be stabilized until budgets were balanced, inflationary policies ended, trade deficits reduced, governmental debts curtailed, banks of issue freed of government interference, and large gold reserves made available to the stabilizing nation. Strong maintained that several nations, including Britain, were close to meeting the conditions necessary for effective stabilization. He wanted to deal with each of these nations separately. He was willing to extend gold credits to the banks of issue of these nations. Indeed, since the United States was then holding most of the world's gold reserve, Strong was anxious to tie other nations to the gold standard to minimize the possibility that the huge stocks of gold in Federal Reserve vaults would lead to domestic inflation. But the governor of the FRBNY also confided to Hoover that the reparation and war debt questions might hamstring his efforts.[49]

Yet Strong was aware of the political pressures affecting the administration's efforts to deal with the war debt and reparation issues. Throughout the winter and spring of 1922 he emphasized to Montagu Norman that American officials were concerned about Europe's financial disorder and sympathetic to central bank efforts to deal with it. But he explained that the political situation in Washington, the attacks of the farm bloc on the administration, the rifts within the Republican party, and the forthcoming elections in November made immediate constructive action impossible. In the meantime Strong urged Norman to encourage European governments to implement sound financial and fiscal policies. Such actions, he emphasized, would favorably impress American officials and hasten American cooperation.[50]

While Strong was laying plans for long-term central bank cooperation, European officials met at Genoa to discuss the problems of European reconstruction. One part of the British plan called for "a unified monetary system based on parities fixed in terms of gold—a system in which domestic economies adjusted in order to maintain international equilibrium." Basically, this was an attempt to restore the prewar system with a few innovations, including the adoption of the gold exchange standard and the return of most continental currencies to gold at new fixed parities. The British proposal also called for continuous

49. Strong to Hoover, 22 April 1922, Strong Papers, 013.1; Strong to James Logan, 12 July 1922, Papers of the Federal Reserve Bank of New York, C797 (hereafter cited as FRBNY Papers).
50. Strong to Norman, 18, 21 February, 22, 28 March 1922, Strong Papers, 1116.3.

central bank cooperation and necessary credit arrangements to limit exchange rate fluctuations. While the French were far from enthusiastic, the Bank of England was nevertheless instructed to call a meeting of central bankers to implement the recommendations.[51]

Strong was hesitant to attend a conference where he might be outvoted. He worried that international obligations might lead to domestic inflation. Nevertheless, he was willing to attend a meeting in London where he could discuss efforts to restore the gold standard and institutionalize central bank cooperation. During July he consulted with Mellon, Hoover, and Harding and found them sympathetic to the idea. The conference, however, never materialized because of the worsening of the reparations crisis and the deterioration of Anglo-French relations.[52]

By the latter part of 1922 government officials and bankers agreed that the best means of dealing with fluctuating exchange rates was through the restoration of the gold standard. The gold standard, it was assumed, was a self-regulating mechanism that once reestablished would insure international monetary stability, promote world commerce, prevent domestic inflation, and automatically reconcile the needs of the national and international economy.[53] Accordingly, President Harding told Congress in December 1922 that ''we would rejoice to help rehabilitate currency systems.''[54] But this aid had to be provided through nonpolitical agencies like the FRBNY. Such an approach avoided formal American governmental involvement in European political and financial affairs, allowed so-called experts (central bankers) to handle complex financial questions on a supposedly apolitical basis, and insured a dominant role for American capital in the struggle for European stability. American officials hoped that through central bank cooperation, Strong would be able to use the nation's enormous gold reserves to rehabilitate foreign currencies and revive world commerce

51. Stephen V. O. Clarke, "The Reconstruction of the International Monetary System," pp. 3–13; Clarke, *Central Bank Cooperation*, pp. 33–35; H. C. MacLean to director, 21 April 1922, RG 151, File 600.2; William Adams Brown, Jr., *The International Gold Standard Reinterpreted*, 1:341–57. The gold exchange standard of the 1920s differed from the prewar gold standard in that many nations held part of their international reserves not in gold but in the foreign exchange of other nations firmly wed to gold.

52. Strong to Norman, 15 May 1922 (and accompanying memoranda), Strong Papers, 1116.3; Strong to Logan, 12 July 1922, FRBNY Papers, C797; Clarke, *Central Bank Cooperation*, pp. 36–38.

53. Chandler, *Benjamin Strong*, pp. 260–61; Clarke, *Central Bank Cooperation*, pp. 27–28. Of course, changes in the international financial environment and escalating domestic pressures precluded the postwar gold standard from functioning in the axiomatic fashion that was anticipated.

54. FR, 1922, 1:xiv–xv.

without risking domestic inflation or entangling the United States government in European political affairs.[55]

Success at these efforts, however, depended on the close cooperation and mutual understanding of central bankers, especially in the United States, Britain, and France. Strong's good relations with Norman and the close ties between J. P. Morgan and Company and British financial houses boded well for Anglo-American cooperation.[56] In fact, during the first half of 1923 British and American bankers worked out a scheme for the rehabilitation of Austrian finances that depended in part on the flotation of a loan in American financial markets.[57]

During this same period Strong made little effort to establish close ties with French bankers or with the Bank of France. His initial task was to tie the stronger European currencies to the gold standard. Yet, given Strong's own long-term plans and the importance that American officials placed on the stabilization of the franc, similar collaborative efforts with the Bank of France were simply a matter of time.[58] There were, however, several preconditions for such action. First, the French had to adopt more conservative financial and fiscal policies. Second, the Harding administration, in cooperation with European governments, had to grapple constructively with the tangled questions of war debts and reparations. Third, Republican officials, in conjunction with private American bankers, had to work out a policy for regulating the outflow of private capital.

Consultation, Voluntarism, and American Loan Policy

By the time the Harding administration assumed office in March 1921 business leaders, agricultural spokesmen, and international bankers agreed that the export of American capital was indispensable for the stabilization of European currencies, the development of American trade, and the reconstruction of devastated Europe.[59] The new presi-

55. The best accounts of Strong's efforts can be found in Chandler, *Benjamin Strong*, pp. 247–449; Clarke, *Central Bank Cooperation*; Richard Meyer, *Bankers' Diplomacy*.

56. Chandler, *Benjamin Strong*, pp. 258–331; Parrini, *Heir to Empire*, pp. 54–58; Michael J. Hogan, *Informal Entente*, pp. 38–77.

57. Frank C. Costigliola, "The Politics of Financial Stabilization," pp. 62–71; Hogan, *Informal Entente*, pp. 60–66.

58. For Strong's recognition of the need to work with France, see Chandler, *Benjamin Strong*, pp. 247–48; Clarke, *Central Bank Cooperation*, pp. 40–41; for Hoover's concern with French financial stabilization, see Hoover to Harding, 4 January 1922, Harding Papers, PCF, Box 5.

59. See, for example, the speech by William G. Baker, in Investment Bankers Asso-

dent immediately began consulting with Hughes, Hoover, Mellon, and Strong about the formulation of an effective foreign loan policy. They concurred that American capital had a vital role in the postwar world, but they considered it unwise for the government itself to engage in foreign loan operations.[60] Instead, they contacted the nation's most prominent bankers and asked them to provide the government with information on all contemplated foreign loans.[61] In this informal manner Republican policymakers hoped to mobilize the financial resources of the private sector in behalf of their own efforts to reconstruct Europe without compromising domestic priorities or incurring dangerous commitments.

The informal consultation between bankers and government officials was intended to reconcile foreign and domestic demands for American capital. Members of the State, Commerce, and Treasury departments were fearful that the outflow of American capital might deprive domestic industry of necessary funding or greatly increase the cost of domestic loans.[62] In July 1921 Hoover and Mellon counseled against the issue of a $10 million loan to the French city of Soissons until credit conditions eased, especially in rural areas. The rising influence of the farm bloc in Congress, the outspoken criticism of Federal Reserve policies, and the divisions within the Republican party impelled policymakers to use the informal consultative procedures to meet internal financial needs and accommodate domestic political circumstances.[63] Even after the credit stringency abated, Hoover continued to worry that foreign demands for American capital might "maintain interest rates against our domestic industry." For the secretary of com-

ciation of America (IBA), *Proceedings of the Annual Convention*, 1918, p. 218; CCUS, "European Finance," November 1919, Kent Papers, Box 4; address by Stephen C. Mason, NAM, *Proceedings*, 1920, p. 115; "Final Declaration," NFTC, *Official Report*, 1921, pp. vii–viii; Wannamaker to Harding, 27 May 1921, Harding Papers, PCF, Box 197.

60. For reference to these deliberations, see the correspondence between Strong and Gilbert, May and June 1921, Strong Papers, 012.5. During 1921–22, the government did facilitate exports through credits extended by the War Finance Corporation (WFC), but this was looked upon as a temporary expedient. See Department of the Treasury, *Annual Report of the Secretary of the Treasury*, 1921, pp. 49–55; ibid., 1922, pp. 37–39.

61. Harding to J. P. Morgan, 10 June 1921, Harding Papers, PCF, Box 88; Harding to Mortimer Schiff, 10 June 1921, ibid.; Gilbert to Strong, 21 May 1921, Strong Papers, 012.5; Morgan to Harding, 6 June 1921, RG 59, 811.51/2981.

62. Cumberland to Dearing, 31 May 1921, RG 59, 811.51/3104.

63. Hoover to Department of State, 14 July 1921, RG 151, File 640; for concern about crowding out domestic borrowers, see also, for example, John Oakwood, "Mass Financing Not Bankers' Way to Aid Europe," *The Annalist* 17 (13 June 1921):655.

merce informal banker-government collaboration constituted a permanent means of efficiently allocating American capital resources.[64]

While cabinet officials concurred on the need to insure that foreign loans did not injure needy domestic borrowers, they disagreed on the wisdom of tying American loans to the sale of American exports. Hoover initially wanted to expand American exports by earmarking the proceeds of foreign loans for expenditure in the United States. Export-oriented manufacturers supported this approach.[65] But a policy of tying American loans to American exports immediately encountered opposition from investment bankers seeking high returns and from officials in the Treasury Department and the FRBNY. Strong and Mellon claimed that all foreign loans eventually redounded to the benefit of American trade. Moreover, Strong worried that any restrictions on foreign loans would exacerbate European exchange problems and retard European currency stabilization. Furthermore, he believed that if the United States wanted to expedite reconstruction efforts abroad, borrowing nations should purchase goods in the cheapest markets.[66] In the end Mellon and Strong succeeded in preventing the inclusion of tie-in clauses in foreign loan transactions.[67]

The controversy over this issue worried many bankers and compounded the difficulties of systematizing informal consultative procedures. By the autumn of 1921 State Department officials became disenchanted with the irregular manner in which banker-government consultation was taking place.[68] Secretary of State Hughes wanted to issue a public statement emphasizing the State Department's desire to be informed in writing about all contemplated loans. Such an announcement, he maintained, would create sufficient pressure to insure the cooperation of the bankers.[69] Hoover, however, opposed this procedure. He feared that a public declaration requesting written infor-

64. Hoover to Hughes, 29 April 1922, RG 59, 800.51/316; see also Grosvenor Jones to Hoover, 5 April 1922, HHCD, Box 375.

65. For Hoover's initial position, see Gilbert to Strong, 21 May 1921, Strong Papers, 012.5; for the position of the NFTC, see Young, Memorandum, 16 May 1922, RG 59, 800.51/481; see also Parrini, *Heir to Empire*, pp. 187–95; Joseph Brandes, *Herbert Hoover and Economic Diplomacy*, pp. 151–63.

66. Strong to Gilbert, 23 May, 13 June 1921, Strong Papers, 012.5; Gilbert to Strong, 21, 28 May, 11, 17 June 1921, ibid.; see also Strong to Hughes, 20 April 1922, HHCD, Box 375; Thomas W. Lamont to Hughes, 31 March 1922, Thomas W. Lamont Papers, Box 94.

67. Eliot W. Wadsworth to Dearing, 24 September 1921, RG 59, 811.51/3016.

68. Cumberland to Dearing, 12 October 1921, ibid., 811.51/2981.

69. Hughes to Hoover, 7 December 1921, ibid., 811.51/3042a; Hughes to Mellon, 7 December 1921, ibid.; see also Dearing to Sumner Welles and Morton D. Carrel, 18 November 1921, ibid., 811.51/2981.

mation about prospective loans would encourage investors to believe mistakenly that the United States government was assuming a measure of responsibility to protect foreign loans. The secretary of commerce insisted that the administration could coordinate private investments with its overall foreign economic policy through informal but direct and systematic contacts with individual bankers and banking committees.[70]

The controversy over regulating foreign loan outflows became more acute during the latter part of 1921 as the flow of gold into the United States, the easier credit policies of the Federal Reserve Board, and the signing of the peace with Germany fostered an environment more conducive to foreign lending and bankers began to compete more intensively for foreign business.[71] It was in this context that Kuhn, Loeb, and Company negotiated a loan with the Department of the Seine without having secured the government's written consent. Hughes was furious. He wrote Otto Kahn, one of the firm's two prominent partners, that Kuhn, Loeb could not expect future assistance from the government.[72] The significance of the incident, however, was that it convinced State Department officials of the necessity of systematizing the procedures of consultation.[73]

In this struggle between the State and Commerce departments over the procedures for implementing banker-government consultation, the former won out. A public statement of the State Department's policy was released on 3 March 1922.[74] This declaration established the basic procedures for subsequent American loan policy in the 1920s. Thereafter, bankers submitted all foreign loan proposals to the Department of State. Appropriate officials in the State, Commerce, and Treasury departments then reviewed these loans according to criteria of public policy. If loans did not meet these criteria, bankers were so informed.

70. Hoover to Hughes, 13 December 1921, ibid., 811.51/3043; Hoover to Hughes, 30 December 1921, ibid., 811.51/3106; IBA, *Proceedings*, 1922, p. 173.
71. For the improving financial environment, see Morgan to Lamont, 20 April 1921, Morrow Papers; "New York Strengthening Position as World Monetary Center," *The Annalist* 17 (17 May 1921):569; for the emerging competition among bankers, see W. C. Huntington to Julius Klein, 23 December 1921, RG 151, File 640; William Wiseman to Otto Kahn, 4 March 1922, Kahn Papers, Box 190.
72. Dearing to secretary, 21 January 1922, RG 59, 851.51/234; Paul Cravath to Hughes, 22 January 1922, ibid., 851.51/224; Hughes to Kuhn, Loeb, and Company, 21, 22, 28 January 1922, ibid., 851.51/225, 223, 235.
73. Dearing to Hughes, 23 January 1922, ibid., 800.51/306; Dearing to Young, 28 January 1922, ibid., 811.51/3106; Young to Dearing, 1 February 1922, ibid., 811.51/3108; FR, 1922, 1:556–57.
74. FR, 1922, 1:557–58.

Although the administration had no legal power to enforce its decisions, bankers were expected to abide by the government's recommendation because they were dependent on the government's aid and goodwill in case of default.[75]

By consulting with bankers prior to the extension of foreign loans, Hughes and Hoover hoped to minimize the likelihood that the United States government would become entangled in foreign political affairs. The two officials recognized that they would be under constant pressure to protect American foreign loans and investments. By reviewing loan transactions and setting certain standards in advance, they hoped to lessen the chances of default and preclude subsequent demands for United States government intervention.[76] Formal review as instituted by the State Department, however, implied some degree of government responsibility to protect those loans that were not disapproved. Ironically, as Hoover and Strong pointed out, a policy originally designed by Hughes to prevent future government entanglements had the potential of having the opposite effect.[77] Yet, Hoover's greater emphasis on voluntarism and self-regulation could not insure the cooperation of the banking community.[78] The dilemma of channeling private American capital toward European reconstruction without engendering too much governmental responsibility for the approved loans was to confound policymakers for years to come. For the meantime, however, State Department officials hoped to solve the dilemma by emphasizing that loans were reviewed strictly according to criteria of public policy and not according to standards of sound business practices.[79]

In April 1922, one month after the State Department's policy was announced, Hoover and his assistants sought to determine the specific criteria of public policy to be used in judging prospective loans. Officials in the Commerce Department emphasized the importance of utilizing scarce capital resources exclusively for "reproductive pur-

75. See Harrison, Memoranda, 8, 10 April 1922, Leland Harrison Papers, Box 7. For the desire of bankers to earn the goodwill of the State Department regarding foreign loans, see, for example, Harris, Forbes, and Company to Hughes, 27 May 1921, RG 59, 800.51/244.

76. Hughes to Hoover, 7 December 1921, RG 59, 811.51/3042a; Hoover, *Memoirs*, 2:86–87; see also Dearing to Welles and Carrel, 18 November 1921, RG 59, 811.51/2981.

77. Hoover to Hughes, 30 December 1921, RG 59, 811.51/3106; Strong to Hughes, 9 June 1922, ibid., 800.51/506.

78. In 1932 Hoover acknowledged that this was the case. See Hoover to secretary of commerce, 9 January 1932, Herbert C. Hoover Presidential Papers, Box 876 (hereafter cited as HHPP).

79. Young to Dearing, 1 February 1922, RG 59, 811.51/3108; FR, 1922, 1:557–58.

poses." Maintaining that the "whole economic and political life [of Europe] is enveloped in an atmosphere of war," Hoover urged that American loans be used "to render impossible that form of statesmanship which would maintain such an atmosphere." Hoover's proposal could be accomplished if nations with unbalanced budgets and unnecessarily high military expenditures were prohibited from floating loans in American financial markets.[80] In accord with this position, during the winter of 1921–22 the secretary of commerce had begun to voice his objections to loans to France. State Department officials, exasperated by the French position at the disarmament conference, came to support Hoover's position.[81] Several loans to French railroads were approved in March and April of 1922 only after French officials indicated that they would cut military expenditures, effect budgetary economies, and support America's right to its fair share of reparation payments.[82]

Within policymaking circles, however, officials in the Treasury Department and the FRBNY continued to insist that the government should not become overly involved in setting guidelines for foreign loans. Such efforts, they claimed, could lead to undesirable political entanglements and unsought international responsibilities.[83] Strong especially objected to Hoover's view that the government should frown upon private loans to nations like France with unbalanced budgets. Given the deplorable state of European currencies, Strong maintained that American loans were essential for both American trade and European stabilization efforts. Moreover, Strong doubted whether restrictions on American loans would have any impact on European budgetary practices. Though sympathetic with the commerce secretary's desire to use American financial power to effect European stability, Strong insisted that this could be done most effectively by using the war debts as a lever. Regulation of capital outflows, in Strong's opinion, was risky

80. Hoover to Hughes, 29 April 1922, RG 59, 800.51/316; see also Jones, Memoranda, 1, 5, 6 April 1922, HHCD, Box 375.

81. Dearing to Fletcher and Hughes, 30 December 1921, RG 59, 851.51/233; Dearing to Fletcher, 17 February 1922, ibid., 851.51/231; Alan G. Goldsmith to Huntington, 22 March 1922, RG 151, File 640.

82. For the French government's assurances, see Huntington to Klein, 10 February 1922, RG 151, File 600; Huntington to BFDC, 9 February 1922, ibid., File 3266; see also Myron T. Herrick to secretary, 28 April 1922, RG 59, 851.51/298; for approval of the loans, see Hughes to Milton E. Ailes, 11 March 1922, Records of the Bureau of Accounts, RG 39, Box 48; Hughes to Lee, Higginson, and Company, 16 March 1922, ibid.

83. Strong to Hughes, 9 June 1922, RG 59, 800.51/506; Mellon to Hughes, 8 July 1922, ibid., 800.51/425.

from a political standpoint and dubious from an economic viewpoint.[84]

These warnings from Mellon and Strong in the spring and summer of 1922 revealed that no clear consensus had yet emerged within the administration on the specific guidelines that the government should use in reviewing loan proposals or on the extent to which the government should get involved in supervising the outflow of American capital. All administration policymakers hoped that the procedures instituted by the State Department in March 1922 would help insure that American loans were used wisely to expand American exports, rehabilitate European currencies, and curtail European arms expenditures. Their objective was to mobilize the capital resources and practical expertise of the private sector in support of the administration's foreign policy goals without engendering congressional interference in decision-making processes, shortchanging the capital needs of the American economy, or entangling the United States government in European political affairs.[85] Whether these procedures were capable of eliciting the effective cooperation of the bankers or of pressuring a major nation like France into permanently altering its military and financial policies remained to be seen. During the latter part of 1922 and throughout 1923, however, these questions became moot as the worsening of the European reparations crisis discouraged foreign lending and focused all attention on the war debt and reparation issues.

War Debts and the Establishment of the World War Foreign Debt Commission

When the Harding administration took office, Republican policymakers were eager to convert the $10 billion in demand obligations owed by the former Allies into long-term obligations. Treasury officials in particular recognized that unsettled foreign debts caused uncertainty and anxiety in international financial and commercial centers. They maintained that until the "financial position [of debtor nations] is made clear, their ability to place loans will be affected, their industrial recovery will be retarded, and our own prosperity will suffer."[86] Therefore, in June 1921 Treasury officials decided to ask Congress for

84. Strong to Hughes, 20 April 1922, HHCD, Box 375; Strong, Memorandum, spring 1922, RG 59, 800.51/316.

85. The goals of the administration's loan policy are expressed most clearly in Jones to Hoover, 5 April 1922, HHCD, Box 375; Hoover to Hughes, 29 April 1922, RG 59, 800.51/316.

86. Department of the Treasury, *Annual Report*, 1921, pp. 42–43.

virtually unlimited authority to negotiate the terms of the refunding agreements. Mellon believed that such extensive discretionary powers would enable him to accommodate the financial needs of debtor nations and thus mitigate the impact of debt payments on exchange rates and American exports.[87]

Mellon, however, was not considering cancellation or even partial cancellation. He was too preoccupied with converting the short-term floating debt, reducing the public debt, and lowering taxes to be generous to the former Allies, even if American trade interests were partly at stake. Both he and the president believed that the recession of 1920–21 was the result of high taxation. Consequently, they were not disposed to relieve foreign debtors at the expense of American taxpayers. Mellon's request for broad authority, therefore, was an attempt to secure discretionary powers that would enable him to reconcile the conflicting demands of trade and fiscal policy without arousing a bitter political controversy.[88]

Congress, however, refused to abdicate control over debt refunding. After a long and acrimonious debate, Congress tied the hands of the Treasury Department, established the five-man World War Foreign Debt Commission (WDC) to conduct negotiations, and called for the repayment of debts within twenty-five years at an annual interest rate of not less than 4.25 percent. Moreover, Congress prohibited the WDC from allowing a debtor to substitute the bonds of another nation for its own obligations to the United States. In fact, the only substantive discretionary power that the WDC retained was over the deferral of interest payments. In setting such harsh terms for repayment congressmen and senators were responding to widespread public pressure for tax reductions, agricultural credits, veterans' compensation, and unemployment relief. At the same time they were manifesting their distrust of the executive branch of the government and asserting their constitutional right to control the government's financial affairs. Democrats, of course, also used the opportunity to denounce their Republican opponents for supposedly responding to the pleas of European debtors while ignoring the legitimate needs of the American people.[89]

Republican policymakers disliked the refunding legislation. They tried to muster support for their original proposal. But rather than risk

87. Melvyn P. Leffler, "The Origins of Republican War Debt Policy, 1921–1923," p. 591.
88. Ibid., pp. 591–92; see also Harding's address to the Senate, 12 July 1921, Senate, *Congressional Record*, 67th Cong., 1st sess., 1921, 61, pt. 4:3597–98.
89. Leffler, "Republican War Debt Policy," pp. 592–95.

a continuous struggle and endless delay, Mellon and Harding eventually acquiesced to the restrictions imposed by Congress. Having recently warned against passage of a popular bonus bill on fiscal grounds and still having to secure congressional approval of important domestic legislation, the president did not wish to risk the political consequences of vetoing the legislation and insisting on generous treatment of European debtors.[90]

Under the terms of the refunding legislation the secretary of the treasury took his seat as chairman of the WDC. To this commission Harding also appointed Hughes, Hoover, Republican Senator Reed Smoot, and Republican Congressman Theodore E. Burton. The WDC began meeting in the spring of 1922 and immediately instructed the Department of State to request foreign governments to send delegations to the United States to enter into debt negotiations.[91] Governor Strong hoped that an exchange of information between the debtors and the WDC would constitute the first step toward educating the American public and altering congressional attitudes about war debts.[92]

In May 1922 the French government agreed to send Jean Parmentier, director of the *Mouvement général des Fonds* of the Ministry of Finance, to the United States to discuss the war debts. Preoccupied with his nation's budgetary deficits and the need to spend billions of francs on reconstructing the devastated regions, Premier Poincaré wanted to gain American sympathy for France's financial predicament. Like most Frenchmen, however, he deplored the terms of the refunding legislation, and he instructed Parmentier to disregard them.[93] During his visit to the United States in July and August, Parmentier reaffirmed France's intent to honor her wartime obligations. But he would not discuss the repayment terms set by Congress. Instead, he presented a comprehensive statistical account of France's precarious financial situation and maintained that repayments, even of accrued interest, would injure the franc and imperil the economic life of his country. Parmentier inquired whether the United States would alter the terms of the existing notes so that the repayment of the principal could be deferred for twenty-five

90. Ibid., pp. 595–96.
91. Mellon to Hughes, 2 June 1922, RG 39, Box 60.
92. Strong to Norman, 21 February 1922, Strong Papers, 1116.3; Strong to Basil Blackett, 18 February 1922, FRBNY Papers, C797; Strong to Logan, 23 June 1922, ibid.
93. FR, 1922, 1:402; for Poincaré's eagerness to send Parmentier, see Harrison to Wadsworth, 3 June 1922, RG 39, Box 60; for Poincaré's instructions, see Harold G. Moulton and Leo Pasvolsky, *War Debts and World Prosperity*, p. 83; for the French press's criticism of the refunding legislation, see "The Shylock Strain in Uncle Sam," *Literary Digest* 72 (18 February 1922):22.

years and interest payments postponed for a certain number of years as well.[94]

During Parmentier's visit no substantive progress was made toward refunding the war debts. American officials gained a clearer understanding of financial conditions in France, expressed sympathy for France's financial plight, and were gratified that France did not support Britain's call for substantial reductions of all intergovernmental debts. Yet, Republican policymakers were unwilling to take any concrete steps to circumvent the refunding terms set by Congress.[95] Hughes and Hoover occasionally intimated that American concessions on the war debts might be forthcoming if the indemnity question were resolved and the French financial situation stabilized. But prior to the 1922 elections the administration refused to countenance any reduction of the war debts, rejected proposals calling for the linkage of the war debt and reparation issues, and insisted that the debts were not responsible for European fiscal and currency problems. With elections forthcoming in November and with large losses anticipated, Republican officials could not be indifferent to legislative restrictions, internal fiscal demands, and domestic political expedients. All of these factors called for a cautious approach to the war debts.[96]

The administration's deference to Congress engendered growing criticism. Many of the nation's business leaders and business organizations demanded that the United States government defer interest payments or cancel part of the war debts to facilitate the stabilization of

94. Wadsworth, Memoranda, 25 July, 2, 17 August 1922, RG 39, Box 60; Gilbert to Mellon, 22 July 1922, ibid.; World War Foreign Debt Commission (WDC), *Minutes of the World War Foreign Debt Commission*, pp. 8–9, 10–12; Department of the Treasury, *Annual Report*, 1922, p. 26.

95. For the reaction of American officials to Parmentier's visit, see Memorandum of conversation between Hughes and Count de Chambrum, 12 August 1922, Hughes Papers, Box 174; Gilbert to Mellon, 22 July 1922, RG 39, Box 60; Mellon to Henry P. Fletcher, 7 September 1922, Fletcher Papers, Box 9; Goldsmith to Hoover, 26 July 1922, HHCD, Box 132. On 1 August 1922, the British stated that Germany and the Continental Allies would have to pay Britain only enough to cover Britain's own war debt obligations to the United States. For some interesting comments on the French reaction, see Andrew McFadyean, *Reparation Reviewed*, pp. 40–45; Logan to Strong, 11 August 1922, FRBNY Papers, C797.

96. For Hughes's view, see FR, 1922, 1:168–69; Hughes to Harding, 8 November 1922, Harding Papers, PCF, Box 45; for Hoover's view, see his Toledo speech in *Commercial and Financial Chronicle* 115 (21 October 1922):1781–82; for the Treasury Department's orientation, see Eliot Wadsworth, "The Inter-Allied Debt Problem and a Stable Monetary System Abroad," pp. 153–54; see also Harding to Fred Starek, 2 November 1922, Harding Papers, PCF, Box 88; "The Allied Debts as a Peace Club," *Literary Digest* 75 (21 October 1922):12–13.

European finances and the expansion of American exports.[97] At the same time American diplomats warned of impending chaos in Europe if the United States government continued to ignore the importance of the debt issue. In October Alanson Houghton, the American ambassador to Germany, implored the secretary of state to cancel the debts on the condition that European governments agree to disarm and maintain peace with one another for fifty years.[98]

Republican officials were neither indifferent to these business and diplomatic warnings nor ignorant of America's self-interest in stabilizing European financial and economic affairs. The dilemma, as Harding succinctly put it, was "how to fully assert a helpful influence abroad without sacrificing anything of importance to our own people."[99] One means to accomplish this objective was to convince the European nations to establish a committee of experts to settle the reparations controversy independently of the war debt question. When Poincaré rejected this approach, Harding and Hughes realized that the United States would have to adopt a more flexible stand on the war debts. Once the elections were out of the way and public concern continued to mount, the president chided Congress for hamstringing effective action. He wrote Senator Lodge that "if Congress really means to facilitate the task of the Government in dealing with the European situation, the first practical step would be to free the hands of the Debt Commission so that helpful negotiations may be undertaken."[100]

The WDC, however, did not wait for a new congressional mandate. When a British delegation arrived in January 1923, the WDC went ahead and negotiated a settlement that disregarded the terms enumerated by Congress. Mellon and Hoover, the two dominant voices within the WDC, wanted an accord that would provide for the repayment of principal, but that would also ease Britain's financial problems, facilitate her return to the gold standard, and promote a flourishing international commerce.[101] As a result the debt agreement with Britain called for the repayment of the debt in full over sixty-two years with interest increasing from 3 to 3.5 percent.[102] Some officials in the

97. Leffler, "Republican War Debt Policy," pp. 586–91.
98. FR, 1922, 1:171–75.
99. Harding to Starek, 2 November 1922, Harding Papers, PCF, Box 88.
100. Senate, *Congressional Record*, 67th Cong., 4th sess., 1922, 64, pt. 1:982; for administration efforts to handle the reparations issue, see pp. 70–79 below.
101. Hoover to Mellon, 6 January 1923, HHCD, Box 367; Wadsworth to Smoot, 10 February 1923, RG 39, Box 113.
102. The text of the agreement can be found in Harold G. Moulton and Leo Pasvolsky, *World War Debt Settlements*, pp. 225–41.

Treasury Department felt that the accord was not lenient enough and did not provide sufficient flexibility in case Britain was unable to meet her payments. Nevertheless, they acknowledged that the WDC had gone as far as Congress would allow.[103] In an address on 7 February 1923 Harding asked Congress to approve the settlement. He stressed the crucial importance of the accord as a reconfirmation of the sanctity of contracts. He also claimed that the settlement was an essential prerequisite of the restoration of the world's financial and economic stability.[104]

The favorable response to this debt settlement indicated that the WDC had struck a popular compromise between the imperatives of fiscal and commercial policy. The WDC had temporarily reconciled the conflicting demands of European stability and domestic politics. Most businessmen and politicians supported the accord because they believed it would facilitate American exports without unduly burdening the American people with additional taxes. It was frequently emphasized that the reduction of interest to between 3 and 3.5 percent reflected the anticipated level of interest rates over a long period of time. Critics, therefore, had difficulty claiming that cancellation had been countenanced and the well-being of the American taxpayer jeopardized. Moreover, the importance of eliminating one major element of uncertainty was widely appreciated in the chaotic international atmosphere engendered by the French occupation of the Ruhr.[105]

Policymakers also realized that the debt settlement with Britain had far-reaching implications for France and the other European debtors. For the first time it was evident that Congress might approve accords that departed from the terms of the original refunding bill. Hoover hoped to manipulate interest rates to accommodate each debtor's capacity to pay and secure European concessions on reparations and disarmament. Likewise, Undersecretary of the Treasury S. Parker Gilbert calculated that the British accord might permit even greater concessions to other debtors, thereby helping to establish the preconditions for the stabilization of European currencies.[106] To prepare the way for subsequent agreements, the administration accepted an amendment to the British accord, proposed by Democratic Senator William J. Harris.

103. Gilbert to Strong, 6 February, 24 April 1923, Strong Papers, 012.5; [Beerits Memorandum], "Funding the Allied War Debts," Hughes Papers, Box 172, p. 4.
104. WDC, *Combined Annual Reports*, pp. 96–100.
105. Leffler, "Republican War Debt Policy," p. 599.
106. Hoover, Memorandum, 4 February 1923, HHPP, Box 871; Gilbert to Mellon, 4, 9 February 1923, RG 39, Box 113; Gilbert "Draft," 20 February 1923, ibid.; Gilbert to Strong, 6 February 1923, Strong Papers, 012.5

This amendment called for the appointment of three Democrats to the WDC. By making the WDC bipartisan the administration sought to take the debt issue out of partisan politics and treat it on an objective basis according to the best advice of experts.[107]

Thus, by early 1923 the machinery for implementing American war debt policy had been established. The bipartisan WDC worked to reconcile conflicting fiscal and commercial imperatives bearing on the debt issue. The WDC endeavored to accommodate both the demands of American taxpayers and the financial needs of Continental debtors, the most important of which was France.

The Reparations Controversy and the "Expert" Approach

Shortly after taking office, circumstances forced Republican officials to focus their attention on the reparations question. Exasperated by German recalcitrance, the French, British, and Belgian governments occupied several Ruhr ports during the spring of 1921. The Germans reacted with a request for American mediation of the reparations controversy. Officials in the Department of State recognized that American interests were at stake. Nevertheless, they did not want to assume the responsibility for fixing the amount of the indemnity. Such action, it was feared, might embroil the United States government in the political affairs of the Old World when neither France nor Germany seemed prepared to be conciliatory. In fact, Louis Loucheur, the French minister of reconstruction, had warned American diplomats that their ability to mediate in the future might be impaired by precipitous action.[108]

While refraining from immediate intervention, Undersecretary of State Henry P. Fletcher and Assistant Secretary of State Leland Harrison began consulting with Roland W. Boyden and James A. Logan, the former unofficial American delegates to the Reparation Commission. A consensus quickly developed among State Department officials that the indemnity should be based on Germany's capacity to pay, that it should be determined by financial experts and not by politicians, and that it should be treated as a business proposition. Boyden claimed that the Reparation Commission possessed sufficient statistical data and independence of judgment to analyze the question of German payment capacity in an objective manner. In May, Hughes sent Boyden and

107. William J. Harris to Harding, 10 February 1923, Harding Papers, PCF, Box 88.
108. Harrison, Memorandum, 21 April 1921, Leland Harrison Papers, Box 9; Logan to Hughes, 19 April 1921, ibid.; FR, 1921, 2:36–58; Walter Allan McDougall, "French Rhineland Policy and the Struggle for European Stabilization," pp. 140–46.

Logan back to Paris as unofficial representatives to the Reparation Commission. The expectation was that they would bolster the power of the commission, revive American influence within it, and force it to adopt a reparations formula based on Germany's capacity to pay.[109]

During the summer and autumn of 1921 Boyden and Logan worked diligently, if not successfully, to get the members of the Reparation Commission, especially the French, to agree to the capacity-to-pay principle. Logan in particular condemned French policies, denounced the London schedule of payments, and appealed for an experts' study of Germany's ability to pay reparations. He sent detailed reports of the deplorable situation to his old friend, Governor Strong of the FRBNY.[110] Strong in turn beseeched Treasury officials to exert American influence in behalf of a settlement within Germany's capacity. The present "situation is no less than monstrous," Strong wrote to Undersecretary Gilbert.[111] Officials in the Treasury and State departments concurred. Like many bankers and businessmen, the officials realized that the reparations quagmire contributed to the fluctuation of European exchange rates, the depreciation of European currencies, the weakening of European purchasing power, and a decline in American exports.[112] But they still wanted to avoid a clash with France over reparations while they were negotiating an arms limitation agreement. Accordingly, Fletcher warned Logan not to be so outspoken in his views.[113]

By the end of 1921, however, American policymakers lost faith in

109. Roland Boyden to Harrison, 25 March 1921, Leland Harrison Papers, Box 2; Harrison to Fletcher, 20 April 1921, ibid., Box 9; Harrison to Castle, 9 May 1921, ibid.; Castle to Ellis Dresel, 19 October 1921, Castle Papers, Box 4; FR, 1921, 1:14–15.

110. Logan to Cecil-Eugène Mauclère, 22 August 1921, FRBNY Papers, C797; Logan to Fletcher, 29 August 1921, ibid.; Logan to Strong, 10 September, 15 October, 3 November 1921, ibid.; see also Dresel to Castle, 1 July, 5, 19 October, 18 November 1921, Castle Papers, Box 4.

111. Strong to Gilbert, 29 September 1921, FRBNY Papers, C797; Strong to Wadsworth, 26 November 1921, ibid.

112. For officials' recognition of the dislocating impact of reparation transfers, see Gilbert to Strong, 24 May 1921, ibid.; Gilbert to Hughes, 8 June 1921, ibid.; Strong to Gilbert, 31 May 1921, ibid.; Strong to Logan, 3 October 1921, ibid.; Hoover to Harding, 4 January 1922, Harding Papers, PCF, Box 5; Castle to Dresel, 9 May 1921, Castle Papers, Box 4; for businessmen's grasp of the importance of the reparations issue, see Special Committee of the CCUS, "European Problems Affecting American Business," Nation's Business 9 (5 October 1921):2–3; Silas H. Strawn, "Can Germany Pay and Not Work?" ibid. (5 June 1922):21–22; Special Committee of the NFTC, "European Conditions," pp. 10 ff.; statement by James Emery in NAM, Proceedings, 1923, pp. 288–89.

113. Fletcher to Logan, 22 October 1921, Leland Harrison Papers, Box 7; Gilbert to Strong, 4 October 1921, FRBNY Papers, C797; Wadsworth to Strong, 18 November, 3 December 1921, ibid.; Castle to Dresel, 2 August 1921, Castle Papers, Box 4.

the Reparation Commission and were considering other means of dealing with European problems. They pondered the wisdom of participating in the forthcoming international economic conference at Genoa. The British had sponsored this meeting with the hope of reviving the German and Russian economies, resuscitating markets, and developing new investment opportunities. But after long and careful deliberation, Harding, Hughes, Hoover, and Culbertson decided that it would not be wise for the United States government to send official delegates to Genoa. They felt that too much emphasis was being placed on the questions of Russian recognition and reconstruction. In addition, the fall of Briand and the apparent disinterest of Poincaré in the conference suggested that the time was not propitious for holding a successful international meeting. Most important, however, Harding also feared that "the nations of the Old World [would] put upon our shoulders the main burden of finding a way out from the present deplorable state of affairs."[114]

Instead of participating in a world economic conference, Republican policymakers sought other means of resolving the reparations controversy according to Germany's repayment capacity. A new opportunity began to develop in November 1921 when the German government requested a $50 million loan from the FRBNY to stabilize the rapidly depreciating mark. Federal Reserve and Treasury officials were sympathetic in principle to the idea of an American loan for this purpose. Indeed, there was an increasing belief that a moratorium on reparation payments, a reform of German financial operations, and the extension of an American loan were prerequisites of the restoration of financial stability not only in Germany but throughout Europe. Mellon, however, wanted private bankers, not the FRBNY, to arrange the loan. Since he knew that American bankers were unlikely to grant a loan until the reparations burden was revised, Mellon and other officials expected to rely upon the financial leverage of the private sector to bring about a reparations settlement according to Germany's capacity to pay.[115] The

114. Harding to Culbertson, 19 December 1921, Culbertson Papers, Box 46; for deliberations regarding the Genoa Conference, see also Culbertson to Harding, 13 December 1921, ibid.; Hoover to Harding, 23 January 1922, HHCD, Box 21; Memorandum of interview between Hughes and Jusserand, 13 February 1922, Hughes Papers, Box 174; Note from French embassy to United States government, 19 February 1922, Harding Papers, PCF, Box 307; Harding to Harvey, 18 February, 16 April 1922, ibid., PPF 60; FR, 1922, 1:389–93; Parrini, *Heir to Empire*, pp. 152–71; for background information on European developments, see Sally Marks, *The Illusion of Peace*, pp. 42–45; McDougall, "French Rhineland Policy," pp. 185–88.
115. Strong to W. P. G. Harding, 4, 7 November 1921, FRBNY Papers, C797;

great advantage of this unofficial, apolitical, and businesslike approach to the reparations crisis was that it neither jeopardized the war debts nor threatened to embroil the United States government in European political affairs.

During the winter and spring of 1922 there was some hope that France would allow the bankers to conduct a study of Germany's capacity to pay reparations. Poincaré, preoccupied with France's financial situation, wanted to balance the budget and stabilize the franc by obtaining a steady flow of reparation payments. But before Germany could make large-scale transfers, she had to terminate her ruinous fiscal and monetary policies and secure private financial aid in the United States. In April 1922 the French approved of the Reparation Commission's appointment of a Bankers' Committee to study the conditions necessary for a successful flotation of a German loan. The proceeds of such a loan were to be used in part to stabilize German finances and in part to pay reparations to France so that the latter could strengthen her own finances.[116] The major impediment to the committee's success was the stipulation that it not modify the terms of the Treaty of Versailles or the provisions of the London schedule of reparation payments agreed upon in May 1921.[117]

American policymakers had great hopes that the Bankers' Committee would urge a solution based upon Germany's repayment capacity. After careful consultation between Republican officials and Governor

W. P. G. Harding to Strong, 5 November 1921, ibid.; Wadsworth to Strong, 18 November 1921, ibid.; Strong to Norman, 25 November 1921, Strong Papers, 116.2; Jay to Strong, 29 November 1921, ibid., 320.115; Casenave to Lamont, 26 November 1921, Thomas W. Lamont Papers, Box 94; Carl Bergmann, *The History of Reparations*, pp. 104–12. For the reparations burden under which Germany was operating, see note 125 below.

116. For Poincaré's motivations and the appointment of the Bankers' Committee, see Logan to Strong, 6, 17 March, 14, 15 April 1922, FRBNY Papers, C797; Logan to Alanson Houghton, 17 May 1922, Fletcher Papers, Box 8; MacLean to director, 17 April 1922, RG 151, File 600.2; MacFadyean to Kent, 8, 28 February 1923, Kent Papers, Box 3; Bergmann, *History of Reparations*, pp. 124–26, 130 ff.; Etienne Weill-Raynal, *Les Réparations allemandes et la France*, 2:166–71; Stephen A. Schuker, *The End of French Predominance*, pp. 14–46.

117. The London schedule of payments agreed upon in May 1921 theoretically called for a total payment of 132 billion gold marks ($33 billion) to the Allies. In reality Allied officials never expected to receive more than 50 billion gold marks ($12.5 billion), a figure that may well have been within Germany's capacity had she been willing to pay. By the spring of 1922, however, German payments had already broken down. The most comprehensive account of the London schedule of payments and its subsequent fate can be found in Weill-Raynal, *Réparations allemandes*, 1:618–702, 2:11–165; see also Sally Marks, "Reparations Reconsidered: A Reminder," pp. 356–65; Schuker, *French Predominance*, pp. 14–28, 181–83.

Strong, the State Department authorized Boyden and Logan to appoint J. P. Morgan as the American member of the Bankers' Committee. It was understood that Morgan would object to any loan so long as the German indemnity remained unchanged. Logan believed that a crisis would develop within the Bankers' Committee. The French, he assumed, would initially oppose any change in the authority and mandate of the committee. Nevertheless, he predicted that Morgan would be able to force Poincaré to reverse his position because of France's desperate financial plight.[118]

When the Bankers' Committee met in late May and early June, Boyden and Logan kept in close contact with Morgan. The New York financier dominated the committee. He followed official American policy, cautioning against linking the war debt and reparation issues. He called for the reform of German finances, the reassessment of the amount of the indemnity to within Germany's capacity to pay, and the cooperation of all the western European nations in the flotation of an international loan. Morgan appealed to the French to allow alterations in the schedule and amount of reparation payments. Such changes, he claimed, were essential to the rehabilitation of German credit. When the Bankers' Committee asked the Reparation Commission to expand the committee's authority in this direction, Boyden argued in behalf of the request.[119] Only the French demurred. Poincaré was prepared to make concessions on the indemnity question, but the French political and financial situation would not allow him to do so without commensurate reductions in the war debts. Since Morgan had demanded unanimity, the French stand meant the termination of the work of the Bankers' Committee.[120]

Despite this setback Harding and his advisers continued to reject all proposals for a comprehensive settlement of the intergovernmental debts. The president insisted that Congress would never allow it. Hoover feared that the United States might become Germany's sole creditor, and he worried that this situation might lead to ominous inter-

118. Logan to Strong, 10 March, 14, 15 April, 5 May 1922, FRBNY Papers, C797; Strong to Logan, 21, 24 April 1922, ibid.; Logan to Harrison, 19 May 1922, Fletcher Papers, Box 8; Logan to Houghton, 17 May 1922, ibid.

119. Logan to Houghton, 17 May 1922, Fletcher Papers, Box 8; Logan to Strong, 2 June 1922, FRBNY Papers, C797; "Report of the Loan Committee to the Reparation Commission," Fletcher Papers, Box 9; Reparation Commission, "Minutes," No. 294, 6, 7 June 1922, ibid.; Weill-Raynal, *Réparations allemandes*, 2:169–82.

120. For Poincaré's position, see Dubois's statement, Reparation Commission, "Minutes," No. 294, 6, 7 June 1922; see also Logan to Harrison, 9 June 1922, Fletcher Papers, Box 9; Fletcher to Hughes, 6 June 1922, ibid.; Schuker, *French Predominance*, pp. 178–79.

national entanglements or unnecessary financial sacrifices.[121] Maintaining that "Europe [could] only be restored through the working of economic forces," Republican officials still sought to take the indemnity issue out of the hands of politicians, who were supposedly ignorant of economic matters and subject to the vagaries of public opinion.[122] In October Hughes instructed the ambassador to France, Myron T. Herrick, to approach Poincaré privately and urge him to convene a committee of financial experts. Herrick explained to the French premier that if he allowed the experts to conduct an impartial study of Germany's capacity to make reparation payments, the experts could be held responsible for recommending a moderate settlement, and he could escape the domestic political repercussions of revision.[123] This argument reflected the belief in American diplomatic circles that, if not for his precarious parliamentary position, Poincaré would be more conciliatory.[124] In November, to strengthen the moderate forces around the French premier, Boyden proposed that, in return for France's acceptance of an indemnity based on the capacity-to-pay principle, Germany demonstrate her "will for peace" by reiterating her acceptance of the Treaty of Versailles, subject to peaceful revisions.[125]

Responding to immense pressures, Poincaré did reappraise the possibility of convening an experts' committee similar to the one that had met in June. In mid-November he invited Morgan to Paris for personal talks. Morgan had been in Europe all summer and had been in contact with American diplomats. He was willing to participate in another impartial committee provided that Poincaré seized the initiative. Before returning to France, Morgan demanded that Poincaré accept not only the general plan outlined by the Bankers' Committee in June but also a prolonged moratorium on reparation payments. The French premier refused to make these concessions as a condition for the financier's

121. For the Harding administration's rejection of plans linking the war debt and reparation issues in June 1922, see Leffler, "Republican War Debt Policy," pp. 596–98.
122. For the quotation, see Herrick to Lamont, 13 September 1922, Herrick Papers, Box 12; see also Boyden, Memoranda, [August 1922], Leland Harrison Papers, Box 2; Boyden to Harrison, 7 August 1922, ibid.
123. [Beerits Memorandum], "The Dawes Plan," Hughes Papers, Box 172, pp. 2–3; FR, 1922, 1:168–69; Herrick to Poincaré, 7 November 1922, Herrick Papers, Box 12.
124. Logan to Strong, 28 July 1922, FRBNY Papers, C797; Herrick to Hughes, 22 December 1922, Herrick Papers, Box 11.
125. See proposed draft of Boyden's letter (on behalf of the Reparation Commission) to German government, 15 November 1922, Fletcher Papers, Box 9; Logan to Hughes, 13, 16 November 1922, ibid.; Boyden to Herrick, 21 November 1922, Herrick Papers, Box 11.

visit to Paris. As a result Morgan returned to the United States, and the possibility of an early convocation of an experts' committee passed.[126]

State Department officials were disappointed with Morgan's intransigent position. William R. Castle, chief of the Division of Western European Affairs, maintained that Morgan did not understand Poincaré's difficult parliamentary position.[127] In effect, Morgan demanded that the French premier make key concessions prior to the meeting of the experts' committee, whereas State Department officials hoped that the findings of the committee would engender a political atmosphere conducive to subsequent French concessions. Although American diplomats had little hope that Poincaré would be able to reverse himself, they nevertheless exhorted Hughes to try once again to break the European deadlock over reparations. The diplomats warned that the German people were desperate, that Western civilization was collapsing, and that social upheaval was imminent. If such conditions were not enough to impel American action, the diplomats also reported that either the continuation of prevailing conditions or the implementation of French sanctions would endanger American economic interests, weaken European purchasing power, and undermine Germany's ability to pay American occupation costs and mixed war claims.[128]

In addition to these warnings from American diplomats, policymakers in Washington were confronted with specific proposals from prominent politicians, agitated businessmen, and concerned governments. Senator Borah, with considerable support from the farm bloc, called for an international economic conference. Business organizations like the CCUS and the Southern Commercial Congress urged a flexible and comprehensive approach to the entire war debt and reparations imbroglio. The German government inquired whether the United States would oversee an agreement between France, Germany, Britain, and Italy in which each promised not to wage war against the other for a generation, unless mandated to do so by a popular referendum.[129]

126. Logan to Hughes, 24 November 1922, Fletcher Papers, Box 9; Logan to Strong, 24 November 1922, FRBNY Papers, C797; FR, 1922, 2:165.

127. Castle to Herrick, 28 November 1922, Herrick Papers, Box 11; see also FR, 1922, 2:165.

128. Houghton to Hughes, 21 November 1922, Hughes Papers, Box 4B; Boyden to Hughes, 9, 22, 28 November 1922, Fletcher Papers, Box 9; Logan to Hughes, 1 December 1922, ibid.; see also FR, 1922, 2:170–77.

129. For the pressures on policymakers, see, for example, *Commercial and Financial Chronicle* 115 (30 December 1922):2847–48; resolution of the CCUS, RG 59, 800.51/428; J. W. Harriman to Harding, 12 December 1922, Harding Papers, PCF, Box 164; Clarence J. Owens to Hughes, 31 October 1922, RG 59, 800.51/433; for the German government's proposal, see FR, 1922, 2:203–5.

The secretary of state rejected these proposals after considering them carefully, discussing them with Harding and Hoover, and exchanging ideas with the French ambassador. So long as it was uncertain how Congress would react to a scaling down of the war debts, it seemed unwise to attend an international conference or link the reparation and war debt issues.[130] Similarly, so long as France wanted the United States to guarantee a nonaggression pact, it seemed pointless to pursue the German proposal for such an agreement. Even those who had once supported guarantees of French security had by now reconsidered the wisdom of American strategic commitments on the Rhine. The prevailing conditions in Europe and the worsening image of France in America discouraged serious reexamination of this matter.[131]

As a result of internal political circumstances and domestic constraints, policymakers felt they had few alternatives before them. Hughes kept urging Ambassador Jusserand to convince Poincaré of the wisdom of an experts' study of Germany's capacity to pay reparations. To insist on more than Germany could pay, Hughes maintained, was countereffective. Such attempts weakened Germany's productive capacity, disrupted her commerce, undermined her social order, and destroyed her incentive to pay.[132] When his arguments failed to elicit a positive response from Poincaré, and when he became exasperated with public criticism of his supposed indifference to European developments, the secretary of state finally decided to present the administration's position publicly. In an address to the American Historical Association in New Haven on 29 December 1922, he reiterated American interest in the reparations controversy, warned against the application of sanctions, and emphasized the utility of an apolitical solution based on an experts' study of Germany's capacity to pay. Furthermore, Hughes expressed his nation's readiness to participate in a settlement along such lines.[133]

Neither Hughes's proposal nor subsequent talks with European lead-

130. Harding to Hughes, 9 November 1922, Harding Papers, PCF, Box 45; Harding to Harriman, 12 December 1922, ibid., Box 164; Hughes to Houghton, 23 October 1922, RG 59, 800.51/432; Hughes to Kent, 8 February 1923, ibid., 800.51/457A; *Congressional Record*, 67th Cong., 4th sess., 28 December 1922, p. 982.
131. FR, 1922, 2:206–10; Frederick H. Gillett to Herrick, 26 December 1922, Herrick Papers, Box 11; Elizabeth Brett White, *American Opinion of France from Lafayette to Poincaré*, pp. 283–96.
132. FR, 1922, 2:187–92, 195–98; [Beerits Memorandum], "Dawes Plan," pp. 5–7.
133. For the speech, see Charles Evans Hughes, *The Pathway of Peace*, pp. 53–58; for Hughes's motivations, see [Beerits Memorandum], "Dawes Plan," p. 8.

ers convinced Poincaré that there was a suitable alternative to the application of sanctions. He disregarded Hughes's initiative and told the Chamber of Deputies that he did not want to permit a committee of bankers to arbitrate the rights of France or influence her destiny. For Poincaré, the reparations issue could not be treated as a purely economic matter. Indeed, from the French viewpoint, the issue encompassed matters of the gravest political and strategic importance. Abandoned by the Anglo-Saxon powers, the French could no longer tolerate repeated Germany violations of the Treaty of Versailles, whether these violations be caused by the impotence of the German government or the intransigence of German industrialists. Faced with persistent German recalcitrance, Poincaré reluctantly opted for military action, which seemed like the only means of preserving treaty rights, gaining access to Ruhr coal, overcoming chronic financial problems, and securing bargaining leverage with France's former allies. During the second week of January 1923, the French premier sent troops into the Ruhr.[134]

Secretary of State Hughes was not surprised that he had been unable to deter French action. He realized that "there are deep-seated convictions as to national interests on each side that must be reckoned with. These are too profound to be affected by mere advice or moral influence." Given the importance of the reparations issue to France, Hughes did not think that the United States government could or should assume responsibility for dictating or arbitrating a resolution to it. "The most this nation could do," he explained to Senator Lodge, "was to endeavor to get the question out of politics, as the statesmen could not agree, and in the hands of an advisory body . . . to deal with intricate economic questions, but of course this could not be done without the consent of France and she would not consent." Thus, it was essential to wait for a change in French public opinion.[135]

By early 1923 American policy on reparations was set, and Republican officials were firmly convinced of its rectitude. The president, the secretary of state, and the secretary of commerce acknowledged that American economic and humanitarian interests were at stake in the reparations dispute, but they did not consider these interests to be of

134. For Poincaré's decision to move into the Ruhr, see Pierre Miquel, *Raymond Poincaré*, pp. 441–60; Denise Artaud, "A propos de l'occupation de la ruhr," pp. 1–21; Schuker, *French Predominance*, pp. 1–180, especially pp. 24–26, 178–79; Mc-Dougall, "French Rhineland Policy," pp. 201–55; Charles S. Maier, *Recasting Bourgeois Europe*, pp. 281–304; Marks, *Illusion of Peace*, pp. 45–51.
135. For the quotations, see Hughes to Samuel H. Church, 7 July 1923, Herrick Papers, Box 13; Hughes to Henry Cabot Lodge, 1 February 1923, Hughes Papers, Box 31; see also [Beerits Memorandum], "Dawes Plan," p. 8; FR, 1922, 2:202–3.

sufficient importance to justify the involvement of the United States government in the political matters attendant to the indemnity issue.[136] This attitude helps to explain Harding's decision to withdraw the remaining American troops on the Rhine.[137] Noting that American economic recovery during 1922 had taken place even while the European situation was deteriorating, Republican officials did not think that vital American interests were at stake.[138] Consequently, they believed that the appointment of a committee of experts afforded the best opportunity to resolve the reparations crisis according to American guidelines. Within such a committee Republican officials expected American financiers and businessmen to utilize American financial power in behalf of an agreement that was based on the principle of Germany's capacity to pay reparations, but that neither compromised the war debts nor embroiled the United States government directly in Europe's political affairs. Thereafter, this position constituted the basic American approach to the reparations issue.

Economic Diplomacy and Franco-American Relations

Between 1921 and 1923 Republican officials did not divorce the United States from European affairs. On the contrary the Harding administration was well aware of the complex network of commercial and financial relationships that linked American well-being to the restoration of European stability. While rejecting political entanglements and strategic commitments in the Old World, Republican policymakers grappled with the problems of war debts, reparations, loans, exchange stabilization, and commercial policy. Insofar as was possible they tried to depoliticize these issues and cultivate an international climate conducive to economic progress. Republican initiatives, however, were not well coordinated because of the absence of a strong president, the diffusion of responsibility within the executive branch, and the not infrequent division of opinion among key officials on what ought to be done to balance the needs of the domestic economy with the requirements of European reconstruction. In addition, Republican efforts were circumscribed by public disillusionment with European affairs, dissen-

136. Harding to Richard W. Child, 9 October 1922, Harding Papers, PPF; Hughes to Lodge, 1 February 1923, Hughes Papers, Box 31; Hoover to Joseph DeFrees, 11 January 1922, HHCD, Box 21.
137. Harding to Fletcher, 24 August 1922, Fletcher Papers, Box 1; Harding to Phillips, 31 August 1922, Harding Papers, PCF, Box 164.
138. See Hoover, "Drafts," January 1922, HHCD, Box 21; Hoover, "Year of Cooperation," pp. 12–13; Department of the Treasury, *Annual Report*, 1923, p. 2.

sion within the Republican party, congressional fears of executive encroachments, divisions among economic interest groups, and the problems besetting the domestic economy.

As a result of these factors the policymaking apparatus put together by Republican officials was complex, cumbersome, and decentralized. The FRBNY was given a large role to play in fostering currency stability and restoring the gold standard; yet, it had no direct control over war debt and reparation issues, the resolution of which were prerequisites of exchange stabilization. Governor Strong did have a good working relationship with officials in the Treasury Department, but the latter were not able to secure unrestricted authority over war debt refunding. Instead, the WDC took charge of the debt issue, though its flexibility was confined by ultimate congressional authority. Similarly, private financiers like Morgan, who were selected as experts to grapple with the reparations issue, were hampered by their inability to deal with the war debts. Moreover, these financiers were equally disturbed by the attempts of Hughes and Hoover to regulate foreign loans. And even when they agreed with high-level Republican officials on the need to increase imports, at least of noncompetitive products, international-oriented bankers were unable to influence the level of tariff duties set by Congress. They hoped, of course, that the Tariff Commission would use the flexible tariff provisions to recommend reductions in the Fordney-McCumber rates. The commission, however, was immediately beleaguered by internal divisions, and Culbertson was unable to scale down the duties.[139] Thus, while the policies that were molded by Republican officials did have considerable merit when analyzed individually and when considered in the prevailing economic and political context, there still remained considerable doubt whether they could be coordinated in behalf of a comprehensive attack on the sources of European instability.

As the Harding administration sought to grapple constructively with European developments, France was most often cited as the great antagonist to American efforts. Republican officials and American bankers and businessmen alluded to France as ''the great, fateful, and menacing question mark.'' This assessment accorded with the growing belief that the controversy over reparations constituted the heart of the European crisis and that France presented the primary opposition to a settlement based on Germany's capacity to pay.[140] In addition, French

139. For Culbertson's problems, see Culbertson to Hoover, 22 March, 5, 7 April 1923, HHCD, Box 294; Culbertson to the president, 1 September 1923, ibid.
140. For the quotation, see Kahn to Felix Warburg, 30 January 1922, Kahn Papers, Box 190; see also Mortimer Schiff, *Europe in March 1922*, p. 9; Herbert C. Hoover and

commercial, financial, and military policies were considered responsible for the deplorable state of European affairs.[141] American policymakers, therefore, believed that before the United States could help resolve European problems the French had an obligation to revise their policies. American assistance in the form of war debt reductions, private loans, and even tariff adjustments awaited French adoption of conservative financial measures, termination of discriminatory trade practices, reduction of military expenditures, and acceptance of the capacity-to-pay formula as the basis of a reparations agreement.

The prevailing attitude among Republican officials reflected their view that while Europe's stabilization significantly served American interests, it was not of vital importance. Hoover maintained that the United States could eventually "reestablish its material prosperity and comfort without European trade."[142] The American contribution to European stability, therefore, was not supposed to be at the expense of domestic priorities; instead, it was to be contingent upon European nations' conforming to American guidelines. Geographic distance, financial predominance, and comparative economic self-sufficiency afforded the United States the opportunity to measure carefully the risks of isolation against the hazards of overcommitment. The French, of course, had no such leeway. Instead, they encountered agonizing choices. They sought access to American financial and commercial markets and wanted America's moral support against Germany. But they did not want to incur additional strategic burdens, financial losses, or political sacrifices to gain American aid. Consequently, the success of economic diplomacy, designed to reconcile the internal and external needs of the American economy without entangling the United States in European political affairs, would depend upon the extent of America's financial leverage over France, the economic efficacy of America's new policymaking apparatus, and the wisdom of American assumptions about the economic determinants of international behavior.

Hugh Gibson, *The Problems of Lasting Peace*, p. 143; Frank A. Vanderlip, *What Next in Europe?*, p. 141; Harding to Phillips, 1 September 1922, Harding Papers, PCF, Box 164; FR, 1922, 2:178–80, 187–92, 195–98.

141. For policymakers' criticism of French commercial, financial, and military policies, see, for example, McClure to Harrison, 17 July 1922, RG 59, 611.0031/188; Tariff Commission, Memorandum on French tariff discrimination, June 1923, ibid.; Klein to Walter S. Tower, 4 January 1922, RG 151, File 600.2; Strong to Wadsworth, 26 November 1921, FRBNY Papers, C797; Hoover to Harding, 4 January 1922, Harding Papers, PCF, Box 5.

142. For the quotation, see Hoover, "Drafts," January 1922, HHCD, Box 21; see also Harding to Starek, 2 November 1922, Harding Papers, PCF, Box 88; Harding to Harvey, 6, 24 April 1922, 3 May 1922, ibid., PPF 60.

[3]

German Rehabilitation
and French Security, 1923–1925

On 10 January 1923 the French and Belgian governments sent a commission of engineers and several infantry and cavalry divisions into the Ruhr to insure German payment of reparations through the supervision of state mines, forests, and other productive facilities. When the Germans responded with passive resistance, French troops moved into Germany in larger numbers, broadened the area of occupation, and established customs barriers between the occupied and unoccupied parts of Germany. The result over the next year was the economic breakdown and financial degeneration of Germany.[1]

The French intervention in the Ruhr constituted a fundamental challenge to the foreign policy of the Harding administration. In the view of Republican officials French policy was aimed at solving French strategic and financial problems through the economic and political emasculation of Germany. With varying degrees of intensity Republican policymakers and American diplomats ridiculed this policy. They believed that the best means of guaranteeing French security and alleviating French financial difficulties was through the consummation of a moderate reparations settlement that would allow for the financial stabilization and economic rehabilitation of Germany. Disregarding the strategic ramifications of such a policy on France, Hughes insisted that "there can be no economic recuperation in Europe unless Germany recuperates. There will be no permanent peace unless economic satisfactions are enjoyed." Both he and Hoover believed that French strategic anxieties and German economic needs could be reconciled. They assumed that a prosperous Germany would be a peaceful and

1. For a summary of developments, see Arnold J. Toynbee, *Survey of International Affairs*, 1920–1923, pp. 189–202; see also ibid., 1924, pp. 268–322.

republican Germany and would willingly pay a reasonable indemnity. Moreover, for Hughes and Hoover, a prosperous Germany constituted the prerequisite of the reconstruction of Europe, the revitalization of the international economy, and the creation of a viable liberal capitalist community.[2]

The problem facing American officials was how to convince the French that a rehabilitated Germany could be reconciled with France's financial and strategic needs. Hughes still believed that his proposal for an experts' study of Germany's capacity to pay reparations provided the best means of accomplishing this objective. Yet, he realized he would have to allow French and German passions to cool before reintroducing his idea.[3] French officials made it clear that they would resent any American initiatives, lest these serve to encourage German supporters of passive resistance.[4] Thus, time would have to elapse before Republican officials could determine whether the mechanisms they had established to resolve the reparations crisis and mobilize capital for European reconstruction were capable of facilitating the financial rehabilitation of Germany and bringing security to France.

Biding Time

As soon as French troops entered the Ruhr, the secretary of state initiated a policy of strict neutrality and watchful waiting. Conforming to a Senate resolution passed on 6 January, the administration hurriedly withdrew American troops from the Rhine. This withdrawal signaled American disapproval of French policy. Though Republican officials were agitated and worried by French action, Hughes scrupulously avoided any statement that might offend either France or Germany.[5] Both the president and the secretary of state recognized that for an indefinite period American power was limited.[6] In fact, Hughes feared

2. For the quotation, see Charles Evans Hughes, *The Pathway of Peace*, p. 55; see also Herbert C. Hoover, *The Memoirs of Herbert Hoover*, 2:182; for various criticisms of French reparations policy by American officials and diplomats, see Department of State, *Papers Relating to the Foreign Relations of the United States*, 1922, 2:188–89 (hereafter cited as FR); see also James Logan to Hughes, 2 February 1923, Fletcher Papers, Box 10; William R. Castle to Alanson Houghton, 12 January 1923, Castle Papers, Box 3.

3. Diary of William Phillips, 8, 12 January 1923, Phillips Papers, Box 1A; Hughes to Samuel H. Church, 7 July 1923, Herrick Papers, Box 13.

4. See, for example, Logan to Hughes, 19 January, 9, 16, 23 February, 16, 23, 29 March 1923, Fletcher Papers, Box 10.

5. For official American reaction to the Ruhr occupation, see FR, 1923, 2:47–52, 192–97.

6. Hughes to Henry Cabot Lodge, 1 February 1923, Hughes Papers, Box 31; Harding

that a precipitous use of American financial pressure might engender French hostility and undermine America's ability to mediate in the future.[7]

There was one additional factor that influenced the administration's impartial and cautious reaction to the Ruhr occupation. American public opinion, rather than being strongly opposed to French policy as Republican officials had anticipated, turned out to be deeply divided on the issue.[8] Hughes summed up the situation to the German ambassador when he said "that the fundamental fact in this country at this time with respect to the controversy between France and Germany [is] that there [is] a radical difference of opinion, and that the Government [is] bound to take this into consideration in anything it might do, and certainly it should not make a perfectly futile gesture." The secretary of state worried that an inopportune American initiative in European politics might alienate an ethnic group in the United States. He feared that the ensuing national dissension might preclude subtle but effective intervention. Consequently, he decided to do nothing until circumstances seemed more propitious.[9]

Hughes's decision to bide time engendered an enormous amount of criticism. Congressmen, journalists, businessmen, and diplomats savagely attacked the administration's alleged indifference to the European situation. Senator Borah denounced official policy and predicted another world war unless vigorous measures were taken. Prominent business leaders like A. C. Bedford of Standard Oil of New Jersey and Frank Vanderlip of the National City Bank of New York echoed similar misgivings. There were recurrent proposals that the United States convene an international conference to deal with the various elements of the European quagmire. The NFTC urged an integrated assault on the problems of war debts, reparations, unbalanced budgets, unstable currencies, and French security. A group of distinguished international lawyers, exasperated by the administration's indecisiveness, called for

---

to Harold DeWolfe Fuller, 2 February 1923, Harding Papers, Presidential Case File, Box 271 (hereafter cited as PCF); see also FR, 1923, 2:55.

7. Memorandum of conversation between Hughes, Otto Wiedfeldt, and Harry Kessler, n.d., Hughes Papers, Box 175.

8. For public opinion, see "Right and Wrong of the Ruhr Invasion," *Literary Digest* 76 (27 January 1923):7–11; "American Public Opinion Concerning the French Seizure of the Ruhr," *The Outlook* 133 (21 January 1923):210–12. This article was sent to Harding by the magazine's president. See Ernest Hamlin Abbott to Harding, 23 January 1923, Harding Papers, PCF, Box 193; see also vote of the National Economic League, *Consensus* 8 (April 1923):57.

9. Memorandum of conversation between Hughes, Wiedfeldt, and Kessler, n.d., Box 175, Hughes Papers.

a strong stand either for or against France. Ambassador Houghton in Berlin also deplored the ambivalent policy of the Department of State. Fearing that French action might strengthen Bolshevik forces in Germany, he warned Hughes that "having destroyed any balance of power in Europe and left France for the moment all powerful, we have simply let loose a great elemental force. . . . It can only be dealt with as a force. And unless it is met by armed force in the shape of armies, it must be met by economic force in the shape of threatened ruin. That is the whole story. France must be met by force. One might as well attempt to reason with the law of gravitation."[10]

Despite this criticism American officials remained certain of their course. The president and the secretary of state found most of the outside recommendations to be self-serving or impractical. Borah's proposal for an international conference, they maintained, was useless so long as Congress restricted the administration's ability to deal with the debt question.[11] Other recommendations calling for the application of financial pressure or the initiation of new efforts to mediate Franco-German differences were considered equally inappropriate. In April 1923 Castle explained to Houghton that any gesture toward mediation would alienate France and therefore fail.[12] In general, policymakers felt that their domestic critics were unaware of the complexity of the European situation, the intensity of French anger, and the pervasive divisions among Americans themselves.[13]

Although the Harding administration decided not to intervene directly in the Franco-German imbroglio, domestic criticism was sufficiently intense and the European situation sufficiently forboding to impel initiatives on related matters. At the same time that the French were occupying the Ruhr, the WDC negotiated a debt settlement with Great Britain.[14] The president immediately followed his request for congressional approval of the debt accord with another message to the

10. Houghton to Hughes, 27 February, 29 January 1923, Hughes Papers, Box 4B; for the other criticisms and suggestions, see William E. Borah to Robert J. Thompson, 5 February 1923, Borah Papers, Box 227; "America Aloof as Europe Burns," *Literary Digest* 76 (10 February 1923):7–9; Special Committee, "Report on European Conditions," National Foreign Trade Council (NFTC), *Official Report of the National Foreign Trade Convention*, 1923, pp. 8–25; Diary of William Phillips, 23 February 1923, Phillips Papers, Box 1A.
11. Hughes to Lodge, 1 February 1923, Hughes Papers, Box 31; Norman Hapgood to Borah, 13 February 1923, Borah Papers, Box 227; Harding to Richard Washburn Child, 16 April 1923, Harding Papers, Presidential Personal File (hereafter cited as PPF).
12. Castle to Houghton, 19 April 1923, Castle Papers, Box 4.
13. Diary of William Phillips, 23 February 1923, Phillips Papers, Box 1A.
14. See chapter 2, pp. 68–69.

Senate calling for American participation in the International Court of Justice at The Hague.[15] In the spring of 1923 the administration also welcomed the efforts of American bankers to cooperate with their British counterparts in rehabilitating Austrian finances and in stabilizing economic and political conditions in that beleaguered central European nation.[16] These initiatives were carefully designed to protect domestic priorities and keep the nation free of political obligations. Hughes, for example, would not consider a formal United States government guarantee of a private loan to Austria because he feared that it might lead to undesirable political entanglements.[17] Similarly, the secretary of state indicated that the United States would not be able to cancel the war debts as part of a general settlement of the European crisis. He did not think that Congress would sacrifice the war debts, accept the tax implications of such action, or adopt the view that European reconstruction was of substantial importance to the United States. He took care to explain that he felt differently, but Congress's wishes could not be disregarded.[18]

Throughout the spring and summer of 1923 the Harding administration bided time, encouraged direct negotiations between the French and Germans, tried to protect immediate American commercial interests in the Ruhr, and waited for France to see the folly of her deeds. American officials were not unsympathetic to France's desire to secure reparations. They repeatedly emphasized that Germany had an absolute obligation to pay to the very limits of her capacity.[19] But the Americans feared that French tactics would prove incapable of securing reparations and destructive to the long-term needs of European stability.[20] Consequently, though Hughes still refused to take any initiative that might offend the French, he did support the efforts of private American businessmen and bankers to drum up national and

15. For the interest of policymakers in the World Court, see [Beerits Memorandum], "Separate Peace with Germany, the League of Nations, and the Permanent Court of International Justice," Hughes Papers, Box 172, pp. 35–37; Herbert C. Hoover, "America's Next Step," *World Peace Foundation Pamphlets* 6 (1923): 61–68; FR, 1923, 1:10–18; Robert K. Murray, *The Harding Era*, pp. 368–71.

16. Michael J. Hogan, *Informal Entente*, pp. 60–66.

17. Ibid., p. 65.

18. Hughes to Fred I. Kent, 8 February 1923, General Records of the Department of State, RG 59, File No. 800.51/457A.

19. See, for example, Castle to Houghton, 22 September 1923, Castle Papers, Box 4; Castle to Robbins, 15 June 1923, ibid.

20. Memorandum of interview between Hughes and Jules Jusserand, 12 July 1923, Hughes Papers, Box 174; Diary of William Phillips, 29 June 1923, Phillips Papers, Box 1A; FR, 1923, 2:64–66.

international support for a solution based on a capacity-to-pay formula. During May, June, and July Fred I. Kent, Bernard Baruch, and John Foster Dulles traveled from one European capital to another, trying futilely to establish a mutually acceptable basis for the initiation of Franco-German negotiations. Poincaré, however, refused to consider any solution to the reparations controversy until the Germans abandoned passive resistance.[21]

Throughout these months Hughes remained convinced that the only possible way to resolve the reparations controversy was through the formation of a committee of experts to evaluate the situation. Circumstances, however, made it difficult for him to reintroduce his proposal. The death of President Harding on 20 August 1923 was one complicating factor. Harding had given his cabinet officers considerable flexibility to mold American diplomatic policy, and he had sympathized with Hughes's desire to find a means of breaking the European deadlock. When Calvin Coolidge succeeded Harding, the new president was similarly inclined to delegate responsibility for foreign affairs. But Coolidge was even more fearful of congressional criticism than his predecessor and, hence, even more reluctant to take risks. At the same time the Japanese earthquake, the Italian-Greek crisis, and the question of Mexican recognition demanded the attention of State Department officials and interfered with their efforts to resolve the worsening European crisis.[22]

The European situation seemed hopeless when on 27 September German Chancellor Gustav Stresemann called an end to passive resistance. Struggling desperately to preserve the economic, political, and administrative unity of the Weimar Republic, Stresemann appealed to Ambassador Houghton for a renewed American initiative along the lines of Hughes's New Haven address.[23] Shortly thereafter, President Coolidge acknowledged that the United States was still committed

21. For the actions of American businessmen and bankers, see the exchange of letters between Fred Kent and Seward Prosser, Kent Papers, Box 4; see also Kent to Houghton, 19 July 1923, ibid., Box 2; Louis Loucheur, *Carnets secrets, 1908–1932*, pp. 130–33, 144; Morris Frommer, "John Foster Dulles," pp. 46–49. For the contact between these businessmen and Republican officials, see, for example, Kent to Hoover, 27 September 1923, Kent Papers, Box 3; Hughes to Kent, 26 October 1923, Hughes Papers, Box 10; see also Hughes's reference to these mediatory efforts in FR, 1923, 2:61–62.

22. Diary of William Phillips, 10 July, 24, 29 August, 11 September 1923, Phillips Papers, Box 1A. For a good, brief analysis of the policymaking orientation of Harding and Coolidge, see Robert K. Murray, *The Politics of Normalcy*.

23. See Houghton to Hughes (including memorandum of conversation between Stresemann, Houghton, and Stephen Porter), 28 September 1923, Hughes Papers, Box 4B. For the New Haven address, see chapter 2, pp. 76–78.

to Hughes's proposal of December 1922. The British then inquired whether the United States would participate formally or informally in an investigation of Germany's capacity to pay. The secretary of state was elated with the British overture. With the aid of Undersecretary William Phillips and Assistant Secretary Leland Harrison, Hughes immediately drafted an *aide-mémoire*, emphasizing that it was "imperative" to design a financial plan that would "prevent economic disaster in Europe, the consequences of which would be world wide." He indicated that the United States government would permit private American citizens to work on an advisory committee appointed by the Reparation Commission to study Germany's capacity to pay. He insisted that there be no link between reparations and war debts, although he acknowledged that Congress might be generous on the war debts if constructive steps were taken by European governments to restore European stability.[24] This approach reflected Hughes's long-standing desire to resolve the reparations crisis along business principles without injecting political considerations, incurring official United States governmental responsibility, or committing the American people to reciprocal sacrifices that they might not be willing to accept.

When Poincaré raised objections to an unrestricted study of Germany's repayment capacity, Hughes became alarmed. Reports from American diplomats that French policy was aimed at dismembering Germany and enhancing French security caused immense consternation in Washington.[25] The secretary warned the French chargé that French security could not be assured in this manner.[26] On 5 November Hughes called in the French ambassador for a "momentous interview." Hughes could no longer maintain his dignified manner, and his voice rose sharply as he lectured Jusserand on the need for an unrestricted inquiry into Germany's capacity to pay reparations. Warning of the politically incendiary situation in Germany and pointing to the actions of the communists in Saxony and the monarchists in Bavaria, he asked whether France would be secure if Germany were dismembered. The secretary did not think so. He maintained that it was an illusion to believe that a divided Germany would guarantee the security of France. Germany, he was certain, would be reunited and France

24. FR, 1923, 2:70–73; Diary of William Phillips, 25 October 1923, Phillips Papers, Box 1A.
25. For the diplomatic warnings, see Logan to Hughes, 25 October 1923, Fletcher Papers, Box 10; see also FR, 1923, 2:77–78.
26. FR, 1923, 2:79–83; see also Diary of William Phillips, 22, 23 October 1923, Phillips Papers, Box 1A.

would have neither security nor reparations.[27] Later that same day in a meeting with his cabinet colleagues, Hoover reiterated that "the French had only one of two courses, to support democratic government in Germany or to face implacable hate and constant danger."[28]

The French began to fear that the United States government might retract the proposal for an experts' inquiry into German finances and withdraw further from European affairs. Hence, Poincaré wrote Herrick that France wanted American cooperation. The French premier maintained that he shared Hughes's desire for a politically tranquil and economically stable Europe. But he did not want to allow a panel of nonpolitical experts to make suggestions on the post-1930 period. Poincaré did not think that an objective basis existed for such calculations, and he worried that subjective estimations would lead to unwarranted reductions of the total indemnity. Unquestionably, the French premier was in a quandary. He was under intense pressure from the French Right to force German dismemberment and to create an independent Rhenish republic. At the same time, he was subject to increasing opposition from the Left, as many Frenchmen began to question the financial and military wisdom of an aggressive policy that isolated France from her former allies without securing tangible results in the form of reparations. Poincaré, himself, was aware of the dangerous implications of that isolation, especially since France's financial weakness was growing more acute each day and French elections were scheduled for the spring.[29]

As a result of these pressures the French premier decided to ascertain whether a frame of reference could be established for a study of the situation by experts that would be acceptable to both France and the United States. On 13 November Louis Barthou raised the matter within the Reparation Commission. Progress at first was very difficult. During the last days of November and first days of December a compromise was worked out. Two committees were established. Their ostensible purpose was not to study Germany's capacity to pay. Rather, the First Committee was to consider how to balance Germany's budget and

27. See Memorandum of interview between Hughes and Jusserand, 5 November 1923, Hughes Papers, Box 174; for Phillips's comments on this "momentous interview," see Diary of William Phillips, 5 November 1923, Phillips Papers, Box 1A.
28. Hoover, *Memoirs*, 2:181–82.
29. FR, 1923, 2:95–97; for the factors influencing Poincaré's behavior, see Logan to Hughes, 25 October, 1 November, 3, 6 December 1923, Fletcher Papers, Box 10; Jules Alfred Laroche, *Au Quai d'Orsay avec Briand et Poincaré*, p. 185; Pierre Miquel, *Raymond Poincaré*, pp. 459–82; Charles S. Maier, *Recasting Bourgeois Europe*, pp. 403–15; Stephen A. Schuker, *The End of French Predominance*, pp. 35–38.

stabilize her currency; the Second Committee was to consider measures for repatriating German capital abroad. In this fashion, the earlier conflict over the chronological limits of an experts' study was sidestepped without politically embarrassing the French premier. Yet, Logan informed Hughes that the French recognized that the formula setting up the study implicitly called for an exhaustive scrutiny of Germany's capacity to pay reparations. In return, Poincaré received assurances that the legality of the Ruhr occupation would not be considered.[30] As a result of these mutual concessions the stage was finally set to test the efficacy of the technical and apolitical approach to the reparations issue long recommended by Republican officials.

Devising the Dawes Plan

Having worked out a possible formula for investigating Germany's capacity to pay reparations, the Department of State proceeded to select the American experts. Officially, of course, the experts were picked by the Reparation Commission. Unofficially, however, the State Department determined the American members of the two committees and cabled their names to the Reparation Commission for public announcement. In choosing the American delegates, the administration was careful not to select anyone who had advocated cancellation of the war debts. The aim of policymakers was to choose delegates who would generate public confidence and stimulate investors' enthusiasm. Thus, the administration chose Charles G. Dawes, a midwest Republican and well-known banker; Owen D. Young, a New York industrialist and Wilsonian internationalist; and Henry M. Robinson, a prominent Pacific coast financier and a vice-president of the CCUS. By selecting men from both parties and from different regions of the nation, Republican officials hoped to avoid any subsequent partisan or sectional recriminations. For the same reason they decided not to select any Wall Street bankers. In addition, Dawes's pro-French reputation, stemming from his wartime duty as chief of supply for the American Expeditionary Forces, and Young's close connections with German industrialists, stemming from his position on the board of directors of General Electric and Radio Corporation of America, increased the prospect of se-

30. Logan to Hughes, 30 November 1923, Fletcher Papers, Box 10; Logan to Hughes, 3, 6 December 1923, ibid., Box 11; Leon Fraser, ''The Evolution of the Terms of Reference of the Committee of Experts,'' 9 January 1924, Records of the United States Participation in International Conferences, Commissions, and Expositions, RG 43, Box 1932.

curing the adherence of both France and Germany to an eventual accord.[31]

Before Young and Dawes departed for Paris, Hughes asked them to come to Washington for discussions. Since they were to be members of the all-important First Committee studying ways to balance Germany's budget and stabilize her currency, the secretary wanted them to be thoroughly acquainted with all information possessed by his department. In Washington Dawes and Young spoke to Hughes, Hoover, and Coolidge.[32] Although specific instructions were not issued, Hoover provided Dawes and Young with several trunks of papers and statistics. To interpret this morass of data and assist quietly in an advisory capacity, Hughes assigned Arthur N. Young, the economic adviser in the State Department. Likewise, Hoover chose Alan Goldsmith, chief of the European Division of the BFDC to aid Dawes and Owen Young. In addition to the appointment of several nongovernmental advisers, Hoover instructed the American commercial attachés in Britain, France, and Germany to participate in the technical labor of the committee. The secretary of commerce had been indignant that Hughes had not consulted him more extensively on the formulation of American reparations policy. Having won Owen Young's confidence, Hoover now hoped that his department would be able to exert a greater influence on the course of events. Although under strict orders to remain as inconspicuous as possible, Hoover's representatives clearly intended to play a major role in the experts' negotiations.[33]

To allow the experts to undertake their work in a favorable atmosphere, Republican policymakers decided to postpone efforts to negotiate war debt refunding agreements. American public opinion, as expressed in the press, was divided on whether the WDC should pressure the French to begin appropriate discussions. By making no reference to this contentious issue, however, Republican officials sought to avoid public controversy in France or the United States that might handicap the work of the experts' committees. American officials wanted to

31. For the appointment of the experts, see Diary of William Phillips, 10, 13, 19, 22 December 1923, Phillips Papers, Box 1A; Hughes to Logan, 13 December 1923, RG 59, 800.51W89/50; Herrick to Hughes, 21 December 1923, Hughes Papers, Box 25; Stuart Crocker to Logan, 28 April 1925, Young Papers, R–14.

32. Hughes to Young, 19 December 1923, Young Papers, R–13; Crocker, Memorandum, 21 March 1925, ibid., R–14.

33. Diary of William Phillips, 29 December 1923, Phillips Papers, Box 1A; Hoover to Hughes, 11 January 1924, Young Papers, R–17; Hughes to Hoover, 12 January 1924, ibid.; Crocker, Memorandum, 21 March 1925, ibid., R–17; see also the Alan Goldsmith-Christian Herter correspondence, Ayres Papers, Box 4.

establish the conditions for a favorable public reception of the experts' report so that they and their counterparts in France might be able to endorse its recommendations without fear of generating political controversy.[34]

Meanwhile, as Dawes and Young voyaged across the Atlantic, they settled upon many of the key elements of a desirable plan for rehabilitating Germany's finances. They believed that German productivity had to be restored, that French economic controls in the Ruhr had to be terminated, and that Germany's economic unification had to be guaranteed. Only after these measures had been taken, they contended, would the German government be able to collect enough taxes to gain the confidence of foreign investors, balance the budget, and pay reparations. Once the Americans arrived in Paris and Dawes was selected as the chairman of the First Committee, he became the publicity agent for the principles he and Young had agreed upon. Dawes repeatedly emphasized the importance of restoring Germany's productivity. Dawes and Young assumed that the return of economic prosperity and political tranquility to Europe depended upon the resuscitation of German economic activity. Moreover, they believed that a "new status quo of economic peace," based on the fiscal and economic unity of the Reich, constituted a firmer guarantee of French security than did the continuing occupation of the Ruhr and the prevailing financial disarray in Germany. Economic peace, Dawes insisted, was the "best antidote for war." Hence, the American experts, like Republican officials, viewed French security and German economic reconstruction as compatible objectives.[35]

Although Dawes and Young believed that the economic unification of Germany was the most important of their principles and indispensable to the success of their plan, they were sensitive to French feelings on this matter. Dawes recognized that "the circumference of the useful activity of our Committee, at least at the inception of our work, is a circle whose radius is the length of the string which ties Parmentier, one of the two French members of our Committee, to Poincaré." Accordingly, the American experts were careful not to discuss the

34. For public opinion, see "The Move to Dun France," *Literary Digest* 79 (15 December 1923):14–15; Arthur N. Young to Leland Harrison, 17 December 1923, RG 59, 800.51W89/60; Calvin Coolidge, *The Talkative President*, pp. 182–84.

35. For the development of the ideas of Young and Dawes, see Crocker, Memorandum, 21 March 1925, Young Papers, R–14; Charles G. Dawes, *A Journal of Reparations*, pp. 30, 116–19, 123–25, 130, 145–46; Rufus Dawes, *The Dawes Plan in the Making*, pp. 72, 214, 236; Logan to Hughes, 22 February 1924, Fletcher Papers, Box 11; Ida M. Tarbell, *Owen Young*, p. 166.

issue of German economic unification in a way that would offend the French. Nor did the Americans raise the matter of the legality of the Ruhr occupation. After meeting with Parmentier on 9 January, Dawes and Young agreed not to determine Germany's total reparations sum lest this prove unacceptable to Poincaré. In fact, to accommodate French public opinion Dawes cleared his opening speech with French officials before delivering it to the assembled experts from Britain, France, Belgium, Italy, and the United States. Similarly, Young prodded his colleagues to avoid acrimony at the onset of their labors and to focus on those principles that were least likely to engender controversy. The French appreciated these conciliatory gestures, and the work of the First Committee began auspiciously in the middle of January 1924.[36]

Young deftly took command of the First Committee. He emphasized the importance of restoring German productivity and steered the experts toward a consensus on how to proceed toward this goal. The committee's first task was to devise a means of stabilizing German currency and balancing the German budget. The experts quickly agreed that to insure currency stability, Germany needed to establish a new, independent gold bank, link the mark to gold, and secure a foreign loan. They also thought that Germany required a temporary moratorium on reparation payments as well as a mechanism to protect her currency when financial transfers were being made.[37] The matter of transfer was especially important to Young. He believed that once Germany collected and deposited gold marks in the new bank in the accounts of the Allied creditors, she fulfilled her obligations. A newly created transfer committee, under the leadership of an agent general for reparations, would be responsible for converting gold marks into foreign currencies when Germany's balance of payments permitted. Accumulation in the new bank of large balances that could not be transferred would demonstrate the unworkability of the plan and justify a revision of the schedule of reparation payments. Meanwhile, the new bank could use the balances to provide credit to needy German borrowers, alleviate the stringent financial conditions in Germany, and rejuvenate the German economy. Thus, by the end of January Young

36. For the quotation, see Dawes, *Journal of Reparations*, p. 13; see also pp. 16–17, 48–51; Crocker, Memorandum, 21 March 1925, Young Papers, R–14; Crocker to Logan, 28 April 1925, ibid.; Young to Gerard Swope, 18 January 1924, ibid., I–67; R. Tileston, "Chronology of the Work of the Committee of Experts of the Reparation Commission," 9 January 1924, ibid., R–6.

37. Crocker, Memorandum, 21 March 1925, Young Papers, R–14; Tileston, "Chronology," 9, 14 January 1924; Dawes, *Journal of Reparations*, pp. 20, 56–57.

had mustered widespread support among all the experts, including Parmentier, for a plan that included a new bank, a foreign loan, a gold currency, and a sophisticated transfer mechanism.[38] Describing Young's means of procedure, Alan Goldsmith wrote his colleagues in the Commerce Department that "Young is a wonder. He has one of the best analytical minds I ever came in contact with. As a matter of fact he and the General [Dawes] make a good team. The General starts a lot of conversation, and gets people talking without reserve. Young sits and classifies, itemises, and card-indexes ideas and data."[39]

Most significantly, Young convinced the other delegates that the best approach to the interrelated tasks of balancing Germany's budget and of facilitating reparation payments was through commensurate taxation. Since Germany's internal debt had been wiped out by inflation, Young believed that the committee of experts should ask the German government to adopt an internal tax policy that would impose a per capita tax burden equal to that which existed in other European nations. Once this tax policy was implemented, Young assumed that there would be surplus revenues available for the payment of reparations. The German government would deposit these funds into the new bank and the transfer committee would convert the gold marks into foreign currencies if possible.[40] Young similarly argued that German railroads and German industries should not benefit from the elimination of their own debts, and that they should carry a financial burden roughly equivalent to that incurred by railroads and industries in other nations. Consequently, he maintained that German reparation payments should come not only from the German budget but also from interest payments and sinking fund charges on specially issued railroad bonds and industrial debentures.[41] In effect then Young introduced the principle of commensurate debt burden as well as the principle of commensurate taxation. By so doing he sought to enlarge the amount of reparation payments that otherwise would have come strictly from budgetary surpluses. He also hoped to eliminate any competitive advantages that German producers and industrialists might enjoy as a

38. Crocker, Memorandum, 21 March 1925, Young Papers, R 14; Memorandum of interview between Crocker and Parmentier, 19 May 1925, ibid.; Goldsmith to Herter, 28 January 1924, Ayres Papers, Box 4.

39. Goldsmith to Herter, 20 January 1924, Ayres Papers, Box 4.

40. Tileston, "Chronology," 23 January 1924; Goldsmith to Herter, 20, 28 January, 4 February 1924, Ayres Papers, Box 4.

41. Memorandum of interview between Crocker and Henry Robinson, 16 May 1925, Young Papers, R-14; Tileston, "Chronology," 30 January–12 February 1924.

result of advantageous tax policies and favorable debt structures.[42]

On 28 January the experts set out for Berlin to study German budgetary and fiscal practices and to determine whether the Germans would agree to the creation of a new bank, the implementation of commensurate taxation, and the establishment of a new transfer mechanism. In the German capital Young tried to escape publicity as he carried on delicate negotiations with German officials and industrialists. With the help of Ambassador Houghton, Young first explained the work of the experts to Chancellor Wilhelm Marx and Foreign Minister Stresemann. These talks proceeded extremely well. Stresemann agreed to the major principles of the plan that the experts had devised. He told Young that if the latter could secure the support of the German industrialists, the German government would go along. Indeed, Stresemann was eager to do whatever was necessary to unite the Ruhr with the rest of Germany and to obtain foreign capital.

Young then met individually with Karl von Siemens and Felix Deutsch. These industrialists were former business acquaintances of Young's and the American had little difficulty convincing them of the wisdom of the experts' proposals. But Hugo Stinnes, whom Young considered to be the "Napoleon of the industrial and financial situation in Germany," was a "harder nut" to crack. The German coal and steel magnate feared that Germany's reparation creditors would use the untransferred balances of gold marks in the new bank to gain control of German industries. Young agreed that this was a danger. Consequently, he was willing to place a limit on the size of the untransferred balances. When this sum was reached, internal payments would cease until additional foreign transfers were made. Young also amended the plan to insure that the untransferred balances would not be used in the purchase of stocks, but would be reserved for ordinary credit purposes. These changes placated some of Stinnes's worst apprehensions. Thus, when Young and the experts left Germany on 13 February, they believed that they had made substantial progress in gaining the approval of prominent German politicians, industrialists, and bankers as well as influential labor and agricultural leaders for their proposals.[43]

But several critical issues remained to be resolved. Many of the tech-

42. Goldsmith to Richard S. Emmett, 26 March 1924, Ayres Papers, Box 4; Goldsmith to Herter, 31 March 1924, ibid. In practice, however, the principle of commensurate taxation was not implemented. See Schuker, *French Predominance*, p. 184.
43. For Young's discussions in Germany, see Tileston, "Chronology," 13 January–18 February 1924; Houghton to Hughes, 19 February 1924, Hughes Papers, Box 31; Dawes, *Journal of Reparations*, pp. 76–77; for Stresemann's feelings, see Gustav Stresemann, *Diaries, Letters, and Papers*, 1:278–83.

nical advisers working with the experts recognized even before the trip to Berlin that though Young had secured an accord between the French, British, and American experts on the general principles of a settlement, there were still enormous differences on how these principles ought to be implemented in practice.[44] Some of the latent distrust emerged on the train to Berlin when the English speaking Anglo-Saxons got together in a separate group from the French, Italian, and Belgian experts.[45] Subsequently, from the middle of February to early April the experts immersed themselves in protracted and often acrimonious discussions over the nature of France's occupation of the Ruhr, the size of the annuities, and the structure of the new bank. Throughout most of these discussions, Dawes and Young tried to mediate the differences between the French and the British. Dawes was determined to come up with a unanimous report; unanimity, he believed, was the essential precondition for the report's eventual acceptance by the governments involved.[46]

Since Dawes and Young placed so much emphasis on the economic reunification of Germany, they were anxious to convince the French to abolish the customs barriers between the Ruhr and the unoccupied parts of Germany and relinquish the deliveries-in-kind and Ruhr revenues they had seized through direct action. If the French were willing to make these concessions, Dawes was prepared to give France tangible guarantees of future payments in the form of railroad bonds, industrial debentures, and specific revenue taxes. During the last week of February Dawes asked Parmentier to ascertain whether Poincaré would agree to remove French economic controls in the Ruhr in exchange for these other forms of financial guarantees. Dawes understood that he was asking Poincaré to make an enormous concession, because the guarantees inherent in the new plan were primarily financial in nature and did not compensate the French for relinquishing the strategic advantages of economic control over the Ruhr. Accordingly, Dawes appealed to his French friends to trust him. He emphasized that the economic unification and financial resuscitation of Germany constituted France's best hope for lasting peace and security. To his gratification, on 29 February Parmentier indicated that Poincaré was willing to eliminate all economic controls as soon as Germany had accepted and implemented the necessary laws and regulations.[47] Most observers

44. Goldsmith to Herter, 4, 9 February 1924, Ayres Papers, Box 4.
45. Tileston, ''Chronology,'' 28 January 1924.
46. Houghton to Hughes, 19 February 1924, Hughes Papers, Box 31.
47. Dawes, *Journal of Reparations*, pp. 82, 99, 104, 116–18, 123–25, 131–33,

believed that the rapid decline of the franc by over 20 percent during December, January, and February contributed to these significant French concessions. On 20 March Poincaré admitted to Ambassador Herrick his great fear that the franc would follow the mark into oblivion.[48]

In return for France's willingness to accept the economic unification of Germany, Dawes was ready to allow the French to continue their military occupation of the Ruhr so long as there was no interference with Germany's economic life.[49] Revealing his strong Francophile sentiments, Dawes calculated that a Germany strong enough to pay might be strong enough to resist payments. Consequently, he approved of France's desire to maintain some aspects of a purely military occupation. According to Dawes, "normal economic functioning [in Germany] and the preservation of this [military] 'status quo' [constituted] France's greatest protection."[50] Some of the American technical advisers, however, wondered whether it was possible to separate economic and military controls. "How to maintain a military occupation, without in any way interfering with Germany's economic unity, and hence her productivity, is a brain racking proposition," commented Alan Goldsmith.[51] Young himself feared that any semblance of military occupation might upset bankers and affect the flotation of a loan to Germany. He contacted Dwight Morrow of J. P. Morgan and Company and inquired if the very presence of French troops in the Ruhr would preclude the raising of foreign capital. Morrow's response was equivocal, but he indicated that the continued military occupation of the Ruhr might not constitute an insuperable impediment to a foreign loan if other conditions were met.[52] As a result Dawes and Young did not make the withdrawal of French troops an integral part of their plan. This satisfied the French but upset the British and, of course, the Germans.

145–49; Logan to Hughes, 22 February 1924, Fletcher Papers, Box 11; Dawes to Morrow, 1 March 1924, Morrow Papers.

48. Herrick to Hughes, 20 March 1924, RG 59, 462.00R294/339; Fletcher to Hughes, 18 February 1924, Fletcher Papers, Box 11; for the depreciation of the franc, see the statistical tables in Alfred Sauvy, *Histoire économique de la France entre les deux guerres*, 1:444–45; for the impact of French financial problems on French foreign policy, see Schuker, *French Predominance*, pp. 89–123.

49. Dawes, *Journal of Reparations*, pp. 99, 73.

50. Dawes to Morrow, 28 February 1924, Morrow Papers.

51. Goldsmith to Herter, 24 February 1924, Ayres Papers, Box 4.

52. Young to Swope, 27 February 1924, Young Papers, I–67; Swope (from Morrow) to Young, n.d., ibid.

On other matters, however, the American experts resisted French pressure. In working out the details of the bank plan, Parmentier wanted to separate the issue department from the banking department and locate the former outside Germany. He feared that in an emergency the Germans might print money in order to finance a war. For similar reasons he requested that Germany's gold reserves be held in a neutral nation. Edwin W. Kemmerer, the Princeton economist who served as a technical adviser to the American experts on the bank plan, successfully rejected these French demands. Parmentier's persistent attempts to insure that the new bank did not serve to abet German political or military objectives convinced Kemmerer that the French "wanted to do everything possible to guarantee their security, regardless of the future of the Germans."[53] In contrast the Americans saw their role as mediating the conflicting demands of the European powers, thereby reconciling French strategic and financial imperatives with the economic and financial needs of Germany.

This mediatory function of the American experts was most clearly evident during March 1924 when the First Committee began to assess Germany's annual reparation payments. Although the principle of commensurate taxation had been accepted, there was much uncertainty about how to apply it, partly because there was so much disagreement about the anticipated size of Germany's budgetary surpluses. The British expert, Sir Josiah Stamp, and the American technical advisers, including Goldsmith, Leonard P. Ayres, Walter E. Tower, and Charles E. Herring, estimated that the maximum annuity that Germany would be able to pay after five years of recuperation was between 1.25 and 2 billion gold marks. Moreover, they claimed that Germany would not have enough of a budgetary surplus during the first two years of the plan to make reparation payments-in-kind or to reimburse the Allies for army occupation costs. They warned that any schedule of payments that did not take this into consideration would "smash up the plan and break the bank." The French, however, refused to accept any postponements in payments-in-kind, and they demanded standard annuities after five years that exceeded 4 billion marks. Confronted with these conflicting demands, Young focused his efforts on arranging a compromise. He ostensibly sided with the French, gained their confidence, acquiesced to their opposition to a moratorium on reparations-in-kind,

53. See Memorandum of interview between Crocker and Edwin W. Kemmerer, 9 May 1925, Young Papers, R-14; see also Memorandum of interview between Crocker and Parmentier, 19 May 1925, ibid.; Tileston, "Chronology," 22 January 1924.

and convinced them to accept a standard annuity of 2.5 billion marks. A prosperity index, which measured Germany's economic growth, permitted upward revisions in her obligations under favorable conditions.[54]

Young's major preoccupation was to establish a plan acceptable to all governments. Since he expected more opposition from France than from either Britain or Germany, he agreed to figures that he acknowledged might be too high. The critical objective, in his mind, was to give the plan a chance. If it proved unworkable, the plan itself incorporated machinery for eventual revision. Meanwhile, it would accomplish the dual objectives of restoring German economic unity and of stabilizing her currency.[55] Indeed, the latter goal was so important that Young and the American technical advisers resisted French and British attempts to delay tying the mark to the gold standard until the pound and the franc had also returned to a gold basis.[56] In Young's view the plan fulfilled immediate American objectives and conformed with the American understanding of Germany's capacity to pay. On the one hand it stabilized the mark, resuscitated German purchasing power, and enabled Germany to resume her central role in the European economy. On the other hand it imposed a heavy enough burden on Germany to assure France a reasonable indemnity and deter German industry from emerging as the dominant force in world commerce.[57]

During the first week in April the experts completed their work and submitted a unanimous report. In addition to recommending a standard annuity of 2.5 billion marks, the experts presented detailed plans for the economic unification of Germany, the establishment of a new central bank, the stabilization of the mark, the flotation of an international loan, and the institution of a sophisticated transfer mechanism.[58] The

54. For the quotation, see Goldsmith to Herter, 9 March 1924, Ayres Papers, Box 4; see also Goldsmith to Herter, 24 February, 3, 17, 24, 31 March 1924, ibid.; Goldsmith to Emmett, 26 March 1924, ibid.; Logan to Hughes, 27 February 1924, Fletcher Papers, Box 11; Dawes, *Journal of Reparations*, pp. 182–86; Houghton to Castle, 6 April 1924, Castle Papers, Box 4.

55. For Young's orientation, see Goldsmith to Emmett, 26 March 1924, Ayres Papers, Box 4; Memorandum of interview between Crocker and Walter S. Tower, 14 May 1925, Young Papers, R–14; Houghton to Castle, 6 April 1924, Castle Papers, Box 4.

56. Dawes, *Journal of Reparations*, p. 164; Memorandum of interview between Crocker and Kemmerer, 9 May 1925, Young Papers, R–14; Stephen V. O. Clarke, *Central Bank Cooperation, 1924–1931*, pp. 60–66.

57. For indications of Young's fears of German competition, see Goldsmith to Herter, 31 March 1924, Ayres Papers, Box 4; Goldsmith to Emmett, 26 March 1924, ibid.

58. For a fine summary of the Dawes Plan, including copies of the experts' reports, see Harold G. Moulton, *The Reparation Plan*.

unanimity of the experts was in large part a result of the financial problems experienced by all European governments and of their desire for American financial support. The French, for example, were unusually conciliatory on such matters as the bank plan, the amount of the annuities, and the abandonment of economic controls in the Ruhr, because of the plight of the franc. When its value fell below four cents in March 1924 and an internal loan failed, the French government was forced to negotiate a $100 million credit with Morgan and Company. The financial weakness of France provided the American experts with considerable leverage over their French colleagues. The British experts also acquiesced to many aspects of the plan because they, too, feared that their opposition might discourage American financial participation in the plan's subsequent implementation. Summing up developments as the experts concluded their work, Herrick wrote President Coolidge that "it is universally conceded that our participation [in the Experts' Report] . . . has made a most profound impression on Europe. . . . The fact that America is the creditor nation and is trusted in all Europe even where she is despised, is a tremendous factor in our favor and also gives us a potential power to straighten out affairs over here."[59]

Completing the Dawes Plan

With a unanimous report finally presented, government officials had to determine whether to endorse the experts' recommendations, and bankers had to decide whether to lend their financial support. The initial response of the Commerce and State Department officials who had worked as technical advisers with the American experts was far from positive. Goldsmith wrote Hoover that the general principles underlying the plan were sound, but that it would not work in practice. He emphasized that the annuities were too high, that the transfer mechanism would cause problems, that the military occupation of the Ruhr would deter the restoration of confidence, and that the administrative controls were too cumbersome. Goldsmith complained bitterly that his own recommendations and those of the other technical advisers had been repeatedly ignored by Young. The result, he insisted, was the imposition of a reparations burden that exceeded Germany's capacity

59. Herrick to Coolidge, 3 April 1924, Herrick Papers, Box 16; for the Morgan credit, see J. P. Morgan and Company to secretary of state, 21 March 1924, RG 59, 851.51/444; for the acquiescence of the British experts, see Tower, "Private Opinions on the Experts' Report," 10 May 1924, RG 43, Box 1933; for an excellent account, see Schuker, *French Predominance*, pp. 89–123, 171–231.

to pay. "Getting such a sum out of Germany . . . seems fantastic," he wrote, even given the most positive expectations of world developments. Although awed by Young's negotiating skill, Goldsmith condemned Young's "horse-trading policy" and his disregard of facts and figures.[60]

Despite these warnings the Coolidge administration immediately endorsed the Experts' Report. The president congratulated Dawes on his efforts and exclaimed that he had represented the "American mind." Insofar as Dawes had generated widespread enthusiasm for a reparations plan based on business principles without injecting the debt issue, he had accomplished exactly what policymakers had expected of him.[61] The favorable editorial reaction in the American press delighted Republican officials and eventually encouraged them to select Dawes as Coolidge's running mate in the 1924 elections. With the Teapot Dome scandal charging "the air in Washington . . . with hatred and malice," the Dawes Plan provided Republicans with a positive achievement, along with lower taxes, to wage the forthcoming campaign.[62] On 22 April Coolidge called upon European governments to accept the Experts' Report and expressed his hope that private American capital would participate in the implementation of the Dawes Plan. According to the president, "sound business reasons exist why we should participate in the financing of works of peace in Europe. . . . It would benefit our trade and commerce, and we especially hope that it will provide a larger market for our agricultural production. . . . We have determined to maintain, and can maintain, our political independence, but our economic independence will be strengthened and increased when the economic stability of Europe is restored."[63] American officials hoped that the Dawes Plan would provide the framework for rehabilitating Germany and for inaugurating a new era of European peace and prosperity, which would constitute the surest guarantees of French security.

American bankers, however, were much less sanguine about the efficacy of the Dawes Plan. Their opinion was of critical importance because the plan depended upon the successful flotation of a foreign loan, the proceeds of which were to be used to help stabilize the mark,

60. Goldsmith to Herter, 24 February, 24 March 1924, Ayres Papers, Box 4; see also the summary confidential cable from Goldsmith and Charles Herring to Hoover, Records of the Bureau of Foreign and Domestic Commerce (BFDC), RG 151, File 3266 (Incoming Confidential Cables).
61. Dawes, *Journal of Reparations*, p. 247.
62. See Diary of William Phillips, 8 March, 10 April 1924, Phillips Papers, Box 2.
63. FR, 1924, 2:14–15.

guarantee budgetary equilibrium, and finance deliveries-in-kind.[64] The reparation experts and the leaders of all the European powers acknowledged that the loan depended upon the cooperation and support of the New York banking firm of J. P. Morgan and Company. But the Morgan partners received the report with grave misgivings. In mid-April Russell Leffingwell, former assistant secretary of the treasury, well-known New York lawyer, and a partner in the prestigious Morgan firm, analyzed the plan and expressed his fears that the payments exceeded Germany's capacity, that the budget might not be balanced, and that the proposed loan was not secure. What most worried Leffingwell and his partners Dwight W. Morrow and Thomas W. Lamont, however, was the fact that reparations-in-kind had not been suspended during the first year of the plan. They feared that Germany would have to use the proceeds of the loan to finance these deliveries or be forced into another default. Either eventuality was disturbing. If the loan were used to finance reparations-in-kind, the mark would be weakened; if another default occurred, sanctions would be applied, the economic rehabilitation of Germany retarded, and the loan endangered.[65]

Before they would contemplate a loan, the Morgan partners presented certain demands. They wanted the loan made the unconditional obligation of the German state and the unqualified first charge on Germany's revenues and assets, thus taking priority over reparation payments. They also desired assurances that the agent general would have sufficient authority to prevent excessive reparation payments and forestall the premature sale of the railway bonds and industrial debentures. Most significant, to protect their investment the Morgan partners demanded that all signatories of the Versailles treaty agree to refrain from taking action against Germany that might impair the service of the loan. With this condition began the onset of the bankers' relentless efforts to force France to abandon her rights to apply sanctions in case of default. In addition, the Morgan partners sought to persuade the French to postpone all payments, including reparations-in-kind, during the first year. Finally, as a means of convincing the American financial community that a new era in European relations was being inaugurated, the bankers insisted that private investors in France, Belgium,

64. Logan to Hughes, 22 February 1924, Fletcher Papers, Box 11.
65. Russell C. Leffingwell, "The Dawes Report," 19 April 1924, Thomas W. Lamont Papers, Box 176; see also Morrow to H. H. Harjes, 18 April 1924, ibid.; Cable from Morgan and Company to Young, 19 April 1924, Young Papers, R–13.

and Italy, as well as those in the United States and Great Britain, partake in the loan.[66]

The bankers' cool reception of the report upset Young. Although all the European governments had indicated support for the Dawes Plan, at least in principle, Young feared that the demands of the Morgan partners might drive the French into opposition. He especially worried about the impact of the bankers' efforts to prohibit future application of sanctions. Just as Dawes had criticized the American technical advisers for their lack of sensitivity to French financial and political realities, Young was concerned that the bankers' disregard of French sensibilities would undermine the painstaking efforts he had made to satisfy the basic requirements of the European powers.[67]

Young, however, did understand the legitimacy of some of the bankers' apprehensions. He recognized that Germany might not be able to meet the schedule of payments written into the Dawes Plan, especially after the first five years. He also grasped the dangers inherent in a renewed use of sanctions. But he felt these issues had been and could be handled without jeopardizing France's cooperation. Young believed that the agent general and the transfer committee would have ample powers to maintain the stability of the mark and protect the loan, especially since cash transfers would be made only when the agent general determined that Germany's balance of payments so permitted. Moreover, Young was convinced that the deliveries-in-kind could be made without endangering the currency or risking sanctions. He pointed out that if Germany acted in good faith but could not meet the schedule of annuities enumerated in the Experts' Report, a new scheme could be devised without affecting the security of the loan. The Dawes Plan was not conceived as a permanent solution to the reparations problem. The plan was a stopgap measure, emphasized Governor Strong of the FRBNY, after discussing it with Young. "It proposes impossible things," Strong concluded, "and sets up alternatives to employ when the impossibility had been demonstrated." Young nevertheless contended that the plan afforded the only prospect of stabilizing the mark, rehabilitating Germany, and restoring Europe to peace and prosperity.[68]

66. Morgan and Company to Young, 19 April 1924, Young Papers, R–13.
67. Young to Herrick, 23 May 1924, Herrick Papers, Box 17; Young to Emile Francqui, 21 April 1924, Young Papers, R–6; Dawes, *Journal of Reparations*, pp. 181–82.
68. For the quotation, see Strong to Pierre Jay, 23, 28 April 1924, Strong Papers, 1000.5; see also Young to Herrick, 23 May 1924, Herrick Papers, Box 17; Young, unfinished letter, 24 July 1924, Young Papers, R–16.

In early May Young returned to the United States and entered into extensive discussions with the Morgan partners, Federal Reserve officials, and Republican policymakers. Governor Strong argued in favor of the administration's launching a full-scale plan for the monetary reconstruction of Europe. He believed that the Dawes Plan could serve as the impetus to introduce central bank cooperation, refund the war debts, and restore the gold standard. Gold was flowing into the United States, threatening inflation, endangering sound credit policies, and undermining foreign purchasing power. This trend could be reversed, Strong maintained, only if the European nations returned to gold.[69]

The bankers, however, remained hesitant about making a loan to Germany under the conditions stipulated in the Experts' Report.[70] Young reiterated that the agent general had extensive powers to protect the new currency and the loan, but they still demurred. Hughes also tried to coax the bankers into cooperation. He indicated that the administration would not object to an American's serving as agent general.[71] He revealed that he sympathized with the bankers' desire to forestall the reimposition of sanctions. Furthermore, he and other Republican officials intimated that after the November elections, they would proceed with a comprehensive effort to restore European financial stability. Meanwhile, they wanted the Dawes Plan put into effect as speedily as possible. "This is the first and essential step," Hughes declared, "to economic recovery abroad in which this country is vitally interested."[72]

While these discussions were under way in Washington and New York, the European governments continued to work out the details for implementing the Dawes Plan and for enforcing it in case of default. Hughes instructed American emissaries in Europe to facilitate the negotiations between the European governments. In fact, Houghton and Logan were already acting as intermediaries in these discussions. The secretary was encouraged by these developments, by the growing spirit of cooperation in Europe, and by the outcome of the French elections

69. Strong to Jay, 23, 28 April 1924, Strong Papers, 1000.5; Strong to Logan, 30 June, 11 July 1924, ibid., 1011.1.
70. For the views of the Morgan partners, see the extensive correspondence for June and early July in Thomas W. Lamont Papers, Box 176; see also Morrow to Lamont, 2 July 1924, Morrow Papers.
71. For the issue of the agent general, see Basil Miles to Logan, 17 May 1924, Herrick Papers, Box 17; Young to Robert Kindersley, 10 June 1924, Young Papers, R–17.
72. For the quotation, see FR, 1924, 2:32; see also ibid., pp. 32–35; for intimations of the administration's monetary policy after the November elections, see Strong to Logan, 10, 30 June 1924, Strong Papers, 1011.1.

in May. He anticipated that the new government of the Cartel des Gauches under Edouard Herriot would be more receptive to the Dawes Plan and easier to deal with. Hughes made plans to utilize his trip to Europe during the summer with the American Bar Association as an opportunity to lobby for a European accord.[73]

At the same time, the secretary of state decided to allow American representatives to attend the London Conference, scheduled to take place in mid-July for the purpose of completing final arrangements on the Dawes Plan. British Prime Minister J. Ramsay MacDonald had laid out an agenda that specifically excluded the questions of war debts and French security. Since Herriot had accepted the agenda, the way was cleared for a settlement of the reparations controversy that did not raise the issues of strategic guarantees and war debt reductions. This prospect delighted Hughes. Nevertheless, in accepting the invitation for Americans to participate in the London Conference, he again reiterated the importance of taking an economic approach to European problems and of subordinating political questions. He stated that the United States government would not guarantee the execution of the Dawes Plan, associate itself with any sanctions, or assume responsibility for the loan to Germany. These matters, he emphasized, would arouse partisan controversy in the United States and engender a destructive legislative-executive struggle over the control of foreign policy. The United States government, Hughes maintained, could play a much more constructive role by rendering disinterested advice, helping to reconcile European positions, and encouraging the mobilization of private capital for European financial stabilization and economic reconstruction.[74]

When leading government officials, bankers, and businessmen converged upon the British capital in July, however, the Morgan partners continued to raise objections to the Dawes Plan. They still doubted whether the French were ready to accept the American view of a stable Europe and a secure France based upon a rehabilitated Germany. They maintained that "the Allies are at the parting of the ways and before asking their friends to lend money to Germany . . . , they must choose

73. For Hughes's actions, see Memorandum of interview between Hughes and Jusserand, 9 May 1924, Hughes Papers, Box 174; Hughes to Frank B. Kellogg, 29 May 1924, ibid., Box 61; Hughes to Herrick, 4 June 1924, ibid., Box 59; Diary of Joseph C. Grew, 1 May 1924, Grew Papers, Box 25; for the role of Logan and Houghton, see, for example, Dawes, *Journal of Reparations*, pp. 247–61; Stresemann, *Diaries, Letters, and Papers*, 1:347–49.
74. FR, 1924, 2:33–35; Memorandum of interview between Hughes and Wiedfeldt, 2 July 1924, Hughes Papers, Box 175; see also Hughes, *Pathway of Peace*, pp. 108–9.

between a rehabilitated Germany with ultimate reparations to them on the one hand, and a broken Germany and what has been called 'security' on the other hand.'' The bankers had their own conception of French security, which Morrow expressed to Hughes in a long letter explaining his firm's reservations about the Dawes Plan. Heretofore, he wrote, ''reparations have been balanced against security, as though the two things are contradictory. I have never believed that this was so. Such an antithesis really defines security as keeping your adversary weak. There is no real security that way. . . . If you mean, however, by security the lessening of the likelihood of future war, it can only measurably come by such a treatment of Germany as will enable her to pay for the damage she has done as quickly and as smoothly as possible.''[75]

In order to expedite the reconstruction of Germany and protect the proposed loan, Lamont stayed in London throughout most of July and conferred with British bankers and European officials. In August J. P. Morgan arrived on the scene to present his firm's views. Morgan and Lamont feared that the prevailing weakness of the new rentenmark, together with the provision for immediate payments-in-kind, would drive Germany into default and invite the renewed application of sanctions. If this occurred, Germany's capacity to pay would be destroyed and the loan endangered. Endeavoring to prevent such eventualities, the Morgan partners wanted to remove the authority to declare a default from the Reparation Commission and place it in the hands of the transfer committee under the aegis of the agent general. They also wanted the French to renounce any rights to impose sanctions in case of default, grant the service of the Dawes loan priority over all other German obligations, and withdraw their troops from the Ruhr at the earliest possible moment.[76]

The demands of Morgan and Company, when combined with those of English bankers and British officials, subjected the new French government of the Cartel des Gauches to unbearable pressures. Herriot was in constant fear that his government would be toppled if he made too many concessions. He was reported to be ''almost hysterical'' about the attacks on him in the press. Most French newspapers were

75. For the quotations, see Morgan and Company to Lamont, 18 July 1924, Thomas W. Lamont Papers, Box 176; Morrow to Hughes, 12 July 1924, Hughes Papers, Box 56.
76. For the views and actions of Morgan and Company, see the extensive correspondence in Thomas W. Lamont Papers, Boxes 176 and 177. A good summary can be found in Lamont to Morgan and Leffingwell, 17 July 1924, ibid., Box 176.

extremely critical of the terms being exacted by the American bankers. Herriot was being asked not only to reduce German reparation payments by a substantial amount but also to renounce France's right and relinquish her ability to apply sanctions when Germany violated the reparation provisions of the Treaty of Versailles. Even moderate Frenchmen like Louis Loucheur advised Herriot not to make concessions regarding reparations and the evacuation of the Ruhr without first securing reciprocal Allied commitments to reduce French war debt payments and guarantee French security.[77]

The French premier was in an awkward position because of his lack of systematic preparation, his support of the Dawes Plan, and his earlier willingness to attend a conference that excluded the consideration of war debts and French security. Moreover, his government's financial problems totally undermined his bargaining power. In order to thwart immediate attacks on the franc and implement a stabilization plan, Herriot and his finance minister, Etienne Clémentel, appealed to the Morgan partners to renew the $100 million credit arranged in March and grant a new long-term loan of a similar amount. The banking firm let it be known that its assistance depended on France's adopting a peaceful foreign policy.[78] Clémentel pleaded with Lamont to be reasonable in his demands. If sanctions were applied against Germany in the future, the French were willing to allow the service of the Dawes loan to take priority over all other German obligations. Clémentel and Herriot requested that the Reparation Commission be allowed to retain authority to declare a default, that France be permitted to take action in case of default, and that French troops be authorized to stay in the Ruhr for two years.[79]

The demands of Morgan and Company stiffened the negotiating position not only of the British, but also of the Germans when the latter

77. For Herriot's fears, see [Beerits Memorandum], "The Dawes Plan," p. 27; Paul Cravath to Kahn, [summer 1924], Kahn Papers, Box 220; Lamont to Morgan and Company, 20 July 1924, Thomas W. Lamont Papers, Box 175; for the reactions of the French press, see "The 'Money Devil' Mixes in the Reparations Row," *Literary Digest* 82 (9 August 1924):7; see also Herriot's references to the bankers in Edouard Herriot, *Jadis*, 2:154–56; Michel Soulié, *La Vie politique d'Edouard Herriot*, pp. 167–72; for Loucheur's attitude, see Loucheur, *Carnets secrets*, pp. 153–54.

78. Leffingwell to Dean Jay, 23 June 1924, Thomas W. Lamont Papers, Box 95; Morgan and Company to Lamont, 1 August 1924, ibid.; Lamont to Morgan and Company, 9 August 1924, ibid., Box 176; for Herriot's problems see also Schuker, *French Predominance*, pp. 124–68, 232ff.

79. Lamont to Morgan and Leffingwell, 17 July 1924, Thomas W. Lamont Papers, Box 176; Lamont to Morgan and Company, 20 July 1924, ibid.; Edward C. Grenfell and Lamont to Morgan and Company, 23 July 1924, ibid.; Lamont to Morrow, 12 September 1924, Morrow Papers.

arrived at the London Conference during the first week of August.[80] The impasse between the bankers and the French, therefore, threatened to wreck the conference. Republican officials in London and Washington observed the trend of events with considerable alarm. Secretary of State Hughes and Secretary of the Treasury Mellon, although not official participants in the conference, visited the British capital during critical stages in the negotiations. They were in frequent contact with Lamont, MacDonald, and Herriot. Both Hughes and Mellon sympathized with Lamont's demands on the French. They wanted to foreclose the possibility of future sanctions, secure a rapid military evacuation of the Ruhr, and insure the rehabilitation of Germany and the safety of the loan. In a well-publicized speech at the Pilgrims' Dinner on 21 July, Hughes emphasized that American investors had to be satisfied before extending the necessary capital to activate the Dawes Plan. At the same time, the secretary of state prodded the Morgan partners to be reasonable and do nothing to break up the conference.[81] He talked to the French premier and stressed the importance of immediately implementing the Dawes Plan. Herriot reiterated his apprehension that if he conceded too much, his government would fall. Hughes said France had no alternative. When he visited Paris, however, Hughes warned Poincaré that if Herriot were toppled on the issue of the Dawes Plan, American interest in European problems would end.[82]

After Hughes left London, American Ambassador Frank B. Kellogg kept trying to arrange the necessary compromises between the clashing parties. In his efforts to mediate between the bankers and the French as well as between the Germans and the French, Kellogg had the continuous aid of Owen Young and James Logan. In the negotiations over the procedures for declaring a default, Logan helped work out an agreement that ostensibly satisfied the French. Though the Reparation Commission retained its authority on the matter of default, an American representative with full voting rights would participate in the deliberations of the commission. Moreover, if the decision of the commission were not unanimous, any delegate could request that the matter be

80. Stresemann, *Diaries, Letters, and Papers*, 1:369, 375.
81. For discussions between the Morgan partners and Mellon and Hughes, see Lamont to Morgan and Leffingwell, 17 July 1924, Thomas W. Lamont Papers, Box 176; Grenfell and Lamont to Morgan and Company, 23 July 1924, ibid.; Leffingwell to Lamont, 22 July 1924, ibid.; Grenfell to Morgan and Company, 21 July 1924, ibid.; Lamont to Morrow, 28 July 1924, ibid.; for Hughes's speech, see Hughes, *Pathway of Peace*, p. 108.
82. [Beerits Memorandum], "Dawes Plan," pp. 25–27; Viscount Edgar Vincent D'Abernon, *An Ambassador of Peace*, 3:83–85.

considered by a newly established arbitral commission, the powerful chairman of which would likewise be an American. Consequently, while the Reparation Commission maintained apparent authority to consider defaults, the bankers were satisfied because a majority vote on the commission was no longer sufficient to initiate sanctions and because an exhaustive procedure of impartial arbitration had been established in which the American opinion was likely to be decisive. Similarly, while the unilateral application of sanctions remained theoretically possible, such sanctions were to be considered only in case of flagrant—that is, intentional—default. If sanctions were ever implemented, the service of the loan was to receive priority over all other obligations.[83]

Morgan and Lamont recognized that in accepting the arbitral commission, France had made a significant concession. Yet, they were still not completely satisfied with the safeguards surrounding the proposed loan. They therefore attached great importance to the selection of an agent general who would be sympathetic to their concerns. Since they bitterly resented what they viewed as the constant efforts of Young and Logan to water down their demands, the Morgan partners resolved that neither of these men should be named as permanent agent general.[84] The selection of someone appropriate to fill this position became so critical that Lamont discussed the issue with Mellon in London while Morrow examined the same matter with Coolidge in Washington. Although the administration refused to assume the responsibility for appointing the agent general, it fully participated in the decision-making process and endorsed Morgan and Company's eventual choice, S. Parker Gilbert.[85] Not coincidentally, Gilbert had been undersecretary of the treasury in 1921 and 1922 and had developed a close rapport and excellent working relationship with Mellon before leaving government

83. For Logan's efforts to work out compromises on key issues, see Inter-Allied Conference, "Minutes of Meetings of First Committee," July 1924, RG 43, Box 1941; see also Young, unfinished letter, 24 July 1924, Young Papers, R–16; for the final agreements, see Allied Powers, Reparation Commission, *The Experts' Plan for Reparation Payments*, pp. 130–61.

84. Morgan, Lamont, Grenfell, and Steele to Morgan and Company, 6 August 1924, Thomas W. Lamont Papers, Box 176; Morgan to Morrow, 8 August 1924, ibid.; Lamont to Morrow, 12 September 1924, Morrow Papers. Young however was accepted as interim agent general.

85. For discussions over the appointment of an agent general and for the selection of S. Parker Gilbert, see Memorandum of interview between Crocker and Logan, 15 May 1925, Young Papers, R–14; Leffingwell to C. F. Whigham, 13 August 1924, Thomas W. Lamont Papers, Box 176; Lamont to Morgan and Company, 12 August 1924, ibid.; Leffingwell to Lamont, 15 August 1924, ibid.; FR, 1924, 2:137–39; Kenneth Paul Jones, "Discord and Collaboration," pp. 118–39.

service to resume his legal practice. Moreover, during the early summer of 1924 Gilbert had represented Morgan and Company in some of the negotiations regarding the proposed loan and had served as a convenient contact between the Morgan partners and the administration.[86] As agent general, Gilbert would have considerable power over German transfer payments, loan service, and budgetary practices. Morgan hoped Gilbert would be able to safeguard the contemplated loan, especially since the administration refused to offer guarantees for its protection.[87]

Even after securing the appointment of an agent general sympathetic to their views, the Morgan partners demanded still more concessions. Lamont wanted the French to evacuate the Ruhr immediately. He believed evacuation would reduce the likelihood of future application of sanctions, especially if Germany defaulted on deliveries-in-kind. Lamont's position encouraged German Foreign Minister Gustav Stresemann and British Chancellor of the Exchequer Philip Snowden to press relentlessly for an immediate withdrawal of French troops from the Ruhr. Kellogg intervened in this dispute, telling Lamont that he was being too intransigent. The ambassador met with Stresemann and Herriot and arranged for an accord that provided for total withdrawal of French troops from the Ruhr within a year and for the immediate evacuation of the Dortmund area.[88]

While Republican officials and American diplomats in London mediated disputes and tried to conciliate all sides, President Coolidge carefully observed developments. He considered the effective implementation of the Dawes Plan to be of substantial economic benefit to the United States and of considerable political interest to the Republican party. He interrupted his work on the presidential campaign in order to be ready to break any deadlocks that might arise in the European negotiations. If the prime ministers could not agree on a procedure for declaring Germany in default, Coolidge was prepared to suggest that the chief justice of the United States arbitrate the matter in future contingencies. Undersecretary of State Joseph Grew noted that

86. Gilbert to Mellon, 18 July 1924, Thomas W. Lamont Papers, Box 176; Leffingwell to Lamont, 18 July 1924, ibid.

87. For the contemplated role of the agent general, see Young to Lamont, 3 September 1924, Young Papers, R–13; Young to Gilbert, 25 September 1924, ibid.

88. For Kellogg's role, see Kellogg to Hughes, 18 August 1924, Hughes Papers, Box 4B; Kellogg to Hughes, 15 October 1924, ibid., Box 61; Lamont to Morgan and Company, 12 August 1924, Thomas W. Lamont Papers, Box 176; Memorandum, [4 August 1924?], ibid.; Stresemann, *Diaries, Letters, and Papers*, 2:394–95.

"we are going as far as we can in every manner without entering into European entanglements."[89] American officials were delighted with the satisfactory outcome of the London Conference, and they immediately endeavored to expedite implementation of the Dawes Plan. In Berlin, Houghton sought right wing support for the London agreements.[90] In New York, Governor Strong had already begun to introduce a Federal Reserve monetary policy aimed at facilitating the sale of Dawes bonds and at stabilizing the mark.[91] Hughes, Grew, and Kellogg encouraged Morgan and Lamont to go ahead with the loan, even though the bankers remained apprehensive that the Germans might someday rebel against the exacting terms of the Dawes Plan.[92] As a result of all these efforts the Morgan partners finally decided to proceed with the loan. On 10 October an agreement was signed at the Bank of England between American, Belgian, French, and British bankers and German financial delegates for an 800,000,000-gold-mark loan to the German government. During the next few days, the loan was oversubscribed in every major financial center.[93]

The flotation of the loan and the implementation of the Dawes Plan were greeted with enthusiasm in the American press and Republican policymaking circles. Virtually all newspapers acclaimed the results of the London Conference and congratulated American officials for their significant role in getting European nations to take this first step toward general European peace.[94] Republicans hoped the implementation of the Dawes Plan, occurring just before the 1924 presidential elections, would pay rich political dividends. Ambassadors Houghton and Kellogg returned to the United States to campaign in behalf of the president and to muster the votes of German-Americans who might have been attracted to the candidacy of Robert LaFollette on the Progressive party ticket.[95] As farm prices moved upward the administration was

89. For Grew's involvement, see Diary of Joseph C. Grew, 27 July–4 August, 1924, Grew Papers, Box 25; Joseph C. Grew, *Turbulent Era*, 1:627–30; see also Coolidge, *Talkative President*, p. 186.
90. Stresemann, *Diaries, Letters, and Papers*, 1:471.
91. Strong to Young, 13 July 1924, Young Papers, R–13.
92. Kellogg to Lamont, 24 September 1924, Hughes Papers, Box 61; Diary of Joseph C. Grew, 22 September 1924, Grew Papers, Box 25; Herbert Feis, *The Diplomacy of the Dollar*, pp. 41–42.
93. Toynbee, *Survey of International Affairs*, 1924, p. 387.
94. "America's Part in the Peace of London," *Literary Digest* 82 (30 August 1924):5–8; "What the Dawes Plan Means to Business Here," ibid., (27 September 1924):12–13.
95. Kellogg to Hughes, 18 September 1924, Hughes Papers, Box 61; Frank C. Cos-

quick to note that the progress toward European financial stabilization initiated by the Dawes Plan was of considerable importance to the American economy. "The effect of a more prosperous Europe," the Treasury Department declared, "means the broadening of our markets . . . and a quickening of our economic development."[96]

What particularly gratified Republican officials was that the expert approach had worked exactly as they had hoped it would. Dawes and Young, bolstered by American financial power, had come up with a plan to stabilize the German currency and revive German productivity that did not jeopardize the war debts, engender domestic political controversy, or compromise America's independence of action.[97] After the American experts had completed their work, the Morgan partners had exerted systematic pressure on the newly elected, relatively inexperienced, and financially troubled government of the Cartel des Gauches. Though Republican officials tried to temper the demands of the bankers and the British somewhat, France was compelled to accept the axiom that an economically revitalized Germany meant a peaceful Germany and a secure France.

Enhancing French Security

Neither Republican officials nor the American experts were foolish enough to believe that the Dawes Plan permanently assured the economic reconstruction of Germany or the security of France. Despite its flaws one of the most important aspects of the plan, as the Commerce Department pointed out, was that it contained "within itself machinery for correction or alteration of details as difficulties arise in its execution."[98] Meanwhile, the plan provided European statesmen and Republican officials with the opportunity to go ahead and make other adjustments to foster European stability. In a testimonial dinner arranged for him on his return from Europe, Owen Young reminded leading New York bankers and businessmen as well as administration officials that "the reconstruction of Germany is not an end in itself, it

tigliola, "The Politics of Financial Stabilization," p. 132; Schuker, *French Predominance*, pp. 287–88.

96. Department of the Treasury, *Annual Report of the Secretary of the Treasury*, 1924, pp. 3–4; see also Department of Commerce, *Annual Report of the Secretary of Commerce*, 1924, pp. 2–7; Coolidge, *Talkative President*, p. 188.

97. See Coolidge's message to Congress, FR, 1924, 1:xix–xx.

98. Department of Commerce, *Annual Report*, 1924, p. 7; see also Goldsmith to Ayres, 19 August 1924, Ayres Papers, Box 4; Young to Lionel Sutro, 16 December 1924, Young Papers, R–17.

is only a part of the larger problem of the reconstruction of Europe.'' The United States, he emphasized, had a continuing role in the process of European restoration, especially in the struggle to stabilize European currencies.[99] Republican officials did not dissent from this view. In late 1924 they were already preparing to negotiate debt settlements on the basis of a new formula that was supposed to accommodate the needs of European debtors.[100] At the same time, Treasury Department officials encouraged Governor Strong to begin making arrangements with the Bank of England to stabilize the pound and other European currencies on a gold basis.[101] Coolidge and Hughes simultaneously sounded out European governments on the possibility of convening another arms limitation conference.[102]

The French preoccupation with security, however, set limits on what could be accomplished. The Dawes Plan had undermined France's ability to enforce the Treaty of Versailles and jeopardized her strategic interests. By accepting a diminution in the powers of the Reparation Commission, agreeing to evacuate the Ruhr, and relinquishing control over a critical sector of the German economy, the French abandoned their ability to safeguard their vital interests through independent military action. French security now depended upon the goodwill of Germany and the aid of her former allies. Unfortunately for France the metallurgical, chemical, and electrical industries that provided the wherewithal for German reparation payments under the Dawes Plan also constituted the industrial infrastructure for a potentially formidable German military machine. France, therefore, was reluctant to make additional readjustments until she gained some leverage over Germany's heavy industry, elicited greater assurances of Germany's good intentions, and secured additional signs of Anglo-Saxon material support. During the latter part of 1924 and early 1925 the French government rejected overtures to attend a new conference on arms limitation, subordinated matters pertaining to debt refunding and currency stabilization, and refused to withdraw troops from the first occupied zone in the Rhineland until Germany abided by the disarmament provisions of the Treaty of Versailles. If the political, financial, and economic stabilization of Europe were to take another step forward, it

99. Owen D. Young and Gerard Swope, *Selected Addresses of Owen D. Young and Gerard Swope*, pp. 147–48.
100. See chapter 4, pp. 123–25.
101. Lester V. Chandler, *Benjamin Strong*, pp. 314–422; see also Clarke, *Central Bank Cooperation*, pp. 71–143.
102. FR, 1925, 1:6–7.

was evident that French strategic apprehensions would have to be taken into consideration.[103]

The American and British financiers, diplomats, and statesmen who had compelled the French to make concessions at the London Conference acknowledged the legitimacy of French fears and recognized the importance of dealing with French anxieties. The British Foreign Office maintained that "the establishment of security was essential to economic and financial recovery."[104] Many American businessmen, bankers, and officials concurred. Even Thomas Lamont, who had exerted such intense pressure on Herriot to make financial and strategic concessions to Germany, insisted that "there can be no solution of the problem of bringing peace back to the earth which leaves French security . . . unprovided for."[105] In other words there was no American objection to the French demand for greater security so long as the definition of security was consistent with the Anglo-Saxon conception of a stable Europe based upon a rehabilitated Germany and so long as the United States was not required to incur strategic obligations.

The real dilemma facing American and British officials was how to protect the legitimate strategic interests of France without overcommitting themselves and freezing the status quo established by the Treaty of Versailles. The British believed that security guarantees, if not carefully circumscribed, might actually discourage French statesmen from making additional concessions that were in the interests of long-term European stabilization. During 1924 and early 1925 the Labour and Conservative governments in Britain successively rejected the Draft Treaty of Mutual Assistance and the Geneva Protocol as a result of pervasive fears that the obligations generated by these agreements would overextend British commitments, especially in eastern Europe where further readjustments were believed imperative.[106] Likewise, Secretary of State Hughes renounced American interest in either of these treaties, lest they impose specific commitments on the United States, infringe upon the nation's freedom of action, undermine tradi-

103. For France's preoccupation with security, see Herriot, *Jadis*, 2:168–94; Ministerial declaration by Paul Painlevé, 22 April 1925, *Le Temps*, Records of the Bureau of Accounts, RG 39, Box 60; Jon Jacobson, *Locarno Diplomacy*, pp. 26–60; for the impact of the Dawes Plan on France's strategic interests, see Schuker, *French Predominance*, especially pp. 295–393; Sally Marks, *The Illusion of Peace*, pp. 53–54.

104. Great Britain, Foreign Office, *Documents on British Foreign Policy, 1919–1939*, Series 1A, 1:8 (hereafter cited as DBFP).

105. Lamont to Herbert Croly, 23 January 1925, Thomas W. Lamont Papers, Box 95.

106. See Jacobson, *Locarno Diplomacy*, pp. 14–26; see also Schuker, *French Predominance*, pp. 249–56, 356, 388–89.

tional neutrality policy, or link the United States to the League of Nations.[107] Although some prominent Americans, like Professor James T. Shotwell, had been instrumental in devising the Geneva Protocol, the Coolidge administration doubted its value because it threatened to generate political controversy and embroil the United States in European political and territorial disputes that were considered unrelated to vital American interests.[108] Most organized public opinion on foreign affairs in the United States as revealed in the peace movement and the business community shared the administration's skepticism of the value of assuming strategic commitments abroad.[109] Hence, Republican officials hoped that some other means could be found to relieve French anxieties.

In January 1925 Stresemann's proposal for a mutual security pact among the Rhineland powers opened up new means to achieve American designs. Stresemann's willingness to sign a nonaggression pact with France, accept the territorial status quo and the demilitarized zone in the west, and arbitrate German grievances in the east satisfied the Anglo-American conception of France's basic security needs. Moreover, the reciprocal nature of the proposed agreement circumscribed France's ability to apply sanctions over such matters as reparations, thereby reinforcing the work of the Dawes Plan. Because the regional orientation of the pact obviated the need for American commitments and placed the burden of maintaining European political order on the European nations themselves, it seemed especially attractive to American officials. Although they believed that a security agreement was prerequisite to the stabilization of Europe, they wanted to remain aloof from the territorial and political controversies that might arise in connection with such an accord. This wish to remain aloof reflected the belief in American military as well as civilian circles that a threat to the prevailing French notion of European security did not necessarily jeopardize vital American interests and therefore did not warrant American guarantees to intervene. In their reviews of the international situation conducted in the middle and late 1920s, Army and Navy analysts never perceived a threat to American strategic interests from Germany,

107. For official United States policy on the Draft Treaty of Mutual Assistance and the Geneva Protocol, see FR, 1924, 1:82–83; FR, 1925, 1:16–20.
108. Charles DeBenedetti, "The Origins of Neutrality Revision," pp. 75–89; for Coolidge's insistence on preserving the nation's independence, see FR, 1924, 1:xix–xx; FR, 1925, 1:xii–xiv.
109. Charles DeBenedetti, "Alternate Strategies in the American Peace Movement in the 1920s," pp. 69–78; Joan Hoff Wilson, *American Business and Foreign Policy, 1920–1933*, pp. 31–64.

despite extensive information gathered by the Military Intelligence Division (MID) about German technical violations of the Treaty of Versailles.[110]

While wishing to avoid strategic embroilments, Republican policymakers remained concerned about the outcome of the European security negotiations. Believing that a mutual security pact might reassure the French and constitute a framework for a stable Europe, American diplomats and officials encouraged European governments to carry the talks to a successful conclusion. From the onset of the negotiations, Ambassador Houghton prodded German and British officials to work out an accord satisfactory to all parties.[111] On 4 May 1925, in a well-publicized speech in London, Houghton recapitulated the extent of recent private American investments in the Old World and warned that new American capital depended upon the development of a more peaceful political environment conducive to the reconstruction of European markets.[112] The State Department was immediately informed that the French viewed Houghton's speech as an American effort to exert financial pressure on France to sign a security agreement.[113] That such suspicions were well founded was confirmed a few weeks later when President Coolidge told the British ambassador that additional American private loans to Europe were contingent upon the consummation of a European security pact.[114]

The financial leverage available to the United States during 1925 was considerable, and American policymakers did not hesitate to use it. The mechanisms of central bank cooperation and banker-government consultation enabled the administration to exert pressure on France and Germany. By the summer of 1925 Germany was again caught in a credit crunch. Stresemann was desperate to attract new American

110. For Stresemann's proposals and his motivations, see Stresemann, *Diaries, Letters, and Papers*, 2:59, 64–70, 79, 143–49, 204, 246; see also Jacobson, *Locarno Diplomacy*, pp. 3–12; Christoph M. Kimmich, *Germany and the League of Nations*, pp. 62–75; for the view of American diplomatic officials, see Fletcher to Kellogg, 19 May, 30 June 1925, Fletcher Papers, Box 12; FR, 1925, 1:23–24; for the analysis of American military officials, see, for example, the annual naval assessments conducted by the War Plans Division (WPD) and sent to the Chief of Naval Operations (CNO), "Estimate of the Situation," annually, Confidential Records of the Secretary of the Navy, RG 80, File L1–1; "Intelligence Summary," 30 October–12 November, 27 November–10 December 1926, 17 September–30 September 1927, Records of the Military Intelligence Division (MID), RG 165.
111. DBFP, 1A, 1:35.
112. Costigliola, "Financial Stabilization," pp. 157–58; see also "America's Peace Ultimatum to Europe," *Literary Digest* 85 (16 May 1925):5–7.
113. George F. Wadley to secretary, 15 May 1925, RG 59, 711.40/21.
114. Jacobson, *Locarno Diplomacy*, p. 5, n. 6.

loans, the growth of which had fallen off during the spring.[115] In July Governor Strong visited Berlin and talked to German officials and bankers. Hjalmar Schacht, director of the Reichsbank, requested that the FRBNY help ease credit conditions by purchasing mark bills. Strong, indicating a desire to cooperate and to establish central bank cooperation, emphasized that Germany first had to sign a security pact.[116] At the same time, officials in the State, Treasury, and Commerce departments agreed to ask private bankers to forego all loans to France and other European debtors until they entered into refunding accords.[117] The French, however, perceived this action as still another manifestation of American efforts to impose a security settlement on Europe. Yet, according to the Belgian ambassador, the French could hardly resist this pressure because of their desperate need for foreign capital.[118]

The financial problems plaguing the French and German governments and the application of American financial pressure were among the important considerations impelling the leaders of both nations to reconcile their differences and come to terms with one another.[119] Yet, the Rhineland Pact and the arbitration agreements signed at Locarno in October 1925 did not eradicate French strategic apprehensions. Germany reaffirmed her intent to refrain from military action and respect the territorial status quo in the west, but made no such commitments regarding her territorial grievances in the east. France secured a British (as well as Italian) guarantee of her border with Germany, but was unable to work out any military arrangements for the implementation of such guarantees. The signatories reaffirmed the binding nature of Articles 42 and 43 of the Treaty of Versailles relating to the demilitarized zone, but Britain became the defender of Germany against a renewed application of sanctions as well as the protector of France against German aggression. As a result of additional understandings Germany agreed to enter the League of Nations. France, however, modified the nature of Germany's obligations under Article 16 of the

---

115. Stresemann, *Diaries, Letters, and Papers*, 2:136–37.
116. Memorandum of discussion at Reichsbank, 11 July 1925, Strong Papers, 1000.6; Strong to Jay, 20 July, 31 August 1925, ibid.; see also Jacques Seydoux, *De Versailles au plan Young*, pp. 313–14.
117. For the institution of the embargo on private loans, see chapter 4, pp. 127–29.
118. Belgium, Commission royale d'histoire, *Documents diplomatiques belges, 1920–1940*, 2:334.
119. For French and German interest in American capital, see Castle to Houghton, 31 August 1925, Castle Papers, Box 2; Stresemann, *Diaries, Letters, and Papers*, 2:202–3; Josef Korbel, *Poland Between East and West*, pp. 168–69; Annelise Thimme, "Stresemann and Locarno," p. 82.

League covenant and weakened the international organization's ability to deter aggression through collective action. To usher in a new era of good will and cooperation, the French agreed to withdraw Allied troops from the Cologne zone in the Rhineland. Such a withdrawal, however, impaired France's capacity to protect French allies in eastern Europe.[120]

From the French perspective then the Locarno treaties did not provide adequate material safeguards. Briand signed them because he recognized that he had to satisfy Anglo-American financiers and accommodate the needs of French industrialists. The commercial provisions of the Versailles treaty were due to expire in 1925. Germany would then regain her commercial sovereignty and tariff autonomy. Thereafter, she would be able to discriminate against French trade and terminate the special treatment enjoyed by a contingent of Alsace-Lorraine products in German markets. French industrialists feared the consequences of these developments. They sought a wide range of agreements that would preserve German markets, limit competition in the international arena, and guarantee supplies of German coal and coke. The Rhineland Pact and arbitration agreements created the political truce indispensable for subsequent cartel agreements and commercial accords that served the needs of important interest groups in both France and Germany. Hence, at Locarno Briand tried to reap Anglo-American good will, attract American capital, and establish the framework for Franco-German collaboration in the economic realm.[121]

French security increasingly depended upon the extent of Germany's satisfaction with the revisionist order being created in Europe. Both the Dawes Plan and the Locarno treaties envisioned changes in the status quo. Such alterations would redound inevitably to Germany's benefit. Whether they would constitute a threat to France's well-being would depend upon the extent to which the expansionist, militarist, and nationalist strains latent in German culture and society would be submerged by the evolution of a prosperous, interdependent, capitalist order among European nations, bound together by technocratic elites sharing corporatist values and a common fear of bolshevism.[122] The

120. Marks, *Illusion of Peace*, pp. 64–74; Kimmich, *Germany and the League*, pp. 64–75; Walter Allan McDougall, ''French Rhineland Policy and the Struggle for European Stabilization,'' pp. 393–96.

121. Maier, *Recasting Bourgeois Europe*, especially pp. 516–45; Schuker, *French Predominance*, pp. 222–29, 359–73; Marks, *Illusion of Peace*, pp. 64–65.

122. Maier, *Recasting Bourgeois Europe*; Schuker, *French Predominance*; Jay L. Kaplan, ''The Internationalist Alternative''; McDougall, ''French Rhineland Policy,'' pp. 394–99.

outcome was unclear in 1925. But many Frenchmen, exasperated with the United States over the continuation of the American loan embargo and the controversy over debt refunding, hoped that a rapprochement with Germany might offset America's financial domination of the Old World. Since the United States refused to assume strategic commitments in Europe and compelled French concessions to Germany, it was altogether logical for Frenchmen to begin questioning the value of American amity and contemplating the advantages of full-scale detente with their former enemy. As the Locarno spirit emerged in Europe, Ambassador Houghton warned the secretary of state that ''we are not popular in Europe just now. Our refusal to join the League of Nations and our insistence upon debt repayments have left us without friends.''[123]

The United States and the Spirit of Locarno

Republican officials recognized that Locarno might unite Europe against the United States.[124] Nevertheless, the Americans welcomed the Locarno agreements because they seemed to constitute a framework for a new era of stability in Europe, an era based on orderly change and the imperatives of modern capitalist economies. In the view of American policymakers, Locarno accomplished the elusive task of enhancing French security without emasculating Germany's economic potential or compromising America's independence of action. Not surprisingly, President Coolidge heralded the agreements and claimed that they confirmed the success of American efforts to get European nations to resolve their own political problems. Now that the European nations had demonstrated a real disposition to help themselves, the president indicated that the United States was ready to help them solve their other problems. Coolidge stressed that the time was ripe to limit land armaments and complete the process of financial stabilization begun with the Dawes Plan.[125]

Most Americans thought of Locarno as another step toward the larger goal of creating a new order of capitalist stability in Europe. Characteristically, Dwight Morrow wrote Thomas Lamont that ''the primary idea of the pact is to allay French fears and thus afford a basis

123. For Houghton's statement, see FR, 1925, 1:12–13; see also Stresemann, *Diaries, Letters, and Papers*, 2:237; for the acrimony over the loan embargo and debt refunding, see chapter 4.

124. Castle to Houghton, 12 November 1925, Castle Papers, Box 2.

125. For the president's view, see Coolidge, *Talkative President*, pp. 207–8; FR, 1925, 1:xii–xiv; FR, 1926, 1:42–44.

for proceeding with the restoration of the political and economic life of Europe."[126] Americans did not worry that the new order might collapse leaving France at the mercy of a bellicose Germany. They saw no immediate threat to American security and believed that efforts to emasculate Germany might arouse her latent militancy and bring about the very developments that everyone wished to avoid. The critical objective from the American standpoint was to make the new order work. The most immediate tasks were to complete a debt refunding accord with France and effect the stabilization of the franc. These efforts had languished while energies had been expended on reconciling French security needs with the economic reconstruction and financial stabilization of Germany.

126. Morrow to Lamont, 5 September 1925, Morrow Papers; for general press response to Locarno, see "Locarno Founds the 'United States of Europe,'" *Literary Digest* 87 (31 October 1925):5–8.

[4]

Toward Monetary Stability, 1924–1926

During the autumn of 1925 American officials were pleased by the course of events in Europe and by the efficacy of their economic, non-political approach toward European affairs. ''There can be no question that Europe is making steady and solid progress,'' Hoover commented. Only those who had witnessed the extent of European economic dislocation in 1919, he insisted, could appreciate the ''tremendous'' advances that had occurred during the last few years.[1] Not yet complacent about economic and political developments in the Old World, however, Republican policymakers were determined to refund the Allied war debts and restore monetary order on the Continent. Officials in the Treasury Department and the FRBNY were especially eager to establish a modified form of the prewar gold standard in order to increase American exports, moderate the flow of gold into the United States, and relieve inflationary pressures at home.[2] While security negotiations were proceeding in 1925, efforts were undertaken to negotiate war debt agreements and stabilize European currencies.

After implementation of the Dawes Plan, American officials and bankers believed that the instability of the franc constituted the most serious impediment to the success of European stabilization programs. Governor Strong maintained that the fluctuating value of the franc disrupted trade, engendered speculative activity in France and Bel-

1. Hoover to Charles Hebberd, 24 November 1925, Herbert C. Hoover Commerce Department Papers, Box 21 (hereafter cited as HHCD).
2. See, for example, Department of the Treasury, *Annual Report of the Secretary of the Treasury,* 1926, p. 212; Benjamin Strong to Andrew Mellon, 10 August 1926, Strong Papers, 1000.7; Garrard Winston, ''American War Debt Policy,'' Records of the Bureau of Accounts, RG 39, Box 220, p. 14; Winston, Address, at the Twenty-first Annual Meeting of the Institute of American Meat Packers, 26 October 1926, Morrow Papers.

gium, and impeded the restoration of the gold standard throughout the Continent. Treasury Undersecretary Garrard Winston agreed that the instability of the franc directly upset efforts to stabilize the Belgian franc and the Italian lira.[3] S. Parker Gilbert, the agent general for reparations, as well as private bankers in New York worried that the decreasing value of the franc would enable French manufacturers and exporters to capture markets formerly held by their German competitors. Gilbert and the bankers feared that depreciation of the franc might retard German recovery, undermine the Dawes Plan, and jeopardize the safety of American loans to Germany.[4]

Before the franc could be stabilized, however, American policymakers believed that the French had to cut expenditures, raise taxes, curtail inflationary practices, clarify war debt obligations, and obtain foreign credits. To pressure the French to go through such a difficult process of financial retrenchment, Republican officials put into operation the policymaking machinery established earlier in the decade to deal with war debts, foreign loans, and exchange stabilization. Believing that debt settlements were indispensable components of a successful stabilization program as well as valuable to American taxpayers, the WDC set out to devise a formula that would accommodate the needs of debtor nations and serve the interests of the American economy. Recognizing that European leaders would be reluctant to risk the political consequences of refunding war debts and reforming financial practices, officials in the State, Commerce, and Treasury departments prepared to urge private bankers to discourage loans to recalcitrant debtor nations. But where there was a stick, there was a carrot. European governments were informed that once they signed and ratified debt agreements, the FRBNY was ready to offer financial aid. Thus between 1924 and 1926 the whole gamut of economic machinery was mobilized to encourage the French and the other former Allies to refund their war debts and stabilize their currencies.[5]

3. Lester V. Chandler, *Benjamin Strong*, p. 360; Winston to Mellon, 14 May 1926, RG 39, Box 220.
4. S. Parker Gilbert to Dwight W. Morrow and Russell C. Leffingwell, 24 September 1926, RG 39, Box 85; "General Conditions Abroad," *Guaranty Survey* 6 (July 1926):11; Morrow, "Memorandum on the Economic and Financial Condition of France," RG 39, Box 220, pp. 13–14.
5. The statements made in this paragraph will be documented in the course of the chapter.

Activating the Capacity-to-pay Formula

The signing of the London accords on reparations in August 1924 convinced American officials that the time was right to pressure the French into refunding their war debts and balancing their budget, essential prerequisites of currency stabilization. On 20 September 1924 Arthur N. Young, economic adviser in the Department of State, wrote Secretary of State Hughes that the Dawes Plan paved the way for a settlement of the war debts. The reparations accord, he insisted, clarified France's fiscal position and her future capacity to pay war debts. Further delays in initiating debt negotiations, he argued, might not only discourage French efforts to undertake necessary financial reforms but also induce a feeling that the wartime obligations were not to be taken seriously. A debt settlement with France, Young emphasized, would establish an essential precedent for similar accords with other European nations, lower taxes within the United States, and reduce the national debt.[6]

Since President Coolidge had already stated his willingness to submit to Congress any plan recommended by the WDC,[7] that organization's immediate task was to establish a satisfactory basis for conducting the debt negotiations. Within the WDC the factors that had influenced policymaking in 1922 and early 1923 still applied. Fiscal demands, popular pressures, and legislative restrictions called for a rigid bargaining posture; commercial imperatives, international financial considerations, and foreign outcries demanded American flexibility and generosity. But the importance of each of these factors had been modified by events. Ratification of the British debt settlement indicated that the legislative branch of government might acquiesce to certain deviations from the original congressional enactment. Moreover, Republican victories in the 1924 elections engendered hopes that the Sixty-ninth Congress might be more responsive to the administration's initiatives than had been the Sixty-eighth. Furthermore, internal developments in 1924, including the passage of the bonus bill, the reduction of taxes, the appearance of budgetary surpluses, and the decrease in the long-term public debt, had altered the domestic situation and opened up the possibility of a more conciliatory Congress on the question of war debts.[8]

6. Arthur N. Young to Charles E. Hughes, 20 September 1924, General Records of the Department of State, RG 59, File No. 800.51W89 France/91.
7. Calvin Coolidge, *The Talkative President*, p. 188.
8. For a survey of political developments and Coolidge's dealings with Congress, see Donald R. McCoy, *Calvin Coolidge*, pp. 193–335.

As far as the European situation was concerned, policymakers recognized that France would not accept and could not afford an agreement along the same lines as the British debt settlement. Within the State Department, Arthur Young warned that it would be foolish to force France to make large payments to the United States before the French budget was balanced and the currency stabilized. The policymakers' goal was to secure a debt agreement that would be fair to American taxpayers and encourage the French to reform their financial practices and stabilize their currency. Young insisted that "the United States would [be making] no sacrifice in accepting a basis less favorable than the British basis." He wrote Hughes that "it cannot be in the interest of this country to make an agreement which would clearly be too onerous to France to carry out. . . . A too harsh settlement is not worth the risk of 62 years of injured relations."[9]

As a result of these external considerations and the changes in the domestic financial situation, the WDC decided to refund the war debts on the basis of the debtor nations' capacity to pay. The Treasury Department, officially in charge of the WDC, explained that the capacity-to-pay principle was designed to allow each debtor nation "to improve its economic position, to bring its budget into balance, and to place its finances and currency on a sound basis." The capacity-to-pay formula was to be applied by adjusting interest rates to fit the special circumstances of each debtor nation. In theory the capacity of a nation to pay its war debts was susceptible to precise determination. Hence, Hoover instructed his experts to conduct an exhaustive examination of the French financial situation. In practice, however, Mellon acknowledged that "the capacity of a nation to pay over a long period of time is not subject to mathematical determination. It is and must be largely a matter of opinion."[10] Mellon's statement suggests that the decision of the WDC to open negotiations on the basis of the capacity-to-pay formula was motivated by a belief that this principle afforded sufficient flexibility to arrive at an accord not only mutually satisfactory to France and Congress but also equally responsive to the conflicting demands of fiscal and commercial imperatives. The difference after all between a 3 percent and a 5 percent interest rate on the French debt of $4,025,000,000 could amount to over $4 billion during a sixty-two-year period.[11]

9. Young to Hughes, 20 September 1924, RG 59, 800.51W89 France/91.
10. For the quotations, see Department of the Treasury, *Annual Report*, 1925, p. 53; ibid., 1926, p. 213; for Hoover's action, see Hoover to secretary of war, 31 December 1924, HHCD, Box 371.
11. World War Foreign Debt Commission (WDC), *Combined Annual Reports of the World War Foreign Debt Commission*, p. 329.

On 1 December 1924 Treasury Secretary Mellon, in behalf of the WDC, informed the French ambassador of the new American negotiating position. Mellon stated that interest rates would be manipulated to accommodate the peculiar economic circumstances of France. In all other respects, he explained, the terms of the British debt settlement would be controlling. Payments on the principal would have to begin immediately, and the entire debt, including interest, would have to be liquidated in sixty-two years. Taking the legalist position of a pragmatic creditor, Mellon reiterated that the principal of the debt could not be cancelled. Two days after Mellon spoke to Jusserand, Coolidge outlined this approach in his annual message to Congress.[12]

In the latter part of 1924 there was some prospect that France would enter into serious negotiations on the basis of her capacity to pay. In November Ambassador Herrick returned to France and found Premier Herriot ready to send Finance Minister Clémentel to the United States to discuss the debt question. Herrick feared that precipitous action might be countereffective, and he persuaded Herriot to postpone Clémentel's visit. Instead, the American ambassador and the French premier began informal talks in the French capital. Herrick reported that the French government wanted ''to do everything that will be agreeable to the United States.'' With the budget still in deficit and confidence waning, Herriot and Clémentel recognized that they had to secure foreign loans to cope with a floating debt of 22 billion francs falling due in 1925. The French leaders wanted to sign a debt settlement and clarify their government's budgetary situation to gain the confidence of American bankers.[13]

Yet, Herriot and Clémentel ignored the American request to conduct negotiations on the basis of the capacity-to-pay formula. Instead, they presented their own plan. It called for a ten-year moratorium on debt payments, interest rates never to exceed .5 percent, and an amortization period of ninety years. Moreover, French payments to the United States were to be made contingent upon Germany's continued fulfillment of her reparation obligations to France. Finally, the Herriot ministry requested that the United States reduce either the interest or the

12. WDC, *Minutes of the World War Foreign Debt Commission*, pp. 60–61; Memorandum handed by Mellon to Jules Jusserand, 1 December 1924, RG 39, Box 60; Department of State, *Papers Relating to the Foreign Relations of the United States*, 1924, 1:xxii (hereafter cited as FR).
13. For Herrick's reports, see Myron T. Herrick to Hughes, 21 November, 12 December 1924, Herrick Papers, Box 16; for a good analysis of French financial problems, see Eleanor Lansing Dulles, *The French Franc, 1914–1928*, pp. 181–93; Robert Murray Haig, *The Public Finances of Post-War France*, pp. 100–21, 226–45.

principal on the $400 million that had been loaned to France in 1919 for the purchase of surplus American war stocks.[14]

The French were disillusioned when the United States government promptly rejected their proposal. Clémentel and Herriot reminded American officials that the war loans had not contributed to the productive capacity of France, that France had endured enormous sacrifices during the conflict, that France had experienced unparalleled financial problems since the war, and that France had already agreed to a reduction of the German indemnity. Consequently, they claimed that France was entitled to American generosity. Clémentel and Herriot reiterated their intention to honor the war debts, but they insisted that France's precarious financial state and their own tenuous political position precluded any accord on the basis of the capacity-to-pay formula.[15]

The problems beleaguering the French government were not well understood by the American public. The American press initially misconstrued Clémentel's position on the war debts as favoring cancellation, and there was an outpouring of anti-French and anticancellationist sentiment in the United States.[16] Although this criticism diminished after Clémentel clarified his position, the recriminations on both sides of the ocean worried American policymakers. Before leaving office Hughes wrote Herrick that he was disturbed by the public furor over the war debts. Acknowledging that the Department of State was not formulating war debt policy and that real power resided with the WDC and ultimately with Congress, the retiring secretary of state recommended that the French send a delegation to the United States to resolve the controversy on the basis of fact, not emotion. "The way out," Hughes wrote Herrick, "is to face the facts; on the other side to dissipate the notion that the debt is one that ought not to be paid or that there is no intention to pay it; on this side, to deal with the economic verities."[17]

Before the Herriot ministry had a chance to send such a mission, it was toppled in the wake of charges that the government had falsified financial statistics. During the ensuing political crisis in early April, American diplomats became alarmed over the unsettled state of politi-

14. FR, 1925, 1:140–43.
15. Ibid., 137–39, 144–45; see also Eliot Wadsworth, Memorandum for the French files, 28 February 1925, RG 39, Box 60; for Herriot's financial and political problems, see Edouard Herriot, *Jadis*, 2:199–225; Michel Soulié, *La Vie politique d'Edouard Herriot*, pp. 213–40.
16. "France to Pay Us by 2015," *Literary Digest* 84 (17 January 1925):5–7; "The Turmoil Over the French Debt," ibid. (7 February 1925):5–8.
17. FR, 1925. 1:146.

cal and financial affairs.[18] News of the worsening situation in France, however, did not lead policymakers in Washington to alter their negotiating position on the war debts. Officials in the Commerce and Treasury departments studied the French financial situation and concluded that the French economy was basically sound, that French financial problems were the result of gross ineptitude, and that the situation would be ameliorated if a debt settlement were signed on the basis of the capacity-to-pay formula. Mellon was impressed by the absence of unemployment and the extent of France's economic activity and industrial progress. Moreover, he maintained that a debt settlement would aid French business by inspiring confidence in France's overall financial situation.[19] Since policymakers in the Treasury, Commerce, and State departments believed that the deteriorating financial and political situation in France reflected a lack of self-discipline, they decided to try to coordinate their loan and war debt policies in an effort to pressure the French to resolve their financial problems and accept the capacity-to-pay formula.

Instituting the Loan Embargo

Since the autumn of 1924 American policymakers had been considering the advisability of imposing an embargo on private loans to France and other recalcitrant debtor nations. On 12 November 1924 J. P. Morgan and Company had informed the Department of State that the French government was seeking a $100 million loan. Although the Morgan partners explained that they had received assurances from Herriot and Clémentel that the French budget would be balanced, the floating debt consolidated, and inflationary policies terminated, officials in the State and Commerce departments questioned the utility of the loan. Grosvenor M. Jones, chief of the Finance and Investment Division of the Department of Commerce, emphasized that the loan was "fundamentally unsound." "A long-term loan of such a huge amount for exchange stabilization," he insisted, "is a confession of fiscal instability." Hughes concurred. But when Herriot promised to

18. Herrick to Parmely Herrick, 3 April 1925, Herrick Papers, Box 18; Chester L. Jones to Julius Klein, 28 April 1925, Records of the Bureau of Foreign and Domestic Commerce (BFDC), RG 151, File 600.
19. Wadsworth, Memorandum for the French files, 28 February 1925, RG 39, Box 60; R. S. Tucker, "Considerations Bearing on the Repayment of the French Debt to the United States," 1 March 1925, ibid., Box 59. The press generally concurred with this view of the French situation. See "French Ability to Pay," *Literary Digest* 84 (24 January 1925):10–11; "France's Financial Plight," ibid. (25 April 1925):5–7.

support an American claim for a small share of the Dawes annuities, policymakers reluctantly decided to offer no objection to the Morgan loan.[20]

Hoover, however, continued to voice strong reservations about the loan. He maintained that it was unsound from an economic viewpoint. He told Assistant Secretary of State Harrison that "the financing operations of these Governments [France, Italy, and Belgium] were mainly covert schemes of finding money for unproductive expenditures, largely for military purposes, and even in the present case . . . much of the money would be used for just these unproductive purposes." The commerce secretary acknowledged that reproductive loans to America's former allies were justified after debt accords had been negotiated. But he asserted that "loans of the character of this one which are for the purposes of covering governments' deficits in places where no effort is being made to settle with us, . . . are the negation of economic reconstruction." Hoover argued that the time was ripe for government officials to consult with private bankers and secure their cooperation in behalf of a loan policy designed to pressure foreign governments into refunding their war debts and balancing their budgets.[21]

When the initial attempts to negotiate a debt agreement according to the capacity-to-pay formula failed, the commerce secretary's position became the prevailing one in policymaking circles. In April officials in the Commerce, Treasury, and State departments agreed to institute a loan embargo. They counseled bankers not to issue loans on behalf of public and private organizations in recalcitrant debtor nations. Coming at a time when the London market was closed to French securities and when the French government desperately needed capital to convert her floating debt and stabilize the franc, the loan embargo was designed to maximize American financial leverage.[22]

A variety of reasons impelled American policymakers in three executive departments to agree on a loan embargo. Some officials, like Assistant Secretary of State Harrison, viewed the embargo as an ef-

20. J. P. Morgan and Company to secretary, 12 November 1924, RG 59, 851.51/495; for Hughes's view, see FR, 1924, 2:72–73; for Coolidge's view, see Joseph C. Grew, Memorandum, 20 November 1924, RG 59, 851.51/507; for the quotation, see Grosvenor M. Jones to Harold Phelps Stokes, 14 November 1925, HHCD, Box 376; for information on the Paris Finance Ministers Conference, where the allocation of the Dawes annuities was discussed, see FR, 1925, 2:133–65.

21. Memorandum of conversation between Harrison and Hoover, 20 November 1924, RG 59, 851.51/506; Hoover to Hughes, 20 November 1924, ibid., 851.51/499 (filed as 800.51/499).

22. Leland Harrison to Frank B. Kellogg, 10 April 1925, ibid., 800.51/507½; for

fective means of securing the money owed the United States as war debts.[23] Other officials, however, had more farsighted considerations in mind. They agreed that the loan embargo would serve as an effective means of negotiating debt accords. They maintained that these debt agreements would contribute to the rehabilitation of European finances, the stabilization of European currencies, and the expansion of world-wide commerce. Hoover was considering these factors, at least in part, when he expressed his misgivings about the Morgan loan to France in November 1924. In April 1925 Frank B. Kellogg, the new secretary of state, made these considerations even more explicit in voicing the department's objection to a proposed loan to the city of Paris.[24] Treasury officials like Mellon and Winston were most eager to force the French into a debt settlement because they believed it would serve as the key to the complete overhauling of French finances. A debt settlement in their opinion would clarify the extent of France's external obligations, expedite the balancing of her budget, and help reestablish the credit of the French government. Treasury officials hoped that a debt agreement would stimulate a series of developments, culminating in the extension of credits from the FRBNY and the stabilization of the franc.[25]

At the same time that executive officials instituted the loan embargo, the FRBNY was helping Britain return to the gold standard through the provision of credits and the exchange of information on discount rates. Within the councils of the Federal Reserve Board, Mellon and Winston endorsed Strong's efforts.[26] Moreover, they hoped that he would undertake similar attempts to foster exchange stability throughout Europe when conditions were propitious. Strong believed that the stabilization of the franc had to constitute the next step in the reconstruction of Europe and that successful negotiation of moderate debt accords was one prerequisite of effective stabilization efforts. Strong and Treasury

---

the Treasury's official announcement of the loan embargo, see Department of the Treasury, *Annual Report*, 1925, pp. 54–55; for the implementation of the embargo regarding prospective French loans, see Harrison, Memorandum, 1 April 1925, 7, 9, 10, 11, 16 June 1925, Leland Harrison Papers, Box 46; for the closing of the British market, see Winston to Mellon, 21 April 1925, RG 59, 800.51W89 France/109.

23. Harrison to Kellogg, 10 April 1925, RG 59, 800.51/507½.

24. Harrison, Memorandum, 1 April 1925, Leland Harrison Papers, Box 46.

25. Winston, "American War Debt Policy," pp. 12–14; Winston to Robert Whitehouse, 12 August 1926, RG 39, Box 47; House, Committee on Ways and Means, *French and Yugoslavian Debt Settlements*, p. 5.

26. See, for example, Diary of Charles S. Hamlin, 7, 10 January 1925, Hamlin Papers, Vol. 10; Chandler, *Benjamin Strong*, pp. 251–331. For Britain's return to the gold standard, see also D. E. Moggridge, *The Return to Gold, 1925.*

Undersecretary Winston discussed these matters thoroughly when their trips to Europe coincided in the spring of 1925. After Winston returned to Washington, Strong continued his travels abroad and maintained an extensive correspondence with the undersecretary. Strong was eager to move ahead with his contribution to the stabilization process once the loan embargo had forced the French to sign a refunding agreement.[27]

Negotiating with Caillaux

As American officials expected, the loan embargo forced the new French government under the leadership of Premier Paul Painlevé to conduct serious negotiations on the war debts. Joseph Caillaux, Painlevé's finance minister, was in the midst of a sensational political comeback after having been disgraced during the war for his pacifist attitudes and purported treasonous activity.[28] Caillaux wanted to balance the budget, convert the enormous short-term floating debt, and stabilize the franc. His entire financial program depended on his being able to secure foreign credits. He realized that the loans he so desperately needed from the United States would not be forthcoming until the debt question was resolved. Consequently, Caillaux told Herrick that he would try to refund the war debts even though he felt constrained by the government's weak parliamentary position and financial troubles. He solicited more precise information about the extension of a possible moratorium, the length of the amortization period, and the level of interest rates. If an acceptable basis for an accord could be established, he was willing to send a commission to the United States to work out a final settlement.[29]

Initially, the WDC reiterated that the terms of the British accord would be controlling, except insofar as interest rates would be adjusted to accommodate the peculiar economic circumstances of France.[30] But after Herrick warned that debt negotiations might have to be postponed indefinitely unless the United States modified its position, Mellon and Winston as spokesmen for the WDC made certain alterations

27. For the above generalizations, see the Winston-Strong correspondence, RG 39, Box 220; see also the materials on Strong's trip to Europe in 1925, Strong Papers, 1000.6.
28. Rudolph Binion, *Defeated Leaders*, pp. 70–102.
29. Herrick to Kellogg, 9, 16 June, 3 July 1925, Herrick Papers, Box 18; FR, 1925, 1:156; for Caillaux's financial program, see Harold G. Moulton and Cleona Lewis, *The French Debt Problem*, pp. 449–543; Haig, *Public Finances*, pp. 114–22; Binion, *Defeated Leaders*, pp. 90–107.
30. FR, 1925, 1:151, 154.

in American policy that paved the way for Caillaux's subsequent visit to the United States. On 2 July they told Emile Daeschner, the new French ambassador, that the amortization period could be extended up to eighty years, that interest payments could be deferred a few years if circumstances warranted it, that a moratorium on payments of principal could be left open for negotiation, and that the probability of reparation receipts could be considered in determining France's overall repayment capacity. This broadening of the American negotiating posture once again revealed the Treasury Department's desire to be as lenient as Congress was likely to permit on the debt issue to achieve the more important goal of stabilizing financial conditions in France and throughout Europe. By holding out the possibility of an initial moratorium on all payments, Mellon and Winston were indicating their desire to accommodate French financial needs while that nation went through the difficult process of stabilizing the franc. They were willing to consider departing from the British precedent because they believed that Caillaux sincerely wished to grapple with the substantive problems facing France. Yet, they recognized that Congress and the other members of the WDC might not be quite as sympathetic. Consequently, Mellon and Winston warned Daeschner that the French would have to prove their incapacity to make debt payments to Congress, which had the final authority to approve or disapprove any accord.[31]

The French ambassador was much impressed by this interview with Mellon and Winston. He reported to his government that the WDC was now well disposed toward a settlement. As a result Caillaux decided to lead a delegation to the United States. But before voyaging to Washington the French finance minister went to London to discuss possible terms for settling France's debt to Britain. He believed the British would be more responsive to French needs than the Americans, especially since the British Foreign Office was then struggling to reconcile the French and German positions on a security treaty. In London Caillaux pleaded for a generous settlement. He requested that French payments to Britain be very small during the first few years of the accord to facilitate the task of rehabilitating French finances. He also desired that French payments to Britain be made contingent upon the receipt of reparation payments from Germany. This arrangement became known as the safeguard clause. Like the British, Caillaux felt certain that

31. Memorandum of conversation between Mellon, Winston, and Daeschner, 2 July 1925, RG 39, Box 60; see also Winston to Mellon, 1 May 1925, ibid.; Winston, Memorandum, 28 May 1925, ibid.

Germany would only be able to pay approximately 50 percent of the annuities provided for in the Dawes Plan. Therefore he hoped that the total amount of French payments to her creditors would not exceed 50 percent of the scheduled reparation transfers.[32]

While Caillaux negotiated in London, American diplomats carefully observed his actions, assessed his overall intentions, and communicated their views to Washington.[33] More important than these official dispatches, however, were the personal letters and reports composed by Strong and sent directly to Winston and Mellon. After consulting with Caillaux, the governor of the FRBNY reported that the French finance minister would negotiate in good faith. Yet, Strong warned that Caillaux's political position was precarious, his internal consolidation loan was failing, and France's domestic debt was in a "fairly perilous position." Acknowledging that France was enjoying "reasonable prosperity," Strong still insisted that the French government would not be able to buy foreign exchange for war debt payments until it resolved its internal financial problems, balanced its budget, and stabilized its currency. He advised Winston and Mellon to be lenient with Caillaux, and he pleaded for moderate payments during the first years of an agreement. Such an accord, he maintained, would expedite the financial rehabilitation of France and facilitate the stabilization of the franc. Otherwise, the governor of the FRBNY predicted the further deterioration of financial conditions, the accession to power of a socialist government, and the implementation of a forced conversion loan or a capital levy, "all calculated to scare the French investor out of his wits."[34]

Winston had great faith in Strong's judgment and believed that the WDC could rely on the accuracy of his observations.[35] But while awaiting Caillaux's visit, the treasury undersecretary solicited reports from other New York bankers and carefully studied Harold G. Moulton's *The French Debt Problem*. Winston collected extensive data not only on financial conditions in France but also on France's budgetary

32. Alanson Houghton to Kellogg, 4 September 1925, RG 39, Box 60; F. A. Sterling to Kellogg, 28 August 1925, RG 59, 800.51W89 France/167.
33. Houghton to Kellogg, 26 August 1925, RG 59, 800.51W89 France/159; Sterling to Kellogg, 28 August 1925, ibid., 800.51W89 France/167; Sheldon Whitehouse to Kellogg, 31 July 1925, ibid., 800.51W89 France/155.
34. For the quotations, see Strong to J. H. Case and Winston, 28 July, 26 August 1925, RG 39, Box 220; see also Strong to Winston, 14, 19, 29 August, 1, 21 September 1925, ibid.
35. Winston to Coolidge, 25 August 1925, RG 39, Box 220.

situation, tax burden, balance of trade, and balance of payments.[36] Winston's impression, like that of Benjamin Strong and Dwight Morrow, was that France was a prosperous country with badly mismanaged finances. He and Mellon increasingly shared Strong's view that a debt settlement should not handicap French efforts to resolve their financial problems and stabilize their currency. Moreover, after their colleagues on the WDC accepted a lenient accord with Belgium, Mellon and Winston became more hopeful that a satisfactory agreement could be reached with France.[37]

They did not count on the strong opposition of Herbert Hoover. Hoover was not oblivious to the benefits to be derived from the stabilization of European finances, but he put an even greater stress than did Mellon, Winston, and Strong on the domestic sources of American prosperity. Hoover was concerned about the tax burden that would fall upon the shoulders of the American people if the WDC agreed to a large reduction of the French debt. Moreover, he did not think that the French had any intention of meeting their obligations, and he assumed that Caillaux had first negotiated with Britain to exert pressure on the United States for greater concessions. Caillaux, Hoover maintained, was only interested in saving his ''political skin'' and securing American credits. Although he acknowledged the accuracy of Caillaux's statistical data, Hoover chose to interpret it in his own way because he was obsessed with the size of French military expenditures, disturbed by the dissipation of French resources in the Riff war in Morocco, and convinced of France's potential ability to pay a large part of the debt. Consequently, Hoover favored the conclusion of a temporary five-year accord. He claimed that a temporary settlement would enable the French to clean up their financial mess and clarify their long-term capacity to pay. More important, in Hoover's opinion a temporary agreement would allow the United States to retain the war debts as a lever to force further arms reductions upon the French. By using the debts in this fashion Hoover believed he could save American taxpayers additional hundreds of millions of dollars a year, because he

36. For the data, see the materials in ibid., Boxes 58, 59, and 220; for Winston's opinion of the Moulton book, see Winston to Mellon, 1 September 1925, ibid., Box 220.
37. Winston to Gerald Fennell, 15 September 1925, ibid., Box 47; Winston to G. E. Roberts, 20 August 1925, ibid., Box 220; Mellon to Richard Olney, 26 August 1925, ibid. Mellon was even thinking of revising the British debt agreement. See Memorandum, 30 September 1925, HHCD, Box 20; for the terms of the Belgian debt accord, see Harold G. Moulton and Leo Pasvolsky, *World War Debt Settlements*, pp. 353–63.

assumed that arms reductions in Europe would enable the United States government to cut its own military expenditures. Aware of the growing public clamor for additional tax reductions and the prevailing anti-French sentiment in the United States, Hoover's position was motivated by political as well as by financial considerations.[38]

Thus, when Caillaux and his delegation of eight prominent French politicians arrived for negotiations during the last week of September 1925, the WDC was divided between those members predisposed to follow Mellon's lead and those inclined to support Hoover's viewpoint.[39] Despite the differences of opinion within the WDC and similar variations of sentiment within the French delegation, considerable progress was made in the ensuing negotiations. The two sides agreed to incorporate the war stocks debt into the political debt and recognize a total debt of $4,025,000,000. They sought to adjust interest rates according to the principle of French capacity to pay. They agreed to amortize the debt over a period of sixty-two to sixty-eight years and provide for two permissible postponements of payments during the first five years of the accord and three thereafter. They delineated the range of annuities during the early years of the settlement. The fact that the French and Americans were able to concur on these points, points that previously had been contested, demonstrated that both parties were negotiating in earnest.[40]

Two very difficult problems, however, did arise. The first revolved around the level of annuities after the first ten or twelve years and, in effect, amounted to a dispute over the total sum France would have to pay the United States. The other related to the French demand for a

38. For Hoover's views, see his daily memoranda on the French debt negotiations, 23 September–1 October 1925, HHCD, Box 20; see also Department of Commerce, *Annual Report of the Secretary of Commerce*, 1925, pp. 31–37; for the demand for further tax cuts, see "Shall We, or Our Children Pay for the War?" *Literary Digest* 87 (24 October 1925):9–10; for the growing anti-French sentiment in the United States, see Elizabeth Brett White, *American Opinion of France from Lafayette to Poincaré*, pp. 272–303.

39. Two of the Democratic members of the WDC, Edward N. Hurley and Richard Olney, supported Mellon's view. Kellogg and Reed Smoot sympathized with Hoover's position. The views of the remaining commissioners, Congressman Charles R. Crisp and Senator Theodore E. Burton, were ambiguous. For divisions within the WDC, see Winston to Morrow, 8 July 1926, Morrow Papers; Martin Egan, Memorandum, 5 October 1925, ibid.; Diary of Charles S. Hamlin, 7 November 1925, Hamlin Papers, Vol. 11; Olney to Winston, 22 October 1925, RG 39, Box 220.

40. For an account of the war debt negotiations, see WDC, *Minutes*, pp. 90–108; see also the excellent series of articles entitled "How French Debt Mission Failed," by Stéphane Lauzanne, the renowned French journalist, in the *Christian Science Monitor*, 6, 8, 9 February 1926, RG 39, Box 61. Lauzanne accompanied the French delegation to the United States and served as an interpreter during informal talks.

safeguard clause. Even on these critical issues, under the impetus of Caillaux and Mellon, both sides tried to accommodate one another. Caillaux boosted his initial proposal of a total repayment of $4,655,-000,000 to a final offer of $6,220,000,000.[41] Meanwhile, an American subcommittee including Mellon and Hoover carefully considered various forms of a general safeguard clause that called for a review of the proposed schedule of payments, if subsequent events demonstrated that these exceeded France's capacity to pay, "taking into account all of its essential elements."[42]

After a week of discussions members of the WDC decided to urge Coolidge to reject the final French offer. Total repayments of $6.25 billion, they realized, meant a long-term interest rate of less than 1 percent, a return they believed would prove unacceptable to Congress and American taxpayers.[43] The WDC members also disapproved of a general safeguard clause. They feared that the French would interpret such a clause to mean that their own payments to the United States ought to be scaled downward, regardless of the overall state of French payment capacity, if the Dawes Plan annuities were reduced. Members of the WDC did not think that German reparation payments constituted the most essential determinant of France's capacity to pay war debts. Nor would they allow the United States to become the de facto creditor of last resort against Germany. If the United States were put in such a position, the WDC members feared that the nation would become immersed in European politics, a situation they wanted to avoid at all costs.[44]

In addition to these substantive factors there were important personal, emotional, and political considerations that accounted for the negative recommendation of the WDC. Hoover, for example, was convinced from the opening of the negotiations that Caillaux was no more than a "roulette table croupier" intent on duping the Americans at every turn. Hoover carefully prepared for each formal meeting of the WDC and systematically cultivated support for his own viewpoint, thereby outflanking Mellon who angrily but quietly demurred. The secretary of the treasury also had reservations about the general safe-

41. WDC, *Minutes*, pp. 93, 105, 107–8; Lauzanne, "French Debt Mission," 9 February 1926.
42. Winston, "American War Debt Policy," pp. 19–20; see also the numerous memoranda on possible safeguard clauses, 29, 30 September 1925, RG 39, Box 61.
43. WDC, *Minutes*, pp. 107–8.
44. Winston, "American War Debt Policy," pp. 19–20; Lauzanne, "French Debt Mission," 8 February 1926.

guard clause and the total amount France was willing to pay. But he did not want to cut off negotiations and resented Hoover's tactical efforts to push through a temporary five-year accord.[45] The secretary of commerce, however, had a natural ally in Senator Smoot, who shared Hoover's primary concern with the tax implications of a lenient debt settlement and who was especially sensitive to the political overtones of the debt issue. Moreover, Smoot worked closely with Senator Borah and transmitted Borah's opinions and prejudices into the proceedings of the WDC, especially Borah's belief that the international bankers wanted to wipe out the war debts to save their own private loans. The views of Borah and Smoot carried weight as a result of their influence in the Senate. The more internationally oriented members of the WDC could not ignore the two senators' opinions: Congress had yet to ratify the Belgian debt settlement, and there was even less support for a generous treatment of the French debt. Indeed, Borah's feeling that France was the least deserving of all the debtors was widely held. The French government's colonial wars in Morocco and Syria, its attitude toward Germany, and its reputed delinquency in imposing necessary taxes had engendered widespread public disaffection in the United States.[46] What made matters worse was the failure of the French delegation to inspire confidence even among the more sympathetic members of the WDC.[47]

When several members of the WDC met with Coolidge on 1 October, the president did not prod them to reverse their decision. Hoover took the opportunity to condemn the last French proposal. Once again he spoke in favor of a temporary five-year accord that called for payments of $40 million annually. When Mellon reluctantly acquiesced to Hoover's position, the issue was settled.[48] The president's style was to let

45. For Hoover's maneuvering and Mellon's resentment, see Memoranda, 23 September–1 October 1925, HHCD, Box 20.

46. For the influence of Smoot and Borah, see Egan, Memorandum, 5 October 1925, Morrow Papers; Lauzanne, "French Debt Mission," 6 February 1926; Pertinax, "Ce Que Fut la Conférence de Washington," L'Echo de Paris, 12 October 1925, RG 59, 800.51W89 France/236; for Borah's views, see his numerous letters, Borah Papers, Boxes 251, 264; for typical anti-French letters to executive officials, see J. W. Breitenstein to Mellon, 11 September 1925, RG 39, Box 47; William E. Weidner to Coolidge, 14 January 1925, ibid., Box 48; John J. Blaine to Coolidge, 24 September 1925, RG 59, 800.51W89 France/192; see also White, American Opinion of France, pp. 272–303.

47. For the actions of the French war debt commissioners that upset the Americans, see Lauzanne, "French Debt Mission," 8, 9 February 1926; Robert Lacour-Gayet, "Le Problème de la dette française envers les Etats-Unis après la première guerre mondiale," p. 19; Hoover, Memorandum, 29 September 1925, HHCD, Box 20; Morrow to Jean Monnet, 10 December 1925, Morrow Papers.

48. See Hoover, Memorandum, 1 October 1925, HHCD, Box 20.

those directly responsible make the final decision on policy. He certainly was not eager to take a strong stand on a foreign policy issue that might alienate Borah, exacerbate legislative-executive relations, and unite southern Democrats and insurgent western Republicans against him, especially when he was preparing new tax proposals for submission to the next session of Congress.[49]

Thus, although the WDC compiled an enormous amount of statistical data on the French economy and finances, its final decision was determined by domestic political and fiscal considerations rather than by an objective analysis of France's capacity to pay. Not that the WDC lacked an economic rationale for its action. Indeed, members of the WDC believed that the French economy was fundamentally sound and that all French problems stemmed from the egregious mismanagement of French finances. They felt that once French budgetary and currency difficulties were solved, France would have the capacity to pay more than the $100 million annuities that Caillaux had offered. But the evidence suggests that the WDC was concerned mostly with arriving at a debt settlement that the American public and Congress would find acceptable. Pressure was still being exerted by the proponents of cancellation and noncancellation. The task of the WDC was to find a compromise between these two extremes, a compromise that would not only be politically acceptable, but that would also reconcile conflicting fiscal and commercial imperatives. Caillaux's offer, though forthright and courageous from the French perspective, did not constitute a suitable basis for compromise in the collective view of the WDC.[50]

Mellon did not wish to see the negotiations fail. He believed there was little likelihood of an affirmative French response to the American proposal of a temporary settlement. Such an accord would leave the debt issue unresolved for five years and would be a constant source of uncertainty afflicting French finances. Mellon therefore invited Caillaux to meet privately with him and Undersecretary Winston to discuss alternate terms. Mellon tried to get the French finance minister to raise the amount of the annuities that France would pay in the latter years of

49. For Coolidge's fear of Borah regarding the debts, see William R. Castle to Houghton, 12 November 1925, Castle Papers, Box 2; for Coolidge's style of leadership, his relations with Congress, and his preoccupation with lowering taxes, see McCoy, *Calvin Coolidge*, pp. 264–86, 301–7; for the anticancellationist inclinations of southern Democrats and progressive Republicans, see Joan Hoff Wilson, *American Business and Foreign Policy, 1920–1933*, pp. 133–35.

50. See, for example, "The Failure to Settle the French Debt," *Literary Digest* 87 (10 October 1925):5–6; "France's Financial Quicksand," ibid. (5 December 1925):10.

the accord. In return Mellon proposed to reduce the amount of the early annuities. Although these changes would have meant a larger total amount of payments, they would have eased France's immediate financial problems, paving the way for stabilization of the franc.[51]

Caillaux refused to alter the French position. He was in a hurry to return to France in time to participate in the annual congress of the Radical-Socialist party so that he could consolidate his own political position. Caillaux had no desire to belabor the debt question when there seemed little chance of obtaining an accord acceptable to the French public. He knew that his own delegation already felt he had gone too far. He also knew that the French press was demanding a safeguard clause. Consequently, Caillaux turned down Mellon's final overtures and returned to France.[52] Despite some progress the major impediments to a Franco-American debt agreement remained to be resolved.

Completing a Debt Settlement

Caillaux's decision not to make additional concessions to the Americans was a popular one in France, but it succeeded neither in keeping him in power nor in stopping the deterioration of his country's financial situation. During 1925 the franc declined from approximately nineteen to twenty-six to the dollar. At the same time, France's internal debt increased by another 3 billion francs and Caillaux's conversion loan failed. To deal with the floating debt, the government had to borrow another 14 billion francs from the Bank of France. Hence, total advances from the bank to the state reached almost 36 billion francs by the end of 1925. Simultaneously, the total note circulation of the Bank of France increased from approximately 41 billion to 51 billion francs. That the French government constantly depended on the Bank of France to help meet maturing short-term obligations indicated that the government had exhausted its own resources and that default on government bonds was a distinct possibility. This situation in turn shattered confidence, contributed to the rapid depreciation of the franc, and intensified the internal political crisis.[53]

51. Mellon to Bérenger, 17 April 1926, RG 39, Box 61.
52. For the factors influencing Caillaux, see Lauzanne, "French Debt Mission," 9 February 1926; Binion, *Defeated Leaders*, pp. 100–4; for the views of the French press, see the summary compilations, RG 59, 800.51W89 France/193–96, 205, 221, 226.
53. For the above figures, see the statistical tables in Dulles, *French Franc*, pp. 455–536, especially pp. 471–75, 485–86, 489, 496, 502, 528; see also pp. 181–93, 244.

A new government was formed in the aftermath of the Locarno talks, with Briand as premier and Loucheur as finance minister. Briand and Loucheur believed that the resolution of the war debt issue was a prerequisite for stabilizing the franc and reestablishing French credit. They did not want a provisional five-year accord, because they felt such an accord would leave the long-term situation beclouded and thereby retard France's financial rehabilitation. Instead, Briand wanted a settlement, perhaps patterned on the generous Italian-American accord signed on 14 November. Such an agreement, he hoped, would not only induce American officials to lift the informal loan embargo but would also convince American bankers of France's earnest intentions to grapple with her financial woes.[54] In late November Robert Lacour-Gayet, the French financial attaché in Washington, was instructed to carry on secret discussions with Treasury officials. At first these talks proved unrewarding. But by January progress had been made, and Briand decided to send Henry Bérenger as a special envoy to work out a settlement.[55]

During the late autumn and winter of 1925–26, American officials were more inclined than ever to resolve the war debt issue with France. Treasury officials, in particular, were eager to complete an agreement based on France's capacity to pay that would facilitate attempts to stabilize all European currencies. Mellon became exasperated with those who opposed his efforts. He emphasized that the debt settlements were "essential to the stabilization of Europe and this stabilization is very nearly as important to us as it is to the European nations. So much of our prosperity depends upon Europe as a customer." Mellon wrote the president that he would not succumb to pressures calling for a tougher approach on the war debts. Although he admitted that generous debt settlements might mean a somewhat heavier tax burden for Americans, Mellon claimed that "the farmer or the laboring man would rather have a market for our surplus in Europe than save a dollar of Federal taxes." As for himself the secretary of the treasury preferred to "have solvent customers in the future which permit me to run a profitable business than to insist upon terms of debt settlement which will again force my customers into bankruptcy."[56]

54. Herrick to Kellogg, 29 October, 1 December 1925, RG 59, 800.51W89 France/ 235, 252; Herrick to Kellogg, 22 December 1925, Herrick Papers, Box 18. For the debt settlement with Italy, see Moulton and Pasvolsky, *War Debt Settlements*, pp. 353–63.
55. Lacour-Gayet, "Dette française," p. 19; WDC, *Minutes*, pp. 187–88, 190; Henry Bérenger, *La Question des dettes*, pp. 19–87.
56. Mellon to Senator Edward I. Edwards, 11 February 1926, RG 39, Box 149; Mel-

The president found Mellon's arguments convincing. Coolidge, too, acknowledged the interrelationships between war debts, currency stability, and American trade. Moreover, with the national debt already reduced by $6 billion (allowing annual savings of $250 million in interest payments), the president maintained that the United States could afford to be more lenient on the war debts and to abide by the capacity-to-pay formula.[57] The dilemma, of course, was how to interpret and implement this formula. As European stabilization efforts encountered substantial difficulties in early 1926, as the French financial situation continued to deteriorate, and as European payment problems attracted more attention, even State and Commerce department officials paid increasing attention to the capacity principle.[58]

But negotiations with Bérenger proceeded slowly during the winter and early spring of 1926. Mellon and Winston were wary of moving too quickly while the Senate postponed ratification of the Italian debt accord and considered the administration's tax proposals. Winston complained bitterly that the Democrats were playing politics with the war debts and seeking support from insurgent Republicans to embarrass the administration. Although a few prominent Democrats like Newton Baker had called for cancellation, some of the staunchest opposition in the Senate to lenient debt settlements emanated from southern Democrats. Mellon warned that he would not apply pressure on the Italian government to resume negotiations if the present accord were rejected. Meanwhile, he sought to muster support in the Senate in favor of ratification of the Italian debt agreement.[59] Finally, on 23 April it was approved. Immediately thereafter, serious talks between the French ambassador and the WDC ensued.

lon to Coolidge, 10 February 1926, Strong Papers, 012.6; see also WDC, *Combined Annual Reports*, pp. 301–2.

57. FR, 1925, 1:xvii–xviii; Coolidge, *Talkative President*, pp. 193–94.

58. See, for example, Hoover to Adolph Ochs, 3 May 1926, HHCD, Box 364; Lamont to Morrow, 29 October 1925, Morrow Papers; Castle to Houghton, 12 November 1925, Castle Papers, Box 2. During the autumn of 1925 policymakers became increasingly alarmed about the extent of American loans to Germany and the possibility of a transfer crisis. See, for example, the materials in RG 39, Box 85; see also RG 151, File 640. Gilbert and Owen Young warned Winston and Hoover about the payment problems caused by American debt and tariff policies. See Gilbert to Winston, 16 October 1925, Strong Papers, 1012.1; Young to Hoover, 5 January 1926, Young Papers, I–73. For the problems faced in stabilizing the Belgian franc, see Chandler, *Benjamin Strong*, pp. 346–47.

59. For the political problems encountered by the administration in securing ratification of the debt settlements, see Winston to Hurley, 23 February 1926, RG 39, Box 149; Mellon to Edwards, 11 February 1926, ibid.; Olney to Coolidge, 1 March 1926, ibid.; Winston to Grew, 14 October 1926, ibid., Box 220; Winston to Strong, 12 February 1926, Strong Papers, 012.6.

Within the week the Mellon-Bérenger accord was signed. In this agreement there was no safeguard clause; the war stocks debt was incorporated into the political debt; the first annuities were set at $30 million; and the total debt of $4,025,000,000 was to be repaid over sixty-two years at an annual average interest rate of 1.64 percent. Although Bérenger read a statement to the WDC expressing his belief that the payment of war debts and reparations were interdependent, France made a key concession in signing an accord that did not include the highly prized safeguard clause. In addition, the French ambassador accepted a schedule of payments that totalled $6,847,674,104 (almost $630 million more than Caillaux had offered). In return for these long awaited French concessions, the WDC agreed to set the first five annuities below $40 million and give France special postponement privileges during the early years of the settlement.[60]

Mellon and Winston worked closely with Bérenger to mold an accord that would be acceptable to the governments of both nations. The American officials explained to the French envoy that an agreement with a safeguard clause would never win favor in the United States. Mellon and Winston advised Bérenger about how to present France's case most convincingly to the WDC, demonstrate that French taxes were higher than American taxes, and correct the mistaken notion that French military expenditures were excessive. Treasury officials were thus able to justify a substantial reduction in interest rates, in effect canceling 52.8 percent of the debt. Mellon and Winston were prepared to go even further and accept payments of only $25 million during the first five years. But they had to settle for somewhat higher initial payments because of the opposition of Hoover and Smoot.[61] In fact, Coolidge accepted the agreement because he believed that the WDC had struck a satisfactory compromise between the nation's internal and external needs. In an off-the-record press conference on 4 May, the president emphasized that the Mellon-Bérenger agreement would re-

60. The final agreement may be conveniently located in Moulton and Pasvolsky, *War Debt Settlements*, pp. 363–74.
61. For Treasury officials' sympathetic negotiations with Bérenger and Lacour-Gayet, see Winston to Lacour-Gayet, 10 February 1926, RG 39, Box 220; Winston to Bérenger, 1 April 1926, ibid., Box 61; Mellon to Bérenger, 17 April 1926, ibid.; Winston, Memorandum, 20 April 1926, ibid.; see also the manner in which Treasury officials presented the French case to the House Ways and Means Committee in House, Ways and Means, *French and Yugoslavian Debt Settlements*, pp. 6, 9–11, 17, 29–30, 35–36. For Commerce Department studies that cast doubt on the accuracy of Bérenger's statistical analysis, see Tucker, "Balance of International Payments of France" and "France's Ability to Invest Abroad," [spring 1926], RG 39, Box 61; for Smoot's demand for higher payments, see WDC, *Minutes*, pp. 244–45.

sult in large payments to the United States treasury and would expedite the rehabilitation of financial conditions throughout Europe.[62]

But prospects for quick ratification of the debt settlement faded quickly. After the House of Representatives voted its approval on 2 June, Mellon told the Senate Finance Committee that it could defer action until the French Chamber of Deputies approved the accord. This strategy reflected the administration's belief that an acrimonious debate in the Senate could be avoided if the French ratified the agreement first.[63] The delay was a costly tactical mistake. Briand decided that the accord was so unpopular in France it could not be submitted immediately to the Chamber of Deputies. French criticism focused on the absence of a safeguard clause, the lack of transfer protection, and the inclusion of a commercialization provision. The latter allowed the United States government to market French obligations and raised the possibility that they could fall into German hands. Briand had instructed Bérenger to sign an agreement in spite of these flaws because he hoped the consummation of an accord would open up American financial markets. Once loans had been secured and the prevailing crisis overcome, he expected to be able to push the Mellon-Bérenger agreement through the Chamber of Deputies. For the time being, however, action had to be deferred and the completed debt settlement left unratified while talks proceeded between French and American bankers.[64]

Contemplating Central Bank Cooperation

As soon as the Mellon-Bérenger agreement was signed, the French began to seek out the loans and credits they so desperately needed. On behalf of the French government Jean Parmentier visited London and spoke to Strong, Winston, Lamont, and other American bankers who were then in the British capital. Parmentier asked Lamont for a $100 million credit from J. P. Morgan and Company. When Lamont refused, Parmentier solicited support from other American banking firms. Most of all he appealed to Strong for aid from the FRBNY. The following

62. Coolidge, *Talkative President*, p. 195.
63. Senate, Committee on Finance, *French Debt Settlement*, p. 2; Castle to Houghton, 12 May 1926, Castle Papers, Box 2; Mellon to Kellogg, 12 June 1926, RG 39, Box 61.
64. For Briand's intentions and the French reaction to the debt settlement, see Bérenger, *Question des dettes*, pp. 32–37; Herrick to Kellogg, 20 May, 3, 17 June 1926, RG 39, Box 61; Herrick to Kellogg, 21 May, 8 June 1926, RG 59, 800.51W89 France/312, 319; Herrick to Coolidge, 11 June 1926, Herrick Papers, Box 19; Damon C. Woods to Kellogg, 21 May 1926, RG 39, Box 62; FR, 1926, 2:92, 94, 96.

week Strong went to Paris and received similar requests from Finance Minister Raoul Péret and from Charles Robineau, governor of the Bank of France. To all these inquiries Strong reacted negatively, and he managed to get the representatives of American banking firms to support his position. The governor of the FRBNY was appalled by the political disarray and financial chaos in France. He deplored the lack of courageous political leadership, denounced the absence of plans to deal with the financial crisis, and criticized the actions of the officials of the Bank of France. He bluntly stated that aid from the FRBNY depended upon all groups in the Chamber of Deputies getting together and developing a coherent and comprehensive program for France's financial rehabilitation.[65]

As a result of his distress with the state of affairs in France, Strong was not upset when the Briand government was overthrown and Péret discharged from the Finance Ministry. On 23 June Briand formed a new government with Caillaux as finance minister. Caillaux immediately changed the leadership of the Bank of France and brought in Émile Moreau as governor and Charles Rist and Pierre Quesnay as his assistants. The new finance minister also indicated that he wanted to reorganize and stabilize French finances according to a plan recommended by a group of independent French experts appointed by the previous ministry. In essence, Caillaux sought to raise taxes, balance the budget, and establish a special fund to amortize the floating debt. To stabilize the franc, he also wanted to ratify the Mellon-Bérenger accord, obtain foreign credits, and insure the independence of the Bank of France. These measures were intended, at least in part, to satisfy Strong and other foreign bankers. Yet, Caillaux encountered enormous political problems. His antipathy to a capital levy antagonized the Socialists; his support for ratification of the debt settlement aroused the opposition of many deputies in the Center and Right of the political spectrum. Moreover, his request for decree powers generated suspicions among all parties in the Chamber; Caillaux's unsavory past now haunted him.[66]

Strong was impressed by Caillaux's efforts. As he traveled through

65. Strong to Jay, 9 May 1926, Strong Papers, 1000.7; Strong to George L. Harrison, 15, 23 May, 7 June 1926, ibid.; Winston to Mellon, 14 May 1926, RG 39, Box 220; Strong and Winston to Mellon, 20 May 1926, ibid.
66. For Caillaux's plans and problems, see Haig, *Public Finances*, pp. 146–59; Edouard Bonnefous, *Histoire politique de la Troisième République*, 4:147–56; Binion, *Defeated Leaders*, pp. 104–6; Herrick to Kellogg, 30 June 1926, 5, 7 July 1926, RG 39, Box 62; Herrick to Kellogg, 16 July 1926, RG 59, 851.51/858.

Europe and vacationed at Antibes, Strong received detailed reports on developments in Paris. Robert Warren, his personal assistant, remained in the French capital and conducted talks with the new officials of the Bank of France. Warren wrote Strong that the new administration in the Bank of France was businesslike and efficient. Warren maintained that Briand and Caillaux sincerely desired to stabilize the franc and ratify the debt agreement despite the political roadblocks. Strong became increasingly concerned about the survival of the existing government. If it were toppled and its plan for stabilization discarded, the prospects for his own stabilization programs throughout Europe would be hurt. Strong confided to Dean Jay, a Morgan partner in Paris, that "it has been one of my feeble ambitions to see the period of monetary reorganization completed before relinquishing the management of the Bank, and I do not hesitate to say that if this opportunity is lost in France it will be one of the disappointments of my life."[67]

Strong wanted to return to Paris to talk to Moreau about the aid that the FRBNY could furnish the Bank of France to effect stabilization. But Strong feared the reactions of Congress and the Federal Reserve Board to his having conversations with officials of a nation that had not yet ratified its debt settlement. Some members of the Federal Reserve Board had already criticized him for his supposedly exaggerated concern with European stability and his purported indifference to the internal ingredients of American prosperity. In addition, Strong did not want to arouse any accusations from United States senators that he was implicitly committing them to ratification. Since he had long been subject to attacks from the farm bloc, he wished to avoid further ridicule and unnecessary publicity. Strong was torn. He sought to help France and expedite the financial rehabilitation of Europe; yet he was aware of the domestic economic and political constraints. As usual he looked to the Treasury Department for advice and aid.[68]

Undersecretary Winston had been with Strong in London when the latter was first approached by the French. He shared Strong's concern for the French situation and agreed to try to explain the importance of Strong's efforts to the Federal Reserve Board. Moreover, Winston conferred with Mellon and reported that the secretary heartily endorsed

67. Strong to Jay, 9 July 1926, Papers of the Federal Reserve Bank of New York (FRBNY), C261.1; Strong to Jay, 2 July 1926, ibid.; for Warren's reports, see Warren to Strong, 30 June, 5, 7 July 1926, Strong Papers, 1000.7.

68. Strong to Winston, 1, 8 July 1926, Strong Papers, 1000.7; Strong to George Harrison, 2 July 1926, RG 39, Box 220; for the acrimony between Strong and members of the Federal Reserve Board, see Diary of Charles S. Hamlin, 28 October 1925, 13 April 1926, Hamlin Papers, Vol. 11.

Strong's goal of bringing about the financial stabilization of Europe. In fact, Mellon encouraged the governor to go to Paris to talk with Moreau.[69] In mid-July Mellon made a significant gesture not only to aid Strong but also to reassure the French government of his support and sympathy. Recognizing that one of the principle French objections to the debt settlement related to Article 7, which gave the United States the right to commercialize French war debt obligations, Mellon wrote Lacour-Gayet that he did not foresee any chance that the United States Treasury would ever make use of this provision. Treasury officials hoped this letter would be used by Caillaux to quell some of the opposition to ratification.[70]

Mellon and Winston might have gone still further to aid and encourage Strong if not for the domestic obstacles they encountered. During July 1926 the multiplication of French and British attacks on American war debt policies and the growing European criticism of American selfishness raised a storm of controversy in the United States, hardened the attitude of those who felt American policies had been generous, and circumscribed the flexibility of those who considered additional concessions desirable. Senator Borah was incensed by the Uncle Shylock accusations of European imperialist nations. State Department officials were both irritated by European ingratitude over American concessions and exasperated by European envy of American prosperity. Hoover was agitated by Europe's indifference to the burden borne by American taxpayers and convinced that the war debt settlements were within the capacity of European nations to pay.[71] Winston not only perceived the uncompromising attitudes of powerful figures within the administration but also assumed that the Democratic opposition would try to exploit the war debt controversy to its own political advantage in the forthcoming congressional elections. Consequently, he felt that the Treasury and the FRBNY had to submit to prevailing political and bureaucratic constraints.[72] Under existing circumstances the Coolidge administration decided to continue the informal ban on for-

69. Winston to Strong, 22 June 1926, Strong Papers, 012.6; George Harrison to Strong, 3 July 1926, RG 39, Box 220.
70. Mellon to Lacour-Gayet, 14 July 1926, RG 39, Box 63; Winston to Philippe Bunau-Varilla, 7 July 1926, ibid., Box 62.
71. For the public controversy, see "The Tiger's Plea for France," *Literary Digest* 90 (21 August 1926):12; for Borah's feelings, see, for example, Borah to William Ingle, 27 July 1926, Borah Papers, Box 264; for the view of the State Department, see, for example, Grew to Frances Peabody, 21 September 1926, Grew Papers, Box 32; for Hoover's appraisal, see Hoover to Kellogg, 28 July 1926, RG 59, 800.51W89/199.
72. Winston to Strong, 16, 21 July, 30 August 1926, Strong Papers, 012.6.

eign loans to France until the debt accord was ratified. The Department of State circulated a memorandum purporting to show that American war debt settlements were more generous than those negotiated by Great Britain. Secretary Mellon issued a public statement defending the agreement with France, justifying the capacity-to-pay formula, and emphasizing the tax implications of additional concessions.[73]

The official American defense of its war debt policies not only complicated Strong's efforts to cooperate with Moreau but also infuriated the French. As the franc fell to two cents, as wholesale prices increased 25 percent in three months, and as the government's ability to redeem the immense short-term floating debt became increasingly doubtful, the United States served as a convenient scapegoat for France's financial debacle. Twenty thousand French veterans and mutilated ex-soldiers paraded down the streets of Paris protesting the Mellon-Bérenger accord. Ambassador Herrick wrote Secretary Kellogg that he was "astonished at the rapid growth of adverse sentiments."[74] Meanwhile, panic struck Paris. Democratic institutions seemed unable to handle the financial crisis. On 17 July the Briand-Caillaux government was toppled. Four days later the Herriot ministry was overthrown. Talk of dictatorship became commonplace. Street fighting seemed possible. French bankers took their families away from Paris. Americans prepared for violent anti–United States outbreaks.[75]

The situation seemed desperate when Poincaré formed his coalition cabinet of National Union and became premier and finance minister on 23 July. Dramatically, the situation was transformed overnight. Fear of the abyss impelled caution and cooperation among almost all groups in the Chamber. Direct taxes were reduced; indirect taxes, increased; the budget, balanced. A special fund for the amortization of the floating debt was established. New legislation was passed insuring greater independence for the Bank of France and providing it with new powers considered indispensable for the stabilization task. Confidence re-

73. For the perpetuation of the loan embargo, see Leland Harrison to Kellogg, 12 July 1926, Leland Harrison Papers, Box 47; for the State Department memorandum, see FR, 1926, 2:100–6; for Mellon's statement, see WDC, *Combined Annual Reports*, pp. 302–6.
74. Herrick to Kellogg, 16 July 1926, Herrick Papers, Box 20; Herrick to Coolidge, 21 July 1926, ibid., Box 19; see also "French Wounds and American Dollars," *Literary Digest*, 90 (24 July 1926):7–8; "Uncle Shylock's Reply to His Critics," ibid. (31 July 1926):5–6; for figures on the value of the franc and on wholesale price increases, see Dulles, *French Franc*, pp. 477, 517, 524.
75. See Strong's vivid description, in Strong to George Harrison, 21 July 1926, FRBNY Papers, C261.1; for the financial and political crisis, see also Alfred Sauvy, *Histoire économique de la France entre les deux guerres*, 1:67–82; Bonnefous, *Troisième République*, 4:155–64.

turned. Capital was repatriated. Wtihin two weeks the franc rose from approximately two to three cents.[76]

On 20 July, the day the franc reached its low point, Strong quietly arrived in Paris to begin talks with Moreau and other officials of the Bank of France. After several days of discussion with Moreau, Strong became impressed with the latter's integrity and determination. Strong indicated his desire to help Moreau through the stabilization process if the new French government devised a comprehensive program for rehabilitating the franc and if it secured the Chamber's approval of the Mellon-Bérenger accord. Recognizing that several members of the incoming Poincaré ministry had previously condemned the debt settlement, the governor of the FRBNY said he would try to get the United States to furnish "a bridge" so that they could retreat from their former position without embarrassment. Although Moreau had some suspicions about Strong's intent to establish New York's dominance in international finance, he nevertheless understood that the American's desire to help stabilize the franc coincided with his own ambitions. Yet, nothing could be done between the central banks until Poincaré clarified his financial program and presented his views on ratification of the debt agreement.[77]

After talking to Moreau, Strong and S. Parker Gilbert traveled to Dinard. There they met secretly with Secretary Mellon, who was beginning a month's vacation in Europe. The three men stayed up late into the night discussing the international financial situation. During this conversation and in subsequent exchanges with Mellon, Strong put forth his entire view of the European situation. European markets, he emphasized, could not be fully restored until European currencies were stabilized. Since the well-being of the American farmer depended on the full recovery of European markets, the solution to the American farm problem awaited the complete rehabilitation of European finances. Low agricultural prices, Strong maintained, were the result of insufficient purchasing power, caused by deranged finances, exchange instability, and restricted trade.

Intimately related to these problems, continued Strong, was the issue of intergovernmental debts. These payments weighed heavily on

76. Haig, *Public Finances*, pp. 161–79; Dulles, *French Franc*, pp. 193–200; Sauvy, *Histoire économique*, 1:83–87; Pierre Miquel, *Raymond Poincaré*, pp. 542–69.
77. Strong to George Harrison, 24 July 1926, FRBNY Papers, C261.1; Strong to Mellon, 30 July, 1 August 1926, Strong Papers, 1000.7; Warren, Memorandum, 31 July 1926, ibid.; for Moreau's views, see Emile Moreau, *Souvenirs d'un gouverneur de la Banque de France*, pp. 50–51.

European finances and interfered with the natural progress of world commerce. Therefore, Strong urged that American war debt policy be conducted in the interests of American trade and the American farmer. He recommended that the United States declare a moratorium on all interest payments for three to five years. Such a moratorium ''would relieve Europe of an immense burden, greatly facilitate financial and monetary restoration, and . . . do more to protect the farmer's market than any other thing that we could do.'' At the end of the moratorium, Strong hoped that it might be possible to revise all the war debt settlements. But before any moratorium could be implemented, he acknowledged that France would have to ratify the existing debt settlement and stabilize the franc. To facilitate these developments, Strong argued that the FRBNY had to be ready to furnish credits and the United States government had to be willing to help Poincaré get the Mellon-Bérenger accord through the French Chamber of Deputies.[78]

Strong was delighted by Mellon's sympathy, understanding, and encouragement. The secretary agreed that American farmers had much to gain from Europe's financial stabilization. He advised Strong to stay in Europe and keep up his efforts to restore the gold standard and institutionalize central bank cooperation. Nothing he could do in New York, Mellon told Strong, was as important to the American people as what he was doing in Europe. Moreover, the treasury secretary indicated that he would support Strong's actions when he returned to Washington and participated in the meetings of the Federal Reserve Board.[79] Finally, Mellon did not ignore Strong's recommendation that he furnish French officials with an excuse to reverse their stand on ratification. He apparently reminded Strong of his letter to Lacour-Gayet promising not to commercialize French war debt obligations.[80] More important, he intimated that he might be willing to accept a safeguard clause in the text of the agreement ratified by the French Chamber of Deputies.[81] While Mellon was discussing such matters in

78. For Strong's meeting with Mellon, see Strong to George Harrison, 26 July, 17 August 1926, FRBNY Papers, C261.1; see also Strong to Mellon, 30 July, 10 August 1926, Strong Papers, 1000.7; Strong to Winston, 3, 30 August 1926, ibid.; Warren, Memoranda, 24, 26 August 1926, ibid.

79. For Mellon's attitudes and actions, see Strong to George Harrison, 3 August 1926, Strong Papers, 1000.7; Strong to Pierre Jay, 9 September 1926, ibid.; Warren, Memorandum, 31 August 1926, ibid.; Mellon to James W. Witherow, 8 July 1926, Morrow Papers.

80. Strong first alluded to this letter in his talk with Moreau on 31 July after his meeting with Mellon. See Warren, Memorandum, 31 July 1926, Strong Papers, 1000.7; see also Moreau, *Souvenirs*, p. 57.

81. Moreau, *Souvenirs*, pp. 57–58, 62.

France, Winston urged President Coolidge to publicly reassure the French that if their capacity to pay were undermined, the United States would not be an exacting creditor. Such a statement, Winston hoped, might induce Poincaré to seek ratification of the debt settlement.[82]

Once again, however, the Treasury Department's ability to help Strong stabilize European currencies and Poincaré secure legislative passage of the debt accord was limited. President Coolidge rebuffed Winston's suggestion that the United States publicly acknowledge the existence of a general safeguard clause. The president told Winston to speak to Kellogg about the matter.[83] But the secretary of state was preoccupied with other issues and generally unsympathetic to extending more generous terms to France. Neither Undersecretary Grew nor Assistant Secretary Harrison were any more inclined to provide additional incentives to secure French ratification of the debt accord. Perhaps they feared the wrath of Borah, with whom they constantly had to deal on the Senate Foreign Relations Committee. Perhaps they honestly believed, as they claimed, that the American people would not tolerate additional concessions to the French. In any case, although responsible for the conduct of foreign relations, the State Department did not support the Treasury Department's efforts to accommodate the French.[84] Nor did Hoover and his assistants in the Commerce Department. Their reluctance to make further concessions stemmed from their belief that foreign trade, while important, was not the key determinant of American prosperity. They believed that too much of the financial burden of World War I was being shifted onto the shoulders of American taxpayers and that a prosperous domestic economy would benefit the European debtors and enhance their ability to pay.[85]

The result of all this was that there was little coordination of policy between the Treasury Department, the FRBNY, and the agent general for reparations on the one hand and the State and Commerce departments on the other.[86] The lack of consensus in the executive branch circum-

82. Winston to Coolidge, 9 August 1926, RG 39, Box 62.
83. Coolidge to Winston, 11 August 1926, ibid.
84. Lewis Ethan Ellis, *Frank B. Kellogg and American Foreign Relations, 1925–1929*, p. 9; see also Kellogg to Hughes, 5 December 1924, 3 January 1925, Hughes Papers, Box 75; Joseph C. Grew, *Turbulent Era*, 1:682–83; Leland Harrison to Kellogg, 12 July 1926, Leland Harrison Papers, Box 47; for Borah's influence, see Ellis, *Kellogg*, p. 235.
85. Hoover to Kellogg, 28 July 1926, RG 59, 800.51W89/199; Department of Commerce, *Annual Report*, 1925, pp. 31–32.
86. Important State Department officials, for example, did not even know of Mellon's letter to Lacour-Gayet regarding the commercialization clause. See Castle to Whitehouse, 19 August 1926, Castle Papers, Box 3.

scribed the maneuverability of Mellon, Strong, and Gilbert. During the latter part of August when they met with Poincaré, Moreau, and other French policymakers, the three Americans felt compelled to reiterate that American financial aid would not be forthcoming until France ratified the debt settlement.[87]

Since Strong still hoped to cooperate with Moreau, he spent several days with the French banker. They discussed the essential elements necessary for the stabilization of the franc, the institutionalization of central bank cooperation, and the extension of Federal Reserve aid. Strong urged the Bank of France to maintain its independence from the government and establish effective means to gain control over financial markets in France. He emphasized that the French government had to reassure foreign creditors by dealing more effectively with the floating debt. Once these tasks had been accomplished, Strong estimated that up to $400 million in loans and credits could be forthcoming from various American sources to help stabilize the franc. Interestingly, Strong gave little attention to the new par value of the franc. This decision was apparently up to the French. As far as Strong was concerned, stabilization was the essential objective. In early September he was increasingly eager for the French to take concrete action so that he could proceed with his efforts to stabilize other currencies, especially the Italian lira and the Belgian franc. Once again Strong felt obligated to warn Moreau that ratification of a debt agreement was prerequisite to full cooperation between the Bank of France and the FRBNY.[88] Thus, it was up to the French to determine whether they should attempt to stabilize the franc on their own, or whether they should ratify the debt agreement and benefit from the aid of the FRBNY.

Stabilizing the Franc

American insistence on debt ratification complicated Poincaré's efforts to stabilize the franc. The French premier still believed that he needed to secure foreign credits in order to complete his stabilization program. But he was uncertain whether he could put together a majority in the

87. For Strong's talks with Moreau, Mellon's meeting with Poincaré, and related matters, see Warren, Memoranda, 23, 24, 25, 26, 28, 31 August 1926, Strong Papers, 1000.7; Strong to Winston, 30 August 1926, ibid.; Strong to George Harrison, 17 August 1926, 2 September 1926, FRBNY Papers, C261.1; Gilbert to Morrow and Leffingwell, 8 October 1926, RG 39, Box 220.
88. Warren, Memoranda, 23, 24, 25, 26, 28, 31 August 1926, Strong Papers, 1000.7; Strong to Jay, 9 September 1926, ibid.; Moreau, *Souvenirs*, pp. 78–83, 87–89, 91–93.

Chamber of Deputies in favor of the debt settlement. Even within his own government there was strong opposition to ratification. Consequently, he began to explore indirect means of securing the foreign credits necessary for stabilization. On 23 August he talked to S. Parker Gilbert about the possibility of commercializing German reparation bonds, 52 percent of the proceeds of which would go to France.[89] During the next week Moreau repeatedly raised the same matter in his talks with Strong.[90]

Strong and Gilbert initially reacted negatively to these French overtures. On 24 August the governor of the FRBNY told Moreau that the legal problems were overwhelming, that the transaction would necessitate the unlikely cooperation of the government of Germany as well as the governments of all the reparation creditors, and that the bonds would not be well received in New York. Strong talked the whole matter over with Mellon and Gilbert during the last days of August. They apparently concurred that the railroad bond scheme was not a constructive option because it might open an unproductive debate throughout Europe about the wisdom of immediately revising the intergovernmental debt settlements.[91]

Despite American objections, the French decided to explore this approach with the Germans. On 17 September Briand met Stresemann at Thoiry, a small French town near the Swiss border, to discuss a comprehensive settlement of outstanding Franco-German differences. French officials hoped to work out an arrangement that would lead to the commercialization of German reparation bonds and the stabilization of the franc. According to the deal contemplated by Briand and Stresemann, France would evacuate the Rhineland, return the Saar to Germany, support the withdrawal of the Inter-Allied Military Control Commission, and allow Germany to purchase Eupen-Malmedy from Belgium. In exchange, Germany would approve the sale of 1.5 billion marks of reparation railroad bonds and pay France 300 million gold

89. For Poincaré's sentiments and the French political situation, see Herrick to Coolidge, 10 August 1926, Herrick Papers, Box 19; William Phillips to Kellogg, 17 September 1926, RG 39, Box 62; Strong to Winston, 30 August 1926, Strong Papers, 1000.7; Gilbert to Morrow and Leffingwell, 8 October 1926, RG 39, Box 220; Moreau, *Souvenirs*, pp. 82–83.

90. Warren, Memoranda, 24, 26 August 1926, Strong Papers, 1000.7; Moreau, *Souvenirs*, pp. 78–79, 82.

91. Warren, Memoranda, 24, 26, 31 August 1926, Strong Papers, 1000.7; Strong to Winston, 30 August 1926, ibid.; Strong to Jay, 9 September 1926, ibid.; Gilbert to Morrow and Leffingwell, 24 September 1926, RG 39, Box 85; Gilbert to Morrow and Leffingwell, 8 October 1926, ibid., Box 220.

marks for the Saar coal mines.[92] Poincaré was apparently willing to consider an agreement along these lines if the evacuation of the Rhineland proceeded gradually and in unison with the total commercialization of German reparation bonds. In this way he hoped to put Germany's reparation obligations in private hands and thereby circumscribe Germany's ability to revise the Dawes Plan. For Poincaré the Thoiry formula constituted a means of stabilizing the franc while locking Germany into the Dawes Plan, avoiding further French dependence on Anglo-American finance, and escaping a political impasse over debt ratification.[93]

As agent general for reparation transfers, S. Parker Gilbert was kept well informed of the reaction of the major European governments to the Thoiry discussions. He cabled his friends at Morgan and Company and his former colleagues in the Treasury Department "that something big and useful" might develop out of the talks. Gilbert envisioned an accord linking a partial mobilization of German bonds to the stabilization of the franc and the ratification of the Franco-American debt settlement. He acknowledged that the sale of German bonds in the United States would constitute, in effect, a loan to France. But he suggested that it might be wise for the United States government to condone such an indirect loan to supply the "sugar coating" necessary to obtain French ratification of the debt agreements and stabilization of the franc. Gilbert anxiously awaited completion of a French stabilization program because the prevailing instability of the franc put pressure on the mark and complicated his own task of managing reparation transfers.[94]

Upon receiving Gilbert's cables, Treasury Undersecretary Winston immediately recognized that important developments were under way in Europe. He asked Dwight Morrow if American financial markets could absorb such a large quantity of German bonds. Winston regretfully admitted that the whole matter was linked to French ratification of the Mellon-Bérenger accord. Although a major step toward Euro-

92. For the Thoiry talks, see Jon Jacobson, *Locarno Diplomacy*, pp. 84–87; Gustav Stresemann, *Diaries, Letters, and Papers*, 3:17–26; Georges Suarez, *Briand*, 6:203–28.

93. For Poincaré's attitudes toward Thoiry, see Gilbert to Morrow and Leffingwell, 8 October 1926, RG 39, Box 220; Memorandum of conversation between Arthur N. Young and Leon Fraser, 11 November 1926, RG 59, 462.00R2962/68; FR, 1926, 2:107; Great Britain, Foreign Office, *Documents on British Foreign Policy*, Series 1A, 2:412 (hereafter cited as DBFP); Moreau, *Souvenirs*, pp. 11, 142.

94. Gilbert to Morrow and Leffingwell, 24 September 1926, RG 39, Box 85; Gilbert to Morrow and Leffingwell, 8 October 1926, ibid., Box 220.

pean political pacification and financial stabilization was in the offing, American policy had been set: no loans to France, direct or indirect, until France ratified the debt settlement. Since this policy had become public knowledge, it was considered politically embarrassing for the administration to change its position. "The psychology of the situation," one State Department official commented, prevented both the marketing of German reparation bonds in the United States and the extension of indirect loans to France until the war debt matter was resolved.[95] But since American policymakers did not want to incur responsibility for blocking the railroad bond scheme, they relied upon the opposition of British and German officials to bury the Thoiry proposals.[96]

Poincaré apparently lost interest in the Thoiry arrangement as he encountered overt British and tacit American opposition. There was no sense in making political and strategic concessions to Germany if the Americans continued to demand prior French ratification of the debt settlement as a condition for marketing the railroad bonds.[97] Moreover, during October and November there was increased questioning throughout France of the wisdom of acquiescing to Germany's demands and of the necessity of relying upon American financial aid to stabilize the franc. According to many Frenchmen, "The wise plan is to make an internal effort to free ourselves from the yoke of Anglo-Saxon finance."[98] Poincaré was inclined to share this view, especially as financial conditions steadily improved. During the autumn of 1926 the foreign exchange reserves of the Bank of France mounted, and the Morgan credit was reestablished. The French government made substantial repayments to the Bank of France, and loans became available from other European countries.[99]

Under these circumstances Poincaré had little incentive to divide his

95. For the quotation, see Arthur N. Young to Kellogg, 11 October 1926, RG 59, 462.00R2962/66½; see also Winston to Morrow, 27 September 1926, RG 39, Box 85; Mellon to Herrick, 17 March 1927, Herrick Papers, Box 22.

96. For British and German attitudes, see Gilbert to Morrow and Leffingwell, 8 October 1926, RG 39, Box 220; Jacobson, *Locarno Diplomacy*, pp. 84–90; DBFP, 1A, 2:409–11, 414, 415–18, 424, 444; Moreau, *Souvenirs*, p. 121.

97. Gilbert to Morrow and Leffingwell, 8 October 1926, RG 39, Box 220.

98. For French public opinion, see Whitehouse to Kellogg, 14 October 1926, RG 59, 800.51W89 France/416; Whitehouse to Kellogg, 22 October 1926, RG 39, Box 62; Herrick to Kellogg, 19 November 1926, Herrick Papers, Box 20; see also Jacobson, *Locarno Diplomacy*, pp. 91–98.

99. For financial developments in France during the autumn of 1926, see Dulles, *French Franc*, pp. 260–64; Sauvy, *Histoire économique*, 1:86–88; see also Chester Lloyd Jones to director, 10 November 1926, RG 151, File 443.3.

government and risk the political consequences of a debate over ratification of the debt agreement with the United States. Indeed, he decided to proceed with a de facto stabilization without American aid. In December 1926 he allowed Moreau to initiate operations to maintain the value of the franc at approximately four cents. Soon thereafter Poincaré informed American officials that France would begin making payments to the United States according to the Mellon-Bérenger schedule, even though the agreement had not yet been ratified.[100] Thus, France, unlike almost all the other continental Allies, overcame the financial crisis of the early 1920s, stabilized her currency, and began making debt payments without the aid of the FRBNY.

Conclusion

With the franc approaching stability, a debt agreement signed, and payments soon to be forthcoming, American officials breathed a sigh of relief. Although the French did not need the aid of the FRBNY, Strong was nevertheless gratified by the excellent working relationship he had established with Moreau.[101] Similarly, although the French had not yet ratified the debt agreement, Mellon was so pleased by developments that he was willing to recommend lifting the loan embargo in order to effect de jure stabilization.[102] In general, American policymakers enthusiastically welcomed the financial recovery of France as prerequisite to the stabilization of European currencies, the growth of world trade, and the expansion of American markets.[103]

American officials had reason to be satisfied with the recent course of financial and economic developments in Europe and the United States. By the end of 1926 almost all European currencies had been stabilized, at least de facto. In addition, European manufacturing production had exceeded its prewar level and risen markedly since 1920. European exports, though still below 1913 levels, had grown substantially since 1921. In France production had climbed approximately

100. For Poincaré's actions and the de facto stabilization of the franc, see Miquel, *Raymond Poincaré*, pp. 569–77; Moreau, *Souvenirs*, pp. 160–68, 182ff.; for Poincaré's decision to make war debt payments, see Department of the Treasury, press release, 1 March 1927, RG 39, Box 47; see also Bonnefous, *Troisième République*, 4:206–8.
101. Strong to George Harrison, 2 September 1926, FRBNY Papers, C261.1.
102. Mellon to Herrick, 17 March 1927, Herrick Papers, Box 22.
103. See, for example, Winston's speech to the Bankers Club of Kansas City, "Currency Stabilization in Europe," 11 October 1926, Morrow Papers; Herbert C. Hoover, *The Future of Our Foreign Trade*, pp. 7–8.

25 percent above its prewar base, and total real national income had increased 33 percent since 1920. Furthermore, economic collaboration between French and German industrialists was becoming more routine.[104] In the United States industrial production had increased 38 percent between 1921 and 1926. Total national income had climbed from approximately 60 to 80 billion dollars. Total domestic exports and imports had grown by over 50 percent in value between 1913 and 1926. While production, income, and trade were increasing, the public debt had been reduced by approximately $7.5 billion. During 1925 and 1926 alone the budget had shown a surplus of over $1 billion.[105] Yet, taxes had been lowered in 1924 and 1926. No wonder, then, Republican policymakers could take considerable pride in their efforts to promote stability in Europe without sacrificing domestic priorities or incurring strategic obligations.

Publicly, American officials did not allude to the differences that existed among themselves. These internal debates focused on the extent to which the United States should incur financial sacrifices to effect European stability. Also disputed was the degree to which the administration should take political risks to placate French anxieties over ratification of the debt agreement and stabilization of the franc. Policymakers exuded confidence that their economic orientation to European affairs was sound and their policymaking machinery adept at reconciling domestic and foreign goals. According to American officials, the interdepartmental regulation of foreign loan outflows had compelled France and other European debtors to balance their budgets and refund their war debts. The officials claimed that the WDC had found an intelligent balance between domestic fiscal needs, foreign financial imperatives, and American economic interests overseas. They credited the FRBNY with facilitating Europe's financial rehabilitation and aiding American commerce without stimulating domestic inflationary pressures.[106]

American policymakers, of course, realized that all of this had not been accomplished without engendering a certain amount of ill will

104. These figures are based on the statistical tables in Ingvar Svennilson, *Growth and Stagnation in the European Economy*, pp. 305, 292, 233; Dulles, *French Franc*, pp. 502, 409; for Franco-German industrial collaboration, see Henri de Peyerimhoff de Fontenelle, "The International Cartel Movement and French Economic Life," pp. 176–85.

105. See the figures in George H. Soule, *Prosperity Decade*, p. 108; Department of Commerce, *Statistical Abstract of the United States*, 1928, pp. 445, 202, 163.

106. See Winston, Address, 26 October 1926, Morrow Papers; Department of the Treasury, *Annual Report*, 1926, pp. 11–12; Department of Commerce, *Annual Report*, 1925, pp. 36–37; ibid., 1926, pp. 13, 50.

abroad. The French in particular resented America's use of financial leverage, criticized the Mellon-Bérenger accord, and complained that American policies were not only antagonistic to French interests but also irreconcilable with the imperatives of European stability.[107] American officials accepted such criticism with a good deal of equanimity. They believed that the French were insensitive to the domestic constraints affecting American policy and unwilling to recognize the extent to which American prosperity benefited all nations.[108] American officials contended that their policies had to be given a chance to work. They assumed that as American loans continued to flow to Europe, central bank cooperation became more routine, and European nations experienced economic growth, existing difficulties would disappear. The burden of the war debts, especially, would become more manageable. Using a picturesque analogy, Winston declared that "a weight may be too heavy for some child to move, but when he grows up he can carry it with ease." In other words the heavy payments expected from European debtors beginning in the 1930s might now seem too burdensome. But as their wealth increased, the European nations would be able to meet their obligations. Hence, time would prove to be the "healer of wounds" and the "solvent of difficulties." If events proved otherwise, American policymakers admitted their readiness to reassess their policies. But the officials did not think they would have to do so. "I, for one," said Winston in late 1926, "have faith to believe that we shall meet and solve the problems of the future as we have solved those of the past."[109]

Although American officials had reason to feel pleased with European developments, they nevertheless attributed too much of the progress to their own efforts. The Americans mistakenly belittled French and European sacrifices and disregarded the latent gap between world productive capacity and world purchasing power. By the end of 1926 it was already evident that additional readjustments would have to

107. See, for example, Whitehouse to Kellogg, 14 October 1926, RG 59, 800.51W89 France/416; Warrington Dawson to Castle, 10 November 1926, RG 39, Box 62; Gilbert to Morrow and Leffingwell, 8 October 1926, RG 39, Box 220.
108. Winston to Morrow, 8 July 1926, Morrow Papers; Grew to Peabody, 21 September 1926, Grew Papers, Box 32.
109. Winston, Address, 26 October 1926, Morrow Papers; Winston, "Currency Stabilization in Europe," 11 October 1926, ibid. From the very beginning of the decade, Hoover had stressed that European economic growth would lighten the burden of the war debts. See Hoover, drafts of letters to Joseph DeFrees, January 1922, HHCD, Box 21. But Hoover was willing to acknowledge the possiblity of revisions. See Hoover to Ochs, 3 May 1926, ibid., Box 364.

be made.[110] The capacity of the United States to play a constructive part in these readjustments was far more questionable than American officials assumed. The events of 1925–26 demonstrated that official American policy toward France and Europe was beset by problems. At home, these problems included the timidity of the administration in dealing with Congress, the difficulty of coordinating policy between the FRBNY and the administration, and the differences of opinion between policymakers in various executive departments. Moreover, American officials underestimated the spiritual and economic toll taken by the Great War and the resentment engendered abroad by the exercise of economic diplomacy. They also placed too much confidence in the functioning of the gold exchange standard and minimized the deflationary pressures it imposed on most European nations. As the financial power of France mounted after 1926 and as French officials felt able to challenge American (and British) policies, many of the potential weaknesses of the American approach toward European stability became apparent.

110. Strong to Mellon, 10 August 1926, Strong Papers, 1000.7.

[5]

Economic Diplomacy Falters, 1927–1928

With Europe apparently on the road to recovery, Republican officials had little incentive to change their nonpolitical, economic approach to European affairs. During 1927 and 1928 their aim was to continue the policies set in motion during the earlier part of the decade—policies designed to foster European stability, augment French security, and increase American trade. The Republicans hoped to convene another disarmament conference, promote the unconditional most-favored-nation principle, systematize the outflow of private capital, arrange a final reparations settlement, and maintain the stability of European currencies. They still sought to achieve these objectives without incurring strategic commitments or generating political entanglements. As a result of the experiences of the early 1920s Republican policymakers assumed that they could rely on the familiar techniques of economic diplomacy to reconcile foreign policy goals with domestic priorities.

These techniques, which had seemed so promising in the earlier part of the decade, began to falter in the more prosperous and relatively stable environment of the late 1920s. One of the most interesting and important factors behind this development was the unanticipated change in Franco-American relations. The reemergence of France as a great financial power impelled American and French policymakers to reappraise their diplomatic viewpoints and discover a greater mutuality of interests. Unfortunately, the uneasy accommodations that ensued were often at the expense of the greater interests of European stability.

Disarmament and Security

The promotion of arms limitation agreements without accompanying security guarantees was a basic component of Republican economic diplomacy. To this end, in early 1926 President Coolidge accepted an invitation to participate at Geneva in the work of the League of Nations–sponsored Preparatory Commission for the Disarmament Conference. Although he would have preferred to convene another arms limitation conference in the United States, Coolidge did not want to obstruct European disarmament efforts or delay an opportunity to limit auxiliary naval craft. He was eager to avert an incipient arms race with Britain and save the taxpayers of the United States and Europe hundreds of millions of dollars a year. By limiting armaments Republican officials hoped to promote peace, protect American strategic interests, and help European governments balance their budgets and stabilize their currencies.[1]

Their substantial interest in fostering the limitation of armaments notwithstanding, Republican officials approached the proceedings at Geneva cautiously. They were intent on safeguarding vital American interests and avoiding entangling commitments. Hence, American policymakers denounced efforts to limit the war-making capacity or armament expenditures of independent nations; they insisted on separate treatment of naval, air, and land armaments; they decried attempts to devise supervisory machinery to enforce disarmament agreements; and they refused to incur commitments to apply sanctions or respect blockades.[2]

This orientation conflicted with the French approach to disarmament questions. Having acquiesced to the Anglo-American policy of reviving Germany economically, the French sought to strengthen the security guarantees inherent in the League covenant and control the latent military capacity of their industrially powerful neighbor. France wanted the industrial capacity and war-making potential of a nation to constitute at least part of the basis for limiting armaments. Because they believed that the viability of their army depended on the ability of their navy to transport troops across the Mediterranean from North Africa, the French insisted on the complete interdependence of land, sea, and air armaments. Furthermore, their experience with German

1. See Department of State, *Papers Relating to the Foreign Relations of the United States*, 1926, 1:42–44, 78–79, 81–120 (hereafter cited as FR); see also Calvin Coolidge, *The Talkative President*, pp. 149–51, 160–61, 207–8.
2. FR, 1926, 1:51–56, 80–100; 1927, 1:163–66.

violations of the disarmament provisions of the Treaty of Versailles impelled the French to demand rigorous enforcement of any future accord. Finally, her concern with preserving the status quo in central and eastern Europe convinced France of the need to enhance the security of her smaller continental allies before limiting armaments or evacuating the second and third zones of the Rhineland.[3]

Although the French and American positions at Geneva contradicted one another, representatives of the two nations did not become involved in a direct confrontation. The American delegates, though extolling the benefits of land disarmament, did not actively concern themselves with this matter, which was of supreme importance to the French. Secretary of State Kellogg stressed that the United States had no more than an "academic interest" in land disarmament and instructed Ambassador Hugh Gibson not to become immersed in discussions over this issue and the related question of strategic guarantees. In fact, both the secretary of state and American military officials were willing to acknowledge the French view that security was an essential precondition for land disarmament. But the Americans maintained that the appropriate strategic guarantees had to be incorporated into regional security accords and could not be provided by the United States.[4] The French in turn accepted reality and no longer expected direct commitments from the United States. Instead, in April 1927 Briand sought a bilateral pact outlawing war between the two nations. He hoped that this pact would enhance the efficacy of European security arrangements by reducing the likelihood of a clash with the United States over the application of American neutrality rights when European nations were acting collectively to deter aggression.[5]

Rather than rely on the United States for outright security guarantees, the French looked to the British to enhance security on the European continent. Although the French did not seek new commitments, they wanted all League members to clarify their intentions and obligations under various articles of the League covenant, especially under Article 16. The French wanted the British to agree to use their navy

3. For the French position, see ibid., 1926, 1:110–11; 1927, 1:163–203; Jon Jacobson, *Locarno Diplomacy*, pp. 104–13; Richard Challener, *The French Theory of the Nation in Arms, 1886–1939*, pp. 137–214, especially pp. 187–90.
4. FR, 1926, 1:78–79, 80–84; Major A. W. Lane, "The Relation Between Regional Security and Regional Disarmament and Between Regional Disarmament and General Disarmament," [1926?], Records of the War Department General and Special Staffs, RG 165, Box 35; C. E. Kilbourne, "Résumé of the Efforts for the Limitation of Land Armaments by International Agreement," 24 May 1933, ibid., pp. 1–2.
5. For Briand's proposal, see FR, 1927, 2:611–13.

to enforce sanctions or implement an economic embargo should the League take action against an aggressor nation. The British were unwilling to accede to the French on this matter. In turn, the French refused to consider British plans for limiting armaments. The resulting impasse between the French and the British deadlocked the work of the Preparatory Commission.[6]

In early 1927, exasperated by the lack of progress in arms negotiations, Coolidge invited Britain, France, Japan, and Italy to join the United States in a separate conference on naval matters.[7] The president's initiative, however, not only failed to break the logjam at Geneva but also complicated the efforts to improve European security arrangements. The French, well aware of their growing financial prowess, refused to attend a conference that focused exclusively on naval issues.[8] Although the naval conference convened in June 1927, without the French and Italians, the British and Americans were unable to reconcile their approaches to limiting cruisers.[9] Both Austen Chamberlain, the British foreign secretary, and Esme Howard, the British ambassador to the United States, concluded that the American desire to have a substantial number of large cruisers reflected a determination to protect America's neutral trade in any future European war. This assessment of American intentions impelled British officials to be more circumspect than ever about assuming precise obligations to enforce a blockade against an aggressor nation. Fearing the prospect of a conflict with the United States over American neutrality rights, British policymakers hesitated to define their commitments under Article 16.[10]

The Geneva Naval Conference highlighted the interrelationships between naval armaments, neutrality rights, and European security arrangements. In a prearranged interview on the morning of 4 November 1927, Henry Wickham Steed, the well-known British journalist, explained these interrelationships to President Coolidge. The Englishman emphasized that European disarmament talks might be expedited if the

6. For French demands and Anglo-French differences, see Great Britain, Foreign Office, *Documents on British Foreign Policy*, Series 1A, 2:26–27, 30, 32–34; 3:364–65, 427–28, 500–2; 4:181, 184–85, 363–64 (hereafter cited as DBFP); see also FR, 1926, 1:108.

7. FR, 1927, 1:1–9.

8. For France's refusal to participate, see ibid., pp. 10–13.

9. Ibid., pp. 46–159; Lewis Ethan Ellis, *Frank B. Kellogg and American Foreign Relations, 1925–1929*, pp. 167–84; Raymond G. O'Connor, *Perilous Equilibrium*, pp. 15–18; Stephen Roskill, *Naval Policy Between the Wars*, 1:498–516; David Carlton, "Great Britain and the Coolidge Naval Disarmament Conference of 1927," pp. 573–98.

10. DBFP, 1A, 3:363–64, 366–69, 538–41, 724–25, 733–34, 736–37; 4:373–74, 392–94, 415–16.

United States government clarified its policy regarding neutrality rights when other nations were acting collectively to deter aggression. The president showed considerable interest in the matter. He indicated that he might support a congressional resolution that renounced American aid to aggressor nations and that expressed American willingness to consult with other nations trying to deter aggression. Coolidge encouraged Steed to talk to Senator Borah about these matters. Steed found the senator receptive to the idea of a congressional resolution along the lines recommended by Coolidge, provided that the United States was not bound by any decision of the League of Nations and retained the right to determine who the aggressor was.[11]

These developments help to explain why Republican officials began to show a growing interest in Briand's proposal to outlaw war. Certainly, the peace movement in the United States was exerting pressure on the administration to make some contribution to world peace. But policymakers began to give serious consideration to Briand's *démarche*, not simply because they wanted to mollify the public but also because they better appreciated the nature of the European impasse over security and disarmament. They did not wish to sign a bilateral pact with France because they suspected Briand's motives, disliked the French alliance system, and saw no reason to single out France for special treatment. Yet, by extending a pact outlawing war to all nations and by promising not to protect trade with violators of such a pact, the United States could mold its neutrality policy to accommodate the needs of League members, especially Britain, when acting under Article 16. In fact, Kellogg initially supported an approach along these lines advocated by Professor James Shotwell and Senator Arthur Capper. Eventually, however, the secretary of state accepted a more restricted approach supported by Borah that called for the renunciation of war but made no reference to trade or neutrality rights.[12]

When the administration came out for a multilateral accord renouncing war as national policy but saying nothing about American neutrality policy in case of violations, Briand lost interest in his initial overture. Nevertheless, after receiving assurances that Kellogg's proposals would not undermine previous treaty commitments, Briand de-

---

11. Ibid., 4:431–32.
12. The standard account of the Kellogg-Briand Pact is Robert H. Ferrell, *Peace in Their Time*; see also Robert James Maddox, "William E. Borah and the Crusade to Outlaw War," pp. 200–220; John Chalmers Vinson, *William E. Borah and the Outlawry of War*; Charles DeBenedetti, "Borah and the Kellogg-Briand Pact," pp. 22–29.

cided to sign the treaty renouncing war.[13] The agreement, signed in August 1928, did not contain any enforcement provisions. But the pact was seen by many European leaders as a step toward American collaboration with European security arrangements. As Austen Chamberlain pointed out, there was no need to secure firm strategic commitments from the United States. It was, he declared,

axiomatic that no United States government would undertake in advance obligations to act in a particular way in some future contingency, nor was it in the least necessary that they should do so. The value of the proposed treaty was not dependent upon such engagements, but would be determined by [whether] . . . the world thought it probable—still more if the world thought it certain—that the United States Government would give no help to the treaty-breaker, but would prevent the citizens of the United States from giving it aid or comfort, then indeed the new treaty would be a formidable guarantee for the maintenance of peace.[14]

The Kellogg-Briand Pact tried to reconcile the French demand for security and the American desire for political aloofness through modifications in American neutrality policy. Such modifications might enable the British to define their obligations under Article 16 more precisely.[15] This definition of British obligations might palliate French strategic anxieties and expedite a land disarmament agreement. The British, therefore, were eager to convene negotiations with the State Department regarding the redefinition of belligerents' rights.[16] Meanwhile, they began talking to the French about working out a compromise agreement on land and naval armaments.

These Anglo-French discussions aroused the suspicions of the American public and ignited the apprehensions of big-navy advocates in the United States. Under these circumstances Republican officials felt compelled to denounce the ensuing Anglo-French compromise as illustrative of British efforts to outmaneuver the United States on the cruiser issue and weaken the American strategic position in the Pacific.[17] American policymakers told the British that discussions over

13. For Franco-American negotiations over the Kellogg-Briand Pact, see FR, 1927, 1:611–30; 1928, 1:1–157; see also Kellogg to Borah, 27 July 1928, Borah Papers, Box 542; Georges Suarez, *Briand*, 6:257–67.
14. For Chamberlain's view, see DBFP, 1A, 5:774–75; for Briand's view, see Belgium, Commission royale d'histoire, *Documents diplomatiques belges, 1920–1940*, 2:486–88, 508–9 (hereafter cited as DDB); Suarez, *Briand*, 6:267–74.
15. DBFP, 1A, 4:551–52, 584–85, 590–92; 5:610–11, 688.
16. Ibid., 4:641–44; 5:604–7, 688.
17. For the Anglo-French compromise and the American reaction, see ibid., 5:654–55, 667–68, 719–20, 770, 776–77, 779–80, 788–93, 795, 808–9; FR, 1928, 1:264–91;

the redefinition of belligerents' rights would have to be postponed until a new administration took office in 1929.[18] In a period of general prosperity, security, and complacency, policymakers decided not to try anything innovative lest it upset vested interests in the navy and further divide the Republican party. Hence, little progress was made on disarmament and security questions, and consummation of the Kellogg-Briand Pact did not provide an opportunity to revise American neutrality policy.

During 1927 and 1928 neither America nor France would compromise neutral rights or strategic interests in order to make a major contribution to long-term European stability. Instead, within the bounds of their respective strategic doctrines, each nation tried to accommodate the needs of the other. American officials did not exert any pressure on the French to limit their land armaments, and the French sought to avoid primary responsibility for challenging the American position on naval matters. Similarly, France no longer sought positive strategic commitments from the United States on the Continent; in turn, the United States did not press the French to abandon their demands for additional safeguards of their security. The Kellogg-Briand Pact reflected the uneasy accommodation reached by American and French officials over security matters when neither side had the financial leverage to elicit major concessions from the other. As a result Franco-American relations were not particularly strained at Geneva during 1927 and 1928. But the uneasy accommodation did little to enhance European stability or augment French security.

The failure of the former Allies to agree at Geneva on an accord limiting their land armaments left Germany disgruntled and provided an excuse for her violations of the peace treaty. During 1926 and 1927 American military officials reported extensively on German transgressions of the armaments provisions of the Treaty of Versailles. The Army's MID accurately assessed Germany's desire to revise the treaty; secure Allied evacuation of the Rhineland; regain the Polish Corridor, Upper Silesia, and Danzig; unite with Austria; and establish some form of economic predominance in central Europe. "Germany is like a young giant in chains," commented the MID, "whose growing . . .

---

see also War Plans Division (WPD) to Chief of Naval Operations (CNO), 10 April 1929, "Estimate of the Situation," Confidential Records of the Secretary of the Navy, RG 80, File L1–1.

18. DBFP, 1A, 5:604–7, 686–89.

powers cause him to expand in one direction as rapidly as constrictions are applied in another."

The meaning of these trends for European peace was not altogether clear. Other developments made it difficult to predict the future course of events. The MID noted, for example, that a "common insecurity" impelled collaboration between France and Germany even while "extreme nationalism" remained rampant in both countries. American intelligence reports stressed the significance of Franco-German cartel agreements, the pervasive fear of bolshevism in France and Germany, and their mutual apprehension of the economic ascendancy of the United States. The MID concluded that Franco-German relations were undergoing a "tremendous amelioration" although many differences had not been resolved. The question remained whether German expansion, certain to recur in some form, would jeopardize European stability, French security, or vital American interests. The weakness of the German military machine, the absence of an imminent threat of war, the growth of Franco-German collaboration in the economic realm, and the occasional criticism within Germany of that nation's secret rearmament led American military observers to think that German revisionism might not necessarily undermine the well-being of the international community or threaten the strategic and economic interests of the United States.[19] The reluctance of American officials to proceed with a revision of their neutrality practices, however, did not constitute the type of innovative and courageous statesmanship that was required to coopt a revisionist Germany and an insecure France into a stable and prosperous liberal capitalist order.

Trade and Tariffs

In July 1928, as negotiations between Kellogg and Briand culminated in the peace pact, Ambassador Herrick voiced considerable cynicism about the treaty renouncing war. "I suppose," he remarked, "treaties are somewhat like children's games. When some child does not want to play any longer, he breaks up the game and that's the end of it." Herrick did not attach much importance to formal agreements, espe-

19. For the reports of the Military Intelligence Divisions (MID) cited in this paragraph and the preceding one, see "Intelligence Summary," 21 August–3 September, 13–21 September, 30 October–12 November, 27 November–10 December, 11 December–24 December 1926, 9 July–22 July, 23 July–5 August, 17 September–30 September 1927, Records of the MID, RG 165.

cially those of a political nature. Like many prominent Americans, he looked to the economic realm for the surest guarantees of peace. "Some day," he emphasized, "the force of economic considerations may become so great . . . that there will be no more war."[20]

During 1927 and 1928 Republican policymakers did not lose sight of the critical economic issues. In February 1927 they accepted an invitation from the League of Nations to participate in the forthcoming world economic conference at Geneva. The agenda of the conference called for a discussion of trade barriers, industrial cartels, and agricultural conditions. Although American officials realized that the conference, scheduled for May, would focus on the European aspects of these issues, they were nevertheless anxious to attend because they recognized the interdependence of the European and American economies. As a creditor nation on both public and private account, Arthur Young pointed out, the United States had a substantial interest in European prosperity. Moreover, the meeting afforded an opportunity to muster European support for the unconditional most-favored-nation trading principle. Fearing that Congress might attack the administration for embroiling the United States in purely European affairs, policymakers once again selected nongovernmental experts to present the American viewpoint without formally committing the administration.[21]

In the view of American officials the conference turned out to be a resounding success. Although no consensus was reached on the advantages or disadvantages of cartels and little meaningful action was taken on agricultural problems, there was general accord on the positive attributes of the unconditional most-favored-nation principle. American policymakers were delighted by the emerging consensus on the need to end trade discrimination, simplify tariff classifications, and stabilize customs regimes. Therefore, they were inclined to disregard the anti-American rhetoric emanating from Geneva. Reviewing the work of the conference for the secretary of state, Arthur Young happily reported that more importance had been attached to the stability of tariff rates than to the level of customs duties. The French principle of reciprocity, then, was in growing disrepute. Young agreed with officials in the Commerce Department and on the Tariff Commission that the time

20. Myron T. Herrick to Robert W. Bliss, 3 July 1928, Herrick Papers, Box 4.
21. Arthur N. Young, Memorandum, 8 January 1927, General Records of the Department of State, RG 59, File 550.M1/62; Hoover to Frank B. Kellogg, 28 January 1927, ibid., 550.M1/55; Wallace McClure, "International Economic Conference," 17, 22 December 1926, 8 January 1927, ibid., 550.M1/191, 61, 44; Leland Harrison, Memorandum, 1 February 1927, ibid., 550.M1/66; Harrison to Kellogg, 14 March 1927, ibid., 550.M1/193.

was ripe to press France to sign a new commercial treaty based on the unconditional most-favored-nation clause.[22]

Before these negotiations could get underway, however, the French embarked on a new commercial policy. As a result of the stability of the franc and the development of closer economic ties with her former enemy, France concluded a de facto most-favored-nation treaty with Germany. At the same time, the French raised minimum import duties on 1700 products and decided on a schedule of maximum rates approximately 400 percent above the minimum duties. By putting a premium on receiving most-favored-nation treatment in the French market, which most American goods did not enjoy, these actions damaged American interests. The French Ministry of Commerce inflicted even greater harm by terminating the privileged status between the maximum and minimum rate schedules enjoyed by many American manufactured items since 1921. Thus, American goods were once again subjected to maximum duties, at rates higher than ever before. What made matters worse was that German goods, heretofore not admitted on favorable terms, were now accorded much more favorable treatment than corresponding American products. In effect, the Franco-German commercial treaty and the concomitant changes in tariff rates meant a substantive increase in the degree of French discrimination against American commerce.[23]

In justifying these actions the French disputed the notion that the nonbargaining, single-column, high-tariff system of the United States constituted equality of treatment. Such equality, the French charged, was equality before a closed door. According to the French, America's high-tariff system precluded imports into the United States. It thus undermined the ability of America's debtors to make payments and contributed to world economic instability.[24] Moreover, the French

22. For reports on the conference, see Young to Kellogg, 20, 28 May, 1 June 1927, ibid., 550.M1/280, 335, 330; Norman H. Davis to Kellogg, 23 May 1927, ibid., 550.M1/314; FR, 1927, 1:240–46; for the views of the Commerce Department and the Tariff Commission regarding a commercial treaty with France, see Henry Chalmers to Hoover, 22 May 1926, Herbert C. Hoover Commerce Department Papers, Box 292 (hereafter cited as HHCD); Tariff Commission and Department of Commerce, Memorandum on French tariff discrimination, June 1926, RG 59, 611.5131/543.
23. Chalmers, "Effect of New French Duties on American Trade," RG 59, 611.5131/679; Sheldon Whitehouse to Kellogg, 2 September 1927, ibid., 651.003/200; Harold R. Enslow, "The Franco-American Tariff Problem," pp. 212–19; Graham Stuart, "Tariff Making in France," pp. 103–5; André Siegfried, "The Development of French Tariff Policy After the War," pp. 164–86.
24. Summary of an interview between Daniel Serruys and Chester L. Jones, 22 March 1927, RG 59, 611.5131/516; Whitehouse to Kellogg (encloses French aide-mémoire), 1 October 1927, ibid., 611.5131/594, 596.

contended that American tariff policies especially hurt French goods. French exports to the United States were subject to considerably higher duties than were American exports to France. Likewise, American tariffs on imports from France were higher than American duties on imports from all other nations. According to the French, this tariff policy in no way constituted equality of treatment.[25] Therefore, Americans could no longer expect equal treatment in the French market until they were ready to make reciprocal concessions (as the Germans had done).[26]

American officials realized that they were faced with a direct challenge to their commercial policy. Although most European governments had endorsed the equality-of-treatment principle, especially as it applied to intra-European trade, they apparently sympathized with French efforts to use discriminatory practices to compel reductions in United States customs duties. Moreover, American diplomats in Paris reported that Frenchmen looked upon themselves as the standard-bearers for all Europe, trying to knock down America's high-tariff walls.[27] Confronted with this bold action, Republican policymakers activated section 317 of the Fordney-McCumber Act and levied penalty duties on French imports.[28]

At the same time, American officials denounced the inequities of French bargaining practices and extolled the virtues of the equality-of-treatment principle. The Americans claimed that there could be little confidence in the stability of trade relations until this principle was applied universally. Furthermore, they rejected charges that French goods were discriminated against in the American market, explaining that French exports to the United States were often luxury items subject to high duties. Finally, they pointed out that if American tariffs were relatively high, so was the per capita purchasing power of the American people. This purchasing power sustained American demand for

25. Paul Claudel to William R. Castle, 28 September 1927, ibid., 611.5131/600. Certain aspects of the French claims were verified by American studies. In 1926, for example, the average rate of duty on imports from France was 46.6 percent while it was only 39.3 percent on imports from all other countries. See Thomas O. Marvin to Kellogg, 7 October 1927, ibid., 611.5131/610.
26. FR, 1926, 2:672–75, 693–95.
27. Whitehouse to Kellogg, 30 September, 5, 6 October 1927, RG 59, 611.5131/612, 607; John Calvin Brown to Castle, 30 September 1927, ibid., 611.5131/602; D. C. Poole to Kellogg, 17 November 1927, ibid., 611.5131/698; see also Frank W. Taussig, "The Tariff Controversy with France," pp. 185, 189–90.
28. Chairman Marvin of the Tariff Commission prepared the data for the imposition of the retaliatory provisions. See Marvin to Kellogg, 23 September 1927, RG 59, 611.5131/582.

foreign goods, especially luxury items, regardless of high customs duties.[29]

The controversy might have worsened except that French officials made it clear that they did not want to become immersed in a protracted dispute over irreconcilable commercial principles. They preferred to focus on short-term expedients that might eventually lead to a more permanent trade detente. The French were prepared to remove the new discriminations against American goods if the United States acceded to certain demands. France wanted the Tariff Commission to proceed, under the flexible provisions of section 315 of the Fordney-McCumber Act, to investigate French complaints that American tariff rates exceeded the differences in the costs of production between the two nations. French officials also requested a reexamination of those administrative procedures and sanitary restrictions that retarded the import of French agricultural and pharmaceutical products into the United States. Finally, the French asked that American customs officials be prohibited from examining the records of French businessmen and manufacturers in French territory.[30]

The French offer of a *modus vivendi* appealed to American policymakers. Although the French had not accepted the unconditional most-favored-nation principle, they seemed ready to bow to American pressure and retreat from their attack on the protectionist-expansionist nature of United States commercial policy. Restoration of the status quo ante regarding tariffs meant that the overall position of American goods in the French market would be better than it had been heretofore. Recent increases in French minimum duty rates usually narrowed and sometimes eliminated the gap between the intermediate rate status once again accorded some American goods and the most-favored-nation status granted the products of America's chief competitors in the French market. Hence, American officials accepted the *modus vivendi* and withdrew the countervailing duties. In turn, the French restored the status quo ante of their tariff policy toward the United States.[31]

29. For the American position, see FR, 1927, 2:672–73, 677–81; McClure, "Memorandum Regarding Franco-American Tariff Controversy," 16 September 1927, RG 59, 611.5131/674.
30. Whitehouse to Kellogg (encloses French *aide-mémoire*), 30 September, 1 October 1927, RG 59, 611.5131/594, 596; FR, 1927, 2:693–95.
31. The French stressed the positive features of their proposals in two *aide-mémoire*. See FR, 1927, 2:693–95, 698–99; see also pp. 691–93, 696–98; United States Tariff Commission to Kellogg, 2 November 1927, RG 59, 611.5131/675; Castle to Wesley Frost, 5 November 1927, Castle Papers, Box 3.

The Franco-American tariff compromise had significant ramifications for long-term European stability. The compromise challenged Republican officials to use existing policymaking machinery to reconcile their seemingly contradictory efforts to expand exports while protecting the domestic market. As the French pointed out, American officials might accomplish this reconciliation either through the use of the flexible tariff provisions or through the revision of administrative procedures. For most of 1928 the French waited to see if the Tariff Commission would use section 315 of the Fordney-McCumber Act to reduce duties on specific French goods and if the Treasury and Agriculture departments would revise their regulations to accommodate French requests.[32]

But the American policymaking apparatus faltered. The Tariff Commission, under Chairman Thomas O. Marvin, was not an independent body committed to unbiased application of the flexible tariff provisions found in the Fordney-McCumber Act. In fact, by 1928 the protectionist predisposition and political orientation of the Tariff Commission had engendered many complaints and precipitated a full-scale congressional investigation of its procedures. William S. Culbertson, former vice-chairman of the commission and principal architect of the flexible tariff provisions, had resigned in a state of disillusionment.[33] Not surprisingly, then, the commission systematically rebuffed French requests for rate reductions. It refused to place much reliance on the data presented by French parties, ignored many French grievances, and focused more attention on finding cases of French discriminatory action against American goods than on applying section 315 impartially. The preliminary investigations of the commission even suggested that duties on many French goods might be too low.[34] At the same time neither the Agriculture Department nor the Treasury Department responded sympathetically to French requests for changes in American

32. For French policy, see Whitehouse to Kellogg (encloses *aide-mémoire*), 2 November 1927, RG 59, 611.5131/657; Claudel to secretary of state, 14 May 1928, ibid., 611.5131/736.

33. William B. Kelly, Jr., "Antecedents of Present Commercial Policy, 1922–1934," p. 22; Taussig, "Tariff Controversy," p. 187; J. Richard Snyder, "Coolidge, Costigan, and the Tariff Commission," pp. 131–48; William S. Culbertson to Hoover, 11 October 1924, HHCD, Box 294; Senate, Select Committee, *Investigation of the Tariff Commission*.

34. United States Tariff Commission to Kellogg, 2 November 1927, RG 59, 611.5131/675; Paul Culbertson, "Summary Statement of the Tariff Negotiations with the French Government in 1927," ibid., 611.003/1664; Marvin to Kellogg, 5 October 1928, 2 January 1929, ibid., 611.5131/746, 757; Kelly, "Commercial Policy," p. 51, n. 147.

sanitary restrictions and customs regulations. State Department and even Commerce Department officials deplored these developments, but they were unable to determine the policies of other departments, which were often responding to pressures exerted by their own constituencies.[35]

The inability of the United States to respond positively to French requests under the *modus vivendi* of 1927 demonstrated the inadequacy of section 315 and the problems inherent in America's nonbargaining, high-tariff legislation of 1922. These shortcomings not only handicapped State Department efforts to disseminate the unconditional most-favored-nation principle but also exacerbated the balance-of-payments problems of many European nations. During 1928 France was not beleaguered by such payments difficulties and enjoyed a healthy currency and flourishing trade despite an unfavorable merchandise balance with the United States. As a result, although the French were not happy with the treatment accorded their goods in the American market, they appeared less inclined to lead a European assault on American tariff barriers.[36] In fact, as the French increased their own duties, espoused a formula for setting tariff rates based on production costs, and concluded de facto most-favored-nation treaties, their commercial policies increasingly resembled those of the United States.[37] Another controversy between the two nations was thus averted. But one of the most prosperous and financially powerful nations in Europe was no longer ready to champion the cause of the Old World against American protectionist-expansionist policies.

Within the United States the clash with France over tariffs, the ensuing compromise, and the ongoing Senate investigation of the Tariff Commission engendered some criticism of the high duties and flexible tariff provisions of the Fordney-McCumber Act. Frank Taussig, the nation's leading tariff authority, questioned the utility of section 315 and called for increased imports. So did a number of internationalist bankers and export-oriented businessmen. Their apprehensions about

35. Chalmers to Young, 7 November 1928, RG 59, 611.5131/755; for interest group pressures that conflicted with French appeals, see, for example, Chester Gray to president, 28 May 1929, ibid., 611.003/1443.
36. Young, "Commercial Treaty Negotiations with France," 26 March 1928, ibid., 611.5131/735.
37. French tariff rates remained lower than American duties, but the direction was the same. Moreover, at the Geneva Economic Conference, the French submitted resolutions that, in effect, justified the tariff principle of cost equalization. See Arnold J. Toynbee, *Survey of International Affairs, 1929*, pp. 96–98; Siegfried, "French Tariff Policy," pp. 177–86.

the negative impact of American trade practices on the international balance sheets of European nations were shared by a few prominent Democrats, among them Cordell Hull and Norman H. Davis. A handful of reputed experts, like Owen D. Young and S. Parker Gilbert, and several officials in the Department of State, including Arthur Young and Wallace McClure, had similar worries.[38]

But in an era of prosperity and complacency their warnings were easily dismissed. For political and economic reasons Coolidge wanted to avoid the uncertainties produced by wholesale tariff revision. Moreover, the president supported the protectionist principle, appointed protectionists to the Tariff Commission, and usually approved their recommendations.[39] Within the administration, responsibility for reviewing long-term American commercial policy was divided between the Tariff Commission and the Commerce, Treasury, and State departments. But given the protectionist orientation of Congress, the political overtones of the tariff issue, and the rancorous state of legislative-executive relations, not a single prominent official wanted to reexamine the impact of American commercial policy on the national or international economy. Even Garrard Winston, the undersecretary of the treasury who worked so extensively on international currency problems, perceived the tariff issue primarily in domestic political terms. Under these circumstances domestic and foreign critics of United States commercial policy had little prospect of effecting significant reductions in American customs duties.[40]

What made any major revision especially unlikely was the emergence of Herbert Hoover as an outspoken advocate of the protectionist principle. Hoover mustered a formidable array of statistical data to demonstrate that the expansionist-protectionist policies of the United States were not inimical to the international economy. Of course, Hoover began with two critical sets of assumptions: protectionism contributed to American prosperity; and American prosperity was prerequisite to a healthy international economy. These beliefs reflected his tremendous confidence in the wellsprings of the national economy, his

38. Taussig, "Tariff Controversy," pp. 186–90; Joan Hoff Wilson, *American Business and Foreign Policy, 1920–1933*, pp. 86–96; Davis to Cordell Hull, 8 January 1925, 24 February 1926, Davis Papers, Box 27; McClure to Young, 10 November 1924, RG 59, 611.0031/233; Arthur N. Young, Memorandum, 24 November 1925, ibid., 611.0031/246; Owen D. Young to Hoover, 5 January 1926, Young Papers, I–73; S. Parker Gilbert to Garrard Winston, 16 October 1925, Strong Papers, 1012.1.
39. Snyder, "Coolidge," pp. 131–48; FR, 1927, 1:xiv.
40. Winston to Dwight W. Morrow, 8 July 1926, Morrow Papers; for congressional attitudes, see Frank W. Fetter, "Congressional Trade Theory," pp. 413–27.

antipathy toward foreign economic systems, and his view that, if necessary, the United States could get along independently of the European economy. Like the typical American manufacturer, perhaps best represented by the NAM, Hoover desired to expand exports, but not at the expense of the protective tariff, which he emphasized was the "fundamental safeguard of the American workman and the American farmer." During the presidential campaign of 1928 he expounded upon these themes with great conviction, evidently feeling that they made good political as well as economic sense.[41]

Given the views of Hoover and Coolidge, the actions of the Tariff Commission, the sentiments of most legislators, and the acquiescence of France, it is not hard to understand why the techniques of economic diplomacy, especially as they applied to commercial policy, began to falter during the latter part of the decade. As 1927 began, the Geneva Economic Conference sparked considerable hope that trade and tariff practices might be handled in the interests of the larger European and world economic community. But these hopes were dashed by the inability and unwillingness of American policymakers to apply section 315 of the Fordney-McCumber Act in a way that either palliated French pride or eased British and German financial problems. The only consolation was the existence of some evidence to support Hoover's view that the revision of American duties was less vital to the functioning of the international economy than the adroit handling of other issues, such as the export of American capital.[42] Unfortunately, however, the mechanisms for dealing with these matters also faltered during 1927 and 1928.

Loans

From the onset of the 1920s Republican policymakers agreed that to expand exports and expedite European reconstruction, it was essential for them to oversee the export of private American capital. These factors accounted for the decision in 1922 to inaugurate an interdepart-

41. See Hoover's campaign speeches in Herbert C. Hoover, *The New Day*, especially pp. 101–2, 70, 128–43; see also [Hoover?], "Draft," [1925?], HHCD, Box 371; "Hoover Denies U.S. Tariff Hits Europe," 23 October 1926, HHCD, Box 656; Hoover to Kellogg, 28 July 1926, RG 59, 800.51W89/199; for the view of the National Association of Manufacturers (NAM), see, for example, NAM, *Proceedings of the Annual Convention*, 1927, pp. 81–82.

42. The best guide to understanding Hoover's reasons for downplaying the impact of high tariffs can be found in the annual studies of the balance of payments conducted by the Bureau of Foreign and Domestic Commerce (BFDC). See Department of Commerce,

mental review of foreign loan offerings. Having instituted such a review, government officials found it convenient to expand the purposes of the review process. In 1925 the Department of State began objecting to loans to nations that had not refunded their war debts. Almost simultaneously, the government started to advise bankers to be more cautious in making loans to Germany, especially to German states and municipalities. Although the regulation of loans presented certain difficulties, American policymakers were willing to put up with these problems, so long as they believed that the review procedures afforded them leverage to accomplish specific diplomatic objectives without generating unwanted political embroilments.[43] Accordingly, in February 1927 the cabinet decided to continue its ban on loans to France until the French ratified the Mellon-Bérenger accord.[44]

The decision to maintain the loan embargo engendered much hostility in the financial community. Wall Street bankers, searching for profits and surfeited with capital, were eager to make loans to France. Between the end of December 1926 and early March 1927 there were at least fifteen inquiries from the nation's leading investment bankers regarding French financing.[45] When the government responded negatively to all these requests, the banking community embarked on a systematic campaign to alter official policy. As a leading member of the American Bankers Association (ABA), Fred Kent presented the bankers' case to Hoover, Kellogg, and Ogden L. Mills, the new undersecretary of the treasury. Kent argued that the loan embargo endangered American trade with France, injured American financial markets, sacrificed the interests of American bankers, diminished government revenues, and hurt Franco-American relations.[46] In addition to protesting

BFDC, *The Balance of International Payments of the United States, 1922–1928, Trade Information Bulletin,* Nos. 144, 215, 340, 399, 503, 552, 625. For a more recent analysis minimizing the dislocating impact of American tariff policy, see M. E. Falkus, "U.S. Economic Policy and the 'Dollar Gap' of the 1920's," pp. 599–623.

43. For the warnings regarding loans to Germany, see FR, 1925, 2:172–87; 1926, 2:201–13; 1927, 2:727–30; for the advantages and disadvantages of the review procedures, see, for example, Arthur N. Young, Memorandum, 2 April 1925, RG 59, 800.51/509½; Harrison to Kellogg, 10 April 1925, ibid., 800.51/507½.

44. Hoover to Coolidge, 21 February 1927, HHCD, Box 369; Arthur N. Young to Harrison, 22 March 1927, RG 59, 851.51/1033.

45. See, for example, Allen Dulles to Arthur N. Young, 23 February 1927, RG 59, 851.51/1001; for inquiries from W. A. Harriman and Company, Aldred and Company, and others, see ibid., 851.51/1033, 1041, 1008, 1023.

46. Fred I. Kent to Kellogg, 4 March 1927, ibid., 851.51/1034; Harrison, Memorandum, 17 March 1927, ibid., 851.51/1033; Kent to Ogden L. Mills, 13 June 1927, Records of the Bureau of Accounts, RG 39, Box 47.

official policy, the bankers found ingenious ways to get around it. Some of them tried to arrange French financing in foreign markets; others sought to purchase French loans already marketed abroad; still others maneuvered to underwrite privately the financing of French corporations.[47] The New York Trust Company estimated that between September 1926 and February 1927, 26 percent of all French loans wound up in American hands. During the next year major shares of three additional French loans went to the United States.[48]

The protests and actions of American bankers combined with other factors to alter the course of American loan policy. State Department officials came to agree with their Treasury colleagues that the loan embargo was countereffective. Since the French no longer needed American capital, the embargo was simply antagonizing the Poincaré ministry and delaying ratification of the debt settlement.[49] More important, State and Treasury officials developed misgivings about the embargo because of their growing apprehensions about the ramifications of the loan review process. The irony of objecting to many sound loans to France while acquiescing to many questionable loans to Germany was a continual source of consternation. Moreover, officials feared the possibility of an exchange crisis in Germany, at which time the British and French governments were sure to try to postpone service on private loans while attempting to extract reparation payments. If such a crisis occurred, Republican officials anticipated enormous pressures from the banking and investment community to safeguard American loans that the administration had cautioned against but not blocked. If Republican officials bowed to these pressures and intervened in the European situation, they were likely to encounter demands from former Allies for decreases in the war debts or pleas from

47. Jones to Hoover, 17 February 1927, HHCD, Box 376; Memorandum of conversation between Harrison, Finletter, and Currier, 17 March 1927, RG 59, 851.51/1068; "Memorandum on French Financing," by Arthur N. Young, 3 May 1927, ibid., 851.51/1108.
48. "The State Department and Foreign Loans," pp. 6–7.
49. For an analysis of the French financial situation circulating in government circles, see Morrow to Coolidge, 21 June 1927, RG 59, 851.51/1129; see also Floyd G. Blair to Mills (includes letter from P. F. Fatzer to G. K. Weeks, 23 February 1927), RG 39, Box 47; Thomas W. Lamont to Kellogg, 29 December 1927, RG 59, 851.51/1263; for the factors influencing American officials to change their position on the French loan embargo, see also Memorandum of conversation between John Calvin Brown, Arthur N. Young, and Castle, 29 September 1927, ibid., 611.5131/601; Robert E. Olds, Memorandum, 4 January 1928, ibid., 851.51/1298; Morrow to Lamont and Dean Jay, 8 July 1927, Morrow Papers; Russell Leffingwell to Lamont, 12 July 1927, Thomas W. Lamont Papers, Box 103.

Germany for American aid in liberating the Rhineland. Responding to such requests would involve either sacrificing the interests of American taxpayers or embroiling the nation in European political affairs. The first option posed serious domestic political problems; the administration's loan review process was already under serious attack from Senator Carter Glass. The second option constituted an undesirable diplomatic course of action. Such ominous alternatives convinced State and Treasury officials of the wisdom of revising existing loan procedures, including the embargo on loans to France and the futile warnings regarding loans to Germany. The loan review process, originally instituted to encourage the productive use of American capital, was damaging the nation's relations with France, threatening to embroil the government in European political affairs, raising the probability of a nasty domestic political controversy, and exacerbating legislative-executive relations.[50]

Throughout 1927, however, Hoover sought to preserve the review process and maintain the embargo on most loans to France. Yet, his position remained enigmatic. While rhetorically supporting the review procedures in general and disapproving of German loans in particular, Hoover opposed clear-cut efforts to stop the latter.[51] Thus, his stand produced the worst possible results: it did not preclude unproductive loans; yet, it engendered the belief that the government had a responsibility to protect loans it did not formally disapprove. Mellon and Kellogg recognized the liabilities of Hoover's position and of existing policy, but they had no better alternatives to offer. Therefore, they sought to end the ban on French loans and to place primary responsibility for examining German offerings onto the German government. When Hoover became involved in the 1928 presidential race and Con-

50. For the growing anxieties about German loans and the impact of these anxieties on the entire loan review process, see, for example, Harrison to Kellogg, 28 January, 1927, RG 59, 800.51/558; Dorsey Richardson to Castle, 10 April 1927, Castle Papers, Box 3; Castle to Richardson, 20 April 1927, ibid.; J. T. M. to Castle, 21 June 1927, RG 59, 800.51/566; Mills to Kellogg, 15 July 1927, RG 39, Box 85; Grosvenor Jones to Hoover, 5 November 1927, Records of the BFDC, RG 151, File 640; Kellogg to American diplomatic officers and certain consular officers, 28 December 1927, RG 59, 800.51/572a; Olds, Memorandum, 4 January 1928, ibid., 851.51/1298; Frank Livesey, "Federal Supervision over the Investment Merits of Foreign Securities," 30 March 1928, ibid., 800.51/599; for Glass's view, see Carter Glass, "Government Supervision of Foreign Loans," pp. 45–51; for policymakers' warnings about German loans, see, for example, Castle to Sullivan and Cromwell, 11 October 1927, RG 59, 862.51P95/40.

51. For Hoover's views on foreign loan policy in the 1920s, see especially Hoover to secretary of commerce, 9 January 1932, Herbert C. Hoover Presidential Papers, Box 876 (hereafter cited as HHPP); Jones to Robert Lamont, 13 July 1929, ibid., Box 871; Castle to Alanson Houghton, 7 January 1926, Castle Papers, Box 2.

gress continued to criticize official policy, Mellon and Kellogg reduced the government's oversight of capital exports and terminated its embargo on most French security offerings in the United States.[52]

During 1928, then, Republican officials curtailed their attempts to regulate the flow of private capital to Europe. The interdepartmental loan review process, relying on the voluntary cooperation of bankers and postulating the financial hegemony of the United States, did not function as officials had hoped. In their search for lucrative profits many bankers—especially those in less prestigious firms—refused to cooperate with the government, ignored its warnings, and circumvented its guidelines. At one time or another almost all key policymakers, including Hoover, Winston, Castle, Harrison, Strong, and Gilbert, became infuriated with the irresponsibility of Wall Street.[53] Rather than increase governmental intervention, however, all of them, with the exception of Hoover, believed that abandoning government guidelines was the best solution since it diminished the possibility of political embroilments abroad and partisan controversies at home. This approach to the problem seemed especially attractive as policymakers perceived the growing financial power of France and appreciated the resentment engendered in that nation by the loan embargo. Although withdrawal of the embargo did have a favorable impact on the French government,[54] it nevertheless signified a larger failure of American diplomacy. Since it came at the time that policymakers relaxed their efforts to control loans to Germany, the end of the loan embargo symbolized the failure of Republican officials to find a means of systematizing the export of private capital for peaceful and productive purposes without engendering unwanted political embroilments in the Old World.

52. For the attempt to place primary responsibility on the German government, see, for example, Wilbur Carr to American Embassy, Germany, 26 September 1927, RG 59, 862.51P95/42; for the differences between Hoover, on the one hand, and Mellon and Kellogg, on the other hand, see *Commercial and Financial Chronicle* 124 (7 May 1927):2687–88; Leffingwell to Lamont, 12, 20 July 1927, Thomas W. Lamont Papers, Box 103; for the end of the embargo on most French loans, see Department of State to interested firms, 13 January 1928, RG 59, 851.51/1282a, 1282b, 1282c. . . .

53. See, for example, Gilbert to Strong, 19 April 1926, RG 39, Box 85; Strong to Gilbert, 24 September 1927, RG 59, 862.51P95/43; Harrison to Kellogg, 28 January 1927, ibid., 800.51/558. Some bankers worried about the irresponsibility of their colleagues. See Ilse Mintz, *Deterioration in the Quality of Foreign Bonds Issued in the United States, 1920–1930*, pp. 54–58, 63–86, especially pp. 67–68; see also Leffingwell to Lamont, 20 July 1927, Thomas W. Lamont Papers, Box 103.

54. Whitehouse to Kellogg, 19 January 1928, RG 59, 851.51/1304.

The faltering of American loan policy was accompanied by a grow-ing rigidity in the handling of the war debts. In 1927 the wDC was disbanded. Having completed negotiations with all the debtors, the administration seemed unwilling to engage in an ongoing review of prevailing agreements. Even Treasury officials feared the confusion and discord that might arise from a full-scale revision of the debt settlements. Mellon maintained that the great virtue of the existing accords was that they introduced an important element of stability after a long and dangerous period of uncertainty.[55]

The French refusal to ratify the Mellon-Bérenger agreement, how-ever, continued to serve as a reference point for the critics of Repub-lican war debt policy. Taking note of French unhappiness with the existing accord, members of the faculties of Columbia and Princeton universities petitioned the administration in late 1926 and early 1927 to revise the debt settlements. At about the same time, several prominent Americans visiting Paris announced their opposition to the existing debt agreements. According to American diplomats, these outbursts tended to stir up latent hostility to American policy and retard French ratification of the debt agreement. Although after 1926 there were only a handful of Americans who called for more lenient treatment of the European debtors, their voices tended to raise illusory hopes of a change in American policy.[56]

With the wDC no longer operating, Hoover and Mellon were the two Republican officials who continued to concern themselves with the war debt issue. As secretary of commerce, self-appointed overseer of the nation's economic life, and presidential aspirant, Hoover began to express strong opposition to further reductions in Allied payments and to linkage of the war debt and reparation issues. In an elaborate memo-randum prepared under his direction in the Department of Commerce, Hoover maintained that "further cancellation is both inequitable and impolitic." The secretary of commerce argued that war debt payments did not constitute a serious burden on foreign budgets because they never exceeded 4 percent of a debtor government's annual expendi-tures. In the case of France war debt payments amounted to only 1.3

---

55. Department of the Treasury, *Annual Report of the Secretary of the Treasury*, 1927, p. 321; see also Winston to Kellogg, 5 July 1928, RG 59, 800.51W89/328.

56. Herrick to Henry B. Joy, 18 March 1927, Herrick Papers, Box 21; George S. Messersmith to Kellogg, 22 March 1927, RG 59, 800.51W89/272; for the decreasing numbers of public critics, see Wilson, *American Business*, p. 147.

percent. Nor did Hoover feel that a foreign country's payment capacity was harmed either by America's protective tariff policy or her merchandise export surplus. In fact, Hoover demonstrated that, on a percentage basis, American imports from Europe were increasing much more rapidly than exports to the Old World. Moreover, the critical variable affecting European capacity, according to Hoover, was the growing importance of the invisible items in America's balance sheet. These invisible items were so important in the case of France that the United States actually had an unfavorable balance of payments with that nation. American tourist expenditures in France and payments to the French merchant marine exceeded the sums accruing to the United States from its merchandise export surplus and its receipt of war debt payments. Statistics of this sort led Hoover to the "inescapable conclusion . . . that the tariff has little or no effect on the ability of Europe to transfer her debt payments to the United States."[57]

Although Mellon was less rigid than Hoover on this issue, he refused to put himself in the vanguard of a cancellationist movement. In January 1928 Mellon spoke to Gilbert about the prospects for war debt revision, should this matter come up during the agent general's attempts to arrange a final reparations accord. Mellon's position was equivocal. Apparently, he did not rule out the possibility of future American concessions. But Mellon remained sensitive to the views of cabinet colleagues and prominent senators. He insisted that European nations take the initiative and agree to a reparations settlement without assurances of reciprocal American concessions. While publicly acknowledging a link between war debts and reparations and privately sympathizing with Gilbert's efforts to revise the Dawes Plan, the secretary of the treasury felt compelled to defend the interests of American taxpayers and emphasize France's capacity to meet her existing obligations. Moreover, with elections forthcoming and Borah declaring himself "utterly opposed to any cancellation," Mellon did not think that Congress would accept a more favorable agreement with France.[58]

57. "Memorandum on War Debt Settlements," 1927, HHCD, Box 365; see also Ray Hall, "French-American Balance of Payments in 1928: Our Unfavorable Position," *The Annalist* 34 (8 November 1929):908.
58. For Mellon's views, see Mellon to Herrick, 17 March 1927, Herrick Papers, Box 22; Mellon to Kellogg, 17 March 1927, ibid.; Department of the Treasury, *Annual Report*, 1927, pp. 320–25; World War Foreign Debt Commission (WDC), *Combined Annual Reports of the World War Foreign Debt Commission*, pp. 59–60; for inferences about Mellon's contacts with Gilbert, see Strong to Gilbert, 3, 27 March 1928, Strong Papers, 1012.2; DBFP, 1A, 4:212–13, 257–58; see also pp. 183–85 below; for Borah's view, see Borah to F. H. Plaistid, 7 January 1927, Borah Papers, Box 276.

Gilbert relayed Mellon's views to Poincaré and found the French premier willing to accommodate American wishes. Poincaré was no longer preoccupied with attacking American war debt policy. Instead, he wanted to arrange a final reparations agreement that would preserve a positive balance or net-creditor status for France when all reparation and war debt obligations were settled. If he could succeed in arranging such an indemnity agreement, Poincaré was prepared to ask the Chamber of Deputies to accept the existing debt accords with the United States and Great Britain. Since the $400 million war stocks debt to the United States would have to be paid in mid-1929 if the Mellon-Bérenger accord were not ratified, Poincaré was increasingly anxious to resolve the ratification question, provided he could first secure a satisfactory reparations settlement.[59]

In effect, the French premier was moving to align the positions of France and the United States, the two nations that claimed a net-creditor status as a result of the intergovernmental war debt obligations.[60] Although Poincaré and other French officials appeared to trust and like Gilbert, Strong, and Mellon, the French recognized that Hoover would probably emerge as the next president. Hoover's strong bias against reopening the war debt issue was well known in European political and financial circles.[61] Anticipating an intransigent American stand, Poincaré sought to protect French interests by reconciling the French and American positions. Poincaré's actions reduced the pressure on the United States government to reappraise its own war debt policies and placed an additional burden on Great Britain and Germany, nations less able to afford financial sacrifices.

As on commercial issues, the French and American positions on war debts became more reconcilable during 1928, but at the expense of European stability. If economic diplomacy were to function successfully, debt agreements had to be readjusted on the basis of a nation's capacity to pay. But the growing influence of Hoover retarded such action. Although Hoover was shrewd enough to support his position

59. For French policy under Poincaré, see DBFP, 1A, 4:212–14; 5:58, 79–80, 190, 267–69, 305, 315, 392–94; Gilbert to Kellogg, 4 October 1928, RG 39, Box 78; Gilbert to Kellogg and Mellon, 23 October 1928, ibid.; Jacobson, *Locarno Diplomacy*, pp. 156–67; Étienne Weill-Raynal, *Les Réparations allemandes et la France*, 3:403–5.

60. Britain, in effect, abandoned her claims as a net creditor in the Balfour note of August 1922.

61. For Poincaré's relationship with Gilbert, see DBFP, 1A, 4:212–14, 320–21; for Moreau's relations with Gilbert and Strong, see, for example, Emile Moreau, *Souvenirs d'un gouverneur de la Banque de France*, pp. 528–29, 566–69; for warnings regarding Hoover's positions, see ibid., p. 567; DBFP, 1A, 5:81, 130.

with elaborate statistical data, his arguments were flawed. He emphasized that imports were increasing relatively faster than exports, but he overlooked the fact that this increase did not keep the absolute gap between exports and imports from widening. He justified American debt policy by depicting France's growing financial strength, but he did not explain that this growth was the result, at least in part, of French monetary and reparation policies that exacerbated financial problems in Great Britain and Germany. He stressed that war debt transfers constituted a small percentage of the foreign trade of debtor nations, but he never carefully assessed the overall payments problems of European nations, especially Great Britain and Germany. Had he done so, he would have been compelled to acknowledge the interrelationships between the war debt and reparation issues. In other words Hoover's use of evidence to prove that American debt policy was not harmful to Europe was selective and misleading.[62]

Yet, few Americans were inclined to challenge Hoover's findings and debate the one policymaker whose reputation was built on his supposed ability to analyze empirical data objectively. Moreover, the prevailing health of the domestic economy and the return of almost all European currencies to the gold exchange standard suggested that Hoover might be correct in his complacent assessment of existing realities. Those financiers who were aware of underlying problems hesitated to speak out lest they be accused of trying to safeguard their private loans at the expense of American taxpayers.[63] Similarly, party leaders feared that if they reversed their positions and acknowledged a link between reparations and war debts, they might be attacked by the opposition.[64] In an election year, with farmers calling for agricultural subsidies, westerners demanding water resource projects, southerners and New Englanders pleading for flood control programs, and big-navy supporters requesting increased armaments expenditures, there were more expedient things to do with the government's revenues than reduce foreign war debt payments or link them to the reparations issue.[65]

62. These generalizations are based on an analysis of Hoover's major statements on United States war debt and tariff policies. See, for example, his "Memorandum on War Debt Settlements," 1927; Hoover, *New Day*, pp. 128–43.

63. William Castle, who supported Hoover's presidential aspirations in 1928, noted that the Morgan partners opposed Hoover's nomination because of his stand on the war debts. Castle then charged that the Morgan partners were trying to enhance bankers' profits. See Castle to Mrs. Parker Maddox, 10 February 1928, Castle Papers, Box 3.

64. S. Parker Gilbert reported this possibility to Ronald Lindsay. See DBFP, 1A, 4:258.

65. For the demands of different interest groups, see Donald R. McCoy, *Calvin Coolidge*, pp. 322–35.

Thus, no influential spokesman, either inside or outside the administration, emerged to challenge Hoover's defense of official war debt policy. As a result efforts to revise the Dawes Plan were greatly complicated.

Reparations

For several years the tact, integrity, and intelligence of S. Parker Gilbert enabled him to oversee the successful operation of the Dawes Plan and gain the confidence of European leaders.[66] The Dawes Plan, however, had never been intended as a permanent solution to the reparations controversy. The plan was supposed to serve as an experiment to determine how much Germany could pay without undermining the stability of her currency. German payments were scheduled to increase gradually over a five-year period until the standard annuity of 2.5 billion marks was reached in 1928–29. A prosperity index would then reveal whether Germany could make payments above the standard annuity. The number of annuities and the total amount of payments were left unsettled. These issues were reserved for subsequent discussions under more favorable political circumstances, when experience would provide some indication of how much Germany could pay and how much the ex-Allies could absorb.[67]

By 1927 Gilbert had grasped the financial weaknesses and political shortcomings of the Dawes Plan and was beginning to consider the merits of a permanent revision. He was especially disturbed by the extravagant financial practices of the German government, the irresponsible monetary policies of the Reichsbank, the maladroit administration of the German railroad system, and the indiscriminate lending by American bankers. The agent general feared that a combination of these factors might touch off a financial crisis and jeopardize German credit. He believed he could safeguard the German financial structure most effectively by arranging a final reparations settlement.[68] This

66. For Poincaré's satisfaction with Gilbert's work, see DBFP, 1A, 4:212–14; for the view of the British Treasury, see ibid., p. 94; see also Lamont to Leffingwell, 30 April 1925, Thomas W. Lamont Papers, Box 103.

67. For the experimental nature of the Dawes Plan, see Owen Young to Nelson Perkins, 29 January 1926, Young Papers, I–13; Allied Powers, Agent General for Reparations, *The Execution of the Experts' Plan, 1925–1926*, pp. 177–79.

68. Gilbert to Morrow, 6 May 1927, Morrow Papers, Gilbert to Strong, 8 September 1927, Strong Papers, 1012.2; Gustav Stresemann, *Diaries, Letters, and Papers*, 3:278–83; DBFP, 1A, 4:82–83, 121, 176–77; Gilbert to Strong, 14 November 1927, Castle Papers, Box 5; Herrick to Kellogg, 27 May 1928, RG 59, 426.00R296/2258; Allied Powers, *Experts' Plan, 1926–27*, pp. 147–49, 172–78, 209–12, 233–53, 315–18.

task had great personal appeal to Gilbert as well. He had grown tired of his job and was eager to undertake new responsibilities, but he wanted to cap his achievements as agent general with a resolution of the reparations controversy.[69]

A successful agreement, according to Gilbert, not only had to stipulate the total amount of the indemnity but also had to grant the German government full responsibility for meeting its obligations. Such a settlement, Gilbert argued, would enhance Germany's economic capacity, since Germans would no longer fear that gains in their productivity, revenues, and savings would be taken away as reparations. With this apprehension allayed, the agent general predicted that German finances would be handled more conservatively, the Reichsbank managed more effectively, and savings increased. Gilbert assumed that a final reparations accord would enable German industrialists to borrow more cheaply and encourage American bankers to loan more prudently. Agreement, moreover, would allow for more amicable political discussions between French and German leaders.[70]

Once the positive attributes of a reparations agreement were clear to him, Gilbert began consulting with Mellon, Strong, Lamont, Morrow, and Owen Young. They all believed that resolution of the reparations issue would mitigate international financial problems, stimulate world commerce, and protect American loans and investments. During 1927 the broad outlines of a comprehensive settlement to the intergovernmental debt problem began to emerge out of their discussions. This settlement proposed reducing German reparation annuities, setting a total indemnity, and terminating the mechanisms established under the Dawes Plan to safeguard the German currency when reparation transfers were made. American financial leaders also suggested commercializing German reparation obligations and marketing them in the world's financial centers, with proceeds used by the former Allies to liquidate at least part of their indebtedness to the United States. The twin goals of the American plan included prepayment of all wartime obligations, at substantial discounts if necessary, and removal of the intergovernmental indebtedness issue from the international political arena.[71]

69. See Charles G. Dawes, *Notes as Vice President, 1928–1929*, p. 157; DBFP, 1A, 5:82, 114–15.

70. Gilbert to Strong, 14 November 1927, Strong Papers, 1012.2; Agent General, Memorandum for the Reparation Commission, 24 February 1928, RG 59, 462.00R296/2162; DBFP, 1A, 5:57–58, 195–201; Allied Powers, *Experts' Plan*, 1926–1927, pp. 315–18.

71. Morrow to Lamont and Leffingwell, 5, 6 May 1927, Thomas W. Lamont Papers,

Gilbert realized the enormous problems of working out such a settlement. With elections coming up in France, Germany, and the United States in 1928, and in England in 1929, no government would likely have the flexibility to make significant concessions. Securing agreement on a reparations sum high enough to satisfy the Allied governments and low enough to gain German approval was bound to be a formidable task. Moreover, the financial problems impeding settlement were almost as difficult as the political ones. A wave of stock market speculation erupted in early 1927, abated for a while, and intensified after January 1928. Under these circumstances commercialization and capitalization of reparation bonds were anything but assured.[72]

Despite these formidable problems, the agent general decided to lay the groundwork for settlement. Gilbert feared that if he did not act quickly, Germany's growing indebtedness might impair her credit and foreclose the possibility of marketing additional reparation bonds.[73] In December 1927 he visited Paris and talked to Poincaré about the nature and timing of an accord. Both men felt it wise for European governments to work out an agreement after the American elections.[74] Such timing might prevent the intergovernmental debt issue from being injected into the presidential campaign. Gilbert and Poincaré reasoned that a newly elected president would thus arrive at the White House without having committed himself on the debt issue. If the new president then witnessed European governments taking forthright action to resolve the reparations question, he might ask Congress for authority to deal with the war debts in a generous manner.[75]

Such were Gilbert's expectations before he voyaged to the United States in late December 1927, discussed the political and financial

Box 113; Lamont to Morrow, 6 May 1927, ibid.; Leffingwell to Lamont, 20 July 1927, ibid., Box 103; Lamont to Robbins, 16 January 1928, ibid., Box 80; Gilbert to Morrow, 16 May 1927, Morrow Papers; Arthur N. Young to Kellogg, 28 November 1927, RG 59, 462.00R296/2054; Owen Young to Basil Miles, 9 January 1928, Young Papers, R–30; Gilbert to Castle, 22 August 1927, Castle Papers, Box 5; DBFP, 1A, 5:358.

72. For the problems of working out an accord, see Lamont to Robbins, 16 January 1928, Thomas W. Lamont Papers, Box 80; Leffingwell to Lamont, 20 July 1927, ibid., Box 103; Gilbert to Morrow, 16 May 1927, Morrow Papers; Gilbert to Pierre Jay, 24, 25 September 1928, Young Papers, R–30; DBFP, 1A, 4:82, 121, 212–14.

73. Gilbert to Strong, 14 November 1927, Castle Papers, Box 5.

74. For reference to the talks between Gilbert and Poincaré, see DBFP, 1A, 4:212–14; for an excellent portrayal of European diplomacy as it related to the issues of reparations, war debts, and the Rhineland occupation, see Jacobson, Locarno Diplomacy, pp. 119–349.

75. This is inferred from Strong to Gilbert, 3, 27 March 1928, Strong Papers, 1012.2; see also DBFP, 1A, 4:320–21.

situation with Mellon, Strong, Lamont, and Morrow, and observed the rising political star of Hoover. This visit convinced Gilbert that he could not offer European leaders assurances regarding future American action on the war debts. But this realization did not dissuade Gilbert from his goal of arranging a reparations settlement. Instead, he proceeded to arrange an accord within the limitations imposed by the American position. This orientation meant that the burden of a reparations agreement would fall entirely on the European powers and not be shared by the United States, at least not in the short run. Either the reparation creditors would have to reduce their demands on Germany, regardless of their own commitments to the United States, or Germany would have to pay a heavier burden than she felt capable of bearing.[76]

Gilbert's answer to this dilemma was straightforward: Germany would have to pay a heavy price for a final accord. Although he envisioned a settlement that would substantially reduce the reparations total of 132 billion marks agreed on in 1921, Gilbert did not think that the average German payment would be more than 20 percent below the standard annuity proposed in the Dawes Plan. Gilbert believed that the advantages to Germany of a final settlement were so evident that even a slight reduction in annual payments would appeal to German leaders. A final reparations accord would reduce the cost of credit, enhance Germany's competitive ability, and stimulate German production and exports. A settlement would also hasten France's withdrawal from the Rhineland. Thus, the short-term burden of a reparations accord would fall principally on Germany, the nation which, according to Gilbert, had the greatest incentive to bear the burden. Neither French nor British officials had much inclination to reduce reparation payments without commensurate American action on the war debts. The agent general realized that such action was impossible for the immediate future.[77] Consequently, as an independent expert, Gilbert was able to put forth the economic merits of a final accord, even if it depended on large German payments; as an American he agreed to work within the confines set by the more sympathetic interpreters of American public opinion in the Treasury, in the FRBNY, and on Wall Street.[78]

76. This is based on DBFP, 1A, 4:257–59, 320; 5:57–59, 79–82, 447; Gilbert to Strong, 10 July 1928, Strong Papers, 1012.2; Memorandum for the Reparation Commission, 24 February 1928, RG 59, 462.00R296/2162.

77. In addition to citations in previous note, see DBFP, 1A, 4:221–23; 5:13–14, 195–201, 385–86.

78. British, French, and German leaders believed that Gilbert first cleared his ideas with Mellon and a few prominent bankers. See ibid., 1A, 4:212–13, 219–20, 302, 320.

Returning to Europe, Gilbert spent all of 1928 preparing the final reparations settlement. He traveled from one European capital to another presenting his viewpoint, warning of the dangers of delay, and elucidating the benefits that would flow from a resolution of the indemnity issue. Poincaré responded sympathetically. He was willing to proceed toward a settlement, even within the framework of the Mellon-Bérenger accord, so long as German reparation payments covered France's war-debt obligations and paid for a portion of reconstruction costs. Since Gilbert's version of a settlement assured France's wishes, there was no friction between the agent general and the French premier. The British were more wary of Gilbert's efforts. Nevertheless, repeatedly assured that Britain's payments would not exceed her receipts, even Winston Churchill, chancellor of the exchequer, agreed to cooperate with Gilbert.[79]

The Germans, of course, objected to the developing plan. A settlement was being devised that would gear indemnity payments to the minimal demands of the Allies. The newly elected government of Hermann Müller rejected this approach and claimed that it placed an intolerable burden on Germany. The Germans demanded the convocation of another experts' committee, including Americans, to enumerate a schedule of annuities within Germany's capacity to pay. Churchill and Poincaré initially objected, but they agreed to such a procedure when Gilbert suggested that the experts would frame an accord that conformed to the minimum requirements of France and Britain. Gilbert sensed that an experts' report was a political necessity for German leaders. He also believed that such a report would facilitate the marketing of German reparation bonds. Though the agent general managed to get all the European governments to support the meeting of another experts' committee, European leaders continued to perceive its function in divergent ways. The British and French viewed the committee as a rubber stamp of their clearly expressed demands. The Germans saw the meeting as an opportunity to enlist the aid of American experts in behalf of a much more moderate agreement. Gilbert made little effort to clear up these divergent expectations. Had he tried, he would have compromised his goal of achieving a final settlement.[80]

79. Gilbert to Jay, 24, 25 September 1928, Young Papers, R–30; DBFP, 1A, 4:354, 5:114–15, 195–202, 311–12, 354–55, 358–62, 385–86, 392–94, 432–36; Fletcher to Kellogg, 13 April 1928, RG 59, 462.00R296/2229; DeSanchez, Memorandum, 21 August 1928, Thomas W. Lamont Papers, Box 103; Weill-Raynal, *Réparations allemandes*, 3:403–14; Jacobson, *Locarno Diplomacy*, pp. 156–57.

80. Jacobson, *Locarno Diplomacy*, pp. 167–235; DBFP, 1A, 5:387, 392–94, 428–29, 432–36, 438–39, 460–62, 469, 483, 521–25, 543.

Gilbert did appeal to the United States government for its cooperation in the work of the experts' committee. Mellon promised that neither he, the secretary of state, nor the president would say anything to undermine Gilbert's efforts to bring about a reparations accord. Moreover, in late October 1928 Kellogg informed Gilbert that the administration would allow private American citizens to participate on the experts' committee.[81] But the extent of official collaboration was circumscribed by domestic political considerations and fear of entanglements in European political affairs. Most Republican officials opposed linkage of the reparation and war debt issues. They worried about embroilment of the United States in reparations-related discussions over evacuation of the Rhineland.[82] Hence, Republicans would not assume any official responsibility to ease Gilbert's task, though some of them sympathized with his efforts.

Gilbert proposed an accord that was acceptable to the United States and France, but suspect to Britain and repugnant to Germany. The most reputed independent expert of the era was thus compelled to accommodate the political forces operating within the two most financially powerful nations. Although he had compromised the precepts of economic diplomacy, based on the use of nonpolitical experts and the application of objective criteria, Gilbert had few options. In a crisis free atmosphere, no government, least of all the American government, was prepared to risk the domestic political consequences of a generous stand on intergovernmental debts.[83] The experts' committee, scheduled to meet in early 1929, still had a chance of harmonizing the divergent expectations of the respective governments, but the prospects for a viable and amicable reparations settlement were not good.

Currency Stabilization

During 1927 and 1928 governments did not do much to lighten the burden of intergovernmental debt payments on the international monetary system. As a result central bankers shouldered much of the re-

81. Mellon to Gilbert, 10 October 1928, RG 39, Box 78; FR, 1928, 2:873–74.
82. FR, 1928, 2:873–74; Coolidge, *Talkative President*, p. 198; Statement by Undersecretary of State Joseph P. Cotton, House, Committee on Banking and Currency, *German Reparation Bonds*, p. 64. The link between a reparations settlement and the evacuation of the Rhineland became apparent during the September 1928 meetings at Geneva between European leaders. See DBFP, 1A, 5:304–7, 312–21, 327–36; see also DDB, 2:528, 537–39.
83. See Vice-President Dawes's comments on the ramifications of the noncrisis atmosphere, in Dawes, *Notes*, pp. 74–77, 156–57, 197–200.

sponsibility for preserving the stability of major European currencies. Although Governor Strong prodded officials in the United States government to be more sensitive to the problems emanating from reparation and war debt payments, his advice was looked upon with suspicion and distrust, especially in the Commerce and State departments.[84] Without allies in the executive branch, except in the Treasury Department, and always fearful of congressional criticism, Strong refrained from attacking official policy and sought to cooperate more closely with European central bankers and the agent general for reparations.

During the early months of 1927 Strong's greatest concerns included the weakness of the pound sterling and the growing friction between Emile Moreau and Montagu Norman, governors of the Bank of France and the Bank of England respectively.[85] The opportunity to deal with these problems came at a meeting of central bankers during the first week of July 1927 at the Long Island home of Undersecretary of the Treasury Ogden Mills. Attending the sessions at the invitation of Strong and Mills were Norman; Hjalmar Schacht, head of the Reichsbank; and Charles Rist, Moreau's close assistant. Participating in some of the discussions were members of the Federal Reserve System's Open Market Investment Committee and several of the partners of J. P. Morgan and Company. Although the gamut of European financial problems was explored, the participants focused most of their attention on finding means to relieve the pressure on sterling. Norman stressed the critical gold shortage facing England and sought aid through the lowering of discount rates in New York.[86]

After the European central bankers departed, members of the Federal Reserve Board met with the officers of the FRBNY, as well as with the directors of other Federal Reserve banks, to debate the merits of lowering discount rates. Strong emphasized the need to lower rates in order to relieve the financial strain on Britain and the rest of Europe. Otherwise, he explained, European central banks would have to raise their discount rates, which would hurt the European economy and

84. See, for example, Livesey to Young, 27 October 1927, RG 59, 862.51P95/ between 29 and 30; for Hoover's disdain for Strong, see Herbert C. Hoover, *The Memoirs of Herbert Hoover*, 3:5–15.

85. Strong to Moreau, 20 June 1927, Papers of the Federal Reserve Bank of New York (FRBNY Papers), C261.1; Moreau to Strong, 5 July 1927, ibid.; Stephen V. O. Clarke, *Central Bank Cooperation, 1924–1931*, pp. 108–23; Henry Clay, *Lord Norman*, pp. 226–37; Moreau, *Souvenirs*, pp. 324–33.

86. For the meetings of the central bankers, see Diary of Charles S. Hamlin, 7, 8, 25 July 1927, Hamlin Papers, Vol. 14; Leffingwell to Lamont, 12 July 1927, Thomas W. Lamont Papers, Box 103; Clarke, *Central Bank Cooperation*, pp. 123–27.

reduce the overseas sale of American agricultural goods. Moreover, Strong argued that domestic considerations, including slackening business conditions, reinforced the international reasons for reducing rates. He acknowledged that the action he recommended might lead to an increase in stock market speculation. Nevertheless, he believed that such speculation was a small risk to take, given the beneficial impact lowered discount rates would have on European finances, American exports, and domestic business.[87]

Between the end of July and the middle of September, all district banks reduced their rates. In addition, the FRBNY and the Bank of France took steps to ease the pressure on sterling and shift the burden of supplying gold from London to New York.[88] The resulting widely acclaimed central bank cooperation, at least for the short run, resuscitated the pound sterling, eased financial conditions in central Europe, fostered American exports, and stimulated the domestic economy.[89] The secretary and the undersecretary of the treasury enthusiastically praised Strong's efforts to promote European financial stability. Mills stressed that this action constituted one of the highlights of Republican foreign policy. "All this," he wrote, "has contributed not only to the stability of Europe but to the prosperity of this country, for the nations of the world must be reestablished on a sound financial basis if our surplus products . . . are to find an export market."[90]

Strong's policy, however, did have significant negative consequences that became evident during 1928. It accelerated the wave of stock market speculation; it intensified the competition between the FRBNY and the Federal Reserve Board for control of policy within the Federal Reserve System; and it encouraged unproductive loans, stimulated enormous gold exports, and raised doubts about the ability of the FRBNY to control the domestic money market.[91] But, perhaps worst of

87. Diary of Charles S. Hamlin, 25, 27 July 1927, Hamlin Papers, Vol. 14; Ogden Mills, "An Explanation of Federal Reserve Policy," *American Review of Reviews* 78 (July–August 1928):260; Owen D. Young, "Recent Federal Reserve Policy," ibid., pp. 252–54; Roy A. Young, "Money Rates and World Prosperity," *Journal of the American Bankers Association* (December 1928):527, 617–19.

88. Clarke, *Central Bank Cooperation*, pp. 127–34; Clay, *Lord Norman*, pp. 236–37.

89. Even Adolph C. Miller, a member of the Federal Reserve Board and a bitter critic of Strong, subsequently admitted that at the time Strong's actions seemed brilliantly successful. See A. C. Miller, "Responsibility for Federal Reserve Policies, 1927–1929," p. 447.

90. Ogden Mills, "Our Foreign Policy," pp. 566, 572; Department of the Treasury, *Annual Report*, 1928, pp. 348–49.

91. For the stock market speculation, see Young, "Federal Reserve Policy," pp. 253–54; for the competition between the FRBNY and the Federal Reserve Board, see

all, Strong's policy intensified the atmosphere of complacency within American policymaking circles. With the pound and the mark temporarily strengthened, Treasury officials were prone to exaggerate the importance of Strong's efforts and overlook the need for war debt revision. At the same time the improvement in European financial conditions in late 1927 and early 1928 may have accentuated Hoover's belief that American war debt and tariff policies were not exacerbating European financial problems.[92]

The negative ramifications of this policy of monetary ease came to haunt the governor of the FRBNY during 1928. Strong agreed that stock speculation had to be curbed, foreign loans restricted, and gold reserves protected. Between January and July he went along with the Federal Reserve Board's desire to increase discount rates from 3.5 to 5 percent. Although Strong worried that the "maintenance of very high rates in New York may ultimately present a real hazard to Europe," he still refused to make "unreasonable sacrifices at home." He would not promise to lower rates during the summer of 1928. Through central bank cooperation Strong had hoped to balance a variety of internal and external considerations. When these proved irreconcilable, he placed his primary emphasis on stabilizing the internal situation.[93] The unfortunate consequence was a setback to stabilization efforts in Europe.

When Strong made his annual trip to Europe in the spring and summer of 1928, he was sick, tired, and preoccupied with domestic priorities. He was also disillusioned by the breakdown of relations between Norman and Moreau. He hoped to patch up differences between the two central bankers. But when Norman showed no interest, Strong's growing sympathy for Moreau became evident. He respected Moreau's candor and appreciated France's financial power. Moreover, Strong and Moreau shared a growing fear of the gold exchange standard and distrusted the ideas of Norman and other English financiers who wanted to downgrade the role of gold in the international financial

---

Diary of Charles S. Hamlin, 7, 13, 16 July 1927, 9 January 1928, Hamlin Papers, Vol. 14; Miller, "Federal Reserve Policies," pp. 442–58; for the unproductive loans, gold exports, and domestic monetary problems, see Franc C. Costigliola, "The Politics of Financial Stabilization," pp. 386–404.

92. Mills, "Foreign Policy," pp. 566, 572; for Hoover's views, see pp. 172–73, 178–81, above.

93. For the quotations, see Strong to Gilbert, 14 July 1928, Strong Papers, 1012.2; for the factors that Strong considered in molding his policies, see Strong to Moreau, 20 June 1927, FRBNY Papers, C261.1; for Federal Reserve policy during the first half of 1928, see the Diary of Charles S. Hamlin, January to July 1928, Hamlin Papers, Vol. 14; Costigliola, "Financial Stabilization," pp. 401–3.

system. With most of the world's gold in their possession, the governors of the Bank of France and the FRBNY had a common interest in trying to restore the prewar gold standard. Their similar perception of national interests, however, distracted them from tackling the larger problems besetting the international economic and monetary system, such as the decline in raw material prices and the lag between world productive and purchasing power.[94]

By the summer of 1928, though Strong still used the jargon of central bank cooperation, his own concerns had become more nationalistic. His preoccupation with domestic financial conditions, his emphasis on gold, and his exasperation with Norman reflected the shift in Strong's interests. The relations between the Bank of France and the FRBNY were closer than ever, because Moreau and Strong often identified with each other's national interests, not because they shared a common approach toward solving European financial problems. Indeed, when he considered the competitive efforts of Britain and France to dominate the financial affairs of central and eastern Europe, Strong was often as disgruntled with Moreau as he was with Norman. Consequently, by mid-1928 Strong believed that the United States had discharged its moral obligation to Europe. He cautioned against "entering into arrangements which might embarrass us . . . politically or financially."[95]

Given Strong's attitude, the prevailing speculative excesses on Wall Street, and the unfolding electoral campaign, it is not surprising that Federal Reserve discount rates were not lowered in mid-1928. In fact, in July the New York rate went above the London rate. This increase initiated another long period of financial strain in Britain and throughout most of Europe, except France. The high rates in New York discouraged foreign loans and combined with the bullish stock market to drain Europe of capital.[96] In October Strong died. His death symbolized the faltering efforts of central bankers to maintain the stability of European currencies when government officials did not assist in a comprehensive effort to solve complex international financial problems, such as the intergovernmental war debts.

94. Strong, Memoranda, 24, 27 May 1928, Strong Papers, 1000.9; Strong to George Harrison, 6, 8 July 1928, ibid.; Moreau, *Souvenirs*, pp. 566–69; Costigliola, "Financial Stabilization," pp. 378–408; Charles P. Kindleberger, *The World in Depression, 1929–1939*, pp. 58–107.

95. Clarke, *Central Bank Cooperation*, p. 144.

96. Ibid., pp. 147–68; D. E. Moggridge, *British Monetary Policy, 1924–1931*, pp. 135–39.

Conclusion

During 1927 and 1928 friction between the United States and France declined. In part, this decline was symbolized by the goodwill engendered in the aftermath of Charles Lindbergh's first transatlantic flight. But in larger measure the reconciliation of the French and American positions on various issues reflected the growing similarity of interests between net-creditor, high-tariff, relatively self-sufficient nations with enormous gold holdings.

Yet, the improvement in Franco-American relations was not necessarily in the best interests of European stability. Increasingly, the two relatively satisfied nations began moving along parallel lines in defense of the status quo. Recognizing the financial strength and legitimate interests of one another, neither government found it desirable to challenge the vital interests of the other. Though each disapproved of the other's policies, the United States government acquiesced to the French view on security and land disarmament, and the French government bowed to the American position on war debts and tariffs. The quasi-official experts working on reparation and currency problems took note of their governments' views, acknowledged the similarity of interests between the two nations, and proceeded within the guidelines set by government policies. Consequently, pressures to reduce intergovernmental indebtedness subsided, plans to weaken the barriers to international trade never came to fruition, suggestions to reform the international financial system were ignored, and proposals to break the security-disarmament deadlock were not fully explored.

The improved relations between France and the United States did not result from conscious American policymaking. Indeed, the most conspicuous aspects of the American decision-making process during this period were its decentralization, excessive optimism, and parochialism. Policy was molded on particular issues by numerous decision makers with different perceptions, constituencies, ambitions, and motivations. Strong, Gilbert, Mellon, and the Morgan partners tried to cooperate with one another on matters pertaining to reparations, currency stabilization, and private loans. But they had little control over debt and tariff policies, which were caught in the impasse between executive and legislative authority. Even within the executive branch, it was unclear which department or commission determined debt and tariff policies. With the dissolution of the WDC, both Hoover and Mellon concentrated on the debt issue. But they leaned toward different positions, with Mellon sympathetic to Wall Street, Hoover sensitive to Main Street, and neither anxious to approach Congress about the matter. The situation was much the same with American trade policy. State, Commerce, and Tariff Commission officials planned strategy to disseminate the unconditional most-favored-nation principle. But they did not engage in a comprehensive interdepartmental review of the impact of American tariff policy on the nation's foreign policy goals. Instead, they preferred to defer to Congress to avoid additional legislative-executive acrimony.

Without a strong chief executive and with no cabinet official coordinating policy and instituting action, many policymakers accepted the assumption that prosperity itself would provide the solutions to the problems besetting the relations between the United States and Europe. Hoover and Mellon maintained that as long as there was peace and stability, trade would increase and economic growth would take place, progressively minimizing the burden of intergovernmental debts. In a similar vein American policymakers often expressed their view that domestic prosperity would breed a large market for foreign goods regardless of tariff barriers. Thus, prosperity and complacency reinforced one another, stultifying the policymaking process and engendering illusions that in the long run undermined both peace and stability. Policymakers forgot that the peace and stability of the mid-1920s resulted from constructive and innovative actions in the early part of the decade. Stability did not rest on lethargy; it demanded systematic if nondramatic action to keep pace with the changes and challenges it engendered.

Republican economic diplomacy faltered because foreign policy initiatives threatened to collide with domestic priorities, stimulate partisan controversies, exacerbate legislative-executive relations, and generate political embroilments abroad. In other words many latent problems were recognized; solutions were discussed and sometimes planned. But the impetus to take forthright action was lacking. Since European problems were no longer seen as grave and the international consequences of inaction no longer considered ominous, policymakers tended to exaggerate the possible risks and discount the probable benefits of diplomatic initiatives. In an era of national security, relative prosperity, and official complacency, the policymaking approaches devised between 1921 and 1923 lost their vitality. Finding their national interests increasingly reconcilable with those of France, American officials felt less pressure to take risks in behalf of European stability.

[6]

Changing Times,
Old Approaches, 1929–1930

During his campaign for the presidency in 1928 Herbert Hoover repeatedly declared that "our country has entered upon an entirely new era." He recognized the creditor status of the United States and emphasized the interdependence of all nations in the technological age. Hoover maintained that through intelligent study, systematic effort, and cooperative action, the American people could play a responsible role in the struggle for world order.[1] Like his predecessors in the presidential office after World War I, Hoover acknowledged the importance of European stability to American self-interest. But he wanted the European nations to assume a larger share of the responsibility for maintaining stability in the Old World. This attitude reflected the growing belief in Republican policymaking circles that Europe had "arrived at a state of financial stability and prosperity" at which it could handle most of its own problems.[2]

This orientation, a product of the halcyon days of the late 1920s, became particularly inappropriate when the western world was buffeted by a succession of financial, economic, and political shocks. Yet much of the diplomacy of 1929 and 1930 was conceived during Hoover's first months in the presidency, prior to the stock market crash and the onset of the Great Depression. Upon taking office, Hoover advocated strengthening the Tariff Commission, supported the use of experts to resolve the reparations issue, and encouraged the convocation of another international conference to limit armaments. Hoover's campaign rhetoric notwithstanding, these foreign policy initiatives were firmly

1. Herbert C. Hoover, *The New Day*, pp. 97–98.
2. See Coolidge's Armistice Day speech, *Commercial and Financial Chronicle* 127 (17 November 1928):2761.

rooted in the diplomatic approaches of the early 1920s. They owed more to the past than to the future. Only in 1931, when a new era was indeed under way, would the president and his advisers feel compelled to reassess the efficacy of economic diplomacy.

The Hawley-Smoot Tariff and American Commercial Policy

On 4 March 1929 Hoover delivered his inaugural address and focused most of his attention on domestic social problems. Although he alluded to "the profound truth that our own progress, prosperity, and peace are interlocked with the progress, prosperity, and peace of all humanity," he made not a single reference to the ongoing attempts of the reparation experts to settle the indemnity issue or to the preparations of European governments to arrange a "final liquidation of the war." The president was preoccupied with internal affairs, and his first order of business was to convene a special session of Congress to secure "agricultural relief and limited changes in the tariff."[3]

In planning for farm relief and tariff revision, Republican officials believed the domestic market afforded the best protection to American industry and agriculture. In April 1929 Secretary of Commerce Robert P. Lamont emphasized the many advantages of the nation's relative self-containment. "A foreign trade that is too large in proportion to domestic production," he warned, "involves a dependence that means risk." Accordingly, the Hoover administration sought internal cures to the country's chronic agricultural problem. The president wanted to create a federal farm board to expedite the efficient marketing of agricultural goods within the United States. He desired increased tariffs on agricultural imports to encourage diversification of crops and reduce dependence on foreign markets. This emphasis on domestic tactics did not mean that the president and his advisers were sympathetic to wholesale increases in the tariff schedule. Hoover emphasized that "it is obviously unwise protection which sacrifices a greater amount of employment in exports to gain a less amount of employment from imports." Only those industries which had experienced a "substantial slackening of activity," he said, were entitled to additional protection. In other words Hoover tried to mold commercial policy by balancing his primary concern for the domestic market with his secondary but substantial desire to expand exports. The means of accomplishing this

3. Herbert C. Hoover, *The State Papers and Other Public Writings of Herbert Hoover*, 1:3–12; for a discussion of European efforts to arrange a final liquidation of the war, see Jon Jacobson, *Locarno Diplomacy*, pp. 287–349.

goal, Hoover told Congress, was to strengthen the Tariff Commission, revitalize the flexible tariff provisions, and reaffirm the principle of equalizing costs of production at home and abroad.[4]

Congress, however, did not respond positively to the president's requests. Willis C. Hawley and Reed Smoot, the powerful chairmen of the House Ways and Means Committee and the Senate Finance Committee respectively, put an even greater emphasis than did Hoover on protecting the domestic market. The vast majority of senators and congressmen disregarded the international economic and financial ramifications of tariff revision. Most of them shared Smoot's belief that "the most striking feature of America's rise to the position of foremost industrial nation in the world is the creation of our immense domestic market." Hardly a word was said during the congressional debates about the complex interrelationships between customs duties, war debt payments, European finances, and international financial stability. Most legislators, regardless of party affiliation, sought higher duties. But Democrats in particular tried to weaken the president's power by authorizing the Tariff Commission to report directly to Congress rather than to the chief executive. As a result the president's request for limited tariff revision became immersed in a whirlwind of partisan controversies, legislative-executive rivalries, sectional jealousies, and personal struggles. In this atmosphere effective presidential leadership broke down. In November 1929 the special session of Congress closed without enacting any tariff legislation.[5]

Throughout the spring of 1929 the State Department had carefully observed the course of tariff revision in Congress. Officials were anxious to secure congressional action that would expedite their efforts to negotiate unconditional most-favored-nation treaties. They feared that the entire commercial policy of the United States would be jeopardized if American duties were raised. The trend toward upward revision, they predicted, would reinvigorate France's opposition to the most-

4. For Lamont's speech, see National Foreign Trade Council (NFTC), *Official Report of the National Foreign Trade Convention*, 1929, pp. 13–14; for Hoover's views, see Hoover, *State Papers*, 1:31–37.
5. For Smoot's view, see Reed Smoot, "Our Tariff and the Depression," pp. 173–82, especially p. 178; for congressional attitudes, see Frank W. Fetter, "Congressional Trade Theory," pp. 413–27; William R. Allen, "Issues in Congressional Tariff Debates, 1890–1930," pp. 340–55; "Majority and Minority Committee Reports on Tariff Bill," *Congressional Digest* 8 (June–July 1929):173–78; see also Elmer E. Schattschneider, *Politics, Pressures, and the Tariff*; Harris Gaylord Warren, *Herbert Hoover and the Great Depression*, pp. 84–94; Frank W. Taussig, *The Tariff History of the United States*, pp. 489–501.

favored-nation principle and drive other nations in western Europe into France's camp.[6]

The assessments of State Department officials were correct. Coming at a time when the reparation experts were working out a final accord, when Poincaré was planning to request legislative ratification of the debt settlements, and when the League of Nations was arranging a tariff truce, the prospects of an upward revision in United States tariffs caused consternation in France. Characteristically, the prominent, nationalist French newspaper *L'Echo de Paris* editorialized that "the American tariff wall is the most vital and most serious problem before the world today." In early June a group of French businessmen met in Paris, bitterly condemned American tariff revisions, and petitioned the government to concert with other European nations in an effort to combat American action. In this atmosphere Briand's idea of the United States of Europe gained increased attention. In fact, the French statesman decided to capitalize on prevailing sentiment and introduce the idea of a European federal union at the tenth assembly of the League of Nations in September 1929. Writing in *Foreign Affairs*, André Siegfried explained that American tariff action impelled European leaders to consider plans for unity to ward off American domination.[7]

President Hoover and his closest advisers realized that American interests would be endangered if the movement toward European union assumed an anti-American orientation.[8] Nevertheless, as the process of congressional tariff making dragged on through the winter and spring of 1930 with seeming indifference to the changing economic climate, executive officials did not act systematically to prevent wholesale tariff revisions from taking place. On several occasions both before and after the stock market crash, Hoover reiterated his unhappiness with contemplated tariff increases. But he exerted his full influence only in

6. Frank B. Kellogg to Willis C. Hawley, 26 February 1929, General Records of the Department of State, RG 59, File 611.003/1172; Wallace McClure, Memorandum, 30 March 1929, ibid., 611.003/1151; Frank Livesey to William R. Castle, 6 April 1929, ibid., 611.003/1513; Theodore W. Marriner, Divisional Economic Memoranda, nos. 1 and 2, 8 May 1929, ibid., 611.003/1524½.

7. For the quotation from *L'Echo de Paris*, see "Shouting Down Our Tariff Wall," *Literary Digest* 102 (20 July 1929):5; see also Norman Armour to Henry L. Stimson, 5 June 1929, RG 59, 611.003/1562; Armour to Stimson, 17, 18 July 1929, ibid., 840.00/91, 92; André Siegfried, "European Reactions to American Tariff Proposals," pp. 13–19. Briand also hoped that the European federal union would enhance French security, especially as Allied troops were withdrawn from the Rhineland. See Sally Marks, *The Illusion of Peace*, pp. 104–5.

8. Castle to Stimson, 6 June 1929, RG 59, 611.003/1916; Stimson to Hoover, 9 June 1929, ibid.; McClure, Memorandum, 23 September 1929, ibid., 840.00/105.

behalf of flexible tariff provisions and a strengthened Tariff Commission. He insisted that through the proper administration of flexible tariff provisions, the Tariff Commission could correct the abuses of congressional logrolling, accommodate changing economic circumstances, and remedy legitimate foreign complaints. Moreover, he contended that for the flexible tariff provisions to operate effectively, the president had to retain ultimate authority to accept or reject the recommendations of the Tariff Commission.[9]

Eventually, Hoover signed the Hawley-Smoot legislation only because in its final form it did incorporate the flexible tariff provisions, the formula for equalizing costs of production, and a revitalized Tariff Commission. Although he recognized that many abuses in rate making had occurred, Hoover minimized their significance because the new legislation was based on assumptions and principles he had long espoused. The protective principle inherent in the policy of equalizing costs of production accorded with his view that tariff protection was the most important of all American economic policies. The flexible tariff provisions in section 336 accorded with his customary emphasis on the use of experts to implement general principles and reconcile conflicting imperatives. Accordingly, Hoover emphasized that the most outstanding feature of the new legislation was the revitalization of the flexible tariff provisions into a form that would expedite the "prompt and scientific adjustment of serious inequities." In general, then, the president's signing of the Hawley-Smoot tariff underscored his faith in the policymaking approaches formulated in the early 1920s. His approval of the legislation attested to his feeling that the domestic market constituted the greatest source of American economic strength and deserved top priority.[10]

European nations responded to Hoover's signing of the tariff bill with widespread disapproval. Percy W. Bidwell, an economist with many years' experience working for the Tariff Commission, noted that "in France our tariff was compared to a declaration of war, an economic blockade." Ambassador Walter Edge forwarded to the State Department a bundle of French newspaper articles revealing the extent

9. Ogden L. Mills, Memorandum for the president, 23 April 1930, Herbert C. Hoover Presidential Papers, Box 296 (hereafter cited as HHPP); Hoover, *State Papers*, 1:102–4, 147–49; Herbert C. Hoover, *The Memoirs of Herbert Hoover*, 2:292–99; Stimson to Felix Frankfurter, 5 February 1930, Frankfurter Papers, Box 103.

10. For Hoover's views, see Hoover, *State Papers*, 1:314–18; Hoover, *Memoirs*, 2:298–99; Hoover, *New Day*, pp. 24–25, 70, 101–2, 129–40; for a fine discussion of American commercial policy and Hoover's role, see Joan Hoff Wilson, *American Business and Foreign Policy, 1920–1933*, pp. 65–100.

of French anger. The French claimed that the upward revision of American tariff rates would retard world trade, precipitate retaliatory action, worsen the Depression in the United States, and exacerbate the difficulty of paying intergovernmental war debts. Within a week after Hoover's approval of the Hawley-Smoot Act, Ambassador Edge was warned that unless duties were lowered on French goods, the *modus vivendi* reached in 1927 would be suspended and the most-favored-nation status accorded many American goods withdrawn.[11] The French waited anxiously to see how the reconstituted Tariff Commission would operate. In December 1930 French Ambassador Paul Claudel formally requested a reappraisal of the duties levied on numerous French goods.[12]

The worsening economic situation in the latter half of 1930, however, foreclosed extensive use of the flexible tariff provisions. In mid-July 1930 Assistant Secretary of State Castle warned Ambassador Edge not to raise too many expectations in France regarding the use of section 336 of the Hawley-Smoot tariff. Castle feared that Tariff Commission studies might actually lead to rate increases.[13] Although the president struggled to appoint competent personnel to the Tariff Commission, tried to expedite its proceedings, and agreed to reduce more duties than he raised, he was able neither to apply the flexible tariff provisions on a large scale nor to palliate European feelings.[14] As world trade contracted and American exports and imports diminished, the flexible tariff provisions fell into increasing disrepute, and the Hawley-Smoot duties were condemned at home and abroad.[15]

Hoover and his closest advisers resented French charges that American trade policies were responsible for the decline in world trade and the multiplication of international financial problems. The president and his supporters emphasized that France and other major nations had raised their tariffs repeatedly throughout the 1920s and had therefore set precedents for the American action. Moreover, they argued that the

11. Percy W. Bidwell, "The New American Tariff," pp. 13–26; Walter Edge to Stimson, 16, 20 June 1930, RG 59, 611.003/2172, 2182; Edge to Stimson, 23 June 1930, HHPP, Box 860.

12. Edge to Stimson, 3 July, 15 December 1930, RG 59, 611.003/2279, 2410.

13. Castle to Edge, 14 July 1930, Castle Papers, Box 3; Edge to Castle, 26 July 1930, ibid.

14. For Hoover's efforts to implement section 336, see "Work of New Tariff Commission to Date, 10 May 1931, Under Section 336, Act of 1930," 15 May 1931, HHPP, Box 296; Stimson to Frankfurter, 5 February 1930, Frankfurter Papers, Box 103; Diary of Henry L. Stimson, 11 May 1931, Stimson Papers.

15. See, for example, Joseph M. Jones, *Tariff Retaliation*; J. Marshall Gersting, *The Flexible Provisions in the United States' Tariff, 1922–1930*.

decline in French and European exports to the United States in 1930 was not the result of higher duties but a consequence of the domestic business downturn. The Commerce Department demonstrated that duties on French imports had increased less than 4 percent in 1930, not nearly enough to cause a serious disruption of French trade with the United States if unaccompanied by other factors. The actual increase in duties on French goods had been greater in 1922 than in 1930; yet, French exports to the United States had increased during the 1920s. Although American purchases of French goods had never exceeded American sales to France, France had still retained a favorable balance of payments during the late 1920s. Facts of this sort convinced Republican officials that the new American tariff duties were neither a significant cause of French commercial problems nor a source of European financial troubles.[16]

The Hoover administration's defense of its policies was superficial. By emphasizing the favorable position of France in the late 1920s, Republican officials downplayed the serious payments problems of Germany and Britain. By alluding to European tariff increases, policymakers disregarded the fact that American rates still remained higher than those in the Old World. By justifying the timing of the tariff act on the basis of prior European action, administration spokesmen ignored the obvious truth that it was an unpropitious time to raise duties, when the international economy was already in a tailspin and the forces of economic nationalism were ready to erupt everywhere. Furthermore, by placing such importance on the flexible tariff provisions, Hoover and his colleagues minimized the problem of collecting appropriate data, downplayed the difficulties inherent in determining the differences in costs of production at home and abroad, and ignored the theoretical possibility that the principle of equalizing costs could prevent all trade if carried to extremes.[17]

Though the loopholes in Hoover's arguments were obvious, a review of the historical context in which he operated suggests that he

16. For the Republican defense of the Hawley-Smoot tariff, see Hoover, *Memoirs*, 2:291; Julius Klein, "The Tariff and the Depression," pp. 498–99; Castle to Edge, 14 July 1930, Castle Papers, Box 3; Department of Commerce, "Effect of New Tariff on Trade with France," July 1930, RG 59, 611.003/2289; Tariff Commission, "Tariff and Trade Relations Between the United States and France," 17 May 1930, ibid., 611.5131/793; Ray Ovid Hall, "French-American Balance of Payments in 1928," p. 908; Hall to Donald Woodward, 30 September 1929, Records of the Bureau of Foreign and Domestic Commerce (BFDC), RG 151, File 600.
17. For an excellent account of the commercial and financial problems facing European nations in the interwar era, see Ingvar Svennilson, *Growth and Stagnation in the*

was not indifferent to the international ramifications of American tariff making. Hoover requested only "limited revisions" in the tariff schedule when other nations were contemplating similar action.[18] He believed that small upward shifts in the duty structure would not hurt European economies. Some of the nation's outstanding tariff experts concurred that European exports to the United States, mostly specialty items and luxury goods, "had a way of persisting in the face of duties very high."[19] He supported the cost-of-production formula when many legislators in both parties desired even more protection and when most businessmen, even export-oriented ones, had yet to champion the reciprocity version of the unconditional most-favored-nation clause.[20] He assumed that the higher tariffs would not constitute a barrier to international recovery. During the first part of 1930 American capital exports did revive, although temporarily, lending some validity to Hoover's view that the creditor status of the United States might be reconcilable with its export surplus, at least for the immediate future.[21] Although the president rejected the advice of leading businessmen and economists and signed the Hawley-Smoot tariff, he did so because he feared that further delays would exacerbate the economic downturn.[22]

These points indicate that Hoover's signing of the tariff legislation was not prompted by a parochial nationalism that denied the importance of European stability to American self-interest. Nevertheless, the Hawley-Smoot tariff did strain Franco-American relations and accel-

---

European Economy, pp. 168–202; for comparative tariff levels, see League of Nations, Economic and Finance Section, *Tariff Level Indices*, p. 15; for the ominous tendency toward higher tariff duties prior to the stock market crash, see League of Nations, Economic Organization, Consultative Committee, *Application of the Recommendations of the International Economic Conference*, pp. 8–30; for the inherent weaknesses of the flexible tariff provisions, see Gersting, *Flexible Provisions*, pp. 172–83; see also Tariff Commission, *Annual Report*, 1929, pp. 17–23.

18. League of Nations, Economic Organization, Consultative Committee, *Application*, pp. 8–30.

19. Frank W. Taussig, "The Tariff Bill and Our Friends Abroad," p. 9.

20. For congressional sentiment, see Fetter, "Trade Theory," pp. 413–27. Although some export-oriented groups, like the NFTC, became increasingly disillusioned with the flexible provisions, there was little support for alternative approaches in the late 1920s. See NFTC, *Official Report*, 1927, 1928, 1929. William W. Nichols, president of the American Manufacturers Export Association, continued to retain his faith in the efficacy of an apolitical tariff commission. See William Wallace Nichols, "Trade Barriers and Customs Duties," pp. 125–26.

21. For figures pertaining to American capital exports, see Cleona Lewis, *America's Stake in International Investments*, pp. 393, 629.

22. Hoover, *State Papers*, 1:318. Even some of the renowned critics of the Hawley-Smoot Act understood Hoover's reasons for signing it. See Owen D. Young to Coolidge, 6 June 1930, Young Papers, I–58.

erate the nationalistic response of all European nations to the problems of the Depression. The French viewed the increase in American duties as a violation of the *modus vivendi* of 1927, a threat to their export interests, and a menace to European economic stability. Officials in the French ministries of Commerce and Agriculture began advocating a return to the special bargaining and reciprocity practices of the early postwar years. Claiming they were no longer bound by the *modus vivendi*, the French sought to increase their own duties or to impose quotas on foreign imports. Although such actions did not become widespread for another year or two, by the end of 1930 it was evident that American and French commercial policies were on a collision course.[23] As both creditor nations struggled to protect their home markets and foist responsibility for maintaining financial equilibrium onto one another, the interests of all Europe were sacrificed.

Thus, Hoover's reaffirmation of the protective principle, his revival of the flexible tariff provisions, and his reinvigoration of the Tariff Commission failed to usher in a new era in the commercial relations between the United States and France or between the United States and western Europe. In fact, his policies revealed a rigid commitment to the established techniques of Republican economic diplomacy. His acceptance of the higher duties indicated that he had rather risk the economic consequences of overprotection than prolong the domestic controversy, weaken his political position, or further exacerbate his relations with Congress. Even more ominous, however, Hoover's action reflected the growing sentiment that European nations, especially France, could and should absorb a larger share of the responsibility for maintaining European stability. This attitude especially influenced the official American approach to the problems of reparations and disarmament.

The Young Plan, the Bank for International Settlements, and American Financial Policy

In the spring of 1929, while Hoover was focusing his attention on farm and tariff legislation and preparing several studies of the nation's social problems, a committee of experts was meeting in Paris to arrange a final settlement of the reparations issue. Coolidge had worked out a procedure whereby the Reparation Commission had appointed the

23. Bidwell, "American Tariff," pp. 13–26; Jones, *Tariff Retaliation*, pp. 155–66.

American experts after the president had indicated his preferences. Coolidge and his advisers had selected Owen D. Young and J. P. Morgan as the principal American experts and Thomas W. Lamont and Thomas Nelson Perkins as alternates. Young's work on the Dawes Plan, his prominence as an international businessman, his reputation as a brilliant negotiator, and his appeal to all European nations had made him a logical first choice. Morgan and Lamont had been selected because American policymakers wanted to involve the nation's foremost international bankers in the formulation of the agreement and the subsequent mobilization of the reparation bonds. Before departing for Paris, both Young and Morgan had met with the outgoing president. Coolidge had reluctantly agreed to allow Young to become chairman of the committee of experts. But the president had emphasized the potential dangers that lay ahead for the American experts. He admonished them to limit their efforts to completing the Dawes Plan and told them to avoid establishing precedents. Coolidge wanted to utilize private experts as Harding and Hughes had used them in 1922 and 1923: to safeguard American war debts, foreclose political embroilments, and foster European financial and political stability through the use of private American capital.[24]

But the task of the experts was destined to be even more difficult than it had been in 1924. Even before the experts convened, Young acknowledged that their work had been severely circumscribed by the discussions Gilbert had carried on with Poincaré and Churchill in 1928.[25] More important, the influence and leverage of the experts were less than they had been five years earlier. This circumstance was in part a consequence of France's remarkable financial rehabilitation, in part a reflection of the substantial recuperation of all Europe. In 1924 France was financially prostrate. A sense of impending catastrophe, engendered by the occupation of the Ruhr and the inflation of the mark, overhung Europe. In such an environment, European leaders

24. For the selection of the American experts and Coolidge's attitude toward them, see Young to Thomas Nelson Perkins, 23 January 1929, Young Papers, R–30; Young to S. Parker Gilbert, 19 November 1928, ibid.; Gilbert to Young, 24 December 1928, ibid.; J. R. C., Memoranda, 22, 24 December 1928, RG 59, 462.00R296/2578, 2588; Castle, Memoranda, 10 January 1929, ibid., 462.00R296/3079, 3081; Calvin Coolidge, *The Talkative President*, p. 199; Charles G. Dawes, *Notes as Vice President, 1928–1929*, pp. 155–57, 175, 190, 221–28; Coolidge to Hoover, 9 April 1929, RG 59, 462.00R296/2775½.
25. Dawes, *Notes*, p. 156; see also Gilbert to Kellogg and Andrew W. Mellon, 23 October 1928, Records of the Bureau of Accounts, RG 39, Box 78.

felt compelled to defer to the recommendations of the experts. In early 1929, however, European officials were looking to the experts, not for viable solutions, but for verification of their own demands.[26]

Additional factors complicating the work of the experts related to the speculative frenzy on Wall Street, the drain of gold from Europe, and the termination of almost all foreign loans by the United States. These developments placed an enormous strain on Britain's financial position, exacerbated credit conditions in Germany, and generated uncertainty about the marketability of the reparation bonds. Officials in the FRBNY and partners in the Morgan firm believed that the discount rate of the FRBNY should be raised quickly and steadily to break the speculative mania. Once speculation had subsided, they wanted the FRBNY to reduce its rates below those in London, thereby affording relief to Britain and Germany and making possible the mobilization of reparation bonds.[27]

But members of the Federal Reserve Board disagreed. They argued that the state of domestic business demanded lower, not higher, rates. They maintained that credit should be regulated according to the needs of business and not as a means of controlling speculation. Adolph C. Miller and Charles S. Hamlin, members of the board, suspected that George L. Harrison, Strong's successor as governor of the FRBNY, was more concerned with international financial stability and the success of a German bond flotation than with domestic economic activity. They feared that his preoccupation with the European situation might provoke a congressional investigation of the Federal Reserve System. Consequently, throughout the period that the experts were meeting in Paris, the Federal Reserve Board voted against hikes in the discount rate of the FRBNY.[28] The mounting influence of the domestically oriented board over the more internationally oriented FRBNY constituted an important obstacle in the path of the reparation experts as they began their work in the middle of February 1929.

Despite the multitude of problems that lay before him, Owen Young was determined to arrange a reparations agreement. Elected chairman

26. Dawes, *Notes*, p. 76; J. Harry Jones, *Josiah Stamp*, p. 244.
27. Diary of Charles S. Hamlin, 4, 5, 6 February 1929, Hamlin Papers, Vol. 15; Russell C. Leffingwell to Lamont, 8 March 1929, Thomas W. Lamont Papers, Box 103; Memorandum of conversation between George Harrison and Mills, 18 May 1929, George L. Harrison Papers, 2013.1; Stephen V. O. Clarke, *Central Bank Cooperation, 1924–1931*, pp. 154–57; Henry Clay, *Lord Norman*, pp. 245–52.
28. For the struggle between Harrison and the Federal Reserve Board and for the thinking of the board, see Diary of Charles S. Hamlin, 5, 8, 14 February, 5, 19, 21, 23, 26, 27, 28 March, 18, 19, 25 April, 9, 20, 23 May 1929, Hamlin Papers, Vol. 15.

of the committee of experts, he immediately elicited the views of his associates. Hjalmar Schacht, the German expert, explained to the committee that Germany's continuing merchandise trade deficit and large foreign loan service necessitated substantial reductions in her reparation obligations. He intimated that Germany could pay only about one billion marks per year and stressed that payments could not be prolonged beyond one generation. Josiah Stamp, the British expert, considered this offer inadequate. Yet, he sympathized with Schacht's worries about Germany's ability to make financial transfers. Consequently, Stamp suggested that Germany's payments be divided into two categories: one had to be paid unconditionally; the other was to be made conditional and afforded some type of transfer protection.

Emile Moreau, the French expert, reacted angrily to Schacht's position and to Stamp's suggestions. Moreau called for annuities of 3.5 to 4.7 billion marks. He also criticized the idea of creating special machinery for transfer protection. Such machinery threatened to obstruct France's desire to capitalize the reparation bonds. Rapid capitalization, the French believed, would deter any future German attempt to renege on reparation payments, lest such an attempt endanger Germany's entire credit structure. Moreover, lump-sum payments stemming from rapid capitalization of the reparation bonds would enable the French government to redeem its foreign loans, liquidate part of its internal debt, or repay its war debts at a substantial discount.[29]

Young was surprised by the gap between the positions of the French and German experts. He was also disturbed by Moreau's uncompromising presentation of the French viewpoint. Rather than dwell on points of contention, Young endeavored to find a means of accommodating all sides. He sought to establish a new banking institution, subsequently called the Bank for International Settlements (BIS). Schacht wanted a new bank that would help finance international trade and aid Germany's quest for new export markets. Both Moreau and Emile Francqui, the Belgian expert, were happy to have such an institution. They assumed that the new bank would hold Germany's obligations and ''throw the color'' of commercialization over the entire indemnity, even if only part of it were immediately capitalized. Morgan and Lamont likewise believed that the institution could serve as trustee for the indemnity and oversee its proper commercialization and effective

29. For the positions of Schacht, Stamp, and Moreau, see Stuart Crocker, ''Notes on the Young Plan,'' pp. 22–66, in Young Papers; Lamont to Leffingwell, 26 February 1929, Thomas W. Lamont Papers, Box 103; Young to president, secretary of state, and secretary of the treasury, 2 March 1929, Young Papers, R–31.

capitalization. Young assimilated all these ideas. In letters to the president, the secretary of state, and the secretary of the treasury, he extolled the idea of a new international bank. He explained that it would preclude the need for an immediate large bond flotation and remove the treatment of intergovernmental debts from political hands. Young believed an international bank would insure payment of debts through the "ordinary machinery of finance" and the "credit forces of the world."[30]

Young had hoped the bank plan would encourage the experts to resolve their differences over the amount of payments.[31] When their discord persisted, he decided to assume the initiative. At meetings in late March and early April, Young acknowledged that the former Allies had to calculate their demands on the basis of their war debt obligations and reconstruction costs. But he emphasized that German payments should increase gradually, so that the largest burden would be borne by Germany when her peacetime economic development enabled her to make the largest financial transfers. Young proposed that Germany pay an average annuity of 1,942 million marks during the first fifteen years of the agreement and 2,452 million marks during the following twenty-two years. For the remaining twenty-one years, Young indicated that German payments should parallel Allied war debt payments. Although this proposal provided the Allies with sufficient resources to meet their respective war debt payments, it did not cover their reconstruction costs. Not surprisingly, the experts from the creditor nations quickly rejected the plan.[32]

While Young struggled to reconcile the positions of the Allied and German experts, he received a stern rebuke from Washington. In a memorandum prepared by Treasury Undersecretary Mills and approved by Hoover, the American experts were accused of sacrificing traditional United States policy of separating war debts and reparations. Mills warned that European nations were preparing to form a united front to press for the reduction of war debts, the effect of which would be to

30. Young to president, secretary of state, and secretary of the treasury, 2, 17 March 1929, Young Papers, R–31; Crocker, "Notes," pp. 41–46; Lamont to Leffingwell, 26 February 1929, Thomas W. Lamont Papers, Box 103.
31. Young to president, secretary of state, and secretary of the treasury, 2 March 1929, Young Papers, R–31.
32. Crocker, "Notes," pp. 73–94; Young, Statement, 28 March 1929, Young Papers, R–33; Chairman, Memorandum addressed to the French, British, Italian, and Belgian groups, 8 April 1929, ibid; Young to president, secretary of state, and secretary of the treasury, 28 March 1929, RG 39, Box 77; Jacobson, *Locarno Diplomacy*, pp. 252–56.

shift Germany's reparations burden onto the shoulders of American taxpayers. The Hoover administration would not tolerate any such reduction or shifting of reparations burdens. The administration would not allow any official in the Federal Reserve System to serve as a director of the BIS, whose sole function, according to American officials, was to distribute intergovernmental debt payments and thus link war debts and reparations. Nor would Republican policymakers consent to any reduction in German payments to the United States for mixed claims or army occupation costs, even if these reductions were considered essential to a new reparations accord. The administration opposed dividing German payments into two categories, one of which corresponded to Allied war debt payments to the United States. In a subsequent message, Secretary of State Henry L. Stimson admonished:

It may well be that the Allied governments as a matter of policy may be unwilling to accept from Germany an amount less than one necessary to discharge their obligations to the United States, but for a group of independent experts to base their proposed terms of settlement on any such factor seems to us wholly illogical and inconsistent with the very task that was assigned to them under the terms of reference. What Germany can pay and how she can best pay is the question for the experts to decide. What the Allied governments are willing to accept is a political question with which the experts should not be concerned.[33]

Young and Morgan were shocked and infuriated by the reprimands from Washington. While Lamont tried to mollify their anger, S. Parker Gilbert correctly hypothesized that official policy was being set in the Treasury with the president's approval. The agent general was not surprised by Hoover's position. Like Morgan and Lamont, Gilbert had little respect or affection for the president. Young, however, had been a long-time admirer of Hoover's. But he, too, found the president's actions incomprehensible. He was especially distressed by the administration's opposition to American participation in the BIS and by its sanctimonious attitude against the linkage of war debts and reparations. On 11 April, after extensive consultation with Morgan, Lamont, and Gilbert, Young reminded the State Department that the American experts were not official representatives of the United States government. He emphasized that there was no way of preventing the former Allies from calculating their reparation demands on the basis of their own

33. For the quotation, see Stimson to Young, 20 April 1929, RG 39, Box 78; see also Department of State, *Papers Relating to the Foreign Relations of the United States*, 1929, 2:1038–40, 1059–62 (hereafter cited as FR).

war debt obligations. But, while asserting his independence and justifying his actions, Young reassured Washington that American interests would not be compromised.[34]

Young's exasperation with official policy, however, was intensified by the worsening situation within the committee of experts. On 17 April Schacht submitted a proposal that called for thirty-seven annuities of 1.65 billion marks. Not only was this offer far below Allied demands, it was made contingent upon the revision of certain provisions in the Treaty of Versailles. Moreau and Francqui were outraged. The following day Pierre Quesnay, general manager of the Bank of France, threatened to withdraw $200 million from Germany. When Schacht refused to alter his offer, a breakdown in the negotiations seemed certain.[35]

Young kept struggling to bring Germany and her creditors together. After the German government instructed Schacht to drop his political demands and bargain in good faith, the German expert asked Young to draw up a new proposal that would meet the minimum demands of the creditors. Young's new offer envisioned thirty-seven gradually rising annuities, averaging 2.05 billion marks. A part of each annuity was to be paid and transferred unconditionally; the payment and transfer of the remaining portion were made conditional. Young projected twenty-two additional annuities, corresponding to the debt payments of the Allies, to be paid after the initial thirty-seven. When Schacht still equivocated, Young prepared to ask the National City Bank and J. P. Morgan and Company to apply pressure. When Schacht demonstrated a more favorable disposition, Young indicated that the FRBNY would support the mark. Finally, on 3 May the German government advised Schacht to accept Young's proposal. Since the Reichsbank had lost $100 million during the preceding two weeks, an agreement seemed necessary to avoid financial chaos.[36]

Germany's acceptance of Young's compromise proposal did not insure the success of the experts' work. The French and Belgian experts

34. FR, 1929, 2:1043–45; Young to secretary, 20 April 1929, RG 39, Box 78; Crocker, "Notes," pp. 94–108, 141–43; Young to Mellon, 13 April 1929, Young Papers, R–30.

35. German group, Memorandum, 17 April 1929, Young Papers, R–33; Crocker, "Notes," pp. 126–40; Lamont to Leffingwell, 29 April 1929, Thomas W. Lamont Papers, Box 103; Jacobson, *Locarno Diplomacy*, pp. 256–62; Clarke, *Central Bank Cooperation*, pp. 165–66.

36. Crocker, "Notes," pp. 160–65, 176–78, 185–86, 190, 199–209; Young, Memorandum, 6 May 1929, Young Papers, R–33; Jacobson, *Locarno Diplomacy*, pp. 258–72; Clarke, *Central Bank Cooperation*, pp. 165–66.

still complained that Young's offer did not meet their minimum demands. While the present capital value of Young's payment schedule was 40 percent above Schacht's initial offer, it remained 7.5 percent below the creditors' last proposal. Moreover, Moreau was incensed by Young's attempt to preserve the small amount of German reparation payments going to the United States for mixed claims and army occupation costs. In addition, Moreau was very disappointed by the official American attitude toward the BIS. He viewed the proposed bank as an indispensable part of any accord, and he believed that if the BIS did not have the support of the Federal Reserve System, it would be substantially weakened.[37] It seemed to the French that they were being asked to bear the major burden of a reparations settlement.

In letters to the secretary of state in early May, Young explained his dilemma. He believed that the former Allies would acquiesce to the schedule of payments he had proposed if they could agree on a satisfactory distribution of the annuities among themselves. But the problem was that each creditor, including the United States, was requesting the same amount it demanded when the total annuity was considerably higher. As a result there was not enough to go around. Young wanted Washington to make some concessions regarding its claims against Germany, thereby making available sufficient sums to meet the requests of the other creditors. If Hoover had enough courage to waive army occupation costs through executive action, Young believed that the deadlock could be broken.[38]

Rather than helping the situation, the Hoover administration almost broke up the work of the experts. On 16 May Stimson announced that the United States government would not allow any official of the Federal Reserve System to serve with the BIS. When Moreau learned of the announcement, he told Gilbert that the talks were over. The anguished Young could find no explanation for the roadblocks being constructed by the Hoover administration. He told American diplomats in Paris to inform Washington that unless a more cooperative attitude was forthcoming, the experts would not be able to reach agreement.[39]

Republican officials were caught in a quandary. Privately, they appreciated Young's efforts and understood the advantages of a repara-

37. FR, 1929, 2:1067–68, 1071–72; Armour to Stimson, 6 May 1929, RG 39, Box 78; Young to Stimson, 9 May 1929, ibid.; Crocker, "Notes," pp. 195–205, 213–23, 245–47; Jacobson, *Locarno Diplomacy*, p. 260.
38. Young to secretary of state, 6, 9 May 1929, RG 39, Box 78.
39. For Stimson's statement, see FR, 1929, 2:1071; for the reaction in Paris, see Crocker, "Notes," pp. 245–50, 258–60.

tions agreement.[40] But they had expected the American experts to have sufficient personal influence and financial leverage to work out a permanent settlement without jeopardizing the war debts or embroiling the United States government in European political affairs. When the outlines of the reparations plan suggested otherwise, the officials had become alarmed. Hoover, Mellon, Stimson, and Mills feared congressional opposition and public criticism, especially when farm relief and tariff revision were under discussion.[41] Nevertheless, upon learning that their policies might prevent an accord, Republican officials decided to modify their position. Stimson informed Young on 17 May that the administration did not oppose the BIS; private American banking firms would be permitted to establish ties with the new institution. After consulting with congressional leaders on 19 May, Hoover not only acquiesced to a reduction in American claims against Germany for army costs but also consented to an extension of German payments toward mixed claims.[42]

These limited concessions provided Young with additional flexibility to work out an agreement. But since every mark was hotly contested by the creditors, Young had to allocate to the United States a smaller share of each German annuity than had been authorized by American officials. He also had to accept a much closer link between war debts and reparations than had been anticipated. As a result the Hoover administration decided to reserve judgment on the official American attitude toward the Young Plan.[43]

Despite the suspicions of American officials, the Young Plan was neither a European plot to embroil the United States in Europe's political affairs nor an effort to impose the financial burden of the war exclusively upon the United States. On the contrary the plan was a complex document that tried to accommodate the diverse economic and political imperatives of several nations. The Young Plan called for the payment of fifty-nine annuities, the last twenty-two coinciding with

40. Diary of Henry L. Stimson, 28 August 1930, Stimson Papers; Mellon to Young, 14 April 1929, Young Papers, R–30; Memorandum of conversation between Stimson and Friedrich Wilhelm von Prittwitz, 6 June 1929, RG 59, 462.00R296/2956.
41. FR, 1929, 2:1038–40, 1059–62, 1071, 1081–82; Mills to Castle, 6 May 1929, RG 39, Box 78; Castle to Stimson, 15 May 1929, RG 59, 462.00R296/3100.
42. FR, 1929, 2:1073, 1075–76; secretary of state, Statement to the press, 19 May 1929, HHPP, Box 871; Crocker, "Notes," p. 273.
43. Armour to secretary, 23 May 1929, RG 39, Box 78; Crocker, "Notes," pp. 273–74; Mellon to Stimson, 24 May 1929, RG 39, Box 78; FR, 1929, 2:1081–82; Castle to Stimson, 23 May 1929, RG 59, 462.00R296/2929; Stimson to American Embassy, Paris, 5 June 1929, RG 39, Box 78.

Allied debt payments. During the first thirty-seven years the average annuity was 20 percent below the standard Dawes Plan annuity, thus affording Germany substantial reductions in payments. In addition, Germany benefited, at least politically, from the termination of foreign controls over the budget, the railroads, and the Reichsbank. In return for these advantages Germany agreed to pay a part of each annuity, amounting to 660 million marks, unconditionally. France received 500 million marks of each unconditional payment, thus satisfying one of her primary objectives. All of Germany's creditors received enough to cover their future war debt payments. But the Young Plan stipulated that, should the Allies secure reductions in their own obligations, a large percentage of those benefits would be passed on to Germany. Finally, the Young Plan provided for the establishment of the BIS. This institution was expected to distribute the reparation annuities, help finance deliveries-in-kind, facilitate international transfers, and promote world commerce. In addition, the BIS was charged with the responsibility of convening a special advisory committee should Germany ever decide to activate the safeguard clause and postpone the conditional payments.[44]

Though they endorsed the Young Plan, the American experts recognized its limitations. Young and Lamont acknowledged that all of the experts had been responsive to the demands of their governments.[45] But since political imperatives and economic realities eventually had to be reconciled if governments were to accept their recommendations, the American experts had few regrets. They felt they had succeeded in framing a document that was economically viable yet politically acceptable.[46] There were, however, many imponderables. The plan was based on a set of interrelated assumptions that the German economy would continue to grow, foreign loans would stimulate German pro-

44. For excellent descriptions of the Young Plan, see Harold G. Moulton and Leo Pasvolsky, *War Debts and World Prosperity*, pp. 188–200; Jacobson, *Locarno Diplomacy*, pp. 272–76; Etienne Weill-Raynal, *Les Réparations allemandes et la France*, 3:438–79; see also Thomas Lamont, "The Final Reparations Settlement," pp. 336–63; Carl Bergmann, "Germany and the Young Plan," pp. 583–97; for the Bank for International Settlements (BIS), see also the essays by the founders of the BIS in Parker Thomas Moon, ed., *The Young Plan in Operation*; BIS, *Annual Report*, 1930–31.

45. For government infringement on the work of the experts, see Hjalmar Schacht, *The End of Reparations*, p. 49; Lamont, "Reparations Settlement," p. 343; Young to secretary of state, 6 May 1929, RG 39, Box 78; Jones, *Josiah Stamp*, p. 245; Jacobson, *Locarno Diplomacy*, pp. 275–76.

46. Lamont, "Reparations Settlement," pp. 336–63; Lamont, Memorandum for Dawes, 30 July 1929, Thomas W. Lamont Papers, Box 180; Young to secretary of state, 6 May 1929, RG 39, Box 78.

ductivity, German exports would eventually exceed imports, German budgetary problems would be resolved, and the relatively large payments demanded after ten years would be paid. Although the stock market crash and the onset of the Depression lay only a few months ahead, almost no one foresaw that these assumptions would be so quickly discredited.[47]

During 1929 and early 1930 American bankers, economists, and financial analysts debated the economic merits of the Young Plan. Some contended that it imposed too heavy a burden on Germany, but even they qualified their criticisms. At the time Germany's economic development seemed impressive, and many of her financial problems appeared soluble. As for the problem of financial transfers, economists hotly debated whether such a problem really existed. Even among those that admitted the problem's existence, some maintained that it would not affect Germany.[48] To contemporary economists, then, the Young Plan appeared a viable, if not altogether satisfactory, solution to a thorny problem.

The immediate question, however, was not the plan's financial viability, but its political acceptability. Government officials in all nations, including the United States, responded without enthusiasm to the Young Plan. In mid-June Young and Lamont returned to the United States, met with the president and the secretary of state, and recounted their efforts to protect American interests. Although Young and Lamont maintained that they had preserved the legal separation between war debt and reparation payments, they emphasized that realistic men had to face the fact that these payments were interdependent. Smooth functioning of the world economy and the prosperity of American commerce, they insisted, depended upon the proper handling and effi-

47. In a recent book Joseph Davis illustrates how few contemporaries foresaw the coming of the Depression. See Joseph S. Davis, *The World Between the Wars, 1919–1939*, pp. 130–86.

48. For the views of economists, see, for example, Alzada Comstock, "Reparation Payments in Perspective," pp. 199–209; John H. Williams, "Reparations and the Flow of Capital," pp. 73–79; James W. Angell, "The Reparations Settlement and the International Flow of Capital," pp. 80–88; William Adams Brown, Jr., "German Reparations and the International Flow of Capital," pp. 89–92; George P. Auld, "The Prospect in Europe," NFTC, *Official Report*, 1928, pp. 15–24; Robert Crozier Long, "The German Transfer Bugaboo," *Journal of the American Bankers Association* (ABA) 21 (August 1928):133–34, 148–49, 151; for the views of American official and unofficial experts working on the Young Plan, see also Lamont to Leffingwell, 21 March 1929, Thomas W. Lamont Papers, Box 103; Arthur N. Young to Kellogg, 2 January 1929, RG 59, 462.00R296/3060; for Lamont's retrospective view, see Lamont to William Mac-Donald, 26 June 1933, Thomas W. Lamont Papers, Box 182.

cient discharge of these intergovernmental obligations. Young and Lamont claimed that the BIS would facilitate the commercialization and depoliticization of all intergovernmental debts. More important, they explained, the BIS would provide a means for institutionalizing central bank cooperation. Such cooperation was necessary to preserve the stability of currencies, protect the gold standard, and create the conditions for a flourishing commerce. Yet, such cooperation was increasingly difficult because of the nationalistic pressures bearing on central bank policy in all nations, especially in the United States where tensions between the FRBNY and the Federal Reserve Board had reached a breaking point. The American experts urged the administration to endorse the Young Plan, accept the reductions in American claims against Germany, and permit Federal Reserve officials to cooperate in the organization of the new banking institution.[49]

Republican policymakers recognized that the Young Plan offered many benefits. Insofar as it fixed the total German indemnity, removed this issue from the arena of international politics, and contributed to financial certainty in Germany and Europe, the Young Plan was welcomed by Hoover and Stimson. But insofar as it highlighted the connection between debts and reparations and raised the possibility that the United States might become embroiled in European politics, the Young Plan was viewed with misgivings in official circles. That Hoover assigned less significance to the international sources of American prosperity than did Young contributed to these misgivings. Young believed that it was "essential to the prosperity of America" to revive agricultural markets abroad; consequently, he magnified the advantages of the BIS. Hoover hoped to solve the farm problem through passage of the Agricultural Marketing Act and through the efficient cultivation of the domestic market.[50] The president, therefore, tended to minimize the international economic advantages of the BIS and worry more about the banking institution's international political ramifications. Hoover's position was not simply a matter of the way he measured national and international priorities. As president he had to be more concerned than either Young or Lamont about domestic criticism and congressional opposition. Louis T. McFadden, chairman of the House Committee on Banking and Currency, was already waging a campaign against addi-

49. Lamont, Memorandum, 25 June 1929, RG 59, 462.00R296/3114; see also Diary of Charles S. Hamlin, 16 July, 9, 12 August 1929, Hamlin Papers, Vol. 16.
50. For Young's view, see Young to Melvin A. Traylor, 6 May 1930, Young Papers, I–226; see also Diary of Charles S. Hamlin, 1 August 1929, Hamlin Papers, Vol. 16; for Hoover's view, see Hoover, *State Papers*, 1:31–35.

tional American involvement in European affairs and was particularly hostile to American participation in the BIS.[51]

As a result of domestic economic and political factors, Republican officials could neither ignore the sacrifices nor dismiss the risks inherent in the Young Plan. Therefore, they pursued a very complex policy. Without undermining the basic elements of the plan or compromising the important functions of the BIS, the officials tried to impose most of the economic sacrifices of a settlement upon European governments. American policymakers attempted to insulate the United States from the political ramifications of an agreement and protect the war debts. Accordingly, while prodding European leaders to sign the Young Plan, Republican officials decided to negotiate a separate treaty with Germany stipulating that nation's obligations to the United States. In other words both Mills and Undersecretary of State Joseph P. Cotton were willing to reduce American claims against Germany to facilitate a reparations settlement. But they did not want to sign a comprehensive agreement that implied official American endorsement of the reparations sum, approval of the Allied division of reparations, or commitment to enforce the plan should it break down. "The importance of our claims," Cotton wrote, "does not justify any such involvement [in the machinery of the Young Plan]."[52] In a similar vein Cotton and Mills worked out a procedure that avoided any official link between the Federal Reserve System and the BIS but that established a system of collaboration between private American banking firms and the new international financial institution.[53]

The French became extremely agitated with these events. In July 1929, before the official American attitude toward the Young Plan had developed and the new British Labour government had announced its viewpoint, Poincaré had sought legislative ratification of the debt settlements. Faced with the maturation of the $400 million war stocks debt on 1 August if the Chamber of Deputies did not approve the

51. See, for example, statement by Louis T. McFadden, in "Should an International Bank be Established?" *Congressional Digest* 8 (August–September 1929):215, 224; House, Committee on Banking and Currency, *German Reparation Bonds*, p. 1.
52. Joseph P. Cotton to Edwin C. Wilson, 6 January 1930, RG 39, Box 80; Ogden L. Mills, "America's Separate Agreement with Germany," in Moon, *Young Plan*, pp. 54–60; for the negotiations with Germany over a separate treaty, see FR, 1929, 2:1083–1106; for Stimson's prodding of the British to end their opposition to the Young Plan, see, for example, Memorandum of conversation between Stimson and the British ambassador, 29 August 1929, RG 59, 462.00R296/3255.
53. Owen D. Young to Gilbert, 8 August 1929, Thomas W. Lamont Papers, Box 180; Young to Lamont, 15, 20 August 1929, ibid.

Mellon-Bérenger agreement, Poincaré argued that the Young Plan fully protected French interests by linking war debt and reparation payments and insuring France's net-creditor status regarding the intergovernmental debts. After a prolonged and acrimonious debate in the Chamber, the deputies went along with Poincaré's request. Having achieved such a magnificent legislative victory, Poincaré resigned from office.[54] As soon as he departed, the French observed a systematic effort by Britain to gain a larger share of the reparation payments. They watched Germany try to secure an immediate and complete evacuation of the Rhineland and the United States attempt to escape all responsibility for a reparations agreement. At the Baden-Baden Conference in October 1929, where international bankers met to frame the BIS, and at the second Hague Conference in January 1930, where European diplomats convened to complete the Young Plan and set a timetable for evacuating the Rhineland, the French fought back. They tried to arrange a closer link between war debts and reparations, gain greater control over the BIS, and minimize the advantages to be derived by the United States from a separate treaty with Germany. In particular, the French combated American attempts to make German payments to the United States unconditional.[55]

Republican officials did not stand by idly. As in the past they relied upon unofficial experts and informal observers to defend American interests. Stimson permitted private American financiers to participate in the Baden-Baden meeting, and he assigned Edwin C. Wilson, a member of the Paris embassy, to the second Hague Conference as an unofficial American observer. Wilson had gained the confidence of Young and Lamont while the experts had been meeting in Paris, and he now worked closely with them. The Americans threatened to sever all ties, even private ones, with the BIS and prevent the marketing of reparation bonds in the United States if the French and British did not abandon their efforts to politicize the BIS, further revise the Young

54. For coverage of the debate in France, see the extensive collection of French documents and newspaper clippings, RG 39, Boxes 58 and 63; see also Poincaré, "Le Plan Young," *Excelsior*, 28 March 1930, ibid., Box 78; Weill-Raynal, *Réparations allemandes*, 3:479–88, 489–92.

55. For Franco-American differences at the second Hague Conference, see Wilson to Stimson, 7, 8, 9, 10, 17 January 1930, RG 39, Box 80; Cotton to Wilson, 7, 10, 13 January 1930, ibid. At Baden-Baden the British constituted the major opposition to American aims, but the French also presented some problems. See De Sanchez to Lamont, 28 November 1929, Thomas W. Lamont Papers, Box 181. For a detailed discussion of developments at the Hague conferences, see Weill-Raynal, *Réparation allemandes*, 3:489–573.

Plan, and link war debt and reparation payments.[56] Since the French were eager to have some form of American participation in the BIS and to capitalize some portion of the reparation bonds in the United States, they eventually succumbed to American pressure (as did the British).[57]

Not surprisingly, Europe's acceptance of the Young Plan and the BIS in January 1930 was greeted with great enthusiasm in the United States. Newspapers acclaimed the settlement of the reparations issue, and bankers and businessmen heralded the new financial institution.[58] In the Hoover administration's view, its reliance on the traditional techniques of Republican diplomacy had paid rich dividends. The reparation experts had brought about an indemnity agreement. Private American bankers had established a new organization to institution-alize central bank cooperation, with Gates W. McGarrah, former chairman of the board of the FRBNY, as its first president. The administration had avoided an acrimonious debate in Congress over the Young Plan, had protected itself from the international political complications that would arise should the plan break down, had maintained intact the traditional American policy of separating war debts and reparations, and had achieved an unofficial, but intimate, American link with the BIS.[59]

Although the brunt of American policies fell on all European governments, the French felt especially burdened because of the political and financial implications of the reparations settlement. To the French, it seemed as if the Americans were trying to safeguard their war debt claims, protect their private investments, and sustain a healthy European market, all at the same time. The French were angered that they

56. For the selection of American financiers for the Baden-Baden meeting, see Cotton to Castle, 10 July 1929, RG 59, 462.00R296/3101; Young to Henry Robinson, 22 July 1929, Young Papers, R–30; Young to Emile Moreau, 5 September 1929, Thomas W. Lamont Papers, Box 181; for American actions at the second Hague Conference, see Cotton to Wilson, 6 January 1930, RG 39, Box 80; Wilson to Cotton, 9 January 1930, ibid.; for Wilson's close ties with the reparation experts, see Perkins to Stimson, 15 July 1929, Young Papers, R–30; Lamont to Ben Joy, 1 August 1929, Thomas W. Lamont Papers, Box 180.

57. For French aims, see Moreau to Morgan, 24 July 1929, Thomas W. Lamont Papers, Box 180; Moreau to Young, 23 July 1929, Young Papers, R–20; Gilbert to Lamont, 3 September 1929, Thomas W. Lamont Papers, Box 181; De Sanchez to Lamont, 10 October, 28 November 1929, ibid.

58. For press reaction, see "The Young Plan Closes the War Books," *Literary Digest* 104 (1 February 1930):12; for the reaction of businessmen and bankers, see, for example, NFTC, *Official Report*, 1930, vii; ABA, Commerce and Marine Division, *Survey of Financial Affairs at Home and Abroad*, pp. 5–6.

59. Hoover personally approved of McGarrah's selection as president of the BIS. See Memorandum of conversation between Harrison and Cotton, 18 December 1929, George L. Harrison Papers, 2011.1.

were being asked, either directly or indirectly, to reduce reparations, pay war debts, and accept the security risks of a revitalized Germany liberated from Allied occupation forces. Consequently, during the debates in the French Chamber of Deputies over the Young Plan, not only were American war debt and tariff policies attacked but so was S. Parker Gilbert for supposedly arranging a reduction in reparations to safeguard American investments.[60]

The negative features of the Young Plan notwithstanding, Premier André Tardieu exhorted the Chamber of Deputies to ratify the Hague agreements. In early 1930 he suspected that German efforts to secure additional American credits, even at ruinous rates, constituted a devious attempt to prevent the flotation of the reparation bonds. Tardieu was therefore anxious to capitalize a portion of the reparation bonds before French troops had to be withdrawn from the Rhineland in June 1930. Like Poincaré, Tardieu assumed that the marketing of the reparation bonds would force the German government to meet its obligations by interlocking Germany's public and private credit.[61]

The Hoover administration, however, frowned upon a large flotation of reparation bonds in the American market. Although officials in the State Department, the Commerce Department, and the FRBNY realized that the stock market crash had encouraged a revival in foreign lending, which was necessary to maintain American exports, they were not eager to have increasingly scarce American capital resources squandered on the sale of reparation bonds, two-thirds of the proceeds of which would go to France. Undersecretary of State Cotton believed that the French were already too powerful financially. According to him the flow of capital from the United States to France would unnecessarily augment French financial strength while doing little to resuscitate the American economy. Consequently, in reviewing French pleas for a bond flotation, the administration decided that no more than one-third of the total flotation should be marketed in the United States, that the American share should be less than $100 million, and that an equal percentage of the bonds should be sold in France. Uncertain of the extent to which American financial markets could absorb reparation bonds and fearing Congressman McFadden's opposition to the sale of these bonds in the United States, Republican officials were again shifting a larger burden of the reparations settlement onto the French. In the

60. See the reports on the debate in the French Chamber, Armour to secretary, 31 March, 15 April 1930, RG 39, Box 78.
61. Wilson to Cotton, 9 January 1930, ibid., Box 80; Armour to Cotton, 24 March 1930, ibid., Box 79; Weill-Raynal, *Réparations allemandes*, 3:593–94, 557–59.

new economic climate even the private American financial contribution to European stability was to be carefully circumscribed. In June 1930 a total of $300 million worth of Young bonds were sold, but only $85 million worth were marketed in the United States.[62]

The American stand on the bond flotation accorded with Hoover's predilections. His initial response to the stock market crash and the economic downturn was to look inward. He consulted with businessmen regarding wage maintenance programs, and he encouraged local and state governments to undertake additional public works projects. He was eager to settle the tariff issue and make credit more readily available. And he wanted to reduce taxes. "Every dollar so returned," he told Congress in December 1929, "fertilizes the soil of prosperity."[63] Because of his domestic preoccupations, Hoover was not inclined to deal generously with the war debts. Although he urged Congress to ratify the Mellon-Bérenger accord, he did not give any consideration to methods whereby France or other European debtors could use the capitalized portion of their indemnity receipts to prepay war debts at substantial discounts. Such plans had been discussed by Gilbert and Owen Young as well as by some Treasury and State Department officials. Hoover, however, had never indicated much interest in these proposals. As budgetary problems mounted during the latter part of 1930, the incentive to follow up a reparations settlement with a quick and generous liquidation of the war debts disappeared.[64]

In handling the war debt, reparation, and currency issues, the Hoover administration accepted the viability of established Republican techniques and shied away from innovative approaches. Though this orientation put a heavier burden on European nations, by 1929 Hoover felt that the Old World had recovered sufficiently to assume such sacri-

62. For the American position on the reparation bonds, see Harrison to Jay E. Crane, 29 March 1930, RG 39, Box 218; Crane to Harrison, 28 March 1930, ibid.; House, Banking and Currency, *Reparation Bonds*; Hall, Memorandum, 13 May 1930, RG 59, 462.00R296BIS/111; see also the detailed memoranda, May 1930, Thomas W. Lamont Papers, Box 181; for the bond flotation, see Weill-Raynal, *Réparations allemandes*, 3:593–600.

63. For the quotation, see Hoover, *State Papers*, 1:142; for Hoover's initial policies, see ibid., 1:133ff., 289–96, 376–80; Albert U. Romasco, *The Poverty of Abundance*, pp. 3–172.

64. For Hoover's support of the work of the World War Foreign Debt Commission (WDC) and of the Mellon-Bérenger agreement, see Hoover, *State Papers*, 1:143–44, 175–76; for plans relating to the prepayment of the war debts, see, for example, Arthur N. Young to secretary, 2 January 1929, RG 59, 462.00R296/3060; D. C. Poole to secretary, 5 October 1928, ibid., 462.00R296/2389½; Winston "American War Debt Policy," pp. 27–28 in RG 39, Box 220. This writer has not found any evidence that Hoover considered such schemes after the marketing of the Young bonds.

fices. And in 1930 he became too absorbed in domestic solutions to the Depression to consider new answers to foreign policy questions. The administration's financial policy toward Europe engendered criticism from more internationally oriented bankers and businessmen, like Lamont, Harrison, and Young. But Hoover's careful balancing of national and international objectives, his emphasis on domestic priorities, and his nonentanglement inclinations coincided with prevailing American sentiment. Even such actions as the private American participation in the BIS and the limited flotation of reparation bonds provoked congressional charges that the administration was focusing too much attention on European affairs. Opposite complaints, of course, emanated from the French and other European governments. In the face of these conflicting accusations Republican officials continued their efforts to make an appropriate American contribution to European stability and French security, without jeopardizing domestic priorities or incurring dangerous commitments. This orientation was underscored by their actions at the London Naval Conference of 1930.

Arms Limitation and French Security: The London Naval Conference

Upon becoming president, Hoover wanted to limit armaments at home and abroad. He realized that the United States was spending more money on armaments than was any other nation in the world. Since Army and Navy officials assessing the international situation reported no imminent threat to American vital interests, Hoover hoped that limiting armaments would reduce the burden of taxation and curtail the waste of human and capital resources without jeopardizing the nation's security. Yet he remained rigidly opposed to the incursion of military commitments abroad. Hoover was not indifferent to the impact of European boundary disputes, revisionist demands, and strategic rivalries on American interests. In fact, the president stated that all of these matters aroused legitimate American concern because they upset international trade patterns, restricted world economic growth, and retarded American overseas sales. But Hoover did not believe these matters justified the assumption of strategic obligations in Europe because they did not affect *vital* American interests.[65]

65. For Hoover's views, see Hoover, *State Papers*, 1:59–60, 101, 125–29, 141; for Army and Navy assessments of the international situation, see War Department General Staff, "Survey of the Military Establishment," 1 November 1929, General Records of the War Department General and Special Staffs, RG 165, War Plans Division (WPD), No. 3345; WPD to Chief of Naval Operations (CNO), "Estimate of the Situation," 10 April 1929, Confidential Records of the Secretary of the Navy, RG 80, File L1–1.

Hoover wanted to use the Kellogg-Briand Pact as a framework for limiting armaments without incurring military obligations. In the spring of 1929 he authorized Ambassador Hugh Gibson to lay a set of conciliatory proposals before the Preparatory Commission for the Disarmament Conference to break the long-standing impasse at Geneva. Gibson emphasized that America's primary concern was with naval armaments. He reiterated that the United States would defer to other nations on matters pertaining to land armaments. He intimated that the Hoover administration was ready to meet the French halfway on a number of important technical issues, including the definition of military effectives. Most important, however, Gibson declared that the United States was prepared to explore new methods of computing the equivalent value of naval vessels. In this way the United States hoped to overcome the problems that had prevented an Anglo-American naval agreement in 1927.[66]

The Hoover administration was fortunate that its disarmament offensive coincided with the coming to power of a Labour government in Great Britain under Prime Minister J. Ramsay MacDonald. The new government was eager to avert an armaments race with the United States and anxious to improve Anglo-American ties. Very quickly MacDonald accepted the principle that the United States was entitled to naval parity with Britain. He slowed British construction of several cruisers, entered into constructive talks with American diplomats, and laid plans for a visit to the United States. These actions not only bred a new spirit of Anglo-American amity but they also expedited agreement on the basic principles of an arms limitation accord and prepared the way for the convocation of a naval conference.[67]

The British prime minister's conciliatory disposition toward the United States contrasted sharply with his government's attitude toward France. At the first Hague Conference in August 1929 Chancellor of the Exchequer Philip Snowden attacked French financial policy, ridiculed the Young Plan, and demanded larger reparation payments for Britain. At the same time, British Foreign Secretary Arthur Henderson injected a new note of acrimony into Anglo-French relations by announcing his government's intention to withdraw British troops from the Rhineland regardless of French wishes. Though the policies of the British Labour government boded well for an Anglo-American naval

66. FR, 1929, 1:88–96.
67. For MacDonald's actions and Anglo-American discussions prior to the London Conference, see Great Britain, Foreign Office, *Documents on British Foreign Policy*, Series 2, 1:3–105 (hereafter cited as DBFP).

agreement, they aroused widespread apprehension in France that the British were downgrading their commitment to Continental affairs. The French, therefore, worried about the ramifications of MacDonald's trip to Washington in October 1929.[68]

During the prime minister's visit Hoover and MacDonald ironed out some remaining differences over naval matters and discussed other issues as well. The president raised the possibility of amending the Kellogg-Briand Pact to make it more potent. He wanted a commission established to investigate disputes, publish pertinent facts, and propose solutions. Hoover sought to expand the rights of neutrals by exempting food ships from interference during times of war. According to Hoover, agreement on this matter would facilitate naval reductions, because many nations were strengthening their navies to enhance their ability to export or import foodstuffs.[69]

MacDonald discussed these matters in a spirit of amity. He was perplexed by Hoover's simultaneous desire to amend the Kellogg-Briand Pact and to reappraise the rights of neutrals. On the one hand the new provision to the treaty renouncing war might enable the governments of Great Britain and the United States to exchange views on the nature of American neutrality rights should Britain be called upon to enforce Article 16 of the League covenant through a naval blockade. On the other hand Hoover's desire to emphasize the rights of neutrals revived British fears that the principal aim of American naval policy was to protect American shipping during periods of European conflict. If food shipments were exempted from seizure, Article 16 would lose some of its effectiveness. The British had hoped that the Kellogg-Briand Pact would lead to a relaxation, not a strengthening, of the definition of the rights of neutrals.[70] Rather than belabor these contentious issues, however, the British prime minister sought to emphasize areas of mutual interest. The joint statement issued at the conclusion of the Hoover-MacDonald talks highlighted the cordial ties between the two statesmen and stressed the opportunities for naval disarmament engendered by the Kellogg-Briand Pact.[71]

68. Viscount Philip Snowden, *An Autobiography*, 2:788–830; Weill-Raynal, *Réparations allemandes*, 3:492–510; Jacobson, *Locarno Diplomacy*, pp. 283–86; DBFP, 2, 1:125–26, 203–4.

69. For the Hoover-MacDonald talks, see DBFP, 2, 1:106–16; Hoover, *Memoirs*, 2:336, 343–45.

70. For MacDonald's reactions to Hoover's proposals, see Hoover, *Memoirs*, 2:346; DBFP, 2, 1:109–12; for the importance of American neutrality policy in British naval considerations, see chapter 5, pp. 161–63.

71. For the joint statement, see Hoover, *State Papers*, 1:108.

Although the French agreed to attend a five-power naval conference, they observed the improvement in Anglo-American relations with trepidation. France feared that, in the course of reconciling their differences, the British and American governments would sacrifice French strategic interests. This prospect seemed especially alarming to the French because they already viewed the forthcoming withdrawal of their troops from the Rhineland as a strategic blow.[72] Throughout the autumn of 1929 the French emphasized their own minimum naval requirements. They demanded sufficient tonnage to have equality with Germany in the Atlantic, parity with Italy in the Mediterranean, and a few additional vessels for the protection of overseas colonies. Emphasizing their special preoccupation with safeguarding the Marseilles-Algiers crossing, which they considered part of their internal mobilization line, the French insisted that they could never accept Italy's demand for total naval equality unless France received additional security guarantees, perhaps in the form of a Mediterranean nonaggression pact.[73]

MacDonald tried to assure the French that their security would not be jeopardized at the naval conference. Knowing that the French deplored broadening the rights of neutrals, the British prime minister maintained that he would not support Hoover's desire to exempt food ships from interference by belligerents. He acknowledged that such a change would weaken Article 16.[74]

Despite MacDonald's assurances, the French realized that the British Labour government was unwilling to assume new commitments. On Christmas morning 1929 Tardieu became so agitated that he called Ambassador Edge and insisted on a meeting that day. When the two men got together, the French premier charged that "you Anglo-Saxons are trying to disarm France to the advantage of Germany and Italy." Alluding to his fears of Germany's military potential, Tardieu reiterated that his government would not reduce its naval construction program unless France received new security guarantees.[75] In other words Tar-

72. For French fears, see DBFP, 2, 1:126–27, 130–31, 173–77; Walter E. Edge, *A Jerseyman's Journal*, pp. 151–52, 155–56; for the withdrawal of French troops from the Rhineland, see Jacobson, *Locarno Diplomacy*, pp. 279–334.

73. For French demands, see FR, 1929, 1:59–61, 261–62, 266–67, 297–307; DBFP, 2, 1:167–72, 180–81, 201.

74. DBFP, 2, 1:137; for French unhappiness with Hoover's proposals to exempt food ships from belligerent interference, see Armour to Stimson, 13 November 1929, RG 59, 700.00112 Freedom of the Seas/13.

75. Edge, *Journal*, pp. 156–57.

dieu rejected the Anglo-American thesis that the Kellogg-Briand Pact provided the necessary security for additional arms reductions.[76]

The British endeavored to satisfy French demands with the completion of a consultative pact. On 29 December, the Foreign Office instructed the British ambassador in Washington to introduce the idea of such a pact to Stimson.[77] When the secretary of state arrived in London at the head of the American delegation, MacDonald explained that he would not be able to offer France new guarantees but indicated that he would sign a consultative pact along the lines of the Four-Power Treaty concluded at the Washington Conference.[78] In subsequent meetings with the French, MacDonald emphasized the advantages of such a treaty. He maintained that a consultative pact would enhance French security, because the problem "was whether the United States would undertake not to support its citizens who get into difficulties as a result of trading with a nation which had broken the Kellogg Pact and was being subjected to economic sanctions."[79] The assumption, of course, was that once having signed a consultative pact, the United States would cooperate with nations trying to deter aggression and would shape its neutrality practices accordingly. MacDonald, of course, did not add that another advantage of a consultative pact, at least from the British perspective, was that it did not augment British strategic commitments on the Continent.

Britain's willingness to sign a consultative treaty, however, did not satisfy the French. They continued to demand new strategic guarantees. When Tardieu arrived at the conference, he presented the French naval program, which called for 240,000 tons of new construction between 1930 and 1936. The French premier explained that this program constituted no menace to Britain or the United States; it was aimed exclusively at meeting the threats posed by Italy and Germany. Tardieu alluded to provisions of the Treaty of Versailles allowing Germany to build six cruisers and six battleships. Given the fact that Germany was embarking on a program to build these cruisers, Tardieu asked MacDonald how he could expect France to limit the number of

---

76. DBFP, 2, 1:173–77; FR, 1929, 1:59–61.
77. DBFP, 2, 1:183; see also pp. 186–87.
78. FR, 1930, 1:3. The Four-Power Treaty, among other things, obligated the signatories (the United States, Britain, France, and Japan) to consult with one another regarding possible action should a nonsignatory threaten their possessions in the Pacific Ocean.
79. DBFP, 2, 1:254.

her own cruisers to seven, especially when Italy was demanding parity with France and challenging French interests in Tunisia, Libya, Abyssinia, and the Adriatic. Tardieu concluded that he would modify the French naval program only in return for a mutual assistance pact in the Mediterranean.[80]

During February and most of March Stimson and the other American delegates observed the impasse between Britain and France with mounting consternation. The British refused to offer new security guarantees to France, yet desired to maintain a navy at least equal in size to the two largest Continental navies. The French naval program, therefore, threatened to force Britain to undertake new construction of her own. This prospect impeded an Anglo-American agreement. On 23 February Stimson wired the State Department that "our first problem is, obviously, to get the French to come down from their original figures."[81] Accordingly, he and Senator Dwight W. Morrow, one of the American delegates, engaged the French in extensive discussion regarding their demand for security. During these talks the French never asked the United States to assume direct obligations in the Mediterranean. Morrow realized that the French were not asking the United States to enter into entangling alliances in Europe. Rather, France wanted the United States to assure Great Britain that American neutrality rights would be suspended when members of the League of Nations were acting collectively to deter aggression. Upon repeated questioning, the French reiterated that a consultative pact was important only insofar as it would affect Britain's willingness to offer firm security guarantees. Standing alone, a consultative pact would not induce the French to modify their naval program.[82]

As the American delegates gained a better appreciation of the French position and realized that the deadlock in the conference threatened even a three-power agreement, Stimson decided to assume the initiative. On 24 March he told the British that if they offered to guarantee French security, the United States would consider signing a consultative pact. If such a pact were accompanied by guarantees from other nations, Stimson felt that France would not be able to interpret it to

80. Ibid., pp. 212–13, 221–25; for an excellent contemporary analysis of France's rivalry with Italy and her naval strategy, see the lecture by Joseph C. Green at the Naval War College, 12 December 1930, RG 59, 740.0011 Mutual Guarantee-Mediterranean/36.
81. FR, 1930, 1:29.
82. Harold Nicolson, *Dwight Morrow*, p. 368; FR, 1930, 1:36–39, 45–46, 52–53, 55–56, 63–65, 72–73, 75–79, 92–95. These dispatches from Stimson to the State Department were forwarded to Hoover. See HHPP, Box 849.

mean that the United States was guaranteeing French security. In other words the secretary was prepared to consult about American neutrality policy if consultation would expedite a new security agreement between France and Britain. But he was unwilling to assume new responsibilities for the United States to guarantee French security. Neither Army nor Navy officials thought such guarantees desirable.[83]

President Hoover was upset by the change in Stimson's position and by the emphasis being placed on a consultative pact. The president did not object to the principle of consultation. But he worried that a consultative pact might be misconstrued to mean that the United States was assuming concrete commitments. Should such misinterpretation occur, Hoover feared that big-navy supporters might muster additional allies to defeat both a consultative pact and an arms limitation treaty. He sounded out friends of the administration on Capitol Hill and found them unexcited about the prospect of a consultative treaty. The president declared that peace groups and newspaper writers who supported the principle of consultation did not represent public opinion. But his reading of public opinion was influenced by his own predilections. Fundamentally, Hoover was suspicious of all attempts, however indirect, to embroil the United States in European politics. "From the very beginning," Undersecretary Cotton wrote Stimson, "his attitude . . . has been against inclusion of any political undertaking as a part of disarmament agreement." Yet, the president did not wish to discredit his secretary of state or undermine Stimson's efforts to effect a naval accord. Although Hoover hoped to defer the question of consultation to a later date, he was nevertheless willing to consider a modified consultative agreement, if it carefully differentiated between the commitments of the United States and Britain and if it specifically foreclosed the use of American military force.[84]

Stimson realized that his initiative of 24 March had caused the president some embarrassment. Stimson thanked Hoover for his "fine sporting spirit." The secretary assured the president that he would

83. DBFP, 2, 1:266–67; FR, 1930, 1:79–81; Henry L. Stimson and McGeorge Bundy, *On Active Service in Peace and War*, pp. 170–71; for views of Army and Navy officials, see Director, WPD, to CNO, "Estimate of the Situation," 15 April 1930, RG 80, File L1–1; extract from Military Intelligence Division (MID) Summary, 3 January 1930, Office of Naval Intelligence (ONI), RG 38, File C–10–g 1999.

84. For the quotation, see FR, 1930, 1:89; for Hoover's attitudes and actions, see pp. 32–33, 39–43, 48–49, 59, 81–83, 85–86, 88–90, 96–97; Hoover, *Memoirs*, 2:348; Lamont to Morrow, 26 March 1930, Thomas W. Lamont Papers, Box 113. Hoover's fears about the ramifications of a consultative pact were shared by some well-known Democratic internationalists. See Norman H. Davis to Hoover, 25 March 1930, HHPP, Box 864.

circumscribe American commitments and not even discuss the specific phrasing of a consultative pact until the British and French had agreed on security guarantees and armament figures. Stimson reasserted that his purpose was to expedite an agreement between the former allies and accommodate "Britain's desire to ascertain the effect [of the use of her fleet] . . . upon United States trade and policy." After a few days Stimson informed Washington that his initiative had produced the desired effect: the British and French had finally begun to talk constructively.[85]

Although the discussions between France and Britain did not satisfy the French quest for additional security guarantees, they did produce a feeling of greater solidarity between the former allies. Thereafter, MacDonald sought to clarify Britain's obligations under existing treaty commitments. Briand was pleased by this development and thanked Stimson "for . . . having given the push that broke the jam."[86] Subsequently, the French agreed to sign four of the five sections of the treaty. Yet this action was only a symbolic gesture of cooperation because France retained her freedom to build additional tonnage. The Franco-Italian naval rivalry was left unresolved. It threatened to force Britain into undertaking new construction, thereby jeopardizing the accord with the United States and Japan.[87]

Despite the potential problems, Republican officials expressed satisfaction with the outcome of the naval conference and immediately requested the Senate to ratify the London agreement. The treaty, in the view of policymakers, fulfilled American objectives: it stopped competitive building in all categories, gave the United States parity with Britain, left American defenses unimpaired, reduced expenditures on armaments, met the needs of the world economic situation and the American recovery effort, and did not entangle the United States in the political affairs of the Old World. Although Hoover was somewhat disappointed that the reductions in tonnage were not greater, he estimated that the agreement would save the world $2.5 billion and be "a great stimulus to world prosperity." He also hoped that the London

85. For the quotations, see FR, 1930, 1:87, 95; see also pp. 84, 92–95; Stimson to Cotton, 27 March 1930, HHPP, Box 849; see also Charles G. Dawes, *Journal as Ambassador to Great Britain*, p. 178.

86. FR, 1930, 1:101; for the Anglo-French talks, see DBFP, 2, 1:276–79, 292–305; see also FR, 1930, 1:101–6.

87. An "escalator clause" permitted Britain to undertake additional construction under certain circumstances. For Stimson's explanation of the agreement and of the obligations of the five powers, see Senate, Committee on Foreign Relations, *Treaty on the Limitation of Naval Armaments*, pp. 7 ff.

treaty would lead to future naval reductions and accelerate other steps toward world peace and stability.[88] For the most part the American press and business community shared Hoover's outlook. In July the Senate ratified the treaty with less than a dozen votes in opposition.[89]

One glaring weakness of the treaty, however, was that it contributed little to European stability. The treaty neither enhanced French security nor limited French armaments. Moreover, Germany grew increasingly agitated by the failure to make greater progress toward limiting land armaments. The only comfort to American officials was that the proceedings at London had clarified French wishes. Before leaving London in April, Briand had reiterated to Stimson that France did not seek security guarantees from the United States but wanted an amendment to the Kellogg-Briand Pact providing for consultation in times of crisis. During the summer of 1930 both Walter Lippmann and André Geraud wrote articles in *Foreign Affairs* explaining that a consultative accord would facilitate Anglo-French understanding on security and contribute greatly to European stability.[90]

Yet, after the London treaty was ratified by the Senate, Republican policymakers did not try to satisfy France's limited demands. Hoover and Stimson sought to mediate Franco-Italian naval rivalries lest these upset the London accords. But they did not want to embroil the United States in European politics and, therefore, avoided pressuring either nation to compromise its views of national self-interest. Rather than allow the United States to assume indirect commitments, Stimson insisted that the English had a greater responsibility to extend political guarantees and iron out Franco-Italian differences. But for the remainder of 1930 the secretary of state did nothing to encourage the British to extend these political guarantees. Bills before the appropriate Senate and House committees that would have provided for consultation and that would have revised American neutrality policy to make it more compatible with European security arrangements did not receive sup-

88. For Hoover's views, see Hoover, *State Papers*, 1:230–33, 236–37, 274ff., 311–12, 348, 351–56; for Stimson's defense of the treaty, see Senate, Foreign Relations, *Limitation of Naval Armaments*, pp. 1–62.

89. "Foes of the Naval Treaty Overwhelmed," *Literary Digest* 106 (2 August 1930):5–6; for business sentiment, see, for example, president of Chamber of Commerce of the United States (CCUS) to Hoover, 1 July 1930, HHPP, Box 865; A. G. Everett, "Navies, Taxes, and International Peace Insurance," *Journal of the American Bankers Association* 23 (August 1930):94–95, 142.

90. For Briand's remarks to Stimson, see FR, 1930, 1:101; see also André Geraud, "The London Naval Conference," pp. 519–33; Walter Lippmann, "The London Naval Conference," pp. 499–519; Hugh Robert Wilson, *Diplomat Between Wars*, pp. 240–41.

port from the administration. Thus, although the United States government prodded French and Italian officials to limit their armament programs, the responsibilities and risks attendant to such action fell principally on the British and French. Characteristically, in October 1930 Hoover bitterly condemned the French for impeding consummation of the five-power London treaty, but made no mention of France's legitimate strategic anxieties.[91]

Even after huge gains by the Nazis in the September 1930 German elections had caused great apprehension in France, the fundamental orientation of Republican diplomacy did not change. Hoover and Stimson recognized the growing seriousness of the European political situation, acknowledged that European governments might repudiate their promises not to resort to war, and realized the complexity of the issues involved. Yet, throughout 1930 both men agreed that American interests in European affairs were not great enough to justify political embroilments. Both maintained that American strategic imperatives were not threatened and that American intervention would not necessarily resolve European differences. Most characteristic, at a critical moment in the London Conference, Stimson had wired Hoover that "we can properly take no leading part [in European disputes]. The parties to the controversies must themselves work out their problems with such friendly help as we can give." France, Stimson acknowledged, was entitled to new guarantees of security. But it was Britain's responsibility to provide them. The proper American role in 1930, even according to one of the great forbears of American internationalism, was to try to foster European stability without incurring such commitments.[92]

Conclusion

During 1929 and 1930 Hoover continued to rely on the techniques of diplomacy established between 1921 and 1923 to reconcile domestic

91. For the State Department's efforts to mediate Franco-Italian differences, see FR, 1930, 1:132–86; for Stimson's attitude, see Stimson and Bundy, *On Active Service*, p. 170; for the administration's failure to support legislation revising American neutrality policy, see Noel H. Field, "The Security Question Since the Peace Conference," December 1931, Davis Papers, Box 17; for Hoover's view of French policy, see Diary of Henry L. Stimson, 17 October 1930, Stimson Papers.
92. For the quotation, see FR, 1930, 1:78; for Stimson's views, see pp. 75–81, 92–95; for Hoover's views regarding political embroilments in Europe and American interests, see Hoover, *State Papers*, 1:235, 239–40, 271, 416–17.

goals and European imperatives. In his handling of all matters linking the interests of the United States and Europe, however, he tended to emphasize domestic priorities. He expected European nations, especially financially powerful France, to bear a larger share of the sacrifices, risks, and responsibilities for preserving European stability. Hoover's policies were motivated by two sets of assumptions. First, he felt that involvement in European political disputes might engender responsibilities that were out of proportion to legitimate American concerns.[93] Second, Hoover was convinced that the United States could "make a very large degree of recovery independently of what may happen elsewhere." In late 1930 Hoover estimated that, even at the reduced levels of American trade, the United States could return to a 97 percent normal business situation if domestic consumption were restored. Thus, his use of the policymaking machinery in a more nationalistic mold reflected his view that the United States was "remarkably self-contained."[94]

Hoover's personal assessment of American economic and strategic needs assumed great importance in 1929 and 1930. As president he exerted a much greater influence on the entire policymaking process than any chief executive since the war. Hoover believed in an active presidency, and he possessed great confidence in his own ability. He was willing to make tough decisions that reflected his own set of values and perceptions. Accordingly, he used established diplomatic techniques in a way that highlighted both his emphasis on domestic economic priorities and his apprehension of European political entanglements. Although this orientation upset a few of the most internationally oriented bankers and businessmen, there was little opposition to the president's policies within the administration. Stimson, Cotton, Mellon, and Mills felt comfortable with the president's overall orientation toward European affairs. Army and Navy officials continued to minimize the importance of European developments and French strategic anxieties.[95] In Congress there was little overt sentiment for either greater American participation in the political affairs of the Old World or greater American economic sacrifices in behalf of

93. Hoover, *State Papers*, 1:234–40, 415–17.
94. Ibid., pp. 376–80, 429.
95. Director, WPD, to CNO, 10 April 1929, 15 April 1930, "Estimate of the Situation," RG 80, File L1–1; War Department General Staff, "Survey of the Military Establishment," 1 November 1929, General Records of the War Department General and Special Staffs, RG 165, WPD No. 3345; extract from MID Summary, 3 January 1930, RG 38, C–10–g 1999.

European stability. If anything the contrary was true. Thus, there was little impetus for the president to devise bold and innovative methods for dealing with European problems. Only the repeated financial shocks of 1931 compelled Hoover to reassess American policies and consider whether new approaches were necessary to meet the problems of a new era.

[7]

Crisis, Action,
and Uncertainty, 1931

During the latter part of 1930 economic and financial conditions in the United States and Europe deteriorated rapidly. President Hoover acknowledged in his second annual message to Congress on 2 December 1930 that during the preceding year manufacturing production had declined 20 percent, factory employment 16 percent, wholesale prices 17 percent, mineral production 10 percent, and department store sales 7 percent.[1] He did not analyze the state of the nation's foreign trade; had he done so, he would have reported that exports had decreased by approximately 35 percent. At the same time, the number of business failures had reached an all-time high of 26,355; the net income of corporations had dropped by over $5 billion; the unemployment rate had jumped from 3.2 to 8.7 percent; and the number of bank failures had increased by almost 500.[2]

The situation in Europe was not much better. For the Continent as a whole, annual manufacturing production in 1930 decreased substantially; but the declines were most precipitous in Germany, Austria, Poland, Belgium, and Great Britain. Declines in the foreign trade of European nations were often more rapid than decreases in production. Between 1929 and 1930 total European exports fell by over $2 billion and European imports by almost $3 billion. Naturally, these steep reductions in production and trade were accompanied by increasing unemployment rates and diminishing per capita incomes. In the United

1. Herbert C. Hoover, *The State Papers and Other Public Writings of Herbert Hoover*, 1:429.
2. Department of Commerce, *Statistical Abstract of the United States*, 1932, pp. 430, 295, 297; 1933, p. 185; Lester V. Chandler, *America's Greatest Depression, 1929–1941*, p. 5.

Kingdom and Germany, for example, unemployment rates increased from approximately 10 to 16 percent and 13 to 22 percent respectively. For the most part economic conditions in France did not deteriorate quite so quickly as in neighboring nations or as in the United States. But by the end of 1930, despite her enormous holdings of gold and foreign exchange, France too was rocked by stock market scandals and bank failures.[3]

The worsening economic and financial situation affected political developments in all western nations and narrowed the options available to policymakers. In Germany, Chancellor Heinrich Brüning sought to govern by decree under Article 48 of the Weimar constitution. Beleaguered by mounting opposition on the Right and the Left, he tried to seize the diplomatic offensive and challenge the Versailles system to gain popular approval and offset the nationalistic appeal of Adolf Hitler's rhetoric. In France the relative political stability that had accompanied Poincaré's financial triumphs of the late 1920s disappeared. After a succession of crises, Pierre Laval emerged at the head of a new government in January 1931. He wanted to conciliate both Germany and Italy. But faced with an uncertain majority in the Chamber of Deputies Laval felt compelled to challenge Brüning's proposal for an Austro-German customs union and suspend the promising naval talks with Italy. Almost everywhere in Europe parliamentary instability and political dissension complicated the task of policymaking, retarded innovative thinking, and precluded bold initiatives to deal with the economic downslide and attendant foreign policy issues.[4]

The situation was similar in the United States. In November 1930 the American people went to the polls and demonstrated their discontent with prevailing conditions. The large Republican majorities in both the Senate and House were virtually wiped out. Hoover had had considerable difficulty dealing with the Republican-dominated Seventy-first Congress. The prospect of grappling with an even more hostile Congress under worsening economic conditions deeply troubled him. His contemptuous attitude toward the legislative branch, his failure to

3. For pertinent statistical information on European production, trade, and unemployment, see Ingvar Svennilson, *Growth and Stagnation in the European Economy*, pp. 304, 312–13, 31; Alfred Sauvy, *Histoire économique de la France entre les deux guerres*, 1:114–20, 462–70, 476–94; see also Charles P. Kindleberger, *The World in Depression, 1929–1939*, pp. 135–48; David Landes, *The Unbound Prometheus*, pp. 359–485, especially pp. 382–83, 390.

4. For a fine account of the political and diplomatic side of the European financial crisis, see Edward Wells Bennett, *Germany and the Diplomacy of the Financial Crisis, 1931*.

present initiatives, and his determination to circumscribe the extent of government spending bred hostility among Republicans and Democrats alike. Although few legislators formulated innovative proposals of their own, the last session of the Seventy-first Congress was filled with rancor as the president fought off raids on the treasury, reaffirmed his opposition to government-sponsored projects at Muscle Shoals, and vetoed the Wagner Bill for the improvement of public employment agencies.[5]

Preoccupied with the struggle over internal matters, neither the president nor Congress contemplated initiatives toward the Old World during the gloomy winter of 1930–31. In the spring Stimson laid plans for a visit to Europe and conferred with Borah on the possibility of consulting with European nations during times of aggression.[6] But Hoover still emphasized the importance of limiting armaments. He did not alter his aversion to entanglements in the Old World and continued to ignore occasional appeals for war debt reductions.[7] Although he began to place increasing emphasis on the international sources of the Depression, he remained skeptical of the efficacy of any measure that imposed sacrifices on the American people. He believed that domestic recovery through domestic action was the key to resuscitating the world economy; a resuscitated world economy would, in turn, benefit the American economy.[8] Until May and June of 1931, then, Hoover did not seem inclined to try anything new. At that time, however, a series of financial developments in central Europe shattered the illusion that the accustomed techniques of economic diplomacy, in conjunction

5. Hoover, *State Papers*, 1:428–532; Jordan A. Schwarz, *The Interregnum of Despair*, pp. 18–71; Albert U. Romasco, *The Poverty of Abundance*, pp. 3–172; Joan Hoff Wilson, *Herbert Hoover*, pp. 122–67; Edgar Eugene Robinson and Vaughn Davis Bornet, *Herbert Hoover*, pp. 134–78.

6. For Stimson's European trip, see Diary of Henry L. Stimson, 21, 22 May 1931, Stimson Papers; see also Stimson to American embassy, Rome, 16 April 1931, General Records of the Department of State, RG 59, File No. 033.1140 Stimson/1; for Stimson's talks with Borah, see Diary of Henry L. Stimson, 14, 20, 22 May 1931, Stimson Papers.

7. For Hoover's preoccupation with arms limitation and his opposition to political entanglements in the Old World, see Department of State, *Papers Relating to the Foreign Relations of the United States*, 1931, 1:493–95 (hereafter cited as FR); see also Diary of Henry L. Stimson, 1 May 1931, Stimson Papers; for occasional calls for war debt reductions, see Fred I. Kent to Hoover, 21 October 1930, Kent Papers, Box 3; Henry Robinson to Hoover, 1 August 1930, Herbert C. Hoover Presidential Papers, Box 871 (hereafter cited as HHPP); "War Debt Reduction and Business Recovery," *Literary Digest* 108 (24 January 1931):38; for Hoover's view of the war debts, see Hoover to Kent, 25 October 1930, HHPP, Box 871; Great Britain, Foreign Office, *Documents on British Foreign Policy*, Series 2, 1:578 (hereafter cited as DBFP).

8. Hoover, *State Papers*, 1:574–75, 580–81; see also Hoover to Kent, 25 October 1930, HHPP, Box 871.

with local and voluntary initiatives at home, could suffice to meet the intensifying crisis.

The Financial Crisis and the Hoover Moratorium

On 6 May 1931 President Hoover had a long talk with the German ambassador on financial conditions in central Europe. Later that day United States Ambassador Frederic M. Sackett, back from Berlin, met with the president and confirmed the bleak picture already drawn by the German envoy. Sackett described the misery of the German people, reported on the widespread political disturbances, and emphasized the extent of the unemployment problem. He concluded that unless something was done, revolution would topple the Weimar Republic. Hoover immediately requested statistical data on the scheduled war debt and reparation payments and on their relationships to the movement of European trade and the cost of European armaments. On 11 May, even before learning of Austria's growing financial difficulties, Hoover confided to Stimson that worldwide economic conditions had deteriorated so rapidly that the intergovernmental debts might now exceed the capacity of debtors to pay. As Hoover received more news about the failure of the Creditanstalt, the credit runs on Austria, and the financial strains on Germany, he contemplated revising the intergovernmental debt settlements in light of the capacity of nations to pay under depression conditions.[9] The critical issue for the president was whether a reduction in debts and a possible revival in trade would have a more salutary impact on the domestic economy than the collection of debts and possible deferment of tax increases.[10]

While Hoover pondered this matter, developments in the Old World caused mounting consternation in administration circles. During the first week of June the emergency credits that had been extended to the Austrian National Bank in late May were exhausted. Meanwhile, the financial crisis flared up in Germany. Within a few days the Reichsbank lost over 150 million reichsmarks in gold, compelling Brüning to visit Britain to seek a revision of the Young Plan. While he sought foreign relief, the German chancellor was subject to intense new criticism at home. Opposition parties denounced his deflationary measures

9. See entries, 6–11 May 1931, "President's Diary of Developments," HHPP, Box 880 (hereafter cited as Hoover Diary).

10. "What Action—or Inaction—on War Debts Will Do," *Literary Digest* 108 (28 March 1931):44–45.

and attacked his decree powers.[11] As the survival of the Weimar Republic came into doubt, Hoover's concern increased because he had always believed that a prosperous and republican Germany was essential to a stable Europe.[12] But European developments were not viewed in isolation from domestic considerations. As Stimson noted in his diary on 2 June, Hoover was growing impatient at the failure of the domestic economy to revive. The president feared that the drift of gold to the United States resulting from the financial disarray in Europe might paralyze "central banking institutions the world over," further restrict international trade, and create additional economic havoc within the United States.[13]

Such portentous events at home and abroad prompted Hoover to discuss the merits of a one-year moratorium on all war debt and reparation payments with Mellon, Mills, and Stimson on 5 June. Although Mellon denigrated the idea, the president prodded his advisers to study the proposal. Hoover contemplated action, but he was too cautious an individual and too aware of the manifold problems before him to move abruptly. A debt moratorium might give his approach to the Depression a more international flavor and gain him new popularity at home and abroad. But a moratorium might engender Democratic opposition and exacerbate Franco-American relations. Therefore, the president sought more precise information on financial conditions in Austria and Germany and the extent of American short-term commitments in those nations.[14]

While Hoover studied the situation, Wall Street bankers became panicky. On 5 June the senior partners at J. P. Morgan and Company discussed the gravity of the crisis. J. P. Morgan emphasized that the United States government had to provide "a life-saver for the world." In the later afternoon Thomas Lamont phoned Hoover to express the firm's apprehensions. Estimating that American financial institutions held about 50 percent of the $2 billion worth of short-term credits in Germany, Lamont contended that many small banks in the United States would become alarmed and call in their credits if Germany declared a moratorium on reparation transfers. The result would be a

11. Kindleberger, *World in Depression*, pp. 152–53; Stephen V. O. Clarke, *Central Bank Cooperation, 1924–1931*, pp. 186–92; Bennett, *Financial Crisis*, pp. 116–31.
12. Herbert C. Hoover, *The Memoirs of Herbert Hoover*, 2:181–82.
13. Diary of Henry L. Stimson, 2 June 1931, Stimson Papers; Hoover Diary, 5 June 1931, HHPP, Box 880.
14. Diary of Henry L. Stimson, 5 June 1931, Stimson Papers; Hoover Diary, 5 June 1931, HHPP, Box 880.

"terrifying crisis." Many American banks, he predicted, would find their assets frozen in Germany. To head off an international crisis, the Morgan partners advised the United States government to invite America's debtors to avail themselves of the postponement clauses in their debt settlements.[15]

Hoover listened politely, raised some objections, and stated that he wanted to talk the situation over with Lamont's former partner, Senator Dwight Morrow. When Morrow met with the president, the senator agreed with Hoover that the crisis had to worsen to insure that a presidential initiative would neither be opposed by the Democrats nor rebuffed by the French.[16] Stimson and Mills disagreed. They were in constant contact with prominent New York bankers and began to share the anxieties overhanging Wall Street. When the Reichsbank lost another 400 million reichsmarks in gold during the second week in June, Stimson and Mills urged immediate action. Stimson wanted to salvage American investments in Germany. He realized that Britain would not aid Germany until the United States was willing to make reciprocal concessions. He told the president that there was no way of avoiding a linkage between war debt and reparation payments. When Hoover postponed action, the secretary of state bemoaned the president's timidity and reproached him for his indecisiveness. Yet, Stimson never explained how the administration could secure French approval of a moratorium or avoid possible charges by Democratic partisans that it was acting in the interests of Wall Street plutocrats.[17]

Hoover wavered because he was uncertain whether a moratorium was necessary. Nor did the president know whether a moratorium would be well received at home or abroad or whether it would be effective. Whereas Lamont and Stimson emphasized that Americans had $1 billion in short-term credits in Germany, Hoover estimated that the figure might be only $300 million.[18] Whereas Governor Harrison of the FRBNY claimed that the situation in Germany was untenable, Hoover learned from Gates McGarrah, president of the BIS, that the

15. Thomas W. Lamont, Memorandum, 5 June 1931, Thomas W. Lamont Papers, Box 98; Lamont to Hoover, 5 June 1931, HHPP, Box 871; Hoover Diary, 5 June 1931, ibid., Box 880.

16. Hoover Diary, 6, 9 June 1931, HHPP, Box 880.

17. For the attitudes and actions of Stimson and Mills, see Diary of Henry L. Stimson, 5–15 June 1931, Stimson Papers; see also Stimson's talks with the British ambassador, DBFP, 2, 2:69–71; for the losses of the Reichsbank, see Kindleberger, *World in Depression*, pp. 152–53.

18. Diary of Henry L. Stimson, 11 June 1931, Stimson Papers.

condition of the Reichsbank was serious but not critical.[19] Moreover, the president feared that either the American public or the French government would disapprove of a unilateral American call for a suspension of all debt and reparation payments. Well aware of the financial strength of France, Hoover did not consider it appropriate to reduce or cancel the debts of a nation that had the capacity to pay. Nor did he think Congress would approve such action. He worried that an American initiative might encourage European nations to postpone essential readjustments of their own and rely upon the United States to assume the major share of the sacrifices necessary to restore European stability.[20]

The president left Washington on 15 June for a brief political trip to the Midwest without having approved any action. Stimson and Mills were disappointed, but Hoover promised to sound out political opinion and reconsider the matter. When he returned on 18 June, Hoover met with his two closest advisers. Since Mills had a better personal rapport with the president, Stimson allowed the treasury undersecretary to present their case. Mills told Hoover that he had spoken to Mellon, who was in London, and that Mellon now endorsed a moratorium. Mills maintained that the present financial crisis could be "tided over," but that it would recur unless "fundamental conditions are dealt with." Germany was certain to invoke the suspension provisions of the Young Plan. Mills predicted that France would subsequently stop payment on the war debts. He therefore concluded that the United States could not remain aloof from the European situation. If the administration did not seize the initiative and declare a moratorium, Mills warned that Republican officials would eventually have to attend a general conference where they would find themselves enmeshed in Europe's economic and political problems. Standing alone, the American officials would then be asked to assume the major responsibility for rehabilitating European finances. Rather than face this scenario, Mills urged the president to declare a suspension of debt payments for two years. Before making the moratorium public, Mills emphasized that Hoover should secure the consent of the Democratic leadership and the approval of the French government. Mellon had told Mills that this latter point was of critical importance. Hoover listened without a trace of

19. Ogden L. Mills to Pierre de Lagarde Boal, 15 June 1931, Mills Papers, Box 109.
20. For Hoover's attitudes, see Hoover Diary, 5–14 June 1931, HHPP, Box 880; Lamont, Memorandum, 5 June 1931, Thomas W. Lamont Papers, Box 98; Diary of Henry L. Stimson, 8–16 June 1931, Stimson Papers.

enthusiasm. "It was like sitting in a bath of ink to sit in his room," Stimson noted in his diary. But Hoover considered the change in Mellon's attitude to be of real significance; the president acknowledged his approval of Mills's recommendations.[21]

Since Congress would have to approve a suspension of payments when it reconvened in December, Hoover asked Charles Dawes and Bernard M. Baruch to help muster Republican and Democratic support for the moratorium. During the next two days Hoover and Mills contacted over forty members of Congress and explained the proposed action. The president and his adviser were gratified by the favorable response.[22] While they were canvassing members of Congress, the press learned of Hoover's contemplated action. At the same time, the situation in Germany suddenly worsened. On 19 June the Reichsbank reported a loss of 90 million reichsmarks. The president hurriedly instructed Stimson to consult with European diplomats. The secretary of state contacted French Ambassador Paul Claudel. Before Claudel was able to consult with his government, Hoover acted. On Saturday, 20 June, the president issued his statement offering to postpone the collection of war debt payments for one year if other governments deferred the war debt and reparation payments due them.[23]

The immediate cause of the moratorium announcement was the renewed crisis in Germany and the threat it posed to the American banking system. Expecting a complete collapse of Germany's credit structure within a day or two, the president wanted to forestall a self-proclaimed moratorium on all German public and private foreign debt payments. Mills subsequently told the House Committee on Ways and Means that the president acted because "the world . . . was confronted with the danger of a major catastrophe of incalculable consequences to the credit structure of the world and to the economic future of all nations." Although the treasury undersecretary denied that the government was acting in behalf of American banks, Herbert Feis, the eco-

21. Diary of Henry L. Stimson, 14–18 June 1931, Stimson Papers; Hoover Diary, 13–18 June 1931, HHPP, Box 880; Mills to Hoover, 18 June 1931, Mills Papers, Box 109; see also the memorandum on Mills's conversation with Andrew Mellon, 18 June 1931, ibid.

22. Hoover Diary, 18–20 June 1931, HHPP, Box 880; Mills to John Foster Dulles, 25 June 1931, Mills Papers, Box 109; for the tally of congressional responses, see the lists in HHPP, Box 880.

23. Diary of Henry L. Stimson, 19, 20 June 1931, Stimson Papers; Hoover Diary, 18–20 June 1931, HHPP, Box 880; for the moratorium announcement, see Hoover, *State Papers*, 1:591–93; for the financial situation in Germany, see Kindleberger, *World in Depression*, p. 153.

nomic adviser in the State Department, confided to Felix Frankfurter that American officials were afraid of the impact of a German collapse on the American banking structure. "It was emergency action," Feis wrote, "to ward off impending catastrophe." Hence, war debt and reparation payments were to be suspended to avoid an imminent default on Germany's private obligations.[24]

In addition to the financial considerations that prompted immediate action, Hoover explained in his moratorium announcement that his intention was "to give the forthcoming year to the economic recovery of the world." The abnormal influx of gold into the United States, he emphasized, disrupted credit arrangements everywhere. The chaotic financial environment, in turn, undermined purchasing power abroad, restricted American exports, and contributed to domestic unemployment and low agricultural prices.[25] The goals of the moratorium were to restore confidence, resuscitate the German economy, preserve the gold standard, and reinvigorate commerce as well as protect private American credits. Since 1929 American businessmen, bankers, and policymakers had realized that the decline in American exports was, at least in part, a result of the decrease in foreign lending. In essence, then, the moratorium was designed as a loan from creditor governments, especially France and the United States, to insolvent debtors and customers.[26]

Insofar as the moratorium was aimed both at preserving German stability and at rehabilitating European finances, there was nothing revolutionary about its goals. Hoover emphasized that the moratorium "is entirely consistent with the policy which we have hitherto pursued. . . . It represents our willingness to make a contribution to the early restoration of world prosperity in which our people have so deep an interest." Though the president had heretofore emphasized the impor-

24. For Mills's statements, see House, Committee on Ways and Means, *Moratorium on Foreign Debts*, 1:4; see also Herbert Feis to Felix Frankfurter, 26 June 1931, Feis Papers, Box 16; Charles G. Dawes, *Journal as Ambassador to Great Britain*, p. 356.

25. Hoover, *State Papers*, 1:592.

26. See the testimony of Mills and Stimson, House, Ways and Means, *Foreign Debts*, 1:2–3, 51–54; Senate, Committee on Finance, *Postponement of Intergovernmental Debts*, pp. 13–15. For the well-recognized interrelationships between loans, currency stability, trade, and the Depression, see, for example, American Bankers Association (ABA), Commerce and Marine Division, *Domestic and Foreign Affairs*, p. 12; James A. Farrell, "The World Outlook," National Foreign Trade Council (NFTC), *Official Report of the National Foreign Trade Convention*, 1931, pp. 10–11; National Association of Manufacturers (NAM), *The Platform of American Industry for 1932*, p. 3; Frederic Feiker to G. A. Harris, 9 July 1931, Records of the Bureau of Foreign and Domestic Commerce (BFDC), RG 151, File 640.

tance of internal palliatives, the moratorium signified his recognition of the dramatic worsening of European financial conditions in the spring of 1931 and the importance of averting a European financial collapse to protect the domestic financial and economic situation. Lest anyone imagine that he felt the United States should assume the primary role in stabilizing Europe, Hoover also stated in his moratorium announcement that he had no intention of embroiling the nation in strictly European affairs or canceling the war debts. Since he still believed that the United States would "make a large measure of recovery irrespective of the rest of the world," the president carefully delimited the extent of American sacrifices. He demanded that European nations assume their share of the financial burdens and urged them to limit their armaments.[27]

Although Hoover was not reassessing foreign policy goals, he was willing to consider a new tactical approach toward the war debts. The moratorium undermined the sanctity of contractual obligations, highlighted the interdependence of war debt and reparation payments, and circumvented the customary reliance on a nonpartisan debt commission. Moreover, Hoover privately conceded that some of the existing debt accords would have to be revised. Mills, in fact, began to study possible means of accomplishing this objective.[28] The moratorium, then, was aimed at relieving the immediate financial crisis and providing time to reassess whether or not a new tactical approach was needed to accomplish the familiar objectives of restoring European stability and American prosperity.

The domestic reaction to Hoover's initiative was much more enthusiastic than the president had anticipated. "The effect on the market had been magical," Stimson noted in his diary. Everything went up—stocks, commodities, and bonds. Bankers, exporters, and manufacturers acclaimed the president's action.[29] Editorials in both Democratic and Republican newspapers endorsed the moratorium proposal. Although misgivings were expressed in the Hearst press and the *Chicago Tribune*, these initial reservations were drowned out by public expressions of support from such unlikely bedfellows as Owen Young, Newton Baker, Norman Davis, Reed Smoot, and William Borah.[30]

27. Hoover, *State Papers*, 1:591–93, 572–83. The quotations are on pp. 593, 574; see also Hoover Diary, 8 May, 2 June 1931, HHPP, Box 880.

28. For the private views of key officials, see Hoover Diary, 8 May, 2 June 1931, HHPP, Box 880; Mills to Dulles, 16 June 1931, Mills Papers, Box 109; Dawes, *Journal as Ambassador*, p. 359.

29. Diary of Henry L. Stimson, 22 June 1931, Stimson Papers.

30. "What the 'Hoover Holiday' Means to the World," *Literary Digest* 110 (4 July

The French Reaction

The positive domestic reaction to the moratorium made the qualified French response all the more disappointing to American officials. The political questions raised by the French angered Hoover; he considered his proposal to be purely economic in nature. Moreover, the president calculated that the French had much more to lose from an economic and social debacle in central Europe than did the United States. Should such a calamity occur, Hoover insisted, "it is the French people whose borders will front on—Bolshevism—not the American." American officials wanted to provide financial aid to Germany, and they did not want to encounter any resistance.[31] When French opposition persisted, Republican policymakers were forced to reappraise the efficacy of their apolitical approach to European affairs and reassess their view of the appropriate risks and responsibilities that different nations should assume in promoting European stability.

French officials were irate that they had not been fully consulted before the moratorium announcement. Premier Laval condemned American "shock-tactics," and Foreign Minister Briand charged that Hoover had acted out of narrow self-interest to save Anglo-American private investments.[32] In strictly financial terms the French were being asked to relinquish more in lost reparation payments than they benefited from postponed war debt obligations. On a per capita basis their intergovernmental debt sacrifices were as great as American sacrifices; yet they had not nearly as much to gain on private account as did American investors.[33] More important, the French deplored the political implications inherent in a postponement of the unconditional annuity owed by Germany. They believed this component of Germany's

1931):5–6; "The Thorns on the Hoover Rosebush," ibid. (11 July 1931):7–8; "The 'Hoover Holiday' and Business Recovery," ibid., pp. 42–44; "The Moratorium," *Journal of the American Bankers Association* 24 (July 1931):19; Edward Hurley to Hoover, 21 June 1931, HHPP, Box 871; Norman H. Davis to Hoover, 24 June 1931, Davis Papers, Box 27; see also the White House's tabulation on press reaction, HHPP, Box 880.

31. For the quotation, see unsigned memorandum [Hoover's handwriting], 24 June 1931, HHPP, Box 880; see also FR, 1931, 1:77–78, 84–85, 93–94, 97.

32. For the French reaction, see Walter E. Edge, *A Jerseyman's Journal*, pp. 191–97; for Laval's subsequent feelings, see Jesse Straus to Cordell Hull, 26 October, 31 December 1934, RG 59, 800.51W89 France/1007, 1019; see also "Europe's Cheers and Jeers for the War-Debt Holiday," *Literary Digest* 110 (4 July 1931):13–14; Bennett, *Financial Crisis*, pp. 168–74; DBFP, 2, 2:107–8, 166–67.

33. William O. Scroggs, "The American Investment in Germany," pp. 324–26; see also Hamilton Fish Armstrong, "France and the Hoover Plan," pp. 23–24.

obligations inviolable under the terms of the Young Plan. They were disgusted that an outside power had had the temerity to intervene unilaterally and call for the abrogation of contractual accords without regard for the legal ramifications of such action. They feared that suspension of the unconditional annuity would encourage Germany to seek political as well as financial changes in the Treaty of Versailles. The French worried that once the unconditional annuity was suspended, no German government would have the courage to reimpose taxes to pay reparations.[34] Hence, the French felt that the Americans were imposing the major financial and political burden for effecting European stability on them.

Laval realized, however, that France could not afford to be isolated from the other powers. Consequently, he and French Finance Minister Etienne Flandin tried to moderate the hostile French reaction as they sought to protect France's interests. Although they accepted the one-year postponement, Laval and Flandin felt it essential to maintain the appearance of unconditional payments to demonstrate that existing agreements had not been abrogated. They demanded that the unconditional annuities be paid, then reloaned through the BIS, not only to Germany but also to other needy central European powers. Moreover, Laval and Flandin stressed that these loans should be made to the German railroads rather than to the German government to preclude additional German expenditures on armaments. The French insisted that the deferred payments be repaid quickly after the moratorium and that certain deliveries-in-kind be continued during the year. Finally, in return for their financial concessions, the French wanted the Germans to stop work on certain battleships, abandon the Austro-German customs union project, and cease penetrating French spheres of influence in central Europe and the Balkans.[35]

The tenacity of the French government's resistance to a suspension of all debt payments for one year angered American officials. Yet, Mills and Stimson urged the president to be conciliatory. Hoover, however, was opposed to concessions. He insisted that all reparation payments, conditional and unconditional, be suspended. The moratorium, he argued, had to benefit Germany, and that nation had to be given adequate time to repay the deferred annuity. The French attitude,

34. Geoffrey Warner, *Pierre Laval and the Eclipse of France*, pp. 31–33; DBFP, 2, 2:107–8, 166–67; Armstrong, "Hoover Plan," p. 26; Dawes, *Journal as Ambassador*, pp. 354–55.
35. For the French position regarding the moratorium, see FR, 1931, 1:44, 47, 57–58, 61–65, 80, 96, 105–8, 133–35, 142–43, 150–59.

the president told Lamont on 29 June, was "intolerable," and he was "fed up" with their "technical and fictitious" reservations. Hoover was unmoved by the political difficulties encountered by Laval. The president emphasized his own political problems; Senator Borah had already warned that concessions to the French might cause him to withdraw his support of the moratorium.[36]

Meanwhile, Mellon traveled to Paris to help Edge with the difficult negotiations. Stimson departed for Europe on 26 June, leaving the Department of State in the hands of William R. Castle, Hoover's personal choice for undersecretary of state after Cotton's death. With Castle overlooking developments, members of the Division of Western European Affairs labored until midnight day after day on the moratorium proposal. They were in constant communication with Mellon and Edge. Yet, the talks dragged on causing the initial positive impact of the moratorium proposal to wear off and the outflow of capital from Germany to resume. Finally, on 5 July Hoover became exasperated. He prepared an ultimatum indicating that if the French remained intransigent, European nations would have to handle the crisis by themselves.[37]

Despite Hoover's attitude, Edge and Mellon in Paris and Mills, Morrow, and Castle in Washington worked tirelessly and tactfully to reconcile the conflicting French and American positions. As a result Hoover eventually accepted a compromise that preserved the essential framework of his proposal. He agreed that Germany should pay her unconditional annuity to the BIS so long as the annuity was reloaned in its entirety to Germany. In addition, the president concurred that France's allies in central Europe should also receive financial aid, but that such aid should be extended through private banking channels. The French, in turn, accepted the one-year moratorium and acceded to the American demand that the entire unconditional annuity be used for the relief of Germany. Both sides compromised and agreed that all suspended payments be repaid over a ten-year period. More technical questions with regard to deliveries-in-kind and French payments into a guarantee fund, as stipulated in the Young Plan, were reserved for

36. For Hoover's attitude and the official American position, see Memorandum of phone conversation between Hoover and Lamont, 29 June 1931, Thomas W. Lamont Papers, Box 98; Hoover, *Memoirs*, 2:72; FR, 1931, 1:55–57, 65–67, 74–82, 88–91, 112–17, 127–28, 133–35; see also Diary of Henry L. Stimson, 22–25 June 1931, Stimson Papers; 24, 25 June 1931, Hoover Diary, HHPP, Box 880.

37. Hoover Diary, 3–6 July 1931, HHPP, Box 880; unsigned memorandum [Hoover's handwriting], 24 June 1931, ibid.; Diary of Jay Pierrepont Moffat, 1–6 July 1931, Moffat Papers.

subsequent deliberations among financial experts of the various nations.[38] This accord, signed on 6 July 1931, ended the immediate dispute between France and the United States but did not terminate the ill will that persisted in both nations.

The Franco-American controversy over the Hoover moratorium illustrated the different approaches of the two nations to postwar Europe and highlighted one of the major policy questions facing Republican officials as they sought to foster European stability without incurring political or military obligations. The American orientation toward Europe was economic. Therefore, the United States had proposed a financial solution to Europe's troubles and had minimized its political ramifications. The French approach, though not devoid of economic considerations, was mainly political. Consequently, even Laval, who was hopeful of effecting some type of rapprochement with Germany, was compelled by political pressures and popular opinion to safeguard France's international political and strategic interests before acceding to purely economic palliatives. To the French, stability still meant enforcement of the Treaty of Versailles; hence, they could not disregard the political ramifications of a moratorium on reparation payments. To the Americans, however, stability depended upon the preservation of a prosperous and republican Germany. When these conflicting approaches collided, something had to give. In the early 1920s the financial prowess of the United States had compelled French concessions. But in 1931 France had considerable financial leverage of her own. American officials had to decide whether they were prepared to accept some responsibility for protecting France's political and strategic interests to secure her adherence to their viewpoint. The Americans were forced to ponder their willingness to enter Europe's political affairs in a constructive and meaningful fashion should the Continent's economic and financial stability depend on it.

Hoover was reluctant to do so. Throughout the painstaking talks with the French over implementation of the moratorium, American officials had known that their bargaining position would be strengthened if they could get the Germans to make certain political concessions to the French. Undersecretary Castle wanted Sackett to pressure German officials into conciliating French opinion either by dropping

38. See the "Basis of Agreement," in FR, 1931, 1:162; see also pp. 114–17, 133–35, 142–43, 150–57; Edge, *Journal*, pp. 197–200; 4–6 July 1931, Hoover Diary, HHPP, Box 880.

the proposed customs union with Austria or by curtailing expenditures on a second pocket battleship.[39] But Hoover cautioned Castle not to allow Sackett to go too far. The president worried about congressional reaction to American intervention in European political affairs; he, too, was reluctant to see the United States enmeshed in the intractabilities of European politics. Hoover expected the British to exert pressure on the Germans, and he denied any interest in French political demands vis-à-vis Germany. As a result Chancellor Brüning and Foreign Minister Julius Curtius did not take Sackett's remonstrances seriously, and the Germans did little to expedite the talks between French and American negotiators.[40]

The moratorium negotiations engendered considerable disillusionment in American policymaking circles. Hoover was disgusted with the French, Castle with the Germans, and Mills with both the French and Germans. "They are all a great crowd to do business with," Mills sarcastically commented to former Treasury Undersecretary Garrard Winston.[41] To Republican officials in Washington, it seemed as if they had taken an enormous political risk and incurred substantial financial sacrifices without reciprocal action being undertaken in Europe. Mellon, Edge, and Sackett kept their Washington colleagues informed about the political situation in France and Germany and the limited options available to Laval and Brüning in early July 1931. But, from Hoover's perspective, his own political problems were as serious as those facing any European leader, and his administration's financial difficulties were as grave as those besetting any European government. Why, the president pondered, should he assume the bulk of the political and financial sacrifices when most of the American press concurred that French recalcitrance had been inexcusable and when many American bankers maintained that Germany was largely responsible for her own financial problems?[42]

39. DBFP, 2, 2:117–18.
40. For American policy toward Germany during the Franco-American dispute over the moratorium, see FR, 1931, 1:49, 84–85, 93, 96–98, 109–10, 129–32; DBFP, 2, 2:107–111, 112, 115, 117–18, 124–25, 133, 141, 144, 156–57; Sackett to William R. Castle, 11 January 1932, Castle Papers, Box 5; see also Bennett, *Financial Crisis*, pp. 177–203.
41. Mills to Garrard Winston, 15 July 1931, Mills Papers, Box 109.
42. For American press reaction to France's position, see "Hoover's Winning Way with Reluctant France," *Literary Digest* 110 (18 July 1931):3–4; for bankers' feelings about German culpability, see, for example, Memorandum of phone conversation between Hoover and Lamont, 29 June 1931, Lamont Papers, Box 98.

The European Financial Crisis
and the London Finance Conference

The recrudescence of the German financial crisis during the first two weeks of July confronted the Hoover administration with difficult questions. What should the administration do if the private sector could no longer be depended upon to make the bulk of the American contribution to European stabilization? What should it do if European nations were no longer willing or able to accept the larger share of the sacrifices and if France, in particular, refused to make concessions similar to those made in the early and mid-1920s? Had the American interest in European stability during the 1920s become so extensive that no option remained for the United States government except to assume new commitments or incur additional burdens? These were the questions that the Hoover administration pondered as the financial underpinnings of the postwar world disintegrated.

The moratorium announcement of 20 June and the extension of a $100 million central bank credit to the Reichsbank five days later did not put an end to the financial crisis. The prolonged Franco-American negotiations over the moratorium generated additional uncertainty and exacerbated the emergency. By 5 July the $100 million credit was exhausted and the liquidity of Germany's banking system came into question. On 9 July Hans Luther, president of the Reichsbank, flew to London, Paris, and Basle seeking funds. Similar appeals for help were made in New York and Washington. In Great Britain the German ambassador warned that additional assistance was imperative for Hoover's initiative to succeed. Otherwise, the ambassador foresaw a wave of financial breakdowns "which will have catastrophic results for the whole of Central Europe."[43]

Observing the deterioration of financial conditions in Europe, Hoover rapidly concluded the moratorium negotiations with France. But he did not believe that the United States government had the resources or the authority to extend additional aid to Germany. After consulting with Mills and Castle, the three men agreed that the continuation of the emergency situation was the result of an "internal banking crisis in Germany" which could "only be resolved by the banking world." As

43. For the quotation, see DBFP, 2, 2:180–81; see also Hans Luther to George L. Harrison, 14 July 1931, Papers of the Federal Reserve Bank of New York (FRBNY Papers), C261.12; Boal, Memorandum, 11 July 1931, RG 59, 462.00R296/449; Bennett, *Financial Crisis*, pp. 218–43; Kindleberger, *World in Depression*, pp. 153–57; Clarke, *Central Bank Cooperation*, pp. 189–99.

was their custom, Republican policymakers sought to place the American responsibility for solving the European crisis onto the private banking community and the Federal Reserve System. Predictably, Hoover asked Eugene Meyer, governor of the Federal Reserve Board, to see what could be done.[44]

American bankers, however, did not want to augment their commitments in Germany. From the beginning of July the FRBNY kept in constant contact with leading New York banking firms. Governor Harrison not only prodded them to maintain their existing credits in Germany, but also encouraged the banks to increase their commitments. Though all of them with the exception of Guaranty Trust agreed to maintain their existing lines of credit, none were prepared to increase their commitments.[45] Lamont, for example, insisted that German officials were acting irresponsibly, that Germans themselves were transferring funds abroad, and that the Reichsbank was not instituting measures previously used to deal with similar problems. Given Germany's recent favorable trade balance, Lamont claimed that there was no reason why Germany should require additional credit.[46]

Harrison accepted the position of the private bankers. He was prepared, however, to extend additional aid from the FRBNY to the Reichsbank, if the Bank of France and the Bank of England did likewise. After European central bankers met at Basle and refused to act until their governments tackled the political underpinnings of the crisis, Harrison reversed himself. He followed the lead of his European counterparts and demanded that public officials assume responsibility.[47]

Hoover, Castle, and Mills understood why American bankers were hesitant to take on new commitments abroad when they were faced with such serious problems at home. Hence, they demanded that the German government make a greater effort to deal with the emergency. Believing that 80 percent of the withdrawals from Germany had been made by Germans themselves, Castle told a press conference on 13

44. For the quotation, see 12 July 1931, Hoover Diary, HHPP, Box 880; see also Diary of Charles S. Hamlin, 12 July 1931, Hamlin Papers, Vol. 19.
45. Harrison, Memorandum, 3 July 1931, George L. Harrison Papers, 2690.2b; J. E. Crane, Memorandum, 15 July 1931, FRBNY Papers, C261.12.
46. Lamont to Martin Egan, 9 July 1931, HHPP, Box 874; Lamont to Morgan partners, London, 9 July 1931, ibid.
47. For Harrison's attitudes and actions, see Memorandum of phone conversation between Harrison and Montagu Norman, 8 July 1931, ibid., Box 874; Harrison, Memorandum, 13 July 1931, George L. Harrison Papers, 3013.1; Harrison to Luther, 15 July 1931, FRBNY Papers, C261.12; for developments at Basle, see Harrison, Memorandum, 13 July 1931, George L. Harrison Papers, 3013.1; FR, 1931, 1:254.

July that the worsening crisis was the result of the German government's failure to impose restrictions on exchange operations.[48] Suspecting that Germany might be trying to maneuver the United States into making fresh commitments, the White House instructed Stimson, who was in Rome, not to go to Berlin. "There is a tendency," Castle wrote, "to burden us with the responsibility of maintaining German credit. We cannot assume this responsibility."[49] The shifting of primary responsibility for restoring stability onto European governments was the natural reflex of the Hoover administration when the private banking community indicated its inability to cope with the crisis.

By mid-July, however, the situation was beyond the grasp of European leaders. The German government temporarily closed German banks, instituted a set of decrees regulating exchange transactions, and raised the discount rate from 7 to 10 percent. These measures somewhat eased the situation in Germany. But repercussions of the crisis began to be felt in London, where budgetary deficits and balance-of-payments problems had already caused considerable anxiety. The realization that substantial amounts of British credits had been frozen in central Europe, together with the publication of the MacMillan report emphasizing the magnitude of London's short-term liabilities, touched off a new wave of speculation. On 15 July the value of sterling dropped below the gold export point, and on the following day the Bank of England reported substantial gold losses. Alarmed by these developments, the British government sought the immediate convocation of an international conference in London.[50]

With German banks closed and troubles spreading to London, Hoover realized that the crisis was approaching monumental proportions. Given information about the extent of outstanding short-term bills, the president later recalled that he never had "received a worse shock. The haunting prospect of wholesale bank failures and the necessity of saying not a word to the American people . . . lest I precipitate runs on our banks left me little sleep. . . . The situation was no longer one of helping foreign countries to the indirect benefit of everybody. It was now a question of saving ourselves."[51] After talking matters over with Castle, Mills, Morrow, and Harrison, Hoover instructed Stimson and

48. Memorandum of press conference, 13 July 1931, HHPP, Box 880; see also FR, 1931, 1:251; Mills to Winston, 15 July 1931, Mills Papers, Box 109.

49. FR, 1931, 1:256.

50. Bennett, *Financial Crisis*, pp. 218–43; Clarke, *Central Bank Cooperation*, pp. 199–203; Kindleberger, *World in Depression*, p. 156.

51. Hoover, *Memoirs*, 3:75.

Mellon to attend the conference in London. This was a new departure by a president who formerly had grave misgivings about allowing official American representatives to attend meetings on primarily European issues.

Laval, however, refused to attend a conference in London unless preliminary talks were held in Paris. Once these talks were arranged, the French premier proposed a ten-year $500 million loan to the Reichsbank, guaranteed by the creditor governments and secured by German customs. Laval told Stimson and British Foreign Secretary Henderson that such a loan would solve the financial crisis, provided that Germany abandon her political demands and allow the lenders to supervise the uses of the loan. Since he and Flandin put forth the French loan plan in moderate tones, emphasized their willingness to be helpful, and carefully explained the political pressures that circumscribed their options, Stimson was impressed. The secretary of state phoned Washington daily and described the French position to Hoover, Mills, and Castle.[52]

In Washington Hoover focused his attention on the European crisis and determined the course of American policy. He met constantly with Mills and Castle and consulted occasionally with Dawes and Morrow, both of whom were invited to the White House during the crisis.[53] Mills was in continual communication with Harrison in New York. Harrison held almost daily meetings with representatives of nearly a dozen leading Wall Street firms. While all but two of them were willing to accept a standstill on existing credits, not a single firm was ready to commit itself to extending new credits, let alone floating new loans.[54] The Morgan partners, in particular, voiced their opposition to new commitments. As a result the president and his advisers concluded that it was impossible to implement the French loan scheme.[55]

Yet, even if American bankers had been willing to consider the French proposal, the president would have opposed it. He maintained

52. Diary of Henry L. Stimson, 15–17 July 1931, Stimson Papers; Memoranda of conversations between Stimson and Hoover, 15, 16 July 1931, RG 59, 462.00R296/4513½, 4525½; Telephone conversation with Secretary Stimson, 17 July 1931, HHPP, Box 874; DBFP, 2, 2:194, 198–99, 201–2, 208.

53. Hoover, *Memoirs*, 3:75; Morrow to Dawes, 18 July 1931, Morrow Papers; Dawes, *Journal as Ambassador*, pp. 360–73.

54. Memoranda, 16, 17 July 1931, George L. Harrison Papers, 2013.1; see also Lamont to Hoover, 27 July 1931, HHPP, Box 114.

55. FR, 1931, 1:268; Memorandum of phone conversation between Mills [or Castle] and Sackett, 17 July 1931, HHPP, Box 874; Memorandum of phone conversation between Hoover and Stimson, 17 July 1931, ibid.; Lamont to Hoover, 18 July 1931, Thomas W. Lamont Papers, Box 98.

that the United States government had already made a $250 million contribution to Germany's rehabilitation through the moratorium and that it had no authority to take additional action and guarantee a foreign bond flotation. With a budget deficit of $1.6 billion and with widespread unemployment, Hoover felt it preposterous to assume that Congress would authorize new sacrifices. Moreover, the president feared that government guarantees would link the United States to France's demands for a long-term political moratorium. Not only was he opposed to an extended political moratorium, but so were American bankers and the British government. Furthermore, Hoover considered the French scheme impractical because it would engender controversy over an entire matrix of issues—the Young Plan, the debt settlements, and the Treaty of Versailles—that could not possibly be settled in a few days.[56]

Consequently, on 17 July Hoover emphasized to Stimson that there was no time to belabor the French proposal. The president felt it imperative that the London Conference deal with the emergency situation as a banking matter: "it arises from the overextension of short-term credits abroad and the loss of confidence resulting in the flight of the mark from Germany." To stop the withdrawals, Hoover had gotten Harrison to arrange a temporary American standstill on existing credits. But American bankers were very fearful that their funds would be frozen in Germany while other foreign lenders hurried to withdraw their credits. Consequently, Hoover proposed the consummation of an international standstill accord. Until the bankers of all nations agreed to maintain their existing credits in Germany, Hoover believed that it was futile to contemplate new loans. He thought that if the standstill were accompanied by rigorous exchange controls, Germany would get through the prevailing crisis. She had a current trade surplus, had benefited from the moratorium, and still had available $1.4 billion in short-term credits. Once the existing emergency was overcome, Hoover predicted that confidence would be restored and German capital repatriated.[57]

Though the president insisted that the London Conference deal with

56. For Hoover's views, formed in talks with Castle and Mills, see Castle to Stimson, 15 July 1931, RG 59, 462.00R296/4497; Memorandum of phone conversation between Hoover and Stimson, 15 July 1931, ibid., 462.00R296/4513½; FR, 1931, 1:268–69, 275–78; for British opposition to the French loan proposal, see, for example, DBFP, 2, 2:204–5.
57. FR, 1931, 1:275–78; Memorandum of phone conversation between Stimson and Hoover, 17 July 1931, HHPP, Box 874.

the financial crisis as an emergency banking matter, he neither over-looked the political dimensions of the situation nor foreclosed the possibility of additional aid to Germany. In a phone conversation on 17 July he told Stimson that, when Brüning arrived in Paris the next day, attention should be focused on eliminating points of political friction between France and Germany. Hoover obviously hoped that Brüning would either reduce German appropriations for battleship construction or withdraw the proposal for a customs union with Austria. The president emphasized that the United States could serve only as a mediator in these political questions. Nevertheless, if the political questions were resolved or submerged and a credits standstill accepted, Hoover intimated that private American credits might be forthcoming, especially if they received priority over reparations. The president confidentially informed Stimson that he might be able to provide Germany with an additional $120 million in government assistance through credits extended by the Farm Board.[58]

When the German chancellor arrived in Paris on Saturday, 18 July, he met with Stimson as well as with Laval and Henderson. Brüning stressed that Germany needed a loan of $400–500 million in addition to an increase in short-term credits. A credits standstill, he emphasized, was not sufficient to meet Germany's problems.[59] Stimson was impressed with Brüning's calm demeanor, moderate tone, and incisive presentation of Germany's case. He was also relieved to see that Brüning did not affront the French nor ostensibly bear any animosity toward them. Stimson believed that Laval and Brüning offered the best hope of ironing out Franco-German differences. In a phone call to Hoover late that night, Stimson put forth the German request for additional funds and spoke sympathetically of the French loan plan.[60]

Hoover suspected that his secretary of state was coming under "the spell of the French" and losing contact with the domestic situation. Emphasizing the weak spots in the American banking system and the underutilization of America's productive capacity, Hoover attacked the loan proposal and ridiculed the French. He argued that "one of the most damaging things has been the reduction of French short-term claims on Germany." He estimated that the French had withdrawn

58. Telephone conversation with Secretary Stimson, 17 July 1931, HHPP, Box 874; FR, 1931, 1:275–78; see also unsigned memorandum [by Hoover?], 18 July 1931, HHPP, Box 878.
59. Diary of Henry L. Stimson, 18 July 1931, Stimson Papers; FR, 1931, 1:287–88; DBFP, 2, 2:195.
60. Telephone conversation with Secretary Stimson, 18 July 1931, HHPP, Box 874.

$200 million and maintained that, if the French really wanted to help, they would put this money back in Germany. France had a larger interest in preserving European stability than did the United States, Hoover claimed, and he would not be "bluffed about that." Therefore, the president insisted that France had to assume larger risks, including the acceptance of a credits standstill, the restoration of credits withdrawn since the moratorium announcement, and the termination of talk about a politically guaranteed loan.[61]

When Stimson arrived in London on 20 July, he received a long dispatch outlining Hoover's reasons for a standstill accord.[62] The secretary of state talked to MacDonald and found that the British prime minister agreed with the president's position.[63] During the conference, which opened that night and continued the next day, Brüning and Curtius again emphasized Germany's need for a sizable long-term loan. Moreover, Mellon and Snowden concurred that Germany needed new funds. But there was no agreement on how to provide Germany with the aid she required. Laval hedged on his loan proposal as it became evident that the German leaders, for domestic political reasons, could not postpone their demands for a peaceful revision of the Treaty of Versailles. Moreover, officials in the Bank of France opposed a long-term loan. Thus, Hoover's contention and Stimson's suspicion that the French loan proposal might be a maneuver to throw responsibility for failure to reach an agreement onto other nations proved correct. Yet no one at the conference had anything constructive to offer that stood a chance of immediate acceptance. Stimson persuasively pressed the case for a credits standstill, which everyone agreed was a necessary but inadequate first step to deal with the full dimensions of the crisis.[64] Finally, after all-day discussions on the twenty-first, the conferees decided that a standstill should be supplemented with two measures. First, the Bank of France, the Bank of England, the BIS, and the FRBNY should agree to renew their $100 million credit to the

61. Hoover Diary, 19 July 1931, ibid., Box 880; Telephone conversation with Secretary Stimson, 18 July 1931, ibid., Box 874; Memorandum of phone conversation between Hoover and Stimson, 19 July 1931, ibid.; Hoover's drafts of dispatches to Stimson and Mellon, 19 July 1931, ibid., Box 878.

62. FR, 1931, 1:180–86.

63. Diary of Henry L. Stimson, 20 July 1931, Stimson Papers.

64. For stenographic notes of the conference meetings, see DBFP, 2, 2:436–57, also pp. 210–11, 218–21; FR, 1931, 1:298–99, 302–6; Ray Atherton to Castle, 20 July 1931, HHPP, Box 874; for the opposition of the Bank of France to Laval's loan plan, see Edge to Castle, 21 July 1931, ibid.; for American suspicions regarding French intentions, see, for example, Edge to Castle, 19 July 1931, ibid.

Reichsbank for three months. Second, European central banks and the FRBNY should agree to rediscount acceptances held by the Reichsbank.[65]

After the day's meetings, Stimson called Hoover and summarized the recommendations. Stimson emphasized that the standstill was an insufficient solution. He pointed out that France could not be asked to restore her credits; even Brüning acknowledged that France had not participated in the recent credit runs on Germany. Furthermore, the secretary of state maintained that the president's information on the severity of the European financial crisis greatly underestimated its dimensions. Britain, he reported, was now in serious trouble as well as Germany.[66]

The president was angered by Stimson's readiness to have the FRBNY discount German bills and his assertion that he had better information than the White House on the European crisis. Hoover claimed that he had carefully assessed the situation and gathered accurate data, both on the dimensions of the crisis and on the amount of American short-term commitments. He and Mills had spoken to Harrison, who was in constant contact with officials at the BIS, the Reichsbank, and the Bank of England. Harrison had been told by excellent sources, Hoover claimed, that Germany could make it through the crisis without additional assistance, if a credits standstill were accepted by all nations. Even the president of the Reichsbank, it was said, acknowledged this claim. Brüning wanted additional assistance, Hoover intimated, not for financial reasons but for political purposes. Moreover, the president stated that Gates McGarrah, Leon Fraser, S. Parker Gilbert, Oliver M. W. Sprague, and Walter W. Stewart, leading experts on German finances, concurred that Germany could pull through. Given these assessments, Hoover told Stimson that the standstill constituted the "full extent of our possibilities" at the present time. When Stimson equivocated, Mills abruptly intervened in the conversation and began speaking to Mellon. Mills emphasized that the United States could not provide aid in the form of rediscounting privileges at the FRBNY. He claimed that the Bank of England was in no position to offer such assistance and hypothesized that Governor Norman was trying to saddle the United States with responsibility for preventing agreement.[67]

65. FR, 1931, 1:305–6.
66. Diary of Henry L. Stimson, 21 July 1931, Stimson Papers; Conversation between Stimson and the president, 21 July 1931, HHPP, Box 874.
67. Conversation between Stimson and the president, 21 July 1931, HHPP, Box 874; Diary of Henry L. Stimson, 21 July 1931, Stimson Papers; Harrison, Memorandum, 20

Hoover and Mills were upset with Stimson for manifesting so little understanding of their problems. Hoover was grappling with many of the same political and financial pressures as those besetting the French and British; yet Stimson, Hoover and Mills felt, was oblivious to the president's predicament.[68] The domestic constraints on the administration's options were manifold: American bankers claimed they could not take on new commitments; Meyer and Harrison refused to consider rediscounting German bills; Senator Carter Glass, cosponsor of the Federal Reserve Act, called such rediscounting operations illegal; and Senator Borah warned against embroilments in European political affairs.[69] To overcome these impediments, Hoover believed that he needed time to convince the American people that European governments were willing to make commensurate sacrifices. Hoover and Mills felt that they had been both generous and wise. They had relinquished $250 million in revenues and had agreed to maintain the largest share of existing credits, now estimated at $600 million, in Germany. Which nation in Europe, they inquired, had made comparable sacrifices during the last few months? Britain, of course, was in terrible straits, as was Germany. But if Germany needed additional help to overcome the immediate crisis, why not expect the French to make the sacrifices? Thus far they had been least affected by the Depression.[70]

When Stimson sat down at the conference table on 22 July, he had instructions to oppose the rediscount proposal. But as Hoover had predicted, it was unnecessary for him to do so. British Chancellor of the Exchequer Snowden and French Finance Minister Flandin immediately interjected their own reservations. Snowden declared that Britain could not assume new obligations. He emphasized that short-term expedients were inappropriate. What was needed, Snowden added, was a resolution of Germany's political grievances and a revision of the war debt and reparation settlements. Stimson rebuffed these recom-

July 1931, George L. Harrison Papers, 3013.1; Gilbert, Memorandum, 21 July 1931, Mills Papers, Box 9.

68. For the tension between Stimson and Hoover, see Diary of Henry L. Stimson, 21 July 1931, Stimson Papers; 20, 21 July 1931, Hoover Diary, HHPP, Box 880.

69. For the domestic constraints, see Mills to Mellon, 21 July 1931, HHPP, Box 874; Draft of cable to Sackett, no signature, 20 July 1931, ibid., Box 878; Diary of Charles S. Hamlin, 17, 20, 21, 29 July 1931, Hamlin Papers, Vol. 19; William E. Borah to Hoover, 23 July 1931, HHPP, Box 874.

70. See, for example, Conversation between Stimson and the president, 21 July 1931, HHPP, Box 874.

mendations. But he did endorse MacDonald's proposals to redistribute the existing short-term credits in Germany and have the French assume a larger share of them. Laval rejected this suggestion. He maintained that Anglo-American financiers had reaped great profits from German loans through the 1920s and now had to accept the consequences of their financial policies. Having acquiesced to the Hoover moratorium, the French government was in no mood to assume additional sacrifices. Unlike in 1923–24 France had the financial power to ward off American pressure. Consequently, the conference closed on 23 July with agreement that the central bank credit of $100 million should be renewed, a standstill of existing credits should be implemented, and a committee to study Germany's long-term needs should be established.[71]

The conference endorsed Hoover's program. The results pleased Laval but disappointed Brüning and embittered Snowden.[72] The Germans and British felt that the fundamental questions had been left unresolved. They were undoubtedly correct. But Hoover and Stimson had never contended that the American proposals were aimed at curing long-term problems. The president, in particular, had argued that it was impossible to deal with major issues in a few days and that short-term expedients were essential to afford government officials time to grapple with the more complex questions.

Hoover's assessment of the negotiating possibilities was correct. Although there was an urgent need for fundamental readjustments, there was no basis for agreement on such matters. Laval could not reduce German reparation payments unless Germany accepted the political status quo and the United States accepted war debt reductions. Brüning, however, could not think of making political concessions until the Young Plan was revised; Hoover could not contemplate a revision of the Mellon-Bérenger accord until France demonstrated her incapacity to pay. Snowden could not assent to further infusions of British capital into Germany until he was assured that war debts and reparations would be wiped out. Given the intractable positions of the various nations and the inability of any single government to compel concessions from the others or assume responsibility for the functioning of the international financial system, a standstill accord constituted

71. For the deliberations at the conference, see DBFP, 2, 2:457–84; see also FR, 1931, 1:306–13.
72. See, for example, Diary of Henry L. Stimson, 22–24 July 1931, Stimson Papers.

the only possible common denominator for dealing immediately with the German liquidity crisis.[73]

Since Hoover insisted that the standstill and moratorium were aimed at providing time for more fundamental financial and political readjustments, his subsequent actions demand close scrutiny. American policy was in a state of flux. On the one hand the standstill and related agreements continued to place the major burden for Europe's stabilization on the private sector and central banks. Similarly, allusions to French financial strength and German financial ineptness suggested that Hoover still expected other nations to assume most of the risks and sacrifices. On the other hand having participated in a conference on European financial problems and having promised to consider more permanent solutions, the administration could not simply withdraw from the reexamination of European needs. Indeed, negotiations were immediately begun to provide governmental credits to Germany through the Farm Board.[74] Whether Republican officials would jettison the old approaches and adopt a new orientation to European affairs remained to be seen.

The British Departure from the Gold Standard, the Laval Visit, and the Reappraisal of American Policy

In midsummer 1931 journalists and reporters emphasized that American foreign policy was in a state of great transition. George R. Holmes of the International News Service considered the participation of Stimson and Mellon in the London Conference reflective of an "epochal change in the foreign policies of the American Government." Likewise, the *Journal of the American Bankers Association* editorialized that "the last vestige, the last pretense, of following Washington's advice to avoid European entanglements [has been] thrown aside. . . . Our isolation is at an end, and we sit in the seats of the mighty." Editorial writers and political commentators focused considerable attention on the American role at the London Conference. They hypothesized that Hoover had benefited politically from the initiatives he had taken. They speculated that if these initiatives generated recovery, American policy toward Europe would be transformed and the president would become a viable candidate in the 1932 elections. Such

73. For the importance of one nation assuming responsibility for the functioning of the international monetary system, see Kindleberger, *World in Depression*.
74. FR, 1931, 2:293–309.

predictions were tempered by an awareness that the program endorsed at the London Conference comprised a number of temporary expedients, which would have to be supplemented by more far-reaching changes in the international economic, financial, and political order. There was no agreement, however, on the role the United States government should play in these changes or the responsibilities it should assume.[75]

Republican policymakers were puzzled about what to do next. Hoover and his advisers scrutinized the press reaction to their summer initiatives and pondered alternatives. They hoped that constructive actions by European governments and American bankers would reverse the economic downturn and convince the American people of the wisdom of the moratorium and standstill. Moreover, such action would afford the policymakers additional latitude to safeguard the $5 billion worth of American investments in Europe and revive American exports to the Old World, exports which had decreased by $1 billion since 1929.[76] With these objectives in mind Stimson stayed in Europe another month. He urged German and British officials to solve their financial problems and lay the political basis for a successful disarmament conference.[77] At the same time, Hoover and Mills disseminated the gospel of self-help at home. The president prodded American bankers to honor the standstill accord, and Mills encouraged Governor Harrison of the FRBNY to extend additional aid to the Bank of England.[78]

It soon became apparent that European officials, central bankers, and private financiers could not or would not shoulder the responsibility for new policies. The French reiterated their unwillingness to limit armaments until they received additional security guarantees.

75. For the quotations, see "Political Effects of the Hoover Adventure," *Literary Digest* 110 (1 August 1931):5–6; "The End of Isolation," *Journal of the American Bankers Association* 24 (August 1931):78–79; see "Germany's Salvation Now 'Up to Germany,'" *Literary Digest* 110 (8 August 1931):7; "Mr. Wiggin's Lusty Child," ibid., 110 (5 September 1931):7.

76. Walter Newton to Robinson, 27 July 1931, HHPP, Box 28; Castle to Berlin Embassy, 27 July 1931, ibid., Box 875; Castle to Edge, 13 August 1931, Castle Papers, Box 3; for indications of the very careful assessment of press sentiment, see Wilbur Carr to Stimson, 25 July 1931, HHPP, Box 875; for the American economic interest in Europe, see Julius Klein, "America's Stake in European Stability," 27 July 1931, Feiker Papers, Box 82.

77. For Stimson's discussions in Europe, see FR, 1931, 1:536–65; also 321–22, 508–9, 516–17; Diary of Henry L. Stimson, 1–7 August 1931, Stimson Papers.

78. Hoover, *Memoirs*, 3:77–78; Harrison, Memorandum, 31 July 1931, George L. Harrison Papers, 2013.1.

The Germans declared their incapacity to meet their obligations under the Young Plan. The British reasserted their inability to assist Germany until they received assurances from the United States that their war debt payments would be scaled down.[79] Simultaneously, private bankers at home and abroad indicated that they had exhausted their resources and would not offer help until governments took appropriate action to reduce intergovernmental debts and resolve outstanding political questions. In the United States internationalists like Lamont and Owen Young emphasized that they had done everything possible to aid Germany and wanted to avoid further involvement in Europe's difficulties.[80]

The British financial crisis, more than any other development, demonstrated the incapacity of central bankers and private financiers to handle prevailing difficulties through traditional methods. During the last two weeks of July the Bank of England lost over $200 million, one-quarter of its international reserves. In usual fashion on 1 August the FRBNY and the Bank of France offered aid in the form of a $250 million credit. Pressure on sterling intensified when a new experts' report predicted another large budgetary deficit. MacDonald and Snowden decided that to cope with the crisis, they had to raise additional funds in New York and Paris, even at the price of succumbing to bankers' demands that they cut expenditures. This policy precipitated a rift within the Labour party and the resignation of the Labour government. A national coalition government, including members of the Labour, Liberal, and Conservative parties, was formed under MacDonald's leadership. At the end of August private French and American bankers agreed to raise another $400 million to help keep sterling on gold. But the prospect of social and political turmoil, rumors of mutiny in the British navy, and the fundamental weakness of the British economy accentuated the pressure on sterling. On 21 September the British government severed the pound from the gold standard.[81]

Britain's suspension of gold payments alarmed American officials; it foreshadowed developments that promised to restrict international

79. For the French position, see, for example, FR, 1931, 1:507; for the German position, see p. 324; for the British position, see DBFP, 2, 2:235–36.

80. See the *Report of the Committee Appointed on the Recommendation of the London Conference*, 1931, Records of the Bureau of Accounts, RG 39, Box 104. The chairman of this committee was Albert H. Wiggin of the Chase National Bank. See also Lamont to Hoover, 27 July 1931, HHPP, Box 114; Young to Lamont, 3 August 1931, Young Papers, I–221.

81. Clarke, *Central Bank Cooperation*, pp. 203–18; Reginald Bassett, *Nineteen Thirty-One*, pp. 54–245.

commerce, curtail American exports, and exacerbate international economic conditions. The fluctuating value of sterling, American policymakers concluded, made it almost "impossible to fix prices or make commitments abroad." Republican officials realized that, before the pound could be stabilized, they must deal in an innovative fashion with the economic, financial, and political issues that linked the interests of Europe, Great Britain, and the United States. The president acknowledged that the FRBNY had done everything possible to afford relief to Britain and that failure to keep the pound at par underscored the need for initiatives, especially regarding the intergovernmental debts. Stimson, back from Europe, found Hoover's attitude refreshing, but he warned the president against separating political and financial issues.[82]

Although Hoover was ready to consider diplomatic initiatives, his primary concern with domestic economic and political considerations delayed immediate action. He feared a request to Congress for additional aid to Europe would not only be rejected in favor of domestic appropriations bills, but would also precipitate a dramatic confrontation between the legislative and executive branches. Congressmen, he predicted, would want to know why he chose to relieve Europe's distress, when he continued to oppose measures affording domestic relief. Rather than face such questioning at a time when the budget deficit for a peacetime year was reaching a record high, Hoover thought it politically expedient to propose internal solutions before trying out innovative foreign policy options.[83]

When the internal repercussions of the British crisis proved more severe than expected, Hoover emphasized domestic palliatives. On 22 September the United States experienced its largest gold withdrawals in history. By the end of October gold outflows and currency withdrawals totaled nearly $1,120 million. The result was a wave of bank failures, over 800 in September and October alone, and a severe credit crunch. Hoover riveted his attention to the domestic crisis and rapidly pushed his plans to liquefy the financial system. With bankers he con-

82. For the ramifications of sterling depreciation, see Allen Klots, Memorandum of conversation at the home of Ogden Mills, 4 October 1931, RG 59, 842.51/410; "Effects of Currency Depreciation on International Trade," [autumn 1931], Feiker Papers, Box 79; for Hoover's views, see Diary of Henry L. Stimson, 8, 12, 13, 16, 18 September 1931, Stimson Papers; Stimson to Dawes, 19 September 1931, RG 59, 842.51/971A; for Stimson's emphasis on the interrelationships between financial and political problems, see Diary of Henry L. Stimson, 8 September–17 October 1931, Stimson Papers.

83. For Hoover's views, see Stimson to Dawes, 19 September 1931, RG 59, 842.51/971A; for the political ramifications of the budgetary situation, see "The Skyrocketing Deficit," *Literary Digest* 110 (19 September 1931):7.

sidered voluntary means of aiding weaker banks and supporting financial markets. With legislators he discussed the re-creation of the WFC, the strengthening of the Federal Farm Loan System, the revision of the Federal Reserve Act, and the possibility of raising taxes. To Hoover's dismay tax hikes seemed necessary not only to boost confidence in conservative financial circles but also to avoid additional government borrowing that might raise interest rates and divert capital from the private sector. Having to contemplate an increase in taxes, Hoover was reluctant to decrease revenues through war debt reductions. Yet, he hoped to preserve the gold standard as the last link between the American and European economies.[84]

The president's growing preoccupation with the internal situation began to discourage Stimson. The secretary of state believed that Hoover's domestic proposals were too radical, and he was unconcerned about their fate at the hands of Congress. He urged Hoover to increase taxes. Most of all Stimson reproached Hoover for postponing attempts to deal with the European crisis.[85] Ironically, while the secretary of state chastised the president for relegating European affairs to secondary importance, the outbreak of hostilities in Manchuria diverted Stimson's attention from the Old World. On 23 September Jay Pierrepont Moffat, the State Department official in charge of preparations for the General Disarmament Conference at Geneva, noted that disarmament had begun to take a "back seat" to the Far Eastern crisis. Thereafter, East Asian affairs were a constant drain on Stimson's energy, even though he recognized that he should be focusing more of his attention on European security issues prior to the opening of the disarmament conference in early 1932.[86]

At the end of September the international financial crisis impelled policymakers to focus attention on European affairs. At the same time, the domestic credit crunch and the Manchurian incident engendered legitimate questioning about the utility of new efforts to deal with the

84. For the domestic monetary crisis, see Lester V. Chandler, *American Monetary Policy, 1928–1941*, pp. 160ff.; for Hoover's plans and actions, see [Hoover], "Program Proposed to Harrison, Mills, Mellon, and Wiggin," 25 September 1931, HHPP, Box 878; see also Diary of Henry L. Stimson, 29 September, 5 October 1931, Stimson Papers; Diary of Charles S. Hamlin, 7, 8 October 1931, Hamlin Papers, Vol. 19; for Hoover's fiscal considerations, see Herbert Stein, "Pre-Revolutionary Fiscal Policy," pp. 215–220.

85. Diary of Henry L. Stimson, 13, 29, 30 September 1931, Stimson Papers.

86. Diary of Jay Pierrepont Moffat, 23 September, 6–8 November 1931, Moffat Papers; Diary of Henry L. Stimson, 9, 13 October, 6 November 1931, Stimson Papers.

debt and disarmament issues.[87] Initiatives might endanger domestic priorities or strategic interests without having a salutary impact on European affairs, unless France was willing to cooperate. Since many of the best informed American officials, diplomats, bankers, and intelligence experts were struck with the preponderance of French power on the Continent, they questioned whether they could formulate solutions that were financially desirable and politically feasible from the American standpoint, yet capable of inducing France to reorient her stand on matters pertaining to reparations, disarmament, and the Polish Corridor.[88] The president did not think so. He had always borne a grudge against the French and was embittered by their reaction to the moratorium and their attempt to extract political concessions from Germany.[89]

Stimson shared some of the president's sentiments. He, too, felt that the French were foolishly aiming for "hegemony" in Europe. He considered their position on reparations, disarmament, and the Polish Corridor to be intransigent and unreasonable. Nevertheless, Stimson empathized with French anxieties and insecurities. He believed that if these feelings were taken into consideration, the French would behave more reasonably and accept necessary revisions in the Treaty of Versailles.[90] He was particularly impressed with Laval because the French premier seemed willing to conciliate Germany, effect a Franco-German rapprochement, and share in the sacrifices necessary to restore European stability. Therefore, when the secretary of state heard on 19 September that Laval wanted to visit the United States and talk to Hoover, Stimson immediately invited the French premier to Washington.[91]

87. As a result of the situation in East Asia, American military officials opposed any new disarmament initiatives. This complicated policymaking toward Europe. See Diary of Jay Pierrepont Moffat, 13, 16, 18, 20, 23, 24 November, 4 December 1931, 6 January 1932, Moffat Papers.

88. See, for example, Moffat, Memorandum, 2 October 1931, RG 59, 033.5111 Laval/257; Klots to Castle, 2 October 1931, ibid., 033.5111 Laval/256½; Gibson to Castle, 7 October 1931, HHPP, Box 861; Lamont to Hoover, 20 October 1931, ibid., Box 18; "Intelligence Summary," 10–23 October 1931, Records of the Military Intelligence Division (MID), RG 165.

89. For Hoover's bitter feelings toward the French, see Diary of Henry L. Stimson, 13 September, 24 October 1931, Stimson Papers.

90. For Stimson's views, see his talks with MacDonald and Jules Henry, FR, 1931, 1:514–17, 524–25.

91. For Stimson's attitude toward Laval, see Diary of Henry L. Stimson, 24 July 1931, Stimson Papers; Memorandum of conversation between Stimson and Friedrich Wilhelm von Prittwitz, 24 September 1931, RG 59, 033.5111 Laval/26; for the origins of Laval's visit, see FR, 1931, 2:237–43.

In preparation for Laval's visit policymakers conducted the most comprehensive reexamination since 1918–19 of American policy toward Europe. Within the Department of State, Stimson formed a committee, including Feis, Moffat, Pierre de Lagarde Boal, and Allen Klots, to study the security-disarmament impasse. The secretary of state also invited Dwight Morrow to join these discussions. When these officials got together in early October, they concurred that France was entitled to security. But "the rub came in the definition of the word 'security.' If the French meant the perpetual freezing of the post war status quo, including the maintenance of unjust and bitterly resented treaty solutions, and a preponderant military force to guarantee it, then we could not agree with them. Our idea of security was a tranquilized Europe, which meant the solution, one by one, and by peaceful means, of the problems that were preventing it from settling down." In effect American policymakers maintained that the French government had to reverse its attitude toward Germany, alleviate German grievances, and proceed with steps toward arms limitation. The Americans understood that such concessions placed an enormous burden on France, and they agreed that France was entitled to additional strategic guarantees, if she accepted the Anglo-American definition of French security.[92]

The key question facing American officials was whether the United States government could and should overcome its traditional antipathy to European embroilments and play a role in relieving French strategic anxieties. Since Laval, Flandin, and Briand sought additional concrete commitments from the British and only requested assurances from American officials that they would not interfere with the application of sanctions,[93] Stimson and Morrow believed that the United States could assume a constructive role in European security arrangements without incurring overseas strategic commitments. A six-page memorandum, written by Stimson's old friend, Charles P. Howland, provided a specific guide. Howland suggested that the United States should determine its future policies according to the principles of the Kellogg-Briand Pact. If American officials agreed that a nation had violated the peace

92. For the quotation, see Moffat, Memorandum, 2 October 1931, RG 59, 033.5111 Laval/257; see also Moffat, Memorandum, 5 October 1931, ibid., 711.0012 Anti-War/1189½; Klots to Castle, 2 October 1931, ibid., 033.5111 Laval/256½; Moffat, Memorandum, 5 October 1931, ibid., 033.5111 Laval/98 1/8; Diary of Henry L. Stimson, 29 September, 1, 2 October 1931, Stimson Papers; Diary of Jay Pierrepont Moffat, 30 September 1931, Moffat Papers.
93. See, for example, FR, 1931, 1:531–32; DBFP, 2:302, 317–18; Edge to secretary, 1 October 1931, HHPP, Box 875.

pact, Howland urged that they deny that nation its belligerent rights, accommodate League efforts to halt aggression, and withhold protection from Americans trying to trade with the aggressor. Howland maintained, and Stimson concurred, that such a policy could be presented in a presidential message without necessitating congressional approval. Since the policy would be linked to the Kellogg-Briand Pact and made contingent upon French cooperation on disarmament issues, American officials believed that it would be well received by the American people. The officials hoped that it would not only alleviate French apprehensions over American policy but also encourage Britain to undertake new commitments on the Continent.[94]

While State Department personnel assessed the European political situation, Mills, Harrison, Meyer, Feis, Stewart, Gilbert, and other bankers and officials examined European financial and economic questions. They discussed reconstruction of viable economic units in central Europe, restoration of trade with Russia, and reduction of tariff barriers. The bankers and officials concurred that action on these matters was desirable. But they realized that prospects for immediate results were negligible, especially in light of the uncertainties engendered by the fluctuation and depreciation of foreign currencies.[95] Hence, at a meeting at the FRBNY on 19 October they focused on the need to revise the debt settlements. Acknowledging the political constraints on American officials, the conferees maintained that Germany should take the first step toward a general debt revision and convoke the special advisory committee provided for in Article 119 of the Young Plan. If European governments successfully tackled the reparations question, the bankers and officials believed that the United States government should offer to renegotiate the war debt agreements. The attraction of this step-by-step approach was that it avoided a general conference on debts and reparations.[96]

On the eve of Laval's visit Hoover met with Stimson, Mills, and Assistant Secretary of State James G. Rogers and discussed the results

94. For Howland's memorandum, see Charles P. Howland, "Note on Security and Disarmament," [September 1931?], HHPP, Box 866; see also Diary of Henry L. Stimson, 29 September, 17 October 1931, Stimson Papers; Moffat, Memorandum, 2 October 1931, RG 59, 033.5111 Laval/257.
95. See, for example, Klots, Memorandum of conversation at home of Ogden Mills, 4 October 1931, RG 59, 842.51/410; James G. Rogers, Memorandum, 22 October 1931, ibid., 611.0031/379; Rogers, "Our Policy Toward Eastern European Tariff Agreements," 22 October 1931, ibid., 662.7131/48; see also Nils Olsen to Feis, 30 October 1931, ibid., 662.7131/42.
96. Feis, Memorandum, 20 October 1931, ibid., 033.5111 Laval/217.

of their extensive studies. The president also talked to Ambassador Hugh R. Wilson and representatives of Morgan and Company. Almost everyone emphasized that France reigned supreme in Europe; hence, they urged the president to cooperate with Laval in framing a program that would restore European stability and American prosperity.[97] Hoover, however, was increasingly preoccupied with the passage of his domestic legislative proposals and had not had sufficient time to think about an international program. In fact, according to Stimson, he had come to regard Laval's visit as a "nuisance." Moreover, he was infuriated by alleged French gold withdrawals from the United States. He maintained that French policies had exacerbated his domestic problems, disillusioned the American people, and circumscribed his options. With Congress to convene soon, he wondered aloud whether it might be easier and wiser to divorce the national from the international economy.[98]

Hoover's speculation was not so much an indication of his preference for an exclusively domestic approach to recovery as it was a reflection of his uncertainty about how to reconcile his domestic program, which he considered of primary importance, with foreign policy initiatives. Eventually, however, he accepted the advice of his financial advisers and agreed to encourage Laval to convene the Young Plan advisory committee as the first step toward a revision of all intergovernmental debt settlements. But he still expressed skepticism about the efficacy of Howland's proposals regarding implementation of the Kellogg-Briand Pact and revision of neutrality practices. According to Stimson, Hoover "was afraid that [Howland's suggestions] would lead us back into sanctions and get us tangled up with League principles."[99]

The growing prospect of war between Germany and Poland diminished any inclination the president might have had to increase American involvement in European political affairs. On 21 October, the day before Laval arrived in Washington, the Polish ambassador met with Hoover, warned that a conflict was imminent, and reiterated his gov-

97. Lamont to Hoover, 20 October 1931, HHPP, Box 18; Diary of Jay Pierrepont Moffat, 17, 18 October 1931, Moffat Papers; Hugh Wilson, Memorandum, 19 October 1931, HHPP, Box 875; Diary of Henry L. Stimson, 20 October 1931, Stimson Papers.

98. Diary of Henry L. Stimson, 30 September, 9, 12, 13, 14, 20 October 1931, Stimson Papers; Egan, Memorandum, 21 October 1931, Thomas W. Lamont Papers, Box 98; Diary of Jay Pierrepont Moffat, 13, 20 October 1931, Moffat Papers. For the reasons behind French gold withdrawals, see Diary of Charles S. Hamlin, 4 November 1931, Hamlin Papers; J. C. DeWilde, "French Financial Policy," pp. 237–39.

99. Diary of Henry L. Stimson, 17, 20 October 1931, Stimson Papers.

ernment's unwillingness to discuss concessions to Germany. When Stimson learned of this interview, he was disgusted. Yet, reports from the American embassy in Poland confirmed that the ambassador had presented the views of his government accurately. The Poles would not even consider establishing more direct communication links between the Reich and East Prussia.[100] This attitude exasperated Hoover and Stimson. They believed that the political questions relating to Germany's eastern boundary constituted a major element in the European crisis. Moreover, they hoped to resolve the problem of the Polish Corridor by proposing the construction of an "elevated causeway internationalized."[101]

When Laval arrived at the White House on the afternoon of 23 October, Hoover plunged into a discussion of the Polish question. The president "said that Central Europe seemed to be the unstable spot of Europe and of the world." He intimated that unless the corridor issue was resolved, it would be hard for him to muster political support for American initiatives. Laval said it was impossible to do anything: "Poland would never consent; she would fight." Laval sought a moratorium on calls for revising the Treaty of Versailles. Stimson interjected that France was endangering herself by trying to preserve French hegemony in Europe. The French premier, however, did not budge from his position. Laval's attitude on the Polish question and his espousal of the traditional French line on German intentions disappointed not only the president but also the secretary of state, who had anticipated a much more flexible posture.[102]

This initial exchange influenced the attitude of Hoover and Stimson during evening discussions, when Laval reiterated that France required "security before she disarmed." He did not ask for American guarantees but noted that a consultative pact "would help very much the possibility of any disarmament." The president stated that a consultative pact was a political impossibility for him; yet, Hoover acknowledged that the United States would never be found on the side of an aggressor nation. Stimson interceded, telling Laval that a consultative pact must never be considered a substitute for French security and

100. FR, 1931, 1:598–600; Castle to Sackett, 23 October 1931, Castle Papers, Box 5; Diary of Henry L. Stimson, 21 October 1931, Stimson Papers.

101. Diary of Henry L. Stimson, 6, 12 October 1931, Stimson Papers.

102. The quotations are all from Stimson's diary account of the discussions. See Diary of Henry L. Stimson, 23 October 1931, Stimson Papers. Hoover reviewed these diary entries and penciled in a few corrections. See Stimson file in Herbert Hoover Post-Presidential Papers, Box 178 (hereafter cited as HHPPP).

should not be discussed in that context, lest it raise illusory expectations that the United States was agreeing to provide armed assistance in the future. Stimson reiterated that a promise of armed assistance was a political impossibility. Laval acknowledged the truth of this statement and did not press the matter.[103] Given the deteriorating state of Polish-German relations, the unaltered position of France on the corridor issue, and the reaffirmation of France's traditional stand on security and disarmament, neither Hoover nor Stimson alluded to the Howland plan in their talks with Laval. Apparently they intended to use the proposal as a trump card during the disarmament conference.[104]

Though no progress was made during the French premier's visit on the questions of disarmament and security, there was considerable accord between Hoover and Laval on financial issues. Both men realized that it was in the common interest of their nations to cooperate in preserving the gold standard and restoring exchange stability. Their first task was to deal with intergovernmental debts. Hoover wanted the BIS to appoint the advisory committee of experts to study Germany's capacity to pay reparations during the Depression. After European governments met to approve the recommendations of the advisory committee, Hoover indicated he would ask Congress to reestablish the WDC. Laval seemed surprised by the president's forthright and specific proposal on how to proceed. In turn, Hoover was gratified by Laval's readiness to provide relief to Germany. To minimize his domestic political problems, however, Laval emphasized that a final communiqué had to be carefully worded to demonstrate that he was not openly repudiating the Young Plan.[105]

The president and the French premier felt satisfied that their talks had led to a frank exchange of views. Laval had safeguarded the French position on security, maintained the integrity of the Young Plan, and reaffirmed the importance of the gold standard. The French press congratulated him on these accounts.[106] Likewise, Hoover and

103. Diary of Henry L. Stimson, 23 October 1931, Stimson Papers.
104. Diary of Henry L. Stimson, 23–25 October 1931, ibid.; see also Diary of Jay Pierrepont Moffat, 17–19 October 1931, Moffat Papers. Although Laval displayed an inflexible attitude on the corridor issue, French officials had been considering possible compromise solutions of this problem for quite some time. See Sally Marks, *The Illusion of Peace*, pp. 94–95. American military intelligence was aware of this. See "Intelligence Summary," 30 January–12 February 1932, MID, RG 165.
105. Diary of Henry L. Stimson, 23, 24 October 1931, Stimson Papers; see also Hoover's subsequent recollection of the talks, Hoover to Stimson, n.d., HHPP, Box 877.
106. For Laval's feelings, see Williamson S. Howell to secretary, 3 November 1931, RG 59, 033.5111 Laval/204; DBFP, 2, 2:317–18; for the reaction of the French press, see

Stimson were gratified by the extent of agreement on financial issues. Since the president still placed primary importance on the economic and financial underpinnings of European stability, he was especially pleased that agreement had been achieved on procedural matters regarding debts and reparations. He predicted that the restoration of sound financial and economic conditions in Germany would quell the social and political ferment in that nation and contribute to stability throughout the Continent. He also hoped that even a temporary settlement of the intergovernmental debt questions might lead to a conference aimed at reestablishing the gold standard and stabilizing the pound.[107]

Laval returned to Europe and prodded Brüning to seek the convocation of the special advisory committee. Suspecting that Americans might saddle the French with the bulk of the sacrifices, Laval tried to circumscribe the experts' study. He emphasized that France would never abandon the unconditional annuities. He insisted that reductions in the conditional payments had to be proportionate to reductions in French war debt payments and that the new arrangements had to be limited to the Depression. He maintained that France could never permit the repatriation of private credits to be accorded priority over the payment of reparations.[108]

Hoover, Stimson, and Castle disapproved of Laval's attempts to circumscribe the results of the advisory committee's inquiry. American officials wanted the advisory committee to recommend far-reaching changes in Germany's obligations, both conditional and unconditional. They hoped that such changes would expedite the renewal of the standstill accord, safeguard American investments, and protect the domestic banking structure.[109] Despite their disappointment with Laval's policy statements, they did not want to renege on their side of the bargain. In late November and early December Stimson, Klots, and Feis urged Hoover to ask Congress to approve the moratorium and recreate the WDC. Mills, noting Britain's special problems, argued that the new

the clippings and summaries in Howell to Department of State, 23, 26, 27 October, 3, 6 November 1931, RG 59, 033.5111 Laval/191, 164, 177, 219, 240.

107. Diary of Henry L. Stimson, 23, 24, 27 October 1931, Stimson Papers.

108. For Laval's actions and statements, see Howell to secretary of state, 4, 5, 6, 13, 18, 19, 30 November, 10 December 1931, RG 39, Box 104; see also DBFP, 2, 2:357–59; Warner, *Pierre Laval*, p. 50.

109. Memorandum of conversation between Stimson and Claudel, 3 December 1931, Castle Papers, Box 11; DBFP, 2, 2:331; Feis to Stimson and Mills, "Note on the Present Status of the International Debt and Reparations Negotiations," 2 November 1931, RG 39, Box 105.

debt accords should not be restricted to the period of the Depression.[110] Accordingly, on 10 December Hoover urged Congress to accept the moratorium and reestablish the WDC. He explained that because several debtors would not be able to meet their obligations during the forth-coming year, the United States had to face the realities of the interna-tional financial situation. At the same time, Mellon indicated that the administration's policy was intended to readjust debts according to the capacity of the debtors to pay.[111]

Congress responded with hostility. There was little enthusiasm for the moratorium and considerable anger at the prospect of recreating the WDC and scaling down the debts. Congressman McFadden accused Hoover of being an agent of the international bankers and called the president an "oriental potentate drunk with power."[112] Many other legislators claimed that the moratorium and debt revision proposals were sinister efforts to rescue the investments of Wall Street bankers at the expense of American taxpayers. The Senate Finance Committee launched an investigation to determine whether international bankers were indeed conspiring against the interests of the American people. Many congressmen charged that the United States should not assume the burden of stabilizing European finances when European govern-ments were dissipating their resources on armaments. The congress-men believed that France, in particular, had a greater capacity to pay the war debts than the United States had ability to cancel. But because they were unable to renege on prior commitments, most legislators voted to approve the moratorium. With virtual unanimity, however, they forbade further revisions or reductions of the war debt obligations. Summing up the views of the American press, the *Literary Digest* concluded that Congress had accurately expressed the sentiments of the American people.[113]

110. Diary of Henry L. Stimson, 4 December 1931, Stimson Papers; Harvey Bundy to Stimson, 7 December 1931, HHPP, Box 53.

111. For Hoover's address, see FR, 1931, 1:xxv; for Mellon's statement, see "Should the United States Further Readjust Foreign Debt Settlements," *Congressional Digest* 11 (January 1932):14; for legislative-executive relations, see Schwarz, *Interregnum*, pp. 172–205.

112. Quoted in Schwarz, *Interregnum*, p. 85.

113. For congressional sentiment, see "Foreign Debt Settlements," pp. 15, 17, 18, 20, 23; House, Ways and Means, *Moratorium on Foreign Debts*, 2:78–90, 94–100; "New Congress Tackles Foreign Debt Problem," *Congressional Digest* 10 (January 1932):13, 29; for the investigation of the Senate Finance Committee, see Senate, Com-mittee on Finance, *Sale of Foreign Bonds or Securities in the United States*; for press sentiment, see "Dawes Plan, Young Plan—Next!" *Literary Digest* 112 (9 January 1932):5.

State Department officials were awed by Congress's bitter reaction. Stimson personally went to Capitol Hill to explain the seriousness of European developments, but his efforts were to no avail. Even friendly senators rebuffed his pleas for support. He became deeply depressed. "Everything is down again. Everybody is blue," Stimson wrote in his diary on 28 December. Given the dissension in Europe and the reaction of Congress, the secretary of state agreed with Hoover that the administration should focus its efforts on the domestic situation. Unless European nations took the initiative to straighten out their own problems, and France, as the dominant Continental power, assumed greater financial sacrifices, Stimson could not contemplate additional American action. He feared that, if the president tried to go any further to promote financial stability in Europe, he would lose all support among the American people. On 29 December Stimson sent an *aide-mémoire* to the French embassy explaining this viewpoint and stating that the United States government could not participate in the forthcoming conference on reparations.[114]

Even those businessmen and bankers most concerned about European stability did not exert much pressure in behalf of initiatives to effect European stability. They agreed that, as important as the foreign market was, the internal fiscal situation, the budgetary deficit, the credit crunch, and the general domestic economic downturn set limits on what the administration could and should do to ameliorate the world crisis. Hoover's desire to readjust debts according to the principle of payment capacity was in step with the recommendations of those most interested in the relationship between the United States economy and the European economy. International bankers, like Lamont and Kahn, told Congress that the $600 million in short-term American credits locked up in Germany did not pose a threat to the banking system. Garrard Winston, the former undersecretary of the treasury who had played such a key role in fostering European currency stabilization in the mid-1920s, cautioned against cancellation of the debts. James A. Farrell, president of the NFTC, reminded members of his organization

114. For Stimson's feelings, see Diary of Henry L. Stimson, 17, 18, 26, 27, 28 December 1931, Stimson Papers; for the *aide-mémoire*, see RG 59, 462.00R296A1/1. The conference on reparations was supposed to discuss the recommendations of the advisory committee. The advisory committee, under pressure from the American delegate, had called for a moratorium on conditional payments and for additional action in light of the intensity of the Depression. For the report, see DBFP, 2, 2:495–508; for Stimson's effort to influence the report, see Diary of Henry L. Stimson, 21 December 1931, Stimson Papers; for the negotiations behind the report, see Merle Cochran to Castle, 10, 15, 24, 28 December 1931, RG 39, Box 104.

that "it should be possible for us to discover means of making our domestic market a stronger stabilizing influence in periods of world depression." Even officials in the BFDC had to acknowledge, however regretfully, that interest in foreign markets had declined as businessmen focused most of their attention on domestic palliatives.[115]

Conclusion

At the end of 1931 Republican policymakers placed primary emphasis on domestic initiatives to foster recovery. The president believed that he had made a valiant effort to use America's dwindling financial strength to meet the needs of the European crisis. In Hoover's view, and in the view of most Americans at the time, his actions constituted a wise effort to measure the importance of European stability against American self-interest and act accordingly. Although Hoover was willing to consider additional initiatives, he wanted assurances that they would be effective. France, he believed, had stymied every effort he had made to reconcile domestic priorities with European imperatives. Therefore, nothing further could be done until France demonstrated to his satisfaction that she was willing to share in the sacrifices and risks necessary to restore European stability. Only then would Hoover be prepared to incur additional short-term sacrifices and risk greater American involvement in Europe's political affairs. Although European instability affected the domestic economy, the president reminded Congress on 8 December that the United States could insulate itself from a total European breakdown and "make a large measure of recovery independent of the rest of the world."[116]

The president's placement of major responsibility for European recovery onto France was deeply and understandably resented in that nation. The French believed that the high-tariff policy of the United States and the ill-considered private American loans to Germany were primarily responsible for the European economic crisis. Therefore, France felt it incumbent upon the United States to assume a larger

115. For the views of Lamont and Kahn, see Senate, Finance, *Foreign Bonds*, pp. 28–36, 137; for Winston's attitude, see "Should America Cancel the War Debts?" *Congressional Digest* 10 (October 1931), p. 253; for Farrell's statement, see "The World Trade Outlook," NFTC, *Official Report*, 1931, p. 13; for the views of officials in the BFDC, see Notes on Saturday morning meeting, 7 November 1931, Feiker Papers, Box 81; Feiker to Matthews, 18 November 1931, ibid., Box 84.

116. For the quotation, see FR, 1931, 1:xiii; for Hoover's feelings, see Byron Price, Oral History Interview, 21 March 1969, pp. 4–6, 11, 20–21, in Herbert Hoover Presidential Library.

share of financial sacrifices in the form of war debt reductions. The favorable balance-of-payments position of the United States indicated to Frenchmen that America had the capacity to absorb greater sacrifices. From the French perspective, the moratorium appeared an arbitrary attempt to serve American self-interest, and Hoover's subsequent inability to recreate the WDC reflected the bankruptcy of American policymaking. What agitated France more than anything else was the apparent indifference of American officials to the strategic and political implications of their financial and disarmament proposals. American claims that France had the capacity to make greater financial sacrifices seemed irrelevant to most Frenchmen. They had to bear the strategic risks of any well-intentioned concession, made for the purpose of salvaging the Weimar Republic, that might ultimately enhance the strength of a resurgent Germany under Nazi control.[117]

In turn, American policymakers considered French attitudes and complaints shortsighted, ungrateful, and contentious. Unsure about what the United States should do next, some of them, like Stimson, Mills, and Feis, considered the Howland memorandum and contemplated new approaches to the war debt–reparations imbroglio.[118] But even the most European-oriented American officials acknowledged an interlocking network of domestic and foreign variables that inhibited new actions. In light of these constraints the traditional Republican orientation, aimed at contributing to European stability without compromising domestic priorities or incurring strategic commitments, did not seem altogether unwise. No one in official circles, for example, was more of an internationalist than Herbert Feis; no one pondered the nature of the interdependence of the domestic and European economies more than he. Yet, in 1931 even he could not endorse American initiatives without reservations. He recognized that the United States might overcommit itself financially and militarily, impairing its domestic resources and dissipating its military strength.[119] Similarly, military

117. For these generalizations about French sentiment, see, for example, André Tardieu, *France in Danger!*, pp. 19–29; Edge to Stimson, 31 December 1931, RG 59, 462.00R296A1/10; "Les Etats-Unis et les dettes," *Le Temps*, 20 December 1931, RG 39, Box 105; for Flandin's view, see also DBFP, 2, 2:380–81.
118. For new approaches to the intergovernmental debt problem, see Mills to Winston, 3, 27 October, 7 November 1931, Mills Papers, Box 109; Diary of Henry L. Stimson, 27 November 1931, Stimson Papers.
119. See, for example, Feis to Frankfurter, 15 July 1931, Feis Papers, Box 16; Feis, Memorandum, "An Economically Independent United States," 11 February 1932, Frankfurter Papers, Box 54. During 1932, however, Feis's stress on international initiatives did increase.

officials who sympathized with French apprehensions, like Admiral Mark L. Bristol, president of the General Board of the Navy, steadfastly opposed American strategic commitments in the Old World.[120] The internationalists of the period did not think that the nation's most vital interests were imperiled in Europe. Military analysts, aware of German revisionist aims, did not foresee an imminent threat to American strategic concerns. Believing that the United States could get along economically without Europe and perceiving no strategic menace in the Old World, civilian and military leaders awaited the outcome of Hoover's domestic proposals and hoped for a change in congressional attitudes and European policies.[121]

120. Mark L. Bristol to Robert M. Scotten, 6 June 1931, Bristol Papers, Box 94; Bristol to James G. MacDonald, 19 June 1931, ibid., Box 104.

121. For Stimson's inclination to strengthen the domestic "defenses," see Diary of Henry L. Stimson, 18, 28 December 1931, Stimson Papers. Shortly before he died in October 1931, Morrow analyzed French security demands, sympathized with them, but still cautioned against the United States assuming strategic commitments in Europe. See Morrow to Gilbert, 3 September 1931, Morrow Papers; for the views of military analysts, see "Intelligence Summary," 21 November–4 December 1931, 1–6 January 1932, RG 165, MID.

[8]

Hoover and the Failure of
Economic Diplomacy, 1932

At the close of 1931 President Hoover temporarily disregarded the European crisis while he sought passage of his domestic program. Although he claimed that events abroad exacerbated conditions in the United States, Hoover did not think that domestic recovery had to wait for an improvement in the international economic and financial situation. On the contrary he emphasized that the "action needed is in the home field and it is urgent." Because he believed that the domestic credit paralysis and the financial situation of American railroads constituted the major impediments to recovery, he called upon Congress to create the Reconstruction Finance Corporation (RFC), strengthen the Federal Land Bank System, and institute a system of Home Loan Discount Banks. Hoover wanted Congress to expand the discount facilities of the Federal Reserve System, revise the banking laws, reappraise the legislation pertaining to the nation's transportation systems, and balance the budget.[1] This program reflected the president's long-term emphasis on properly regulating internal credit and effectively stimulating the domestic construction industry to insure American prosperity.[2] The temporary subordination of international concerns to domestic

1. Herbert C. Hoover, *The State Papers and Other Public Writings of Herbert Hoover*, 2:83, 46, 51, 56–93, 102–6, 148, 162–63, 172; see also Hoover to Thomas W. Lamont, 21 November 1931, Thomas W. Lamont Papers, Box 98.
2. For the relationship between the Home Loan Discount Banks and the residential construction industry, see Hoover, *State Papers*, 2:32, 40; for Hoover's earlier stress on regulating credit and stimulating domestic construction, see, for example, Department of Commerce, *Annual Report of the Secretary of Commerce*, 1922, pp. 16, 31–32; 1925, p. 32; essay by Ellis W. Hawley, in *Herbert Hoover and the Crisis of American Capitalism*, edited by J. Joseph Huthmacher and Warren L. Susman, pp. 16–17, 24–25.

priorities accorded with Hoover's view that foreign trade constituted "a small portion of our national activities." It was a valuable portion but not nearly so important as the preservation and cultivation of the domestic market.[3]

In early 1932 Hoover's preoccupation with his domestic legislative proposals made him hesitant to launch foreign policy initiatives, especially with regard to the intergovernmental debts. At the time congressional disclosures of corruption on Wall Street would have ignited a nasty controversy between the executive and legislative branches had the administration tried to assume a flexible stand on the war debt question. The administration's critics would have excoriated Hoover for sacrificing the interests of American taxpayers to salvage the private loans of wily international financiers. Wishing to avoid any acrimony that might jeopardize Hoover's domestic program, Secretary of State Stimson told European ambassadors that their respective governments would have to resolve the reparations controversy by themselves at the forthcoming Lausanne Conference.[4]

Simultaneously, the Hoover administration decided to play an inactive role during the opening stages of the General Disarmament Conference at Geneva. Stimson realized that French and German officials could not begin to resolve their respective claims for security and equality before the May elections in France. Consequently, the secretary of state and the president decided to defer presentation of a detailed American program until a more propitious moment.[5] Only at the last moment did they put together a delegation that included professional diplomats Hugh Gibson and Hugh R. Wilson, former Democratic Undersecretary of State Norman H. Davis, and Senator Claude Swanson. When the conference convened in early February, Stimson permitted Gibson to emphasize the importance of limiting military effectives and reducing offensive land armaments. But Gibson was not allowed to embroil himself in the critical political issues.[6]

3. Hoover, *State Papers*, 2:362, 104.

4. For Stimson's talks with European ambassadors, see, for example, Memorandum of conversation between Henry L. Stimson and Friedrich Wilhelm von Prittwitz, 11 January 1932, General Records of the Department of State, RG 59, 462.00R296A1/41; for a cogent summary of the findings of congressional inquiries, see Vincent P. Carosso, *Investment Banking in America*, pp. 322–51; for the impact of the Senate hearings, see Herbert Feis to Stimson, 7 January 1932, RG 59, 800.51/672.

5. Memorandum of conversation at the White House, 5 January 1932, Davis Papers, Box 20; Diary of Jay Pierrepont Moffat, 9–15 January 1932, Moffat Papers; Memorandum of phone conversation between Stimson and Charles G. Dawes, 21 December 1932, Herbert C. Hoover Presidential Papers, Box 866 (hereafter cited as HHPP).

6. For the selection of the American delegation, which also included Mary Emma Woolley, see Diary of Henry L. Stimson, 13, 14 December 1932, Stimson Papers; Diary

With the president focusing on domestic priorities and the secretary of state preoccupied with the Far Eastern crisis,[7] the ramifications of American policies were especially hard for the French to bear. The prospect that war debt revisions would have to take place according to a capacity-to-pay formula distressed the French because they had the greatest ability to pay.[8] More important, the American emphasis on limiting offensive land armaments exposed France's vulnerable position at the Geneva Conference. Since Germany was already disarmed in many offensive categories, the United States was in effect asking France to move toward Germany's level. Stimson insisted that "Germany could not be kept indefinitely waiting [for Allied disarmament] under an implied moral obligation [in Article 5 of the Treaty of Versailles]."[9] The American understanding of the German position, however, was not accompanied by an alteration in the American disposition to guarantee French security. American military officials continued to emphasize France's military superiority. They did not foresee the rapidity of Germany's future rearmament and showed no inclination to buttress France's strategic interests.[10]

As the United States turned toward domestic concerns, French officials adopted a tougher public stance, a posture which American diplomats viewed as a sign of France's mounting apprehension. At Geneva Premier Tardieu called for the creation of an international security force, the internationalization of civilian aviation, and the systematic organization of security guarantees. These demands reflected the French reaction to developments in Germany, where Adolf Hitler challenged Paul von Hindenburg for the presidency of the tottering republic and Brüning demanded cancellation of all reparations and disarmament of the former Allies. Although Tardieu tried to counter German ambitions in central and eastern Europe by promoting a Danubian federation under

---

of Jay Pierrepont Moffat, 17, 22, 28 December 1931, 8 January 1932, Moffat Papers; for the events leading up to Gibson's speech, Department of State, *Papers Relating to the Foreign Relations of the United States*, 1932, 1:1–30 (hereafter cited as FR); for Gibson's aloofness from political issues, see also Diary of Jay Pierrepont Moffat, 3 March 1932, Moffat Papers.

7. For Stimson's continued preoccupation with the Far Eastern crisis, see Diary of Henry L. Stimson, February and early March 1932, Stimson Papers.

8. Walter E. Edge to Stimson, 2 February 1932, Records of the Bureau of Accounts, RG 39, Box 106.

9. House, Committee on Foreign Affairs, *General Disarmament Conference*, pp. 32–33, 25.

10. "Intelligence Summary," 21 November–4 December 1931, 1–16, 16–29 January, 7–20 May 1932, Records of the Military Intelligence Division (MID), RG 165; War Plans Division (WPD) to Chief of Naval Operations (CNO), 21 April 1932, "Estimate of the Situation," Confidential Records of the Secretary of the Navy, RG 80, File L1–1.

French tutelage, he encountered strong Italian and British opposition.[11] Under these circumstances the French premier sought to reconcile French and American differences. He explained the French position to American diplomats and asked for assurances that the United States would not interfere with League actions against an aggressor nation. Tardieu expressed hope that Washington would send a representative to the Lausanne Conference and appealed for American aid in financing his Danubian scheme.[12]

The overtures of the French premier affected American perceptions and policies. In late March Davis returned to Washington convinced of France's goodwill and intent on persuading the administration to alter its policies. Although he encountered substantial resistance, he was able to stimulate a full reassessment of the American stand at Geneva. Abatement of the crisis in East Asia allowed Stimson to spend more time thinking about European affairs. Moreover, Herbert Feis, the secretary's economic adviser, began to emphasize that an increase in domestic credit would not suffice to promote recovery so long as international trade was stifled. Believing that domestic economic upswings were aborted by low agricultural and raw material prices set in international markets, both Feis and Davis supported foreign policy initiatives to foster European stability, aid American exports, and hasten domestic recovery.[13]

Hoover listened carefully to Davis's arguments. By the end of March many of the president's domestic proposals had been enacted, and he was again prepared to tackle European problems. Even while he had temporarily placed primary emphasis on domestic initiatives, Hoover had never discounted altogether the value of promoting stability abroad. In fact, he had always sought to foster stability in the Old World so

11. For Tardieu's proposals at Geneva, see John Wheeler Wheeler-Bennett, *The Pipe Dream of Peace*, pp. 13–16; for Franco-German competition in central and eastern Europe, see Edge to Stimson, 25 March, 3 May 1932, RG 59, 462.00R296A1/142, 149; Frederick M. Sackett to William R. Castle, 6 April 1932, ibid., 462.00R296A1/142½; for the impact of Nazi political gains, see, for example, Edge to Stimson, 3 May 1932, RG 39, Box 105. At the same time, the publication of the papers of Gustav Stresemann, the former German foreign minister, had a terrible impact on French public opinion. See, for example, Robert T. Pell to Moffat, 26 May 1932, RG 59, 762.00/59.

12. FR, 1932, 1:56–59; American Embassy, Paris, to Stimson, 23 March 1932, RG 39, Box 105.

13. For Davis's talks in Washington, see Diary of Jay Pierrepont Moffat, 28 March–4 April 1932, Moffat Papers; Diary of Henry L. Stimson, 30 March–5 April 1932, Stimson Papers; see also Herbert Feis to Davis, 22 April 1932, Feis Papers, Box 15; Davis to Feis, 13 June 1932, ibid.; Feis to Felix Frankfurter, 12, 25 February 1932, ibid., Box 16; Frankfurter to Feis, 10 June 1932, ibid.; Feis, Memorandum, 8 March 1932, Frankfurter Papers, Box 54.

long as domestic priorities were not compromised or strategic commitments incurred. If the machinery set up to accomplish these goals had not worked effectively in the past, it was time to consider alternative tactics. Hoover's inclination was to give a major public address championing the cause of disarmament. But, advised to take a low-key approach, he quietly reviewed the European situation and decided to send Stimson to Geneva for private talks with European officials.[14] Thereafter, between mid-March and mid-August Republican policymakers reassessed old policies, considered new approaches, and launched initiatives in a continuing effort to balance domestic and foreign economic policies and reconcile strategic imperatives in East Asia with a disarmament program in Europe.

Land Disarmament and French Security

By mid-March Davis and Gibson were convinced that the United States had sufficient prestige, power, and respect to push through a disarmament agreement. But the American delegates recognized that success depended upon their ability to present a plan that truly enhanced French security. Hence, they wanted to assuage France's fear of invasion by abolishing offensive armaments and restoring the superiority of defensive weaponry. Such a plan, they believed, could be coupled with regional guarantees of French security. Moreover, Gibson and Davis hoped that by abolishing offensive weapons, they might relieve French anxieties about the long-term implications of Germany's demand for equality of rights. If all nations renounced offensive land weapons, Germany would never be able to lay claim to them and French defenses would remain invulnerable. Thus, the aim of the American delegates was to find a means of reconciling France's desire for security with Germany's clamor for equality without imposing new strategic commitments on the United States. To make their proposal more appealing to France and other nations, Davis and Gibson also wanted the United States government to accept budgetary limitations on arms expenditures and acquiesce to the abolition of naval and military aviation.[15]

14. Diary of Henry L. Stimson, 30 March–7 April 1932, Stimson Papers; Memorandum of conversation between Stimson and Gibson, 2 April 1932, HHPP, Box 867; Diary of Jay Pierrepont Moffat, 31 March 1932, Moffat Papers; Hoover, *State Papers*, 2:158; Jordan Schwarz, *The Interregnum of Despair*, pp. 106–34.

15. FR, 1932, 1:59–67; see also the unsigned memoranda for N. Davis, March 1932, Davis Papers, Box 20; George S. Simonds to Douglas MacArthur, 15 March 1932, Simonds Papers, Box 42.

American military officials, however, maintained that the program favored by the American delegates would weaken America's armed strength. Admiral William V. Pratt, chief of naval operations, pleaded against the abolition of naval aviation, which he claimed was a great strategic asset, especially against Japanese submarines. Though Army Chief of Staff Douglas MacArthur was prepared to consider the abolition of military aircraft, as well as tanks and heavy mobile artillery, he joined Pratt in rejecting budgetary limitation. Secretary of State Stimson was torn between his desire to expedite a disarmament agreement in Europe and his commitment to build up American military strength in the Pacific. Therefore, he accepted the Navy's position on military aviation and budgetary limitation but told Davis that he would allow Gibson to present an American plan for the abolition of offensive land armaments.[16]

Although this limited step forward did not satisfy the American delegates, it did signify a new orientation in American policy. On 11 April Gibson appeared before the general commission of the disarmament conference and called for the abolition of tanks, heavy mobile artillery, and poisonous gas. These were aggressive weapons, he stated, that engendered fears of invasion. Their elimination, he predicted, would enhance the security of all nations, save enormous sums of money, and expedite the economic rehabilitation of Europe.[17] By assuming the initiative in the matter of land armaments, the Hoover administration was taking on a new role. Heretofore, Republican policy had focused on naval armaments and disregarded land armaments. But by the spring of 1932 the two had become interlocked, and the General Board of the Navy was refusing to consider additional limitation of naval weaponry until land and air armaments were also stabilized.[18]

Unfortunately, Gibson's speech infuriated Tardieu. The French premier condemned the American position as self-serving. He wondered why battleships were not considered offensive weapons and reaffirmed France's demand for guarantees and an international security force. He and Joseph Paul-Boncour, one of the French delegates to the conference, exposed serious flaws in the American proposal. The plan did not clearly distinguish between offensive and defensive armaments; it

16. Diary of Jay Pierrepont Moffat, 29 March–4 April 1932, Moffat Papers; FR, 1932, 1:62–67; for the Navy's opposition to budgetary limitation, see Admiral Mark L. Bristol to secretary of navy, 26 October 1931, General Records of the Navy Department, Office of the Secretary, RG 80, Box 92; MacArthur to Simonds, 7 April 1932, Simonds Papers, Box 42.
17. For Gibson's address, see FR, 1932, 1:75–83.
18. General Board to secretary of navy, 23 January 1932, RG 80, Box 92.

did not consider the interdependence of land, sea, and air armaments; it did not provide for enforcement machinery. The French feared that once they destroyed their offensive armaments, the Germans would gain a great strategic edge because of their ability to outproduce the French in a future arms race. Moreover, the French were wary of a plan that sought to abolish all tanks and mobile artillery, since such weapons constituted an integral part of their defensive strategy. Davis, Gibson, and Wilson had overlooked this critical point.[19]

While the French were attacking the American proposal at Geneva, Stimson arrived in Paris. Again, he realized that the French electoral campaign precluded the serious consideration of a disarmament program. Once he reassured Tardieu that he would not generate public discussion of controversial issues, the French premier treated Stimson cordially.[20] French officials in Paris and Geneva expressed their growing anxiety about French security. In particular, they criticized the United States for dissuading Britain from assuming additional commitments on the Continent. Such accusations infuriated Gibson and Wilson. Stimson, however, responded calmly. He reiterated that the United States did not oppose regional security accords and placed no obstacles in the path of the British. He stated that if the British provided guarantees in return for French disarmament, the United States would be prepared to consult during times of crisis to adjust American neutrality practices. Once the secretary of state got Prime Minister MacDonald and Foreign Secretary John Simon to admit that American policy had no bearing on Britain's reluctance to extend additional guarantees, Tardieu had a much better grasp of both the American and British positions.[21]

Stimson's visit to Geneva did not break the disarmament deadlock. But, believing in the importance of a political rapprochement between the French and Germans, he arranged for Gibson and Davis to visit London to lay the groundwork for direct Franco-German negotiations.[22] When the American delegates arrived in the British capital and con-

19. For the French reaction, see FR, 1932, 1:85–103; Walter E. Edge, *A Jerseyman's Journal*, 213–16; André Tardieu, *France in Danger!*, pp. 77–83; Mary Emma Woolley, *Life and Letters of Mary Emma Woolley*, pp. 143–44; Diary of Henry L. Stimson, 15 April 1932, Stimson Papers.
20. Stimson to Hoover, 25 April 1932, HHPP, Box 867; Diary of Henry L. Stimson, 15 April 1932, Stimson Papers.
21. Diary of Henry L. Stimson, 15–28 April 1932, Stimson Papers; FR, 1932, 1:104–8; Great Britain, Foreign Office, *Documents on British Foreign Policy*, Series 2, 3:516–17 (hereafter cited as DBFP).
22. Diary of Henry L. Stimson, 26, 29 April 1932, Stimson Papers.

ferred with Stanley Baldwin, the acting prime minister, they found him desperately worried about the European situation and anxious to cut British military expenditures. He was considering a revolutionary proposal aimed at abolishing battleships, submarines, military aviation, heavy mobile guns, and tanks. After talking to Baldwin, Gibson and Davis returned to the Continent and met with Tardieu in Paris and Herriot in Lyon. Since the latter was likely to become premier following the victory of the Left in the French elections, the American delegates were especially delighted by his liberal orientation toward the world and his interest in the Geneva proceedings. They also welcomed his readiness to consider peaceful changes in the Treaty of Versailles, provided he could have the support of Britain and the United States.[23]

The interviews with Baldwin, Tardieu, and Herriot convinced the American delegation that the time was ripe for the United States to make a major breakthrough in the disarmament talks. In a long dispatch on 28 May Gibson reminded Stimson that, despite the American rhetoric about the benefits of disarmament, the United States was well behind most of the other powers when it came to concrete proposals for arms limitation. Regarding military aviation, Gibson stressed, the position of the United States was especially weak. Most other nations wanted to abolish all land-based and naval aviation to enhance security. Gibson, maintaining that budgetary problems in France might compel a new leftist ministry to accept a bold program even without security guarantees, pleaded for a more flexible American posture. All nations, including the United States, had to share in the losses and gains of a comprehensive disarmament plan. Only such a general program, Davis confided to friends, could prevent the loss of foreign trade and investments.[24]

The pressure exerted by the American delegation intensified the rift that had been growing since March between Gibson and Davis on the one hand and the Navy, Army, and State departments on the other. The General Board of the Navy rejected French plans for the internationalization of civilian aviation and the creation of an international police force. The latter was considered especially repugnant because it was likely to perpetuate the status quo, "result in grave injustice, and give

23. FR, 1932, 1:117–44; see also Andrew W. Mellon to Stimson, 14 May 1932, RG 59, 740.0011 Mutual Guarantee-Mediterranean/39.

24. FR, 1932, 1:145–50; Davis to Lamont, 20 April 1932, Davis Papers, Box 20; Woolley, *Life and Letters*, pp. 146–47.

rise to violent repercussion.''[25] While the American civilian delegates at Geneva struggled to come up with viable alternatives to the French proposals, the Navy continued to oppose the abolition of military aviation, frown upon the limitation of the size of military aircraft, attack the establishment of enforcement machinery, and denounce substantive alterations in the London and Washington naval treaties. The Army, moreover, joined the Navy in rejecting any form of budgetary limitation on military expenditures. Stimson, meanwhile, was sympathetic to the Navy's viewpoint. He was worried about the East Asian situation and strongly opposed attempts to weaken the American fleet.[26]

In late May the president entered the conflict between the Geneva delegation and the Navy, Army, and State departments. As a result of domestic fiscal considerations Hoover came out firmly in support of a new, more far-reaching disarmament plan. Fearful of the cancellationist demands emanating from the Lausanne Conference, alarmed by the worsening economic conditions, worried by growing budgetary deficits, and distraught about Congress's refusal to pass his revenue legislation, Hoover wanted to press the cause of disarmament in order to reduce military expenditures, cut budgetary deficits, and save taxpayers at home and abroad billions of dollars. Under great pressure from the president, Stimson relaxed his opposition to disarmament initiatives. In turn, Hoover agreed to tailor some of his own ideas to meet American strategic needs in the Pacific. Since he did not believe that Japan challenged vital American interests in Asia, the president insisted on concrete naval reductions to lighten the burden on the budget.[27]

When the American delegates received Hoover's disarmament plan on 19 June, they were jubilant. Declaring that "it was better than our best hopes," Gibson and Davis immediately sounded out MacDonald

25. Bristol to secretary of navy, 6 April, 5 March 1932, RG 80, Box 92.
26. For the views of the Navy, see Bristol to secretary of navy, 26 October, 17 December 1931, 7, 23 January, 5 March, 1 June 1932, ibid.; for the Army's position, see MacArthur to Simonds, 7 April 1932, Simonds Papers, Box 42; for Stimson's feelings, see Diary of Henry L. Stimson, 19, 21 April 1932, Stimson Papers; for the views of other State Department officials, see Jay Pierrepont Moffat, *The Moffat Papers*, pp. 67–70.
27. For Hoover's linkage of budgetary and disarmament issues, see FR, 1932, 1:180–82, 186–87, 189–91; for his budget address and the legislative-executive impasse, see Hoover, *State Papers*, 2:197–203; Schwarz, *Interregnum*, pp. 104–41; for the differences between Hoover and Stimson, see Moffat, *Papers*, pp. 68–71; FR, 1932, 1:180–86; for Stimson's views, see pp. 153–57, 166–68; for Hoover's view of the Far East situation, see Hoover to Stimson, 3 June 1936, Herbert C. Hoover Post-Presidential Papers, Box 178 (hereafter cited as HHPPP).

and Herriot, both of whom were at Lausanne discussing a reparations settlement. The British and French leaders, however, refused to endorse the American initiative without consulting their respective cabinets. The American delegates phoned this news to Washington and implored Hoover to wait a few days before presenting his proposals. They alluded to the unofficial conversations underway at Geneva among the French, British, and American delegates, and they warned that these promising talks might be undermined by the precipitous introduction of a new plan. Hoover feared that if he waited, he would wind up issuing his plan during the Democratic convention scheduled for the last week in June. The president stated that he did not want to be accused of political expediency. Perhaps recalling the dramatic impact of Hughes's proposals at the Washington Conference in 1921, Hoover wanted to present his plan without press leaks or prior diplomatic haggling. Hoping for an enthusiastic public response, Hoover released his plan to the press on 22 June. At the same time, Gibson presented it to a hastily reconvened meeting of the general commission.[28]

The president's plan called for the abolition of all tanks, chemical warfare, large mobile guns, and bombing planes. It divided land armies into two parts—a police component and a defense component—and called for a 33 percent cut in the latter. The president also advocated a 33 percent reduction in battleships and submarines and a 25 percent decrease in aircraft carriers, cruisers, and destroyers. The thrust of his plan, Hoover argued, was to augment the security of nations by reducing the threat of invasion engendered by offensive armaments. Consequently, he excluded all fixed fortifications from limitation. Hoover believed that cutting armaments as he proposed "would be the most important world step that could be taken to expedite economic recovery."[29]

The Hoover plan was a serious effort to inject life into the disarmament talks. It represented an attempt by the president not only to overcome the obstacles to a disarmament agreement presented by American military spokesmen but also to accommodate some of the demands of France without embroiling the United States in European political affairs. By calling for a reduction in battleships and aircraft

28. For the reaction of the American delegates, see Woolley, *Life and Letters*, p. 148; FR, 1932, 1:189; for the exchanges between the American delegates, Hoover, and Stimson, see pp. 186–214; Memorandum of phone conversation, 21 June 1932, Davis Papers, Box 20; for the private and unofficial talks underway at Geneva, see DBFP, 2, 3:527–53.

29. For Hoover's disarmament plan, see FR, 1932, 1:212–14.

carriers and advocating the abolition of bombing planes (without making the latter proposal contingent upon the abolition of submarines), Hoover risked incurring the wrath of big-navy supporters.[30] He championed qualitative reduction of land armaments and, therefore, went further than many Army officials in the War Plans Division (WPD) thought appropriate.[31] By insisting on real arms reductions and developing a formula for computing effectives that provided an element of equality to Germany, Hoover's proposals grappled with that nation's demands. Yet, his plan recognized the interdependence of land, sea, and air armaments, excluded stationary fortifications from limitations, avoided any increment in German armaments, and resisted pleas to abolish submarines—proposals designed to respond constructively to French demands. By immersing the United States in the momentous problems of European land armaments and linking them to the matter of naval reductions, Hoover demonstrated his administration's readiness under emergency conditions to reappraise earlier tactics. Nevertheless, his continued antipathy to military sanctions and strategic commitments and his persistent emphasis on the financial benefits of arms limitation revealed that the fundamental principles of economic diplomacy remained intact.

That its supporters wildly acclaimed it while its detractors responded in a guarded and equivocal fashion illustrated the broadmindedness of Hoover's plan. Within the United States the press welcomed the president's proposals.[32] At Geneva the response was more enthusiastic than either Gibson or Davis had anticipated. The American delegates phoned Hoover and Stimson and exclaimed that "it has been without doubt the biggest day we have ever had." Many of the delegations from smaller nations hailed the American initiative. The willingness of the United States to reduce its fleet and abolish military aviation foreclosed charges that the proposals were self-serving. Hence, the French

30. For the Navy's position on battleships, aircraft carriers, submarines, and bombing planes, see Bristol to secretary of navy, 7, 11, 23 January, 5 March, 1 June 1932, RG 80, Box 92.

31. For some of the reservations of the Army WPD, see C. E. Kilbourne to chief of staff, 3 January 1933, Records of the Adjutant General's Office, Central Files, 1926–1939, RG 94, Box 82; Kilbourne, "Resumé," 24 May 1933, Records of the War Department General and Special Staffs, RG 165, Box 35; see also WPD, "Comments in Comparison of Important Plans Now Before the Disarmament Conference," 6 February 1933, HHPP, Box 867.

32. "World Reaction to the New Hoover Arms Plan," *Literary Digest* 114 (2 July 1932):7; *Army and Navy Journal* 69 (25 June 1932):1012. For a more critical evaluation of Hoover's plan, see, for example, Christopher Thorne, *The Limits of Foreign Policy*, pp. 315–20.

and British were put on the defensive. Paul-Boncour, recently appointed the French minister of war, had serious private reservations but publicly felt obliged to demonstrate his sympathy for the American plan. Herriot, moreover, admitted that Hoover had tried to accommodate France on several important matters such as the interdependence of armaments and the legitimacy of expenditures on fortifications.[33]

In private discussions the French voiced their displeasure. They objected to the abrupt introduction of new proposals without prior consultation; they disliked the absence of budgetary limitations; and they complained about the naval clauses, which, if implemented, would reduce their existing naval superiority over Italy. Moreover, Herriot objected to the provisions relating to military effectives because they were based on demographic criteria. They also imposed reductions on France, disregarded the quasi-military organizations in Germany, and ignored the problem of national coalitions. Most significant, the French denounced the absence of enforcement machinery, demanded on-the-spot inspection of arms limitations provisions, and pleaded for regional security guarantees and a consultative agreement with the United States.[34]

Despite these reservations Herriot and French delegate Henry de Jouvenel told Davis that they wanted to cooperate with the Anglo-Saxon nations. Indeed, Herriot's efforts at Lausanne to reconcile relations with Great Britain reflected his earnest desire to institute a new era of harmonious relations with that nation. He wished to follow a parallel course with the United States, and he knew that his reaction to the Hoover plan would be considered indicative of his true intentions. Herriot implored Davis to understand France's predicament, surrounded as she was by two lunatic ["fous"] nations, Germany and Italy. He referred to Brüning's successors in Germany, to speeches by Chancellor Franz von Papen and General Kurt von Schleicher demanding revisions in the Treaty of Versailles, and to an article by Benito Mussolini glorifying war. "How can any French Chief of Government," Herriot inquired of Davis, "no matter how deeply and sin-

33. For the reaction at Geneva, see FR, 1932, 1:215–18; see also Simonds to MacArthur, 27 June 1932, Simonds Papers, Box 42; for the official French reaction, see FR, 1932, 1:222–23, 243–44; for Paul-Boncour's feelings, see Joseph Paul-Boncour, *Entre deux guerres*, 2:379; Edouard Herriot, *Jadis*, 2:335–37.
34. For French objections and demands, see DBFP, 2, 3:558–60, 565–66, 567, 570–78; FR, 1932, 1:222–23, 231, 234, 247–48, 311–12; France, Ministère des Affaires Etrangères, *Documents diplomatiques français*, Series 1, 1:44, 66–68, 153–57, (hereafter cited as DDF).

cerely committed to peace and disarmament he may be, convince the French people that they are secure when their neighbors are guilty of like extravagances?"[35]

American policymakers were not oblivious to France's growing predicament. With the demise of the Brüning government in early June, State Department officials became increasingly apprehensive about developments in Germany, noticeably more sensitive to the impact of these developments on France, and somewhat less revisionist in their own orientation. Still believing in the legitimacy of Germany's demand for juridic equality, these officials strongly opposed German rearmament.[36] At the same time, they admonished the French to face realities. France was not going to obtain additional security guarantees from either Britain or the United States, Davis bluntly told Henry de Jouvenel. Consequently, the French had to decide whether they felt more secure trying to preserve their current military superiority over Germany or whether they would feel greater safety by reducing their armaments, endeavoring to bind Germany voluntarily to certain new limitations, and counting on British and American goodwill should Germany abrogate these new commitments. American officials understood that this was an extraordinarily difficult decision beset with many imponderables. But it was the choice that French officials had to make. Davis hoped that France would gamble on a more conciliatory approach and endorse the Hoover plan.[37]

Meanwhile, American policy did not remain static. Responding to French criticism, Stimson departed from precedents, overruled the objections of military officials, and agreed to the principle of on-the-spot inspection along French lines.[38] Though he persisted in fending off French proposals for global budgetary limitations on military expenditures, which the Army and Navy found repugnant, the secretary of state did acquiesce to certain forms of budgetary limitation, provided these complemented efforts to place quantitative limits on spe-

35. Memorandum of conversation between Herriot and Davis, 29 July 1932, Davis Papers, Box 20; see also FR, 1932, 1:234–46, 243–44; for Herriot's efforts at Lausanne, see John W. Wheeler-Bennett, *The Wreck of Reparations*, pp. 210–53.

36. For State Department attitudes towards developments in Germany, see FR, 1932, 1:315–16, 2:295–323; Pierre de Lagarde Boal, "The Hitherto Unpublished Stresemann Papers," 9 June 1932, RG 59, 762.00/59; Thorne, *Limits of Foreign Policy*, pp. 318, 322–23.

37. FR, 1932, 1:234–36.

38. Ibid., p. 249; DDF, 1, 1:136; Bristol to secretary of navy, 29 June 1932, RG 80, Box 92.

cific categories of armaments.[39] Moreover, Stimson accepted certain modifications in the Hoover proposals regarding land effectives, heavy mobile artillery, and military aviation. As a result of these concessions a compromise resolution was passed by the general commission on 23 July, recording recent progress and enumerating specific principles to guide future action.[40]

The secretary of state believed that the United States should go further to alleviate French anxieties. When he learned in late June that the failure of the Hoover plan to mention consultation was one of the principal reasons for Paul-Boncour's objections, Stimson determined to resolve this issue once and for all. With the help of Davis and Senator Swanson, the secretary got the Democrats to approve the principle of consultation in their campaign platform. This action took the issue out of partisan politics and enabled Stimson to contemplate a unilateral declaration of America's willingness to confer in times of crisis. Assured by the French that this announcement would be a great contribution, the secretary labored diligently on a speech that he considered of enormous importance for both European and Asian affairs. Although Hoover insisted on modifying the speech and deleting some of its tougher language, Stimson presented his views in a major address to the Council on Foreign Relations on 8 August. In effect, Stimson declared that in times of European crisis the United States would consult about the application of American neutrality rights should Britain be called upon to use her navy to enforce sanctions. Three days later, in his speech accepting the Republican nomination, Hoover reaffirmed America's willingness to consult ''in times of emergency to promote world peace.''[41]

The statements of Stimson and Hoover attracted considerable attention in France. Herriot was elated. He summoned a group of journalists

39. For military objections to budgetary limitations, see Bristol to secretary of navy, 29 June 1932, RG 80, Box 92; Kilbourne, ''Resumé,'' 24 May 1933, Records of the War Department General and Special Staffs, RG 165, Box 35; FR, 1932, 1:326–27; for the talks at Geneva and limited American concessions, see pp. 295–304, 320–21.

40. For the negotiations and compromises leading to the 23 July resolution, see FR, 1932, 1:225–322. The Army WPD objected to Stimson's compromises, see Kilbourne, ''Resumé,'' 24 May 1933, Records of the War Department General and Special Staffs, RG 165, Box 35; Simonds to MacArthur, 2 August 1932, Simonds Papers, Box 42.

41. For Stimson's speech, see FR, 1932, 1:575–83; for circumstances leading up to speech, see pp. 182–84, 215–18, 223–25, 244–45, 249–51; Diary of Henry L. Stimson, 29, 30 June, 14 July–10 August 1932, Stimson Papers; Memorandum of conversation between Stimson and Paul Claudel, 21 June 1932, RG 59, 711.0012 Anti-War/1269; Stimson to Swanson, 22 June 1932, ibid.; Davis to Cordell Hull, 23 June 1932, ibid.; for Hoover's speech, see Hoover, *State Papers*, 2:260.

to his office and applauded the secretary of state's attempt to reconcile America's desire for independent action with Europe's need for international cooperation. Now that the United States had made a sincere effort to satisfy French needs, Herriot felt that he had new leverage to appeal to the French Right and military establishment for reciprocal concessions. The French premier did not think that the new American policies alone constituted a sufficient basis for limiting French armaments. But the announcement of the Hoover disarmament plan and the American willingness to consult in times of crisis provided additional impetus for reappraising France's policy orientation and for reconsidering such demands as the creation of an international security force.[42]

Herriot's appraisal of the situation was correct. As a result of the worsening domestic economic situation, mounting budgetary problems, and ominous developments in Germany, the Hoover administration had considered new tactics and had proposed initiatives in an attempt to break the disarmament deadlock. Hoover, of course, reiterated his opposition to binding military commitments and condemned the use of force to deter aggression.[43] Nevertheless, he was willing to inject the United States into European armaments questions to help reconcile Franco-German differences. He stated that the United States would consult with European governments in times of crisis, hoping to expedite European security accords. He was prepared to place additional limitations on America's military strength to enhance the chances of a European armaments agreement. These were not radical departures from the past, but they represented new attempts to make a contribution to European stability without incurring military commitments.

At the time no high-level official thought it desirable to provide France with strategic guarantees. Stimson opposed a treaty that even implied a promise of military assistance.[44] His stand accorded with the views of Army and Navy officials who designed American policy at Geneva; they simply did not think that American strategic interests were at stake in the discussions over French security. Both the Navy's General Board and its WPD sneered at French efforts to freeze the status quo, assumed that Germany would regain her prewar influence in world affairs, and focused primary attention on East Asian develop-

42. For Herriot's reaction to Hoover's plan and Stimson's speech, see Edge to Stimson, 29 July 1932, Davis Papers, Box 17; Norman Armour to Stimson, 10, 12 August 1932, RG 59, 711.0012 Anti-War/1278, 1274; Edge to Stimson, 19 August 1932, ibid., 711.0012 Anti-War/1320.

43. Hoover, *State Papers*, 2:260.

44. Diary of Henry L. Stimson, 29 June 1932, Stimson Papers.

ments.[45] The Army showed more sensitivity to France's dilemma but did not consider America's vital interests to be intertwined with those of France.[46] Given the military establishment's perceptions, it is understandable that civilian officials refused to alter fundamentals and simply revised tactics. But the tactical changes on disarmament matters illustrated a comprehensive attempt to grapple with the problems plaguing the United States, France, and Europe in the spring and summer of 1932.

War Debts and Reparations

When Davis returned to the United States in March, he not only stimulated a reassessment of the administration's position on disarmament but also generated a reconsideration of official American attitudes toward the intergovernmental war debts. Once Stimson decided to go to Geneva, he realized he would have to answer European inquiries regarding the American stand on war debts and reparations. In early April he discussed these matters with Mills and Hoover. Although they realized that the war debt agreements would have to be revised, they were hesitant to propose specific action, because they felt certain that the Democrats would exploit the issue in the forthcoming political campaign. Mills, however, did suggest that Germany's reparation obligations be scaled down to no more than $250 million a year for twenty-five years. He knew that this suggestion would not meet Germany's demand to end all payments, but he proposed that the war-guilt clause of the Treaty of Versailles be withdrawn as an appropriate quid pro quo.[47]

Stimson had still not decided on a war debt formula that might be acceptable to the former Allies and palatable to Congress when he began the trip to Geneva, crossing the Atlantic on the same ship with Thomas W. Lamont. The New York banker had developed more concrete ideas on what needed to be done, and his views greatly influenced

45. For the General Board's attitude, see Bristol to secretary of navy, 6 April 1932, RG 80, Box 92; General Board to secretary of navy, 18 January 1933, Records of the General Board of the Navy, File 438–2, Serial No. 1521 AA; WPD to CNO, 21 April 1932, "Estimate of the Situation," RG 80, File L1–1.

46. For the views of Army officials, see Kilbourne, "Resumé," 24 May 1933, Records of the War Department General and Special Staffs, RG 165, Box 35; see also the materials in Simonds Papers, Box 42; Maxime Weygand, *Mémoires*, 2:389–90.

47. Diary of Henry L. Stimson, 7, 8 April 1932, Stimson Papers; for Hoover's plans for revising the war debts, see also Ogden L. Mills to Hoover, 18 March 1932, HHPP, Box 876.

the evolution of official policy. Before departing for Europe, Lamont and several of his associates had met with Emmanuel Monick, the French financial attaché. They had pleaded for a reparations settlement that reduced, but did not cancel, indemnity payments. They had warned against an attempt to raise the war debt issue until after the forthcoming elections. Congressmen, Lamont had claimed, could not appear before their constituents, ask for their endorsement of tax increases, and then justify the reduction of foreign payments. When the secretary of state reached Geneva, he repeated these arguments to MacDonald and other European leaders. He advised against cancellation of all reparations, warned against linking the war debt and indemnity issues, and counseled against expecting an equal reduction of all intergovernmental obligations.[48]

While Stimson expressed these views in Geneva, the French sought out Lamont in Paris. They wanted to know whether the British were portraying the American position accurately when they stated that the United States wanted all reparation payments cancelled. Tardieu indicated his willingness to disavow the Young Plan, reduce the indemnity, and alter the terminology of reparations. But he would not cancel all indemnity payments because he feared that such action would lead to the abrogation of other treaty commitments. In short, Tardieu and Flandin wanted reassurances that the United States would not place the total burden of war debt revision upon the French.[49]

Lamont stated that the British were not portraying American opinion correctly. The American people, he stressed, did not want reparations cancelled. If he ruled the world, Lamont acknowledged, he might prefer an end to intergovernmental debts. But in real life governments had to respond to public opinion, and neither the American nor French people were ready for cancellation. A realistic approach, he asserted, would provide a three-year moratorium on indemnity payments. For several years thereafter, if economic conditions permitted, there might be annual payments of $50 million to $100 million. A wise and generous settlement along these lines, Lamont claimed, would influence American public opinion and encourage reciprocal action on the war debts after the elections.[50]

From Paris Lamont went to London, where he discovered that the

48. Diary of Henry L. Stimson, 5, 27, 29 April 1932, Stimson Papers; DBFP, 2, 3:123; Lamont, Memorandum, 7 April 1932, Thomas W. Lamont Papers, Box 95.
49. Lamont to J. P. Morgan, Russell C. Leffingwell, and S. Parker Gilbert, 19 April 1932, RG 59, 462.00R296A1/154½; Lamont to J. R. Carter, 4 May 1932, ibid.
50. Lamont to Morgan, Leffingwell, and Gilbert, 19 April 1932, ibid.

British, in fact, were advocating total cancellation. They believed that Germany could not recover economically unless reparations were wiped out. Moreover, they feared that, unless reparations were cancelled, Germany might declare a total moratorium on private as well as public debts, thereby retarding Britain's financial recuperation. Lamont, however, disagreed with these views. After consulting with Norman Davis and Andrew Mellon, the ambassador to Great Britain, Lamont wrote a memorandum for the use of top British policymakers. In his memorandum, Lamont encouraged cooperation with France and counseled against action on the war debts until the American elections were over. He most emphatically warned against cancelling reparations. In the United States, he said, such action would be interpreted as a European prelude to repudiating the war debts. Furthermore, Lamont doubted whether cancellation would "lead the Germans to be one whit more circumspect or anxious to handle their commercial obligations properly. Germany would have received a wonderful example of the money value of evading obligations and might well be encouraged to pursue that policy in other directions."[51]

After Lamont returned to the United States, he met with Hoover and Mills and discussed the war debt–reparations imbroglio with them.[52] Thereafter, Hoover and Stimson adopted Lamont's approach as official American policy. When the British continued to press for total cancellation, State Department officials entered the controversy. On 1 June Stimson summoned the British ambassador and emphasized his opposition to cancellation. During the next week, he presented the American position to other European emissaries. On 8 June, partly in response to a French request, he issued a public statement to the same effect.[53]

Stimson's representations of the American viewpoint illustrated both a continuity in American objectives and a change in American tactics. As in the 1920s, the United States wanted a moderate reparations settlement that would help rehabilitate German finances, safeguard American investments, and stimulate American exports. The United

51. Lamont, "Memorandum re Reparations and Debts," 5 May 1932, ibid.; Lamont to Stimson, 23 May 1932, ibid.
52. Lamont to Stimson, 23 May 1932, ibid.; Lamont to Theodore G. Joslin, 13 May 1932, Thomas W. Lamont Papers, Box 98.
53. Feis, Memorandum, 27 May 1932, RG 59, 462.00R296A1/157½; FR, 1932, 1:673–75; Memorandum of conversation between Stimson and Claudel, 3 June 1932, RG 59, 462.00R296A1/183; Stimson, Statement, 8 June 1932, ibid., 462.00R296A1/158½; for Stimson's frustration with Britain, see Memorandum, 2 June 1932, George L. Harrison Papers, 2011.1; for the identity of views between Stimson and Lamont, see Stimson to Lamont, 27 May 1932, Thomas W. Lamont Papers, Box 181.

States still opposed cancellation of reparations lest it undermine the sanctity of agreements, enhance Germany's competitive ability in world markets, and set an unfortunate precedent regarding the treatment of other intergovernmental obligations. But Republican policymakers no longer called upon independent experts to devise a schedule of annuities that conformed to Germany's long-term capacity to pay. The Depression had discredited the reputation of businessmen and had dissipated faith in economic expertise. Hence, it was up to the politicians themselves to grapple with issues that had always been as much political as economic.[54]

When the Lausanne Conference on reparations finally convened in mid-June 1932, American opposition to cancellation bore heavily on the proceedings. The French constantly alluded to the American position to buttress their own arguments against cancellation. French Finance Minister Louis Germain-Martin repeatedly emphasized that the French delegation was convinced "that complete cancellation at Lausanne would be the best means of creating a spirit of hostility in the United States on the Debts question." After considerable acrimony the British finally acceded to the French (and American) position. Herriot felt that Stimson's attitude was of considerable importance in eliciting the British concession.[55]

But the American influence extended beyond the decision not to cancel reparations. Having agreed that some reparations would have to be paid, the French, British, and Germans immersed themselves in a protracted dispute over the amount and nature of the payments. After more than three weeks of discussion, they agreed on an accord that bore striking similarity to many of Lamont's recommendations. The terminology of reparations was eliminated, the Hague agreements and Young Plan discarded, and a three-year moratorium instituted. After this period, if economic conditions permitted, the BIS was authorized to market up to three billion reichsmarks in bonds. However, if these bonds could not be sold within fifteen years, they were to be cancelled. In any case Germany's total obligations were reduced from approximately $25 billion to $2 billion. The sum was less than the French demanded. But during the conference Herriot argued that all he wanted

54. Even the bankers were happy to see government officials grappling with the reparations problem. See Leffingwell to Lamont, 14 June 1932, Lamont Papers, Box 103.
55. For France's presentation of the American position, see DBFP, 2, 3:222–23, 239; for Herriot's appreciation of American help, see Armour to Stimson, 11 June 1932, RG 59, 462.00R296A1/172; Memorandum of conversation between Claudel and Stimson, 13 October 1932, ibid., 462.00R296A1/349.

was a payment that would serve as the basis for a subsequent offer to the United States.[56]

At Lausanne, French, British, and German leaders agreed to an indemnity settlement that conformed to American prescriptions.[57] But the French refused to implement the agreement until the former Allies resolved their war debt problems with their respective creditors. Mac-Donald reluctantly capitulated to Herriot's demand and agreed to sign a Gentleman's Agreement on 2 July. This confidential accord stated that ratification of the Lausanne agreements would be deferred until the former Allies satisfactorily readjusted their war debt obligations with one another and with the United States.[58]

American officials had warned the French and British against taking such action. Hoover worried that the Democrats would use the debt issue to embarrass him in the forthcoming presidential race. Editorial opinion in the United States was reacting angrily to reports of a secret deal involving the war debts, and the Democratic convention had passed a resolution opposing cancellation. Feis and Stimson tried to arrange a deal with leading Democrats to keep the war debts out of the campaign.[59] Such an agreement had not been reached when Democratic Senator Kenneth McKellar launched a congressional attack on the administration's alleged conspiracy to reduce the war debts. A few days later, when the Gentleman's Agreement was leaked to the press and the British intimated that the United States had agreed to scale down the war debts, Hoover blew up. Stimson and Castle warned that a vitriolic response might hamstring subsequent revision. After the president calmed down, he wrote a public letter to Senator Borah, denying that he had been consulted about the Gentleman's Agreement

56. For the discussions at Lausanne, see DBFP, 2, 3:188–446; for the final accords, see Harold G. Moulton and Leo Pasvolsky, *War Debts and World Prosperity*, 354–66; for Herriot's argument, see DBFP, 2, 3:256.

57. See, for example, Memoranda of conversations between Stimson and Claudel, 8, 28 July 1932, RG 59, 462.00R296A1/238, 289.

58. For Herriot's view of the Lausanne talks, see Herriot, *Jadis*, 2:307–49; for Mac-Donald's concession, see pp. 345–47; Henry Bérenger, "Les Résultats de Lausanne," *La Révue de Paris*, RG 59, 462.00R296A1/292; for the Gentleman's Agreement, see Wheeler-Bennett, *Reparations*, pp. 272–73.

59. For press opinion, see "A 'Rubber' Check from Europe for Uncle Sam," *Literary Digest* 114 (2 July 1932):5; for the efforts of Feis and Stimson, see Feis to Davis, 25 June 1932, Feis Papers, Box 15; Diary of Henry L. Stimson, 12 July 1932, Stimson Papers; Colonel Edward M. House to Franklin D. Roosevelt, 25 July 1932, House Papers, general correspondence; for the Democratic plank opposing cancellation, see Arthur M. Schlesinger, Jr., ed., *History of United States Political Parties*, 3:1969.

and insisting that the United States would not be influenced or intimidated by concerted European action.[60]

The administration's great consternation over the secret accord stemmed from the fact that it had provoked an outcry in the press and in Congress, provided the Democrats with a possible campaign issue, and complicated the task of revision. How could the administration convince the American people to be generous to the scheming and sinister French? Were not the French immune from the Depression, weighed down with gold, and enjoying general prosperity? So they were popularly (but mistakenly) portrayed. If such were the case, were not the French better able to pay than the Americans to cancel?[61] Several New York bankers insisted that a carefully orchestrated publicity campaign could alter such popular conceptions.[62] But Stimson and Mills were skeptical. They maintained that "while the Kansas farmer was in trouble and we couldn't pay any money to him it was folly to talk of giving up hundreds of millions to foreign sufferers."[63] Even if Senator Borah's positive reaction to the Lausanne agreements did constitute one auspicious political sign, other senators, including Republican stalwarts like Reed Smoot and George Moses, remained bitterly opposed to revision.[64]

Domestic financial factors and partisan political considerations reinforced one another and circumscribed foreign policy decision making. Like the majority of the nation's businessmen, the president saw the war debts as a secondary, although not inconsequential, matter in the greater struggle to restore prosperity. Hoover still believed that balancing the budget was the most important thing he could do to restore confidence and encourage business investment. He was therefore reluctant to scale down the war debts and reduce government revenues. Locked in a bitter struggle with Congress and constantly engaged in attacks on Democratic profligacy, Hoover was easy prey to

60. For the letter to Borah, see Hoover, *State Papers*, 2:235; for the events leading up to the letter, see Diary of Henry L. Stimson, 8, 11–14 July 1932, Stimson Papers; Castle to Hoover, 9 July 1932, Castle Papers, Box 14; see also Wheeler-Bennett, *Reparations*, pp. 236–38.
61. See Claudel's assessment, DDF, 1, 1:16–17.
62. Lamont, Memorandum, 12 July 1932, Thomas W. Lamont Papers, Box 98; Martin Egan to Lamont, 14 July 1932, ibid.; Gilbert to Stimson, 20 July 1932, RG 59, 800.51W89/550½.
63. Memorandum of conversation between Shepard Morgan and Stimson, 8 June 1932, RG 59, 800.51W89/533½; see also DDF, 1, 1:59–61.
64. For Borah's view, see Diary of Henry L. Stimson, 14, 24 July 1932, Stimson Papers; DDF, 1, 1:100–2; for the view of other senators, see DDF, 1, 1:16–17.

charges that he preferred to aid foreign debtors than help domestic sufferers.[65] Because of Hoover's political problems, Mills told the French financial attaché that no action could be taken until after the elections. Acknowledging the economic benefits of the Lausanne accords, Mills nevertheless stated that, with taxes as high as they were, Hoover could not approach the electorate with an appeal to reduce the war debts.[66]

The French were willing to defer their request for revision of the debt agreement until November, but they were eager to secure reciprocal concessions. Despite the negative image of France in America, Herriot had taken courageous action at Lausanne. Though he had connected reparations and debts, he was facing economic and political realities. Though he had made action in one realm contingent upon action in another, he was doing nothing different than Hoover had done in declaring his moratorium in June 1931. The French had good reason to feel that they had gone far to satisfy the wishes of American policymakers, especially since conditions in France were not nearly so optimistic as most Americans believed. Budgetary deficits were increasing and the unfavorable balance of trade loomed ominous. Hence, Herriot anxiously awaited Hoover's next move.[67]

The first sign of a change in American policy appeared in Hoover's acceptance speech on 11 August at the Republican convention. The president announced his readiness to trade debt payments for a "tangible form of compensation such as the expansion of markets for American agriculture and labor."[68] Faced with rising trade barriers and proliferating exchange controls, the president was intimating that he might take a quid pro quo approach to the war debts. This attitude marked a shift from the Republicans' previous stress on having a commission of experts study the matter according to a payment ca-

65. For Hoover's relations with Congress, see Schwarz, *Interregnum*, pp. 142–78; for Hoover's position on matters pertaining to the budget and relief, see Hoover, *State Papers*, 2:197–203, 206, 214–16, 222–26, 228–37; for business opinion on the relative importance of balancing the budget, settling the war debts, and other action in stimulating recovery, see the survey in "Business Wants Fiscal Economy," *Nation's Business* 20 (November 1932):14; see also "Chamber Favors Balanced Budget," ibid. (July 1932):13; Silas Strawn, "How Business Views the Budget Crisis," ibid. (June 1932):38; see also numerous articles and editorials in *Journal of the American Bankers Association* (ABA) 24 (1931–1932).
66. DDF, 1, 1:169.
67. For a balanced contemporary assessment of French financial and commercial circumstances, see J. C. DeWilde, "French Financial Policy," pp. 233–35; see also Martin Wolfe, *The French Franc Between the Wars, 1919–1939*, pp. 77–104.
68. Hoover, *State Papers*, 2:256–57.

pacity formula and independently of other issues. Whether it offered the possibility of reconciling foreign demands for relief with Congress's antipathy to debt revision was still unknown. In light of French and British actions at Lausanne, the president's suggestion signified a willingness to explore new approaches to the old dilemma of aiding the rehabilitation of European finances and resuscitating American trade without undermining the administration's fiscal program and political needs.[69]

The French knew that action was pending, but the extent of the revisions and the conditions under which they would take place had to be left in doubt until November.[70] In the meantime the domestic political process took precedence over the international economic and financial situation. Ironically, both France and the United States were moving toward one another. But the progress was slow, the obstacles great, and the suspicions mutual. Faulty policy implementation had made matters worse than they had to be. The Hoover administration had angered the French by acting unilaterally and arbitrarily in declaring a debt moratorium. Likewise, the Anglo-French Gentleman's Agreement had antagonized Americans because of its secrecy and suspected duplicity.

Commercial and Financial Policies

While the Republican approach to the issues of disarmament and war debts was being reappraised in the spring and summer of 1932, there was an accompanying reexamination of commercial and financial policies. The precipitous drop in total American exports by almost $3 billion between 1929 and 1931 and the abandonment of the gold standard by over twenty nations by the onset of 1932 demonstrated the failure of simultaneous Republican attempts to expand exports, preserve exchange stability, and safeguard the domestic market.[71] As currencies depreciated, exchange controls proliferated, and preferential treaties multiplied, Democratic congressmen assailed the chief executive's use

69. Hoover also expressed some kind words about Lausanne. See ibid., pp. 271–73; for additional indications that Republican officials were contemplating a more lenient attitude on the debts, see DBFP, 2, 3:125, 132–33; Mills to Foster Kennedy, 7 July 1932, Mills Papers, Box 111; Castle to William Taylor, 17 July 1932, Castle Papers, Box 3.
70. DDF, 1, 1:168–69.
71. For statistics on American trade, see Department of Commerce, *Statistical Abstract of the United States*, 1933, pp. 397–407; for a list of nations that had departed from the gold standard, see Lester V. Chandler, *America's Greatest Depression, 1929–1941*, p. 105.

of the flexible tariff provisions, State Department officials questioned the efficacy of a nonbargaining approach to commercial negotiations, and the president himself acknowledged the incapacity of central bankers to preserve the gold standard.[72] With all the elements of Republican commercial policy under attack from one source or another, the French aggravated the situation by expanding their quota system, escalating their discrimination against American goods, and promoting a customs union among the Danubian nations.[73] As a result American officials felt compelled to hasten their reassessment of commercial and financial policies.

The expansion of the French quota system during the winter of 1932 served as the initial catalyst to American action. French quotas on industrial goods were assigned after consultation between French and other European producers of a particular product. American manufacturers were excluded from these talks; predictably, American goods were discriminated against. American businessmen bitterly protested the discriminatory arrangements and Commerce Department and State Department officials responded to their appeals for help. Castle threatened to utilize the retaliatory provisions in section 338 of the Hawley-Smoot tariff if American grievances were not redressed. American officials feared that France's use of a quota system to rectify balance-of-payments problems might lead to its adoption throughout Europe and constitute a challenge to open and competitive trade.[74]

Eager to win American goodwill prior to the Lausanne Conference, the French bowed to American pressure and signed an agreement eliminating the most ostensible forms of discrimination in the assignment of quotas on industrial goods. Thereafter, American industrial products were guaranteed the same relative share of the French market as they had enjoyed during a base period. But the accord did not apply to agricultural products. It did nothing to prevent the proliferation of

72. For Democratic criticism, see "Tariff, Politics and the 72nd Congress," *Congressional Digest* 11 (March 1932):65; for misgivings in the State Department, see Feis to William S. Culbertson, 3 February 1932, Feis Papers, Box 15; for Hoover's admission, see chapter 7, p. 259.
73. For French commercial policy, see Joseph M. Jones, Jr., *Tariff Retaliation*, pp. 139–55; Frank Arnold Haight, *A History of French Commercial Policies*, pp. 165–70; DeWilde, "French Financial Policy," p. 24.
74. For the discriminatory nature of the French quota system, see F. W. Allport to director, Economic and Trade Notes, 531, 27 January 1932, Bureau of Foreign and Domestic Commerce (BFDC), RG 151, File 47.0; for the American reaction, see FR, 1932, 2:195–262; Diary of Jay Pierrepont Moffat, 14–17 April 1932, Moffat Papers; Castle to Sackett, 22 April 1932, Castle Papers, Box 5.

new quotas and ignored the mounting number of French tariff deviations from the *modus vivendi* of 1927. Hence, United States officials remained disgruntled with the French treatment of American commerce. They expressed their desire to negotiate an unconditional most-favored-nation commercial treaty subjecting all American goods to the French minimum duty schedule.[75] In exchange, Stimson inquired whether the French might be satisfied with the passage of legislation protecting French dress models in the United States.[76]

The meagerness of this proposed concession demonstrated that Republican commercial tactics no longer had any realistic possibility of relieving European grievances, resuscitating America's export trade, or easing European payments problems. In 1932 American exports to France more than doubled American imports from France.[77] This trade surplus occurred while American tourist expenditures rapidly decreased. Thus, the invisible items, including overseas loans, that had helped provide an ephemeral equilibrium in the 1920s were no longer operating to offset America's merchandise surplus with France and other European nations. At the same time, the rapid decrease in raw material prices meant that European nations had greater difficulty than ever earning dollars through the sale of their goods in Latin America and Asia. Under these circumstances it was natural for Britain to move toward imperial preferences, for Germany to impose exchange controls and seek out preferential trade partners in eastern and central Europe, and for France to assign quotas and demand substantial concessions in return for an unconditional most-favored-nation treaty.

Recognizing that the flexible provisions of the Hawley-Smoot legislation, based on equalizing costs of production, did not provide sufficient latitude to win concessions from France and other key trading partners, some State Department officials advocated substantial changes in American commercial policies. Herbert Feis, for example, called for a reduction in American tariff duties and linkage of the reciprocity formula to the unconditional most-favored-nation principle.[78] Neither the president nor Congress, however, was prepared to

75. For the quota agreement and the lukewarm reaction to it, see FR, 1932, 2:222–34; Henry Chalmers to Allport, 18 June 1932, RG 151, File 47.0.
76. FR, 1932, 2:231.
77. See the statistical computations in "United States Trade with France," RG 59, 611.5131/1517½.
78. Feis to Culbertson, 3 February 1932, Feis Papers, Box 15; Feis, Memorandum, Frankfurter Papers, Box 54; see also Wallace McClure to James G. Rogers, 24 September 1931, RG 59, 611.0031/399.

accept such advice. Although some Democrats assailed the Hawley-Smoot rates, most simply wanted to emasculate presidential powers under the flexible provisions. In May, Hoover defeated such an attempt and reiterated his conviction that the domestic market had to be protected through the cost-of-production formula. He believed that high tariffs were the natural consequence of the industrialization process, that they represented the universal drive to national self-sufficiency, and that they were the by-product, rather than the source, of worldwide economic dislocation. Failing to assess the impact of prevailing duties on European payments problems, exchange controls, or commercial practices, Hoover claimed that a policy of reciprocal tariff concessions was likely to breed trade wars and jeopardize the interests of American farmers. Unlike Feis, who contended that an expansion of foreign markets was crucial to the recovery of the agricultural sector, the president insisted that the best way to help the American farmer was to maintain or increase protection of the domestic market. Therefore, he refused to modify the long-standing Republican policy of protectionism to win trade concessions, expand exports, or ease payments problems abroad. As a result trade negotiations with France languished.[79]

Hoover, however, did respond more constructively to French attempts to establish a Danubian customs union. On 14 March 1932 he met with Assistant Secretary of State Rogers. They agreed to raise no objections to a customs union among Danubian nations, even though a customs union would discriminate against the trade of nonmember nations and violate the unconditional most-favored-nation principle. During the next three weeks Castle and Stimson repeatedly told European diplomats that the United States favored a Danubian customs union, so long as it did not include preferences for any of the major European powers. The Italian ambassador protested that the customs union would lead to French financial hegemony, and the Swedish minister warned that the exclusion of Germany would be a fatal weakness. Castle nevertheless insisted that the old Austro-Hungarian empire had to be reconstituted economically. Stimson told the Austrian minister that, although the United States government had no money to finance a Danubian federation, he hoped that such a federation would be consummated and that the trade preferences extended by one Danu-

79. For congressional attitudes toward the tariff, see "Tariff, Politics, and the 72nd Congress," pp. 65–66; see also Feis to Culbertson, 3 February 1931, 6 May 1932, Feis Papers, Box 15; Feis to Walter Lippmann, 5 May 1932, ibid., Box 20; for Hoover's attitude, see Hoover, *State Papers*, 2:181–86; Hoover to Robert P. Lamont, 20 July 1932, RG 151, File 400.

bian nation to another would be substantial. American policymakers did not want to get embroiled in Franco-German rivalries in this region. But they did favor a customs union, which they claimed would reduce artificial trade barriers and expedite financial recovery.[80]

In May, however, as the Danubian customs union floundered and economic conditions at home and abroad deteriorated, Hoover encouraged Stimson to consider a British request for the convocation of a world economic and monetary conference. The president hoped that a conference of leading government officials might lead to collaborative efforts to increase commodity prices and restore world-wide confidence. Stimson telephoned Prime Minister MacDonald on 25 May and discussed the wisdom of convening an international conference. The secretary maintained that governments might be able to join together and combat tariff discrimination, establish a number of comparatively free trade areas, and limit exchange fluctuations. During their meeting at Lausanne, British and French officials agreed on the need for such a conference. Shortly thereafter, Stimson reaffirmed the administration's willingness to partake in the necessary preparatory meetings provided that the silver issue was included in the agenda for the conference.[81]

Although the goals of Republican commercial and financial policies remained constant during the spring and summer of 1932, the tactics were in a state of transition. Hoover still wanted to expand American exports and foster European financial stability without compromising protectionist duties and other domestic priorities. Therefore, he insisted that tariff rates, war debts, and reparations be excluded from the agenda of the forthcoming World Economic Conference.[82] Yet, the willingness of the administration to attend such a conference signified a change in Republican tactics. During the 1920s Republican officials had refused to participate officially in world economic conferences at Genoa and Geneva. Financial problems had been handed over to central bankers, and commercial questions had been set aside for resolution by the Tariff Commission within the framework of established policy. Since the Depression had discredited the ability of private experts and nonpolitical commissions to effectively reconcile internal

---

80. "Decision and Recommendations in Respect of the Grain Preferential Treaties," 15 March 1932, RG 59, 640.0031 Danube/184; Diary of Henry L. Stimson, 15 March 1932, Stimson Papers; FR, 1932, 1:846–61.

81. Stimson to Mellon, 26 May 1932, HHPP, Box 876; Hoover, Memorandum, 25 May 1932, ibid.; for the Anglo-French agreement at Lausanne, see Wheeler-Bennett, *Reparations*, pp. 270–71; for the subsequent arrangements, see FR, 1932, 1:814–19.

82. FR, 1932, 1:817–18.

and external priorities, policymaking had become much more central-
ized. Hoover and Stimson increasingly acknowledged the need for
high-level government officials to join together and devise solutions to
pressing economic and financial issues. Thus the president and secretary of state were willing to consider new tactics, participate in a world
economic conference, and reappraise the efficacy of commercial principles, such as the world-wide application of the equality-of-treatment
formula.

Political Interlude

Once the presidential campaign got underway in the autumn of 1932,
the reformulation of diplomatic strategy took a back seat to political
considerations. Conscious of the pervasive anti-French attitudes among
the American people and convinced that most Americans sought relief
through domestic action, the president did not want to jeopardize the
small chance he might have to be reelected by unleashing foreign
policy initiatives.[83] In his campaign speeches Hoover repeatedly emphasized the European origins of the Depression but did not stress the
importance of European stability to American recovery. Instead, his
emphasis was on domestic priorities, especially on the protection of
the domestic market.[84] Stimson and some of his colleagues in the State
Department often expressed frustration with the president's orientation. Yet, they could not alter his attitudes, in part because they, too,
realized the difficulty of overcoming the parochial economic interests
and ingrained political prejudices of many Americans. Even Herbert
Feis privately acknowledged that political constraints precluded progress on foreign policy matters until after the elections. Accordingly, he
and Stimson cautioned the French to defer new proposals on the war
debts. Although Wall Street bankers advocated immediate relief of
hard-pressed foreign debtors, Hoover's eyes were on Main Street businessmen, who were manifesting a growing indifference to foreign
trade developments.[85]

83. For the growing importance of political considerations and the exasperation with
the European situation, see Diary of Henry L. Stimson, 12–26 July 1932, Stimson Papers; for the extent of anti-French sentiment, see DDF, 1, 1:16–17, 183–85, 350–52.
84. Hoover, *State Papers*, 2:247–65, 293–480.
85. For the views of Stimson and Feis, see Feis to Frankfurter, 30 July, 12 August
1932, Feis Papers, Boxes 33 and 16; Diary of Henry L. Stimson, 26 July 1932, Stimson
Papers; Memorandum of conversation between Stimson and Claudel, 28 July 1932,
RG 59, 800.51W89 France/700; for the view from Wall Street, see Lamont to Hoover,
4 August 1932, Thomas W. Lamont Papers, Box 98; for the diminishing interest in

The French were careful to do nothing on the war debts to agitate Hoover before November. Jules Henry, the French chargé, warned his government that future American policy would be guided by public opinion, that France's reputation in America had never been worse, and that it was imperative to alter the image of France as a rich, greedy, and vindictive nation. Herriot took such advice seriously. In his view the debt issue was subordinate to the larger questions of French security. He believed that it was extremely misguided to antagonize American opinion when Anglo-American goodwill was increasingly vital to France's economic and strategic well-being.[86]

In particular, Herriot was anxious to convince Americans of the growing menace from across the Rhine. At the end of August the German government said it would no longer participate in the disarmament conference until Germany was accorded equality. Yet, the German definition of equality was in flux. No longer content with the demand for juridic equality, in which her existing arms limitations would be written into a new treaty lasting a specific number of years, Germany called for the right to possess certain armaments that she was presently denied but that other nations showed no intention of relinquishing. Moreover, Germany wanted to alter the period of training in the Reichswehr and establish a special militia. These demands alarmed the French. Though Herriot deferred action on the war debts, he could not wait until November to enlist American aid in his campaign to keep German armaments within the bounds set by the Treaty of Versailles. In Paris, French officials expressed their concerns to Ambassador Edge, and, in Washington, Jules Henry explained the worsening diplomatic situation to Stimson and Castle.[87]

American officials were sympathetic. "The Germans are getting heady," Stimson noted in his diary on 7 September. "The Old Prussian spirit is coming up, and now we have a very dangerous sore spot in the world." The secretary believed Germany was entitled to juridic equality. But he was strongly opposed to German rearmament lest it

---

foreign trade, see the reports flowing into Washington from the district offices of the BFDC: J. S. Goff to Frederick M. Feiker, 8 August 1932, RG 151, File 400; T. L. Gaukel to Feiker, 5 August 1932, ibid.; John H. Farrell, "Selling Abroad," 9 August 1932, ibid.; J. E. Wrenn to Feiker, 19 August 1932, ibid.

86. For Henry's view, see DDF, 1, 1:182–85; for Herriot's orientation, see pp. 648–49, 683–85; see also his speech to the Chamber of Deputies on 12–13 December 1932, RG 59, 800.51W89 France/808.

87. DDF, 1, 1:242–43, 290–91, 312–13, 316–17, 354–56; see also FR, 1932, 1:426–30, 458.

intensify political unrest in Europe and jeopardize the Washington and London naval treaties. Stimson prepared an *aide-mémoire* outlining his antipathy to Germany's new demands. When he showed a draft of it to Hoover, however, the president strongly objected. Claiming that Germany's demand for equality had broad popular appeal and fearing the impact of Stimson's *aide-mémoire* on his political campaign, the president berated the position of the secretary of state at a cabinet meeting on 20 September. As a result a weak statement was released to the press inviting Germany back to the conference, advocating disarmament by stages, and disclaiming direct American interest in Germany's recent demands.[88]

Jules Henry accurately reported to Herriot that political considerations prevented the State Department from taking a stronger stand.[89] This state of affairs disappointed the French premier but did not alter his determination to reconcile Franco-American differences. Within the highest councils of the French government, Herriot insisted that France had to make a greater effort to accommodate the Americans and British. He urged France to agree to some arms reductions along the lines envisioned in the Hoover plan. He suggested molding France's security requirements to complement America's revised stand on consultation (and perhaps on neutrality). Herriot pleaded with French military officials to relax their opposition to disarmament and accept the proposition that security accompany disarmament, not precede it. He admitted that he had no faith in Germany's good intentions. Moreover, he was aware of Germany's superior ability to raise an army and prepare for war. This consideration was all the more reason, he emphasized, for supporting the Hoover plan, which envisioned no substantive change in Germany's armed strength. There were risks inherent in such a course of action. Herriot acknowledged these risks, but he maintained that there was no alternative. If France did nothing, Germany would rearm and France would find herself isolated.[90]

Herriot refused to accept Germany's demand for equality without parallel recognition of France's right to security. But he did submit a "maximum plan" to the disarmament conference in early November that tried to reconcile French security requirements with American disarmament proposals. On the one hand the plan tried to satisfy the

88. Diary of Henry L. Stimson, 7, 15, 16, 17, 20 September, 20 October 1932, Stimson Papers; see also FR, 1932, 1:424–26, 431–32, 442–43, 449–50; DDF, 1, 1:282–83.
89. DDF, 1, 1:342–43, 356–57.
90. Ibid., pp. 435–37, 439–62, 476–90, 499–503, 509–25, 544–53, 560–84, 614–41.

French Right and the French military by providing for the establishment of an international force, the conclusion of mutual assistance treaties, and the disposal of existing weapons that would be prohibited by treaty to the League of Nations. On the other hand the plan tried to satisfy the Hoover administration by calling for the standardization and reduction of Continental armies, by contemplating the eventual reduction of armaments, and by providing for the security of France without obligating the United States to use force to deter aggression. Herriot wanted a triple American commitment to consult, to refuse to recognize the fruits of aggression, and to refrain from trading with or financing an aggressor nation.[91]

For the time being, however, the Hoover administration was unable to provide Herriot with aid or encouragement. Although Davis prodded French officials to be as conciliatory as possible, his attention was focused temporarily on naval matters that were of secondary importance to the French government. In Washington, Stimson told Claudel that public opinion and congressional attitudes prevented him from incorporating elements of his August speech into a formal consultative pact. Moreover, Castle indicated that the campaign prevented Hoover from giving the more technical aspects of disarmament adequate attention.[92]

Electoral considerations not only delayed new attempts to deal with the war debt and disarmament issues but also undermined efforts to consummate a new commercial treaty. In mid-September Herriot indicated that he was prepared to consider American requests for de facto most-favored-nation treatment. State Department officials immediately renewed their search for administrative concessions that might encourage the French to apply minimum duties to all American goods.[93] At the same time, however, Hoover continued to champion protective duties and ignored recommendations emanating from the Treaty Division of the Department of State in favor of a change in the nonnegotiable tariff structure of the United States. Evidently believing that his defense of the tariff was good politics, Hoover maintained that "there is no measure in the whole economic gamut more vital to the American

91. For the French plan, see FR, 1932, 1:180–86.
92. For Davis's talks with French officials, especially regarding naval matters, see ibid., pp. 348–50, 458, 468, 473, 535–74; DDF, 1, 2:85–87; for Stimson's view on consultation, see 1, 1:435–37; FR, 1932, 1:359–60; for Castle's view, see p. 540. Meanwhile, however, the American delegates expressed dissatisfaction over the new French plan. See FR, 1932, 1:389–93, 398–401.
93. Edge to Stimson, 16 September 1932, RG 59, 611.5131/853, 854; Stimson to J. T. Marriner, 30 September 1932, ibid., 611.5131/869; Rogers to Marriner, 6 October 1932, ibid., 611.5131/880.

workingman and farmer today than the maintenance of a protective tariff.'' Raising tariffs to aid the farmer, he intimated, was even more important than expanding exports to help the manufacturer.[94] Whatever such rhetoric may have done for Hoover's lackluster campaign, it convinced the French that they would be foolhardy to consummate a treaty with a protectionist Republican administration. Expecting a Republican defeat at the polls, Herriot decided to hold off additional French concessions until the Democrats took office and there was a prospect of gaining reciprocal concessions.[95]

Although electoral considerations precluded initiatives from top American policymakers, such considerations did not prevent Herbert Feis from developing his own program for recovery. As coordinator of the technical preparations for the economic conference, he began to meet weekly with economists in various government departments and at the Federal Reserve Board. Studies conducted by his intergovernmental group of experts reinforced his growing conviction that recovery could not be effected ''by policies that take account solely of domestic resources. . . . The road to recovery if it is planned in that direction will be arduous to the point of critically testing our ability to maintain the present system. This is primarily because American economic and financial interest had deeply and substantially interwoven itself with that of other countries.'' In Feis's opinion the World Economic Conference provided an opportunity to allocate ''immediate risks and sacrifices'' evenly among nations and to arrange cooperative international action aimed at increasing prices and resuscitating private economic activity throughout the world. Feis and his group of experts called for the restoration of stable currencies, increased cooperation of banking systems in different nations, and better coordination of monetary policy. They sought the elimination of exchange controls and the reduction of foreign indebtedness. They advocated the institution of a tariff truce, a gradual decrease in customs duties, and the acceptance of preferential trade agreements within specific regions.[96]

Feis wanted to devise a coherent set of recommendations that could be used to mold the course of official policy toward the World Eco-

94. Hoover, *State Papers*, 2:351, 310–11; see also pp. 360–62, 384–85, 418–19, 461–63; for the recommendations of the Treaty Division, see Treaty Division, Memorandum, November 1932, RG 59, 611.0031/419½; Treaty Division, ''Reciprocity and the Most-Favored-Nation Clause,'' October 1932, ibid., 550.S1/231½.

95. Marriner to Stimson, 1, 5, 11, 16, 18 October 1932, RG 59, 611.5131/873, 877, 883, 886, 891.

96. Feis, Memorandum, 15 October 1932, ibid., 550.S1/231; Feis to Frankfurter, 27 September 1932, Frankfurter Papers, Box 54.

nomic Conference. Prior to the election he was unable to get either Hoover or Stimson to give serious consideration to his group's proposals.[97] At the end of October he accompanied the American experts Edmund E. Day and John H. Williams to a preparatory conference at Geneva. After several days of discussions, Feis found that many of the delegates were routine functionaries bound by their governments' instructions. They could agree only in a general way on the need to stabilize currencies, reduce trade barriers, curtail exchange controls, and raise commodity prices. The meeting, therefore, proved unproductive. Feis realized that a second preparatory meeting would be needed to arrange the agenda for the conference. He hoped that during the interim the experts would be able to consult with their governments and develop more constructive ideas.[98]

Feis returned to Washington assuming that the end of the electoral campaign would allow American policymakers to turn their attention once again to the reformulation of diplomatic tactics and policies. In September he and Felix Frankfurter had already foreseen the possibility of an interregnum, during which policy might drift and conditions worsen. They hoped that some collaboration might be arranged between the incoming and outgoing administrations.[99] Little did they think that Hoover would take the initiative to expedite such collaboration. But circumstances immediately after the election impelled him to do so. With the campaign over, the outgoing president was prepared to make one last attempt to reshape the mechanisms of economic diplomacy to promote European stability without compromising domestic priorities.

The Interregnum

On 9 November 1932, the day after the election of Franklin D. Roosevelt, Governor Harrison of the FRBNY telephoned Mills and warned against letting policy drift during the interregnum. He suggested that the president formulate a comprehensive economic and financial program that would elicit bipartisan support. Harrison said that he was going to contact Owen Young, the most likely Democratic candidate

97. Feis to Frankfurter, 13 October 1932, Feis Papers, Box 33. I have found no evidence that Stimson or Hoover studied Feis's proposals.
98. Feis to Frankfurter, 2 November 1932, Frankfurter Papers, Box 54; FR, 1932, 1:837–40; American Embassy, Paris, to Department of State, 2 December 1932, HHPP, Box 878.
99. Frankfurter to Feis, 30 September 1932, Feis Papers, Box 33.

for secretary of state, to ascertain whether the president-elect would prod Democratic leaders in Congress to cooperate with Hoover on revenue, banking, and war debt matters.[100]

Mills initially told Harrison that Republican policy had been repudiated at the polls, and it was up to the Democratic leadership in Congress to assume the initiative. During the next two days, however, he became alarmed when the British and French ambassadors presented formal diplomatic notes and requested both the suspension of the December war debt installment and the revision of existing accords. Mills called Harrison back and confidentially reported what had been occurring in Washington. The governor of the FRBNY said that he and Young felt that Hoover should write Roosevelt a public letter elucidating the major financial problems before the nation and soliciting his cooperation. Young doubted whether the president-elect would cooperate; the open letter, he hoped, would pressure him to do so. Mills momentarily chuckled at the prospect of seeing Roosevelt confronted publicly with the difficult debt issue. Then, he earnestly told Harrison that he would try to get Hoover to deal with the problem in the broadest public interest.[101] During the next few days Mills and Stimson phoned Hoover, who was on the West Coast, and exhorted him to confer with the president-elect on future policy toward the European debtors.[102]

Hoover was not inclined to cooperate with Roosevelt. He felt that his Democratic opponent had distorted his policies and sullied his reputation during the campaign. With congressmen "coming back [to Washington] redhot against any concession," Hoover was not impressed by Stimson's advice to take a magnanimous stand on the war debts. The issue was political dynamite. For Hoover to respond in a conciliatory manner to the debtors, he needed Roosevelt to keep the Democrats in line. But Hoover feared that the president-elect might humiliate him further if he tried to pursue a moderate course on the war debts. Only with much trepidation, therefore, did he accept Mills's and Stimson's advice and invite Roosevelt to the White House to discuss the matter.[103]

100. Harrison, Memorandum, 11 November 1932, George L. Harrison Papers, 2012.2.

101. Ibid.; for the British and French notes, see FR, 1932, 1:727–28, 754–56.

102. Diary of Henry L. Stimson, 10–16 November 1932, Stimson Papers.

103. Diary of Henry L. Stimson, 10–22 November 1932, ibid. The quotation is from the entry on 16 November. For Hoover's anger over Democratic campaign tactics, see Hoover, State Papers, 2:319, 364–73, 390 ff.; for Hoover's invitation to Roosevelt, see pp. 483–86; Memorandum of conversation between Hoover and Roosevelt, 17 November 1932, HHPP, Box 877; Hoover to Roosevelt, 17 November 1932, ibid., Box 156.

In preparing for his meeting with Roosevelt and in laboring over an answer to the British and French notes, the president consulted with officials in the State, Treasury, and Commerce departments. The advice emanating from each department was influenced by that department's particular concerns. Secretary of Commerce Roy D. Chapin was eager to find new ways of expanding exports. He wanted to trade the war debts for new market opportunities and feared that foreign defaults might precipitate a wave of domestic defaults, thus disrupting all contractual and business arrangements. Though Mills was anxious to secure the stabilization of sterling and recognized the need to reduce the debt in order to bring stabilization about, he was also worried about the mounting deficit and preoccupied with laying plans for refunding the national debt. These domestic and organizational imperatives made him less flexible than Stimson, who was concerned exclusively with foreign policy and more inclined to empathize with foreign requests on the debt issue to ease his task on other diplomatic questions. Stimson understood, for example, that a tough stand on the debts might topple Herriot from power, disrupt Anglo-French cooperation, and set back the disarmament conference. His own concerns occasionally impelled him to attack his cabinet colleagues as politically motivated. Yet, his diary entries indicate that he often came to appreciate the arguments raised by Mills and almost never had enough technical knowledge or political understanding to demonstrate how the administration could overcome the fiscal impediments and congressional objections to a generous treatment of the war debts.[104]

Given the diverse concerns of Hoover's advisers and the overall difficulty of the situation, the consensus of opinion that emerged was remarkable. All agreed that revisions of the debt settlements were urgent. All agreed that the debt issue had to be linked to the disarmament and economic conferences and used as a lever to secure commercial concessions, currency stability, and armament reductions. One outstanding point of contention, however, centered on British and French requests for a postponement of the December war debt installment. Stimson alone seemed willing to contemplate an affirmative response to these inquiries.[105]

104. Diary of Henry L. Stimson, 14 November–4 December 1932, Stimson Papers; Memorandum of conversation between Stimson and Lamont, 28 November 1932, RG 59, 800.51W89/598½; Roy D. Chapin to Hoover, 21 November 1932, HHPP, Box 877; Chapin to Stimson, 21 November 1932, RG 59. 800.51W89/592½; Mills to Hoover, 15 November 1932, HHPP, Box 877; Mills to Young, 16 December 1932, Mills Papers, Box 9; Allen Klots, Memorandum, 15 November 1932, RG 59, 800.51W89/603½.

105. See n. 104.

Hoover reflected on the critical issues before him and presented his ideas to Roosevelt and Raymond Moley, Roosevelt's chief adviser, on 22 November during a long discussion at the White House. The president summarized the major components of American war debt policy as it had existed since the days of the Wilson administration. He then expressed his opposition to a postponement of the December installment. He feared that a continuation of the existing moratorium might undermine "the integrity of the debt," establish an indirect link to the Lausanne accords, and eventually shift the burden of German reparation payments onto American taxpayers.

Yet, Hoover also worried about the prospect of foreign defaults and believed that revision would expedite world recovery and promote international cooperation. He stated that it would be wise to revise the debt accords if the United States could secure stabilization of foreign currencies, reduction of trade barriers, and curtailment of armament expenditures. To bring about such a comprehensive settlement, Hoover stressed the need to establish a united front between the incoming and outgoing administrations and Congress. Such unity was possible if Roosevelt would collaborate in the appointment of delegates to the economic conference and if members of Congress were included among those delegates. Hoover emphasized that in the selection of such a delegation, he would be guided by Roosevelt's wishes. The president realized that no conclusion to the negotiations could be reached until Roosevelt took office.[106]

When Roosevelt refused to cooperate with the president and when congressional leaders responded coolly to Hoover's analysis and proposals, the administration had to deal on its own with European pleas for postponement and revision. In formal notes to French and British diplomats on 23 November, Hoover denied the debtors' requests for immediate postponement. The president summarized the traditional American stand on the war debts but acknowledged the need for revision.[107] The British and French, however, were so distraught by

106. In the Hoover papers there are two unsigned memoranda of the 22 November meeting, both of which appear to have been written by Hoover. See [Hoover?], Memoranda, 22 November 1932, HHPP, Boxes 29 and 156; see also the account by Raymond Moley, *After Seven Years*, pp. 67–79.

107. For Roosevelt's refusal to cooperate, see chapter 9, pp. 317–19; for the response of congressional leaders, see Diary of Henry L. Stimson, 23 November 1932, Stimson Papers; for the notes to Britain and France, see FR, 1932, 1:732–34, 756–57. The note to Britain was more conciliatory because Stimson revised it after the British ambassador protested. See Diary of Henry L. Stimson, 23 November 1932, Stimson Papers.

the recapitulation of old policies and the demand for payment of the December installment that they virtually ignored the administration's expressed readiness to partake in a revision of the existing debt accords.[108] On 1 December they again appealed for postponement. The French did not contest the legality of the American position. They justified their request on the basis of Bérenger's unofficial reservations in 1926, the Hoover moratorium, the Laval-Hoover communiqué, and the Lausanne agreements. More ominous, the British claimed payment incapacity, threatened default, and warned that American demands might lead to the repudiation of the Lausanne agreements and the disruption of Anglo-French collaboration.[109]

British and French pleas made an impression on Republican officials. Stimson, Mills, Chapin, and Harrison reassessed the possibility of postponing the December installment and explored methods of easing transfer problems. They feared that if Britain defaulted, sterling would depreciate, commodity prices would decline, and movements of capital would be deranged. Germany would be encouraged to default on her private obligations, and Congress would be dissuaded from considering permanent revisions. Hoover appreciated these considerations, but his options were circumscribed by congressional opinion. Since Britain demanded equal treatment for France and Congress was not ready to countenance a debt postponement for all the wartime Allies, Hoover had to find some way of easing British transfer problems without arousing latent anti-French sentiment in Congress and engendering another legislative-executive deadlock.[110] Finally, on 6 December the president announced that he would not suspend the December installment. Instead, he indicated that he would recommend "methods

108. Memorandum of conversation between Stimson and Lamont, 28 November 1932, rg 59, 800.51W89/598½; Lamont to Paris partners, 28 November 1932, ibid.
109. For the French and British notes, see FR, 1932, 1:734–39, 758–770; for the French position, see also DDF, 1, 2:114–16, 191–201; Marriner to Stimson, 14, 15, 25 November 1932, rg 59, 800.51W89 France/728, 741, 739; for the British position, see Memoranda of conversations between Stimson and Lamont, 28, 30 November 1932, hhpp, Box 877; Hugh Wilson to Stimson, 6 December 1932, rg 59, 800.51W89 France/750.
110. Diary of Henry L. Stimson, 30 November–8 December 1932, Stimson Papers; Memoranda of conversations between Stimson and Lamont, 28, 30 November 1932, hhpp, Box 877; Mills to Richard F. Warren, 1 December 1932, Mills Papers, Box 111; Federal Reserve Bank of New York (frbny), Confidential memorandum for the secretary of the treasury, "Suggestions for Statement to Ways and Means Committee Regarding Acceptance of Negotiable Notes from Great Britain on Account of War Debt Payment due December 15," 3 December 1932, hhpp, Box 877; Stimson to Hoover, 1 December 1932, ibid.; see also Claudel's comments on congressional sentiment, DDF, 1, 2:71–77.

to overcome temporary exchange difficulties in connection with this payment from nations where it may be necessary.''[111] Thereafter, another set of notes, more conciliatory than ever before, was sent to the British and French governments emphasizing the prospect of permanent revision once the December installment was paid. Monick, the heretofore skeptical French financial attaché, became convinced that the president wanted to help the European economic and political situation but was constrained by congressional authority.[112]

Herriot's political problems, however, were even more serious than Hoover's. French opinion was against payment; yet Herriot did not want to default. He believed his entire policy of seeking close cooperation with the Anglo-Saxon powers was at stake. By early December he learned that Britain would pay the debt installment if compelled to do so. Therefore, despite Britain's loyal efforts to secure equal treatment for all the debtors, France was to be stranded when the crunch came. Herriot understood the British dilemma, but he was angered and embittered by the predicament in which he was placed by American intransigence. Still, he struggled valiantly to obtain legislative approval of payment with reservations. Herriot made this approval a matter of confidence in his government. He was defeated and removed from power. On 15 December the French did not pay the debt installment; the British did.[113]

The French default did not put an end to Republican efforts to resolve Franco-American differences and devise methods for a systematic assault on economic and financial problems at home and abroad. Hoover and Stimson realized that the positions of the two governments were not irreconcilable and that payment might still be obtained through tact and conciliation. The president privately requested key senators to refrain from attacking France. In addition, Hoover allowed Stimson to write an amiable letter to Herriot expressing the administration's goodwill and declaring its readiness to negotiate permanent revisions if the overdue debts were paid. For the moment the restraint of the American press and American politicians afforded the administration time to work out the troublesome issues.[114]

111. Hoover, *State Papers*, 2:502–3.
112. For the notes to the French and British governments, see FR, 1932, 1:739–40, 771–75; for Monick's view, see DDF, 1, 2:226–28.
113. For Herriots's sentiments, see DDF, 1, 2:191–201; Herriot, *Jadis*, 2:355–57; for detailed reports on the debate in the Chamber, see Edge to Stimson, 10, 13, 14 December 1932, RG 59, 800.51W89 France/754, 760, 762, 763.
114. Diary of Henry L. Stimson, 15–17 December 1932, Stimson Papers; Memorandum of conversation between Stimson and Claudel, 16 December 1932, RG 59,

Meanwhile, Stimson, Mills, Harrison, and Feis prodded Hoover to resolve the war debt question with Britain and help stabilize the pound. During 1932 they had come to believe that the stabilization of foreign currencies, especially of sterling, was a necessary precondition for the increase in commodity prices upon which they now claimed domestic recovery depended. Mills maintained that "once currencies and exchanges are stabilized, the artificial trade barriers that have been set up to protect exchanges should automatically come down, world prices will almost inevitably rise and there is real ground for belief that a general forward impulse might result." More detailed studies, completed by the FRBNY and circulated among top officials in the executive branch, demonstrated that American farm prices, especially the prices of wheat and cotton, fluctuated in direct relation to sterling. As the pound had depreciated in early autumn, the prices of key American commodities had also decreased and the gains made in late summer had been sacrificed. Thus, the FRBNY argued that artificial domestic attempts to raise prices would not succeed. Convinced that "the major movements of prices are world, not domestic phenomena," Federal Reserve officials advocated a revision of the war debt accords and contended that "in attempting to reverse the downward movement of prices, measures of an international character will, on the whole, be more effective than purely domestic measures."[115]

Such considerations prompted Hoover to make one last effort to break the logjam on the major problems facing the United States, France, and Europe. During the week following the 15 December installment date, he corresponded with Roosevelt and addressed Congress. Emphasizing that "the most urgent economic effort still before the world is the restoration of price levels," the president called for international cooperation to stabilize currencies. Hoover stressed the need to curtail military expenditures and balance budgets. The war debts, in his opinion, were not so important as these other problems. Since other nations believed otherwise, the president was willing to treat the war debts in conjunction with these other issues, provided that

800.51W89 France/770½; DDF, 1, 2:253, 269, 273–74; "Excerpts of Editorial Comment throughout the Country on the French War Debt Default," 15 December 1932, RG 59, 800.51W89 France/775; Moffat to Davis, 19 December 1932, Davis Papers, Box 41.

115. Mills to Young, 16 December 1932, Mills Papers, Box 9; FRBNY, Confidential memorandum for the secretary of the treasury, "The Reconsideration of War Debts," 12 December 1932, HHPP, Box 877; see also FRBNY, "Suggestions for Statement to Ways and Means Committee," 3 December 1932, ibid.; Stimson, Memorandum of special press conference, 19 December 1932, RG 59, 800.51W89/627½; Feis, Memorandum, 15 October 1932, ibid., 550.S1/231.

the debts were not cancelled and that the United States received adequate "compensations." Once again, Hoover advocated the creation of a commission, including members of Congress and delegates to the arms conference, to discuss the war debts and related economic issues on an individual basis with foreign governments. These discussions would lay the basis for the resolution of the debt problem and the successful conclusion of the disarmament and economic conferences. Yet, Hoover emphasized that, though preparations should begin immediately, negotiations would be consummated only after the president-elect took office. "I wish especially to avoid any embarrassment to your work," he wrote Roosevelt, "and thus have no intention of committing the incoming administration to any particular policy prior to March 4."[116]

The French ambassador correctly informed his government that Hoover was going as far as he could to meet French needs. The new commission called for by the president, Claudel noted, was very different from the old WDC. Moreover, the president seemed to have abandoned his customary emphasis on the capacity-to-pay formula.[117] Many of the old techniques of economic diplomacy appeared to have been jettisoned. Hoover no longer relied on central bankers or private experts to examine each problem on its own merits. Instead, he called for a linkage approach, recognized the need to participate in international economic conferences, accepted the use of politicians in supposedly expert capacities, and acknowledged the interrelationship between economic, financial, and political issues.[118]

The alterations in Hoover's foreign policies were constructive steps forward, appropriately recognized as such by some of his severest critics within the administration.[119] The president perceived, quite rightly, that Congress was unlikely to accept unilateral American con-

116. Hoover, *State Papers*, 2:547–58. There is no evidence that Hoover was trying to trap Roosevelt or sabotage his policies. Only after conditions greatly deteriorated in January and February did Hoover seek a specific endorsement of policy from the president-elect.

117. DDF, 1, 2:281–82. In explaining Hoover's position to Claudel on 16 December Stimson omitted any reference to the payment capacity formula. See Memorandum of conversation between Stimson and Claudel, 16 December 1932, RG 59, 800.51W89 France/770½.

118. For references to the changes in the techniques of diplomacy, see, for example, Moffat to Hull, 31 August 1933, Hull Papers, Box 63; Mills to Richard Olney, 30 November 1932, Mills Papers, Box 111.

119. Stimson to Harvey Bundy, 21 December 1932, RG 59, 800.51W89 France/797½.

cessions on the war debts.[120] He also realized, equally incisively, that revision of the war debt agreements would have little impact on the international crisis if not accompanied by action in other spheres.[121] Thus, his decision to treat the debt issue in conjunction with the disarmament and economic conferences was a sensible means of trying to cope simultaneously with the international economic crisis and the domestic political impasse. By trading debt payments for the stabilization of currencies, Hoover hoped to eliminate exchange controls, revive international commerce, stimulate American exports, and raise commodity prices. By trading debt payments for some limitation of armaments, he hoped to ease budgetary problems in all nations, including the United States. Hoover hoped that if Congress perceived this coordinated effort to deal constructively with international issues and recognized the tangible advantages of such an effort, it would respond generously with regard to the war debts. Moreover, to enlist bipartisan congressional support and to demonstrate to foreigners that meaningful discussions could ensue, the president sought Roosevelt's cooperation in the selection of a negotiating team.[122]

For various reasons the president-elect chose not to collaborate with Hoover. Moreover, Roosevelt let it be known to the French that after he took office he would handle the outstanding problems between the two nations in a conciliatory manner.[123] The French and British, impressed by the deadlock between the incoming and outgoing administrations, refused to negotiate seriously with the discredited president.[124] Thereafter, the diplomatic initiative rested with Roosevelt. On 21 December Hoover, Mills, and Stimson had a long conversation and decided to forego any more initiatives. Afterwards, Stimson drove Mills home, and they agreed "that it was pretty much the end of the era."[125]

120. For the intensity of congressional sentiment, see the comments of French diplomats, DDF, 1, 2:71–72, 77, 253–54, 307, 317–18.
121. The American experts to the preparatory meeting of the World Economic Conference had enumerated the matrix of economic problems that begged for solutions. See FR, 1932, 1:839–40.
122. The above analysis is based on the documents in Hoover, *State Papers*, 2:547–58.
123. DDF, 1, 2:344–45, 414–18, 353–54; for an analysis of Roosevelt's actions, see chapter 9, pp. 317–29.
124. Diary of Henry L. Stimson, 21 December 1932, 3, 4 January 1933, Stimson Papers; Stimson to Edge, 27 December 1932, RG 59, 800.51W89 France/785; see also DDF, 1, 2:270–71, 293–96, 309–10, 341–42; Edge to Hoover, 4, 5 January 1933, HHPP, Box 877.
125. Diary of Henry L. Stimson, 21 December 1932, Stimson Papers.

Conclusion

The era of Republican foreign policy came to a close with the techniques of economic diplomacy revised but with its goals and principles intact. Some of the president's advisers, like Stimson, Harrison, and Feis, had become convinced of the need to launch foreign policy initiatives to boost commodity prices. But Hoover hesitated to act because he wanted to expedite Europe's stabilization without compromising domestic priorities. On 10 December 1932 he told the Gridiron Club that, although international cooperation was desirable, it must not be effected at the expense of the American people. In other words Hoover was still not willing to jeopardize domestic priorities, like balancing the budget and protecting the domestic market, to placate French demands, hasten Europe's recovery, increase world prices, or promote American exports. Although he may have been willing to abandon the capacity-to-pay formula and link debt concessions to other foreign policy matters, he still opposed foreign demands for debt cancellation, expected other nations to make the key concessions, and maintained that the United States could get along independently of the rest of the world if necessary.[126]

At the same time, Hoover continued to treat disarmament as an essentially economic and financial problem. He had little inclination to supplement his arms proposals with efforts to satisfy French demands for security guarantees. In December, after Davis helped get Germany to return to the disarmament conference, American diplomats claimed that the United States government could aid matters at Geneva by formalizing a new stand on consultation and neutrality.[127] American military leaders, however, denigrated such suggestions and ridiculed French policies. They argued that further diplomatic attempts to satisfy French arms demands would damage American strategic interests. It is doubtful whether Hoover was aware of the technical intricacies that prompted Army officials to denounce French arms limitation proposals. But in the context of the European military situation in the early 1930s, he shared their indifference toward France's strategic anxieties.

126. Hoover, *State Papers*, 2:544, 592–94; Memorandum for the secretary of state from the president, 27 January 1933, HHPP, Box 29; Hoover, Memorandum, 13 January 1933, HHPP, Box 880.
127. For Davis's efforts at mediating a compromise between French and German officials, see FR, 1932, 1:472–528; for the recommendation that the United States seize the initiative, see Wilson to Davis, 15 December 1932, Hugh R. Wilson Papers, Box 1.

Consequently, the president would not depart from his long-standing aversion to strategic commitments in the Old World.[128]

Despite his concern about the international economy and despite his realization of the need for systematic action on the debt, disarmament, and currency issues, Hoover no longer had the capacity to reconcile domestic needs and European imperatives. His sensitivity to partisan politics, his preoccupation with domestic priorities, and his antipathy toward France, which burst out anew in January, precluded any fundamental reorientation of American diplomacy.[129] Although he had sought to reshape the techniques of economic diplomacy and harmonize American and French policies to promote European stability and American recovery, Hoover had failed to do so. Whether Roosevelt would have more success would depend on his ability and inclination to recast domestic priorities and reinterpret strategic imperatives in a way that made them more reconcilable with French needs. The French had great hopes. But since the Hoover administration had already gone further in this direction than most Americans thought appropriate, the prospects were dim.

128. For the criticism of military officials, see Kilbourne to MacArthur, 30 November 1932, 3 January 1933, RG 94, Box 82; Lt. Colonel George V. Strong to MacArthur, 1, 15 December 1932, ibid.; see also General Board to secretary of navy, 18 January 1933, Records of the General Board, File 438–2, Serial No. 1521 AA. Hoover, however, did not ask Congress for authority to control the shipment of armaments to help preserve world peace. The French appreciated this gesture. Hoover, *State Papers*, 2:565–66, 599; Diary of Henry L. Stimson, 9, 10 February 1933, Stimson Papers.

129. See Memorandum for the secretary of state from the president, 27 January 1933, HHPP, Box 29; Hoover, Memorandum, 13 January 1933, ibid., Box 880; Hoover, Memorandum, 21 January 1933, ibid., Box 778; Diary of Henry L. Stimson, 21 January 1933, Stimson Papers.

[9]

Roosevelt and the Dilemmas of Policymaking, 1933

On election eve 1932 Franklin D. Roosevelt sat in front of the fireplace at his home in Hyde Park and talked to his closest confidants about the presidential campaign, the economic crisis, growing unemployment, and the downward trend in domestic prices.[1] Conditions abroad were no more encouraging than those at home. In Asia the Japanese were expanding their gains in Manchuria and northern China. In Europe the persistent economic and political crises showed no signs of abating. In fact, financial and economic problems seemed to be spreading to France, Belgium, and other gold bloc nations. Not far ahead lay mounting political controversies and parliamentary upheavals in those countries. Meanwhile, in Germany the National Socialists, under the leadership of Adolf Hitler, were on the threshold of obtaining power. The world situation could hardly have seemed bleaker. During the electoral campaign Roosevelt had not presented a coherent or systematic program for generating recovery at home or promoting stability abroad. Instead, he had assailed ''the 'Four Horsemen' of the prevailing Republican leadership: The Horsemen of Destruction, Delay, Deceit, and Despair.''[2] Within a week after his election, however, the president-elect was compelled to make some important decisions regarding specific policy matters.

The Interregnum

In November the president-elect, despite his antipathy toward the president, accepted Hoover's invitation and decided to visit the White

1. Frank B. Freidel, *Franklin D. Roosevelt*, 3:369.
2. Ibid., pp. 339–71; for Roosevelt's campaign speeches, see Franklin D. Roose-

House with Moley.[3] For almost a week prior to the meeting, Roosevelt's entourage studied the war debt question. Rexford Tugwell initially wanted to link all the key issues: armaments, war debts, tariffs, currency stabilization, and commodity controls. Roosevelt argued that linking these issues was unwise. He felt that the war debts were primarily a political issue and that public and congressional opinion was opposed to cancellation. In his view the war debt problem had to be kept separate from the other questions. Acceding to Roosevelt's viewpoint, Tugwell discussed the matter more extensively with Moley and Adolf Berle, another member of the "Brain Trust." They decided that European debtors had the capacity to meet the December installments, that a moratorium on payments was not necessary, and that cancellation was a bankers' scheme to salvage private loans and short-term credits. Moley, Tugwell, and Berle believed that recovery could be promoted through internal palliatives; hence, they were reluctant to propose an international initiative that might upset Congress and undermine support for their domestic plans.[4]

When Roosevelt met with Hoover on 22 November, he agreed with the president's opposition to a new moratorium. Roosevelt shared Hoover's antipathy toward total cancellation and supported his determination to keep separate the war debt and reparation issues. The president-elect concurred with Hoover's desire to conduct future negotiations on an individual basis with each debtor nation. But Roosevelt did not respond enthusiastically to Hoover's desire to establish a special commission to consider war debt revision in conjunction with other important questions. Instead, Roosevelt maintained that negotiations should be pursued through normal diplomatic channels. The president-elect did not want to incur the political liabilities of a generous stand on the war debts and jeopardize his future relations with Congress.[5]

---

velt, *The Public Papers and Addresses of Franklin D. Roosevelt*, 1:621–865; for a view that attributes greater coherence to Roosevelt's campaign, see Elliot A. Rosen, *Hoover, Roosevelt, and the Brains Trust.*

3. Roosevelt, *Public Papers*, 1:876–77; Memorandum of phone conversation between Hoover and Roosevelt, 17 November 1932, Herbert C. Hoover Presidential Papers, Box 877 (hereafter cited as HHPP); Roosevelt to Hoover, 17 November 1932, ibid., Box 29.

4. Rexford G. Tugwell, *In Search of Roosevelt*, pp. 205–13; Rexford G. Tugwell Diary, 20 December 1932; Raymond Moley, *The First New Deal*, pp. 22–27; Adolf Berle, *Navigating the Rapids, 1918–1971*, pp. 77–80; see also Rosen, *Brains Trust*, pp. 115–211.

5. For the meeting between Hoover and Roosevelt, see Hoover, Memorandum, 22 November 1932, HHPP, Box 29; see also Raymond Moley, *After Seven Years*, pp. 72–77.

After the December payments crisis was over, Stimson wanted to begin negotiating permanent revisions with those nations that had met their obligations. He assumed that these discussions would be prolonged and complicated. If they were to be successful and lead to an increment in domestic prices and a resumption of economic activity, Stimson believed that the war debt revisions would have to be linked to the stabilization of foreign currencies and the lifting of trade restrictions. Stimson assumed that it would take Roosevelt months to become knowledgeable about these difficult problems. The secretary feared that in the interim recovery might be set back. He decided that it was in the national interest to collaborate with the incoming administration and familiarize Roosevelt and his advisers with these issues as soon as possible. Accordingly, he prodded Hoover to try once again to secure Roosevelt's cooperation. Reluctantly, the president accepted Stimson's advice. On 17 and 20 December Hoover invited Roosevelt to join him in selecting a commission that would discuss war debts and related issues with governments that had paid their December installments. Hoover emphasized that final decisions would be left to Roosevelt.[6]

When Hoover's letters arrived at Hyde Park, Tugwell and the president-elect were discussing the agenda for the upcoming economic conference with the American delegates to the preparatory meeting, Edmund E. Day and John H. Williams. Tugwell insisted that Roosevelt reject collaboration with the outgoing administration. Since the first meeting between Hoover and Roosevelt on 22 November, Tugwell and Moley had given additional thought to the war debts issue and had become increasingly opposed to concessions to the debtor nations. Convinced that the bankers were trying to deceive the American

6. Diary of Henry L. Stimson, 13, 16, 17 December 1932, Stimson Papers; Roosevelt, *Public Papers*, 1:877–79, 881–82. In his most recent volume, Frank Freidel has provided a comprehensive account of the Hoover-Roosevelt relationship during the interregnum. Two assumptions appear to underlie Freidel's view: first, Hoover sought from the onset to commit Roosevelt to the Hoover program; second, Roosevelt already had his own plans for recovery. See Freidel, *Franklin D. Roosevelt*, 4:18–195. Although Freidel does a marvelous job highlighting the mutual suspicions that permeated the Hoover-Roosevelt relationship, his two generalizations are debatable. Hoover obviously distrusted Roosevelt's intentions. Nevertheless, only in February 1933, when the banking situation was reaching crisis proportions, did he ask Roosevelt to endorse conservative fiscal and monetary policies. Until then he repeatedly emphasized that Roosevelt could oversee the outcome of the policy studies undertaken by the proposed commission. Roosevelt refused to cooperate not because he had determined upon a clear-cut policy, as had Moley and Tugwell, but because he distrusted Hoover, wished to keep his options open, and desired to avoid a controversy with Congress. Although this account will not focus on the Hoover-Roosevelt relationship, it is important to keep these points in mind.

people, Roosevelt's advisers suspected that supporters of international initiatives were trying to divert the incoming administration from undertaking domestic reforms. Moreover, Tugwell's talks with Day and Williams had convinced him that the prospects for a successful conference were not very good.[7]

Roosevelt's replies to Hoover's inquiries generally conformed to Tugwell's prescriptions. In letters written on 19 and 21 December the president-elect emphasized that the war debt, economic, and disarmament issues required "selective treatment," although he acknowledged "that in the ultimate outcome a relationship of any two or of all three may become clear." Roosevelt supported Hoover's views on limiting offensive armaments but warned against submerging preparations for the economic conference in conversations over war debts and disarmament. Emphasizing that he could not accept joint responsibility without commensurate authority, Roosevelt maintained that Hoover did not need his aid and could appoint a fact-finding commission to survey the debt issue without seeking congressional authorization. Roosevelt expressed considerable apprehension that any action on his part to collaborate with Hoover might be interpreted by foreigners as a policy commitment. Hence, he advised Hoover to proceed on his own without binding the incoming administration.[8]

Moley momentarily believed that this exchange of letters reflected Roosevelt's commitment to a nationalist road to recovery.[9] But the president-elect began to waver as he became more familiar with the arguments of individuals who believed that international initiatives had to constitute part of a comprehensive recovery program. Lewis Douglas, an Arizona congressman who was soon to become Roosevelt's first budget director, called the president-elect from Washington on 20 December. He explained the reasons why Hoover and Stimson sought to link the war debts with the economic conference and why they had requested the appointment of a special commission to undertake the negotiations. Douglas urged Roosevelt to reconsider the course of action recommended by Moley and Tugwell. At the same time, Norman Davis returned from his work at Geneva. Davis convinced the president-elect of the need to continue the preparations for the economic conference without delay. Reinforcing Davis's arguments was Felix Frankfurter, who arrived at Hyde Park on 22 December and prodded

7. Tugwell Diary, 20–24 December 1932; Tugwell, *In Search of Roosevelt*, pp. 214–15; Moley, *New Deal*, pp. 37–41.
8. Roosevelt, *Public Papers*, 1:879–81, 883–84.
9. Moley, *New Deal*, p. 42.

Roosevelt to cooperate more closely with Stimson. In a "Dear Frank" letter about a week later Thomas Lamont encouraged the president-elect to adopt a clear policy on the war debts, prepare a generous lump-sum settlement with each debtor nation, and arrange a special deal with the French providing for the payment of their defaulted December installment after his inauguration.[10]

The advice offered by Douglas, Davis, Frankfurter, and Lamont appealed to Roosevelt. While Moley, Berle, and Tugwell may have been convinced that the Democrats did not have to attach much significance to foreign initiatives and European problems, Roosevelt had not entirely discarded his internationalist inclinations. At the same time that he rebuffed Hoover's overtures, Roosevelt took numerous steps that revealed his differences with Moley and Tugwell and highlighted his personal uncertainty about the direction of his administration. He decided to appoint Cordell Hull secretary of state, instructed Day and Williams to return immediately to Europe for the second preparatory meeting of the economic conference, and contemplated possible revision of the debt settlements.[11] At the same time, Roosevelt followed Lamont's advice and tried to make arrangements with the French for them to pay their December installment after his inauguration. Moreover, on 11 January the president-elect met privately with French Ambassador Claudel. Roosevelt indicated that he foresaw no problems in reconciling his policies with those of France. He stated that he would carry on private talks with all the debtors, regardless of whether they paid in December. He suggested that a *modus vivendi* might be arranged for the June installment and expressed his willingness to negotiate reciprocal trade concessions. Finally, the president-elect conveyed a good deal of sympathy for France's strategic anxieties and promised to do everything possible to enhance French security.[12]

10. For Douglas's actions, see Diary of Henry L. Stimson, 21 December 1932, Stimson Papers; Tugwell Diary, 20 December 1932; for Davis's role, see ibid., 24–27 December 1932; for Frankfurter's efforts, see Diary of Henry L. Stimson, 22 December 1932–9 January 1933, Stimson Papers; Hoover, Memorandum, 23 December 1932, HHPP, Box 156; [Felix Frankfurter?], Memorandum, 4 January 1933, Feis Papers, Box 16; for Lamont's letter and views, see Thomas W. Lamont to Roosevelt, 4 January 1933, Thomas W. Lamont Papers, Box 127; [Lamont?], "A Possible Approach to the War Debt Problem," [late December 1932?], ibid., Box 135; Lamont, "The Problem of the War Debts," January 1933, ibid., Box 136; Rosen, *Brains Trust*, pp. 362–79.

11. Freidel, *Franklin D. Roosevelt*, 4:102–13, 142–47; Tugwell Diary, 25, 26, 27, 29 December 1932, early January 1933.

12. France, Ministère des Affaires Etrangères, *Documents diplomatiques français, 1932–1939*, Series 1, 2:414–17 (hereafter cited as DDF); for matters regarding the war debts, see also, pp. 309–10, 344–45, 353–54, 556.

Roosevelt's willingness to consult with Stimson was another indication that the president-elect had not yet decided upon an exclusively nationalist road to recovery. During a long conversation at Hyde Park on 9 January, Stimson carefully explained the reasons for linking the revision of the war debt settlements with the preparations for the economic conference. Since Stimson felt that Roosevelt had demonstrated incredible naiveté in rejecting Hoover's proposals, the secretary emphasized the psychological importance of the war debts as an obstacle to progress at the economic conference. He warned Roosevelt that Britain was unlikely to agree to the stabilization of sterling without a prior accord on the war debts. The president-elect restated his opposition to the appointment of a commission like the one recommended by Hoover. But Roosevelt indicated that he would be willing to carry on private talks with prominent individuals from Great Britain and other debtor nations.[13]

Stimson returned to Washington pleased by his meeting with Roosevelt. The secretary presented the president-elect's views to Hoover and inquired whether it might be possible to accommodate Roosevelt's desire to confer with representatives of debtor nations. Initially, Hoover voiced strong misgivings. But after a few days he decided to turn the question over to the president-elect. If Roosevelt wished, Hoover was willing to invite a British delegation to the United States to begin talks with the new administration as soon as it assumed office. Yet Hoover emphasized that the debts should not be divorced from other issues lest the United States lose an opportunity to secure desirable concessions in related areas.[14]

Stimson immediately phoned Roosevelt and asked whether Hoover's ideas were acceptable. The secretary reiterated that the war debts could be used as a lever to secure the stabilization of foreign currencies and could therefore play an important role in raising domestic and world prices. Unless the incoming administration intended to join in the race for national inflation, Stimson stressed that the war debts should not be abandoned without reciprocal concessions. Asserting that he did not want to become involved in competitive devaluations, Roosevelt agreed with the secretary's orientation. Accordingly, the president-

13. Diary of Henry L. Stimson, 9 January 1933, Stimson Papers; for Stimson's previous appraisal of Roosevelt's position, see Diary of Henry L. Stimson, 20 December 1933, ibid.
14. Diary of Henry L. Stimson, 9–13 January 1933, ibid.; Hoover, Memorandum for the secretary of state, 10 January 1933, HHPP, Box 29; Hoover, Memorandum, 15 January 1933, ibid.

elect decided to meet with Hoover on 20 January to draft an invitation to the British regarding the conduct of preliminary talks over the war debts and the economic conference.[15]

As Roosevelt listened more attentively to the views of Stimson, Davis, Frankfurter, and others who believed in the importance of international as well as domestic initiatives, Moley worried that he was losing his influence with the president-elect. He had not been consulted when Roosevelt arranged his first interview with Stimson, and he did not understand why the Department of State had been offered to Hull. "Hull's approach to economic problems," Moley subsequently wrote, "was completely contrary to the proposed New Deal policy of placing emphasis on domestic recovery." The point of course was that Roosevelt was not nearly so certain as Moley about the orientation of his administration. Hence, Moley endeavored to reassert his influence and prevent a deal on the war debts that would arouse domestic controversy and jeopardize his internal proposals.[16]

When Roosevelt journeyed to Washington for his talks with Stimson and Hoover on 19 and 20 January, Moley was ready to use his influence to dissuade the president-elect from linking the war debts to other issues. Moley bitterly assailed Norman Davis for prodding Roosevelt in this direction. Roosevelt's chief adviser accused Davis of conspiring with the Republicans to cancel the war debts, entrap the incoming administration, and create a deadlock between Roosevelt and Congress.[17] At the White House meeting on 20 January, Moley insisted that the war debt negotiations be kept distinct from all other economic issues. He wanted to prevent the slightest intimation that concessions would be made on the war debts in return for the stabilization of sterling. Though Moley boldly asserted his point of view, Roosevelt equivocated. Stimson became irritated and asked the president-elect if he favored a quid pro quo approach to the war debt issue. Roosevelt favored such an approach and added that the two issues were twins, that talks about each should go on separately, and that resolution of each issue should be conditioned on resolution of the other.

Stimson found Roosevelt's a fuzzy position, but Hoover worked out a compromise. The British would be informed in separate sentences

15. Diary of Henry L. Stimson, 15 January 1933, Stimson Papers; see also Stimson, Memorandum, 15 January 1933, HHPP, Box 29; Feis to Frankfurter, 15 January 1933, Feis Papers, Box 33.

16. For the quotation, see Moley, *New Deal*, pp. 91–92; see also, pp. 42–61, 341; Raymond Moley, Oral History Interview, 13 November 1967, pp. 3–7, Herbert Hoover Presidential Library.

17. Moley, *New Deal*, pp. 49–53; Tugwell Diary, 17, 22 January 1933.

that the incoming administration would be willing to discuss debts and other pertinent economic problems. Roosevelt consented to Hoover's plan. As far as the president-elect was concerned, Stimson could personally inform the British that the new administration considered the war debt and stabilization issues "indissolvable." The secretary's task, therefore, was to tell the British ambassador that Roosevelt was ready to receive a British delegation to discuss the war debts in early March. In the course of these discussions Roosevelt expected to raise other issues and secure a quid pro quo for American concessions on the war debts.[18]

When Roosevelt and Moley departed, Stimson, Hoover, and Mills tried to draw up an *aide-mémoire* for the British ambassador. Stimson phoned Roosevelt for his approval just as he was leaving for Warm Springs, Georgia. Now, however, the president-elect emphasized the importance of keeping the two issues separate and avoiding a commitment on the debts. He offered to send Moley to the State Department to help draft the diplomatic note. When Moley arrived, he insisted that the British be informed that forthcoming negotiations on war debts would be kept separate from other economic issues. Stimson was furious but eventually capitulated.[19]

Moley thought he had won an enormous victory. He immediately tried to capitalize upon it and asked Roosevelt if he could take charge of foreign economic policy. When Roosevelt consented, Moley assigned the task of preparing for the talks with Britain to Tugwell. Moley felt confident that he had regained his influence with Roosevelt and that a firm decision had been made to subordinate international initiatives and concentrate on domestic priorities. Moley showed no interest in exploring whether his own ill-defined domestic plans could be reconciled with a constructive international program.[20] When Tugwell put together a group of experts, including Walter W. Stewart and James Paul Warburg, to study international economic and financial problems, one of the first things they wanted to know was the Democrats' blueprint for domestic rehabilitation. Neither Stewart nor Warburg was irrevocably opposed to inflationary policies or to a departure

18. For the meeting at the White House, see Diary of Henry L. Stimson, 20 January 1933, Stimson Papers; Hoover, "Conference on January 20, 1933, between President Hoover and Governor Roosevelt," HHPP, Box 29; Moley, *After Seven Years*, pp. 97–101; Tugwell Diary, 22 January 1933. The word indissolvable is from the Hoover memorandum.
19. Tugwell Diary, 22 January 1933; Diary of Henry L. Stimson, 20 January 1933, Stimson Papers; Moley, *New Deal*, pp. 54–58.
20. Moley, *New Deal*, pp. 59–61; Tugwell Diary, 23 January 1933.

from the gold standard. But they emphasized that it was useless to study foreign policy options until they were informed of Roosevelt's domestic priorities. Stewart and Warburg tried without success to discern the outlines of future policy. Tugwell became perplexed and frustrated; Moley was unable or unwilling to tell him what the president-elect was contemplating.[21]

Roosevelt was not talking because his mind was not made up. Moley was mistaken when he concluded that he had won Roosevelt over to a nationalist strategy. Ironically, while Moley was celebrating his triumph over the internationalists, William C. Bullitt, Roosevelt's secret envoy, was visiting London and Paris reassuring British and French leaders of Roosevelt's desire to cooperate with them.[22] From Warm Springs the president-elect advised Stimson against sending a tough diplomatic note to the French government demanding payment of the December installment. Roosevelt did not want to "kick the French in the eye" and foreclose the possibility of future collaboration on international monetary and commercial issues.[23] On 29 January Roosevelt met with Ronald Lindsay, the British ambassador. The president-elect stated that he looked forward to arranging a comprehensive settlement with Britain and that he wanted to meet with leading British statesmen immediately after his inauguration. Roosevelt told the ambassador that he was contemplating cancellation of all interest payments and that he cared little about the legality of the debt issue or the capacity of the debtor nations to pay. When Lindsay explained that Britain had to have a debt settlement that complemented the Lausanne accords, Roosevelt stressed the domestic political constraints that restricted his flexibility. Nevertheless, he described his desire to increase trade, effect a silver agreement, limit armaments, and arrange a political accommodation in Europe. Roosevelt sounded like a man who had important differences with the British but who desired to reconcile those differences and cooperate in a comprehensive effort to foster European stability, increase world prices, and expedite America's recovery.[24]

21. Tugwell Diary, 23 January–10 February 1933; James Paul Warburg Oral History Memoir and Diary, January and February 1933, pp. 67–91; James Paul Warburg, *The Long Road Home*, pp. 106–13.

22. William C. Bullitt, *For the President, Personal and Secret*, pp. 26–28.

23. See Memoranda of phone conversations between Stimson and Roosevelt, between Stimson and Moley, and between Harvey Bundy and Moley, 17, 24–27 January 1933, General Records of the Department of State, RG 59, File 800.51W89/676 1/7–6/7; see also Diary of Henry L. Stimson, 24–31 January 1933, Stimson Papers; Roosevelt to Stimson, 27 January 1933, RG 59, 800.51W89 France/835.

24. Great Britain, Foreign Office, *Documents on British Foreign Policy*, Series 2, 5:748–51 (hereafter cited as DBFP).

Yet, Roosevelt did not prepare for the task that lay ahead of him. On 3 February he told Stimson that he wanted to begin discussions with the British in early March on matters pertaining to tariffs, gold, disarmament, and exchange controls. Stimson emphasized that these were enormously complicated topics that required exhaustive study. He warned Roosevelt to take matters more seriously and urged him to designate individuals who could prepare themselves for the forthcoming negotiations. The secretary was eager to provide appropriate information and to help in every way possible. But Roosevelt departed the following day for an extended yacht cruise without indicating to Moley or Tugwell the direction he wanted their foreign policy studies to take.[25]

Since Moley was not interested in foreign policy, Tugwell was left to face his group of experts without instructions. He quickly became exasperated and was pleased when Moley put Bernard Baruch in charge of the foreign policy preparations. But when Tugwell talked to Baruch on 12 February, he found that the renowned financier did not know what needed to be done. Baruch asked Tugwell to prepare the background studies. Tugwell agreed, but Moley instructed him to "keep clear" of the State Department, except for informal talks with Feis. Warburg was also ordered not to consult with members of the incumbent administration, with anyone associated with Morgan and Company, or with anyone at the FRBNY. By 15 February Tugwell was so frustrated that he decided not to proceed without better authorization. Everyone waited for the president-elect to return to New York.[26]

While Roosevelt had been sailing for ten days with Vincent Astor, the financial situation had taken a dramatic turn for the worse. Hoover had become panicky. For the first time, on 18 February he asked Roosevelt directly to reassure the nation that he would balance the budget, maintain the government's credit, and refrain from inflationary policies. Although Hoover thought that he was asking the president-elect to abandon "90% of the so-called new deal,"[27] he was actually overestimating the extent to which Roosevelt had made up his mind about future policy. At the time the president-elect was firmly wed to a conservative fiscal policy and had every intention of balancing the budget. As far as monetary policy was concerned, Roosevelt was

25. For the Stimson-Roosevelt exchange, see Diary of Henry L. Stimson, 3 February 1933, Stimson Papers; for the subsequent foreign policy preparations by Tugwell, see Tugwell Diary, February 1933.
26. Tugwell Diary, 4–15 February 1933; Warburg Diary, 7 February 1933, p. 87.
27. Herbert C. Hoover, *The Hoover Administration*, pp. 338–41.

considering embargoing gold and implementing inflationary measures, but his mind was not made up. On 23 February he met with the group of experts working on international issues and remained noncommittal. Even Feis, then an enthusiastic supporter of Roosevelt's, acknowledged that "a certain amount of uncertainty overshadowed the sense of purpose in this meeting."[28]

Roosevelt had not resolved to embark upon an independent and nationalistic monetary policy. On 17 February, the day before he received Hoover's letter, the president-elect had asked to see Emmanuel Monick, the French financial attaché. Obviously worried about the deteriorating conditions at home and abroad, Roosevelt told Monick that the future of western civilization depended on close cooperation between the three great democracies. The president-elect maintained that French and American views on monetary and economic matters were so similar that he could foresee the two nations standing side by side during future negotiations. Clearly, Roosevelt not only shared the French view on the importance of currency stabilization and the restoration of the gold standard but also wanted their help in putting pressure on the British to stabilize the pound. Roosevelt's views became more apparent a few days later when he talked separately with the British and French ambassadors. Roosevelt's conversation with Lindsay did not approach the warmth, cordiality, and sincerity of his conversation with Claudel. This discrepancy could only be explained by the contrasting French and British views on currency stabilization. Claudel was exhilarated as Roosevelt outlined the possibility of cooperating on commercial, monetary, and disarmament problems. The French ambassador informed the Quai d'Orsay, the French Foreign Ministry, that the ideas of Wilsonian internationalists would finally be implemented.[29]

Roosevelt's rhetoric, however, was not accompanied by systematic preparation. Tugwell's group of experts more or less disbanded when Baruch departed to attend to other matters. Warburg became so discouraged by the absence of leadership that he considered breaking off his relationship with the incoming administration. Roosevelt asked Tugwell to brief Hull on policy developments, but the president-elect did not meet with the secretary designate. Thus when Hull met with the British and French ambassadors on 27 February, they found him

28. For Roosevelt's thoughts and actions during the interregnum, see Freidel, *Franklin D. Roosevelt*, 4:3–195. Freidel accurately describes the ambivalence in Roosevelt's thinking and then tries to impose a greater degree of consistency than existed at the time. For the quotation, see Feis to Frankfurter, 23 February 1933, Feis Papers, Box 16; see also Warburg Diary, mid-February, pp. 90–91.

29. DDF, 1, 2:651–53, 684–86, 670–71; DBFP, 2, 5:770–71.

anxious to promote international cooperation but poorly informed of Roosevelt's plans. Hull admitted to Stimson that he did not know Roosevelt's intentions, and he appealed for help. Stimson bemoaned the fact that so much time had been lost in preparing the transition. Everything was disorganized; the department was in a state of upheaval; the banks were closing; the crisis seemed unparalleled; and still, the future course of American policy toward France and western Europe was hardly discernible.[30]

For almost four months Roosevelt refused to collaborate with the outgoing administration. At the same time, he failed to establish an orderly decision-making process and neglected to give direction to the foreign policy studies undertaken by Tugwell. The president-elect did not analyze how his internationalist inclinations might be reconciled with internal economic pressures and domestic political considerations. Initially, he simply wished to keep his options open. But by mid-January, rather than appraising the merits of the options before him, he began to vacillate, sometimes listening to Moley, sometimes to Stimson, always a bit inscrutable about his own intentions. By allowing Moley to oversee foreign economic policy, Roosevelt compounded his own problems. Moley did not sympathize with the internationalist predilections of the president-elect and made no attempt to explore the feasibility of reconciling Roosevelt's domestic and foreign policy goals.[31]

The explanation of Roosevelt's behavior rests within his personality and style of leadership. He was not inclined to think through complex problems in a systematic fashion. His habitual manner was to accept conflicting advice. His exuberant self-confidence and ingratiating optimism led him to believe that he could always work out a tactful compromise or an expedient solution when the crunch came.[32] Thus during the interregnum when he was not obligated to determine a

30. Tugwell Diary, 26, 27 February 1933; Warburg Diary, late February 1933, pp. 90–91; Diary of Henry L. Stimson, 25 February–3 March 1933, Stimson Papers; DDF, 1, 2:702–3; DBFP, 2, 5:773–75; for Roosevelt's uncertain course and his refusal to act during the February crisis, see also Freidel, *Franklin D. Roosevelt*, 4:182–95.

31. For Moley's xenophobic nationalism, see Warburg, *Long Road Home*, pp. 113–16; Herbert Feis, *1933*, pp. 100–3; Tugwell Diary, [early January 1933], 7, 13 February 1933; for a more favorable view of Moley's "intranationalism," see Rosen, *Brains Trust*, pp. 148–49, 348–49, 363–80.

32. This view of Roosevelt is based upon my reading of some of the major works on the New Deal, especially Freidel, *Franklin D. Roosevelt*; William E. Leuchtenburg, *Franklin D. Roosevelt and the New Deal*; James MacGregor Burns, *Roosevelt*; Arthur M. Schlesinger, Jr., *The Age of Roosevelt*; Ellis Hawley, *The New Deal and the Problem of Monopoly, 1933–1939*; Paul K. Conkin, *The New Deal*; Rexford G. Tugwell, *The Democratic Roosevelt*.

course of policy and when his usual approach to policymaking was reinforced by his distrust and dislike for Hoover, he was more than happy to defer tough decisions. Meanwhile, he engendered enormous hopes, at least in France, of a new era of unparalleled cooperation.[33]

This is not to say that if Roosevelt had accepted the approach advocated by Hoover and Stimson he would have been able to harmonize his domestic and foreign policies. Nationalist and autarchic pressures throughout Europe and the British Empire as well as in the United States reduced the prospects for international cooperation. But systematic preparation and preliminary negotiation might have clarified options, eliminated erroneous impressions, and avoided exaggerated expectations. The French, for example, were willing to make concessions to the United States, especially on commercial matters. But their minimum demand was a debt settlement that did not jeopardize the Lausanne accords. The British felt even more strongly than the French about preserving the reparations agreement. In addition, they refused to stabilize the pound without prior assurances regarding the reduction of tariffs, the lifting of exchange controls, the resumption of foreign lending, and the better distribution of gold reserves.

The French and British positions were tough but not inflexible. In late January Day and Williams returned from the second preparatory meeting considerably encouraged about the prospects for the economic conference. Similarly, Governor Harrison of the FRBNY believed that the evolving British position opened up the possibility for eventual agreement. Both the French and British had considerable incentive to seek accord with the United States. The accession to power of the Nazis impelled the French government of the Cartel des Gauches to try to revive the coalition that had triumphed over Germany in 1918. Likewise, the possibility of a currency war with the United States continually induced the British to study ways of resolving their differences with the Americans.[34]

Had Roosevelt agreed to preliminary negotiations or ordered his

33. For the hopes engendered in France, see, for example, DDF, 1, 2:293–96, 309–10, 341–42, 344–45, 353–54, 505–8, 556, 614–16, 651–53, 684–86; see also "France's Roosevelt Expectations," *Literary Digest* 115 (21 January 1933):13.

34. For the French and British positions elucidated in this paragraph and the preceding one, see DDF, 1, 2:328–30, 356–57, 386–87, 516–19, 658–59, 665–68, 700–1, 793–94; 3:1–12; DBFP, 2, 5:753–69; Andrew W. Mellon to Stimson, 2 February 1933, RG 59, 841.51/1137; Frederick M. Sackett to Stimson, 9 February 1933, ibid., 841.51/1140; John H. Fuqua, "The British Attitude Towards a Return to the Gold Standard," 23 March 1933, ibid., 841.51/1147; for the views of Day and Williams, see Diary of Henry L. Stimson, 31 January 1933, Stimson Papers; for Harrison's opinion, see George L. Harrison to Feis, 9 February 1933, Feis Papers, Box 17.

advisers to prepare more thoroughly, he would have better understood the problems inherent in reconciling his domestic objectives with a cooperative approach toward international recovery. As it was he let events take their course.[35] When he assumed office, he was confronted with an unparalleled crisis at home and a worsening situation abroad. On 4 March, the day of his inauguration, most domestic banks were closed. The following day Hitler was given full powers to govern by decree. The American people awaited vigorous leadership that would extricate the country from the Great Depression. The French government awaited international initiatives that would confirm Roosevelt's Wilsonian heritage. If Roosevelt were to fulfill the divergent expectations as he hoped to do, he would have to move quickly on both the national and international fronts.

Policymaking in the Early New Deal

When Roosevelt took office, he was determined to assert bold leadership.[36] He immediately submitted banking and economy bills to a specially convened session of Congress. Although the legislative proposals conferred upon the president unprecedented powers to deal with the banking crisis, regulate gold exports, and cut expenditures, they were quickly passed by both houses of Congress. As Roosevelt had anticipated, his readiness to act rapidly met with almost universal approval. Even the business community, demoralized and dispirited, was prepared to follow the lead of a confident and self-assured president.[37]

In his inaugural address Roosevelt emphasized that internal imperatives had to assume priority, at least temporarily, over international questions.[38] Once the economy and banking bills were passed, the question before the administration was what to do next. Everyone concurred that there had to be a rise in prices, but the question was how to bring higher prices about. Moley pressed for "action on many [domestic] fronts" to inspire confidence and release the natural forces of recovery. Tugwell advocated the importance of structural domestic

35. Freidel, *Franklin D. Roosevelt*, 4:175–95; Tugwell, *In Search of Roosevelt*, p. 217; Tugwell Diary, 29 January 1933.

36. See his inaugural address in Roosevelt, *Public Papers*, 2:11–15.

37. For Roosevelt's actions, see Freidel, *Franklin D. Roosevelt*, 4:196–254; Leuchtenburg, *Franklin D. Roosevelt*, pp. 41–48; Schlesinger, *Age of Roosevelt*, 2:1–13; Susan Estabrook Kennedy, *The Banking Crisis of 1933*, pp. 152–78; for the reaction to Roosevelt's initial actions, see "Business Looks at Roosevelt," *Business Week*, 1 March 1933, p. 1; "Sledge Hammer Blows at the Depression," *Literary Digest* 115 (25 March 1933):3.

38. Roosevelt, *Public Papers*, 2:13–14.

reforms. But some leading members of the administration believed that prices would not rise without initiatives to promote European and world stability. If the prices of key commodities like wheat, cotton, copper, and silver were set in international markets and affected by the value of sterling, as export-oriented businessmen, international bankers, and Republican officials had always insisted, domestic initiatives alone could not do the job. Thus Hull, Feis, Davis, and Bullitt pushed for reciprocal tariff concessions, lifting of exchange restrictions, stabilization of sterling, and limitation of armaments. Warburg and Douglas supported these international initiatives but insisted that they be reconciled with domestic measures to expand credit, rehabilitate industry, increase public works, and revive lending. Uncertain how to proceed Roosevelt let his advisers embark in different directions and explore divergent approaches. The emphasis was on speed, movement, quick answers, and pragmatic solutions.[39]

The president was still vacillating. On the one hand he decided to keep Congress in session. Responding to the wave of enthusiasm that greeted his proposals and recognizing the unique opportunity that awaited him, Roosevelt chose to move ahead on the home front. He submitted a farm bill and assigned priority to the passage of legislation on securities regulation, banking reform, railroad rehabilitation, and regional planning in the Tennessee valley.[40] At the same time, he called in the British and French ambassadors. Expressing his deep concern over developments in Germany, Roosevelt intimated his belief that Hitler was a madman and reaffirmed his interest in fostering European stability. He suggested that MacDonald and Herriot come to Washington to engage in preliminary talks prior to the economic conference. He believed that visits by foreign dignitaries might influence public opinion and enable him to take a more flexible stand on the war debts. As another indication of his belief in the importance of international initiatives, in early April Roosevelt announced his intent to ask Congress for new trade legislation.[41]

39. For Moley's views, see Moley, *New Deal*, pp. 338–39, 355–56; for Tugwell's views see, for example, Tugwell, *In Search of Roosevelt*, pp. 222–24, 230 ff.; for the views of the "internationalists," see Warburg Diary, March and April 1933, vols. 2 and 3; for the absence of any overall planning during the special session of Congress, see Moley, *New Deal*, pp. 338–39; Tugwell, *Democratic Roosevelt*, pp. 261–62, 273–74; Freidel, *Franklin D. Roosevelt*, 4:300–8. All writers agree on the pragmatic bent of Roosevelt's leadership. For basically sympathetic accounts, see those by Schlesinger and Freidel. For accounts that highlight some of the confusion and inconsistencies, see the volumes by Hawley and Conkin.

40. Freidel, *Roosevelt*, 4:300–19; Warburg Diary, 4 April 1933.

41. For Roosevelt's talks with the French and British ambassadors, see DDF, 1,

Claudel's reports on his first encounters with Roosevelt, Hull, and other leading Democratic officials were enthusiastic. On 10 March he informed the Quai d'Orsay that domestic issues were temporarily taking precedence in the United States but that France had a unique opportunity to reap American goodwill and reconcile important policy differences with the United States government. A week later, after speaking to the president, Claudel wrote reassuringly that his earlier impressions of Roosevelt's sympathetic understanding of France's problems had been confirmed. The prospect was real, he reported, that the United States would sign a consultative pact, join the World Court, and modify its demands for immediate French disarmament. In addition, Claudel felt that America might reduce her tariffs, suspend the June debt installment, and support France on the question of currency stabilization. In light of these possibilities Claudel exhorted Foreign Minister Paul-Boncour to arrange for payment of the December debt installment. What France refused to give to Hoover, Claudel emphasized, she might give to Roosevelt; what France denied to a prosperous America, she might relinquish to an impoverished America.[42]

Premier Edouard Daladier and Paul-Boncour wished to reciprocate Roosevelt's assertions of goodwill for France. The Frenchmen were eager to enter into preliminary talks with the president and encouraged the British to do likewise. The French appointed André de Laboulaye ambassador to the United States because of his earlier friendship with the Roosevelt family. Although Herriot had reservations about undertaking a mission to the United States, he agreed to make the trip.[43] In addition, Paul-Boncour and Daladier examined the possibility of paying the December installment. When the Socialists objected and Laval and Tardieu protested, Paul-Boncour indicated that he needed new assurances of future American generosity before he could get the Chamber of Deputies to go along with him. The French government, therefore, despite serious parliamentary problems, earnestly wished to establish close ties with the new Democratic administration.[44]

2:770, 823; 3:94, 148–49; DBFP, 5:776–78, 781–88; Freidel, *Franklin D. Roosevelt*, 4:374–77; for his allusion to trade legislation, see p. 316.

42. DDF, 1, 2:735–36, 767, 771; 3:94, 148–49.

43. Ibid., 3:132–33, 137, 220; J. Theodore Marriner to Cordell Hull, 5 April 1933, RG 59, 800.51W89 France/871; for the appointment of de Laboulaye, see Joseph Paul-Boncour, *Entre deux guerres*, 2:377; for Herriot's reservations and anxieties, see Marriner to Hull, 8 April 1933, RG 59, 550.S1 Washington/359; Memorandum of conversation between Edouard Herriot and Davis, 13 April 1933, Davis Papers, Box 9.

44. For the Daladier ministry's reassessment of the debt issue, see DDF, 1, 2:739–40; 3:98–100; Marriner to Hull, 13, 15 March 1933, RG 59, 800.51W89 France/860, 885;

Meanwhile, the domestic crisis and pressures within the United States made it difficult for Roosevelt to establish an orderly policy-making process that reconciled his assertions of goodwill toward France with his domestic programs. Improvising as he went along in the domestic and foreign spheres, Roosevelt generally did not confide in either Secretary of State Hull or Undersecretary of State William Phillips. As a result both of these men resented Moley, who had been appointed assistant secretary of state, and who they believed was privy to the president's secret wishes. Moley cultivated this image, took control of foreign economic policy from his nominal superiors, and occasionally kept important information from them. But Moley was much more concerned with domestic developments. He therefore allowed Warburg, Feis, and Bullitt to do most of the work regarding financial, commercial, and political relations with Europe. He did not, however, provide them with guidelines on what needed to be done, and he often treated them and their work cavalierly.[45]

Feis and Warburg grew increasingly frustrated as they sought to conduct informal talks with French and British diplomats without the explicit support of their superiors.[46] Their problems were complicated by the technical nature of the discussions on monetary stabilization, exchange controls, commercial restrictions, central bank policy, and war debt revision. Feis and Warburg needed considerable expert advice. Yet Moley and Roosevelt still forbade Warburg from consulting with either George Harrison of the FRBNY or Arthur A. Ballantine, former undersecretary of the treasury. Warburg sought help in Roosevelt's Treasury Department, but no one there had been put in charge of international financial questions. Secretary William Woodin tried to help, but he did not really grasp the intricate nature of the problems. Likewise, although Hull supported Feis's attempts to expand trade, he made no systematic effort to counter the protectionist forces within the administration. Nor was Hull able to provide concrete suggestions on how to handle the formidable problems that lay ahead. On 3 April Feis

---

for the opposition, see Tardieu, "Les Six Jours," *L'Illustration*, 29 April 1933, ibid., 500.S1 Washington/412; Memorandum of conversation between Davis and Pierre Laval, 11 April 1933, Davis Papers, Box 9.

45. For Moley's influence on the decision-making process, see Warburg Diary, 10, 24, 25, 29 March, 7 April 1933, pp. 137–41, 220–21, 223, 226–28, 247–48, 280, 387; see also Feis to Schlesinger, 24 December 1958, and Schlesinger to Feis, 8 January 1959, Feis Papers, Box 26; Feis to Frankfurter, 17 April 1933, Frankfurter Papers, Box 54; Feis, *1933*, 99–103, 110–11.

46. Warburg Diary, 24, 25, 28, 30 March 1933, pp. 223, 244, 272–78, 303–10; Feis to W. Walton Butterworth, 30 March 1933, Feis Papers, Box 12.

confided to Frankfurter that, as far as the preparations for the economic conference were concerned, "there could hardly be worse difficulty and confusion than exists."[47]

Nevertheless, Warburg, Feis, and Bullitt were intent on going as far as they could to make the forthcoming conference a success. In late March they began informal discussions with French and British diplomats over the outlines of a comprehensive plan to stimulate world economic recovery.[48] Feis worked mostly on commercial matters. He developed a program calling for the conclusion of a tariff truce, the reduction of tariffs by approximately 10 percent through multilateral action, and the negotiation of bilateral treaties based on the unconditional most-favored-nation principle. The general objectives of Feis's program were to link the principles of reciprocity and equality, cut American customs duties by executive agreement, and eliminate all discriminatory practices, including quotas, subsidies, and license agreements. Warburg and Hull were pleased by Feis's efforts, but Moley's reaction was ambivalent.[49] Since everyone agreed, however, that the expansion of world trade depended upon monetary stabilization, that issue quickly took precedence over commercial matters.[50]

Although Warburg had no formal position in the administration, he was asked by Moley to take charge of international financial questions. Warburg was not able to ascertain what type of program Moley wanted him to devise; so he worked out a plan that he believed was in accord with the president's desire to increase prices. Warburg recommended the development of a uniform, but lower, legal reserve ratio in order to expand credit. He advocated inclusion of limited amounts of silver in bullion reserves to raise the price of silver. He called for uniform buying and selling points for gold, with a spread of about .5 percent, to prevent the constant and often irrational movement of the precious metal. He urged formulation of a coordinated policy among central banks to insure the availability of sufficient credit and synchronization of government expenditure programs to rehabilitate depressed industries. Warburg also believed that it was important to restore the gold

47. Feis to Frankfurter, 3 April 1933, Feis Papers, Box 16; see also Warburg Diary, 15, 30 March, 3, 7, 11 April 1933, pp. 154, 156, 310, 313–14, 345, 387, 438; Feis, *1933*, pp. 98–99.
48. Warburg Diary, 23, 28, 29 March 1933, pp. 208–9, 272, 280–83; Feis to Frankfurter, 3 April 1933, Feis Papers, Box 16.
49. For Feis's work and the reaction to it, see Warburg Diary, 27 March, 7, 10, 11 April 1933, pp. 261, 388–89, 417–19, 433–36; Moley, *New Deal*, pp. 355–56; see also Meeting of Interdepartmental Reciprocity Group, 1 March 1933, RG 59, 611.0031/428.
50. Warburg Diary, 10 April 1933, p. 419.

standard in some form and to remove exchange controls. Yet, his ideas on these issues were not rigid, and he recommended that the United States temporarily maintain its embargo on gold shipments, establish a stabilization fund, and allow the dollar to weaken somewhat in relation to sterling. He believed that these actions would induce the British to agree to currency stabilization, which he viewed as prerequisite to the expansion of commerce.[51]

When Warburg began discussing his program with Kenneth Bewley and Emmanuel Monick, the British and French financial attachés, he was delighted that there existed substantial areas of agreement.[52] Warburg quickly recognized, however, that no accord could be reached with Britain and France on a cooperative international economic and monetary program unless the debt issue was resolved. On 12 April he and Monick sat down to tackle this problem. Warburg's plan called for a reaffirmation of the amount of principal that made up the war debts and the cancellation of interest on the debts. It advocated the determination of the present value of future payments at an agreed-upon interest base and the mobilization of the present value for immediate use in the United States. Everyone who studied the plan considered it ingenious. It was a means, Warburg noted, "of financing a debt rather than paying it off. It was a method of mobilizing a debt—making the proceeds available to the creditor, without making the debtor put cash on the barrel-head." Because the plan looked better than it was and therefore might have appealed to Congress, Warburg liked to call it his "bunny." Moley, Feis, Hull, and Bullitt were enthusiastic about it. Senator Key Pittman, chairman of the Senate Foreign Relations Committee, maintained that Congress would accept it.[53]

While Warburg and Feis were hard at work preparing recommendations on financial and commercial matters, Roosevelt appointed Norman Davis chairman of the American delegation to the disarmament conference. Davis returned to Europe in late March and carried on exploratory talks in London, Paris, and Berlin. He still hoped to establish a basis for concluding a disarmament accord. He assumed that

51. Ibid., 24, 28, 30 March, 2, 3, 7, 17 April 1933, pp. 223, 277, 280–83, 303–12, 318–19, 331–42, 352, 390–93, 489–90; see also Franklin D. Roosevelt, *Franklin D. Roosevelt and Foreign Affairs*, 1:35–39.
52. Warburg Diary, 28 March, 12 April 1933, pp. 271–72, 441; see also Feis to Frankfurter, 3 April 1933, Feis Papers, Box 16.
53. For the detailed formulation of the bunny, see Warburg Diary, 12 April 1933, pp. 440–49; for the quotation, see p. 448; for the reaction to the plan, see ibid., 13, 14, 17 April 1933, pp. 454, 460–61, 479, 481; see also Feis to Frankfurter, 17 April 1933, Frankfurter Papers, Box 54.

Hitler's accession to power did not fundamentally alter the European situation and looked sympathetically upon MacDonald's disarmament plan and Mussolini's four-power proposal. Davis concluded that the major roadblock to a disarmament accord remained France's preoccupation with security.[54]

Yet, Davis reported that Daladier's security demands were in transition. The French premier realized that without an agreement Germany would rearm, the British and Americans would blame France for the failure of the conference, and the French would be left alone to deal with Germany at a time when France's growing financial problems precluded large-scale rearmament. As a result there was reason for Daladier to gamble on a disarmament agreement, provided that it included effective enforcement procedures and allowed France to rearm as soon as German violations were reported. With such an agreement, France's prevailing arms superiority over Germany would not be greatly jeopardized. In the meantime France would have tested Germany's true intentions and earned Anglo-American goodwill. Given this evolving attitude, Davis believed that France would be more flexible about the type of guarantees she wanted. On the eve of Herriot's and MacDonald's visits, Davis stressed that the United States could make a substantial contribution to the European political situation by agreeing to consult in times of crisis and by renouncing the rights of neutrality when European nations were acting collectively to deter aggression. These recommendations were supported by other career diplomats in Europe and were endorsed by Stimson, whose advice Hull solicited.[55]

The work of Davis, Warburg, and Feis represented the continuation

54. For Davis's talks in Europe, see the numerous memoranda in Davis Papers, Box 9; see also Department of State, *Papers Relating to the Foreign Relations of the United States*, 1933, 1:79–99 (hereafter cited as FR). The MacDonald plan called for the development of consultative procedures, the standardization of armies, the quantitative and qualitative limitation of tanks and artillery, the abolition of military aircraft, the supervision of civilian aviation, the granting of juridic equality to Germany, and the extension of the London naval accords to include Italy and France. See FR, 1933, 1:43–54; for the negotiations over Mussolini's four-power proposal, see DBFP, 2, 5:358–73; for Hitler's plans and actions in the foreign policy realm, see Gerhard L. Weinberg, *The Foreign Policy of Hitler's Germany*, pp. 1–52, 159–65.

55. For Davis's reports and recommendations, see FR, 1933, 1:90–101; for French policy, see DDF, 1, 3:238–42, 262–64, 285–86, 295–96, 306–8; FR, 1933, 1:82–84; numerous Memoranda of Davis's conversations with Herriot, André François-Poncet, Laval, Paul Painlevé, Daladier, and Pierre Cot, 6, 9, 10, 11, 15, 19, 21 April 1933, Davis Papers, Box 9; for Stimson's endorsement, see Roosevelt, *Foreign Affairs*, 1:56–57; for the views of other career diplomats, see Hugh Robert Wilson, *Disarmament and the Cold War in the Thirties*, pp. 26–27; Hugh Robert Wilson, *Diplomat Between Wars*, pp. 284–87; FR, 1933, 1:31–33.

of American efforts to contribute to European stability without incurring strategic commitments or compromising domestic priorities. Even the internationalists in the Roosevelt administration were opposed to the assumption of contractual military obligations to preserve peace and stability. Davis emphasized that his recommendations did not imply strategic commitments. Hull, Warburg, and Bullitt were sympathetic to the idea of consultation but were intent on remaining aloof from European strife.[56] In a similar manner internationalist economic spokesmen in the early days of the New Deal did not want to unleash foreign policy initiatives that might jeopardize domestic economic and financial priorities. They insisted that domestic economic goals like the rise in the internal price structure could be promoted by collaborative efforts in the international realm. Warburg fashioned his monetary proposals in a way that provided for moderate depreciation of the dollar, the undertaking of a large public works program, and implementation of an easy credit policy. Similarly, his complex proposal for dealing with the debts was aimed at insuring that "the principal amounts of the foreign debts are immediately made available to the United States government to spend in whatever way it sees fit to combat the depression or, if it so chooses, to retire existing debt."[57]

The striking characteristic of the Warburg, Feis, and Davis proposals was their complicated and sophisticated nature. If such proposals were going to work, they required careful study and systematic refinement. If they were going to be accepted by foreign governments, exhaustive consultation among governments was necessary. If these proposals were going to be approved by Congress, a tactful campaign of political education and subtle arm twisting was essential. Proponents of these measures were well aware that their success was not assured. What continued to worry Warburg, Feis, and others was the chaotic state of the American policymaking process and the capricious manner in which Roosevelt approached key decisions.

In the weeks before MacDonald and Herriot arrived, communication among policymakers did not improve. State Department officials, including Warburg, generally had access to the president only through Moley. Yet, Moley remained preoccupied with domestic affairs. He

56. For the views of Davis, Warburg, Bullitt, and Hull, see FR, 1933, 1:96–97, 124–26; Warburg Diary, 10, 21 April 1933, pp. 415, 528–29; see also Howard Jablon, "The State Department and Collective Security, 1933–1934," pp. 248–63.

57. For Warburg's views, see Warburg Diary, 12, 14, 18, 19 April 1933, pp. 444–46, 460–61, 500, 510–15; see also Feis to Frankfurter, 17 April 1933, Frankfurter Papers, Box 54.

did not take the time to study foreign policy options, became bored with technical details, and wandered off during important meetings.[58] When he arranged for the president to see his foreign economic advisers on 30 March and 4 and 13 April, Roosevelt indicated substantial accord with what they were doing and encouraged them to proceed. But the president did not ask Congress for discretionary authority to deal with the war debts and intimated that he might approve tariff increases to offset the processing taxes recommended by some of his agricultural advisers. Not surprisingly, Warburg and Feis doubted whether the president was giving serious consideration to their proposals; Moffat felt equally uneasy about the president's treatment of disarmament questions; and Bullitt regretted that the president had not capitalized upon his popularity by securing the necessary powers to resolve the war debt imbroglio.[59]

Some of the worst apprehensions of Roosevelt's foreign economic advisers were confirmed on 18 April, when the president suddenly informed them that he was taking the United States off the gold standard, allowing the dollar to depreciate, and considering various senatorial inflationary schemes. Warburg, Feis, and Douglas were troubled not so much over the departure from gold as over the prospect of uncontrolled inflation. They viewed Roosevelt's inclination to manipulate the value of the dollar with anxiety, not because they were irrevocably committed to the existing gold standard and prevailing exchange rates, but because they accurately foresaw that dollar manipulation was not likely to be effective in the long run. Considering the nation's favorable balance of payments, the dollar may have been overvalued internally (in terms of the debt burden), but it was not overvalued on the international exchanges. The president's advisers knew the fate of western civilization was not at stake, but they were deeply concerned about the prospects for the economic conference. The president had not forewarned them about this action, and their preparations had proceeded on different assumptions. Not even Moley had known the decision was forthcoming. To some of Roosevelt's loyal but skeptical advisers, it seemed another indication of his shortsighted experimentation, "monetary insouciance," and haphazard policymaking.[60]

58. Warburg, *Long Road Home*, pp. 121–22; Feis, *1933*, 100–2, 110–11; Feis to Frankfurter, 3 April 1933, Feis Papers, Box 16.

59. Warburg Diary, 29, 30 March, 4, 7, 13, 18 April 1933, pp. 280–81, 309–11, 365–68, 386, 452–54, 494; Jay Pierrepont Moffat, *The Moffat Papers*, pp. 92–93; for the possibility of tariff increases, see Freidel, *Franklin D. Roosevelt*, 4:310, 317.

60. Warburg Diary, 17, 18, 26 April 1933, pp. 490–515, 584–85; Feis, *1933*, pp. 108–31. In a letter by Arthur Schlesinger, Jr., to Feis, the renowned biographer of

Roosevelt, of course, acted in response to enormous political pressures and substantial gold losses.[61] Having taken the unanticipated step toward an independent monetary policy, he immediately tried to reassure everyone that he was not jettisoning an internationalist approach. On 19 April, he informed the press that he viewed himself as a quarterback leading his team toward one goal—a rise in commodity prices—although he did not know the order of the plays. For the present he hoped his actions would allow the dollar to find its "natural" level and thus stimulate an increase in prices. He also thought that his dramatic action would highlight the need of all nations to stabilize their currencies. Accordingly, he "absolutely" reaffirmed his intent to get the world back on a gold standard. On the same day, he met with the new French ambassador, Laboulaye. The president emphasized his interest in European affairs, his concern with the armaments conference, and his hope for reciprocal tariff reductions.[62] Roosevelt was not dissembling. He sincerely wanted to promote international cooperation while he tried to expedite domestic recovery. But by taking precipitous action, responding to immediate pressures, and foresaking careful preparation and deliberation, he was arousing concern about his ability to reconcile his internationalist inclinations with his domestic priorities.[63] With MacDonald and Herriot scheduled to arrive during the last week in April, however, the president still had an opportunity to delineate an effective international program.

The MacDonald and Herriot Visits

While MacDonald and Herriot were in Washington, the president articulated an internationalist course of action. As usual he was ingratiating and full of goodwill. He especially charmed the French delegation by attempting to greet them in their native tongue.[64] Substantively, Roosevelt spent most of his time discussing disarmament matters. For the most part he put forward the views of Norman Davis. He supported

---

Roosevelt acknowledged he had underestimated the president's "monetary insouciance." See Schlesinger to Feis, 8 January 1959, Feis Papers, Box 26.

61. For Roosevelt's action, see Roosevelt, *Public Papers*, 2:166; Warburg Diary, 18 April 1933, pp. 493–500; Moley, *New Deal*, pp. 298–304; Freidel, *Franklin D. Roosevelt*, 4:320–39.

62. Roosevelt, *Public Papers*, 2:137–41; DDF, 1, 3:245–46.

63. For the reaction in France and Britain to Roosevelt's actions, see, for example, Marriner to Hull, 21 April 1933, RG 59, 800.51W89 France/880; Ray Atherton to Hull, 20 April 1933, ibid., 550.S1/674.

64. Warburg Diary, 24 April 1933, pp. 560–61.

the MacDonald plan and emphasized the need to limit offensive armaments. But to the great satisfaction of the French, the president supported implementation of effective and continuous control machinery
and agreed that the supervisory provisions of the British plan would
have to be strengthened. Moreover, Roosevelt indicated that he was
opposed to German rearmament. Most significant, he declared his
readiness to renounce American rights of neutrality when other nations
were acting collectively to deter aggression, so long as the United
States retained the right to decide independently when and where aggression had occurred. In return for these concessions Roosevelt told
Herriot that he expected progress toward the limitation of land and
naval armaments.[65]

While Roosevelt outlined a course of cooperation on disarmament
matters, he left most of the discussions on economic issues to his
advisers. To the extent that he did address himself to these matters,
however, the president demarcated a course of action in accord with
the prescriptions of his internationalist advisers. Roosevelt emphasized
his interest in arranging a tariff truce that would last for the duration of
the economic conference. He hoped such a truce would lead to a reduction in customs duties, a curtailment of commercial restrictions, and an
end to discriminatory practices.[66] Roosevelt also expressed sympathy
for war debt revision and promised MacDonald to ask Congress for
authority to deal with this problem. Roosevelt emphasized to Herriot
that a French payment of the December installment would have a
positive impact on congressional opinion.[67] In addition, the president
authorized Warburg to negotiate a tripartite de facto stabilization agreement that would temporarily hold the dollar at about a 15 percent
discount. Finally, Roosevelt endorsed Warburg's efforts to devise a
long-term program aimed at re-creating a modified gold standard, cor-
relating central bank policies, synchronizing government expenditures,
lifting exchange restrictions, reducing tariffs, and raising the price of
basic commodities, especially silver.[68]

65. Memorandum of conversation at the White House between Roosevelt, Herriot,
Laboulaye, and William Phillips, 26 April 1933, RG 59, 550.S1 Washington/38; DDF,
1, 3:314–17, 326–27, 337–38; FR, 1933, 1:102–4, 106–12. For the MacDonald disarmament plan, see n. 54 above.
66. For Roosevelt's interest in the tariff truce, see Memorandum of conversation between Herriot and Roosevelt, 27 April 1933, RG 59, 550.S1/707; "Les Entretiens de
Washington," L'Information, ibid., 550.S1 Washington/575.
67. DBFP, 2, 5:792–93; Memorandum of conversation between Roosevelt and Herriot, 27 April 1933, RG 59, 550.S1/707.
68. For Warburg's plans, including a de facto stabilization accord, and Roosevelt's
attitude, see Warburg Diary, 21–27 April 1933, pp. 525–97.

Warburg's discussions with the technical experts who accompanied MacDonald and Herriot were fruitful but inconclusive. The major problem, especially for the French, was that they had not expected to be asked to make specific commitments during their visit.[69] Nevertheless, when confronted with a depreciating dollar, they immediately sought a de facto stabilization of the pound, the dollar, and the franc. When Warburg indicated that the United States was willing to go along with de facto stabilization, provided that a large tripartite equalization fund was established to discourage speculation, the French demurred. They feared the losses that might be incurred in a common stabilization fund, especially as long as the United States refused to make commitments regarding its long-term monetary policy. In addition, the French were fearful of becoming embroiled in a dispute between the British and the Americans over the rates of stabilization. Frederick Leith-Ross, the British expert, felt that a 15 percent discount for the dollar was much too large given the favorable payments balance of the United States. But neither he nor Charles Rist, the French expert, outwardly rejected Warburg's proposal. On 26 and 27 April they indicated that their governments would take the proposal under advisement.[70]

As far as Warburg's long-term plans were concerned, however, considerable progress was made. Both Rist and Leith-Ross commented favorably on Warburg's desire to reform and revitalize the gold standard, establish uniform reserve policies, and lower the reserve ratio. They appreciated Warburg's efforts to correlate central bank policies, synchronize government expenditures, and raise the price of silver. Rist had reservations regarding the coordination of open market operations and the use of government bonds as cover for note circulation. But Warburg did not consider these reservations important in light of French willingness to alter certain restrictions in their capital market. When Rist departed on 29 April, he earnestly expressed his goodwill toward Warburg and apologized for the absence of agreement on de facto stabilization. Rist asked for the submission of a formal proposal on this matter and declared his hopes for more definitive agreements at the economic conference.[71]

Roosevelt expressed satisfaction with his talks with the British and French. In his view these conversations kept open the prospects of

69. Memorandum of conversation between Davis and Herriot, 13 April 1933, Davis Papers, Box 9.
70. DDF, 1, 3:322–23, 328, 456–57; Warburg Diary, 23, 26–29 April 1933, pp. 545, 576–77, 580–81, 590–93, 599–601, 607–10.
71. Warburg Diary, 22–29 April 1933, pp. 535–36, 551–60, 564–65, 568–69, 591–93, 600–1, 607–8.

fulfilling his foreign policy goals without foreclosing a rapid rise in domestic prices. As he met with other foreign delegations, the president released a flood of optimistic communiqués. Journalists conveyed these hopeful assessments to the public.[72] With commodity prices and stock values rising again, there was widespread public confidence in the administration. Roosevelt attributed the favorable turn in the economic tide to his departure from the gold standard. Yet, on 7 May in his second fireside chat the president acknowledged that through internal initiatives "we can get . . . a fair measure of prosperity . . . , but it will not be permanent unless we can get a return to prosperity all over the world." Roosevelt emphasized that his domestic policies had to go hand in hand with efforts to limit armaments, reduce trade barriers, stabilize currencies, and improve international relations. "The international conference," he concluded, "must succeed. The future of the world demands it."[73] Despite his rhetoric Roosevelt's handling of major issues during the next few weeks revealed his continuing inability to shape a comprehensive and consistent course.

A Period of Uncertainty

Of all the problems facing Europe, Roosevelt became most concerned about the possible failure of the disarmament conference. In late April the German delegation announced its opposition to the MacDonald plan, and in early May Baron Constantin von Neurath, the German foreign minister, indicated Germany's intent to rearm and enlarge the Reichswehr. At Geneva there was talk of the conference breaking up and of war immediately erupting. Hence, Europe anxiously awaited Hitler's forthcoming statement on German policy.[74] But before any of the European governments made a major step forward, Roosevelt intervened. First, he reaffirmed American support of the British proposals. Unwilling to allow another plan to be scuttled through endless amendments, he demonstrated considerable courage in overruling the technical objections of his own military establishment to the MacDonald plan. On 6 May Roosevelt met with Hjalmar Schacht, president of the Reichsbank, and stated his opposition to German rearmament. With much fanfare and excitement Roosevelt prepared a message for

72. For the cheerful assessments, see Moley, *New Deal*, p. 400; Roosevelt, *Foreign Affairs*, 1:87; Roosevelt, *Public Papers*, 2:145–47, 149–51; "White House Planning for a New World War," *Literary Digest* 115 (6 May 1933):7.

73. Roosevelt, *Public Papers*, 2:167.

74. There is an excellent unsigned memorandum on security and disarmament issues, 1933–36, in Box 23 of the Davis Papers that captures the atmosphere of the time.

delivery to the chiefs of state of all the major nations. On 16 May he called upon them to accept the MacDonald plan, contemplate additional steps toward disarmament, stay within present treaty limitations, and enter into a new nonaggression pact.[75]

Roosevelt's message reflected his internationalism, his desire to forestall an armaments race, and his interest in preserving European peace and stability. His action was heralded in the American press; most editors acclaimed him for assuming leadership in world affairs. Indeed, his message apparently had a restraining influence on Hitler's speech the following day. But the French immediately recognized a glaring omission in the president's grandiose gesture. He made no allusion to his earlier promises to consult in times of crisis or to revise American neutrality policy. Privately, the French were reassured that the administration was not backtracking on its previous commitments. But Roosevelt had let pass a good opportunity to educate the American people on the obligations, however limited, they had to accept to make the conference a success.[76]

Roosevelt's omission was unfortunate, because a resolution (H.J. 93) authorizing the president to impose a discretionary embargo at the outbreak of foreign hostilities was pending before the Senate Foreign Relations Committee and meeting considerable opposition. At stake was the question of whether the president would secure congressional endorsement of a policy of neutrality revision. Roosevelt, however, seemed unaware of the importance of mobilizing support for the resolution. On 10 May he appeared before a press conference, minimized the importance of consultation, and avoided all mention of neutrality revision. Although he instructed Davis to put forward the new American position at Geneva, it was still uncertain whether the president would put his own prestige and influence behind the proposals.[77] No

75. For the administration's support of the MacDonald plan, see FR, 1933, 1:124–25; for the opposition of the War and Navy departments, see C. E. Kilbourne to chief of staff, 5 June 1933, Records of the Adjutant General's Office, RG 94, Box 82; Claude Swanson to Hull, 15 June 1933, Records of the General Board of the Navy, File 438–2, Serial No. 1521–LL; for Roosevelt's talk with Schacht, see Memorandum of conversation between Roosevelt and Hjalmar Schacht, 6 May 1933, RG 59, 550.S1/408; for the president's address to world leaders, see FR, 1933, 1:143–45; see also Freidel, *Franklin D. Roosevelt*, 4:398–403.
76. For the press response, see "Mr. Roosevelt's Arms Plan to Save the World," *Literary Digest* 115 (27 May 1933):3–4; for its effect on Hitler, see FR, 1933, 1:152–53; for the French reaction, see pp. 147–48; DBFP, 2, 5:246–47, 268; Memorandum of conversation between Phillips and Laboulaye, 17 May 1933, Davis Papers, Box 21.
77. For the press conference, see Roosevelt, *Foreign Affairs*, 1:108–11; for the legislative situation, see FR, 1933, 1:365–66; for the instructions to Davis, see p. 150.

one expected Roosevelt to endorse the idea of collective security. The question was whether the president would link his advocacy of disarmament with concrete efforts to alter neutrality practices and thereby abet European security arrangements.

Along with expediting the proceedings at Geneva, Roosevelt told MacDonald and Herriot in April that he was eager to arrange an immediate tariff truce to curtail the restrictions on world commerce and increase commodity prices set in world markets. Herriot retorted that his government agreed with the principle of a tariff truce but wanted to retain the right to implement tariff legislation pending before the Chamber and to raise duties to offset the impact of foreign depreciation. Roosevelt acquiesced. Even when French objections delayed immediate implementation of the truce, the president instructed American diplomats to continue their attempts to elicit French and British approval.[78]

Though American diplomats fumed at the obstructions presented by the French and British to a tariff truce, the Roosevelt administration's actions betokened a questionable commitment to commercial liberality. In late May Feis accurately reported this paradox to Frankfurter. The president's emerging interest in the National Industrial Recovery Act (NIRA) highlighted the inconsistency between rhetoric and action. It was generally assumed, for example, that if the NIRA were enacted, tariffs would have to be increased to prevent foreign goods from underselling the artificially fixed prices of American products. Accordingly, the proposed tariff bill was revised to provide for the possible increase as well as decrease of customs duties. Indeed, the Agricultural Adjustment Act (AAA) already included contingency provisions for raising tariffs. These developments cast doubt on the president's often expressed interest in reducing commercial impediments.[79]

As Roosevelt remained indifferent to the emerging contradictions between his internationalist aspirations and his domestic programs, Warburg became exasperated. On 23 May he noted that there were "two warring camps [within the administration] with no umpire settling the results between them." He decided to raise the matter with the president. But Roosevelt indicated to reporters on 24 and 31 May that

78. For the French reaction to the tariff truce, see DDF, 1, 3:331–32, 355–57, 372–73, 392–93, 454–55; for Roosevelt's acquiescence, see p. 366; for continued attempts to effect a tariff truce, see Hull to Davis, 28 April 1933, RG 59, 550.S1/697; Davis to Hull, 12, 13, 16, 23 May 1933, ibid., 550.S1/768, 769, 776, 878; DDF, 1, 3:479–82, 486–87.

79. Feis to Frankfurter, 28 May 1933, Frankfurter Papers, Box 54; for Roosevelt's emerging interest in the NIRA, see Freidel, *Franklin D. Roosevelt*, 4:418–35.

he did not know whether he would present a tariff bill to Congress. Thus, up to the day the American delegation departed for London the uncertainty about Roosevelt's trade policy persisted. Press comments on the confusion only hinted at the deep-seated uneasiness within the State Department. Undersecretary Phillips expressed shock at the haphazard way in which policy was being formulated. Hull and Feis concurred.[80]

The uncertainty over the molding of commercial policy was minor compared to the confusion that characterized the formulation of monetary policy. Roosevelt repeatedly stated that he wanted to achieve currency stability and restore a modified gold standard.[81] But as the dollar depreciated in value and prices rose, the president began to question the wisdom of concluding a de facto stabilization accord. On 1 May he indicated that he was content to leave things alone for a while, especially since the United States had gained an important tactical negotiating advantage by placing responsibility for inaction onto the French.[82]

During the second week in May, however, rumors began circulating of an impending French departure from the gold standard. This prospect aroused fears of widespread monetary disorder and competitive devaluations. Secretary of the Treasury Woodin told Governor Harrison of the FRBNY that the administration did not want France to go off gold. Woodin asked Harrison to contact officials at the Bank of France and invite them to submit suggestions on how to prevent violent exchange-rate fluctuations. Moley was furious when he learned that Woodin had talked to Harrison about stabilization problems. Moley told Woodin that Harrison could do nothing without consulting Warburg. Recognizing that nobody in the government had been put in charge of stabilization questions, Moley assigned the task to Dean Acheson, newly appointed undersecretary of the treasury. Acheson conferred with Harrison and Warburg, and the three agreed on the desirability of a de facto stabilization accord. But on 12 May Roosevelt stated that he did not want anything done until Oliver Sprague returned from London and assumed his position as special assistant to the secretary of the treasury.[83]

80. Warburg Diary, 23, 26, 29 May 1933, pp. 804–6, 820–21, 847–48, 854; Roosevelt, *Foreign Affairs*, 1:162–65, 194; Cordell Hull, *The Memoirs of Cordell Hull*, 1:247–49, 353; Feis to Frankfurter, 28 May 1933, Frankfurter Papers, Box 54; for uncertainty on how the trade bill and the recovery act could be reconciled, see "Recovery Problems," *Business Week* (31 May 1933):5.
81. Roosevelt, *Public Papers*, 2:159, 167, 185–86.
82. Warburg Diary, 28 April, 1, 2 May 1933, pp. 600–1, 619, 628–29.
83. Ibid., 8, 10, 12 May 1933, pp. 689, 693, 701–2, 707, 715–17; Jay E. Crane,

Everything was still unsettled when Monick informed Warburg on 15 May that his government was ready to discuss establishment of a tripartite stabilization fund. Upon learning of this development Roosevelt decided to enter into stabilization talks. These discussions were scheduled to take place in London at the opening of the economic conference but were to go on independently of it.[84] Accordingly, on 16 May in his widely publicized message to world leaders, Roosevelt reiterated the importance of stabilizing currencies.[85] But having delivered this address he again lost interest in the matter. Not until the last moment did he select Sprague and Harrison to carry on the stabilization negotiations. Likewise, Warburg was about to sail for London before he was asked to coordinate the stabilization talks with the work at the conference. For almost ten days prior to leaving, Warburg had endeavored without success to get Moley and Roosevelt to give serious consideration to the stabilization issue. When he departed on 1 June, Warburg assumed that the president favored a temporary stabilization agreement. He also knew that Roosevelt was capable of scuttling the entire conference over this matter.[86]

Overhanging all the preparations for the economic conference remained the debt question. Personally, Roosevelt wanted to postpone the June installment and revise the debt accords. He realized, however, that such actions would engender considerable domestic opposition.[87] As a result he continued to equivocate on the debt issue. During the first week in May, the president permitted Warburg to explain the bunny to British and Italian experts; Roosevelt himself refused to discuss the bunny with visiting foreign dignitaries. Nevertheless, on 8 May the president confided to Warburg that he might still ask Congress for authority to renegotiate the debts. Two days later at a news conference, Roosevelt refused to say whether or not he considered a resolution of the debt question vital to the success of the economic conference.[88]

The debt problem of course would not go away. After the French

Memorandum, 8 May 1933, George L. Harrison Papers, 2012.3; Harrison, Memorandum, 8 May 1933, ibid.; L. W. Knoke, Memorandum, 8 May 1933, Papers of the Federal Reserve Bank of New York (hereafter cited as FRBNY Papers), 261.3.

84. Warburg Diary, 15, 17 May 1933, pp. 730, 735, 738, 755; Harrison, Memorandum, 17 May 1933, George L. Harrison Papers, 2012.2; Crane, Memorandum, 18 May 1933, FRBNY Papers, 261.3.

85. Roosevelt, *Foreign Affairs*, 1:126.

86. Warburg Diary, 22 May–1 June 1933, pp. 774–877.

87. See Ambassador Lindsay's comments, DBFP, 2, 5:748–49.

88. Warburg Diary, 1–8 May 1933, pp. 623–24, 628–31, 652, 658–59, 667–70, 680–81; Roosevelt, *Public Papers*, 2:174.

indicated their desire for a stabilization agreement on 15 May, Warburg and Bullitt hoped to make such an agreement contingent upon French acceptance of the bunny. Roosevelt again equivocated, forbidding mention of the bunny in formal notes to the French but allowing Bullitt to discuss the plan unofficially. On 23 May Warburg acknowledged that he did not know what Roosevelt intended to do. Indeed, the president's mind was still not made up. In a letter to MacDonald on 22 May Roosevelt emphasized that the conference could be successful "without reference to the debts at all." But he reaffirmed his desire to help the situation, perhaps by arranging for a partial payment of the June installment.[89]

Almost a month had passed since the British prime minister and the former French premier had come to Washington at the president's request. Little progress had been made toward defining a firm American position on the crucial issues linking American and European interests. As far as the United States policymaking process was concerned, the great imponderable remained the president's own predilections. Roosevelt evidently attached priority to domestic recovery. But to what extent he believed that the achievement of European stability and French security were preconditions for the restoration of domestic prosperity remained to be seen. Moley subsequently indicated that by mid-May Roosevelt's intentions had become clear. At the time Roosevelt's foreign policy advisers were not so certain, although they did realize that Moley had lost interest in international affairs.[90] Actually, throughout most of May, even as he became more committed to the AAA and NIRA and his control of Congress diminished somewhat, Roosevelt continued to articulate a sincere interest in promoting European stability. There was, however, little systematic attempt to assess how well the measures being taken in the domestic sphere might coincide with contemplated foreign policy. Nor was there a continuous effort to educate the American people or Congress about the need for a comprehensive program of national and international action. When the crunch came and decisions could no longer be postponed, therefore, Roosevelt had to choose between distinct courses of action.

89. For the continued uncertainty over the war debts, see Warburg Diary, 17, 18, 22, 23 May 1933, pp. 751–54, 761–63, 776, 783; Roosevelt, *Foreign Affairs*, 1:153–54.
90. See Moley, *New Deal*, pp. 398–410; for comments on Moley's attitude, see Warburg Diary, 23, 24 May 1933, pp. 783, 807–11.

Beginning in the last week of May domestic and foreign developments compelled the president to make a number of critical decisions regarding American policy toward France and western Europe. First, the Senate Committee on Foreign Relations amended the arms embargo resolution and forced Roosevelt to decide how far he would go to aid the disarmament conference. Then the departure of the American delegation for the economic conference obligated Roosevelt to determine whether or not he would ask Congress for new commercial legislation. Soon thereafter, the 15 June debt-installment date forced a decision on how to handle the matter of payment. Finally, the stabilization talks in London and the onset of the economic conference compelled Roosevelt to resolve his position on monetary policy.

On 22 May at Geneva, Davis publicly presented the revised American stand on disarmament, supervision, consultation, and neutrality. The speech received enormous publicity in the United States and was heralded as marking a turning point in American foreign policy.[91] Two days after Davis's speech, within the Committee on Foreign Relations, Senator Hiram W. Johnson offered an amendment, aimed at undermining H.J. 93, that would obligate the president to impose an embargo on arms shipments to all belligerents in a conflict. Secretary Hull had known for some time that such action was pending. Nevertheless, he had declined to argue the administration's case before the committee. Instead, he sent a minor official to read a prepared statement. The committee remained unswayed. On 24 May Senator Pittman informed Roosevelt that the arms embargo legislation would not pass without the Johnson amendment. Roosevelt acquiesced to the changes desired by Johnson and instructed Democratic leaders in the House to accept the revised bill. When Hull heard of the president's decision, he warned Roosevelt that the legislation conflicted with Davis's promises at Geneva. The president reconsidered his action, withdrew his approval of the Johnson amendment, and deferred the matter until the next session of Congress.[92]

The administration's handling of the arms embargo bill typified its approach to foreign affairs during the early months of the New Deal. The Department of State was divided between supporters and oppo-

91. For Davis's speech, see FR, 1933, 1:154–59; for press reaction, see "A Farewell to Isolation," *Literary Digest* 115 (3 June 1933):3–4.
92. Robert A. Divine, "Franklin D. Roosevelt and Collective Security, 1933," pp. 54–58; FR, 1933, 1:365–78; Roosevelt, *Foreign Affairs*, 1:184, 198.

nents of a discretionary embargo. When a policy decision was made, Hull provided little leadership. Meanwhile, the president, as evidenced by his initial willingness to acquiesce to the Johnson amendment, was only partly aware of the significance of developments, ill-informed about the details of proposed legislation, and inclined to follow the politically expedient course. Neither he nor the secretary of state had done much to prepare the legislative and political groundwork for a discretionary embargo. Thus, they felt compelled to submit to the demands of a few key senators, especially Johnson. Rather than risk a divisive battle in Congress, chance the alienation of several progressive senators, and jeopardize passage of the NIRA and other domestic measures, they chose to abandon their position on disarmament and neutrality.[93]

Davis's speech, therefore, signified the high point of American attempts to foster European political stability and enhance French security in the interwar era. Not for many years thereafter would Roosevelt come so close to collaborating politically with the European democracies. His refusal or inability to push the discretionary embargo through Congress dashed the hopes of American diplomats at Geneva. Allen Dulles, one of the experts with the American delegation, confided to Walter Lippman that if Roosevelt could not get Congress to follow him on neutrality legislation, then it was time for American diplomats to leave Geneva. Davis exhorted Hull to inform the American people that the abandonment of traditional neutrality imposed few risks and offered great opportunities. But no more American initiatives were forthcoming. The conference dragged on without the anticipated American assistance.[94]

Although the decision not to battle with the Senate over the Johnson amendment reflected a downgrading of the administration's efforts to foster European stability, it cannot be considered responsible for the failure of the disarmament conference. Once Hitler had consolidated power in Germany, all disarmament efforts were doomed to fail, especially since the British were neither ready to increase their commitments on the Continent nor willing to implement effective supervisory measures. The General Disarmament Conference would have collapsed

93. For comments on Roosevelt's action, see Divine, "Collective Security," pp. 57–59; Freidel, *Franklin D. Roosevelt*, 4:454–58. Since early May Moffat had been worrying about the consequences of Roosevelt's handling of the disarmament issue. See Moffat, *Papers*, p. 94.

94. Allen Dulles to Walter Lippmann, 30 May 1933, Davis Papers, Box 43; Davis to Hull, 15 June 1933, ibid.; see also Memorandum on disarmament and security, pp. 29–32, ibid., Box 23.

regardless of the actions taken by the United States.[95] But Roosevelt's attitude toward the Johnson amendment was correctly perceived as the first ominous sign of the administration's inclination to withdraw from European affairs. On 1 June Laboulaye informed Paul-Boncour that the proponents of economic nationalism and political isolationism were gaining influence within the administration. He was uncertain whether Roosevelt would have the determination to resist their efforts. The next few weeks, he realized, would be decisive.[96]

During the last week in May while Roosevelt was grappling with the Johnson amendment, Warburg began working on final instructions for the American delegation to the economic conference. The president had assigned no one to this task, and Moley had indicated total indifference. Warburg nevertheless assumed the initiative, formulated policy options on currency questions, and asked Feis to devise similar resolutions on commercial matters. On Friday, 26 May, members of the American delegation met with Roosevelt, Moley, and Baruch to discuss Warburg's instructions. The president expressed satisfaction with Warburg's work and specifically endorsed the resolution to reduce tariffs. Warburg emphasized that this endorsement meant that the president would have to ask Congress for authority to decrease American duties. Baruch objected. He said that raising tariffs was essential to the effective functioning of the AAA and the proposed NIRA. Since the issue was left unsettled, Warburg sought to clarify matters when the same group reconvened on 29 May. He read a memorandum stating that the aim of American policy was to reduce trade barriers, except for the possible implementation of compensatory duties necessitated by the farm bill. Roosevelt concurred. Warburg felt satisfied "that we would not be preaching one gospel [at the economic conference] while the cohorts of protectionism were carrying out another behind our backs."[97]

Warburg's optimism, however, was ill-founded. Administration of the key domestic programs was falling into the hands of Baruch's high-tariff followers, George Peek and Hugh Johnson. Meanwhile, the delegation that Roosevelt put together for the economic conference was divided between proponents of high and low tariffs. Once all the

95. For British attitudes toward security commitments and supervisory machinery, see DBFP, 2, 5:265, 282, 326, 333–34, 376–77, 601–6, 609–10, 614–24; for Hitler's foreign policy, see Weinberg, *Hitler's Germany*, pp. 1–52, 159–65.

96. DDF, 1, 3:616–21.

97. Warburg Diary, 23, 24, 26, 29 May 1933, pp. 783–99, 807–11, 820–21, 847–50.

prominent advocates of low tariffs were on their way to London, no one remained in Washington to resist protectionist pressures in Congress and counter the influence of Moley and Baruch within the administration. When the Senate Finance Committee tried to alter the NIRA to prohibit imports that would undermine the efficacy of the proposed legislation, Roosevelt was able to weaken the amendment. But he decided that it was not a propitious time to ask Congress for authority to reduce tariffs. He wanted the NIRA passed and Congress adjourned. Rather than risk a prolonged battle, he wired Hull that the political situation precluded the passage of a reciprocal trade bill.[98]

Thus, the expectations of the American delegates were shattered. Hull was bitterly disappointed. "I left for London with the highest of hopes," he later commented, "but arrived with empty hands." Warburg was angered. "It makes a monkey out of the tariff section of our instructions," he noted in his diary, "and casts doubt on our whole economic setup." Thereafter, the American delegates performed shamefully. Hull exerted no leadership. Pittman and Feis battled publicly over the direction of American commercial policy. The rest of the world looked on with amazement as the American delegation disintegrated into individualized factions.[99]

For almost two months the president had reaffirmed his commitment to commercial liberality. In fact, this commitment seemed to constitute the major aspect of his economic internationalism. But by failing to submit appropriate legislation to Congress in April, as was his original intention, he sacrificed the opportunity to secure the flexible authority that might have enabled him to reconcile his domestic priorities with his internationalist inclinations. Until the latter part of May he was still able to push most of his proposals through Congress without encountering much difficulty. On 17 May *Business Week* reported that, although the tariff proposal would stir more opposition than any of the other New Deal measures, it would unquestionably be approved.[100] Yet, the president still deferred action. When he was suddenly faced

98. Hull, *Memoirs*, 1:249–52; Moley, *New Deal*, pp. 420–25; Freidel, *Franklin D. Roosevelt*, 4:449–50, 466–67.

99. For the quotations, see Hull, *Memoirs*, 1:255; Warburg Diary, 9 June 1933, p. 884; for the performance of the American delegation at London, see Feis, *1933*, pp. 172–258; for Hull's leadership, see Bullitt, *For the President*, pp. 34–35. Only after the bombshell address did Hull take charge in an effective way. For a contemporary view of the disorganization in the American delegation, see "Why Stabilization Prospects Fade at London," *Literary Digest* 116 (1 July 1933):5.

100. "Ticklish Tariff," *Business Week* (17 May 1933):4; for Roosevelt's legislative successes until the latter part of May, see Freidel, *Franklin D. Roosevelt*, 4:444.

with a critical choice, he opted for a nationalist program and chose not to submit a trade bill to Congress.

By itself, passage of the reciprocal trade bill would not have reversed the trend toward autarchy nor ushered in a new era of international economic cooperation. But there were some indications that a forthright gesture by the United States might have had a favorable impact on France and Britain. Despite all their misgivings about the tariff truce, the French accepted it with a few specific qualifications and refrained from imposing compensatory tariff duties to offset the impact of dollar depreciation. Similarly, the British, although increasing their own duties and signing preferential treaties with sterling bloc nations, were still hoping for a quick reversal in American high-tariff policies. In April MacDonald had appealed to Roosevelt unsuccessfully for a 10 percent reduction in the Hawley-Smoot duties. Both Britain and France, with substantial merchandise deficits, expected the United States to assume the leadership in reducing tariffs. Therefore, when on the eve of the conference Roosevelt reneged on his earlier assurances to secure authority to reduce duties on a reciprocal basis, he upset any lingering possibility for working out collaborative arrangements on commercial matters.[101]

Some international cooperation, however, might still have been achievable had agreement been reached on war debt and monetary issues. Unfortunately, Roosevelt's position on the war debts also toughened as both the June installment date and the time for congressional adjournment approached. On 31 May the president repudiated his earlier stand and declared that he would not discuss war debt revision with the French until they paid the December installment. Although Laboulaye was very eager to discuss the bunny, Roosevelt told the French that if their overdue debts were paid, France would be treated on the same basis as Great Britain. As for the latter nation, Roosevelt wrote MacDonald on 7 June that "a number of perplexing problems must be met by the Congress before they can adjourn and the presence of these problems on their calendar makes it impossible to present to

101. For French actions, see Davis to Hull, 16 May 1933, RG 59, 550.S1 Monetary Stabilization/2; Davis to Hull, 16 May 1933, ibid., 550.S1/776; for British interest in tariff reductions, see Fuqua, "The British Attitude towards a Return to the Gold Standard," 23 March 1933, ibid., 851.51/1147; for MacDonald's request, see Warburg Diary, 25 April 1933, p. 566; see also DBFP, 2, 5:763, 767; for the impact of Roosevelt's action, see Hull, *Memoirs*, 1:251–53. After Roosevelt decided not to secure trade legislation, he still prodded Hull to press for tariff reductions. But with his hands tied, Hull had little chance to be successful.

them any proposal concerning debts." The president denied, however, that this decision constituted a barrier to international cooperation.[102]

Roosevelt's decision not to ask Congress for authority to handle the war debts was significant. The French and British had reiterated that war debt revision was prerequisite to effective international economic cooperation. They had made concessions on reparations at Lausanne, and they demanded that the United States reciprocate on the war debts. In several letters to the president following his visit to Washington, MacDonald had emphasized that the British viewed American action on the debts as a measurement of American goodwill and American intentions to pursue an internationalist course. Thus Moley and Tugwell were denying reality when they dismissed the importance of the war debts and considered cancellation a bankers' idea.[103] Although the debts may not have been a critical impediment to recovery from a financial viewpoint, they were of fundamental political and psychological importance. That they were so important had been made unmistakably clear to Democratic officials. Yet, neither Hull nor Moley endeavored to tackle the problem constructively, and Warburg lacked sufficient political clout to influence congressional opinion.[104]

In retrospect it seems that Roosevelt made a tactical mistake in letting matters drift on the debt issue. Since autumn 1932 numerous individuals and groups throughout the nation had begun to advocate the necessity of war debt revision.[105] Aware of the latent support for

102. For Roosevelt's letter, see Roosevelt, *Foreign Affairs*, 1:210–11; see also p. 208; for his policy toward France, see p. 193; DDF, 1, 3:659–60; Memorandum of conversation between Phillips and Laboulaye, 31 May 1933, RG 59, 800.51W89 France/909.
103. The French let the British take the lead in pressing the debt issue. See DBFP, 2, 5:749, 753–58, 769–70, 774, 781, 790–93; DDF, 1, 3:491–92, 516–19, 658–59, 665–68, 700; for MacDonald's letters, see Roosevelt, *Foreign Affairs*, 1:100, 201–4; for Moley's and Tugwell's view, see Moley, *New Deal*, pp. 412–13; Tugwell, *Democratic Roosevelt*, p. 260.
104. For the manner in which Hull and Moley approached the debts, see Moley, *New Deal*, pp. 411–19; Hull, *Memoirs*, 1:247. The British expert, Leith-Ross, considered Moley to be singularly ignorant of the most elementary facts. See DBFP, 2, 5:798, 801–3. There is no indication in the Warburg diaries that he made any effort to influence congressional attitudes.
105. These included not only bankers like Leffingwell and Lamont but also businessmen like Alfred P. Sloan and Lamar Fleming, farm spokesmen like Henry A. Wallace and Louis J. Taber, labor leaders like D. B. Robertson, and politicians like Alfred E. Smith, Frank O. Lowden, and even Senator Borah. See, for example, the activities of the newly formed organization, entitled the Committee for the Consideration of Inter-Governmental Debts, RG 59, 800.51W89/703, 704, 706; see also Fleming to Castle, 22 November 1932, ibid., 800.51W89/605; for Borah's stand, see "No 'Swap' on the Debt Says Chamberlain," *Literary Digest* 115 (18 February 1933):10; see also DDF, 1, 2:639–40; for the viewpoint of the Chamber of Commerce, see Henry I. Harri-

revision, Felix Frankfurter had written Roosevelt in January 1933 that public opinion was "more liquid than it has ever been and more ready to be led."[106] But advocates of revision who offered their services to the administration were met with official indifference. When Congressman Edward W. Pou, chairman of the House Committee on Rules, informed Roosevelt that a large majority of the House would give him flexible authority if he assumed the initiative, there was apparently no presidential response. Although some Republican and Democratic opponents of revision did speak out, the British ambassador was struck by the mildness of the antirevisionist campaign. Having failed to cultivate a constituency in favor of revision, Roosevelt was confronted in early June with a possible legislative impasse; the NIRA might have been jeopardized and the adjournment of Congress postponed. Given the immense pressures at the time, the path of least resistance was one leading to economic nationalism and political isolationism.[107]

To reconcile policy on internal and external matters demanded a type of self-discipline and long-term planning inconsistent with the tenor of the early New Deal. Absence of these characteristics was especially apparent in Roosevelt's handling of the currency stabilization issue. On 10 June, Warburg, Sprague, and Harrison began their stabilization discussions in London with British and French officials. Initially, the British seemed uninterested in an agreement. The French, however, demanded a stabilization accord. Although they desired permanent stabilization, the French were willing to accept a de facto agreement designed to limit currency fluctuations during the lifetime of the conference itself. Warburg, Sprague, and Harrison were satisfied with the French position. The Americans devised a temporary arrangement to level out exchange fluctuations without determining fixed and

---

man to Hoover, 18 November 1932, 1 February 1933, RG 59, 800.51W89/611, 673; see also, for example, Report of the Subcommittee of the American Asiatic Association on the settlement of the war debts, 18 January 1933, ibid., 800.51W89/674.

106. Frankfurter to Roosevelt, 28 January 1933, Frankfurter Papers, Box 256.

107. For official indifference to the efforts of the advocates of revision, see Frederic Coudert to Roosevelt, 24 May 1933, RG 59, 800.51W89/733; see also ibid., 800.51W89/703, 704; for Pou's letter, see Edward W. Pou to Roosevelt, 1 May 1933, Roosevelt Papers, Official File 212; for congressional sentiment against revision, see Freidel, *Franklin D. Roosevelt*, 4:437–38; for Lindsay's appraisal, see DBFP, 2, 5:796–97; for Roosevelt's growing problems with Congress, see Freidel, *Franklin D. Roosevelt*, 4:444–53; "Whittling Down Roosevelt Economy," *Literary Digest* 115 (17 June 1933):3–4. Roosevelt, however, never seems to have explored the validity of Senator Pittman's view that Congress would accept the bunny. See Warburg Diary, 17 April 1933, pp. 477, 481. Evidence that the bunny might have constituted a means of grappling with the opponents of revision is evident in Everett M. Dirksen to Roosevelt, 16 May 1933, RG 59, 800.51W89/732.

permanent rates. Federal Reserve officials believed that a temporary stabilization accord would enhance the work of the economic conference, facilitate efforts to reduce commercial barriers, and permit moderate domestic price increases. They did not feel that such an accord would foreclose subsequent dollar depreciation. Sprague and Warburg cabled Roosevelt that their plan was "exceedingly vital in the sense that the work of the Conference . . . is unmeasurably hindered not only by the fluctuations but even more by the feeling on the part of the other nations that America is an entirely unknown, uncertain and perhaps indifferent factor."[108]

Roosevelt vetoed this plan. During the concluding days of Congress, he had laid aside Warburg's earlier dispatch and was subsequently shocked to hear rumors of an impending stabilization agreement. As soon as there were leaks to the press about a de facto accord, stock and commodity prices declined. Roosevelt, Moley, and Woodin were alarmed by the sudden reversal in prices and angered by the lack of information they had received.[109] The president informed Sprague and Warburg on 17 and 20 June that he did not agree that a temporary accord was vital to the success of the conference. He wanted full freedom to take whatever action was necessary to maintain domestic prices. He worried that Britain and France might either interpret or implement the agreement in ways contrary to the interests of the United States. In any event the president believed that a four-dollar rate for the pound suggested by Warburg was too low. Roosevelt emphasized that there was too much concern with de facto stabilization and encouraged the American delegates to focus the attention of the conference on issues of greater importance, like a balanced budget.[110] The president then left Washington, visited his sons at Groton, and embarked upon a ten-day cruise, during which time he could not be reached by telephone.[111]

In London Warburg acquiesced to Roosevelt's wishes and informed

108. For the quotation, see FR, 1933, 1:648; for the London stabilization talks, see pp. 642–48; Warburg Diary, 10–16 June 1933, pp. 885–92, 896–900, 904–7, 909–13, 927; Harrison to W. Randolph Burgess, 16 June 1933, Goldenweiser Papers, Box 4; Harrison to Eugene Black, 8 July 1933, ibid.; Burgess, "Reasons for a Plan of Temporary Stabilization," ibid.; Knoke, Memoranda, 12, 13 June 1933, FRBNY Papers, 261.3.

109. Roosevelt, Foreign Affairs, 1:239–41; Knoke, Memorandum, 16 June 1933, FRBNY Papers, 261.3; Sproul, Memorandum, 17 June 1933, ibid.; Moley, New Deal, pp. 428–29; Warburg, Long Road Home, p. 132; for the trend of commodity prices, stock prices, and exchange rates, see Charles P. Kindleberger, The World in Depression, 1929–1939, pp. 222–23.

110. FR, 1933, 1:645–46, 649–650.

111. For Roosevelt's actions after the adjournment of Congress, see Freidel, Franklin D. Roosevelt, 4:470–75.

the French and British that the United States would not enter into a temporary agreement. Georges Bonnet, the French finance minister, was enraged. Warburg managed to calm Bonnet by stating that the rejection of the temporary accord did not mean that the United States was abandoning the goal of currency stabilization or foreclosing the possibility of future cooperation in behalf of permanent monetary and fiscal policies to boost world economic activity. During the next few days, from 23 June to 26 June, tempers cooled and progress was made toward reforming the operation of the gold standard and providing it with increased elasticity. But on 26 June the continued fluctuation and depreciation of the dollar began to weaken the guilder and engender fears that the rest of Continental Europe would be driven from the gold standard. MacDonald told Hull that if abandonment of the gold standard occurred, the tariff truce might be undermined, competitive devaluations might ensue, and the conference might be wrecked. The French were alarmed. They deplored the disunity within the American delegation and complained that they could communicate with the Americans only through the British. Nevertheless, to salvage the conference and preserve the gold bloc they agreed to settle for nothing more than a declaration that would have committed the United States and Britain to the principle of exchange stability and the goal of eventual reestablishment of the gold standard.[112]

When Moley arrived in London and grasped the reasonableness of the French position, he urged Roosevelt to acquiesce to a modified form of the innocuous French declaration. He could not reach the president by telephone, but he spoke to Baruch, Acheson, and Harrison—all of whom were at the home of Secretary Woodin in New York. They all supported the declaration and cabled Roosevelt that the departure of Continental nations from the gold standard would lead to a rapid rise in the value of the dollar and a fall in domestic prices. Temporary stabilization, they claimed, complemented Roosevelt's domestic and foreign goals, as did the statement regarding the ultimate reestablishment of the gold standard.[113]

Roosevelt, however, was no longer interested in trying to reconcile internal and external priorities. As the conference verged on collapse, he remained inaccessible. Incoming cables from London had to be

112. Warburg Diary, 21–29 June 1933, pp. 978–82, 989–97, 1007, 1023–25, 1030–35, 1041–44; FR, 1933, 1:652–55, 658–59; DDF, 1, 3:775–76, 794–95, 798–99.
113. Moley, *New Deal*, pp. 452–61; FR, 1933, 1:661–72; Roosevelt, *Foreign Affairs*, 1:253–54; Harrison, Memorandum, 28 June 1933, George L. Harrison Papers, 2013.3b.

relayed to him through the Department of State, a cumbersome process causing several mix-ups. At the same time, Roosevelt made no effort to consult directly with Woodin, Acheson, Douglas, Harrison, or Baruch. The president wrote out his instructions, sent them to Phillips for transfer to London, and requested the undersecretary to ascertain the reaction of his financial advisers. Arriving at Campobello Island with his family and a small group of reporters during the last days of June, the president had with him only Louis Howe and Henry Morgenthau, Jr., to offer advice. When Moley's first message of a proposed declaration arrived, the president seemed exasperated with the stabilization issue and expressed his pent-up frustrations with European machinations. He wrote his "bombshell" address without studying the final proposed declaration that arrived from London with Moley's endorsement, without consulting his best-informed advisers, and without fully grasping the consequences of his action.[114]

In his bombshell message of 2 July, which for all practical purposes broke up the conference, Roosevelt condemned the emphasis on exchange stability. Rather than dissipate energies on specious and temporary expedients to effect the stabilization of currencies, the president suggested that all nations focus greater attention on balancing their budgets and servicing their debts. What was of real importance, he said, was for every nation to have a sound internal economic system. This goal could be achieved by developing national currencies with a constant purchasing power.[115]

Roosevelt was giving notice that the internal price structure had become his exclusive economic preoccupation. He was beginning to flirt with the theories of George F. Warren, economics professor at Cornell University. Warren believed that prices could be increased simply by depreciating the paper dollar in terms of gold. The fact that prices had recently declined whenever rumors circulated of an imminent stabilization accord lent a superficial plausibility to this analysis. Roosevelt could not resist Warren's theory. It held out the promise of a financially simple and politically expedient road to economic recovery.[116]

114. For Roosevelt's attitudes and actions, see Freidel, *Franklin D. Roosevelt*, 4:470–89; Moley, *New Deal*, pp. 460–92; Henry Morgenthau, Jr., *From the Morgenthau Diaries*, 1:64–66; Charles Hurd, *When the New Deal Was Young and Gay*, pp. 149–71.

115. FR, 1933, 1:669–70, 673–74.

116. For Roosevelt's preoccupation with increasing domestic prices, see Morgenthau, *Diaries*, pp. 61–77; see also Elmus R. Wicker, "Roosevelt's 1933 Monetary Experiment," pp. 864–79.

The bombshell address revealed that Roosevelt was abandoning the struggle to achieve European stability. Internal goals not only had priority over foreign policy objectives but were to be pursued regardless of their impact on European developments. Warburg, Acheson, and others warned him that he was making a big mistake. They emphasized that his domestic objectives could not be accomplished without some form of cooperation with the European powers. They maintained that acceptance of a temporary stabilization agreement and commitment to an eventual return to the gold standard were necessary complements to internal recovery measures. Their arguments were to no avail. Roosevelt seemed content with his action and the public's response.[117]

The president denied that he was embarking upon a nationalist course. He instructed Hull to keep the conference from adjourning and endeavored to place responsibility for failure upon the French. To Hull Roosevelt explained that he made his message a bit harsh "because I felt . . . that Conference was getting into [a] stage of polite resolutions about temporary stabilization only and that it was time to be realistic and work toward main objectives."[118] But what were these objectives? Did the advocate of a New Deal at home really believe that the solution to the world economic crisis depended upon balanced budgets and conservative fiscal policies? These were the themes that he emphasized time and again.[119] What areas were still available for international collaboration? Roosevelt had already foreclosed the possibility of American cooperation on war debts, trade questions, and security matters. He seemed unaware that his previous decisions left little room for international cooperation except on currency issues.[120] He disregarded the widely held belief that the greatest impediments to expanded world

117. For the arguments of Warburg and Acheson, see Roosevelt, *Foreign Affairs*, 1:253–54, 325–26; Warburg, *Long Road Home*, pp. 142–50; Dean Acheson, *Morning and Noon*, pp. 165–82; Wicker, "Monetary Experiment," pp. 872–79; for press reaction to the bombshell address, see "The Roosevelt Way with the London Conference," *Literary Digest* 116 (15 July 1933):6; for Roosevelt's subsequent reflections on the bombshell, see Freidel, *Franklin D. Roosevelt*, 4:489.
118. FR, 1933, 1:681; for Roosevelt's views, see also pp. 685–94; for his animus toward France, see pp. 669–70.
119. Ibid., pp. 655, 673–74; Roosevelt, *Foreign Affairs*, 1:265–66; Warburg Diary, 26 May 1933, p. 820.
120. In a thoughtful article, James R. Moore suggests that there still might have been room for cooperation on global public works. Yet this seems unlikely given Roosevelt's stress on balanced budgets. See James R. Moore, "Sources of New Deal Economic Policy," p. 744. After the bombshell address, the American delegates did try to get the conference to take some action toward reducing tariff barriers. But their efforts were hampered by the administration's failure to foresee how the NIRA and AAA could be reconciled with reduced tariffs. See FR, 1933, 1:676–748.

commerce—exchange restrictions, quotas, and import licenses—could not be eliminated until there was greater stability in exchange rates.[121] Roosevelt may have been reluctant to admit it, but Moley accurately summed up American strategy when he said that it was aimed at leaving Continental Europe "out in the cold."[122]

The French and British realized the significance of Roosevelt's actions. They understood that since the latter part of May, he had approached a crossroads, decided to take an independent road to recovery, and left Europe to grapple with its own problems. Resentment in the Old World was intense.[123]

The French in particular were terribly disillusioned. They had welcomed Roosevelt's electoral victory with enthusiasm. They had heard him say that he would lower American tariff barriers, revise American neutrality policy, restore stability in exchange rates, and treat their debt on the same terms as the British.[124] Daladier and Paul-Boncour, within the limits of their political power, tried to reciprocate. They did not impose compensatory duties on American imports.[125] They promised to pay the overdue debts as soon as Roosevelt postponed the June installment and agreed to renegotiate future payments. Having sacrificed reparation payments, the French could hardly do more.[126] French officials acquiesced to the departure of the dollar from the gold standard, sought a de facto stabilization agreement, and requested only a general reaffirmation of American faith in the gold standard and exchange stabilization. They understood Roosevelt's desire to raise domestic prices and did not object to a devaluation of the dollar so long as there was a quick return to exchange stability.[127] They modified their demands for security guarantees, accepted the new American emphasis on supervisory machinery, and for the first time enumerated specific

121. Both American and French experts agreed that monetary stabilization was a precondition for reducing commercial barriers. See, for example, Warburg Diary, 7, 10 April 1933, pp. 389–419; Memorandum of conversation between Rist and Nicholas Roosevelt, 17 May 1933, RG 59, 550.S1/829.

122. FR, 1933, 1:692.

123. For the reaction of French and British leaders to the bombshell address, see, for example, Warburg Diary, 3, 4 July 1933, pp. 1081–82, 1089–93; FR, 1933, 1:681–83, 214–18; Roosevelt, *Foreign Affairs*, 1:290–92; Stimson to Hoover, 31 July 1933, Herbert Hoover Post-Presidential Papers, Box 178.

124. For a few examples of the impressions gained by French diplomats, see DDF, 1, 3:414–17, 651–53, 684–86, 735–36, 823.

125. Davis to Hull, 16 May 1933, RG 59, 550.S1 Monetary Stabilization/2.

126. DDF, 1, 3:98–100, 315, 473–74.

127. For French views on monetary policy, see ibid., 5–12, 288, 482–83, 700–1, 775–76, 794–95; Davis to Hull, 15 May 1933, RG 59, 550.S1/775; Jesse Straus to secretary, 13 June 1933, ibid., 550.S1/1039.

areas of arms reductions.[128] From their viewpoint, the French had made an earnest attempt to meet Roosevelt halfway. In mid-May after Herriot had reported on his visit to the United States, Paul-Boncour acknowledged that there seemed to be a mutuality of interest in stimulating recovery and organizing peace with security.[129] Then in successive thrusts Roosevelt crushed French hopes for neutrality revision, tariff reductions, war debt postponement, and currency stabilization. The French were now on their own to try to deal with Hitler, insure their security, and cope with the unprecedented economic crisis.

Conclusion

The summer of 1933 signified a turning point in American foreign policy. For all practical purposes American efforts to harmonize domestic and foreign policies and contribute to European stability and French security, without compromising domestic priorities or incurring strategic commitments, ceased. In September Davis returned to Geneva hoping to arrange a disarmament agreement. Once Germany left the conference, however, he was instructed to stay out of European politics. American officials thought it more important to isolate the United States from a probable European war than to assume risks in the pursuit of a disarmament accord. Hence, no more pressure was exerted upon the French to limit their armaments; nor was there any further attempt to discuss consultative procedures in the event war should erupt.[130] At the same time, lingering hopes for cooperation in the international economic realm faded. When a British delegation arrived in Washington to discuss the war debts in the autumn, Roosevelt refused to incur the political risks of drastically curtailing payments. The talks collapsed.[131] Simultaneously, the president began tinkering with the gold content of the dollar and foreclosed the possibility of a quick resolution of the currency stabilization issue.[132] The Democratic

128. Both American and British diplomats commented upon the moderation of French demands at Geneva, especially in light of developments in Germany. See FR, 1933, 1:183–84, 191–93; DBFP, 2, 5:247–48, 259–60, 268–69; for French policy, see especially DDF, 1, 3:401–2, 676–91.

129. DDF, 1, 3:473–74.

130. For Davis's efforts at Geneva in the autumn of 1933, see FR, 1933, 1:209–301, especially pp. 273–74, 296–97, 299–300; for the aims and fears of American officials, see also Wilson, *Disarmament*, pp. 40, 43–44; Wilson, *Diplomat Between Wars*, pp. 295–96; Moffat, *Papers*, pp. 106–8; Dulles, Memorandum, 27 October 1933, Davis Papers, Box 23.

131. Acheson, *Morning and Noon*, pp. 183–86; FR, 1933, 1:842–47.

132. Feis, *1933*, pp. 279–306; Morgenthau, *Diaries*, pp. 69–77.

administration had embarked upon a course of economic nationalism and political isolationism.[133]

Given the explosive developments in the Old World and the unparalleled distress at home, Roosevelt abandoned the struggle to devise policies and mechanisms that might have proven capable of reconciling his domestic and foreign priorities. When he had assumed office, he had hoped to foster European stability and enhance French security as part of his program of expediting domestic recovery. He had no clear blueprint in mind on how he might accomplish his goals, but he did believe that action in the foreign field had to complement domestic programs. But domestic pressures took on a momentum of their own. Improvising new legislative programs as they emerged from the minds of his nationalist advisers and their progressive allies in Congress, Roosevelt was never able to assimilate, coordinate, and harmonize all the strategies for promoting recovery. Believing that bold action and imaginative experimentation would stimulate confidence, he wished to avoid a confrontation with Congress that might engender a legislative-executive impasse. Thus, he postponed his requests for authority on war debts, reciprocal tariffs, and discretionary neutrality until so late in the session that everyone was eager for adjournment and the president was satisfied to emerge with his domestic programs intact.

Meanwhile, the unfolding events in Europe—the rising tone of Nazi belligerency, the development of a sterling bloc, and the French refusal to pay the December debt installment—cast doubt on whether action taken by the United States would reverse the trend toward economic autarchy and European political disintegration.[134] Thus, the incentives to battle Congress over foreign policy issues and impose a rigorous co-ordination of policy upon the growing bureaucracy were not as great as they might have been in more normal times. Under these circumstances Roosevelt acquiesced to Congress's indifference to European affairs, submitted to the economic nationalism of the monetary inflationists, and fell victim to his own pragmatism.

Reciprocal tariff agreements, war debt reductions, and exchange stabilization accords would not have sufficed to extricate the United States (or Europe) from the Depression. Domestic initiatives were imperative, but Roosevelt's domestic programs were not able to insure

133. Although Roosevelt did ask for passage of the trade bill in 1934, this was implemented in a very conservative manner. See Paul A. Varg, "The Economic Side of the Good Neighbor Policy," pp. 47–72.

134. Moore, "New Deal Economic Policy," pp. 728–44.

the peace, prosperity, and tranquility of the United States. Roosevelt soon realized this fact. By the mid-1930s the administration was seeking reciprocal trade agreements and stabilization accords with France and other European nations. But by then the pall of Nazism hung over Europe, and the fervor of political isolationism precluded effective collaboration with France and other western European democracies.

[10]

Conclusion

Between 1919 and 1933 the United States was continuously involved in the struggle to reconstruct and stabilize western Europe. Economic imperatives, humanitarian instincts, and ideological impulses compelled American officials to take an active interest in European affairs. These officials wanted to rehabilitate Germany, stabilize European currencies, and foster American exports. To accomplish these objectives, they recognized the need to alleviate French strategic anxieties, resolve the war debt and reparation controversies, systematize the export of private American capital, and reformulate American commercial practices.

There were, however, important constraints circumscribing America's participation in the struggle for European stability. Domestic economic, fiscal, and monetary priorities affected the foreign policy decision-making process and produced significant gaps between the conceptualization of diplomatic goals and the implementation of foreign policy. Similarly, the desire to remain aloof from European political controversies affected the range of foreign policy options available to American officials. Moreover, partisan political rivalries and legislative-executive struggles precluded the cancellation of war debts, the abandonment of protectionism, and the assumption of strategic obligations, even had Republican officials wanted to resort to such tactics.

The willingness of policymakers to work within these constraints, however, reveals a good deal about the nature of American foreign policy in the 1920s and early 1930s. Preoccupation with certain domestic economic priorities suggests that policymakers did not consider export expansionism the only answer, or even the most important solution, to latent economic problems. When foreign sales could be promoted without jeopardizing internal priorities, policymakers did so eagerly and enthusiastically. But when the imperatives of European reconstruction and the demands of American export interests called for a reduction in the war debts, a decrease in government revenues, a lowering of tariff rates, or an inflationary monetary policy, government officials were hesitant to make the necessary domestic sacrifices. For Herbert Hoover, the internal market and the domestic construction industry remained the major determinants of American prosperity; for Andrew Mellon, the reduction of taxes constituted the key to America's domestic economic growth; and, for Benjamin Strong, the maintenance of a noninflationary domestic monetary policy was even more critical to the health of the American economy than was the well-being of the international monetary system. When the tactics necessary to promote the health of the domestic economy clashed with those necessary to revitalize the international economy and America's export trade, the former usually prevailed. Thus, the answers to American economic problems were not externalized by American officials; solutions were sought through various domestic palliatives, although these remained conservative and traditional in nature.

The decision to forego strategic commitments abroad reveals that American officials did not consider the nation's vital interests, either strategic or economic, to be at stake in Europe. With Germany's military power emasculated, policymakers saw no imminent strategic threat to America's national security and did not wish to become embroiled in disputes over such matters as the Rhineland occupation and the Polish Corridor. In the context of the times these issues appeared to affect France's vital interests but not those of the United States. American officials feared that the extension of strategic commitments to France might obligate the United States to guarantee French security without necessarily altering French behavior toward Germany. Through such obligations the United States might have become responsible for preserving a status quo perceived as inherently unstable. Given this danger the economic and financial benefits that might have accrued as a result of a possible diminution in French strategic anxieties did not seem to outweigh the risks of becoming ensnarled in Europe's chronic political problems or traditional Franco-German rivalries. American policymakers put a higher priority on remaining strategically uncommitted than on capturing European markets or promoting European stability. But their determination to avoid military obligations in Europe did not mean that they saw the world through an idealistic prism. Given the state of military technology, Germany's relative disarmament, and France's military predominance, even American military leaders remained unconcerned about strategic developments in the Old World. Civilian and military officials preferred to remain out of controversies recognized as conflict-producing but which, in the absence of a strategic threat and a totalitarian ideology, did not seem to jeopardize American national security.

It is misleading, however, to think that policymakers simply chose domestic priorities over European commitments or sought to remain strategically unentangled rather than economically involved in European affairs. The entire thrust of American diplomacy in the post–World War I era was aimed at reconciling conflicting imperatives. By studying the policymaking process, one can see how government officials struggled to harmonize discordant foreign policy goals and how they sought to reconcile internal and external economic objectives. For the most part, these men worked hard to overcome both domestic political constraints and congressional assertions of authority in order to enable the United States to assume responsibilities in Europe that they considered proportionate to American economic and strategic interests.

After Wilson failed to engender a national consensus on the need to assume carefully circumscribed political commitments in Europe, Republican officials adopted a primarily economic orientation to European affairs. Believing that a prosperous Germany would be the best safeguard of French security and assuming that a financially sound Europe would be a peaceful Europe, the Republicans focused their major efforts on promoting Germany's economic restoration and expediting Europe's financial stabilization. To avoid partisan controversy at home and strategic entanglements abroad and to prevent the politicization of economic issues, they allocated a great deal of responsibility to the private sector and quasi-official institutions. The reparations issue was handed over to independent experts, private bankers were expected to meet Europe's capital requirements, and the FRBNY was authorized to play the key role in stabilizing foreign currencies. Recognizing that not all issues could be removed from government hands, Republican officials also endeavored to establish expert mechanisms within the executive branch and to devise objective criteria for the settlement of war debts, the adjustment of tariff rates, and the regulation of capital outflows. To deal with French anxieties without incurring strategic commitments of their own, Republican officials encouraged the consummation of regional security pacts.

There was logic in the way in which Republican officials approached each of the major problems linking American and European interests. But looking at the American decision-making apparatus as a whole, one can see that it was a cumbersome process, overly decentralized, and full of pitfalls. There was no institutionalized way of synchronizing the work of the WDC with that of the reparations experts or of coordinating the efforts of the FRBNY with those of the Tariff Commission. In fact, within the Tariff Commission the protectionist inclinations of Thomas Marvin triumphed over the more international orientation of William Culbertson. Within the WDC the fiscal and political concerns of Hoover received somewhat greater emphasis than the commercial arguments of Mellon. Within the Federal Reserve System, the domestic preoccupations of the Federal Reserve Board began to outweigh the internationalist leanings of the FRBNY. Theoretically nonpolitical commissions and objective criteria were used in a manner that highlighted domestic imperatives. As a result the major burden for Europe's stabilization was placed upon European governments themselves, especially upon the French, who were asked not only to share in the usual economic and financial sacrifices but also to accept the strategic implications of a revitalized Germany. Indeed, the assumption that a prosperous Germany would be a peaceful neighbor to France was questionable from its inception, but its validity was never fully tested because of the onset of the Depression.

The primacy of domestic concerns and the antipathy to strategic obligations shaped the reaction of Republican officials to the economic setbacks that occurred after 1929. Hoover's initial response to the Depression was to proceed with the revitalization of traditional Republican techniques. Only in 1931, when the breakdown of the international monetary system had occurred and the incapacity of traditional techniques to handle prevailing problems had become manifest, did he and Stimson consider new initiatives. Announcing a debt moratorium, the president contemplated revision of the war debt settlements and encouraged French Premier Laval to tackle the reparations issue. At the same time, Stimson tried to calm French strategic anxieties by prodding the British to assume new commitments in Europe and assuring them that they needn't worry about the implications of American neutrality policy. But the secretary of state did not want the United States to incur military obligations in Europe. He found no means of formalizing his assurances to the British and was unable to coax them to expand their own obligations on the Continent. Meanwhile, Hoover was unable to take action on the war debts. When he asked Congress to recreate the WDC, he encountered intractable opposition. Congress rebelled at the prospect of reducing government revenues and imposing a heavier burden on American taxpayers. With businessmen clamoring for relaxation of the antitrust laws, a balanced budget, cheap credit, and a minimum increase in taxes, there was little support for international initiatives that might upset these domestic priorities. Accordingly, Hoover decided to focus his efforts on securing passage of his domestic legislative proposals.

As economic conditions worsened during 1932, both the goals and tactics of Republican economic diplomacy came into question. Within Republican policymaking circles, officials in the State Department and the FRBNY increasingly emphasized the importance of foreign policy initiatives regardless of whether these initiatives generated greater foreign competition in the domestic market or imposed additional burdens on American taxpayers. Believing that domestic price increases were constantly aborted by the depreciation of foreign currencies, these officials in the State Department and the FRBNY wanted to revise the intergovernmental debt accords, reduce trade barriers, and stabilize currencies. Outside administration circles, during the interregnum, Moley, Tugwell, and Berle urged Roosevelt to focus all his energies on domestic solutions and reject the Republicans' emphasis on the international causes of the Depression. In the midst of the raging controversy over the relative importance of domestic and international solutions, Hoover abandoned his primary reliance on independent experts and nonpolitical mechanisms and interjected himself into European land disarmament questions. He acknowledged a link between the war debts and other issues, contemplated a comprehensive debt settlement that accommodated political imperatives at home and abroad, and appealed for Roosevelt's cooperation. Although his political opponents suspected that he was now adopting an exclusively internationalist approach to recovery, this view was an incorrect assessment of Hoover's intentions. He still believed in the primacy of the domestic market and the importance of a balanced budget. But since he also continued to assume that Europe's stabilization would serve American interests, he was anxious to devise new tactics to abet Europe's recovery without jeopardizing his domestic priorities or incurring strategic obligations. During his last year in office, then, Hoover changed tactics but did not alter his fundamental orientation to European affairs.

Roosevelt, like Hoover, was immediately enveloped in a conflict over the relative efficacy of nationalist and internationalist solutions to the Depression. He distrusted Hoover's emphasis on linking all major international questions to one another. Roosevelt did not want to arouse political controversy over the war debts issue and feared that he might become entrapped in discredited Republican policies. Roosevelt was eager to launch his own foreign policy initiatives to expedite Europe's recovery and enhance France's security. But during the hectic first months of the New Deal, Roosevelt was unable to develop mechanisms and instruments that would allow him to harmonize his domestic programs with his foreign policy goals. His advisers often worked at cross-purposes with one another. As a result in May, June, and July 1933 Roosevelt was confronted with a sequence of decisions on disarmament, trade, debt, and currency questions. On each one he chose the more nationalist option.

These decisions highlighted the difficulty of formulating tactics capable of promoting both domestic and foreign policy goals. Given the intensity of political pressures, the extent of domestic economic duress, and the inhospitable international environment, it was natural for Roosevelt to focus on domestic objectives. In so doing he gave less priority to the issues of European stability and French security. Having acquiesced to the nationalistic and isolationist onslaught, Roosevelt temporarily accepted the views that the United States could recover economically regardless of developments in Europe and remain aloof from a European war. As a result for several years constructive attempts to promote European stability and enhance French security ended.

When American officials again turned their attention to reconstructing a stable Europe in the aftermath of the Second World War, the experience of that conflict and the severity of the Depression radically altered their orientation. The length and depth of the Great Depression led to a greater emphasis on the international sources of American prosperity, a larger governmental role in the domestic economy, a gradual weakening of the forces of fiscal conservatism, and a slow erosion of protectionist sentiments. At the same time, the struggle against one aggressive totalitarian nation and the prospect of having to contain another altered American attitudes toward foreign entanglements. This complex set of developments caused policymakers to be more willing to incur strategic obligations abroad, expand the role of the government in foreign economic policy, and alter the relative balance of priorities between foreign economic goals and domestic imperatives. The result was a much more successful effort to stabilize western Europe. Whether this foreign policy success set precedents for a dangerous overcommitment of the United States in world affairs and an unnecessary subjugation of domestic priorities remains a matter of controversy. The dilemma of finding a desirable balance between internal and external goals without overcommitting the United States in matters of nonvital importance continues as a challenge to policymakers.

The period 1919 to 1933 remains of great interest to students of American foreign policy because it constituted a transitional phase in the evolution of American diplomacy. During that time policymakers grasped the growing interdependence of the world economy and sought to establish a stable liberal capitalist community in western Europe. During that time also policymakers carefully weighed the risks of involvement against the dangers of isolation and studiously considered the domestic repercussions of tactical efforts to expand exports. In the pre-Nazi, pre-Keynesian, pre-atomic era, policymakers understandably questioned the advantages of strategic commitments abroad and allowed fiscal imperatives and protectionist sentiments to influence the molding of foreign economic policy. What is so instructive about this period and what has been overlooked in many former studies is the extent to which government officials sought to reconcile their internal and external economic priorities and endeavored to balance their desire for America's political aloofness with their quest for Germany's rehabilitation and their concern for France's security. Ultimately, they failed in their task. But a study of their efforts should help elucidate the difficulties that policymakers encounter as they ponder the wisdom and efficacy of overseas commitments, struggle to coordinate foreign and domestic policy, and attempt to restrain the forces of partisan politics and parochial nationalism.

Bibliography

Manuscript Collections

Amherst, Massachusetts
  Amherst College Library
    Dwight W. Morrow Papers.
Cambridge, Massachusetts
  Baker Library
    Thomas W. Lamont Papers.
  Houghton Library
    Joseph C. Grew Papers.
    Jay Pierrepont Moffat Papers.
    William Phillips Papers.
Cleveland, Ohio
  Western Reserve Historical Society
    Myron T. Herrick Papers.
Columbus, Ohio
  The Ohio Historical Society
    Warren G. Harding Papers.
Hyde Park, New York
  Franklin D. Roosevelt Library
    Franklin D. Roosevelt Papers.
    Rexford G. Tugwell Diary.
New Haven, Connecticut
  Sterling Library
    Edward M. House Papers.
    Henry L. Stimson Papers.
    Paul M. Warburg Papers.
New York, New York
  Columbia University Library
    James Paul Warburg Oral History
      Memoir and Diary.
  Federal Reserve Bank of New York
    Papers of the Federal Reserve Bank
      of New York.
    George L. Harrison Papers (copies).
    Benjamin Strong Papers.
Princeton, New Jersey
  Princeton University Library
    Otto Kahn Papers.
    Fred I. Kent Papers.

Van Hornesville, New York
  Owen D. Young Library
    Stuart Crocker Diary: Notes on the
      Young Plan.
    R. Tileston: Chronology of the Work
      of the Committee of Experts of
      the Reparation Commission.
    Owen D. Young Papers.
Washington, D.C.
  Library of Congress
    Leonard P. Ayres Papers.
    William E. Borah Papers.
    Mark L. Bristol Papers.
    Bainbridge Colby Papers.
    William S. Culbertson Papers.
    Norman H. Davis Papers.
    Herbert Feis Papers.
    Henry P. Fletcher Papers.
    Felix Frankfurter Papers.
    Emmanuel Goldenweiser Papers.
    Charles S. Hamlin Papers.
    Leland Harrison Papers.
    Charles Evans Hughes Papers.
    Cordell Hull Papers.
    Robert Lansing Papers.
    Russell C. Leffingwell Papers.
    Ogden L. Mills Papers.
    George S. Simonds Papers.
    Woodrow Wilson Papers.
  National Archives
    Frederick M. Feiker Papers.
    Robert P. Lamont Papers.
West Branch, Iowa
  Herbert Hoover Presidential Library
    William R. Castle Papers.
    Herbert C. Hoover Commerce De-
      partment Papers.
    Herbert C. Hoover Presidential Pa-
      pers.

Herbert C. Hoover Post-Presidential Papers.
Raymond Moley Oral History Interview.
Byron Price Oral History Interview.
Hugh Robert Wilson Papers.

Unpublished United States Government Documents

Washington, D.C.
National Archives
Department of Commerce. Records of the Bureau of Foreign and Domestic Commerce. Record Group 151.
Department of the Navy. Confidential Records of the Secretary of the Navy. Record Group 80.
_____. General Records of the Department of the Navy. Record Group 80.
_____. Records of the Office of Naval Intelligence. Record Group 38.
Department of State. General Records of the Department of State. Record Group 59.
_____. Records of the American Commission to Negotiate Peace. Record Group 256.
_____. Records of the United States Participation in International Conferences, Commissions, and Expositions. Record Group 43.
Department of the Treasury. General Records of the Department of the Treasury. Record Group 56.
_____. Records of the Bureau of Accounts. Record Group 39.
Department of War. Records of the Adjutant General's Office. Record Group 94.
_____. Records of the Military Intelligence Division. Record Group 165.
_____. Records of the War Department General and Special Staffs. Record Group 165.
United States Senate. Records of the United States Senate. Record Group 46.
Washington Navy Yard.
Records of the General Board of the Navy.

Published United States Congressional Documents

Congressional Record. 66th to 72d Congress. 1919–33.
House of Representatives
Committee on Banking and Currency. *Hearings on H.R. 8404: Exchange Stabilization.* 67th Cong., 1st sess., 1921.
_____. *Hearings under H.R. Res. 364: German Reparation Bonds.* 71st Cong., 2d sess., 1930.
_____. Staff Report of the Subcommittee on Domestic Finance. *Federal Reserve Structure and the Development of Monetary Policy, 1915–1935.* 92d Cong., 1st sess., 1971.
Committee on Foreign Affairs. *Hearings on H.J. Res. 163: General Disarmament Conference.* 72d Cong., 1st sess., 1932.
Committee on Ways and Means. *Hearings on H.J. Res. 80: Extension of Maturity Date for Indebtedness of France for War-Surplus Supplies.* 71st Cong., 1st sess., 1929.
_____. *Hearings on H.J. Res. 11848 and H.R. 11948: French and Yugoslavian Debt Settlements.* 69th Cong., 1st sess., 1926.
_____. *Hearings on H.R. 6585: French Debt Settlement.* 71st Cong., 2d sess., 1929.
_____. *French Debt Settlement.* House Report No. 26. 71st Cong., 2d sess., 1929.
_____. *Hearings on H.J. Res. 123: Moratorium on Foreign Debts.* 72d Cong., 1st sess., 1931.

————. *Settlement of the Indebtedness of French Republic to the United States.* House Report no. 1338. 69th Cong., 1st sess., 1926.
Senate
  Commission of Gold and Silver Inquiry. *Foreign Currency and Exchange Investigation.* 67th Cong., 4th sess., 1925.
  Committee on Finance. *Hearings Relative to the French Debt Settlement.* 69th Cong., 1st sess., 1926.
  ————. *Hearings on H.J. Res. 147: Postponement of Intergovernmental Debts.* 72d Cong., 1st sess., 1931.
  ————. *Hearings on S. 2135: Refunding of Foreign Obligations.* 67th Cong., 1st sess., 1921.
  ————. *Refunding of Obligations of Foreign Governments.* Senate Report no. 400. 67th Cong., 2d sess., 1922.
  ————. *Hearings Pursuant to S. Res. 19: Sale of Foreign Bonds or Securities in the United States.* 72d Cong., 1st sess., 1931–32.
  Committee on Foreign Relations. *Hearings on the General Pact for the Renunciation of War.* 70th Cong., 2d sess., 1928.
  ————. *Treaty of Peace with Germany.* 66th Cong., 1st sess., 1919.
  ————. *Treaty on the Limitation of Naval Armaments.* 71st Cong., 2d sess., 1930.
  Committee on the Judiciary. *Loans to Foreign Governments.* Senate Document no. 86. 67th Cong., 2d sess., 1921.
  Select Committee on the Investigation of the Tariff Commission. *Investigation of the Tariff Commission.* 69th Cong., 1st–2d sess., 1926–28.

Published United States Government Documents

Washington, D.C.: Government Printing Office
Bureau of the Census. *Historical Statistics of the United States, Colonial Times to 1957.* 1960.
Conference on Unemployment. *Report of the President's Conference on Unemployment.* 1921.
Department of Agriculture. *Annual Report of the Secretary of Agriculture.* 1925–29.
Department of Commerce. *Annual Report of the Secretary of Commerce.* 1922–33.
————. Bureau of Foreign and Domestic Commerce. *The Balance of International Payments of the United States. Trade Information Bulletin* nos. 144, 215, 340, 399, 503, 552, 625, 698, 761, 803, 814, 819. 1922–33.
————. *Commerce Yearbook.* 1921–33.
————. *European Tariff Policies Since the War.* By Henry Chalmers. *Trade Information Bulletin* no. 228. 1924.
————. *Foreign Tariff Legislation.* 1921.
————. *Statistical Abstract of the United States.* 1919–33.
————. *The United States in the World Economy.* By Hal B. Lary. 1943.
Department of State. *Conference on the Limitation of Armament.* 1922.
————. *Papers Relating to the Foreign Relations of the United States*, 1920–33. 1935–49.
————. *Papers Relating to the Foreign Relations of the United States: The Paris Peace Conference, 1919.* 13 vols. 1942–47.
Department of the Treasury. *Annual Report of the Secretary of the Treasury.* 1921–29.
Tariff Commission. *Annual Report of the Tariff Commission.* 1923–30.
————. *Depreciated Exchange and International Trade.* 1922.
————. *Reciprocity and Commercial Treaties.* 1919.
World War Foreign Debt Commission. *Combined Annual Reports of the World War Foreign Debt Commission with Additional Information Regarding Foreign Debts Due the United States.* 1927.
————. *Minutes of the World War Foreign Debt Commission*, 1922–26. 1927.

Additional Published Documents

Allied Powers. Agent General for Reparations. *The Execution of the Experts' Plan: 1st–3d Year.* 3 vols. Berlin: Office for Reparation Payments, 1924–27.
Allied Powers. Reparation Commission. *The Experts' Plan for Reparation Payments.* Paris: 1926.
Bank for International Settlements. *Annual Report.* Basle: 1930/31–1932/33.
Belgium. Commission royale d'histoire. *Documents diplomatiques belges, 1920–1940.* 3 vols. Vol. 1, *Période 1920–1924.* Vol. 2, *Période 1925–1931.* Brussels: Ch. de Visscher et F. Vanlangenhove, 1964.
Burnett, Philip Mason, ed. *Reparation at the Paris Peace Conference from the Standpoint of the American Delegation.* 2 vols. New York: Columbia University Press, 1940.
France. Ministère des Affaires Etrangères. *Documents diplomatiques: Conférence de Londres (16 juillet–16 aôut 1924).* Paris: Imprimerie Nationale, 1925.
————. *Documents diplomatiques: Conférence de Washington (juillet 1921–février 1922).* Paris: Imprimerie Nationale, 1923.
————. *Documents diplomatiques: Documents relatifs aux négociations concernant les garanties de sécurité contre une agression de l'Allemagne (10 janvier 1919–7 décembre 1923).* Paris: Imprimerie Nationale, 1924.
————. *Documents diplomatiques français, 1932–1939.* Series 1, vols. 1–3. Paris: Imprimerie Nationale, 1964–67.
Great Britain. Foreign Office. *Documents on British Foreign Policy, 1919–1939.* Edited by J. P. T. Bury, Rohan Butler, Douglas Dakin, M. E. Lambert, W. N. Medlicott, and Ernest L. Woodward. Series 1, vols. 5, 8–10, 15, 16, 19. Series 1A, vols. 1–6. Series 2, vols. 2–6. London: Her Majesty's Stationery Office, 1947–75.
League of Nations. Documents of the Preparatory Commission for the Disarmament Conference. *Minutes of the Fourth Session of the Preparatory Commisson for the Disarmament Conference and the First Session of the Committee on Arbitration and Security.* Geneva: 1928.
————. Economic and Finance Section. *Tariff Level Indices.* Geneva: 1927.
————. Economic and Financial Organization. *Memorandum on International Trade and Balance of Payments, 1912–1926.* Geneva: 1927.
————. Economic Organization. Consultative Committee. *Application of the Recommendations of the International Economic Conference.* Geneva: 1929.
Mantoux, Paul, ed. *Les Délibérations du conseil des quatre, 24 mars–28 juin 1919.* 2 vols. Paris: Editions du centre national de la recherche scientifique, 1955.

Autobiographies, Diaries, Letters, Memoirs, Speeches, and Personal Accounts

Acheson, Dean. *Morning and Noon.* Boston: Houghton Mifflin Co., 1965.
Allen, Henry T. *My Rhineland Journal.* Boston: Houghton Mifflin Co., 1923.
Baker, Ray Stannard. *Woodrow Wilson and World Settlement.* 3 vols. Garden City, N.Y.: Doubleday, Page and Co., 1922.
Baruch, Bernard. *The Making of the Reparation and Economic Sections of the Treaty.* New York: Harper and Brothers, 1920.
Bérenger, Henry. *La Question des dettes.* Paris: Hachette, 1933.
Berle, Adolf. *Navigating the Rapids, 1918–1971: From the Papers of Adolf Berle.* Edited by Beatrice Berle and Travis Jacobs. New York: Harcourt, Brace Jovanovich, 1973.
Bullitt, William C. *For the President, Personal and Secret: Correspondence Between Franklin D. Roosevelt and William C. Bullitt.* Edited by Orville H. Bullitt. Boston: Houghton Mifflin Co., 1972.
Butler, Nicholas Murray. *Across the Busy Years: Recollections and Reflections.* 2 vols. New York: Charles Scribner's Sons, 1940.

Caillaux, Joseph. *Mes Mémoires*. 3 vols. Vol. 3, *Clairvoyance et force d'âme dans les épreuves, 1912–1930*. Paris: Plon, 1947.

Chamberlain, Austen. *Down the Years*. London: Cassell and Co., 1935.

_____. *The Life and Letters of the Right Hon. Sir Austen Chamberlain*. Edited by Charles Petrie. 2 vols. London: Cassell and Co., 1939–40.

Clemenceau, Georges. *Grandeur and Misery of Victory*. Translated by F. M. Atkinson. New York: Harcourt, Brace and Co., 1930.

Coolidge, Calvin. *The Autobiography of Calvin Coolidge*. New York: Cosmopolitan Book Corporation, 1929.

_____. *The Talkative President: The Off-the-Record Press Conferences of Calvin Coolidge*. Edited by Howard H. Quint and Robert H. Ferrell. Amherst: University of Massachusetts Press, 1964.

D'Abernon, Viscount Edgar Vincent. *An Ambassador of Peace: Lord D'Abernon's Diary*. 3 vols. Vol. 2, *The Years of Crisis, June 1922–December 1923*. Vol. 3, *The Years of Recovery, January 1924–October 1926*. London: Hodder and Stoughton, 1929–30.

Dawes, Charles G. *Journal as Ambassador to Great Britain*. New York: Macmillan Co., 1939.

_____. *A Journal of Reparations*. New York: Macmillan Co., 1939.

_____. *Notes as Vice President, 1928–1929*. Boston: Little, Brown and Co., 1935.

Dawes, Rufus. *The Dawes Plan in the Making*. Indianapolis: The Bobbs-Merrill Co., 1925.

Dewey, Charles S. *As I Recall It*. Washington: Williams and Heintz Lithograph Corporation, 1957.

Edge, Walter E. *A Jerseyman's Journal: Fifty Years of American Business and Politics*. Princeton: Princeton University Press, 1948.

Goldsmith, Alan G. *Economic Problems of Western Europe*. n.p., 1923.

Grew, Joseph C. *Turbulent Era: A Diplomatic Record of Forty Years, 1904–1945*. Edited by Walter Johnson. 2 vols. Boston: Houghton Mifflin Co., 1952.

Herriot, Edouard. *Jadis*. 2 vols. Vol. 2, *D'une guerre à l'autre, 1914–1936*. Paris: Flammarion, 1952.

Hoover, Herbert C. *Addresses Delivered During the Visit of Herbert Hoover, President-Elect of the United States, to Central and South America, November–December 1928*. Washington: Pan America Union, 1929.

_____. *American Individualism*. Garden City, N.Y.: Doubleday, Page and Co., 1922.

_____. *The Future of our Foreign Trade*. Washington: Government Printing Office, 1926.

_____. *The Hoover Administration: A Documented Narrative*. Edited by William Starr Myers and Walter Hughes Newton. New York: Charles Scribner's Sons, 1936.

_____. *The Memoirs of Herbert Hoover*. 3 vols. Vol. 1, *Years of Adventure, 1874–1920*. Vol. 2, *The Cabinet and the Presidency, 1920–1933*. Vol. 3, *The Great Depression, 1929–1941*. New York: Macmillan Co., 1951–52.

_____. *The New Day: Campaign Speeches of Herbert Hoover*. Stanford: Stanford University Press, 1928.

_____. *The State Papers and Other Public Writings of Herbert Hoover*. 2 vols. Vol. 1, *March 4, 1929 to October 1, 1931*. Vol. 2, *October 1, 1931 to March 4, 1933*. Edited by William Starr Myers. New York: Doubleday, Doran and Co., 1934.

_____, and Gibson, Hugh. *The Problems of Lasting Peace*. New York: Doubleday, Doran and Co., 1942.

House, Edward M. *The Intimate Papers of Colonel House*. Vol. 4, *The Ending of the War: June 1918–August 1919*. Edited by Charles Seymour. Boston: Houghton Mifflin Co., 1928.

_____, and Seymour, Charles, eds. *What Really Happened at Paris: The Story of the Peace Conference, 1918–1919, by the American Delegates*. New York: Charles Scribner's Sons, 1921.

Houston, David F. *Eight Years with Wilson's Cabinet, 1913–1920*. 2 vols. Garden City, N.Y.: Doubleday, Page and Co., 1926.

Hughes, Charles Evans. *The Autobiographical Notes of Charles Evans Hughes*. Edited by David Danelski and Joseph Tulchin. Cambridge, Mass.: Harvard University Press, 1973.

————. *The Pathway of Peace*. New York: Harper and Brothers, 1925.

Hull, Cordell. *The Memoirs of Cordell Hull*. 2 vols. Vol. 1. New York: Macmillan Co., 1948.

Lamont, Thomas W. *Across World Frontiers*. New York: Harcourt, Brace and Co., 1951.

Lansing, Robert. *The Big Four and Others of the Peace Conference*. Boston: Houghton Mifflin Co., 1921.

————. *The Peace Negotiations: A Personal Narrative*. Boston: Houghton Mifflin Co., 1921.

Laroche, Jules Alfred. *Au Quai d'Orsay avec Briand et Poincaré, 1913–1926*. Paris: Hachette, 1957.

Lloyd George, David. *Memoirs of the Peace Conference*. 2 vols. New Haven: Yale University Press, 1939.

————. *The Truth About Reparations and War Debts*. Garden City, N.Y.: Doubleday, Doran and Co., 1932.

Loucheur, Louis. *Carnets secrets, 1908–1932*. Edited by Jacques De Launay. Brussels: Brepols, 1962.

McAdoo, William G. *Crowded Years: The Reminiscences of William Gibbs McAdoo*. Boston: Houghton Mifflin Co., 1931.

MacArthur, Douglas. *Reminiscences*. New York: McGraw Hill Book Co., 1964.

Miller, David Hunter. *The Drafting of the Covenant*. 2 vols. New York: G. P. Putnam's Sons, 1928.

Mitchell, Charles E. *Back to First Principles*. n.p., 1922.

Moffat, Jay Pierrepont. *The Moffat Papers: Selections from the Diplomatic Journals of Jay Pierrepont Moffat, 1919–1943*. Edited by Nancy H. Hooker. Cambridge, Mass.: Harvard University Press, 1956.

Moley, Raymond. *After Seven Years*. New York: Harper and Brothers, 1939.

————. *The First New Deal*. New York: Harcourt, Brace and World, 1966.

Moreau, Emile. *Souvenirs d'un gouverneur de la Banque de France: Histoire de la stabilization du franc, 1926–1928*. Paris: M. T. Génin, 1954.

Morgenthau, Henry, Jr. *From the Morgenthau Diaries*. Edited by John Morton Blum. 3 vols. Vol. 1, *Years of Crises, 1928–1938*. Boston: Houghton Mifflin Co., 1959.

Paul-Boncour, Joseph. *Entre deux guerres: Souvenirs sur la III République*. 3 vols. Vol. 2, *Les Lendemains de la victoire, 1919–1934*. Paris: Plon, 1946.

Poincaré, Raymond. *Au Service de la France*. 11 vols. Vol. 11, *A La Récherche de la paix, 1919*. Paris: Plon, 1974.

Roosevelt, Franklin D. *Franklin D. Roosevelt and Foreign Affairs*. 3 vols. Vol. 1, *January 1933–February 1934*. Edited by Edgar G. Nixon. Cambridge, Mass.: Harvard University Press, 1969.

————. *The Public Papers and Addresses of Franklin D. Roosevelt*. 13 vols. Vol. 1, *The Genesis of the New Deal, 1928–1932*. Vol. 2, *The Year of Crisis, 1933*. Edited by Samuel I. Rosenman. New York: Random House, 1938.

Schiff, Mortimer. *Europe in March 1922*. n.p., 1922.

————. *Some Present Day Problems*. n.p., 1924.

Seydoux, Jacques. *De Versailles au plan Young: réparations–dettes interalliées– réconstruction européene*. Paris: Plon, 1932.

Snowden, Viscount Philip. *An Autobiography*. 2 vols. London: Ivor Nicholson and Watson, 1934.

Stimson, Henry L., and Bundy, McGeorge. *On Active Service in Peace and War*. New York: Harper and Brothers, 1948.

Stresemann, Gustav. *Essays and Speeches on Various Topics*. Translated by C. R. Turner. London: Thornton Butterworth, 1930.

_____. *Gustav Stresemann: His Diaries, Letters, and Papers*. Edited and translated by Sir Eric Sutton. 3 vols. London: Macmillan and Co., 1935–40.

Strong, Benjamin. *Interpretations of Federal Reserve Policy in the Speeches and Writings of Benjamin Strong*. Edited by Warren Randolph Burgess. New York: Harper and Brothers, 1930.

Suarez, Georges. *Briand: sa vie – son oeuvre avec son journal et de nombreux documents inédits*. 6 vols. Vols. 5 and 6, *L'Artisan de la paix*. Paris: Plon, 1941–52.

Tardieu, André. *The Truth about the Treaty*. Indianapolis: Bobbs-Merrill Co., 1921.

Tugwell, Rexford G. *The Brains Trust*. New York: Viking Press, 1968.

_____. *The Democratic Roosevelt: A Biography of Franklin D. Roosevelt*. New York: Doubleday and Co., 1957.

_____. *In Search of Roosevelt*. Cambridge, Mass.: Harvard University Press, 1973.

Wallace, Henry C. *Our Debt and Duty to the Farmer*. New York: Century Company, 1925.

Warburg, James Paul. *The Long Road Home: The Autobiography of a Maverick*. New York: Doubleday and Co., 1964.

Weygand, Maxime. *Mémoirs*. 3 vols. Vol. 2, *Mirages et réalité*. Paris: Flammarion, 1957.

Wilson, Hugh Robert. *Diplomat Between Wars*. New York: Longmans, Green and Co., 1941.

Wilson, Woodrow. *The Public Papers of Woodrow Wilson*. 6 vols. Vols. 5 and 6, *War and Peace*. Edited by Ray Stannard Baker and William E. Dodd. New York: Harper and Brothers, 1920.

Woolley, Mary Emma. *Life and Letters of Mary Emma Woolley*. Edited by Jeannette Marks. Washington: Public Affairs Press, 1925.

Young, Owen D., and Swope, Gerard. *Selected Addresses of Owen D. Young, chairman of the Board of Directors and Gerard Swope, president, General Electric Company*. Edited by General Electric Company. New York: General Electric Company, 1930.

Journals, Proceedings, and Publications of Business Organizations

American Bankers Association. *Journal of the American Bankers Association*. 1921–1933.

_____. *The Problems of Economic Restoration*. New York, 1925.

_____. Commerce and Marine Division. *Domestic and Foreign Affairs: A Report of Developments Bearing upon the Commerce of the United States*. New York, 1929.

_____. *Survey of Financial Affairs at Home and Abroad*. New York, 1930.

American Farm Bureau Federation. *Report of the Executive Secretary*. Chicago, 1921–33.

Bankers Magazine. 1921–29.

Business Week. 1932–33.

Chamber of Commerce of the United States. *International Trade Conference*. New York, 1919.

_____. *Nation's Business*. 1921–33.

_____. *Policies of the Chamber of Commerce of the United States, 1925*.

Commercial and Financial Chronicle. 1921–33.

Guaranty Trust Company of New York. *Guaranty Survey*. 1925–27.

International Chamber of Commerce. *Proceedings of the Second Congress*. Brochure no. 32. Paris, 1923.

Investment Bankers Association of America. *Proceedings of the Annual Convention*. Chicago, 1918–28.

National Association of Manufacturers. *The Platform of American Industry*. New York, 1928, 1932.

————. *Proceedings of the Annual Convention*. New York, 1920–28.
National City Bank of New York. *Monthly Letter*. 1926.
The National Economic League. *Consensus*. 1922–24, 1930–33.
National Foreign Trade Council. *The American Trade Balance and Probable Tendencies*. New York, 1919.
————. *Official Report of the National Foreign Trade Convention*. New York, 1921–33.
Stuart, Charles E. *European Conditions in Their Relation to International Trade and Export Credits*. National Foreign Trade Council. New York, 1935.

Other Periodicals

Army and Navy Journal, 1932–33.
Congressional Digest, 1922–33.
Literary Digest, 1919–33.
American Review of Reviews, 1925–29.

Contemporary Articles and Books

Angell, James W. "The Reparations Settlement and the International Flow of Capital." *American Economic Review* 20 (March 1930, Supplement):80–88.
Armstrong, Hamilton Fish. "France and the Hoover Plan." *Foreign Affairs* 10 (October 1931):23–33.
Aubert, Louis. "Security: Key to French Policy." *Foreign Affairs* 11 (October 1932):122–36.
Auld, George P. "Does High Investment Hamper the Repayment of Our Loans and Investments Abroad." *Annals of the American Academy of Political and Social Science* 139 (January 1929):181–203.
Bergmann, Carl. "Germany and the Young Plan." *Foreign Affairs* 8 (July 1930):583–97.
————. *The History of Reparations*. Boston: Houghton Mifflin Co., 1927.
Bidwell, Percy W. "New American Tariff: Europe's Answer." *Foreign Affairs* 9 (October 1930):13–26.
Boyden, Roland W. "Relation Between Reparations and the Inter-Allied Debts." *Academy of Political Science Proceedings* 12 (January 1928):819–26.
Brown, William Adams, Jr. "German Reparations and the International Flow of Capital." *American Economic Review* 20 (March 1930, Supplement):89–92.
"Burden of Armaments: A Major Obstacle to Recovery." *New York Trust Company Index* 12 (August 1932):153–59.
Capper, Arthur. "The Farmer and Foreign Trade." *Foreign Affairs* 9 (July 1931):638–46.
————. "Making the Peace Pact Effective." *Annals of the American Academy of Political and Social Science* 144 (July 1929):59–65.
Carter, John. "America's Present Role in World Affairs." *Current History* 35 (November 1931):161–66.
[Castle, William R.] "Two Years of American Foreign Policy." *Foreign Affairs* 1 (March 1923):1–24.
Collings, Harry T. "The Foreign Investment Policy of the United States." *Annals of the American Academy of Political and Social Science* 126 (July 1926):71–79.
Comstock, Alzada. "Reparation Payments in Perspective." *American Economic Review* 20 (June 1930):199–209.
Coolidge, Calvin. "Promoting Peace Through Limitation of Armaments." *Ladies' Home Journal* 48 (May 1929):3–4, 93.
————. "Promoting Peace Through Preparation for Defense." *Ladies' Home Journal* 48 (April 1929):3–4, 65.

————. "Promoting Peace Through Renunciation of War." *Ladies' Home Journal* 48 (June 1929):6, 160–61.

Culbertson, William S. *International Economic Policies: A Survey of the Economics of Diplomacy.* New York: D. Appleton and Co., 1925.

Davis, Norman H. "Peace and World Trade." *Academy of Political Science Proceedings* 13 (January 1929):301–9.

de Fontenelle, Henri de Peyerimhoff. "The International Cartel Movement and French Economic Life." *A Picture of World Economic Conditions in the Summer of 1929.* New York: National Industrial Conference Board, 1929.

Dernburg, Bernhard. "Germany's Economic Restoration and the Dawes Plan." *Current History* 25 (March 1927):785–91.

DeWilde, J. C. "French Financial Policy." *Foreign Policy Reports* 8 (December 1932):232–42.

Dubois, Louis. *Dettes de guerre et réparations: les accords français de Washington et de Londres et le plan Dawes.* Paris: Union des intérêts économiques, 1929.

Dulles, Allen W. "The Disarmament Puzzle." *Foreign Affairs* 9 (July 1931):605–16.

————. "Progress Toward Disarmament." *Foreign Affairs* 11 (October 1932):54–65.

————. "Some Misconceptions about Disarmament." *Foreign Affairs* 5 (April 1927):413–24.

Dulles, John Foster. "Allied Debts." *Foreign Affairs* 1 (September 1922):116–32.

————. "Our Foreign Loan Policy." *Foreign Affairs* 5 (October 1926):33–48.

Edwards, George W. "American Policy with Reference to Foreign Investments." *American Economic Review* 14 (March 1924, Supplement):31–35.

————. "Foreign Investment Policies and Their Relation to International Peace." *Annals of the American Academy of Political and Social Science* 126 (July 1926):95–97.

————. "Government Control of Foreign Investments." *American Economic Review* 18 (December 1928):684–701.

Ellsworth, D. W. "German Crisis and the Domestic Bank Situation." *The Annalist* 38 (July 1931):3–4.

Enslow, Harold. "The Franco-American Tariff Problem." *Annals of the American Academy of Political and Social Science* 141 (January 1929):212–19.

Fay, H. van V. "Commercial Policy in Post-War Europe." *Quarterly Journal of Economics* 41 (May 1927):441–71.

Feis, Herbert. "After Tariffs, Embargoes." *Foreign Affairs* 9 (April 1931):398–408.

————. "The Export of American Capital." *Foreign Affairs* 3 (July 1925):668–86.

Frey, John Philip. "Foreign Loans and National Prosperity." *American Federationist* 35 (July 1928):792–98.

Geraud, André. "The London Naval Conference: A French View." *Foreign Affairs* 8 (July 1930):519–33.

Glass, Carter. "Government Supervision of Foreign Loans." *Academy of Political Science Proceedings* 12 (January 1928):45–51.

Hall, Ray Ovid. "French-American Balance of Payments in 1928: Our 'Unfavorable' Position." *The Annalist* 34 (November 1929):908.

————. "The United States Balance of Payments for 1927 and 1928." *The Annalist* 34 (August 1929):302, 310.

Hipwell, H. Hallam. "Trade Rivalries in Argentina." *Foreign Affairs* 8 (October 1929):150–55.

Houghton, Alanson B. "Disarmament and Depression." *Nation* 133 (23 December 1931):695.

Kahn, Otto. *Of Many Things.* New York: Boni and Liveright, 1926.

————. *Reflections of a Financier: A Study of Economic and Other Problems.* London: Hodder and Stoughton, 1921.

Kellogg, Frank B. "Some Foreign Policies of the United States." *Foreign Affairs* 4 (January 1926, Special Supplement):i–xvii.

Keynes, John Maynard. *The Economic Consequences of the Peace*. London: Macmillan and Co., 1919.
Klein, Julius. "Foreign Loans and National Prosperity." *American Federationist* 35 (September 1928):1054–58.
———. "The Tariff and the Depression." *Current History* 34 (July 1931):497–99.
Klotz, Louis Lucien. *Les Dettes de guerre interalliées*. Boulogne-Sur-Seine: Impr. d'Etudes sociales et politiques, 1925.
Lamont, Thomas. "The Final Reparations Settlement." *Foreign Affairs* 8 (April 1930):336–63.
Layton, Walter T. "Europe's Future Role in World Trade." *Academy of Political Science Proceedings* 12 (January 1928):161–62.
Lechartier, G. "French Policy and Disarmament." *Academy of Political Science Proceedings* 12 (July 1926):35–40.
Leffingwell, Russell C. "War Debts." *Yale Review* 12 (October 1922):22–40.
Lenroot, Irvine L. "Disarmament and the Present Outlook for Peace." *Annals of the American Academy of Political and Social Science* 126 (July 1926):142–45.
Lippmann, Walter. "Lausanne Agreements and American Recovery." *Fortune* 6 (September 1932):50–57.
———. "The London Naval Conference: An American View." *Foreign Affairs* 8 (July 1930):499–519.
———. "Public Opinion and the Renunciation of War." *Academy of Political Science Proceedings* 13 (January 1929):243–47.
Long, Breckenridge. "Limitations Upon the Adoption of any Foreign Investment Policy by the United States." *Annals of the American Academy of Political and Social Science* 126 (July 1926):92–94.
McFadyean, Andrew. *Reparation Reviewed*. London: Ernest Benn, 1930.
Miller, A. C. "Responsibility for Federal Reserve Policies, 1927–1929." *American Economic Review* 25 (September 1935):442–58.
Mills, Ogden. "Our Foreign Policy: A Republican View." *Foreign Affairs* 6 (July 1928):555–72.
Moon, Parker Thomas, ed. *The Young Plan in Operation*. New York: Academy of Political Science, 1931.
Morgan, Shepard. "Constructive Functions of the International Bank." *Foreign Affairs* 9 (July 1931): 580–92.
Myers, William Starr. "The Kellogg Pact—The Question of Sanctions." *Annals of the American Academy of Political and Social Science* 144 (July 1929):60–61.
Nichols, William Wallace. "Trade Barriers and Customs Duties." *Proceedings of the Academy of Political Science* 12 (January 1928):125–26.
Robinson, Henry M. "Are American Loans Abroad Safe?" *Foreign Affairs* 5 (October 1926):49–56.
———. "Some Lessons from the Economic Conference." *Foreign Affairs* 6 (October 1927):14–22.
Rogers, James Harvey. "Foreign Markets and Foreign Credits." *Recent Economic Changes in the United States*. Report of the Committee on Recent Economic Changes. Vol. 2. New York: McGraw-Hill Book Co., 1929.
Roosevelt, Franklin D. "Our Foreign Policy: A Democratic View." *Foreign Affairs* 6 (July 1928):573–86.
Schacht, Hjalmar. *The End of Reparations*. Translated by Lewis Gannett. New York: Jonathan Cape and Harrison Smith, 1931.
Scroggs, William O. "The American Investment in Germany." *Foreign Affairs* 10 (January 1932):324–26.
Seligman, E. R. A. "World Peace and Economic Stability." *Academy of Political Science Proceedings* 13 (January 1929):197–203.
Shotwell, James T. "The Problem of Disarmament." *Annals of the American Academy of Political and Social Science* 126 (July 1926):51–55.

————. *War as an Instrument of National Policy and Its Renunciation in the Pact of Paris*. New York: Harcourt, Brace and Co., 1929.

Siegfried, André. "The Development of French Tariff Policy After the War." *A Picture of World Economic Conditions at the Beginning of 1929*. New York: National Industrial Conference Board, 1929.

————. "European Reactions to American Tariff Proposals." *Foreign Affairs* 8 (October 1929):13–19.

Smoot, Reed. "Our Tariff and the Depression." *Current History* 35 (November 1931):173–81.

"The State Department and Foreign Loans." *New York Trust Company Index* 8 (February 1928):3–7.

Stimson, Henry L. "Bases of American Foreign Policy During the Past Four Years." *Foreign Affairs* 11 (April 1933):383–96.

Stresemann, Gustav. "The Economic Restoration of the World." *Foreign Affairs* 2 (June 1924):552–58.

Stuart, Graham. "Tariff Making in France." *Annals of the American Academy of Political and Social Science* 141 (January 1929):98–106.

Sullivan, Mark. "President Hoover and the World Depression." *Saturday Evening Post* 205 (11 March 1933):3–5; (18 March 1933):10–11.

Tardieu, André. *France in Danger! A Great Statesman's Warning*. Translated by Gerald Griffin. London: Denis Archer, 1935.

Taussig, Frank W. "The Tariff Bill and Our Friends Abroad." *Foreign Affairs* 8 (October 1929):1–12.

————. "The Tariff Controversy with France." *Foreign Affairs* 6 (January 1928):177–91.

Toynbee, Arnold J. *Survey of International Affairs*, 1920–23, 1924–33. London: Oxford University Press, 1925–34.

Underwood, Oscar W. "The Tariff as a Factor in American Trade." *Foreign Affairs* 1 (March 1923):25–35.

Vanderlip, Frank A. *What Next in Europe?* New York: Harcourt, Brace and Co., 1922.

Van Norman, Louis E. "Present Tendencies in the Investment of American Capital in Europe." *Annals of the American Academy of Political and Social Science* 126 (July 1926):87–91.

Wadsworth, Eliot. "The Inter-Allied Debt Problem and a Stable Monetary System Abroad." *Academy of Political Science Proceedings* 10 (January 1923):153–54.

Williams, John H. "Reparations and the Flow of Capital." *American Economic Review* 20 (March 1930, Supplement):73–79.

Woll, Matthew. "The Effect on American Workers of Collecting Allied Debts." *Annals of the American Academy of Political and Social Science* 126 (July 1926):42–45.

Young, Arthur N. "Loan Policy of the Department of State." *Far East Review* 24 (March 1928):102–3.

Secondary Sources: Articles and Books

Abrahams, Paul P. "American Bankers and the Economic Tactics of Peace, 1919." *Journal of American History* 56 (December 1969):572–83.

Adams, Frederick C. *Economic Diplomacy: The Export-Import Bank and American Foreign Policy, 1934–1939*. Columbia: University of Missouri Press, 1976.

Adler, Selig. *The Isolationist Impulse: Its Twentieth Century Reaction*. New York: Abelard-Schuman, 1957.

————. *The Uncertain Giant, 1921–1941: American Foreign Policy Between the Wars*. New York: Macmillan Co., 1965.

Albrecht-Carrié, René. *France, Europe, and the Two World Wars*. New York: Harper and Row, 1961.

Allen, William R. "Issues in Congressional Tariff Debates, 1890–1930." *Southern Economic Journal* 20 (April 1954):340–55.

Ambrosius, Lloyd E. "Wilson, Clemenceau, and the German Peace Problem." *Rocky Mountain Social Science Journal* 12 (April 1975):69–81.

––––––. "Wilson, the Republicans, and French Security after World War I." *Journal of American History* 59 (September 1972):341–52.

––––––. "Wilson's League of Nations." *Maryland Historical Magazine* 65 (Winter 1970):369–94.

Armstrong, Hamilton Fish. *Peace and Counterpeace: From Wilson to Hitler.* New York: Harper and Row, 1971.

––––––, ed. *The Foreign Policy of the Powers.* New York: Harper and Brothers, 1935.

Artaud, Denise. "A propos de l'occupation de la Ruhr." *Révue d'histoire moderne et contemporaine* 17 (Janvier–Mars 1970):1–21.

––––––. "Le Gouvernement américain et la question des dettes de guerre au lendemain de l'armistice de Rethondes, 1919–1920." *Revue d'histoire moderne et contemporaine* 20 (Avril–Juin 1973):201–29.

Bailey, Thomas A. *Woodrow Wilson and the Great Betrayal.* New York: Macmillan Co., 1945.

––––––. *Woodrow Wilson and the Lost Peace.* New York: Macmillan Co., 1944.

Bankwitz, Philip C. P. *Maxime Weygand and Civil-Military Relations in Modern France.* Cambridge, Mass.: Harvard University Press, 1967.

Bassett, Reginald. *Nineteen Thirty-One: Political Crisis.* London: Macmillan and Co., 1958.

Beard, Charles, and Beard, Mary. *The Rise of American Civilization.* New York: Macmillan Co., 1927.

Bemis, Samuel Flagg. "The Shifting Strategy of American Defense and Diplomacy." *Virginia Quarterly Review* 24 (Summer 1948):321–36.

Bennett, Edward Wells. *Germany and the Diplomacy of the Financial Crisis, 1931.* Cambridge, Mass.: Harvard University Press, 1962.

Best, Gary Dean. *The Politics of American Individualism: Herbert Hoover in Transition, 1918–1921.* Westport, Conn.: Greenwood Press, 1975.

Binion, Rudolph. *Defeated Leaders: The Political Fate of Caillaux, Jouvenel, and Tardieu.* New York: Columbia University Press, 1960.

Birdsall, Paul. *Versailles Twenty Years After.* New York: Reynal and Hitchcock, 1941.

Birn, Donald S. "Open Diplomacy at the Washington Conference of 1921–1922: The British and French Experience." *Comparative Studies in Society and History* 12 (July 1970):297–319.

Bogart, Ernest Ludlow. *War Costs and Their Financing: A Study of the Financing of the War and the After-War Problems of Debt and Taxation.* New York: D. Appleton and Co., 1921.

Bonnefous, Edouard. *Histoire politique de la Troisième République.* 2d ed. 7 vols. Vol. 3, *L'Après-guerre (1919–1924).* Vol. 4, *Cartel des gauches et union nationale (1924–1929).* Paris: Presses Universitaires De France, 1968–73.

Bonnet, Georges. *Le Quai d'Orsay sous trois républiques, 1870–1961.* Paris: A. Fayard, 1961.

Boyle, Andrew. *Montagu Norman.* London: Cassell and Co., 1967.

Braested, William R. *The United States Navy in the Pacific, 1909–1922.* Austin: University of Texas Press, 1971.

Brandes, Joseph. *Herbert Hoover and Economic Diplomacy: Department of Commerce Policy, 1921–1928.* Pittsburgh: University of Pittsburgh Press, 1962.

Bretton, Henry L. *Stresemann and the Revision of Versailles: A Fight for Reason.* Stanford: Stanford University Press, 1953.

Brinton, Clarence Crane. *The Americans and the French.* Cambridge, Mass.: Harvard University Press, 1968.

Brown, William Adams, Jr. *The International Gold Standard Reinterpreted, 1914–1934*. 2 vols. New York: National Bureau of Economic Research, 1940.

Brunn, Geoffrey. *Clemenceau*. Cambridge, Mass.: Harvard University Press, 1943.

Bryn-Jones, David. *Frank B. Kellogg: A Biography*. New York: G. P. Putnam's Sons, 1937.

Buckley, Thomas H. *The United States and the Washington Conference, 1921–1922*. Knoxville: University of Tennessee Press, 1970.

Buehrig, Edward H. *Woodrow Wilson and the Balance of Power*. Bloomington: Indiana University Press, 1955.

Burks, David D. "The United States and the Geneva Protocol of 1924: A New Holy Alliance?" *American Historical Review* 64 (July 1959):891–905.

Burner, David B. *Politics of Provincialism: The Democratic Party in Transition*. New York: Alfred A. Knopf, 1970.

Burns, James MacGregor. *Roosevelt: The Lion and the Fox*. New York: Harcourt, Brace and Co., 1956.

Cairns, John C. "A Nation of Shopkeepers in Search of a Stable France." *American Historical Review* 79 (June 1974):710–43.

Carlton, David. "Great Britain and the Coolidge Naval Disarmament Conference of 1927." *Political Science Quarterly* 83 (December 1968):573–98.

—————. *MacDonald versus Henderson: The Foreign Policies of the Second Labour Government*. New York: Humanities Press, 1970.

Carosso, Vincent P. *Investment Banking in America*. Cambridge, Mass.: Harvard University Press, 1970.

Carroll, John M. "The Paris Bankers' Conference of 1922 and America's Design for a Peaceful Europe." *International Review of History and Political Science* 10 (August 1973):39–48.

Challener, Richard. *The French Theory of the Nation in Arms, 1866–1939*. New York: Columbia University Press, 1955.

Chandler, Lester V. *American Monetary Policy, 1928–1941*. New York: Harper and Row, 1971.

—————. *America's Greatest Depression, 1929–1941*. New York: Harper and Row, 1970.

—————. *Benjamin Strong: Central Banker*. Washington: Brookings Institution, 1958.

Chastenet, Jacques. *Histoire de la Troisième République*. 7 vols. Vol. 5, *Les Années d'illusions, 1918–1931*. Paris: Hachette, 1960.

—————. *Raymond Poincaré*. Paris: René Julliard, 1948.

Chatfield, Charles. *For Peace and Justice: Pacifism in America, 1914–1941*. Knoxville: University of Tennessee Press, 1970.

Clarke, Stephen V. O. *Central Bank Cooperation, 1924–1931*. New York: Federal Reserve Bank of New York, 1967.

Clay, Henry. *Lord Norman*. London: Macmillan and Co., 1957.

Conkin, Paul. *The New Deal*. New York: Thomas Y. Crowell Co., 1967.

Connor, James R. "National Farm Organizations and United States Tariff Policy in the 1920s." *Agricultural History* 32 (January 1958):32–43.

Costigliola, Frank C. "The Other Side of Isolationism: The Establishment of the First World Bank, 1929–1930." *Journal of American History* 59 (December 1972):602–20.

—————. "The United States and the Reconstruction of Germany in the 1920's." *Business History Review* 50 (Winter 1976):477–502.

Craig, Gordon A., and Gilbert, Felix, eds. *The Diplomats, 1919–1939*. Princeton: Princeton University Press, 1953.

Cuff, Robert D. *The War Industries Board: Business-Government Relations during World War I*. Baltimore: Johns Hopkins University Press, 1973.

Current, Richard N. *Secretary Stimson: A Study in Statecraft*. New Brunswick, N.J.: Rutgers University Press, 1954.

Curti, Merle E. *Peace or War: The American Struggle, 1636–1936*. New York: W. W. Norton and Co., 1936.

Davis, Joseph S. *The World Between the Wars, 1919–1939: An Economist's View*. Baltimore: Johns Hopkins University Press, 1975.

DeBenedetti, Charles. "Alternative Strategies in the American Peace Movement in the 1920's." *American Studies* 13 (Spring 1972):69–81.

———. "Borah and the Kellogg-Briand Pact." *Pacific Northwest Quarterly* 63 (January 1972):22–29.

———. "The Origins of Neutrality Revision: The American Plan of 1924." *Historian* 35 (November 1972):75–89.

De Conde, Alexander, ed. *Isolation and Security: Ideas and Interests in Twentieth-Century American Foreign Policy*. Durham, N.C.: Duke University Press, 1957.

Degler, Carl N. "The Ordeal of Herbert Hoover." *Yale Review* 52 (June 1963):563–83.

Dingman, Roger. *Power in the Pacific: The Origins of Naval Arms Limitation, 1914–1922*. Chicago: University of Chicago Press, 1976.

Divine, Robert A. "Franklin D. Roosevelt and Collective Security, 1933." *Mississippi Valley Historical Review* 48 (June 1961):42–59.

———. *The Reluctant Belligerent: American Entry into World War II*. New York: John Wiley and Sons, 1965.

———. *Roosevelt and World War II*. Baltimore: Johns Hopkins University Press, 1969.

Dollar, Charles M. "The South and the Fordney-McCumber Tariff of 1922: A Study in Regional Politics." *The Journal of Southern History* 39 (February 1973):45–67.

Downes, Randolph C. *The Rise of Warren Gamaliel Harding, 1865–1920*. Columbus: Ohio State University Press, 1970.

Dulles, Eleanor Lansing. *The French Franc, 1914–1928: The Facts and Their Interpretation*. New York: Macmillan Co., 1929.

Dulles, Foster Rhea. *America's Rise to World Power, 1898–1954*. New York: Harper and Brothers, 1955.

Duroselle, Jean-Baptiste. *From Wilson to Roosevelt: Foreign Policy of the United States, 1913–1945*. Cambridge, Mass.: Harvard University Press, 1963.

———. "The Spirit of Locarno: Illusions of Pactomania." *Foreign Affairs* 50 (July 1972):52–64.

Earle, Edward M. "A Half-Century of American Foreign Policy: Our Stake in Europe, 1898–1948." *Political Science Quarterly* 64 (June 1949):168–88.

Ekirch, Arthur A., Jr. *The Civilian and the Military*. New York: Oxford University Press, 1956.

Ellis, Lewis Ethan. *Frank B. Kellogg and American Foreign Relations, 1925–1929*. New Brunswick, N.J.: Rutgers University Press, 1961.

———. *Republican Foreign Policy, 1921–1933*. New Brunswick, N.J.: Rutgers University Press, 1968.

Escholier, Raymond. *Souvenirs parlés de Briand*. Paris: Hachette, 1932.

Eyck, Erich. *A History of the Weimar Republic*. Translated by Harlan P. Hanson. 2 vols. Vol. 1, *From the Collapse of the Empire to Hindenburg's Election*. Vol. 2, *From the Locarno Conference to Hitler's Seizure of Power*. Cambridge, Mass.: Harvard University Press, 1962–63.

Fabre-Luce, Alfred. *Caillaux*. Paris: Gallimard, 1933.

Falkus, M. E. "U.S. Economic Policy and the 'Dollar Gap' of the 1920's." *Economic History Review* 24 (November 1971):599–623.

Fausold, Martin L., and Mazuzan, George T., eds. *The Hoover Presidency: A Reappraisal*. Albany, N.Y.: State University of New York Press, 1974.

Feis, Herbert. *The Diplomacy of the Dollar: First Era, 1919–1932*. Baltimore: Johns Hopkins University Press, 1950.

———. *1933: Characters in Crisis*. Boston: Little, Brown, 1966.

Felix, David. "Reparations Reconsidered with a Vengeance." *Central European History* 4 (June 1971):171–79.

———. *Walter Rathenau and the Weimar Republic: The Politics of Reparations*. Baltimore: Johns Hopkins University Press, 1971.

Ferrell, Robert H. *American Diplomacy in the Great Depression: Hoover-Stimson Foreign Policy, 1929–1933*. New Haven: Yale University Press, 1957.

———. *Peace in Their Time: The Origins of the Kellogg-Briand Pact*. New Haven: Yale University Press, 1952.

Fetter, Frank W. "Congressional Trade Theory." *American Economic Review* 23 (September 1933):413–27.

Fischer, Fritz. *Germany's Aims in the First World War*. New York: W. W. Norton and Co., 1967.

Fleming, Denna Frank. *The United States and the League of Nations, 1918–1920*. New York: G. P. Putnam's Sons, 1932.

———. *The United States and World Organization, 1920–1933*. New York: Columbia University Press, 1938.

Floto, Inga. *Colonel House in Paris: A Study of American Policy at the Paris Peace Conference, 1919*. Denmark: Universitets-forlaget i Aarhus, 1973.

Freidel, Frank B. *Franklin D. Roosevelt*. 4 vols. Vol. 1, *The Apprenticeship*. Vol. 2, *The Ordeal*, Vol. 3, *The Triumph*. Vol. 4, *Launching the New Deal*. Boston: Little, Brown and Co., 1952–73.

Fry, Michael D. *Illusions of Security: North Atlantic Diplomacy, 1918–1922*. Toronto: University of Toronto Press, 1972.

Fuess, Claude M. *Calvin Coolidge*. Boston: Little, Brown and Co., 1940.

Furnia, Arthur H. *The Diplomacy of Appeasement: Anglo-French Relations and the Prelude to World War II, 1931–1938*. Seattle: University of Washington Press, 1960.

Galambos, Louis. "The Emerging Organizational Synthesis in Modern American History." *Business History Review* 44 (Autumn 1970):270–90.

Gardner, Lloyd C. "American Foreign Policy, 1900–1921: A Second Look at the Realist Critique of American Diplomacy." *Towards A New Past: Dissenting Essays in American History*. Edited by Barton J. Bernstein. New York: Pantheon Books, 1968.

———. *Economic Aspects of New Deal Diplomacy*. Madison: University of Wisconsin Press, 1964.

Garraty, John A. *Henry Cabot Lodge: A Biography*. New York: Alfred A. Knopf, 1953.

———, ed. *Interpreting American History: Conversations with Historians*. 2 vols. New York: Macmillan Co., 1970.

Gatzke, Hans. *Stresemann and the Rearmament of Germany*. Baltimore: Johns Hopkins University Press, 1954.

Gelfand, Lawrence E. *The Inquiry: American Preparations for Peace, 1917–1919*. New Haven: Yale University Press, 1963.

George, Alexander L., and George, Juliette L. *Woodrow Wilson and Colonel House: A Personality Study*. New York: John Day Co., 1956.

Gersting, J. Marshall. *The Flexible Provisions in the United States' Tariff, 1922–1930*. Philadelphia: University of Pennsylvania Press, 1932.

Gilbert, Charles. *American Financing of World War I*. Westport, Conn.: Greenwood Press, 1970.

Girard, Jolyon P. "Congress and Presidential Military Policy: The Occupation of Germany, 1919–1923." *Mid-America* 56 (October 1974):211–21.

Glad, Betty. *Charles Evans Hughes and the Illusions of Innocence: A Study in American Diplomacy*. Urbana: University of Illinois Press, 1966.

Gleason, John Philip. "The Attitude of the Business Community Toward Agriculture During the McNary-Haugen Period." *Agricultural History* 32 (April 1958):127–38.

Graebner, Norman Arthur, ed. *An Uncertain Tradition: American Secretaries of State in the Twentieth Century*. New York: McGraw-Hill Book Co., 1961.

Grassmuck, George L. *Sectional Biases in Congress on Foreign Policy.* Johns Hopkins University Studies in Historical and Political Science, ser. 68. Baltimore: Johns Hopkins University Press, 1951.

Greer, Guy. *The Ruhr-Lorraine Industrial Problem.* New York: Macmillan Co., 1925.

Griswold, Alfred Whitney. *The Far Eastern Policy of the United States.* New York: Harcourt, Brace and Co., 1938.

Haig, Robert Murray. *The Public Finances of Post-War France.* Social and Economic Studies of Post-War France, vol. 1. Edited by C. J. H. Hayes. New York: Columbia University Press, 1929.

Haight, Frank Arnold. *A History of French Commercial Policies.* New York: Macmillan Co., 1941.

Hall, Ray Ovid. *International Transactions of the United States: An Audit and Interpretation of Balance-of-Payments Estimates.* New York: National Industrial Conference Board, 1936.

Hawley, Ellis. "Herbert Hoover, the Commerce Secretariat, and the Vision of an 'Associative State,' 1921–1928," *Journal of American History* 61 (June 1974):116–40.

————. *The New Deal and the Problem of Monopoly, 1933–1939.* Princeton: Princeton University Press, 1965.

————. "Secretary Hoover and the Bituminous Coal Problem, 1921–1928." *Business History Review* 42 (Autumn 1968):247–71.

Hewes, James E. "Henry Cabot Lodge and the League of Nations." *Proceedings of the American Philosophical Society* 114 (August 1970):245–55.

Hicks, John D. *Rehearsal for Disaster.* Gainesville: University of Florida Press, 1961.

————. *Republican Ascendancy, 1921–1933.* New York: Harper and Brothers, 1960.

Himmelberg, Robert F. *The Origins of the National Recovery Administration: Business, Government, and the Trade Association Issue, 1921–1933.* New York: Fordham University Press, 1976.

Hirsch, Felix. "Stresemann, Ballin, und Die Vereinigten Staaten." *Vierteljahrshefte Für Zeitgeschichte* 3 (January 1955):20–36.

Hoag, Charles Leonard. *Preface to Preparedness: The Washington Disarmament Conference and Public Opinion.* Washington: American Council on Public Affairs, 1941.

Hofstadter, Richard. *The American Political Tradition and the Men Who Made It.* New York: Alfred A. Knopf, 1948.

Hogan, Michael J. *Informal Entente: The Private Structure of Cooperation in Anglo-American Economic Diplomacy, 1918–1928.* Columbia: University of Missouri Press, 1977.

————. "The United States and the Problem of International Economic Control." *Pacific Historical Review* 44 (February 1975):84–103.

Howard, Michael. *The Continental Commitment: The Dilemma of British Defense Policy in the Era of the Two World Wars.* London: Maurice Temple Smith, 1972.

Hughes, Judith M. *To the Maginot Line: The Politics of French Military Preparation in the 1920's.* Cambridge, Mass.: Harvard University Press, 1971.

Hurd, Charles. *When the New Deal Was Young and Gay.* New York: Hawthorn Books, 1965.

Huthmacher, J. Joseph, and Susman, Warren I., eds. *Herbert Hoover and the Crisis of American Capitalism.* Cambridge, Mass.: Schenkman Publishing Co., 1973.

Iriye, Akira. *After Imperialism: The Search for a New Order in the Far East, 1921–1931.* Cambridge, Mass.: Harvard University Press, 1965.

Israel, Fred L. *Nevada's Key Pittman.* Lincoln: University of Nebraska Press, 1963.

Israel, Jerry, ed. *Building the Organizational Society: Essays on Associational Activities in Modern America.* New York: Free Press, 1972.

Jablon, Howard. "The State Department and Collective Security, 1933–1934." *Historian* 33 (February 1971):248–63.

Jackson, John Hampden. *Clemenceau and the Third Republic.* New York: Macmillan Co., 1948.

Jacobson, Jon. *Locarno Diplomacy: Germany and the West, 1925–1929*. Princeton: Princeton University Press, 1972.

James, Dorris Clayton. *The Years of MacArthur*. 2 vols. Vol. 1, *1880–1941*. Boston: Houghton Mifflin Co., 1970.

Johnson, Claudius O. *Borah of Idaho*. Seattle: University of Washington Press, 1936.

Jones, J. Harry. *Josiah Stamp, Public Servant: The Life of the First Baron Stamp of Shortlands*. London: Sir Isaac Pitman and Sons, 1964.

Jones, Joseph M. *Tariff Retaliation: Repercussions of the Hawley-Smoot Bill*. Philadelphia: University of Pennsylvania Press, 1934.

Jones, Kenneth Paul. "Discord and Collaboration: Choosing an Agent-General for Reparations." *Diplomatic History* 1 (Spring 1977):118–39.

Jordan, W. M. *Great Britain, France, and the German Problem, 1918–1939*. New York: Oxford University Press, 1943.

Kaufman, Burton I. *Efficiency and Expansion: Foreign Trade Organization in the Wilson Administration, 1913–1921*. Westport, Conn.: Greenwood Press, 1974.

————. "The Organization Dimension of United States Economic Foreign Policy, 1900–1920." *Business History Review* 46 (Spring 1972):17–44.

Kelly, William B., Jr. "Antecedents of Present Commercial Policy, 1922–1934." *Studies in United States Commercial Policy*. Edited by William B. Kelly, Jr. Chapel Hill: University of North Carolina Press, 1963.

Kennan, George F. *American Diplomacy, 1900–1950*. Chicago: University of Chicago Press, 1951.

Kennedy, Susan Estabrook. *The Banking Crisis of 1933*. Lexington: University of Kentucky Press, 1973.

Kimmich, Christoph M. *Germany and the League of Nations*. Chicago: University of Chicago Press, 1976.

Kindleberger, Charles P. "Origins of United States Direct Investment in France." *Business History Review* 48 (Autumn 1974):381–413.

————. *The World in Depression, 1929–1939*. Berkeley: University of California Press, 1973.

King, Jere C. *Foch versus Clemenceau: France and German Dismemberment, 1918–1919*. Cambridge, Mass.: Harvard University Press, 1960.

Koistinen, Paul A. C. "The 'Industrial-Military Complex' in Historical Perspective: The Inter-War Years." *Journal of American History* (March 1970):819–39.

Korbel, Josef. *Poland Between East and West: Soviet and German Diplomacy Toward Poland, 1919–1933*. Princeton: Princeton University Press, 1963.

Kottman, Richard N. "Herbert Hoover and the Smoot-Hawley Tariff: Canada, A Case Study." *Journal of American History* 62 (December 1975):609–35.

————. *Reciprocity and the North Atlantic Triangle, 1932–1938*. Ithaca, N.Y.: Cornell University Press, 1968.

Kuehl, Warren F. *Seeking World Order: The United States and International Organization to 1920*. Nashville, Tenn.: Vanderbilt University Press, 1969.

Kuznets, Simon. *Economic Change: Selected Essays in Business Cycles, National Income, and Economic Growth*. New York: W. W. Norton and Co., 1953.

Lacour-Gayet, Robert. "Le Problème de la dette française envers les Etats-Unis après la première guerre mondiale (1917–1932)." *Révue d'histoire diplomatique* 75 (Janvier–Mars 1961):10–24.

Landes, David. *The Unbound Prometheus: Technological Change and Industrial Development in Western Europe from 1750 to the Present*. Cambridge: Cambridge University Press, 1970.

Larmour, Peter J. *The French Radical Party in the 1930's*. Stanford: Stanford University Press, 1964.

Leffler, Melvyn P. "American Policy Making and European Stability, 1921–1933." *Pacific Historical Review* 46 (May 1977):207–28.

———. "The Origins of Republican War Debt Policy, 1921–1923: A Case Study in the Applicability of the Open Door Interpretation." *Journal of American History* 59 (December 1972):585–601.

———. "Political Isolationism, Economic Expansionism, or Diplomatic Realism: American Policy toward Western Europe, 1921–1933." *Perspectives in American History* 8(1974):413–61.

Leith-Ross, Sir F. W. *Money Talks: Fifty Years of International Finance*. London: Hutchinson Publishing Group, 1968.

Leopold, Richard W. *Elihu Root and the Conservative Tradition*. Boston: Little, Brown and Co., 1954.

Leuchtenburg, William E. *Franklin D. Roosevelt and the New Deal*. New York: Harper and Row, 1963.

———. *The Perils of Prosperity, 1914–1932*. Chicago: University of Chicago Press, 1958.

Levin, N. Gordon, Jr. *Woodrow Wilson and World Politics*. New York: Oxford University Press, 1968.

Lewis, Cleona. *America's Stake in International Investments*. Washington: Brookings Institution, 1938.

Link, Arthur S. *Wilson the Diplomatist*. Baltimore: Johns Hopkins University Press, 1957.

Link, Werner. *Die amerikanische Stabilisierungspolitik in Deutschland, 1921–1932*. Dusseldorf: Droste Verlag, 1970.

Lloyd, Craig. *Aggressive Introvert: A Study of Herbert Hoover and Public Relations Management, 1912–1932*. Columbus: Ohio State University Press, 1972.

Lougheed, Alan, and Glynn, Sean. "A Comment on the United States Economic Policy and the 'Dollar Gap' of the 1920's." *Economic History Review* 26 (November 1973):692–94.

Maddox, Robert James. *William E. Borah and American Foreign Policy*. Baton Rouge: Louisiana State University Press, 1969.

———. "William E. Borah and the Crusade to Outlaw War." *Historian* 29 (February 1967): 200–20.

Maier, Charles S. *Recasting Bourgeois Europe: Stabilization in France, Germany, and Italy in the Decade After World War I*. Princeton: Princeton University Press, 1975.

Marcus, John. *French Socialism in the Crisis Years, 1933–1936*. New York: Frederick A. Praeger, 1958.

Marks, Sally. *The Illusion of Peace: International Relations in Europe, 1918–1933*. New York: St. Martins Press, 1976.

———. "Reparations Reconsidered: A Reminder." *Central European History* 2 (December 1969):356–65.

———, and Dulude, Denis. "German-American Relations, 1918–1921." *Mid-America* 53 (October 1971):211–26.

May, Ernest R. "An American Tradition in Foreign Policy: The Role of Public Opinion." *Theory and Practice in American Politics*. Edited by William H. Nelson. Chicago: University of Chicago Press, 1964.

———. "The Development of Political-Military Consultation in the United States." *Political Science Quarterly* 70 (June 1955):161–80.

May, Henry F. "Shifting Perspectives on the 1920's." *Mississippi Valley Historical Review* 43 (December 1956):405–27.

Mayer, Arno. *Politics and Diplomacy of Peacemaking: Containment and Counterrevolution at Versailles, 1918–1919*. New York: Alfred A. Knopf, 1967.

McConnell, Grant. *Private Power and American Democracy*. New York: Alfred A. Knopf, 1966.

McCoy, Donald R. *Calvin Coolidge: The Quiet President*. New York: Macmillan Co., 1967.

McKay, Donald C. *The United States and France*. Cambridge, Mass.: Harvard University Press, 1951.

McKenna, Marion Cecilia. *Borah*. Ann Arbor: University of Michigan Press, 1961.

Mellon, William Larimer. *Judge Mellon's Sons*. Pittsburgh: privately published, 1948.

Meyer, Richard. *Bankers' Diplomacy: Monetary Stabilization in the Twenties*. New York: Columbia University Press, 1970.

Mickesell, Raymond F. *United States Economic Policy and International Relations*. New York: McGraw-Hill Book Co., 1952.

Miller, Francis, and Hill, Helen. *The Giant of the Western World: America and Europe in a North-Atlantic Civilization*. New York: William Morrow and Co., 1930.

Mintz, Ilse. *Deterioration in the Quality of Foreign Bonds Issued in the United States, 1920–1930*. New York: National Bureau of Economic Research, 1951.

Miquel, Pierre. *La Paix de Versailles et l'opinion publique française*. Paris: Flammarion, 1972.

————. *Raymond Poincaré*. Paris: A. Fayard, 1961.

Moggridge, D. E. *British Monetary Policy, 1924–1931: The Norman Conquest of $4.86*. Cambridge: Cambridge University Press, 1972.

————. *The Return to Gold, 1925: The Formulation of Economic Policy and Its Critics*. Cambridge: Cambridge University Press, 1969.

Moore, James R. "Sources of New Deal Economic Policy: The International Dimension." *Journal of American History* 61 (December 1974):728–44.

Morgenthau, Hans J. "Another 'Great Debate': The National Interest of the United States." *American Political Science Review* 46 (December 1952):961–89.

————. "The Mainsprings of American Foreign Policy: The National Interest vs. Moral Abstraction." *American Political Science Review* 44 (December 1950):833–54.

Morison, Elting E. *Turmoil and Tradition: A Study of the Life and Times of Henry L. Stimson*. Boston: Houghton Mifflin Co., 1960.

Motherwell, Hiram. *The Imperial Dollar*. New York: Brentano, 1929.

Mott, Thomas Bentley. *Myron T. Herrick, Friend of France*. Garden City, N.Y.: Doubleday, Doran and Co., 1929.

Moulton, Harold G. *The Reparation Plan: An Interpretation of the Reports of the Expert Committees Appointed by the Reparation Commission, November 30, 1923*. New York: McGraw-Hill Book Co., 1924.

————, and Lewis, Cleona. *The French Debt Problem*. New York: Macmillan Co., 1925.

————, and Pasvolsky, Leo. *War Debts and World Prosperity*. Washington: Brookings Institution, 1932.

————. *World War Debt Settlements*. New York: Macmillan Co., 1926.

Murray, Robert K. *The Harding Era: Warren G. Harding and His Administration*. Minneapolis: University of Minnesota Press, 1969.

————. *The Politics of Normalcy: Governmental Theory and Practice in the Harding-Coolidge Era*. New York: W. W. Norton and Co., 1972.

————. *Red Scare: A Study in National Hysteria, 1919–1920*. Minneapolis: University of Minnesota Press, 1955.

Myers, William Starr. *The Foreign Policies of Herbert Hoover*. New York: Charles Scribner's Sons, 1940.

Nearing, Scott, and Freeman, Joseph. *Dollar Diplomacy: A Study in American Imperialism*. New York: B. W. Huebsch and the Viking Press, 1926.

Nelson, Harold I. *Land and Power: British and Allied Policy on Germany's Frontiers, 1916–1919*. London: Routledge and Kegan Paul, 1963.

Nelson, Keith L. *Victors Divided: America and the Allies in Germany, 1918–1923*. Berkeley: University of California Press, 1975.

Newman, William J. *The Balance of Power in the Interwar Years, 1919–1939*. New York: Random House, 1968.

Nichols, Jeannette P. "Roosevelt's Monetary Diplomacy in 1933." *American Historical Review* 56 (January 1951):295–318.

Nicolson, Harold. *Dwight Morrow*. New York: Harcourt, Brace and Co., 1935.

Noble, George B. *Policies and Opinions at Paris, 1919: Wilsonian Diplomacy, the Versailles Peace, and French Public Opinion*. New York: Macmillan Co., 1935.

Noggle, Burt. *Into the Twenties: The United States from Armistice to Normalcy*. Urbana: University of Illinois Press, 1974.

Northedge, F. S. *The Troubled Giant: Britain among the Great Powers, 1916–1939*. London: G. Bell and Sons, 1966.

O'Connor, Raymond G. *Perilous Equilibrium: The United States and the London Naval Conference of 1930*. Lawrence: University of Kansas Press, 1962.

Offner, Arnold A. *The Origins of the Second World War: American Foreign Policy and World Politics, 1917–1941*. New York: Praeger, 1975.

Ogburn, William F., and Jaffe, William. *The Economic Development of Post-War France: A Survey of Production*. Social and Economic Studies of Post-War France, vol. 3. Edited by C. J. H. Hayes. New York: Columbia University Press, 1929.

Osgood, Robert E. *Ideals and Self-Interest in America's Foreign Relations*. Chicago: University of Chicago Press, 1953.

Palmer, James E. *Carter Glass: Unreconstructed Rebel*. Roanoke, Va.: Institute of American Biography, 1938.

Parrini, Carl P. *Heir to Empire: United States Economic Diplomacy, 1916–1923*. Pittsburgh: University of Pittsburgh Press, 1969.

Paul, Randolph E. *Taxation in the United States*. Boston: Little, Brown and Co., 1954.

Pelling, Henry. *Winston Churchill*. New York: E. P. Dutton and Co., 1974.

Perkins, Dexter. *Charles Evans Hughes and American Democratic Statesmanship*. Boston: Little, Brown and Co., 1956.

Pontecorvo, Giulio. "Investment Banking and Security Speculation in the Late 1920's." *Business History Review* 32 (Summer 1958):166–91.

Post, Gaines, Jr. *The Civil-Military Fabric of Weimar Foreign Policy*. Princeton: Princeton University Press, 1973.

Pratt, Julius W. *Cordell Hull, 1933–1944*. 2 vols. *The American Secretaries of State and Their Diplomacy*, vol. 12. Edited by Robert H. Ferrell and Samuel Flagg Bemis. New York: Cooper Square Publishers, 1964.

Pruessen, Ronald W. "John Foster Dulles and Reparations at the Paris Peace Conference, 1919: Early Patterns of Life." *Perspectives in American History* 8 (1974):381–410.

Pusey, Merlo John. *Charles Evans Hughes*. 2 vols. New York: Macmillan Co., 1951.

Rader, Benjamin G. "Federal Taxation in the 1920's: A Re-Examination." *Historian* 33 (May 1971):415–35.

Renouvin, Pierre. *Les Crises du XXᵉ Siècle*. 2 vols. Vol. 1, *De 1914 à 1929*. Vol. 2, *De 1929 à 1945. Histoire des rélations internationales*, vols. 7 and 8. Edited by Pierre Renouvin. Paris: Hachette, 1957–58.

Rhodes, Benjamin D. "Herbert Hoover and the War Debts." *Prologue* 6 (Summer 1974):130–44.

———. "Reassessing Uncle Shylock: The United States and the French War Debt, 1917–1929." *Journal of American History* 55 (March 1969):787–803.

Robinson, Edgar Eugene, and Bornet, Vaughn Davis. *Herbert Hoover: President of the United States*. Stanford: Hoover Institution Press, 1975.

Rogers, James Harvey. *The Process of Inflation in France, 1914–1927*. Social and Economic Studies of Post-War France, vol. 2. Edited by C. J. H. Hayes. New York: Columbia University Press, 1934.

Romasco, Albert U. *The Poverty of Abundance: Hoover, the Nation, the Depression*. New York: Oxford University Press, 1965.

Rosen, Elliot A. *Hoover, Roosevelt, and the Brains Trust: From Depression to New Deal*. New York: Columbia University Press, 1977.
———. "Intranationalism vs. Internationalism: The Interregnum Struggle for the Sanctity of the New Deal." *Political Science Quarterly* 81 (June 1966):274–97.
Roskill, Stephen. *Naval Policy Between the Wars: The Period of Anglo-American Antagonism, 1919–1929*. London: William Collins Sons and Co., 1968.
Rowland, Benjamin, ed. *Balance of Power or Hegemony: The Interwar Monetary System*. New York: New York University Press, 1976.
Sauvy, Alfred. *Histoire économique de la France entre les deux guerres*. 2 vols. Vol. 1, *De L'armistice à la dévaluation de la livre*. Paris: A. Fayard, 1965.
Schattschneider, Elmer E. *Politics, Pressures, and the Tariff: A Study of Free Enterprise in Pressure Politics, as Shown in the 1929–1930 Revision of the Tariff*. New York: Prentice-Hall, 1935.
Schlesinger, Arthur M., Jr. *The Age of Roosevelt*. 3 vols. Vol. 1, *The Crisis of the Old Order*. Vol. 2, *The Coming of the New Deal*. Vol. 3, *The Politics of Upheaval*. Boston: Houghton Mifflin Co., 1957–58.
———, ed. *History of United States Political Parties*. 4 vols. Vol. 3, *1910–1945: From Square Deal to New Deal*. New York: Chelsea House Publishers, 1973.
Schmidt, Royal J. *Versailles and the Ruhr: Seedbed of World War II*. The Hague: Martinus Nijhoff, 1968.
Schofield, Kent. "The Public Image of Herbert Hoover in the 1928 Campaign." *Mid-America* 5 (October 1969):278–93.
Schuker, Stephen A. *The End of French Predominance: The Financial Crisis of 1924 and the Adoption of the Dawes Plan*. Chapel Hill: University of North Carolina Press, 1976.
Schwarz, Jordan. *The Interregnum of Despair: Hoover, Congress, and the Depression*. Urbana: University of Illinois Press, 1970.
Selsam, J. Paul. *The Attempts to Form an Anglo-French Alliance, 1919–1924*. Philadelphia: University of Pennsylvania Press, 1936.
Shideler, James H. *Farm Crisis, 1919–1923*. Berkeley: University of California Press, 1957.
Simonds, Frank H. *American Foreign Policy in the Post-War Years*. Baltimore: Johns Hopkins Press, 1935.
Sklar, Martin J. "Woodrow Wilson and the Political Economy of United States Liberalism." *Studies on the Left* 1 (1960):17–47.
Smith, Daniel M. *Aftermath of War: Bainbridge Colby and Wilsonian Diplomacy, 1920–1921*. Philadelphia: American Philosophical Society, 1970.
———. *The Great Departure: The United States and World War I, 1914–1920*. New York: John Wiley and Sons, 1965.
Smith, Gene. *The Shattered Dream: Herbert Hoover and the Great Depression*. New York: William Morrow and Co., 1970.
Smith, Rixey, and Beasley, Norman. *Carter Glass: A Biography*. New York: Longmans, Green and Co., 1939.
Smith, Robert Freeman. "American Foreign Relations. 1920–1942." *Towards a New Past: Dissenting Essays in American History*. Edited by Barton J. Bernstein. New York: Pantheon Books, 1968.
———. "Republican Policy and the *Pax Americana*, 1921–1932." In *Colony to Empire*. Edited by William A. Williams. New York: John Wiley and Sons, 1972.
Snyder, J. Richard. "Coolidge, Costigan, and the Tariff Commission." *Mid-America* 50 (April 1968): 131–48.
———. "Hoover and the Hawley-Smoot Tariff: A View of Executive Leadership." *Annals of Iowa* 41 (Winter 1973):1173–89.
———. "William S. Culbertson and the Formation of Modern Commercial Policy, 1917–1925." *Kansas Historical Quarterly* 35 (Winter 1969):396–410.

Sontag, Raymond. *A Broken World, 1919–1939*. New York: Harper and Row, 1971.
Soule, George H. *Prosperity Decade: From War to Depression, 1917–1929*. Economic History of the United States, vol. 8. Edited by Henry David et al. New York: Rinehart and Co., 1947.
Soulié, Michel. *La Vie politique d'Edouard Herriot*. Paris: Colin, 1962.
Sprout, Harold, and Sprout, Margaret. *Toward a New Order of Sea Power: American Naval Policy and the World Scene, 1918–1922*. Princeton: Princeton University Press, 1940.
Stein, Herbert. "Pre-Revolutionary Fiscal Policy: The Regime of Herbert Hoover." *The Journal of Law and Economics* 9 (October 1966):189–223.
Steward, Dick. *Trade and Hemisphere: The Good Neighbor Policy and Reciprocal Trade*. Columbia: University of Missouri Press, 1975.
Stone, Ralph. *The Irreconcilables: The Fight Against the League of Nations*. New York: W. W. Norton and Co., 1970.
Stromberg, Roland N. *Collective Security and American Foreign Policy: From the League of Nations to NATO*. New York: Frederick A. Praeger, 1963.
_____. "Uncertainties and Obscurities about the League of Nations." *Journal of the History of Ideas* 33 (January–March 1972):139–54.
Svennilson, Ingvar. *Growth and Stagnation in the European Economy*. Geneva: United Nations Economic Commission for Europe, 1954.
Tarbell, Ida M. *Owen Young: A New Type of Industrial Leader*. New York: Macmillan Co., 1932.
Tate, Merze. *The United States and Armaments*. Cambridge, Mass.: Harvard University Press, 1948.
Taussig, Frank W. *International Trade*. New York: Macmillan Co., 1927.
_____. *The Tariff History of the United States*. 1931. Reprint. New York: Augustus M. Kelley, 1967.
Thimme, Annelise. "Stresemann and Locarno." *European Diplomacy Between Two Wars, 1919–1939*. Edited by Hans W. Gatzke. Chicago: Quadrangle Books, 1972.
Thompson, John M. *Russia, Bolshevism, and the Versailles Peace*. Princeton: Princeton University Press, 1966.
Thorne, Christopher. *The Limits of Foreign Policy: The West, the League, and the Far Eastern Crisis, 1931–1933*. New York: G. P. Putnam's Sons, 1972.
Timmons, Bascon N. *Portrait of an American: Charles G. Dawes*. New York: Henry Holt and Co., 1953.
Trani, Eugene P., and Wilson, David L. *The Presidency of Warren G. Harding*. Lawrence: The Regents Press of Kansas, 1977.
Trask, David F. *General Tasker Howard Bliss and the "Sessions of the World," 1919*. Philadelphia: American Philosophical Society, 1966.
_____. *The United States in the Supreme War Council: American War Aims and Inter-Allied Strategy, 1917–1918*. Middletown, Conn.: Wesleyan University Press, 1961.
Tulchin, Joseph. *The Aftermath of War: World War I and U.S. Policy Toward Latin America*. New York: New York University Press, 1971.
Turner, Henry A. *Stresemann and the Politics of the Weimar Republic*. Princeton: Princeton University Press, 1963.
Vallentin-Luchaire, Antonina. *Stresemann*. Translated by Eric Sutton. New York: Ray Long and Richard R. Smith, 1931.
Varg, Paul A. "The Economic Side of the Good Neighbor Policy: The Reciprocal Trade Program and South America." *Pacific Historical Review* 45 (February 1976):47–72.
Vinson, John Chalmers. *The Parchment Peace: The United States Senate and the Washington Conference, 1921–1922*. Athens: University of Georgia Press, 1955.
_____. *Referendum for Isolation: Defeat of Article Ten of the League of Nations Covenant*. Athens: University of Georgia Press, 1961.

———. *William E. Borah and the Outlawry of War*. Athens: University of Georgia Press, 1955.

Walworth, Arthur C. *America's Moment, 1918: American Diplomacy at the End of World War I*. New York: W. W. Norton and Co., 1977.

———. *Woodrow Wilson*. 2 vols. Vol. 1, *American Prophet*. Vol. 2, *World Prophet*. New York: Longmans, Green and Co., 1958.

Wandycz, Piotre S. *France and Her Eastern Allies: French-Czechoslovak-Polish Relations from the Paris Peace Conference to Locarno*. Minneapolis: University of Minnesota Press, 1962.

Warner, Geoffrey. *Pierre Laval and the Eclipse of France*. New York: Macmillan Co., 1968.

Warren, Harris Gaylord. *Herbert Hoover and the Great Depression*. New York: Oxford University Press, 1959.

Weill-Raynal, Etienne. *Les Réparations allemandes et la France*. 3 vols. Vol. 1, *Des Origines jusqu'à l'institution de l'état des payements (novembre 1918–mai 1921)*. Vol. 2, *L'Application de l'état des payements, l'occupation de la Ruhr, et l'institution du plan Dawes (mai 1921–avril 1924)*. Vol. 3, *L'Application du plan Dawes, le plan Young, et la liquidation des réparations (avril 1924–1936)*. Paris: Nouvelles Editions Latines, 1947.

Weinberg, Gerhard L. "The Defeat of Germany in 1918 and the European Balance of Power." *Central European History* 2 (September 1969):248–60.

———. *The Foreign Policy of Hitler's Germany: Diplomatic Revolution in Europe, 1933–1936*. Chicago: University of Chicago Press, 1970.

Weinstein, Edwin A. "Woodrow Wilson's Neurological Illness." *Journal of American History* 57 (September 1970):324–51.

Werth, Alexander. *The Twilight of France, 1933–1940*. New York: Harper and Brothers, 1942.

Wheeler, Gerald E. *Admiral William Veazie Pratt, U.S. Navy: A Sailor's Life*. Washington: Department of the Navy, 1974.

———. *Prelude to Pearl Harbor: The United States Navy and the Far East, 1921–1931*. Columbia: University of Missouri Press, 1963.

Wheeler-Bennett, John Wheeler. *Disarmament and Security Since Locarno*. New York: Macmillan Co., 1932.

———. *The Pipe Dream of Peace: The Story of the Collapse of Disarmament*. New York: William Morrow and Co., 1935.

———. *The Wreck of Reparations*. New York: William Morrow and Co., 1933.

White, Elizabeth Brett. *American Opinion of France from Lafayette to Poincaré*. New York: Alfred A. Knopf, 1927.

White, William Allen. *A Puritan in Babylon: The Story of Calvin Coolidge*. New York: Macmillan Co., 1938.

Wicker, Elmus R. "Federal Reserve Monetary Policy, 1922–1933: A Reinterpretation." *Journal of Political Economy* 73 (August 1965):325–43.

———. *Federal Reserve Monetary Policy, 1921–1932*. New York: Random House, 1966.

———. "Roosevelt's 1933 Monetary Experiment." *Journal of American History* 57 (March 1971):864–79.

Williams, Benjamin Harrison. *Economic Foreign Policy of the United States*. New York: McGraw-Hill Book Co., 1929.

Williams, William A. *The Contours of American History*. Cleveland: World Publishing Co., 1961.

———. "The Legend of Isolationism in the 1920's." *Science and Society* 18 (Winter 1954):1–20.

———. "A Note on Foreign Policy in Europe in the 1920's." *Science and Society* 22 (Winter 1958):1–20.

_____. *The Tragedy of American Diplomacy.* Cleveland: World Publishing Co., 1959.
Willoughby, William Franklin. *Financial Condition and Operations of the National Government, 1921–1930.* Washington: Brookings Institution, 1931.
Willson, Beckles. *America's Ambassadors to France (1777–1927).* New York: Frederick A. Stokes Co., 1928.
Wilson, Hugh Robert. *Disarmament and the Cold War in the Thirties.* New York: Vantage Press, 1973.
Wilson, Joan Hoff. *American Business and Foreign Policy, 1920–1933.* Lexington: University Press of Kentucky, 1971.
_____. *Herbert Hoover: Forgotten Progressive.* Boston: Little, Brown and Co., 1975.
_____. *Ideology and Economics: U.S. Relations with the Soviet Union, 1918–1933.* Columbia: University of Missouri Press, 1974.
Wiltz, John E. *From Isolation to War, 1931–1941.* New York: Thomas Y. Crowell Co., 1968.
Wimer, Kurt, and Wimer, Sarah. "The Harding Administration, the League of Nations, and the Separate Peace Treaty." *Review of Politics* 29 (January 1967):13–24.
Winters, Donald L. *Henry Cantwell Wallace as Secretary of Agriculture, 1921–1924.* Urbana: University of Illinois Press, 1970.
Wolfe, Martin. *The French Franc Between the Wars, 1919–1939.* New York: Columbia University Press, 1951.
Wolfers, Arnold. *Britain and France Between Two World Wars: Conflicting Strategies of Peace from Versailles to World War II.* New York: Harcourt, Brace and Co., 1940.
Yates, Louis Allmond Richard. *United States and French Security, 1917–1921: A Study in American Diplomatic History.* New York: Twayne Publishers, 1957.
Zahniser, Marvin R. *Uncertain Friendship: American-French Relations through the Cold War.* New York: John Wiley and Sons, 1975.

Unpublished Studies

Boyle, Thomas Edward. "France, Great Britain, and German Disarmament: 1919–1927." Ph.D. dissertation, State University of New York at Stony Brook, 1972.
Carr, Kathryn. "The Diplomatic Career of Myron T. Herrick." Master's thesis, Ohio State University, 1934.
Clarke, Stephen V. O. "The Reconstruction of the International Monetary System: The Attempts of 1922 and 1933." Mimeographed. New York: Federal Reserve Bank of New York, 1972.
Costigliola, Frank C. "Anglo-American Rivalry in the 1920's." Paper read at the Annual Meeting of the Organization of American Historians, 1974, at Denver. Mimeographed.
_____. "The Politics of Financial Stabilization: American Reconstruction Policy in Europe, 1924–1930." Ph.D. dissertation, Cornell University, 1972.
Coston, Glenn Howard. "The American Reaction to the Post–First World War Search of France for Security: A Periodical and Period Piece Study, 1919–1930." Ph.D. dissertation, University of Georgia, 1971.
Dockhorn, Robert Bennett. "The Wilhelmstrasse and the Search for a New Diplomatic Order, 1926–1930." Ph.D. dissertation, University of Wisconsin, 1972.
Frommer, Morris. "John Foster Dulles: His Thoughts, Attitudes, and Actions toward Europe, 1919–1933." Master's thesis, Ohio State University, 1969.
Irvin, Thomas Casey. "Norman H. Davis and the Quest for Arms Control, 1931–1938." Ph.D. dissertation, Ohio State University, 1963.
Kaplan, Jay L. "The Internationalist Alternative: Economic and Ideological Aspects of French Security Policy, 1919–1925." Paper read at the Conference on European Security in the Locarno Era, October 1975, at Mars Hill, N.C. Mimeographed.

Koerselman, Gary Harlan. "Herbert Hoover and the Farm Crisis of the Twenties: A Study of the Commerce Department's Efforts to Solve the Agricultural Depression, 1921–1928." Ph.D. dissertation, Northern Illinois University, 1971.

McDougall, Walter Allan. "French Rhineland Policy and the Struggle for European Stabilization: Reparations, Security, and Rhenish Separatism, 1918–1924." Ph.D. dissertation, University of Chicago, 1974.

Merrill, Milton Rees. "Reed Smoot, Apostle in Politics." Ph.D. dissertation, Columbia University, 1950.

Schoenthal, Klaus Ferdinand. "American Attitudes toward Germany, 1918–1932." Ph.D. dissertation, Ohio State University, 1959.

Swerczek, Ronald Emil. "The Diplomatic Career of Hugh Gibson, 1908–1938." Ph.D. dissertation, University of Iowa, 1972.

Van Meter, Robert H. "Herbert Hoover and the Economic Reconstruction of Europe, 1918–1921." Paper read at the Hoover Centennial Seminars, 1974, at the Herbert Hoover Presidential Library. Mimeographed.

_____. "The United States and European Recovery, 1918–1923: A Study of Public Policy and Private Finance." Ph.D. dissertation, University of Wisconsin, 1971.

Wilson, Joan Hoff. "Hoover's Agricultural Policies, 1921–1928." Paper read at the Hoover Centennial Seminars, 1974, at the Herbert Hoover Presidential Library. Mimeographed.

Wilson, John R. M. "Herbert Hoover and the Armed Forces: A Study of Presidential Attitudes and Policy." Ph.D. dissertation, Northwestern University, 1971.

Woodard, Nelson Eugene. "Postwar Reconstruction and International Order: A Study of the Diplomacy of Charles Evans Hughes, 1921–1925." Ph.D. dissertation, University of Wisconsin, 1970.

Wyly, Theodore Dawson. "Foreign Relations of the United States with France from 1919 to 1929." Ph.D. dissertation, Fletcher School of Law and Diplomacy, 1964.

Index

A

Acheson, Dean: and currency stabilization, 344, 355, 356, 357
Agent general for reparation payments: role of, 93, 102, 103, 104, 106, 109; selection of, 109–10. *See also* Gilbert, S. Parker
Agricultural Adjustment Act, 343, 346, 349
Agricultural Marketing Act, 213
Agriculture: and U.S. tariff legislation, 29
American Bankers Association: and loan embargo, 174
American Bar Association, 105
American Economic Association, 27
American Historical Association, 77
Anglo-French arms compromise, 163–64
Arms limitation, 32–33, 35, 159–65, 219–28, 277–88, 301–3, 314, 334–36, 338–39, 341–43, 347–49. *See also* Coolidge, Calvin; Davis, Norman H.; France; Hoover, Herbert C.; Hughes, Charles Evans; Roosevelt, Franklin D.; Stimson, Henry L.; United States
Army, U.S. *See* Department of War
Article 10 (of League Covenant), 5, 6, 11, 12, 13, 16, 17, 18, 31, 32, 38. *See also* League of Nations; Wilson, Woodrow
Article 16 (of League Covenant): French demands for clarification of, 160, 161, 163; and British obligations, 221, 222
Astor, Vincent, 325
Austria: rehabilitation of finances, 58; U.S. stabilization of, 86; and the Depression, 231; and 1931 financial crisis, 234, 235
Austrian National Bank, 234

Austro-German customs union, 232, 242, 251
Ayers, Leonard P., 98

B

Baden-Baden Conference (1929), 215
Baker, Newton, 140; and Hoover moratorium, 240
Balance of payments: problems of, in Europe, 171, 172, 200, 297, 298; of United States, 337
Baldwin, Stanley, 279–80
Ballantine, Arthur A., 332
Bank for International Settlements, 205, 211, 215, 216, 291; and financial crisis of 1931, 252–53
Bank of England, 55, 57, 111, 113; reports gold losses, 248; and 1931 financial crisis, 252–53, 258
Bank of France, 55, 58, 143, 147, 150, 153; and note circulation, 138; and new management, 143; and central bank cooperation, 189; and 1931 financial crisis, 252, 258; and currency stabilization, 344
Bankers, American: and 1931 financial crisis, 247, 249, 250, 254, 257, 258, 263; and revision of war debt agreements, 293. *See also* Loan embargo; Loans, foreign; Morgan & Co., J. P.; Wall Street
Bankers' Committee (1922), 73–74
Banking crisis (1933), 329
Barthou, Louis, 89
Baruch, Bernard M., 87; urges Wilson to compromise, 16; and reparations, 20; and Hoover moratorium, 238; and 1933 foreign policy preparations, 325, 326; and Roosevelt's foreign economic policy, 349, 350, 355, 356

Bavaria, 88
Bedford, A. C., 84
Belgium, 70, 121–22, 137, 316
Belligerents' rights, 163, 164
Bérenger, Henry: and war debts, 139, 140–41, 142
Berle, Adolf, 317, 366
Bewley, Kenneth, 334
Bidwell, Percy W., 198
Bliss, Tasker H., 10
Boal, Pierre de Lagarde: and French security, 262
Bolshevism: containment of, 3; fear of, 8, 165, 234, 241
Bonnet, Georges, 355
Bonus bill, 66
Borah, William E., 13, 233; attacks Wilson, 13; and French security, 36; and European stability, 41; and desire for economic conference, 76, 85; and denunciation of official policy, 84; and war debts, 136, 137, 145, 149, 179, 292, 293; and U.S. neutrality rights, 162; and Hoover moratorium, 240, 243; and 1931 financial crisis, 254
Boyden, Roland W., 70, 71, 74, 75
Brandegee, Frank B., 12, 13
Briand, Aristide: and the U.S., 31, 33, 37; and Washington Naval Conference, 35; and Cannes Conference, 37; and departure from office, 72, 139, 143, 146; and Locarno treaties, 118; and war debts, 139, 142; and formation of new ministry, 143; and Thoiry talks, 151–52; and United States of Europe, 197; and Hoover moratorium, 241; and French security, 262; and London Naval Conference, 226, 227
Bristol, Mark L., 271–72
Brüning, Heinrich: and government by decree, 232; and revision of Young Plan, 234; and political problems, 234–35; and Hoover moratorium, 244–45; and 1931 financial crisis, 251, 252, 253, 255; and reparations, 275; and arms limitation, 275; and departure from office, 284–85
Bullitt, William C: and international cooperation, 324; and foreign economic policy, 330, 332–33, 334, 337, 346; and antipathy to strategic obligations, 336
Bureau of Foreign and Domestic Commerce, 44, 270

Burgess, William, 44
Burton, Theodore, E., 66, 134n
Business Week, 350

C
Caillaux, Joseph, 130; and war debts, 130–32, 133, 134–35, 137, 138, 141, 143, 145
Cannes Conference (1922), 37
Capper, Arthur, 162
Cartel des Gauches, 104, 106, 112, 328. *See also* Herriot, Edouard
Castle, William R., 85, 181; and reparations, 76; and foreign loans, 177; and U.S. commercial policy, 199, 298–99; and Hoover moratorium, 243, 244–45; and 1931 financial crisis, 246–49; and war debts, 267, 292; and opposition to French quotas, 296
Central bank cooperation, 55–58, 104, 129, 144, 146, 147, 148, 150, 154, 156, 188–91, 213, 216, 333; and 1931 financial crisis, 247, 252–53, 255, 256, 257, 258; and failure of, 296
Chamber of Commerce of the United States, 27, 76; and U.S. commercial policy, 49
Chamber of Deputies, French: and reciprocity formula, 52; and war debts, 142, 143, 147, 148, 151; and Young Plan, 215, 217
Chamberlain, Austen, 161, 163
Chapin, Roy D., 307, 309
Chicago Tribune, 240
Churchill, Winston, 186, 203
Claims, mixed war: of U.S., 76, 209, 210, 214
Claudel, Paul: and U.S. tariffs, 199; and Hoover moratorium, 238; and appraisal of Hoover's policies, 312; and assessment of Roosevelt's policies, 326, 331; and war debts, 331
Clemenceau, Georges: and French security, 5–6, 7–8, 9–10, 16–17; and League of Nations, 6; and struggle with Wilson, 6, 8; and Anglo-American Guarantee Pact, 7–8, 9, 16–17; and separate Rhenish republic, 7; and concessions at peace conference, 9; and Allied unity, 17; and Rhineland, 17
Clémentel, Etienne: and Dawes Plan, 107; and war debts, 125–26; and American loans, 127

Colby, Bainbridge, 21–22
Commerce Ministry, French, 167
Commercial policy. *See* France; United
States
Committee on Banking and Currency,
U.S. House of Representatives, 54
Committee on Finance, U.S. Senate: and
U.S. commercial policy, 46, 47, 48;
and war debts, 142; and onset of
investigation of Wall Street, 268; and
National Industrial Recovery Act, 350
Committee on Foreign Relations, U.S.
Senate, 149, 342, 347
Committee of the Judiciary, U.S. Senate,
25
Committee on Ways and Means, U.S.
House of Representatives: and war
debts, 23, 24; and tariffs, 44, 45, 48
Congress, U.S.: and war debts, 24, 65,
66, 69, 80, 86, 123, 124, 131, 136,
137, 140, 146, 179, 268–69, 294,
306, 308, 309, 312–13, 334, 353n,
365–66; and foreign loans, 26, 176–
77; and reversal of Wilson's veto, 28;
and commercial policy, 29, 172, 173,
196, 297–98; and nonentanglement in
European affairs, 166; and European
stability, 229; and the Depression,
232–33, 259; and Hoover moratorium,
238; and 1931 financial crisis, 259
Consultation. *See* Consultative pact
Consultative pact, 223, 224, 225, 226,
227, 265–66, 284, 286, 314, 331,
335, 342, 347, 359
Coolidge, Calvin, 100; and policymaking, 87; and reparations, 87–88,
202–3; and Dawes Plan, 101, 110,
111–12; and European stability, 101,
111–12, 113, 119; and support of
Dawes, 101; and agent general, 109;
and arms limitation, 113, 119, 159,
161; and Geneva Protocol, 115; and
European security, 116, 119; and war
debts, 123, 125, 135, 136–37, 140,
141–42, 148–49; and currency stabilization, 140, 141–42; and U.S. neutrality rights, 162; and U.S. commercial policy, 172, 173
Cotton, Joseph P., 225; and Bank for
International Settlements, 214; and
final reparations settlement, 214; and
Young bonds, 218; and European stability, 229; and his death, 243
Council on Foreign Relations, 286

Cravath, Paul, 20
Creditanstalt, 234
Crisp, Charles R., 134n
Culbertson, William S., 365; and U.S.
commercial policy, 45–51; and tariff
levels, 80; and resignation from Tariff
Commission, 170
Cumberland, W. W., 45
Currency stabilization, 54–58, 121–57
passim, 187–91, 295; and Dawes Plan,
112–13, 121; and Roosevelt adminis-
tration, 333–34, 339, 340, 344–45,
353–57, 359, 360, 361. *See also*
Central bank cooperation; Exchange
fluctuations; Federal Reserve Bank of
New York; Strong, Benjamin
Curtius, Julius, 245, 252
Customs duties. *See* Tariffs; United
States: and commercial policy

D
Daeschner, Emile, 131
Daladier, Edouard: and war debts, 331;
and French security, 335; and
Roosevelt, 358
Danubian federation, 275–76, 296,
298–99
Davis, Norman H.: urges Wilson to
compromise, 16; and reparations, 20;
and war debts, 24, 288, 290; and U.S.
commercial policy, 172; and Hoover
moratorium, 240; and Geneva Disarmament Conference, 274–86 *passim*,
303, 314, 334–36, 338, 342, 347,
348, 359; and London Economic Conference, 319; and foreign economic
policy, 330; and French security,
335–36, 347, 348
Davis, O. K., 49
Dawes, Charles G., 90, 103; and reparations, 91, 92, 93, 94, 96, 101, 112;
and French security, 92, 96, 97; and
German rehabilitation, 92, 96, 97; and
selection as vice-presidential candidate, 101; and Hoover moratorium,
238; and 1931 financial crisis, 249
Dawes Plan, 121, 122; formulation of,
90–100; and bankers' reaction to,
101–2, 103, 105–6; and European
negotiations, 104–5; and loan, 111;
and French security, 112, 113–14,
115, 118–19; and war debts, 123, 135;
and portion for U.S., 128; and likelihood of fulfillment of, 132; and Thoiry

proposals, 152; and revision of, 182–87, 203. *See also* Reparations; Young Plan

Day, Edmund E., 305, 318, 319, 320, 328

Democratic party, 44, 70; and war debts, 140, 145, 292, 293; and Hoover moratorium, 235; and principle of consultation, 286; and U.S. commercial policy, 297–98

Department of Agriculture, U.S.: and Franco-American trade, 170–71

Department of Commerce, U.S.: records of, xi; and commercial policy, 45, 48, 50, 53; and foreign loans, 59, 61, 62–63, 122, 127, 128; and reparations, 91, 100; and Dawes Plan, 112; and war debts, 127, 140, 149, 307; and Franco-American trade, 166–67, 171; and opposition to French quotas, 296. *See also* Hoover, Herbert C.

Department of the Navy, U.S.: records of, xi; and French security, 33–34, 229, 287–88, 314–15; and Germany, 115–16; and U.S. national security, 219; and strategic guarantees, 225; and arms limitation, 280–81, 285

Department of State, U.S.: records of, xi; and reparations, 21–22, 70, 71, 74, 76, 87, 90, 100; and commercial policy, 45, 48, 51, 52, 170–71, 196–97, 297, 303, 344; and foreign loans, 59, 60, 61, 62, 63, 64, 122, 127, 128, 174, 175, 176; and war debts, 66, 126, 127, 140, 145, 146, 149, 218, 307; and currency stabilization, 129; and Geneva Disarmament Conference, 280–81, 285; and opposition to French quotas, 296; and arms embargo, 347–48; and European stability, 366

Department of the Seine, 61

Department of the Treasury, U.S., 332; and records of, xi; and reparations, 21, 71, 72; and war debts, 22–24, 64–65, 69, 80, 124, 127, 131, 149, 178, 218, 307; and government loans, 26; and foreign loans, 59, 60, 61, 63, 122, 127, 128, 175, 176; and European stability, 112; and currency stability, 113, 121, 129, 131, 139, 144, 145, 149; and Franco-American trade, 170–71. *See also* Mellon, Andrew W.; Mills, Ogden; Winston, Garrard

Department of War, U.S.: records of, xi; and Germany, 115–16; and U.S. na-

tional security, 219; and strategic guarantees, 225; and French security, 229, 287–88, 314–15; and U.S. strategic interests, 272; and arms limitation, 280–81, 283, 285

Deutsch, Felix, 95

Division of Western European Affairs: and Hoover moratorium, 243

Domestic priorities, U.S. *See* Economic diplomacy; Hoover, Herbert C.; Roosevelt, Franklin D.; United States

Douglas, Lewis, 319, 320; and recovery program, 330; and U.S. departure from gold, 337

Draft Treaty of Mutual Assistance, 114

Dulles, Allen, 348

Dulles, John Foster, 20, 87

du Maurais, Baron, 25

E

East Asia. *See* Manchurian crisis

Economic diplomacy, 38, 79, 81, 157, 158, 180–81, 187, 195, 202, 228–30, 233–34, 271–72, 273, 283, 335–36, 364; defined, x; generates resentment, 155–57; falters, 158–93 *passim*; and need for reappraisal of, 241, 244; and Hoover, 276–77; in transition, 287–88, 294–95, 299–300, 312, 314–15, 366; ceases, 359. *See also* United States: and European stability; United States: and policymaking process

Edge, Walter E., 27, 301; and tariff revision, 198–99; and London Naval Conference, 222; and Hoover moratorium, 243, 245

Edge banks, 28

Elections, 17, 89, 110–11, 184; of 1932, and U.S. policymaking, 300–305

Emergency Agricultural Credits Act, 44

Emergency Tariff Act, 43–44

European stability: *See* Currency stabilization; Harding, Warren G.; Hoover, Herbert C.; Stimson, Henry L.; United States

Exchange fluctuations, 19, 29, 54, 57, 71. *See also* Currency stabilization

Exchange stabilization. *See* Currency stabilization

Expert committees: and Dawes Plan, 89–90, 91, 92, 93, 98; and revision of Dawes Plan, 186, 187; and final reparations settlement, 202–10 *passim*

Experts' Report (1924), 99–100

F

Far Eastern crisis. *See* Manchurian crisis
Farm Board, 251, 256
Farrell, James A., 269
Federal Farm Loan System, 260
Federal Land Bank System, 273
Federal Reserve Act, 27, 260
Federal Reserve Bank of New York, 55, 57, 80, 365; and records of, xi; and foreign loans, 60, 63; and reparations, 72, 204, 208; and currency stabilization, 121, 122, 129, 144, 145, 148, 150, 155, 364; and 1931 financial crisis, 247, 252–53, 258, 259; and international initiatives to overcome the Depression, 311; and European stability, 366. *See also* Central bank cooperation; Harrison, George L.; Strong, Benjamin
Federal Reserve Board, 61; and criticism of, 59; and currency stabilization, 129, 144, 188–89; and opposition to Strong, 146; and rivalry with Federal Reserve Bank of New York, 189, 190, 204, 213, 365; and final reparations settlement, 204
Federal Reserve System, 189, 190, 191, 247, 273, 365; and Bank for International Settlements, 214; and Young Plan, 209
Feis, Herbert, 325; and Hoover moratorium, 238–39; and 1931 financial crisis, 263; and war debts, 267, 271, 292, 300, 311, 334; and European stability, 271, 276, 300; and U.S. commercial policy, 297, 298; and French security, 262; and London Economic Conference, 304–5, 350; and recovery program, 304, 330, 333; and Roosevelt's foreign economic policy, 326, 332–37, 343, 344, 349
Financial crisis of 1931, 234–72 *passim*
Flandin, Etienne: and Hoover moratorium, 242; and 1931 financial crisis, 249, 254; and French security, 262; and war debts, 289
Fletcher, Henry P., 70, 71
Foch, Ferdinand, 9, 10
Fordney Bill, 44, 45, 46, 47, 48
Fordney-McCumber Act, 48, 50, 51, 80; and use of flexible provisions, 169, 170, 171, 173; and use of section 317, 53, 168
Foreign Affairs, 197, 227

Foreign loans. *See* Loans, foreign
Foreign Office, British, 114, 131
Four-Power Treaty, 223
Fourteen Points, 7, 13
Franc, 28; weakness of, 29, 97, 100, 138, 146; and European currency stability, 121, 122, 129; and strengthening of, 147, 153, 157. *See also* Currency stabilization
France: security of, ix, xi, 3–18, 31–40 *passim*, 77, 82, 88–89, 92, 101, 105–7, 113–14, 116, 117–19, 159–65, 192, 220–24, 227, 228, 244, 277, 279, 284–87, 301–3, 314, 365; and Rhineland occupation, 9, 14–15, 70, 113, 118, 363; and reparations, 22, 73, 74, 78, 83, 96–97, 98, 100, 203, 205; and war debts, 22, 24, 66, 123–56 *passim*, 177, 180, 275, 289, 291–92, 294, 295, 301, 306, 307, 308–9, 310, 313, 328, 352; and need for American loans, 25–26, 28, 125, 127, 128, 130, 139, 142, 150, 153–54, 175; and the U.S., 33, 81, 270–71, 331; and Washington Naval Conference, 35–37; and commercial policy, 51–52, 167–71, 296–97, 304; and currency stabilization, 121–22, 123, 124, 125, 129, 138, 143, 146, 150, 153–54, 340, 344–45, 353, 355, 358; and Dawes Plan, 106, 107, 112, 186, 187; and arms limitation, 159–61, 164–65, 220–21, 222–24, 226, 227, 257; and Hawley-Smoot tariff, 196–97, 198–99, 201–2; and Young Plan, 214–17, 219; and the Depression, 232; and Hoover moratorium, 235, 239, 241–44; and 1931 financial crisis, 249, 250, 257; and Geneva Disarmament Conference, 275, 278–79, 283–84, 286–87; and tariff truce, 343, 351; and disillusionment with Roosevelt, 358–59
Franco-German commercial treaty, 167
Francqui, Emile, 205, 208
Frankfurter, Felix, 305, 333, 343; and international initiatives, 319–20; and war debts, 352–53
Fraser, Leon, 253

G

Garner, James, 24
General Board of the Navy, 278, 280–81. *See also* Department of the Navy, U.S.

General Disarmament Conference at Geneva. *See* Geneva Disarmament Conference
Geneva Disarmament Conference (1932–33), 274–88 *passim*, 301–2, 341, 342, 343, 347–50, 359
Geneva Economic Conference (1927), 166–67, 171n, 173, 299
Geneva Naval Conference (1927), 161
Geneva Protocol, 114
Genoa Conference (1922), 56, 72, 299
Gentleman's Agreement (1932), 292–93, 295
George, David Lloyd, 7, 24
Germain-Martin, Louis, 291
Germany: reintegration of, as U.S. diplomatic goal, ix, 4–5, 7, 10, 12–13, 15, 18, 36, 37, 38, 39, 82–83, 101, 114, 120, 244, 364, 368; and reparations, 70, 72, 73, 95, 208; and proposal of nonaggression pact, 76, 77; and Dawes Plan, 107–8, 182, 183, 184, 185, 186; and arms limitation, 164–65, 227; and financial problems, 181, 204, 215; and evacuation of Rhineland, 215; and the Depression, 231–32, 234; and 1931 financial crisis, 234, 235, 236, 237, 238, 243–59 *passim*; and Geneva Disarmament Conference, 277, 301
Geraud, André, 227
Gibson, Hugh: and arms limitation, 160; and proposals to the preparatory commission, 220; and Geneva Disarmament Conference, 274–83 *passim*
Gilbert, S. Parker: and war debts, 69, 152, 218; and selection as agent general, 109–10; and franc stabilization, 122, 147, 150, 152; and warning of payments crisis, 140n; and reparations, 151; and Thoiry proposals, 152; and U.S. trade policy, 172; and foreign loans, 177; and efforts to revise Dawes Plan, 179, 182–87; and final reparations settlement, 203, 207, 209, 217; and 1931 financial crisis, 253, 263
Glass, Carter: and war debts, 23; and government loans, 26; attacks loan supervision process, 176; and 1931 financial crisis, 254
Gold exchange standard. *See* Gold standard
Goldsmith, Alan: and reparations, 91, 94, 98, 100–101; and German eco-

nomic unity, 97; and criticism of Dawes Plan, 100
Gold standard, 55, 56, 57, 68, 80, 104, 121, 122, 129, 148, 157, 181, 190–91, 239, 258, 260, 266, 267, 295, 296, 333–34, 355, 357
Great Britain: and Washington Naval Conference, 35; and war debts, 67, 68–69, 133n, 289, 290, 292, 306, 307, 308–9, 310, 313, 324, 352; and occupation of Ruhr ports, 70; and Dawes Plan, 106, 107, 186, 187; and French security, 114, 117, 160–61, 163, 220–21, 222–24, 226; and return to gold standard, 129; and U.S. neutrality rights, 161, 163–64, 221, 222, 223; and financial problems, 181, 188–89, 204; and Bank for International Settlements, 215–16; and Young Plan, 220; and Kellogg-Briand Pact, 221; and arms limitation, 224; and the Depression, 231–32; and 1931 financial crisis, 248, 250, 254, 255, 258; and Geneva Disarmament Conference, 283–84, 348–49; and Lausanne Conference, 289, 290, 291; and currency stabilization, 328, 353, 358; and commercial policy, 351
Great War. *See* World War I
Grew, Joseph C.: and Dawes Plan, 110–11; and war debts, 149
Guarantee Pact. *See* Treaty of Guarantee
Guaranty Trust Co., 247

H
Hague Conferences (1929, 1930), 215, 220; and agreements revised, 291
Hamlin, Charles S., 204
Harding, Warren G.: and French security, 12; and foreign economic policy, 30; and position on Treaty of Versailles, 31–32, 38; and European stability, 32, 36, 38, 40–43, 79; and commercial policy, 43, 46, 47–48, 50, 51, 53; and currency stabilization, 54, 57; and war debts, 65, 66, 68, 69, 85; and reparations, 68, 72, 74–75, 77, 78–79, 203; and withdrawal of American occupation troops, 79, 83; and Ruhr occupation, 83, 85, 86; and death of, 87
Harris, William J., 69–70
Harrison, George L.: and final reparations settlement, 204, 219; and 1931 financial crisis, 236, 247, 248–49,

250, 253, 254, 257, 263; and opposition to policy of drift, 305–6; and war debts, 309, 311; and currency stabilization, 332, 344, 345, 353–54, 355, 356

Harrison, Leland, 70, 128; and reparations, 87; and loan embargo, 128–29; and war debts, 149; and foreign loans, 177

Hawley, Willis C., 196

Hawley-Smoot tariff, 196–202, 296, 297, 351

Hearst press, 240

Henderson, Arthur, 220, 249, 251

Henry, Jules, 301, 302

Herrick, Myron T., 97, 126; and reparations, 75; and Experts' Report, 100; and war debts, 125, 130; and reports on anti-American sentiment in France, 146; and Kellogg-Briand Pact, 165–66

Herring, Charles E., 98

Herriot, Edouard: and Dawes Plan, 105, 106–7, 108; and war debts, 125–26, 291, 292, 294, 301, 310; and ministry overthrown, 126, 146; and American loans, 127–28; and French security, 284–85, 286–87, 301, 302–3; and Geneva Disarmament Conference, 280, 282, 284–85, 286–87, 302–3; and Lausanne Conference, 284, 291–92, 294; and commercial policy toward the U.S., 303, 304; and meeting with Roosevelt, 330, 331, 335, 336, 338–39, 340, 343, 346

Hindenburg, Paul von, 275

Hitchcock, Gilbert, 16

Hitler, Adolf, 232, 275, 316, 329, 330, 335, 341, 342, 348, 359

Holmes, George R., 256

Home Loan Discount Banks, 273

Home Market Club, 43

Hoover, Herbert C.: urges Wilson to compromise, 16; advises reservations, 28; and position on Treaty of Versailles, 31–32; and criticism of French military expenditures, 36, 128, 133; and European stability, 40, 81, 121, 194, 201, 229–30, 235, 244–45, 246, 252, 261, 266–67, 270, 273–74, 276–77, 287, 300, 314; and exports, 44, 54–55; and balance of payments, 50; and imports, 50; and currency stabilization, 54–55, 57, 129, 133, 267, 311; and opposition to government loans, 55; and foreign loans,

59–61, 62, 63, 80, 128, 174, 176, 177; and war debts, 66, 67, 68, 69, 124, 128, 133–34, 135–36, 141, 145, 149, 156n, 178–79, 180–81, 182, 192–93, 218, 233, 234, 365; and reparations, 74–75, 77, 78–79, 91, 185, 194; and French security, 82, 89, 227–28, 265–66, 314; and U.S. commercial policy, 172–73, 178–79, 180–81, 194–202, 297–300, 303–4; and complacency, 181, 190, 193; and Federal Reserve Bank of New York, 189–90; and arms limitation, 194, 219, 221, 226–27, 233, 274, 277, 278, 281–83, 287–88, 302, 303, 314; and domestic priorities, 195, 198, 218, 219, 228–29, 233, 259–60, 263–64, 269, 270, 273–74, 275, 276–77, 293, 298, 300, 314, 363, 366; and farm relief, 195, 210; and attitudes toward France, 202, 229, 241, 242–43, 261, 270, 315; and economic diplomacy, 202, 305, 312–15, 366; and Young Plan, 206–7, 209–10, 213, 216, 217–19; and Bank for International Settlements, 207, 213; and the Depression, 218, 219, 229, 233, 235, 273, 276–77, 300, 311–12, 314–15; and antipathy to strategic commitments, 219, 225, 228, 229, 233, 244–45, 283, 287, 314–15; and MacDonald's visit, 220–21; and American neutrality rights, 221, 227, 264; and Kellogg-Briand Pact, 221; and consultative pact, 225, 265–66, 286, 287; and Congress, 232–33, 293–94, 306, 312–13; and debt moratorium, 235–46; and 1931 financial crisis, 246–61; and Laval's visit, 263–65; and Polish Corridor, 264–65; and revision of war debt agreements, 266, 267, 268, 269, 274, 288, 290, 292–95, 306–13, 321; and Lausanne Conference, 290–91, 295n; and London Economic Conference, 299, 300, 305; and Roosevelt, 305, 306, 308, 311–13, 318, 325

Hoover moratorium, 234–45, 246, 255, 256, 267, 268, 294, 295, 365

Hoover disarmament plan, 281–84, 285, 286, 287, 302

Hornbeck, Stanley K., 51, 53

Houghton, Alanson: and war debts, 68; and fear of Bolshevism, 85; and support of action against France, 85; and

reparations, 87, 95; and Dawes Plan, 104, 111; and campaign for Coolidge, 111; and security negotiations, 116; and meaning of Locarno, 119
House of Representatives, U.S., 44, 142, 353. *See also* Congress, U.S.
House, Edward M., 5–6, 16
Howe, Louis, 356
Howland plan, 262–63, 264, 266, 271
Howard, Esme, 161
Hughes, Charles Evans, 123, 125; and position on Treaty of Versailles, 31–32; and Washington Naval Conference, 33, 34–35, 282; and French security, 36, 82, 88–89; and European stability, 40; and commercial policy, 47, 51; and foreign loans, 59, 60, 61, 62, 80, 127–28; and war debts, 66, 67, 68, 86, 88, 126; and reparations, 70, 75, 76, 77, 78, 83, 86–87, 88, 91, 203; and reaction to Ruhr occupation, 78, 83–84; and Germany's recuperation, 82–83, 88, 108; and Austrian loan, 86; and Dawes Plan, 104–5, 108, 111; and arms limitation, 113; and opposition to strategic commitments, 114–15
Hull, Cordell, 348; and U.S. commercial policy, 172; and appointment as secretary of state, 320, 322; and ignorance of Roosevelt's policies, 326–27; and foreign economic policy, 330, 332–33, 334, 344, 350; and French security, 335, 336; and arms limitation, 347–48; and London Economic Conference, 350, 351n; and war debts, 352
Hurley, Edward N., 134n

I

Inflation: fear of, ix, 19, 27, 56, 57, 58, 121, 337
Intergovernmental debts. *See* Hoover moratorium; Reparations; War debts
International Court of Justice at The Hague. *See* World Court
International Trade Conference (1919), 25
Investment Bankers Association, 27
Irreconcilables: and Wilson, 13, 14; and Harding, 32
Italy, 139, 140

J

Japan, 281

Jay, Dean, 144
Johnson, Hiram W., 13; and arms embargo, 347, 348, 349
Johnson, Hugh, 349
Jones, Grosvenor M., 127
Journal of the American Bankers Association, 256
Jouvenel, Henry de, 284, 285
Jusserand, Jules, 36, 53, 77, 88, 125

K

Kahn, Otto, 27, 61, 269
Kellogg, Frank B., 146; and role at London Conference, 108, 110; and campaign for Coolidge, 111; and foreign loans, 129, 174, 176, 177; and war debts, 134n, 149; and arms limitation, 160; and U.S. neutrality rights, 162; and revision of Dawes Plan, 187
Kellogg-Briand Pact, 160, 162–63, 164, 165–66; contemplated amendments to, 220, 221, 227; and French security, 223
Kemmerer, Edwin W., 99
Kent, Fred I., 87, 174
Kies, W. S., 28
Kitchin, Claude, 24
Klots, Allen, 262, 267
Klotz, Louis-Lucien, 22
Knox, Philander C., 13
Kuhn, Loeb & Co., 61

L

Laboulaye, André de: appointed ambassador, 331; appraises Roosevelt's policy, 349; and war debts, 351
Labour government, Britain. *See* MacDonald, J. Ramsay
Lacour-Gayet, Robert, 139, 145
LaFollette, Robert, 13, 111
Lamont, Thomas W., 269; and reparations, 20; and foreign loans, 27, 142; and Dawes Plan, 102, 107, 108, 109, 110, 111, 183, 185; and French security, 114; and Young Plan, 203, 207, 211, 212–13, 219; and Bank for International Settlements, 205, 213, 215–16; and Hoover moratorium, 235–36; and 1931 financial crisis, 247, 258; and Lausanne Conference, 289–91; and revision of war debt agreements, 288–90, 319–20
Lamont, Robert P., 195
Lansing, Robert: concern with Bolshevism, 8; and condemnation of

Anglo-American Guarantee Treaty, 10; and withdrawal of peace commissioners, 14
Laurent, Theodore, 28
Lausanne Conference (1932), 269, 274, 276, 281, 282, 284, 288–92, 293, 296, 299, 352; and agreements, 309
Lauzanne, Stéphane, 134n
Laval, Pierre, 365; and his policy orientation, 232; and Hoover moratorium, 241–42, 243, 245; and 1931 financial crisis, 249, 251, 252, 255, 261; and visit to U.S., 261–67; and French security, 262; and revision of Young Plan, 266–67; and war debts, 331
League of Nations, x, 5, 6, 7, 18, 38, 115; and Saar, 9; and German entrance into, 117; and French security, 160–61; and tariff truce, 197
L'Echo de Paris, 197
Leffingwell, Russell C., 26, 102
Leith-Ross, Frederick, 340, 352
Lindbergh, Charles, 192
Lindsay, Ronald, 324, 353
Lippmann, Walter, 227, 348
Literary Digest, 34, 268
Loan embargo, 117, 119, 127–30, 139, 145–46, 152–53, 154, 174–76, 177
Loans, foreign: and exports, 19, 28, 29, 58, 60, 63, 64; and domestic inflation, 26–27; to France, 27, 63, 64, 107, 127; and currency stabilization, 54, 58, 60, 63, 64; and supervision of, 58–64, 122, 128, 155, 173–77, 364; and European arms expenditures, 64, 128; to Germany, 72, 73, 74, 122, 140n, 174, 175–76, 177, 249–56
Locarno treaties, 117–18; and impact on French financial situation, 139; and war debts, 131
Lodge, Henry Cabot: and reservations, 13, 16, 17n; and commercial policy, 51
Logan, James A., 70, 71, 74; and Dawes Plan, 104, 108
London Conference (1924), 105–11, 114; and war debts, 123
London Economic Conference (1933), ix, 313n; and preparations for, 299–300, 318–19, 328, 332–38, 340–45, 349–50; and American behavior at, 350, 354–57
London Finance Conference (1931), 248–57
London Naval Conference (1930), 219, 222–28

London Schedule of Payments, 71, 73, 74
Loucheur, Louis, 7, 70, 107, 139
Luther, Hans, 246

M
MacArthur, Douglas: and Geneva Disarmament Conference, 278
McClure, Wallace M., 45, 51, 53, 172
McCormick, Vance C., 20
MacDonald, J. Ramsay, 346; and London Conference, 105, 108; and arms limitation, 220–21; and France, 220, 222–23, 226; and 1931 financial crisis, 252, 255, 258; and French security, 279; and Geneva Disarmament Conference, 281–82; and revision of war debt agreements, 292, 352; and meeting with Roosevelt, 330, 335, 336, 338, 339, 340, 343, 346; and request for reduction in U.S. tariffs, 351; and currency stabilization, 355
MacDonald disarmament plan, 335, 338–39, 341, 342
McFadden, Louis T.: and hostility to Bank for International Settlements, 213–14, 217; and denunciation of Hoover, 268
McGarrah, Gates W., 216, 253; and 1931 financial crisis, 236
McKellar, Kenneth, 292
MacMillan Report, 248
Manchurian crisis, 260, 275, 276, 316
Marvin, Thomas O., 44, 170, 365
Marx, Wilhelm, 95
Mediterranean nonaggression pact, 222, 224
Mellon, Andrew W.: and currency stabilization, 54, 57, 129, 131, 137–38, 139, 144–45, 147, 148, 150, 154; and foreign loans, 59, 60, 64, 72, 176, 177; and taxes, 65, 363; and war debts, 65, 66, 68, 124–54 passim, 178, 179, 180, 192–93, 365; and reparations, 72–73; and Dawes Plan, 108, 109, 179, 183, 185, 187; and complacency, 190, 193; and central bank cooperation, 189, 190; and Young Plan, 210; and European stability, 229; and Hoover moratorium, 235, 237–38, 243, 245; and 1931 financial crisis, 248–49, 252, 253; and revision of war debt agreements, 268, 290
Mellon-Bérenger agreement, 140–42, 143, 146, 147, 148, 152, 154, 156,

174, 178, 180, 186, 215, 218, 255
Meyer, Eugene: and 1931 financial crisis, 247, 254, 263
Military Intelligence Division, U.S. Army, 116; appraises German intentions, 164–65. *See also* Department of War, U.S.
Miller, Adolph C., 189, 204
Millerand, Alexandre, 14–15, 22, 37
Mills, Ogden: and loans to France, 174; and central bank cooperation, 188–89, 190; and currency stabilization, 189, 311; and Young Plan, 206–7, 210, 214; and Bank for International Settlements, 214; and European stability, 229; and Hoover moratorium, 235, 236, 237–38, 240, 242, 243, 245; and 1931 financial crisis, 246–47, 248–49, 253, 254, 257, 263; and revision of war debt agreements, 267–68, 271, 288, 293, 294, 306, 307, 309, 311, 313; and cooperation with Roosevelt, 305–6
Moffat, Jay Pierrepont: and Geneva Disarmament Conference, 260, 337, 348; and French security, 262
Moley, Raymond: and war debts, 308, 317, 318–19, 322, 323, 324, 352; and domestic priorities, 319, 322, 323, 324, 325, 327, 329, 332, 336, 366; and foreign economic policy, 323, 325, 327, 332, 333, 336–37, 344, 345, 346, 349, 350, 354, 358; and London Economic Conference, 354, 355, 356
Monick, Emmanuel, 289; appraises Hoover's war debt policy, 310; meets with Roosevelt, 326; confers with Warburg, 334, 345
Moreau, Emile, 143; and franc stabilization, 144, 145, 146, 147, 150, 151, 153–54; and friction with Norman, 188, 190–91; and Young Plan, 205, 208, 209
Morgan, J. P., Jr., 80; and Bankers' Committee, 74, 75; and Poincaré, 75–76; and Dawes Plan, 106, 109, 110, 111; and Young Plan, 203, 207; and Bank for International Settlements, 205; and 1931 financial crisis, 235
Morgan & Co., J. P., 58, 188; and credit to French government, 100, 107; and Dawes Plan, 101–2, 103, 104, 105–6, 107, 108, 109, 110, 111, 112; and French security, 105–6; and loans to

France, 127–28, 129; and Hoover, 181; and Young Plan, 204, 208; and 1931 financial crisis, 235–36, 249
Morgan partners. *See* Morgan & Co., J. P.
Morgenthau, Henry, Jr., 356
Morrow, Dwight W.: and Dawes Plan, 97, 102, 106, 109, 183, 185; and French security, 106, 119–20, 224, 262, 272n; and French finances, 133; and Hoover moratorium, 236, 243; and 1931 financial crisis, 248–49
Moses, George, 293
Moulton, Harold G., 132
Müller, Hermann, 186
Muscle Shoals, 233
Mussolini, Benito, 284; and Four Power Proposal, 335

N
National Association of Manufacturers, 27; and tariff protection, 173
National City Bank, 208
National Foreign Trade Council, 43, 84; and French security, 34; and commercial policy, 49
National Industrial Recovery Act, 343, 346, 348, 349, 350, 353
National Socialist [Nazi] party, 228, 271, 316, 361
Neurath, Constantin von, 341
Neutrality rights, 160–64, 165, 314, 335, 342, 347–48. *See also* Great Britain; Hoover, Herbert C.; Stimson, Henry L.; United States
New York Stock Exchange, 25
New York Trust Company, 175
Nichols, William W., 201
Norman, Montagu, 54, 56, 58, 253; and British financial problems, 188, 190–91. *See also* Central bank cooperation; Moreau, Emile; Strong, Benjamin
Norris, George W., 13

O
Occupation costs: American, 76, 209, 210, 214
Olney, Richard, 134n
Open Market Investment Committee, 188

P
Painlevé, Paul, 130
Papen, Franz von, 284
Paris Peace Conference, ix, 3, 5–10, 20, 22, 38

Parmentier, Jean: and war debts, 66–67; and reparations settlement, 92–93, 94, 96, 98; and American loans, 142

Paul-Boncour, Joseph, 349; and Geneva Disarmament Conference, 278, 284, 286; and war debts, 331; and Roosevelt, 358–59

Peace, separate: with Germany. *See* Treaty of Berlin

Peek, George, 349

Péret, Raoul, 143

Perkins, Thomas Nelson, 203

Phillips, William, 88, 332, 344, 356

Pichon, Stephen, 7

Pittman, Key: and war debts, 334, 353n; and arms embargo, 347; and London Economic Conference, 350

Poincaré, Raymond, 232; opposes Clemenceau's concessions, 9, 10; becomes premier, 37–38, 146; and French security, 37; and Treaty of Versailles, 37; and reparations, 68, 73, 74, 75, 76, 77, 78, 87–96 *passim*; and war debts, 66, 147, 149, 153–54, 180, 197, 214–15; and Genoa Conference, 72; and Ruhr occupation, 78, 90; and French financial weakness, 97, 100; and Dawes Plan, 108; and financial measures, 146–47; and foreign loans, 150–51, 152; and franc stabilization, 150, 151, 152, 153–54; and Thoiry proposals, 151–52, 153; and loan embargo, 175; and revision of Dawes Plan, 180, 184, 186; and Young Plan, 203, 214–15, 217

Poland: and the Depression, 231; and Germany, 264–65, 266

Policymaking process. *See* United States

Polish Corridor, 261, 264–65, 363

Pou, Edward W., 353

Pratt, William V., 278

Preparatory Commission for the Disarmament Conference, 159–65, 220

President's Committee on Unemployment, 41

Press, France: condemns Wilson, 8; and attitude toward Harding administration, 31; and American ratification of Treaty of Versailles, 17. *See also* France: and the U.S.

Press, United States. *See* United States: and opinion of France

Progressive party, 111

Q

Quai d'Orsay, 331

Quesnay, Pierre, 143, 208

Quota system. *See* France: and commercial policy; United States: and commercial policy

R

Radical-Socialist party, 138

Rathbone, Albert, 23

Reciprocal trade legislation. *See* Roosevelt, Franklin D.: and commercial policy

Reciprocity. *See* United States: and commercial policy

Reconciling foreign and domestic priorities. *See* Economic diplomacy; United States: and policymaking process

Reconstruction Finance Corporation, 273

Reed, James A., 25

Reichsbank, 182, 183, 208; suffers losses, 234, 236, 238; and 1931 financial crisis, 253

Reichswehr, 301, 341

Reparation Commission, 88, 89, 90, 106, 107, 108, 109, 113, 202; and U.S. policy toward, 20–21, 22, 70, 71–72, 74

Reparations, 80, 81, 261, 364; discussed at Paris Peace Conference, 8, 20; and exports, 19, 71; and capacity-to-pay principle, 20, 22; and currency stabilization, 56, 58, 71, 80; and war debts, 73, 74, 76, 77, 79, 88, 101, 107, 185, 187; and Lausanne Conference, 291–92. *See also* Dawes Plan; Expert committees; France; United States; War debts; Young Plan

Republican party, 51, 80, 110, 164

Rhenish republic, 6–7, 89

Rhineland: occupation of, 8, 9, 118, 363; demilitarization of 7, 8–9. *See also* France

Rhineland Pact, 117, 118. *See also* Locarno treaties

Rist, Charles, 143, 188, 340

Robineau, Charles, 143

Robinson, Henry M., 90

Rogers, James G., 263–64, 298

Roosevelt, Franklin D., ix, x, xi; and election of, 305; and refusal to cooperate with Hoover, 308, 313, 317–19, 321, 327; and the world crisis, 316;

and the preparations for London Economic Conference, 317, 318, 319, 321, 327, 330, 340–41; and war debts, 317, 319, 320, 321, 322–23, 324, 330, 337, 339, 345–46, 351–53, 359, 366–67; and Congress, 318n, 346, 348, 350, 353, 360; and alternate routes to recovery, 319–20, 321, 322–24, 325–26, 327–29, 338, 346, 350, 356–57, 360, 366–67; and France, 320, 326, 328; and French security, 320, 342–43, 348, 367; and domestic priorities, 324, 325, 329, 330, 346, 356–57, 359–61, 366–67; and policymaking process, 324–25, 326, 327–30, 332, 336–38, 340–41, 343, 346, 347–48, 353, 355–61, 366–67; and gold standard, 325–26, 337–38, 341, 344; and commercial policy, 330, 337, 339, 343–44, 349–51, 361; and arms limitation, 334, 338–39, 341–43, 347–48, 349, 359; and currency stabilization, 339, 344–45, 353–58, 359, 361; and neutrality rights, 339, 342–43, 347–48
Ruhr: French occupation of, 69, 78, 82, 93, 96, 97; evacuation of, 110, 113

S

Saar, 8, 9, 151
Sackett, Frederic M.: reports to Hoover, 234; and Hoover moratorium, 244–45
Safeguard clause, 131, 135, 138, 141, 142, 148–49
Saxony, 88
Schacht, Hjalmar, 117, 188; and Young Plan, 205, 208, 209; and meeting with Roosevelt, 341–42
Schleicher, Kurt von, 284
Schlesinger, Arthur, Jr., 337–38n
Security, French. See France; Great Britain; Hoover, Herbert C.; Roosevelt, Franklin D.; United States
Senate, French: Wilson addresses, 3
Senate, U.S.: Wilson's struggle with, x, 13, 14, 15, 17–18; and war debts, 140, 142; and London Naval Treaty, 226–27. See also Congress, U.S.
Shotwell, James T., 162; and Geneva Protocol, 114–15
Siegfried, André, 197
Siemens, Karl von, 95
Simmons, Furnifold, 16
Simon, John, 279

Smoot, Reed, 47, 50, 196; and war debts, 66, 134n, 136, 141, 293; and Hoover moratorium, 240. *See also* Hawley-Smoot tariff
Snowden, Philip: at London Conference, 110; and Young Plan, 220; and 1931 financial crisis, 252, 254, 255, 258
Socialist party, France, 331; and opposition to Caillaux, 143
Soissons, 59
Southern Commercial Congress, 76
Sprague, Oliver M. W.: and 1931 financial crisis, 253; and currency stabilization, 344, 345, 353–54
Stamp, Josiah, 98, 205
Standstill agreement, 249, 250, 251, 252, 253, 255–56, 257
Steed, Henry Wickham, 161–62
Stewart, Walter W.: and 1931 financial crisis, 253, 263; and Roosevelt's recovery program, 323–24
Stimson, Henry L.: and Young Plan, 207, 209, 210, 213; and Bank for International Settlements, 210; and consultative pact, 223, 224–26, 265–66, 286, 303; and French security, 224–25, 227–28, 261, 262–63, 264, 265–66, 286, 287, 335, 365; and arms limitation, 226, 260, 274, 275, 276, 278, 279, 281, 285–86, 301–2; and U.S. strategic commitments, 226, 227–28, 365; and U.S. neutrality rights, 227–28, 279, 286, 365; and European stability, 229, 261; and trip to Europe in 1931, 233, 243; and Hoover moratorium, 235, 236, 237–38, 240, 242; and 1931 financial crisis, 248–49, 251, 252, 253, 254–55, 257, 259–61; and Polish Corridor, 264–65; and revision of war debt agreements, 267–68, 269, 271, 288, 289, 290, 292, 293, 300, 306, 307, 309, 310, 311, 313, 319, 321; and Lausanne Conference, 274; and Manchurian crisis, 260, 275; and U.S. commercial policy, 297, 298–99, 300; and London Economic Conference, 299, 300, 305; and currency stabilization, 311, 321, 322, 323; and collaboration with Roosevelt, 318, 321–22, 323, 325; and policymaking process, 365
Stinnes, Hugo, 95
Stock Market: speculation, 184, 190, 191, 204

Strategic commitments: antipathy to. *See* Hoover, Herbert C.; Stimson, Henry L.; United States

Stresemann, Gustav, 276n; calls end to passive resistance, 87; and reparations, 87, 95; and London Conference, 110; and Locarno treaties, 115, 117; and need for American loans, 116–17; and Thoiry talks, 151–52

Strong, Benjamin: and currency stabilization, 54, 55–56, 57, 58, 113, 121, 129–30, 132, 142–43, 144, 147–48, 150, 154, 188–91; and fear of inflation, 56, 57, 58, 104, 190, 363; and foreign loans, 59, 60, 62, 63–64, 142–43, 177; and war debts, 63, 66, 132, 133, 143–44, 147–48, 150, 151; and reparations, 71, 74; and Treasury Department, 80, 147, 148, 149, 188–89; and Dawes Plan, 103, 104, 111; and European security negotiations, 116–17; and his relations with Commerce and State departments, 149, 188; and revision of Dawes Plan, 183, 185. *See also* Central bank cooperation; currency stabilization; Moreau, Emile; Norman, Montagu

Supreme Allied Council, 14

Swanson, Claude: and Geneva Disarmament Conference, 274, 286

T

Tardieu, André: and French security, 6–7, 222–24, 275–76, 278–79; and Hague agreements, 217; and Lausanne Conference, 276; and U.S. neutrality policy, 276, 279; and war debts, 289, 331

Tariff Commission, U.S., 44, 45, 46, 48, 50, 51, 52, 53, 80, 172, 299, 365; and Franco-American trade, 52–53, 80–81, 166–67, 169, 170, 172, 173; and Senate investigation of, 170, 171; and Hawley-Smoot tariff, 198, 199

Tariffs, 80; and currency depreciation, 19, 30; and domestic manufacturers, 19, 30; and foreign trade, 19, 29, 30; and currency stabilization, 42, 49, 54; and imports, 42, 43, 50; and war debts, 199. *See also* Fordney-McCumber Act; Hawley-Smoot tariff; United States: and commercial policy

Tariff truce. *See* Roosevelt, Franklin D.: and commercial policy

Taussig, Frank, 171

Teapot Dome scandal, 101

Thoiry: negotiations at, 151–52; and U.S. view of, 152–53

Tower, Walter E., 98

Transfer committee, 93, 94, 95, 103, 106. *See also* Dawes Plan

Treaty of Berlin (1921), 32–33, 37

Treaty of Guarantee, Anglo-American, x; proposed by Lloyd George, 7; and Wilson's views of, 9, 10–11, 12–13, 15; and Clemenceau's suspicions of, 16–17; and Poincaré's view of, 37; and Harding administration's attitude toward, 38

Treaty of Versailles, x, 73, 75; and Article 429, 9; and Articles 42 and 43, 11, 13, 117; defeated in Senate, 14; and French reaction to American repudiation of, 14; and German violations of, 15, 37, 78, 107, 115–16, 159–60, 164–65; and debate over, precludes economic policymaking, 18–30; undermined by Dawes Plan, 113; and commercial provisions, 118; and impact of Hoover moratorium on, 242, 244; and possible revision of, 250, 252, 261. *See also* Clemenceau, Georges; Paris Peace Conference; Wilson, Woodrow

Tugwell, Rexford: and recovery program, 317, 318, 319, 329–30; and war debts, 317, 318–19, 352; and foreign policy studies during interregnum, 325, 326, 327; and domestic priorities, 366

U

Unconditional most-favored-nation trading principle, 43–53 *passim*, 166–67, 168, 193, 196, 197, 297, 298, 333. *See also* United States: and commercial policy

United States: and antipathy to strategic obligations, ix, xi, 77, 79, 114, 115–16, 159, 160, 163, 164, 262, 275, 277, 287, 362–68; and domestic priorities, ix, 19, 42–43, 81, 190, 191, 269–70, 362–63, 365, 366, 368; and European stability, ix, x, 40–43, 57, 79–81, 86, 114, 115, 119–20, 154–57, 192–93, 241, 244–45, 246, 271, 359, 362–68 *passim*; and German reintegration, ix, 36, 37, 38–39, 82–83, 101, 114, 120, 244, 364, 368; and policymaking process, xi, 43, 79–81, 87, 149–50, 155, 157, 172–73, 192–93, 229, 277, 290–91, 293, 299–300, 311–12, 332, 335–36, 346, 362–68; and French security, 3–13, 18, 31–40 *passim*, 77, 82–83, 85, 88–89, 92, 101, 114, 115, 116, 119–20, 160, 162, 163, 164–65, 192, 224–25, 227–28, 244, 262–63, 275, 277, 285, 287–88, 314–15, 348, 359, 363, 364, 368; and reparations, 20–22, 70–79, 82–90; and war debts, 22–25, 64–70, 91–92, 120–42 *passim*, 178–82, 192–93, 234–45, 266–70, 292–95, 306–13, 321–24, 345–46, 351–53; and foreign loans, 26–29, 58–64, 174–77; and commercial policy, 29–30, 43–54, 80, 168–73, 192–93, 195–202, 295–300; and arms limitation, 32–39, 159–65, 219–28, 277–88, 301–2, 334–35, 341–43, 347–49; and view of German military potential, 33–34, 39; and opinion of France, 35–36, 77, 80–81, 126, 136, 293, 300, 301, 303; and currency stabilization, 54–58, 121–57 *passim*, 187–91, 353–61, 364; and reaction to Ruhr occupation, 78–79, 82–86; and Dawes Plan, 101, 105, 111–12; and Locarno negotiations, 116–20; and neutrality rights, 160, 161–65, 262–63, 264; and Geneva Economic Conference, 166–67; and revision of Dawes Plan, 183, 185, 187; and Young Plan, 202–19; and Bank for International Settlements, 216, 219; and Franco-Italian naval rivalry, 227–28; and Depression, 231; and elections in, 232; and Lausanne Conference, 291, 292, 293; and German rearmament, 275, 285

V

Vanderlip, Frank, 84
Versailles Peace Conference. *See* Paris Peace Conference
Viviani, René: mission to U.S., 31–32

W

Wagner Bill, 233
Wallace, Hugh, 14
Wall Street: and opposition to loan embargo, 174–75, 177; and 1931 financial crisis, 235–36; and corruption on, 274; and revision of war debt agreements, 300

Warburg, James Paul: and recovery program, 323–24, 330, 333–34, 336; and foreign economic policy, 325–26, 332–37, 340, 343, 344, 345, 346, 349, 350, 353–55, 357; and war debts, 334, 336, 345, 352; and antipathy to strategic obligations, 336
Warburg, Paul M., 24, 28
War debts: and budget balancing, 19; and commerce, 19, 64–65, 67–68, 69–70, 121, 139, 147–49, 294, 307, 313; and taxes, 19, 23, 42, 65, 69, 70, 86, 123, 133–34, 135, 136, 137, 139–40, 141, 146, 149, 218, 234, 260, 274, 289, 294, 365–66; and reparations, 42, 67, 74, 76, 77, 131, 134–35, 140–41, 148–49, 178, 179, 181, 206–7, 208, 210, 212, 215, 236–37, 240, 241–44, 255, 259, 263, 264, 266–67, 288–92, 294, 365; and currency stabilization, 56, 58, 65, 67, 69, 80, 122, 123, 128–29, 132–33, 143–50, 191, 310–11, 321–22; and foreign loans, 64, 127–30, 175, 284; and arms limitation, 68, 133–34, 234, 240, 307, 312, 313; and criticism of U.S. policy toward, 178, 181–82, 216–17; and U.S. banking structure, 238–39, 240; and London Economic Conference, 312, 313, 321, 322, 345–46. *See also* France; United States
War Finance Corporation, 26, 28, 44, 59n, 260
Warren, George F., 356
Warren, Robert, 144
Washington Naval Conference (1921–22), 33–40
Weimar Republic, 87, 234, 235
White, Henry, 10
White, William Allen, 46
Wiggin, Albert H., 258n
Williams, John H., 305, 318, 319, 320, 328
Wilson, Edwin C., 215
Wilson, Hugh R., 274, 279
Wilson, Woodrow, ix, x, 364; and French security, 3–18 *passim*; and reintegration of Germany, 4–5, 7, 10, 12–13, 15, 18, 38; and League of Nations, 5, 12, 17, 18, 19; and debate over Treaty of Versailles, 13, 14, 15, 16, 17, 19; and cerebral thrombosis, 14, 18n; and anger with France, 15; and postwar reconstruction, 18–19; and reparations, 20–21; and war debts, 23, 24,

25; and tariffs, 29, 30. *See also* Paris Peace Conference
Winston, Garrard: and currency stabilization, 122, 129–30, 131, 144–45, 152–53, 156; and war debts, 129, 130–31, 132–33, 137, 140, 141, 145, 148–49, 152, 156, 269; and U.S. commercial policy, 172; and foreign loans, 177
Woodin, William: and currency stabilization, 332, 344, 354, 355, 356
Woolley, Mary Emma, 274n
World Court, 85–86, 331
World Disarmament Conference (1932–33). *See* Geneva Disarmament Conference
World Economic Conference (1933). *See* London Economic Conference
World War I, 3; and U.S. underestimates impact of, 157
World War II, 367
World War Foreign Debt Commission, 65, 66, 68, 69, 70, 80, 91, 240, 312, 365; and British debt agreement, 85; and capacity-to-pay formula, 122, 123–24, 125, 126, 130–31, 137, 155; and French debt, 132, 134–37, 140–41, 155; and debt accord with Belgium, 133; and disbandment of, 178; and proposal to reestablish, 267–69

Y

Young, Arthur N.: and reparations, 91; and war debts, 123, 124; and U.S. commercial policy, 172; and Geneva Economic Conference, 166–67
Young, Owen D., 90; and reparations, 91, 92, 93, 94, 95, 96, 98–99; and European stability, 92; and French security, 92, 97; and German rehabilitation, 92, 93, 96, 99, 112–13; and Morgan partners, 97, 103, 104, 109; and Dawes Plan, 103, 108, 112; and warning of payments crisis, 140n; and U.S. commercial policy, 172; and revision of Dawes Plan, 183; and Young Plan, 203–13 *passim*, 219; and Bank for International Settlements, 205–6, 207, 213, 215–16; and war debts, 218; and Hoover moratorium, 240; and 1931 financial crisis, 258; and encouragement of Hoover-Roosevelt cooperation, 305–6
Young Plan: formulated, 202–19; and revision of, 234, 237, 250, 255, 263, 264, 266, 267, 269n, 288, 289, 290, 291; and impact of Hoover moratorium on, 241–42